THE POLITICAL ECONOMY
OF DEVELOPMENT
AND UNDERDEVELOPMENT

FIFTH EDITION

THE POLITICAL ECONOMY OF DEVELOPMENT AND UNDERDEVELOPMENT

Charles K. Wilber

Economics Department
University of Notre Dame

Kenneth P. Jameson

Economics Department
University of Utah

McGraw-Hill, Inc.
New York St. Louis San Francisco Auckland Bogotá
Caracas Lisbon London Madrid Mexico Milan
Montreal New Delhi Paris San Juan Singapore
Sydney Tokyo Toronto

The Political Economy of Development and Underdevelopment

2 3 4 5 6 7 8 9 0 DOC DOC 9 0 9 8 7 6 5 4 3 2

ISBN 0-07-070186-5

This book was set in Palatino by The Clarinda Company.
The editors were Scott D. Stratford and Sheila H. Gillams;
the production supervisor was Friederich W. Schulte.
The cover was designed by Charles A. Carson.
R. R. Donnelley & Sons Company was printer and binder.

Library of Congress Cataloging-in-Publication Data

The Political economy of development and underdevelopment. —5th ed.
     / [edited by] Charles K. Wilber, Kenneth P. Jameson.
          p.   cm.
     ISBN 0-07-070186-5
          1. Economic development.   2. Developing countries—Economic
     conditions.   I. Wilber, Charles K.   II. Jameson, Kenneth P.
     HD82.P546   1992
     330.9172'4—dc20   91-15252

330.9172
P769
1992

ABOUT THE
AUTHORS

Charles K. Wilber received his B.A. and M.S. from the University of Portland and his Ph.D. from the University of Maryland. He has taught at Multnomah College, Portland, Oregon (1958–1960); Catholic University, Ponce, Puerto Rico (1960–1961); Trinity College, Washington, D.C. (1961–1964); The American University, Washington D.C. (1964–1975); and since 1975, at the University of Notre Dame. He was Chair of the Economics Department from 1975 to 1984. He has been a consultant to the Peace Corps, Interamerican Development Bank, George Meany Center for Labor Studies, and the United States Bishops' Committee on Catholic Social Thought and the U.S. Economy. His major research areas are economic development, economic ethics, and economic methodology. He has published over 50 articles in economics journals and a number of books including: *The Soviet Model and Underdeveloped Countries* (University of North Carolina Press, 1969); and with Kenneth Jameson, *An Inquiry into the Poverty of Economics* (University of Notre Dame Press, 1983) and *Beyond Reaganomics: A Further Inquiry into the Poverty of Economics* (University of Notre Dame Press, 1990).

Kenneth P. Jameson received his B.A. from Stanford University and his M.S. and Ph.D. from the University of Wisconsin–Madison. He has taught at the University of Notre Dame (1970–1989); the University of Utah, since 1989; Universidad Nacional San Augustin, Arequipa, Peru; the Catholic University of Peru in Lima; and the Development Studies Program in Washington, D.C. He began his work in development in the villages of Peru in 1964 as a member of the Peace Corps. Since that time he has researched and traveled extensively in Latin America and the Caribbean and has consulted in Peru, Bolivia, Panama, Guyana, the Dominican Republic, Jamaica, and Paraguay. His major research areas are economic development, economic methodology, and macroeconomics. He has published over 50 articles in a variety of development journals, primarily on issues of agriculture and development and on the macro-financial elements in development. He has also published a number of books.

v

I have a dream that one day every valley shall be exalted,
every hill and mountain shall be made low, the rough
places will be made plain, and the crooked places will
be made straight, and the glory of the Lord shall be
revealed, and all flesh shall see it together.

Martin Luther King, Jr.
The March on Washington
August 1963

For all those with dreams and who share our bias for hope about development, that
the lessons of the past and the tensions of the present may resolve into the
fulfillment of the dream.

CONTENTS

PREFACE TO THE FIFTH EDITION

The decade of the 1960s was marked by an optimism that world poverty could be conquered by economic growth. The 1970s saw that hope dashed by growing unemployment and inequality and the intractability of absolute poverty in the Third World. The first edition of this book charted that disillusionment.

The 1970s witnessed the birth of a new optimism to replace the old. The pursuit of "growth with equity" or a strategy of targeting "basic human needs" would succeed where economic growth failed. The second edition of this book captured the beginnings of this movement.

The 1980s ushered in a period of greater caution. World poverty will not be eliminated with simple economic panaceas. Resource shortages (particularly of energy), rising protectionism in the industrial world, militarism in the Third World, the international arms race, the structure of the world economy all make the design of development strategies a complex problem in political economy rather than a simple economic issue.

The fourth edition updated the continuing debate among the contending schools of thought, highlighted the international debt crisis along with the attendant stabilization and readjustment programs, and charted the resurgence of free market economics with its attack upon "development" economics.

This fifth edition is published at the beginning of the last decade of the twentieth century, a time when the old verities are collapsing. The cold war is ending, the Eastern European countries are moving from centrally planned economics of the Second World to market-oriented underdeveloped countries of the Third World. Regional conflicts are moving to center stage in the international political arena with the most notable example being the Gulf War of 1991 and the subsequent chaos in the area. The "bias for hope," replaced in the 1980s with a narrow concentration on technical issues, may fade even further in Africa, Asia, and Latin America if the developed countries' development efforts become focused on aiding the Eastern European countries, and the continuing military engagements in the Middle East have never encouraged development.

This edition focuses on the complex problems and even more complex solutions of human development within this changing international political context. There are no easy answers, but if progress is to be made against the poverty that afflicts the majority of humankind the "bias for hope" must be rekindled and combined with serious analysis of problems and solutions. We hope this book is a contribution to that rekindling and analysis.

Once again, we are indebted to many people for the valuable help they have given us in preparing this fifth edition. They provided critiques of the fourth edition, suggested new readings, and encouraged us to go ahead. We particularly want to thank James H. Weaver of The American University. His ideas have become so entangled with ours that it is no longer possible to sort out ownership.

Solomon Namala contributed mightily in the initial stages of article selection, while David Plante helped in the final stages of the book.

Our thanks to Scott Stratford and Sheila Gillams of McGraw-Hill whose good humored professionalism helped surmount the many barriers to getting the book out in a timely and competent manner.

Charles K. Wilber
Kenneth P. Jameson

PREFACE TO THE
FIRST EDITION

Economists assume that the problem of a more human society is solved by expertise, by know-how. Since they assume that the question of the nature of a good society is already answered, the issue becomes one of solving certain practical problems. The good society is simply assumed to be an idealized version of the United States economy, that is, a consumer society. The key to a consumer society is growth of per capita income. Thus the vast bulk of the development literature has focused on growth rates as the *deus ex machina* to solve all problems. Even much of the socialist writing on development argues that the superiority of socialism over capitalism lies in faster growth rates.

There is much to be said for this approach because some minimum level of food, clothing, shelter, recreation, etc., is necessary before a person can be free to be human. However, the emphasis on consumption and growth of per capita income has not led to a decrease of poverty in the underdeveloped world. If anything it has increased. A thin layer has prospered while the vast majority of the population sinks ever deeper into the backwater of underdevelopment. Therefore, during the past several years a new look has been taken at the meaning of development. Dudley Seers, Mahbub ul Haq, Ivan Illich, and others have questioned the emphasis on chasing the consumption standards of the developed countries via economic growth. Instead they argue for a direct attack on poverty through employment and income redistribution policies. Denis Goulet and Paulo Freire argue that development must include "liberation" from oppression, cultural as well as political and economic.

Both of these positions have merit, and they are not necessarily mutually exclusive. That is, the study of political economy should lead one to ask whether stressing the importance of rapid economic growth has to mean that the growth will consist of movies, bikinis, deodorants, key clubs, and pollution. An analysis of political economic systems should lead one to see why growth has meant luxuries being produced for some while others go hungry.

This book is about economic development and underdevelopment, and is designed to be used with a standard textbook in advanced undergraduate and beginning graduate courses. The readings emphasize the *political economy* rather than the narrowly *economic* approach and issues.

Many of the readings are excellent examples of radical political economy. Political economy recognizes that man is a social being whose arrangements for the production and distribution of economic goods must be, if society is to be livable, consistent with congruent institutions of family, political, and cultural life. As a result, a political economy analysis must incorporate such noneconomic influences as social structures, political systems, and cultural values as well as such factors as technological change and the distribution of income and wealth. The readings are radical in the sense that they are willing to question and evaluate the most basic institutions and values of society.

While I hope that the work presented here is objective, there is no artificial stance of neutrality. I am committed to certain values that undoubtedly influence the choice of questions asked and the range of variables considered for selection. In general, my system of values posits material progress (at least up to some minimum level), equality, cooperation, democratic control of economic as well as political institutions, and individual freedom as positive goods. It should be noted that there may be contradictions among these criteria, and thus society is faced with choices. With these values in mind the reader can judge the degree of objectivity attained.

It is a pleasure to acknowledge my indebtedness to those who have helped me shape my ideas on economic development and underdevelopment. First of all I want to thank Professors W. Michael Bailey, James H. Weaver, Celso Furtado, Branko Horvat, E. J. Mishan, Ronald Müller, Brady Tyson, Albert Waterston, and Irving Louis Horowitz—critics, colleagues, and friends. Some of my greatest debts are to those whom I know only through their writings—Karl Polyanyi and R. H. Tawney. Their example of scholarship and social commitment has been a guide and inspiration. I want to thank Sandy Kelly for her invaluable help in editing and typing, and Bob Devlin for his assistance in research and editing. Barbara Conover and Nancy Perry, editors at Random House, have been invaluable in seeing the book through to publication.

My greatest debt, however, in this as in all my endeavors, is to my wife, Mary Ellen, and our children: Kenneth, Teresa, Matthew, Alice, Mary, Angela, and Louie. I owe all to their love and encouragement.

Charles K. Wilber

PART ONE

THEORY AND METHOD IN ECONOMIC DEVELOPMENT

Political, economic, and social change are the undeniable realities of the modern world. There are certainly few if any "undiscovered" tribes of untouched natives left in the world, and the controversy over whether the Tasaday in the Philippines were simply a public relations ploy casts further doubt. Improvements in transportation and communication have increased the pace of social change and have extended it to areas normally outside of any mainstream. A major contributor has been the generalized acceptance of the inevitability and in most cases of the desirability of change. Countries which long resisted external influences have begun to accede to the inevitability of change. For example, Albania is moving away from its fierce postwar independence and Burma (Mayanmar) appears to be opening both politically and economically.

Development economics was spawned during the 1940s and 1950s by the acceptance of the inevitability of political, social, and economic change. The problem of the lagging countries of Eastern Europe was the genesis of much of its initial work, and then the success in rebuilding Europe and Japan emboldened development economists to extend their horizon to the rest of the world. Development work incorporated an optimism that change could be for the better and that conscious reflection on and control over change, often through national governments and international organizations, could harness change and bring about development. The accomplishments are undeniable.

Growth of GNP throughout the world accelerated, infant mortality decreased dramatically, and life expectancy increased rapidly; access to education was extended far beyond what would have been imaginable in 1945. Data from the *World Development Report, 1990* (table 3.1) give a more precise sense of the changes in developing countries:

	1965	1975	1985
Consumption per capita (1985 PPP dollars)	590	780	985
Life expectancy (years)	51	57	62
Primary net enrollment rate (percent)	73	74	84

As A. K. Sen points out in his article, the factors which development economics highlighted and the policies advocated had an important and positive role in these changes. Albert Hirschman (1983) pointed out that the optimism of development economics often gave policymakers and others the courage to confront social change, to support it, and to attempt to move it in a positive direction.

That optimism has proved naive; for in the words of development economist Paul Streeten, "Every solution created another problem." Sen (1985) notes the problems of fast growth and slow social change, as well as the difficulty of defining development correctly. Development economics has had to learn that "all good things do not go together," that rapid growth and economic development may be accompanied by severe political problems such as the emergence of authoritarian governments, a problem which was compounded by the mediocre economic performance of the 1980s. This was a lost decade for Latin America and Africa in terms of economic development. For example, according to the Inter-American Development Bank, income per person in Latin America actually fell from an average of $2,512 in 1980 to $2,336 in 1988. Many of the articles in this book will focus on the failures of development and will examine the political economy of those failures.

The loss of momentum, of hope in development, and of courage to proceed stimulated free market or laissez-faire economists to attack development economics, attributing slackening development to the interference of government in the normal functioning of the economy, in particular to distortion of the resource allocation role of prices. The article by Lal is a clear statement of this position and a resounding attack on what he terms the *dirigiste dogma* or the massive intervention by government to supplant the price mechanism.

Lal's stance has gained wide acceptance among economists who work on Third World countries. In part this is a reflection of the World Bank's growing role in research on economic development. Lal's article appeared in their journal, *Finance and Development*. To document the weight of the World Bank in development thinking we tabulated the authors of articles which appeared between 1984 and

1986 in the five major journals of economic development. Authors affiliated with the World Bank were the most published in the development field, accounting for 1.6 times as many article pages in these journals as authors of the most productive independent research organization, the Institute of Development Studies at Sussex University in Britain. Adding the articles by the staff of the International Monetary Fund, the World Bank's sister institution in Washington, raises their joint production to 2.25 times that of Sussex. The importance of the World Bank and its numerous economists has given a major impulse to the Lal approach to development.

Helleiner describes the general World Bank approach to development in his article, without a great deal of sympathy. Indeed, he characterizes it as "conventional foolishness," and finds much that is objectionable, though he refrains from noting that the postwar decade of poorest development performance, the 1980s, was the decade the Bank's program was implemented most widely. He notes a series of discrepancies and inconsistencies which lead him to see Lal's approach as foolishness, and he suggests that any such simplification will surely be unable to deal with the complexities of economic development. Much of this case is built upon the mixed economy (government plus the private sector) strategy undertaken by the two unquestioned development success stories, Korea and Taiwan.

Both he and Sen end their articles by setting out an agenda for development studies in the coming years. They agree that there is much work still to be done, and that we can indeed understand and encourage development, though not with the ease and success that development economists had naively assumed in the early years. They implicitly suggest the need for a careful "political economy of development" as represented in the articles of this book.

Their optimism differs from Lal who sees the unfettered operation of the price system leading inevitably to successful economic development. The article by Howard Wiarda provides a very different stance toward development which rejects both of the other approaches. Wiarda wrote long before the weakening of the state in the USSR allowed the outbreak of ethnic strife in Armenia and Azerbaijan, before the Islamic mujahadeen were able to force the withdrawal of Russian forces from Afghanistan, and before tribal rivalries led to a destructive civil war in Liberia. Those events resulted from the same forces noted by Wiarda and represented a rejection of the main elements of the Western capitalist and the Russian state socialist models of development. Many of the examples cited by Wiarda are reactionary, that is, efforts to turn the clock back and to reject changes which have come from outside. As such they will fail. However, Wiarda finds many positive elements in tribalism, Islamic fundamentalism, and Latin American corporatism; he is certainly correct in positing that they will be factors to be incorporated into any development process of the 1990s.

The political economy of development has in some sense come full circle. The development of Eastern Europe, one of its first concerns, is again a primary focus. At this point variants of the Lal model are being implemented in Eastern Europe, despite Helleiner's characterization as conventional foolishness. There are again success stories to build on, most notably Korea and Taiwan, and there are development policies and approaches that give reason for hope. One major difference is that we have learned that the naive belief in a simple and automatic process of development is certainly unwarranted. Solutions do bring problems, reactions to change do occur, and development can't be reduced to a simple formula; it must be studied as the political economy of development and underdevelopment. The variety and challenge of the development process must attract us. The crucial question is whether the acceptance of social change and the belief that it can be positive can energize development efforts, rather than lead to reaction or disillusion. Only the experience of the 1990s will tell.

REFERENCES

Hirschman, Albert. "The Rise and Decline of Development Economics." In his *Essays in Trespassing: Economics to Politics and Beyond.* Cambridge: Cambridge University Press, 1981.

Streeten, Paul. "A Problem to Every Solution: Development Economics Has Not Failed." *Finance and Development*, 22, 2 (June 1985): 14–16.

World Bank. *World Development Report, 1990.* Oxford: Oxford University Press, 1990.

1

Development: Which Way Now?

Amartya Sen

I. THE PROMISE AND THE DEFAULT

"Development economics is a comparatively young area of inquiry. It was born just about a generation ago, as a subdiscipline of economics, with a number of other social sciences looking on both skeptically and jealously from a distance."[1] So writes Albert Hirschman, but the essay that begins so cheerfully turns out to be really an obituary of development economics—no longer the envy of the other social sciences. In this illuminating essay, aptly called "The Rise and Decline of Development Economics," Hirschman puts his main thesis thus:

> our subdiscipline had achieved its considerable lustre and excitement through the implicit idea that it could slay the dragon of backwardness virtually by itself or, at least, that its contribution to this task was central. We now know that this is not so.[2]

The would-be dragon-slayer seems to have stumbled on his sword.

There is some plausibility in this diagnosis, but is it really true that development economics has no central role to play in the conquest of underdevelopment and economic backwardness? More specifically, were the original themes in terms of which the subject was launched really so far from being true or useful? I shall argue that the obituary may be premature, the original themes—while severely incomplete in coverage—did not point entirely in the wrong direction, and the discipline of development eco-

Presidential Address of the Development Studies Association given in Dublin on 23 September 1982. In preparing the final version of the paper, I have benefited from the comments of Carl Riskin, Louis Emmerij, Albert Hirschman, Seth Masters, Hans Singer, and the editorial referees of this Journal, and from the discussions following my DSA address, and also that following a talk I gave on a related theme at the Institute of Social Studies in the Hague on 11 October 1982. Published in *Economic Journal*, 93 (December 1983), pp. 745–62. Copyright © 1983 by The Royal Economic Society. Reprinted by permission of Cambridge University Press.

nomics does have a central role to play in the field of economic growth in developing countries. But I shall also argue that the problematique underlying the approach of traditional development economics is, in some important ways, quite limited, and has not—and could not have—brought us to an adequate understanding of economic development. Later on, I shall take up the question as to the direction in which we may try to go instead.

There is a methodological problem in identifying a subject—or a sub-discipline as Hirschman calls it—with a given body of beliefs and themes rather than with a collection of subject matters and problems to be tackled. But Hirschman is certainly right in pointing towards the thematic similarities of the overwhelming majority of contributions in development economics. While some development economists such as Peter Bauer and Theodore Schultz have not been party to this thematic congruence, they have also stood outside the mainstream of what may be called standard development economics, as indeed the title of Peter Bauer's justly famous book, *Dissent on Development*,[3] indicates. The subdiscipline began with a set of favourite themes and the main approaches to the subject have been much moulded by these motifs. Clearly, the subject cannot live or die depending just on the success or failure of these themes, but the main approaches would need radical reformulation if these themes were shown to be fundamentally erroneous or misguided.

Hirschman identifies two major ideas with which development economics came into being, namely "rural underemployment" (including so-called disguised unemployment") and "late industrialisation." The former idea led naturally to a focus on utilisation of underemployed manpower and to acceleration of capital accumulation. The latter called for an activist state and for planning to overcome the disadvantages of lateness through what Hirschman calls "a deliberate, intensive, guided effort." The subject expended a lot of time in developing "new rationales . . . for protection, planning, and industrialisation itself."[4]

While there have been differences in assertion and emphasis *within* the mainstream of the subdiscipline, it is fair to say that in terms of policy the following have been among the major strategic themes pursued ever since the beginning of the subject: (1) industrialisation, (2) rapid capital accumulation, (3) mobilisation of underemployed manpower, and (4) planning and an economically active state.[5] There are, of course, many other common themes, e.g., emphasis on skill formation, but they have not typically been as much subjected to criticism as these other themes, and there is thus much to be said for concentrating on these four.

These themes (especially the need for planning, but also the deliberate fostering of industrialisation and capital accumulation and the acceptance of the possibility of surplus labour) are closely linked to criticisms of the traditional neoclassical models as applied to developing countries. Hirschman calls this eschewal of "universal" use of neoclassical economics the rejection of "monoeconomics." Monoeconomics sounds perhaps a little like a disease that one could catch if not careful. I shall avoid the term, though some would no doubt have thought it quite appropriate to characterise universal neoclassical economics as a contagious affliction.

It was argued by development economists that neoclassical economics did not apply terribly well to underdeveloped countries. This need not have caused great astonishment, since neoclassical economics did not apply terribly well anywhere else. However, the role of the state and the need for planning and deliberate public action seemed stronger in underdeveloped countries, and the departure from traditional neoclassical models was, in many ways, more radical.

The discrediting of traditional development economics that has lately taken place, and to which Hirschman made reference, is undoubtedly partly due to the resurgence of neoclassical economics in recent years. As Hirschman (1981) rightly notes, "the claim of development economics to stand as a separate body of economic analysis and policy derived intellectual legitimacy and nurture from the prior success and parallel features of the Keynesian Revolution" (p. 7). The neoclassical resurgence against Keynesian economics was to some extent paralleled by the neoclassical recovery in the field of economic development. The market, it was argued, has the many virtues that standard neoclassical analysis has done so much to analyse, and state intervention could be harmful in just the way suggested by that perspective.

The neoclassical resurgence has drawn much sustenance from the success of some countries and the failure of others. The high performance of economies like South Korea, Taiwan, Hong Kong, and Singapore—based on markets and profits and trade—has been seen as bringing Adam Smith back to life. On the other hand, the low performance of a great many countries in Asia, Africa, and Latin America has been cited as proof that it does not pay the government to mess about much with the market mechanism. Recently, doubts raised about the record of China, and the vocal desire of the Chinese leadership to make greater use of material incentives, have been interpreted as proof that even a powerful socialist regime cannot break the basic principles on which the market mechanism is founded.

The attack on state activism and planning has been combined with criticism of some of the other features of traditional development economics. It has been argued that enterprise is the real bottleneck, not capital, so that to emphasise capital accumulation and the creation of surplus—as was done for example by Maurice Dobb (1951; 1960) and Paul Baran (1957)—was to climb the wrong tree. The charge of misallocation of resources has been levelled also against industrialisation, especially for the domestic market. Hirschman (1981) notes: "By itself this critique was highly predictable and might not have carried more weight than warnings against industrialisation emanating from essentially the same camp ten, or twenty, or fifty years earlier." But—as he goes on to say—the effectiveness of this critique was now greater for various reasons, including that fact that "some of the early advocates of industrialisation had now themselves become its sharpest critics" (p. 18). Hirschman refers in this context to some "neo-Marxist" writings and the views of some members of the so-called dependency school. Certainly, the particular pattern of industrial expansion in Latin America provides many examples of exploitative relations with the metropolitan countries, particularly the United States of America, and the internal effects were often quite terrible in terms of fostering economic inequality and social distortion. But to move from there to a rejection of industrialisation as such is indeed a long jump.

I should explain that Hirschman, from whom I have been quoting extensively, does not in many cases endorse these attacks on the policy strategies of traditional development economics. But he provides excellent analyses of the arguments figuring in the attacks. I believe Hirschman is more hesitant in his defence of traditional development economics than he need have been, but his own reasons for rejecting that tradition—to which he himself has of course contributed much[6]—rests primarily on the argument that development economics has tended to be contemptuous of underdeveloped countries, albeit this contempt has taken a "sophisticated form." These countries have been "expected to perform like wind-up toys and 'lumber through' the various stages of development single-mindedly'. As Hirschman (1981) puts it, "these countries were perceived to have only *interests* and *no passions*" (p. 24).[7]

I believe this diagnosis has much truth in it. But I also believe that, contemptuous and simplistic though development economics might have been in this respect, the main themes that were associated with the origin of development economics, and have given it its distinctive character, are not rejectable for that reason. I shall argue that they address common problems, which survive despite the particular passions.

II. TRADITIONAL THEMES IN THE LIGHT OF RECENT EXPERIENCES

Growth is not the same thing as development and the difference between the two has been brought out by a number of recent contributions to development economics.[8] I shall take up the complex question of the content of economic development presently (in Sections III–V below). But it can scarcely be denied that economic growth is one aspect of the process of economic development. And it happens to be the aspect on which traditional development economics—rightly or wrongly—has concentrated. In this section I do not assess the merits of that concentration (on which more later), but examine the appropriateness of the traditional themes, given that concentration. Dealing specifically with economic growth as it is commonly defined, the strategic relevance of these themes is examined in the light of recent experiences. How do these theories—formulated and presented mainly in the forties and fifties—fare in the light of the experiences of the sixties and the seventies?

The World Development Report 1982 (henceforth *WDR*) presents comparative growth data for the period 1960–80 for "low-income economies" and "middle-income economies," with a dividing line at US$410 in 1980. Leaving out small countries (using a cut-off line of 10 million people) and excluding the OPEC countries which have had rather special economic circumstances during the seventies, we have fourteen countries in the low-income category for which data on economic growth (GNP or GDP) are given in *WDR*. Correspondingly, there are eighteen such countries in the middle-income category. Table 1 presents these data. For three of the low-income countries, namely China, Bangladesh and Afghanistan, the GNP growth figures are not given in *WDR* and they have been approximately identified with GDP growth. In interpreting the results, this has to be borne in mind, and only those conclusions can be safely drawn which would be unaffected by variations of these estimates within a wide range.

The fourteen low-income economies vary in terms of growth rate of GNP per capita during 1960–80 from *minus* 0.7% in Uganda to 3.7% in China. The top three countries in terms of economic growth are China (3.7%), Pakistan (2.8%), and Sri Lanka (2.4%). (Note that China's preeminent position would be unaffected even if the approximated growth figure is substantially cut.) In the middle-income group, the growth performance again varies a great deal, ranging from *minus* 10% for Ghana to 8.6% for Romania. The top three countries in terms of economic growth are Romania (8.6%), South Korea (7.0%), and Yugoslavia (5.4%).

How do these high-performance countries compare with others in the respective groups in terms of the parameters associated with the main theses of traditional development economics? Take capital accumulation first. Of the three top growth-performers, two also have the highest share of gross domestic investment in GDP, namely Sri Lanka with 36% and China with 31%. Pakistan comes lower, though it does fall in the top half of the class of fourteen countries.

Turning now to the middle-income countries, the top three countries in terms of growth are also the top three countries in terms of capital accumulation, namely Yugoslavia with 35%, Romania with 34%, and South Korea with 31%. Thus, if there is anything to be learned from the experience of these successful growers regarding the importance of capital accumulation, it is certainly not a lesson that runs counter to the traditional wisdom of development economics.

It might, however, be argued that to get a more convincing picture one should look also at failures and not merely at successes. I don't think the cases are quite symmetrical, since a failure can be due to some special "bottleneck" even when all other factors are favorable. Nevertheless, it is not

TABLE 1

Country	GNP Per Head		1980 Gross Domestic Investment (% of GDP)	1980 Share of Industry in GDP (%)
	1980 Value ($)	1960–80 Growth (%)		
Low-income				
Bangladesh	130	1.3*	17	13
Ethiopia	140	1.4	10	16
Nepal	140	0.2	14	13
Burma	170	1.2	24	13
Afghanistan		0.9*	14	—
Zaire	220	0.2	11	23
Mozambique	230	−0.1	10	16
India	240	1.4	23	26
Sri Lanka	270	2.4	36	30
Tanzania	280	1.9	22	13
China	290	3.7*	31	47
Pakistan	300	2.8	18	25
Uganda	300	−0.7	3	6
Sudan	410	−0.2	12	14
Middle-income				
Ghana	420	−1.0	5	21
Kenya	420	2.7	22	21
Egypt	580	3.4	31	35
Thailand	670	4.7	27	29
Philippines	690	2.8	30	37
Morocco	900	2.5	21	32
Peru	930	1.1	16	45
Colombia	1,180	3.0	25	30
Turkey	1,470	3.6	27	30
S. Korea	1,520	7.0	31	41
Malaysia	1,620	4.3	29	37
Brazil	2,050	5.1	22	37
Mexico	2,090	2.6	28	38
Chile	2,150	1.6	18	37
South Africa	2,300	2.3	29	53
Romania	2,340	8.6	34	64
Argentina	2,390	2.2	—	—
Yugoslavia	2,620	5.4	35	43

*Based on GDP growth figures per head (*World Development Report 1982*, tables 2 and 17).

SOURCE: *World Development Report 1982*, tables 1–5. The countries included are all the ones within the 'Low-income' and 'Middle-income' categories, other than those with less than 10 million population, members of OPEC, and countries without GNP or GDP growth figures.

useless to examine the cases of failure as well, especially with respect to capital accumulation, since it has been seen in traditional development economics to be such a *general* force towards economic growth.

The three worst performers in the low-income category in terms of growth rate are, respectively, Uganda with *minus* 0.7%, Sudan with *minus* 0.2%, and Mozambique with *minus* 0.1%. In terms of capital accumulation, Uganda's rank is also the worst there, with only 3% of GDP invested. Mozambique is the second lowest investor, and Sudan the fifth lowest.

What about growth failures in the middle-income countries? The worst performers in terms of growth rate are Ghana with *minus* 1%, Peru with 1.1%, and Chile with 1.6%. As it happens these countries are also respectively the lowest, the second lowest, and the third lowest accumulators of capital in the category of the middle-income countries.

So both in terms of cases of success and those of failure, the traditional wisdom of development economics is scarcely contradicted by these international comparisons. Quite the contrary.

Hans Singer (1952) in his paper entitled "The Mechanics of Economic Development," published thirty years ago, seems to be almost talking about today's worst case of growth failure in the combined category of low-income and middle-income countries, namely Ghana. Using the Harrod-Domar model with an assumed capital-output ratio, Singer argues that a country with 6% savings and a population growth rate of 1.25% will be a "stationary economy." While Ghana has managed an investment and savings ratio of just below 6% (5% to be exact) it has had a population growth between 2.4 and 3.0% during these decades as opposed to Singer's assumption of 1.25%. Rather than being stationary, Ghana has accordingly slipped back, going down at about 1% a year. The Harrod-Domar model is an oversimplification, of course, but the insight obtained from such reasoning is not altogether without merit.

I turn now to the theme of industrialisation. In the category of low-income countries, the top performers—China, Pakistan, and Sri Lanka—happen to be among the four countries with the highest share of industries in GDP. In the middle-income group, the top growers—Romania, South Korea, and Yugoslavia—are among the top five countries in terms of the share of industries in GDP.[9]

The picture at the other end, i.e. for countries with growth failures, is certainly less neat than at the top end in this case, or at either end in the case of capital accumulation. It is, however, certainly true that Uganda, which occupies the bottom position in the low-income category in terms of growth rate, also has the bottom position in terms of the share of industries, and similarly Ghana, with the lowest record of growth in the middle-income group, also has the lowest share of industries in that group. But the positions of second and third lowest are not quite so telling. In the low-income category, low-performing Sudan and Mozambique have middling industrial ratios. In the middle-income group, the second-lowest growth performer, Peru, has the third *highest* ratio of industries in that group, though the third-lowest growth performer, Chile, has a middling industrial ratio. The picture is, thus, a bit more muddled at the lower end of growth performance.[10]

Altogether, so far as growth is concerned, it is not easy to deny the importance of capital accumulation or of industrialisation in a poor preindustrial country. Turning to the thesis of underemployment and the role of labour mobilisation, there have been several powerful attempts at disestablishing the thesis of "disguised unemployment," e.g., by Theodore Schultz (1964), but they have not been altogether successful.[11] Furthermore, what is really at issue is the crucial role of labour mobilisation and use, and not whether the opportunity cost of labour is exactly zero.[12] It is worth noting, in this context, that the high-growth performers in both groups have distinguished records of labour-using economic growth, and some (e.g., China and South Korea) have quite outstanding achievements in this area. While they have very different political systems, their respective successes in labour mobilisation have been specially studied and praised.[13]

The question of planning and state activism is a field in which comparative quantitative data are particularly difficult to find. But some qualitative information is of relevance. Of the three top growing economies in the low-income group, one—China—is obviously not without an active state. While Pakistan is in no way a paradigmatic example of determined state planning, it has been frequently cited as a good example of what harm government meddling can do.[14] The third—Sri Lanka—has been recently studied a great deal precisely because of its active government intervention in a number of different fields, including health, education, and food consumption.

In the middle-income group, of the three top performers, Romania and Yugoslavia clearly do have a good deal of planning. The third—South Korea—has had an economic system in which the market mechanism has been driven hard by an active government in a planned way. Trying to interpret the South Korean economic experience as a triumph of unguided market mechanism, as is sometimes done, is not easy to sustain. I have discussed this question elsewhere,[15] and I shall not spend any time on it here. I should only add that, aside from having a powerful influence over the direction of investment through control of financial institutions (including nationalised banks), the government of South Korea fostered an export-oriented growth on the secure foundations of more than a decade of intensive import substitution, based on trade restrictions, to build up an industrial base. Imports of a great many items are still prohibited or restricted. The pattern of South Korean economic expansion has been carefully planned by a powerful government. If this is a free market, then Walras's auctioneer can surely be seen as going around with a government white paper in one hand and a whip in the other.

The point is not so much that the government is powerful in the high-growth developing countries. It is powerful in nearly *every* developing country. The issue concerns the systematic involvement of the state in the *economic* sphere, and the pursuit of *planned* economic development. The carefully planned government action in, say, China or Sri Lanka or South Korea or Romania, contrast—on the whole strongly—with the economic role of the government in such countries as Uganda or Sudan or Chile or Argentina or Ghana.

This examination of the main theses of traditional development economics has been too brief and tentative, and certainly there is no question of claiming anything like definitiveness in the findings. But, in so far as anything has emerged, it has not gone in the direction of debunking traditional development economics; just the contrary.

Before I move on to develop some criticisms of my own, I should make one last defensive remark about traditional development economics. The general policy prescriptions and strategies in this tradition have to be judged in terms of the climate of opinion and the overall factual situation prevailing at the time these theories were formulated. Development economics was born at a time when government involvement in deliberately fostering economic growth in general, and industrialisation in particular, was very rare, and when the typical rates of capital accumulation were quite low. That situation has changed in many respects, and, while that may suggest the need to emphasise different issues, it does not in any way invalidate the wisdom of the strategies then suggested.

The point can be brought out with an example. In the 1952 paper of Hans Singer from which I have already quoted, one of the conclusions that Singer emphasised is the need to raise the then existing rate of saving. He argued, with some assumptions about production conditions, that to achieve even a 2% rate of per capita growth, with a population growing at 1.25% per year, "a rate of net savings of 16.25% is necessary," and that "this rate of saving is about three times the rate actually observed in underdeveloped countries" (Singer, 1952, pp. 397–8). The current average rate of saving is no longer a third of that figure, but substantially *higher* than the figure. The weighted average ratio of gross domestic saving for low-income developing countries is estimated to be about 22%, and that for middle-income developing countries about 25%; and, even after deducting for depreciation, Singer's target has certainly been exceeded. And, even with a faster growth of population than Singer anticipated, the weighted average of GDP growth rates per capita has been about 2.5% per year for low-income countries and more than 3% per year for middle-income countries over the seventies.[16]

The point of policy interest now is that, despite these *average* achievements, the performances of different countries are highly divergent. There is still much relevance in the broad policy themes which traditional development economics has emphasised. The strategies have to be adapted to the particular conditions and to national and international circumstances, but the time to bury traditional development economics has not yet arrived.

III. FAST GROWTH AND SLOW SOCIAL CHANGE

I believe the real limitations of traditional development economics arose not from the choice of means to the end of economic growth, but in the insufficient recognition that economic growth was no more than a means to some other objectives. The point is not the same as saying that growth does not matter. It may matter a great deal, but, if it does, this is because of some associated benefits that are realised in the process of economic growth.

It is important to note in this context that the same level of achievement in life expectancy, literacy, health, higher education, etc., can be seen in countries with widely varying income per capita. To take just one example, consider Brazil, Mexico, South Korea, China, and Sri Lanka.[17]

China and Sir Lanka, with less than a seventh of GNP per head in Brazil or Mexico, have similar life expectancy figures to the two richer countries (see Table 2). South Korea, with its magnificent and much-eulogised growth record, has not yet overtaken China or Sri Lanka in the field of longevity, despite being now more than five times richer in terms of per capita GNP. If the government of a poor developing country is keen to raise the level of health and the expectation of life, then it would be pretty daft to try to achieve this through raising its income per head, rather than going directly for these objectives through public policy and social change, as China and Sri Lanka have both done.

Not merely is it the case that economic growth is a means rather than an end, it is also the case that for some important ends it is not a very efficient means either. In an earlier paper (Sen, 1981b) it was shown that had Sri Lanka been a typical developing country, trying to achieve its high level of life expectancy not through direct public action, but primarily through growth (in the same way as typical developing countries do), then it would

TABLE 2

Country	Life Expectancy at Birth 1980 (Years)	GNP per Head, 1980 (US Dollars)
Brazil	63	2,050
China	64	290
Mexico	65	2,090
South Korea	65	1,520
Sri Lanka	66	270

have taken Sri Lanka—depending on assumptions—somewhere between 58 years and 152 years to get where it already now happens to be.[18] It might well be the case that "money answereth all things," but the answer certainly comes slowly.

IV.   ENTITLEMENTS AND CAPABILITIES

Perhaps the most important thematic deficiency of traditional development economics is its concentration on national product, aggregate income, and total supply of particular goods rather than on "entitlements" of people and the "capabilities" these entitlements generate. Ultimately, the process of economic development has to be concerned with what people can or cannot do, e.g., whether they can live long, escape avoidable morbidity, be well nourished, be able to read and write and communicate, take part in literary and scientific pursuits, and so forth. It has to do, in Marx's words, with "replacing the domination of circumstances and chance over individuals by the domination of individuals over chance and circumstances."[19]

Entitlement refers to the set of alternative commodity bundles that a person can command in a society using the totality of rights and opportunities that he or she faces. Entitlements are relatively simple to characterise in a pure market economy. If a person can, say, earn $200 by selling his labour power and other saleable objects he has or can produce, then his entitlements refer to the set of all commodity bundles costing no more than $200. He can buy any such bundle, but no more than that, and the limit is set by his ownership ("endowment") and his exchange possibilities ("exchange entitlement"), the two together determining his overall entitlement.[20] On the basis of this entitlement, a person can acquire some capabilities, i.e. the ability to do this or that (e.g., be well nourished), and fail to acquire some other capabilities. The process of economic development can be seen as a process of expanding the capabilities of people. Given the functional relation between entitlements of persons over goods and their capabilities, a useful—though derivative—characterisation of economic development is in terms of expansion of entitlements.[21]

For most of humanity, about the only commodity a person has to sell is labour power, so that the person's entitlements depend crucially on his or her ability to find a job, the wage rate for that job, and the prices of commodities that he or she wishes to buy. The problems of starvation, hunger, and famines in the world could be better analysed through the concept of entitlement than through the use of the traditional variables of food supply and population size. The intention here is not, of course, to argue that the supply of goods—food in this case—is irrelevant to hunger and starvation, which would be absurd, but that the supply is just one influence among many; and, in so far as supply is important, it is so precisely because it s the entitlements of the people involved, typically through prices. ultimately, we are concerned with what people can or cannot do, and this links directly with their "entitlements" rather than with overall supplies and outputs in the economy.[22]

The failure to see the importance of entitlements has been responsible for millions of people dying in famines. Famines may not be at all anticipated in situations of good or moderate overall levels of supply, but, notwithstanding that supply situation, acute starvation can hit suddenly and widely because of failures of the entitlement systems, operating through ownership and exchange. For example, in the Bangladesh famine of 1974, a very large number died in a year when food availability per head was at a peak—higher than in any other year between 1971 and 1975. The floods that affected agriculture did ultimately—much later than the famine—reduce the food output, but its first and immediate impact was on the rural labourers who lost jobs in planting and transplanting rice, and started starving long before the main crop that was affected was to be harvested. The problem was made worse by forces of inflation in the economy, reducing the purchasing power especially of rural labourers, who did not have the economic muscle to raise their money wages correspondingly.[23]

Entitlements may not operate only through market processes. In a socialist economy entitlements will depend on what the families can get from the state through the established system of command. Even in a nonsocialist economy, the existence of social security—when present—makes the entitlements go substantially beyond the operation of market forces.

A major failing of traditional development economics has been its tendency to concentrate on supply of goods rather than on ownership and entitlement. The focus on growth is only one reflection of this. Extreme concentration on the ratio of food supply to population is another example of the same defective vision.[24] Recently the focus has shifted somewhat from growth of *total incomes* to the *distribution of incomes*. This may look like a move in the right direction, and indeed it is. But I would argue that "income" itself provides an inadequate basis for analysing a person's entitlements. Income gives the means of buying things. It expresses buying power in terms of some scalar magnitude—given by one real number. Even if there are no schools in the village and no hospitals nearby, the income of the villager can still be increased by adding to his purchasing power over the goods that are available in the market. But this rise in income may not be able to deal at all adequately with his entitlement to education or medical treatment, since the rise in income as such guarantees no such thing.

In general, one real number reflecting some aggregate measure of market power can scarcely represent so complex a notion as entitlement. The power of the market force depends on relative prices and, as the price of some good rises, the hold of income on the corresponding entitlement weakens. With nonmarketability, it slips altogether. In the extreme case, the entitlement to live, say, in a malaria-free environment is not a matter of purchase with income in any significant way.

In dealing with starvation and hunger, the focus on incomes—though defective—is not entirely disastrous. And of course it is a good deal better than the focus on total food output and population size. The weighting system of real income and cost-of-living pays sufficient attention to food in a poor community to make real income a moderately good "proxy" for entitlement to food in most cases.[25] But when it comes to health, or education, or social equality, or self-respect, or freedom from social harassment, income is miles off the target.

V. POLITICAL COMPLEXITIES

To move from concentrating on growth to supplementing that with an account of income distribution is basically an inadequate response to what is at issue. It is also, in effect, an attempt to refuse to come to terms with the complexity of entitlement relations. The metric of income, as already discussed, is much too crude. Indeed, entitlements related even to purely economic matters, e.g., that to food, may actually require us to go beyond the narrow limits of economics altogether.

Take the case of famine relief. A hungry, destitute person will be *entitled* to some free food *if* there is a relief system offering that. Whether, in fact, a starving person will have such an entitlement will depend on whether such a public relief operation will actually be launched. The provision of public relief is partly a matter of political and social pressure. Food is, as it were, "purchased" in this context not with income but with political pressure. The Irish in the 1840s did not have the necessary political power. Nor did the Bengalis in the Great Bengal Famine of 1943. Nor the Ethiopians in Wollo in the famine of 1973. On the other hand, there are plenty of examples in the world in which timely public policy has averted an oncoming famine completely.

The operation of political forces affecting entitlements is far from simple. For example, with the present political system in India, it is almost impossible for a famine to take place. The pressure of newspapers and diverse political parties makes it imperative for the government in power to organise swift relief. It has to act to retain credibility. No matter how and where famine threatens—whether with a flood or a drought, whether in Bihar in 1967–8, in Maharashtra in 1971–3, or in West Bengal in 1978—an obligatory policy response prevents the famine from actually occurring.

On the other hand, there is no such relief for the third of the Indian rural population who go to bed hungry every night and who lead a life ravaged by regular deprivation. The quiet presence of nonacute, endemic hunger leads to no newspaper turmoil, no political agitation, no riots in the Indian parliament. The system takes it in its stride.[26]

The position in China is almost exactly the opposite of this. On the one hand, the political commitment of the system ensures a general concern with eradicating regular malnutrition and hunger through more equal access to means of livelihood, and through entitlements vis-à-vis the state; and China's achievements in this respect have been quite remarkable. In a normal year, the Chinese poor are much better fed than the Indian poor. The expectation of life in China is between 66 and 69 years in comparison with India's miserable 52 years. On the other hand, if there is a political and economic crisis that confuses the regime and makes it pursue disastrous policies with confident dogmatism, then it cannot be forced to change its policies by crusading newspapers or by effective pressure from opposing political groups.

It is, in fact, now quite clear that in China during 1959–61 there were deaths on a very large scale due to famine conditions. The extent of the disaster has only recently become evident, even though there are still many uncertainties regarding the exact estimation of extra mortality.[27] Important mortality data were released in 1980 by Professor Zhu Zhengzhi of Beijing University,[28] indicating that the death rate rose from about 10.8 per thousand in 1957 to an average of 16.58 per thousand per year during 1958–61. This yields a figure of extra mortality of 14–16 million in China in the famine-affected years—a very large figure indeed. It is, in fact, very much larger than the extra mortality (calculated in the same way) even in the Great Bengal Famine of 1943 (namely about 3 million[29]), the largest famine in India in this century.

In 1981 the noted economist Sun Yefang released some further mortality data,[30] referring to "the high price in blood" of the economic policy pursued at that time. He reported that the death rate per thousand had risen to as high as 25.4 in 1960, indicating an extra mortality of 9 million in that year alone. His figures for the four years also yield a total of around 15 million extra deaths during the Chinese famine of 1959–61.[31] Others have suggested even higher mortality.[32]

These are truly staggering figures. Even if we take a level quite a bit below the lower limit of the estimates, the sudden extra mortality caused by the famine[33] would still be on a scale that is difficult to match even in preindependent India (and there has of course been no famine in India since independence).

Is it purely accidental that a famine—indeed one on an enormous scale—could take place in China while none has occurred in postindependent India? The contrast is particularly odd when viewed in the context of the undoubted fact that China has been very much more successful than India in eliminating regular malnutrition. There may well be an accidental element in the comparative records on famines, but as already noted, on a number of occasions potentially large famines have been prevented in India through quick, extensive, and decisive government intervention. Reports on deaths from hunger reach the government and the public quickly and dramatically through active newspapers, and are taken up vigorously by parties not in power. Faced with a threatening famine, any government wishing to stay in office in India is forced to abandon or modify its ongoing economic policy, and meet the situation with swift public action, e.g., redistribution of food within the country, imports from abroad, and widespread relief arrangements (including food for work programs).

Policy failures in China during the famine years (and the Great Leap Forward period), which have been much discussed in China only recently, relate not merely to factors that dramatically reduced output, but also to distributional issues, e.g., interregional balances, and the draconian procurement policy that was apparently pursued relentlessly despite lower agricultural output.[34] Whatever the particular policy errors, the government in power was not forced to reexamine them, nor required to face harrowing newspaper reports and troublesome opposition parties. The contrast may not, therefore, be purely accidental.

In an interesting and important speech given in 1962—just after the famine—Chairman Mao made the following remarks to a conference of 7,000 cadres from different levels: "If there is no democracy, if ideas are not coming from the masses, it is impossible to establish a good line, good general and specific policies and methods. . . . Without democracy, you have no understanding of what is happening down below; the situation will be unclear; you will be unable to collect sufficient opinions from all sides; there can be no communication between top and bottom; top-level organs of leadership will depend on one-sided and incorrect material to decide issues, thus you will find it difficult to avoid being subjectivist; it will be impossible to achieve unity of understanding and unity of action, and impossible to achieve true centralism."[35] Ralph Miliband (1977), who has provided an illuminating and far-reaching analysis of the issue of democracy in capitalist and socialist societies from a Marxist perspective, points out that Mao's "argument for 'democracy' is primarily a 'functional' one" (pp. 149–50), and argues that this is an inadequate basis for understanding the need for "socialist democracy."[36] That more general question certainly does remain, but it is worth emphasising that even the purely "functional" role of democracy can be very crucial to matters of life and death, as the Chinese experiences of the famine of 1959–61 bring out.[37]

Finally, it is important to note that the protection that the Indian poor get from the active news distribution system and powerful opposition parties has very severe limits. The deprivation has to be dramatic to be "newsworthy" and politically exploitable (see Sen, 1982c). The Indian political system may prevent famines but, unlike the Chinese system, it seems unable to deal effectively with endemic malnutrition. In a normal year when things are running smoothly both in India and China, the Indian poor is in a much more deprived general state than his or her Chinese counter-part.[38]

VI.   CONCLUDING REMARKS

I shall not try to summarise the main points of the paper, but I will make a few concluding remarks to put the discussion in perspective.

First, traditional development economics has not been particularly unsuccessful in identifying the factors that lead to economic growth in developing countries. In the field of causation of growth, there is much life left in traditional analyses (Section II).

Secondly, traditional development economics has been less successful in characterising economic development, which involves expansion of people's capabilities. For this, economic growth is only a means and often not a very efficient means either (Section III).

Thirdly, because of close links between entitlements and capabilities, focusing on entitlements—what commodity bundles a person can command—provides a helpful format for characterising economic development. Supplementing data on GNP per capita by income distributional information is quite inadequate to meet the challenge of development analysis (Section IV).

Fourthly, famines and starvation can be more sensibly analysed in terms of entitlement failures than in terms of the usual approach focusing on food output per unit of population. A famine can easily occur even in a good food supply situation, through the collapse of entitlements of particular classes or occupation groups (Section IV).

Fifthly, a study of entitlements has to go beyond purely economic factors and take into account political arrangements (including pressure groups and news distribution systems) that affect people's actual ability to command commodities, including food. These influences may be very complex and may also involve apparently perplexing contrasts, e.g., between (1) India's better record than China's in avoiding famines, and (2) India's total failure to deal with endemic malnutrition and morbidity in the way China has been able to do (Section V). Whether the disparate advantages of the contrasting systems can be effectively combined is a challenging issue of political economy that requires attention. Much is at stake.

NOTES

1. Essay 1 in Hirschman (1981).
2. Hirschman (1981), p. 23.
3. Bauer (1971). See also Schultz (1964) and Bauer (1981). For a forceful critical account without breaking from traditional development economics, see Little (1982).

4. Hirschman (1981), pp. 10–11.
5. See Rosenstein-Rodan (1943), Mandelbaum (1945), Dobb (1951), Datta (1952), Singer (1952), Nurkse (1953), and Lewis (1954, 1955).
6. See particularly Hirschman (1958, 1970).
7. For the conceptual framework underlying the distinction, see Hirschman (1977).
8. See, for example, Streeten (1981). See also Grant (1978), Morris (1979), and Streeten et al. (1981).
9. An additional one in this case is South Africa, and its industrial share is high mainly because mining is included in that figure. In fact, if we look only at manufacturing, South Africa falls below the others.
10. The rank correlation coefficient between per capita growth and the share of gross domestic investment in GDP is 0.72 for middle-income countries, 0.75 for low-income countries, and 0.82 for the two groups put together. On the other hand, the rank correlation coefficient between per capita growth and the share of industries is only 0.22 for middle-income countries, even though it is 0.59 for the low-income countries and 0.68 for the two groups put together.
11. My own views on this are presented in Sen (1975). See also Sen (1967), and the exchange with Schultz following that in the same number of [Economic Journal].
12. See Marglin (1976), chapter 2. Also Sen (1975), chapters 4 and 6. See also Fei and Ranis (1964).
13. See Little (1982). See also the important study of Ishikawa (1981), which discusses the empirical role of labour absorption in different Asian economies.
14. For example, Little et al. (1971).
15. Sen (1981b), and the literature cited there, especially Datta-Chaudhuri (1979).
16. See tables 2, 5, and 17 of the *World Development Report 1982*.
17. Taken from *World Development Report 1982*, table 1. The 1982 Chinese census indicates a higher expectation of life—around 69 years. The Sri Lankan figure of 66 years relates to 1971, and the current life expectancy is probably significantly higher.
18. See Sen (1981b), pp. 303–6. See also Jayawardena (1974), Marga Institute (1974), Isenman (1978), Alailima (1982), Gwatkin (1979).
19. Marx and Engels (1846); English translation taken from McLellan (1977), p. 190.
20. The notion of "entitlements" is explored in Sen (1981a). It is worth emphasizing here, to avoid misunderstandings that seem to have occurred in some discussions of the concept, that (1) "exchange entitlement" is only a *part* of the entitlement picture and is incomplete without an account of ownership or endowment, and (2) "exchange entitlement" includes not merely trade and market exchange but also the use of production possibilities (i.e., "exchange with nature").
21. Capabilities, entitlements, and utilities differ from each other. I have tried to argue elsewhere that "capabilities" provide the right basis for judging the advantages of a person in many problems of evaluation—a role that cannot be taken over either by utility or by an index of commodities (Sen, 1982a, pp. 29–38, 353–69). When we are concerned with such notions as the well-being of a person, or standard of living, or freedom in the positive sense, we need the concept of capabilities. We have to be concerned with what a person can do, and this is not the same thing as how much pleasure or desire fulfilment he gets from these activities ("utility"), nor what commodity bundles he can command

("entitlements"). Ultimately, therefore, we have to go not merely beyond the calculus of national product and aggregate real income, but also that of entitlements over commodity bundles viewed on their own. The focus on capabilities differs also from concentration on the mental metric of utilities, and this contrast is similar to the general one between pleasure, on the one hand, and positive freedom, on the other. The particular role of entitlements is *through* its effects on capabilities. It is a role that has substantial and far-reaching importance, but it remains derivative on capabilities. On these general issues, see Sen (1982a, d, 1983) and Kynch and Sen (1983).

22. See Sen (1981a, b), Arrow (1982), Desai (1983).

23. See Sen (1981a), chapter 9. Other examples of famines due to entitlement failure without a significant—indeed any—reduction of overall food availability can be found in chapter 6 (the Great Bengal Famine of 1943) and chapter 7 (the Ethiopian famine of 1973–4); see also chapter 7 (the Sahelian famines of the 1970s). On related matters, see also Sen (1976, 1977), Ghose (1979), Alamgir (1978, 1980), Chattopadhyay (1981), Oughton (1982), Ravallion (1983). See also Parikh and Rabar (1981) and Srinivasan (1982). Also the special number of *Development*, Aziz (1982).

24. On this and related issues, see Aziz (1975), Taylor (1975), Griffin (1978), Sinha and Drabek (1978), Spitz (1978), Lappé and Collins (1979), George and Paige (1982), Rao (1982).

25. However, the index of real income will continue to differ from the index of food entitlement since the price deflators will not be the same, though the two will often move together. A problem of a different sort arises from *intra*-family differences in food consumption (e.g., through 'sex bias'), as a result of which both the real income and the food entitlement of the family may be rather deceptive indicators of nutritional situations of particular members of the family. On this issue, see Bardhan (1974), Sen (1981c), Kynch and Sen (1983), and Sen and Sengupta (1983).

26. See Sen (1982b, c).

27. See Aird (1982), pp. 277–8.

28. Zhu Zhengzhi (1980), pp. 54–5. These data have been analysed by Coale (1981). See also Bernstein (1983b).

29. See Sen (1981a), appendix D. In both cases the death rate immediately preceding the famine-affected year is taken as the bench mark in comparison with which the "extra" mortality in famine-affected years are calculated.

30. Sun Yefang (1981) and People's Republic of China (1981).

31. See Bernstein (1983a, b).

32. See Bernstein's (1983b) account of the literature. See also Aird (1980). For a description of the intensity of the famine in a particular commune (the Liyuan Commune in Anhui province), see Research Group of the Fen Yang County Communist Party Committee (1983). "The commune's population of 5,730 people in 1957 had dropped to 2,870 people in 1961. More than half died of starvation [e si] or fled the area. . . . In 1955, the Houwang production team was a model elementary cooperative. The village had twenty-eight families, a total of 154 people. . . . fifty-nine people starved to death [e si], and the survivors fled the area" (p. 36).

33. The number of deaths due to a famine must not be confused with the number actually dying of starvation, since most people who die in a famine tend to die from other causes (particularly from diseases endemic in the region) to which they become more susceptible due to undernutrition, and also due to break-down of sanitary arrangements, exposure due to wandering, eating noneatables, and other developments associated with famines. See Sen (1981a), pp. 203–16.
34. See Bernstein (1983b), who also argues that the harsh procurement policies in China did not have the ideologically "anti-peasant" character that similar poli-cies in the USSR did during 1932–3, but reflected "erroneous" reading of the level of output and of the economic situation.
35. Mao Zedong (1974), p. 164.
36. Miliband goes on to argue: "Much may be claimed for the Chinese experience. But what cannot be claimed for it, on the evidence, is that it has really begun to create the institutional basis for the kind of socialist democracy that would effectively reduce the distance between those who determine policy and those on whose behalf it is determined" (p. 151).
37. The Soviet famines of the 1930s and the Kampuchean famine of more recent years provide further evidence of penalties of this lacuna.
38. The crude death rate in China in 1980 was reported to be 8 per thousand in con-trast with India's 14 (*World Development Report 1982*, table 18, p. 144). Only in famine situations did the reported death rate in China (e.g., 25.4 reported in 1960) exceed that in India.

REFERENCES

Aird, J. "Reconstruction of an Official Data Model of the Population of China." U.S. Department of Commerce, Bureau of Census, May 15, 1980.

———. "Population Studies and Population Policy in China." *Population and Development Review*, 8 (1982): 267–297.

Alailima, P. J. "National Policies and Programmes of Social Development in Sri Lanka." Mimeographed, Colombo.

Alamgir, M. *Bangladesh: A Case of Below Poverty Level Equilibrium Trap.* Dhaka: Bangladesh Institute of Development Studies, 1978.

———. *Famine in South Asia—Political Economy of Mass Starvation in Bangladesh.* Cambridge, Mass.: Oelgeschlager, Gunn and Hain, 1980.

Arrow, K. J. "Why People Go Hungry." *New York Review of Books*, 299 (July 15, 1982): 24–26.

Aziz, S. (ed.). *Hunger, Politics and Markets: The Real Issues in the Food Crisis.* New York: NYU Press, 1975.

———. (ed.). "The Fight against World Hunger." Special number of *Development*, 1982, p 4.

Baran, P. A. *Political Economy of Growth.* New York: Monthly Review Press, 1957.

Bardhan, P. "On Life and Death Questions." *Economic and Political Weekly*, 9 (1974): 1293–1304.

Bauer, P. *Dissent on Development.* London: Weidenfeld and Nicolson, 1971.

———. *Equality, the Third World, and Economic Delusion.* Cambridge, Mass: Harvard University Press, 1981.

Bernstein, T. P. "Starving to Death in China." *New York Review of Books*, 30 (June 6, 1983a): 36–38.

———. "Hunger and the State: Grain Procurements During the Great Leap Forward; with a Soviet Perspective." Mimeographed, East Asia Center, Columbia University.

Chattopadhyay, B. "Notes towards an Understanding of the Bengal Famine of 1943." *Cressida*, 1 (1981).

Coale, A. J. "Population Trends, Population Policy, and Population Studies in China." *Population and Development Review*, 7 (1981): 85–97.

Datta, B. *Economics of Industrialization*. Calcutta: World Press, 1952.

Datta-Chaudhuri, M. K. "Industrialization and Foreign Trade: An Analysis Based on the Development Experience of the Republic of Korea and the Philippines." ILO Working Paper WP II-4, ARTEP, ILO, Bangkok, 1979.

Desai, M. J. "A General Theory of Poverty." Mimeographed, London School of Economics, 1983. To be published in *Indian Economic Review*.

Dobb, M. H. *Some Aspects of Economic Development*. Delhi: Delhi School of Economics, 1951.

———. *An Essay on Economic Growth and Planning*. London: Routledge, 1960.

Fei, J. C. H., and Ranis, G. *Development of the Labour Surplus Economy: Theory and Practice*. Homewood, Ill.: Irwin, 1964.

George, S. and Paige, N. *Food for Beginners*. London: Writers and Readers Publishing Cooperative, 1982.

Ghose, A. "Short Term Changes in Income Distribution in Poor Agrarian Economies." ILO Working Paper WEP 10-6/WP 28, Geneva, 1979.

Grant, J. *Disparity Reduction Rates in Social Indicators*, Washington, D.C.: Overseas Development Council, 1978.

Griffin, K. *International Inequality and National Poverty*. London: Macmillan, 1978.

Gwatkin, D. R. "Food Policy, Nutrition Planning and Survival: The Cases of Kerala and Sri Lanka." *Food Policy*, November 1979.

Hirschman, A. O. *The Strategy of Economic Development*. New Haven, Conn.: Yale University Press, 1958.

———. *Exit, Voice, and Loyalty*. Cambridge, Mass.: Harvard University Press, 1970.

———. *The Passions and the Interests*. Princeton: Princeton University Press, 1977.

———. *Essays in Trespassing: Economics to Politics and Beyond*. New York and Cambridge, England: Cambridge University Press, 1981.

Isenman, P. "The Relationship of Basic Needs to Growth, Income Distribution and Employment—The Case of Sri Lanka." Mimeographed, World Bank, 1978.

Ishikawa, T. *Essays on Technology, Employment and Institutions in Economic Development*. Tokyo: Kinokuniya, 1981.

Jayawardena, L. "Sri Lanka." In *Redistribution with Growth*, H. Chenery et al. (eds.). London: Oxford University Press, 1974.

Kynch, J., and Sen, A. K. "Indian Women: Survival and Well-Being." Mimeographed, 1983. To be published in *Cambridge Journal of Economics*.

Lappé, F. M., and Collins, J. *Food First: Beyond the Myth of Scarcity*. New York: Ballantine Books, 1979.

Lewis, W. A. "Economic Development with Unlimited Supplies of Labour." *Manchester School* (1954): 139–191.

————. *The Theory of Economic Growth.* Homewood, Ill.: Irwin, 1955.

Little, I. M. D. *Economic Development: Theory, Policy and International Relations.* New York: Basic Books, 1982.

————. T. Scitovsky, and Scott, M. *Industry and Trade in Some Developing Countries.* London: Oxford University Press, 1971.

McLellan, D. (ed.). *Karl Marx: Selected Writings.* Oxford: Oxford University Press, 1977.

Mandelbaum (Martin), K. *The Industrialization of Backward Areas.* Oxford: Blackwell, 1945.

Mao Tse-tung (Zedong). *Mao Tse-tung Unrehearsed, Talks and Letters: 1956–71,* S. R. Schram (ed.). London: Penguin Books, 1974.

Marga Institute. *Welfare and Growth in Sri Lanka.* Colombo: Marga Institute, 1974.

Marglin, S. A. *Value and Price in the Labour Surplus Economy.* Oxford: Clarendon Press, 1976.

Marx, K., and Engels, F. *The German Ideology.* New York: International Publishers, (1846). 1947.

Miliband, R. *Marxism and Politics.* London: Oxford University Press, 1977.

Morris, M. D. *Measuring the Condition of the World's Poor: The Physical Quality of Life Index.* Oxford: Pergamon Press, 1979.

Nurkse, R. *Problems of Capital Formation in Underdeveloped Countries.* Oxford: Blackwell, 1953.

Oughton, E. "The Maharashtra Drought of 1970–73: An Analysis of Scarcity." *Oxford Bulletin of Economics and Statistics,* (1982): 169–197.

Parikh, K., and Rabar, F. (eds.). *Food for All in a Sustainable World.* Laxenburg: IIASA, 1981.

People's Republic of China. *Foreign Broadcast Information Service,* no. 58, March 26, 1981.

Rao, V. K. R. V. *Food, Nutrition and Poverty in India.* Brighton: Wheatsheaf Books, 1982.

Ravallion, M. *The Performance of Rice Markets in Bangladesh During the 1974 Famine.* Mimeographed, University of Oxford, 1983.

Research Group of the Feng Yang County Communist Party Committee. "An Investigation into the Household Production Contract System in Liyuan Commune." *New York Review of Books,* 30, 16 (June 1982): 36–38. Translated from *Nongye Jingji Congkan* (Collected Material on Agricultural Economics), November 25, 1980.

Rosenstein-Rodan, P. "Problems of Industrialization in Eastern and Southeastern Europe." *Economic Journal,* 53 (1943): 202–211.

Schultz, T. W. *Transforming Traditional Agriculture.* New Haven, Conn.: Yale University Press, 1964.

Sen, A. K. "Surplus Labour in India: A Critique of Schultz's Statistical Test." *Economic Journal,* 77 (1967): 154–161.

————. *Employment, Technology and Development.* Oxford: Clarendon Press, 1975.

————. "Famines as Failures of Exchange Entitlement." *Economic and Political Weekly,* 11 (1976): 1273–1280.

————. "Starvation and Exchange Entitlement: A General Approach and Its

Application to the Great Bengal Famine." *Cambridge Journal of Economics,* 1 (1977): 33–59.

———. *Poverty and Famines: An Essay on Entitlement and Deprivation.* Oxford: Clarendon Press, 1981a.

———. "Public Action and the Quality of Life in Developing Countries." *Oxford Bulletin of Economics and Statistics,* 43 (1981b): 287–319.

———. "Family and Food: Sex Bias in Poverty." Mimeographed, Oxford Institute of Economics and Statistics, (1981c). To be published in *Rural Poverty in South Asia,* P. Bardhan and T. N. Srinivasan (eds.).

———. *Choice, Welfare and Measurement.* Oxford: Blackwell; and Cambridge, Mass.: MIT Press, 1982a.

———. "Food Battles: Conflict in the Access to Food." Coromandel Lecture, December 13, 1982. Reprinted in *Mainstream,* January 8, 1983.

———. "How Is India Doing?" *New York Review of Books,* 29 (Christmas Number, (1982c): 41–45.

———. *Commodities and Capabilities.* Hennipman Lecture, April 1982. Amsterdam and New York: North-Holland, 1985.

———. "Poor, Relatively Speaking." *Oxford Economic Papers,* 35 (1983) 153–169.

———, and S. Sengupta. "Malnutrition of Rural Children and the Sex-Bias." *Economic and Political Weekly,* 18 (1983).

Singer, H. W. "The Mechanics of Economic Development." *Indian Economic Review,* 1952. Reprinted in *The Economics of Underdevelopment,* A. N. Agarwala and A. P. Singh (eds.), London: Oxford University Press, 1958.

Sinha, R., and Drabek, A. G. (eds.). *The World Food Problem: Consensus and Conflict.* Oxford: Pergamon Press, 1978.

Spitz, P. "Silent Violence: Famine and Inequality." *International Social Science Journal,* 30 (1978).

Srinivasan, T. N. "Hunger: Defining It, Estimating Its Global Incidence and Alleviating It." Mimeographed, 1982. To be published in *The Role of Markets in the World Food Economy,* D. Gale Johnson and E. Schuh (eds.).

Streeten, P. *Development Perspectives.* London: Macmillan, 1981.

———, with S. J. Burki, Mahbub ul Haq, N. Hicks, and F. Stewart. *First Things First: Meeting Basic Needs in Developing Countries.* New York: Oxford University Press, 1981.

Sun Yefang. Article in *Jingji Guanli* (Economic Management), no. 2 (February 15, 1981). English translation in People's Republic of China, 1981.

Taylor, L. "The Misconstrued Crisis: Lester Brown and World Food." *World Development,* 3 (1975): 827–837.

Zhu Zhengzhi. Article in *Jingji Kexue,* no. 3, 1980.

2

The Misconceptions of "Development Economics"

Deepak Lal

Ideas have consequences. The body of thought that has evolved since World War II and is called "development economics" (to be distinguished from the orthodox "economics of developing countries") has, for good or ill, shaped policies for, as well as beliefs about, economic development in the Third World. Viewing the interwar experience of the world economy as evidence of the intellectual deficiencies of conventional economics (embodied, for instance, in the tradition of Marshall, Pigou, and Robertson) and seeking to emulate Keynes' iconoclasm (and hopefully renown), numerous economists set to work in the 1950s to devise a new unorthodox economics particularly suited to developing countries (most prominently, Nurkse, Myrdal, Rosenstein-Rodan, Balogh, Prebisch, and Singer). In the subsequent decades numerous specific theories and panaceas for solving the economic problems of the Third World have come to form the corpus of a "development economics." These include: the dual economy, labor surplus, low level equilibrium trap, unbalanced growth, vicious circles of poverty, big push industrialization, foreign exchange bottlenecks, unequal exchange, "dependencia," redistribution with growth, and a basic needs strategy—to name just the most influential in various times and climes.

Those who sought a new economics claimed that orthodox economics was (1) unrealistic because of its behavioral, technological, and institutional assumptions and (2) irrelevant because it was concerned primarily with the efficient allocation of given resources, and hence could deal neither with so-called dynamic aspects of growth nor with various ethical aspects of the alleviation of poverty or the distribution of income. The twists and turns that the unorthodox theories have subsequently taken may be traced in four major areas: (1) the role of foreign trade and official or private capital flows in promoting economic development; (2) the role and appropriate form of

From *Finance and Development*, 22 (June 1985), pp. 10–13.

industrialization in developing countries; (3) the relationship between the reduction of inequality, the alleviation of poverty, and the so-called different "strategies of development"; and (4) the role of the price mechanism in promoting development.

The last is, in fact, the major debate that in a sense subsumes most of the rest, and it is the main concern of this article; for the major thrust of much of "development economics" has been to justify massive government intervention through forms of direct control usually intended to supplant rather than to improve the functioning of, or supplement, the price mechanism. This is what I label the *dirigiste dogma*, which supports forms and areas of *dirigisme* well beyond those justifiable on orthodox economic grounds.

The empirical assumptions on which this unwarranted *dirigisme* was based have been repudiated by the experience of numerous countries in the postwar period. This article briefly reviews these central misconceptions of "development economics." References to the evidence as well as an elucidation of the arguments underlying the analysis (together with various qualifications) can be found in A. O. Hirschman's *Essays in Trespassing* (Cambridge, 1981).

DENIAL OF "ECONOMIC PRINCIPLE"

The most basic misconception underlying much of development economics has been a rejection (to varying extents) of the behavioral assumption that, either as producers or consumers, people, as Hicks said, "would act *economically;* when the opportunity of an advantage was presented to them, they would take it." Against these supposedly myopic and ignorant private agents (that is, individuals or groups of people), development economists have set some official entity (such as government, planners, or policymakers) which is both knowledgeable and compassionate. It can overcome the defects of private agents and compel them to raise their living standards through various *dirigiste* means.

Numerous empirical studies from different cultures and climates, however, show that uneducated private agents—be they peasants, rural-urban migrants, urban workers, private entrepreneurs, or housewives—act economically as producers and consumers. They respond to changes in relative prices much as neoclassical theory would predict. The "economic principle" is not unrealistic in the Third World; poor people may, in fact, be pushed even harder to seek their advantage than rich people.

Nor are the preferences of Third World workers peculiar in that for them too (no matter how poor), the cost of "sweat" rises the harder and longer they work. They do not have such peculiar preferences that when they become richer they will not also seek to increase their "leisure"—an assumption that underlies the view that there are large pools of surplus labor in developing countries that can be employed at a low or zero social opportunity cost. They are unlikely to be in "surplus" in any meaningful sense any more than their Western counterparts.

Nor are the institutional features of the Third World, such as their strange social and agrarian structures or their seemingly usurious informal credit systems, necessarily a handicap to growth. Recent applications of neoclassical theory show how, instead of inhibiting efficiency, these institutions—being second best adaptations to the risks and uncertainties inherent in the relevant economic environment—are likely to enhance efficiency.

Finally, the neoclassical assumption about the possibilities of substituting different inputs in production has not been found unrealistic. The degree to which inputs of different factors and commodities can be substituted in the national product is not much different in developed or developing countries. Changes in relative factor prices do influence the choice of technology at the micro level and the overall labor intensity of production in Third World economies.

MARKET VS. BUREAUCRATIC FAILURE

A second and major strand of the unwarranted *dirigisme* of much of development economics has been based on the intellectually valid arguments against laissez-faire. As is well known, laissez-faire will only provide optimal outcomes if perfect competition prevails; if there are universal markets for trading all commodities (including future "contingent" commodities, that is, commodities defined by future conditions, such as the impact of weather on energy prices); and if the distribution of income generated by the laissez-faire economy is considered equitable or, if not, could be made so through lump-sum taxes and subsidies. As elementary economics shows, the existence of externalities in production and consumption and increasing returns to scale in production, or either of them, will rule out the existence of a perfectly competitive utopia. While, clearly, universal markets for *all* (including contingent) commodities do not exist in the real world, to that extent market failure must be ubiquitous in the real world. This, even ignoring distributional considerations, provides a prima facie case for government intervention. But this in itself does not imply that any or most forms of government intervention will improve the outcomes of a necessarily imperfect market economy.

For the basic cause of market failure is the difficulty in establishing markets in commodities because of the costs of making transactions. These transaction costs are present in any market, or indeed any mode of resource allocation, and include the costs of excluding nonbuyers as well as those of acquiring and transmitting the relevant information about the demand and supply of a particular commodity to market participants. They drive a wedge, in effect, between the buyer's and the seller's price. The market for a particular good will cease to exist if the wedge is so large as to push the lowest price at which anyone is willing to sell above the highest price anyone is willing to pay. These transaction costs, however, are also involved in acquiring, processing, and transmitting the relevant information to design public policies, as well as in enforcing compliance. There may, consequently, be as many instances of bureaucratic as of market failure, making it impossible to attain a full welfare optimum. Hence, the best that can be expected in the real world of imperfect markets and imperfect bureaucrats is a second best. But judging between alternative second best outcomes involves a subtle application of second-best welfare economics, which provides no general rule to permit the deduction that, in a necessarily imperfect market economy, particular *dirigiste* policies will increase economic welfare. They may not; and they may even be worse than laissez-faire.

FORETELLING THE FUTURE

Behind most arguments for *dirigisme,* particularly those based on directly controlling quantities of goods demanded and supplied, is the implicit premise of an omniscient central authority. The authority must also be omnipotent (to prevent people from taking actions that controvert its diktat) and benevolent (to ensure it serves the common weal rather than its own), if it is to necessarily improve on the working of an imperfect market economy. While most people are willing to question the omnipotence or benevolence of governments, there is a considerable temptation to believe the latter have an omniscience that private agents know they themselves lack. This temptation is particularly large when it comes to foretelling the future.

Productive investment is the mainspring of growth. Nearly all investment involves giving hostages to fortune. Most investments yield their fruits over time and the expectations of investors at the time of investment may not be fulfilled. Planners attempting to direct investments and outputs have to take a view about future changes in prices, tastes, resources, and technology, much like private individuals. Even if the planners can acquire the necessary information about current tastes, technology, and resources in designing an investment program, they must also take a view about likely changes in the future demand and supply of myriad goods. Because in an uncertain world there can be no agreed or objective way of deciding whether a particular investment gamble is sounder than another, the planned outcomes will be better than those of a market system (in the sense of lower excess demand for or supply of different goods and services) only if the planners' forecasts are more accurate than the decentralized forecasts made by individual decision makers in a market economy. There is no reason to believe that planners, lacking perfect foresight, will be more successful at foretelling the future than individual investors.

Outcomes based on centralized forecasts may, indeed, turn out to be worse than those based on the decentralized forecasts of a large number of participants in a market economy, because imposing a single centralized forecast on the economy in an uncertain world is like putting all eggs in one basket. By contrast, the multitude of small bets, based on different forecasts, placed by a large number of decision makers in a market economy *may be* a sounder strategy. Also, bureaucrats, as opposed to private agents, are likely to take less care in placing their bets, as they do not stand to lose financially when they are wrong. This assumes, of course, that the government does not have better information about the future than private agents. If it does, it should obviously disseminate it, together with any of its own forecasts. On the whole, however, it may be best to leave private decision makers to take risks according to their own judgments.

This conclusion is strengthened by the fact, emphasized by Hayek, that most relevant information is likely to be held at the level of the individual firm and the household. A major role of the price mechanism in a market economy is to transmit this information to all interested parties. The "planning without prices" favored in practice by some planners attempts to supersede and suppress the price mechanism. It thereby throws sand into one of the most useful and relatively low-cost social mechanisms for transmitting information, as well as for coordinating the actions of large numbers of interdependent market participants. The strongest argument against centralized planning, therefore, is that, even though omniscient planners might forecast the future more accurately than myopic private agents, there is no reason to believe that ordinary government officials can do any better—and some reason to believe they may do much worse.

It has nevertheless been maintained that planners in the Third World can and should directly control the pattern of industrialization. Some have put their faith in mathematical programming models based on the use of input-output tables developed by Leontief. But, partly for the reasons just discussed, little reliance can be placed upon either the realism or the usefulness of these models for deciding which industries will be losers and which will be winners in the future. There are many important and essential tasks for governments to perform (see below), and this irrational *dirigisme* detracts from their main effort.

REDRESSING INEQUALITY AND POVERTY

Finally, egalitarianism is never far from the surface in most arguments supporting the *dirigiste dogma*. This is not surprising since there may be good theoretical reasons for government intervention, even in a perfectly functioning market economy, in order to promote a distribution of income desired on ethical grounds. Since the distribution resulting from market processes will depend upon the initial distribution of assets (land, capital, skills, and labor) of individuals and households, the desired distribution could, in principle, be attained either by redistributing the assets or by introducing lump-sum taxes and subsidies to achieve the desired result. If, however, lump-sum taxes and subsidies cannot be used in practice, the costs of distortion from using other fiscal devices (such as the income tax, which distorts the individual's choice between income and leisure) will have to be set against the benefits from any gain in equity. This is as much as theory can tell us, and it is fairly uncontroversial.

Problems arise because we lack a consensus about the ethical system for judging the desirability of a particular distribution of income. Even within Western ethical beliefs, the shallow utilitarianism that underlies many economists' views about the "just" distribution of income and assets is not universally accepted. The possibility that all the variegated peoples of the world are utilitarians is fairly remote. Yet the moral fervor underlying many economic prescriptions assumes there is already a world society with a common set of ethical beliefs that technical economists can take for granted and use to make judgments encompassing both the efficiency and equity components of economic welfare. But casual empiricism is enough to show that there is no such world society; nor is there a common view, shared by mankind, about the content of social justice.

There is, therefore, likely to be little agreement about either the content of distributive justice or whether we should seek to achieve it through some form of coercive redistribution of incomes and assets when this would infringe other moral ends, which are equally valued. By contrast, most moral codes accept the view that, to the extent feasible, it is desirable to alleviate abject, absolute poverty or destitution. That alleviating poverty is not synonymous with reducing the inequality of income, as some seem still to believe, can be seen by considering a country with the following two options. The first option leads to a rise in the incomes of all groups, including the poor, but to larger relative increases for the rich, and hence a worsening of the distribution of income. The second leads to no income growth for the poor but to a reduction in the income of the rich; thus the distribution of income improves but the extent of poverty remains unchanged. Those concerned with inequality would favor the second option; those with poverty the first. Thus, while the pursuit of efficient growth may worsen some inequality index, there is no evidence that it will increase poverty.

SURPLUS LABOR AND "TRICKLE DOWN"

As the major asset of the poor in most developing (as well as developed) countries is their labor time, increasing the demand for unskilled labor relative to its supply could be expected to be the major means of reducing poverty in the Third World. However, the shadows of Malthus and Marx have haunted development economics, particularly in its discussion of equity and the alleviation of poverty. One of the major assertions of development economics, preoccupied with "vicious circles" of poverty, was that the fruits of capitalist growth, with its reliance on the price mechanism, would not trickle down or spread to the poor. Various *dirigiste* arguments were then advocated to bring the poor into a growth process that would otherwise bypass them. The most influential, as well as the most famous, of the models of development advanced in the 1950s to chart the likely course of outputs and incomes in an overpopulated country or region was that of Sir Arthur Lewis. It made an assumption of surplus labor that, in a capitalist growth process, entailed no increase in the income of laborers until the surplus had been absorbed.

It has been shown that the assumptions required for even underemployed rural laborers to be "surplus," in Lewis' sense of their being available to industry at a constant wage, are very stringent, and implausible. It was necessary to assume that, with the departure to the towns of their relatives, those rural workers who remained would work harder for an unchanged wage. This implied that the preferences of rural workers between leisure and income are perverse, for workers will not usually work harder without being offered a higher wage. Recent empirical research into the shape of the supply curve of rural labor at different wages has found that—at least for India, the country supposedly containing vast pools of surplus labor—the curve is upward-sloping (and not flat, as the surplus labor theory presupposes). Thus, for a given labor supply, increases in the demand for labor time, in both the industrial and the rural sectors, can be satisfied only by paying higher wages.

The fruits of growth, even in India, will therefore trickle down, in the sense either of raising labor incomes, whenever the demand for labor time increases by more than its supply, or of preventing the fall in real wages and thus labor incomes, which would otherwise occur if the supply of labor time outstripped the increase in demand for it. More direct evidence about movements in the rural and industrial real wages of unskilled labor in developing countries for which data are available has shown that the standard economic presumption that real wages will rise as the demand for labor grows, relative to its supply, is as valid for the Third World as for the First.

ADMINISTRATIVE CAPACITIES

It is in the political and administrative aspects of *dirigisme* that powerful practical arguments can be advanced against the *dirigiste dogma*. The political and administrative assumptions underlying the feasibility of various forms of *dirigisme* derive from those of modern welfare states in the West. These, in turn, reflect the values of the eighteenth-century Enlightenment. It has taken nearly two centuries of political evolution for those values to be internalized and reflected (however imperfectly) in the political and administrative institutions of Western societies. In the Third World, an acceptance of the same values is at best confined to a small class of Westernized intellectuals. Despite their trappings of modernity, many developing countries are closer in their official workings to the inefficient nation states of seventeenth- or eighteenth-century Europe. It is instructive to recall that Keynes, whom so many *dirigistes* invoke as a founding father of their faith, noted in *The End of Laissez-Faire:*

> But above all, the ineptitude of public administrators strongly prejudiced the practical man in favor of *laissez-faire*—a sentiment which has by no means disappeared. Almost everything which the State did in the 18th century in excess of its minimum functions was, or seemed, injurious or unsuccessful.

It is in this context that anyone familiar with the actual administration and implementation of policies in many Third World countries, and not blinkered by the *dirigiste dogma*, should find the oft-neglected work, *The Wealth of Nations,* both so relevant and so modern.

For in most of our modern-day equivalents of the inefficient eighteenth-century state, not even the minimum governmental functions required for economic progress are always fulfilled. These include above all providing public goods of which law and order and a sound money remain paramount, and an economic environment where individual thrift, productivity, and enterprise is cherished and not thwarted. There are numerous essential tasks for *all* governments to perform. One of the most important is to establish and maintain the country's infrastructure, much of which requires large, indivisible lumps of capital before any output can be produced. Since the services provided also frequently have the characteristics of public goods, natural monopolies would emerge if they were privately produced. Some form of government regulation would be required to ensure that services were provided in adequate quantities at prices that reflected their real resource costs. Government intervention is therefore necessary. And, given the costs of regulation in terms of acquiring the relevant information, it may be second best to supply the infrastructure services publicly.

These factors justify one of the most important roles for government in the development process. It can be argued that the very large increase in infrastructure investment, coupled with higher savings rates, provides the major explanation of the marked expansion in the economic growth rates of most Third World countries during the postwar period, compared with both their own previous performance and that of today's developed countries during their emergence from underdevelopment.

Yet the *dirigistes* have been urging many additional tasks on Third World governments that go well beyond what Keynes, in the work quoted above, considered to be a sensible agenda for *mid-twentieth-century* Western polities:

> the most important *Agenda* of the State relate not to those activities which private individuals are already fulfilling, but to those functions which fall outside the sphere of the individual, to those decisions which are made by no one if the State does not make them. The important thing for governments is not to do things which individuals are doing already, and to do them a little better or a little worse; but to do those things which at present are not done at all.

From the experience of a large number of developing countries in the postwar period, it would be a fair professional judgment that most of the more serious distortions are due not to the inherent imperfections of the market mechanism but to irrational government interventions, of which foreign trade controls, industrial licensing, various forms of price controls, and means of inflationary financing of fiscal deficits are the most important. In seeking to improve upon the outcomes of an imperfect market economy, the *dirigisme* to which numerous development economists have lent intellectual support has led to policy-induced distortions that are more serious than, and indeed compound, the supposed distortions of the market economy they were designed to cure. It is these lessons from accumulated experience over the last three decades that have undermined development economics, so that its demise may now be conducive to the health of both the economics and economies of developing countries.

3

Conventional Foolishness and Overall Ignorance: Current Approaches to Global Transformation and Development

G. K. Helleiner
University of Toronto

INTRODUCTION

As I sat down to prepare some notes for this occasion, I began to realize that it is a far easier matter to give the summary paper at the end of a conference than it is to give a so-called keynote address at its beginning. At the end of a meeting, one is invariably stimulated by new ideas, newly aware of inter-connections between old ones, and there are always lots of fresh papers and outrageous discussants' remarks from which one can draw quotations. A keynote speaker has particular problems when he is not altogether clear as to the precise meaning of the prescribed conference theme; and they become even greater if, upon running through the conference program, he discovers only limited overlap between the topics of the papers and the announced overall theme. I am therefore going to take what some of you will probably see as excessive liberties with my assignment.

Although some think we have come quite a long way, I believe that historians are likely to be impressed more by our continuing foolishness and ignorance than by our progress during the Post-Second-War period. Foolishness and ignorance are no doubt quite evenly spread among our

Text of the keynote address to the Fourth Annual Conference of the Canadian Association for the Study of International Development given at the University of Windsor, June 7, 1988. From *Canadian Journal of Development Studies*, 10, 1 (1990), pp. 107–120.

various disciplines; but I have a comparative advantage in those of economics. Moreover, most influential, if not necessarily most helpful, in recent policymaking and writing on development in recent decades, most people think, have been those in my own profession of economics. I therefore shall concentrate my fire upon economics. I hope that colleagues in other disciplines may be encouraged to undertake parallel curmudgeonly activities in their own areas of comparative expertise.

I want to speak, then, of some currently conventional approaches in development economics and policymaking, and the frequent foolishness or ignorance that underlies them. I am not sure whether what I am about to say truly constitutes a keynote address, as billed in the program. Let me, in any case, tell you what I intend to do. That way, those who are unhappy with all or parts of my program can more effectively plan their departure. In the first half of my remarks, I intend to deliver myself of some general blasts about some current problems of "structural adjustment." These may be seen as very unconventional to some, but are, by now, fairly conventional for me and, I know, for some of my friends here. I shall include in this section a plea for greater terminological clarity concerning the major subject of our deliberations here. These comments probably amount, more or less, to what was expected of me. The second half of my time will be devoted to personal ruminations about some longer-term development issues which are newer to me. They include a reconsideration of our most fundamental measuring-sticks in development studies, and the relevance of recent experiences and new perceptions to some very old measurement and development debates. On these matters, again, I shall be appealing primarily to the economists and statisticians among us; but I hope that others who are often much affected by what economists are thinking or doing in developing countries may also find these reflections interesting, if only as further evidence of the limitations of the economics profession.

I. IMMEDIATE ISSUES: STRUCTURAL ADJUSTMENT

The announced theme for this conference is *"Global* transformation and Development." The program's list of papers, however, suggests that, to the extent that the papers relate to the theme at all, authors are primarily concerned with *national* "restructuring" or "structural adjustment"—which certainly sounds a lot less ambitious.

International aid and financial communities are also abuzz with discussions of developing countries' "adjustment" at the national level. That is reason enough for independent academics to try to shed light on these issues. Evidently, the "restructuring" and "structural adjustment" now being discussed is *not* the same as the "structural change" that development analysts of my generation spoke so much of in the 1950s and 1960s. What we had in mind in discussion of this sometimes somewhat fuzzy concept related to the production structure, institutions, and other prerequisites of sustained economic growth. Industrialization and/or the deployment of more productive technology were seen as central to structural change and what Kuznets called "modern economic growth" (1966).

Is there today an agreed meaning of "structural adjustment" in the developing countries? I know what I mean by it. My meaning relates purely to external balance of payments problems and the necessity of restructuring production toward exports and import substitutes in response to a worsening prospect of external imbalance. Is that what the U.S. government or the World Bank typically mean? I am afraid not. When they use the term they have in mind across-the-board economic "liberalization" in the sense of an increased role for markets and a reduced role for the state, and increased external "openness," both to trade and to capital flows and other inputs. They thereby introduce further highly controversial and political elements to policy debates that originated purely in short- to medium-term balance of payments crisis. The developing countries originated the logic of "growth-oriented adjustment" to solve balance of payments and debt difficulties, long before U.S. Treasury Secretary James Baker, and thereafter everyone else, began to speak of it in late 1985. But when they spoke of the need for growth, they, unlike Baker and the World Bank, attached no controversial excess "liberalization" baggage to it. No doubt some of the authors of the national restructuring or adjustment papers for this conference use these terms in ways that accord neither with my balance of payments–oriented version nor with the Washington market-oriented version.

Still more would view conflict on conceptions of the "*global* transformation" of our conference title. Does it relate to the distribution of global assets, income, and power? to Brundtland style environmental and sustainability objectives? to UNIDO objectives for the relocation of global industrial activity? to the implications of the massive technical innovations in bioengineering, electronics, transport, and information systems, among others? to the sexual revolution, still hardly started at the global level? Each of these have been by themselves subject enough for many conferences.

I cannot refrain from the comment that, at the level of global transformation, I can see no greater current foolishness than that of conventional governmental approaches to the Third World's debt crisis. Human suffering is prolonged and the restoration of normal growth processes delayed by continuing official resistance to forgiving a penny of Paris Club debt (official debt incurred primarily in connection with our export promotion) or assisting in the conversion to more appropriate levels and terms of the Third World's commercial debt. It is not true that writing down the debt will do appreciable harm to the international financial system *or* that it will put an end to future financial flows to developing countries *or* that everything will turn out for the best if governments simply stand aside and wait for matters to resolve themselves. On the contrary, resolute intergovernmental action to deal with the terribly damaging "overhang" of Third

World debt would do *far* more for human welfare—both in rich countries and in poor—than the bilateral trade agreements that currently so preoccupy our leaders. If all goes according to plan, according to the best estimates of the Economic Council of Canada, the U.S.-Canadian free trade agreement will raise Canadian GNP by 2½% by 1998 (Economic Council, 1988). What a devastating reflection on our provincialism and myopia is this figure, and the intensity of governmental efforts and public debate about the agreement, when set beside the enormity of the Third World's debt crisis, and its implications, not least for Canada itself.

Most of the papers at this conference, as I have said, however, appear to relate to *national* "adjustment" or "restructuring" issues. Let us seek terminological clarity at least at that level. If we cannot agree as to a common usage of the "structural adjustment" terminology in our analyses—and, frankly, I think we ought to try hard, at least in scientific discourse, to do so—let us all agree, in our discussions here, to begin by defining our terms. Only then can we be sure, in what has become a very confused and heated debate, what it is we are agreeing or disagreeing about.

Conventional Washington advice notwithstanding, there is room for considerable political and professional disagreement on such matters as:

1. The basic objectives of development including such "political" and "ideological" matters as the role of the state and income distribution
2. The efficacy of alternative strategies and policy instruments in securing overall growth and development
3. The appropriate pace and sequencing of policy reforms, and, in particular, their technical and political sustainability

Needless to say, there is also room for argument concerning the appropriate degree of external intrusion into matters of domestic policy.

The World Bank, the principal repository of today's conventional wisdom in development strategy, states its primary emphasis as follows:

1. Mobilization of domestic resources through fiscal, monetary, and credit policies (including interest rates)
2. Improving efficiency of allocation and resource use in the public sector (including rationalization and divestiture of public enterprises)
3. Trade regime reforms
4. Other pricing reforms
5. "Institutional reforms supportive of adjustment with growth" (Michalopolous, 1987, p. 39)

In the short run, this translates into monetary and fiscal orthodoxy, appropriate real exchange rates, positive real interest rates, and liberal approaches on external account. As far as longer-term development strategy is concerned, the Bank urges: export expansion and eventual overall outward orientation, in the capital as well as current account; the liberalization of import barriers and an approach toward unified import incentives; and maximum reliance upon markets rather than government ownership or direction in the domestic economy. The prime emphasis is on price incentives and "getting the prices right," and the underlying presumption is that, even in a world of pervasive imperfections, markets can normally be trusted to achieve that objective better than governments. Even in the world of the second-best, its approach is consistently to liberalize that which can be liberalized.

My own foremost instinct is to resist generalizations as to the nature of desirable change at the national, regional, community, or even family level. In a policy environment such as that which today pervades the capitals of the Western world, this is not nearly as trite a proposition as it may sound. Nor, in a world of intensified donor conditionality and financially desperate Third World governments is it as innocuous in its implications as it may appear. A struggle is necessary today to allow a variety of developmental approaches and aspirations. The only weapon with which we can fight effectively is hard evidence that challenges the simplistic nostrums of the fundamentalists of economic, political, and other doctrines.

I thus see foolishness in overideological approaches to the resolution of the growth difficulties of Latin American and African countries, suggesting that reduction of the role of government and raising that of the magical marketplace will achieve what decades of previous effort have not. Mercifully, the peaks of that kind of foolishness have now probably been passed, with the retreat perhaps sped by its new association not only, as before, with "voodoo economics" but also with astrology.

Those who have dominated recent decision making in Washington also argue that the credibility and therefore the sustainability of policy reform, especially in other people's countries, is enhanced by strong action at the outset. Smaller, more gradual, changes are likely, in this view, to be easily rolled back and indicate a lack of governmental commitment. This is *still* the conventional Washington wisdom of developing country adjustment.

It can obviously equally be argued that targets and policy changes that are modest, but firm and realistic, are likely to be more credible and sustainable than large changes that are, to a degree, "leaps into the unknown." Attempts at "forced marches" toward large-scale policy change surely strain governmental capacity and strengthen the impression, dangerous in local politics, that the policy program is externally imposed rather than internally generated.

Washington ambitions for the Bank in respect of the *breadth* of coverage of their recommended policy package are no less controversial. It is difficult to disagree with the assessment by Feinberg (1986), recently quoted with approval by Mahmadou Touré of Senegal: "A long list of requirements either holds an entire programme hostage to a secondary issue or is open to highly subjective assessment" (Touré, 1987; p. 505). Moreover, when one Bank mission after another descends with detailed piecemeal recommendations upon a country (Ghana has been receiving over forty such missions per year recently), there is bound to be a certain amount of confusion, inconsistency, and, of course, recipient annoyance. The borrowing government's absorptive capacity for external advice is limited, maintenance of a domestic consensus on policy change is difficult, and it is almost certainly counterproductive to "overload the political circuits" (Sachs, 1987, p. 294).

Let me address some of the specifics of the issues in dispute.

A.   Distribution and Poverty Objectives

In the new emphasis on improved policies for overall efficiency, purveyors of the conventional wisdom have noticeably downgraded their previous concern for equity and the alleviation of poverty. The high social costs of global slowdown and the availability of alternative policies for overcoming some of them have now been demonstrated (Cornia et al., 1987). Only recently, however, has more than lip service been paid in Washington to the social impact of adjustment programs, and even now serious policy attention to these issues is limited to a relatively few countries. Difficulties in agreeing upon appropriate approaches and finding reliable data can explain some of the failures in this area; but, if there had been more will, more progress would undoubtedly have been made. At a minimum, the distributional implications of agreed programs should be understood. It has even been persuasively argued that at least one of the reasons why Korea, Taiwan, and Japan could be so effective in the efficiency-oriented restructuring that led them into their successful industrial export experience was that they had *previously* achieved reasonable equity in income distribution through major land reforms and other measures (Sachs, 1987, pp. 299–302 and 321–2).

B.   Prices, Markets, and Government

The World Bank and IMF are committed by their articles of agreement to liberal, market-oriented approaches to international economic affairs. Direct controls over foreign exchange earnings and expenditures are explicitly forbidden by the IMF except in stipulated circumstances (which include authorization for capital controls), and the World Bank is mandated to encourage and rely upon private capital flows to the maximum degree possible. Appropriate pricing—particularly in respect of the exchange rate—and incentives for individual and corporate enterprise are important elements in development policy. But there are other important elements as well. Both the IMF and the Bank were created to overcome "market failures," and their very existence is testimony to the postwar founding states' recognition of the important role to be played by government in pursuit of universally agreed social goals. It is therefore somewhat surprising to find these institutions emphasizing the universal virtues of the market in the developing countries to the degree to which they have recently done. The role of the state in development processes *has* at times been oversold and governments *have* frequently been overambitious and/or incompetent. But the "market fundamentalism" of much of Washington's recent advice cannot have been based upon a sophisticated understanding of political and economic requirements for development, or experience in varieties of "successful" countries.

There can certainly be wide agreement that governments should be selective in their activities and, where possible, more efficient. Divestment of public enterprises is undoubtedly appropriate in many cases; as a universal prescription, however, it is of dubious merit. Market imperfections and failures, distributional and "noneconomic" objectives, and political pressures of various kinds will continue to generate significant government interventions in developing countries' economies. The political and economic efficacy of markets and governments varies across countries and in individual countries over time. The complexities in this realm are dramatically illustrated by the fact that two articles were recently published, within months of one another, in leading U.S. journals, presenting econometric findings that were diametrically opposed: one showed that the size of government in GNP was associated with more rapid growth (Ram, 1986), the other that it was associated with slower growth (Landau, 1986). Policy generalizations based on ideologically rooted "priors" can only be viewed with skepticism.

The very meaning of the term "liberalization" can be ambiguous. It may refer either to "getting prices right" or to reduction in the degree of governmental intervention; the two are not synonymous, since the former may be achieved, as to some degree in Korea, with an activist state no less than via greater laissez-faire. "Liberalization" of either kind is possible, and may be appropriate in a variety of different spheres.

C.   Import Liberalization

The debate over the appropriate nature, degree, and timing of *trade* liberalization is probably the most active. World Bank missions typically recommend the earliest and fullest possible import liberalization, beginning with the replacement of quantitative import restrictions by tariffs, thereby creating both government revenue and greater transparency of incentives, and thereafter reduction in the levels and dispersion of tariffs. Gradualist approaches have generally been favoured by the more pragmatically oriented in the liberal camp and many have noted the importance of favourable macroeconomic conditions (capital inflow, terms of trade, weather, etc.) in the timing of successful major policy changes. The World Bank itself has recently argued:

> The more ambitious and long-lasting liberalizations—in Portugal, Greece, Spain, Israel, Chile and Turkey—all started with macroeconomic stabilization. The countries which have tried to liberalize trade in the midst of macroeconomic crisis have failed . . . (World Bank, *WDR*, 1987, p. 109).

The link between export expansion and import liberalization is also important, and one that remains controversial. Advocates of "shock" treatment for the trade regime—as well as other reforms—are at present in the ascendancy in Washington. A leading World Bank economist recently put the case:

> Experience . . . suggests that future reforms ensure that export expansion programs be accompanied by import liberalization. . . . Experience . . . does *not* in our view suggest that import liberalization should be undertaken only after export reforms have increased the supply of foreign exchange (Michalopoulos, 1987, p. 45).

But this is a difficult case to make in terms of empirical evidence. The "lessons" from East Asian experience in respect of the transition from stabilization to liberalization, if they are transferable at all, are, to the contrary, the following:

1. There is likely to be a long time interval between stabilization and successful exporting or liberalization effort
2. Substantial external financial assistance is likely to be an essential element in successful transition
3. Import liberalization is likely to follow successful exporting with a fairly long time lag, and is *not* an essential or typical part of successful export promotion efforts
4. The public sector is likely to play an important role in the shift into successful industrial exporting (Sachs, 1987, pp. 303–10)

Beyond eventual—not necessarily immediate—"tarification" of quantitative restrictions, on which most can agree, further efforts toward "liberalization" and laissez-faire are considerably more controversial. There exist respectable orthodox arguments for nonuniform incentive structures as "second-best" policies for a "second-best" world. Modern trade theory has knocked the struts from under the conventional arguments for the uniformity of treatment that free trade achieves. Krugman has recently put a new and more theoretically sophisticated case for liberal (or free) trade. Abandoning the traditional comparative advantage arguments based upon the assumption of efficient markets, he posits instead a world in which the sophisticated trade (and other) interventions, for which "the new trade theories" call, are likely to be extremely informationally demanding, difficult to implement, low in their returns, and subject to hijacking by special interests. *Simple* policy rules, he argues, are best "in a world whose politics are as imperfect as its markets" (1987, p. 143). This stands previously conventional approaches on their head. Whereas political influences used to be blamed for the inability of governments to pursue "rational" free trade policies, now political factors are deployed to defend free trade policies against the new, economic arguments for sophisticated intervention. But his advocacy of simple policy rules would permit lots of alternatives short of overall free trade, including, say, across-the-board industrial protection, a strictly limited number of further infant industry subsidies, and across-the-board incentives for nontraditional exports.

D.   Export Expansion

No one quarrels with the aspiration of expanding exports from foreign exchange constrained economies. The prospect of all of the developing countries simultaneously expanding export volume in similar products, whether primary or manufactured, however, must raise some concerns. Primary product prices are likely to suffer and protectionist barriers to manufactures to increase in consequence of concerted efforts at export growth. Even Bhagwati, among the most enthusiastic and influential of trade liberalizers, although he believes modern "export pessimism" to be unjustified, acknowledges that the international economic environment may be an important determinant of the efficacy of outward-oriented policies (1987, pp. 260 and 269–83).

The keys to successful expansion of exports are realistic exchange rates and sustained governmental support, not import liberalization and laissez-faire. It is noteworthy that the export promotion policies of Korea were successfully undertaken by a thoroughly *dirigiste* government simultaneously employing tight import controls and a tightly regulated capital market. "The Asian experience . . . suggest(s) . . . that successful development might be helped as much by raising the quality of public sector management as by privatizing public enterprises or liberalizing markets" (Sachs, 1987, p. 294).

The efficacy of export subsidies as an important weapon of trade policy also emerges as an important area for debate. Granting the greater administrative ease of currency devaluation for the purpose of rectifying anti-export bias, there may nonetheless be an important case for targeted/selective export subsidies for infant industry export promotion. Such selective export promotion was an important element in Korean penetration of overseas markets for its manufactured exports (Westphal, 1981). WIDER research on alternative stabilization programs has also noted the efficacy of targeted export subsidies as an important short-term stabilization policy instrument (Taylor, 1987).

E.   Openness to External Private Capital

Controls over external private portfolio capital flows—whether inward or outward—are fairly universally seen as desirable in low-income countries. Experimentation with financial openness in the Southern Cone of Latin America had generally unhappy consequences. Policies toward direct foreign investment remain, however, a matter of some controversy. Increased incentives and receptivity to foreign investors (including the much-touted "debt-equity swaps") may simply generate quasi-rent for them if, as much of the recent evidence suggests, their investment decisions are based primarily on more fundamental and long-run factors (Moran, 1986). In recent years direct investment in developing countries, which was always highly concentrated in the same countries that attracted commercial bank lending, dropped just as far and as fast as that lending; and it is unlikely to resume until the overall economic outlook in these countries improves. Quite apart from the sensitivities of many countries regarding foreign ownership and control of domestic industries, and however desirable increased equity or equity-like finance might be, the elasticity of response by direct foreign investors to improved investment incentives in developing countries is, for the present, likely to be low.

F.   Financial Liberalization and Interest Rates

The role of interest rates in developing countries remains controversial. Increased real rates may improve the allocative efficiency of investment, reduce capital flight, and even attract savings from abroad in economies with relatively developed financial markets. The IMF's own research department concludes, however, that "despite the amount of research expended on the interest responsiveness of savings in general, and in developing countries in particular, it is still uncertain whether an increase in interest rates will, on balance, raise the savings rate" (Khan and Knight, 1985, p. 14).

Differences in behavioural responses in this sphere appear to be linked in a predictable fashion to the stage of financial development of different areas or countries. Because of capital market imperfections (severe constraints on liquidity and borrowing by private firms and individuals), private consumption and savings do not respond as much to real interest rate changes in low-income countries as in higher-income ones. A recent IMF study's results imply that "the effective mobilization of domestic savings through changes in savings incentives is likely to require changes in the real interest rates, which, given the existing constraints, may prove unfeasible, especially in low-income developing countries" (Rossi, 1988, p. 126).

There also remains some uncertainty as to the implications of segmented and imperfect capital markets. Conventional analysis has often assumed away the extensive network of informal (or curb) credit markets. Yet careful modelling of real/financial interactions in Korea, allowing for the distinction between "curb" and regulated financial markets there, generated "unconventional" results from orthodox monetary and interest rate policies: higher (regulated) interest rates and monetary restraint led, in combination, to a serious slowdown in investment and growth, the effects of which exceeded any positive effects for household savings (Van Wijnbergen, 1983).

Nor are the advantages of financial liberalization for overcoming "financial repression" unambiguously favourable. Painful experience with overenthusiastic financial liberalization in the Southern Cone has bred a new respect for governmental supervision and control of the domestic financial system, and caution in respect of external capital market "opening" (Diaz-Alejandro, 1985).

II.   LONGER-TERM ISSUES: MEASUREMENT AND SUSTAINABILITY

Let me use the rest of my time to address some longer-term issues in development economics, and development studies more generally, that have recently been emerging or *re*emerging in policy discussions.

The first is one to which that late and great curmudgeon in development economics, Dudley Seers, directed major attention in the late 1960s and early 1970s: "What," he asked in 1972, "are we trying to measure?" His question, following earlier reflections on the meaning of "development," related to overall measures of economic development, and it was part of an effort that some described at the time as "dethroning GNP" (Seers, 1969, 1972). Twenty years later, I am not sure that there has been a satisfactory answer. And yet the 1980s have brought terrible new urgency to the basic question he asked.

Seers' main concern was with the proper consideration of poverty, unemployment, and equality in the measurement of overall development. Subsequent thinking generated suggestions for different ways of calculating overall economic growth rates—allowing equal weight for the income growth of each individual (instead of recording each extra dollar of total income as equal, regardless of who earns or receives it, as current GNP estimation procedures require), or even introducing "poverty weights" so as to assign higher weight to increases in the income of those at the bottom end of the income distribution than to those of the more fortunate at higher levels. These suggested alterations of estimating procedures were, in my judgment, good ideas. With the reduced fashion for distributional concern in the major industrialised countries in the 1980s, they have been more or less forgotten. But they remain good ideas. The renewed interest and debate in the latter half of the 1980s over the poverty and distributional implications of stabilization and adjustment programs—"adjustment with a human face"—provides an opportunity for their resurrection. The Ghanaian economy is said to be growing again; yet the suffering of the poorest and most vulnerable continues, and donors construct a PAMSCAD ("Program to Mitigate the Social Consequences of Adjustment"). And the poverty impact of the recession of the early 1980s, continued balance of payments and debt crises in subsequent years, and declining net international resource transfers (negative 6–7% of GDP in Latin America in recent years) is only now being fully understood. I therefore suggest a conscious effort, once again, to introduce distributional components into our commonest measures of economic performance, both at the national and the global level. (At the global level, the relatively good performance of poor and populous China and India may make global poverty-sensitive aggregate performance indicators for the 1980s look *better* than many think.)

The treatment of poverty and income distribution is important, but it is not the only aggregative measurement problem. And many others, of course, have addressed these and other measurement issues. The UN Research Institute for Social Development, for instance, developed a whole set of socioeconomic indicators of development in the 1960s (UNRISD, 1970). Adelman and Morris (1967) also made early efforts to incorporate noneconomic variables into overall measures of development. Another Morris fixed on only three indicators—infant mortality, literacy, and life expectancy—and proclaimed his "physical quality of life" (PQLI) index (1978), which was effectively popularised by Washington's Overseas Development Council. And these few references barely scratch the surface of the relevant literature. (Baster, 1972, is a good reference to the early literature on development indicators.)

On one aspect of the development question the social scientists most concerned with the measurement of development have, until very recently, had *very* little to say. And the time has come for them to say a little more. It has been left to physical scientists, environmentalists, and ecologists to worry about "sustainability." The Brundtland Commission Report and other events have forced many more of us to devote attention to this hitherto relatively neglected dimension of development. Before Brundtland, increasing concern was expressed in many quarters about the longer-run implications of short-term survival strategies in ecologically fragile parts of the developing world, notably in drought-prone Africa. The short-term cutbacks necessitated by the trauma of the 1980s in most of sub-Saharan Africa and Latin America intensified these concerns. What would be the longer-run consequences of failure to maintain current social infrastructure—roads, buildings, schools, hospitals, etc.—not to speak of directly productive capital stock? And, even more frightening, what would be the longer-run consequence of failure to provide minimal nutrition for pregnant women and children in their crucial early years? Brundtland's concern for the environment expands these questions to the infinitely broader realm of planetary equilibrium.

That any of these "sustainability" issues should be seen as "new" to measurement-minded social scientists is, on the face of it, very odd. In the first place, those who specialize in national income accounting describe their favourite summary indicator as *Gross* National Product for a reason. The GNP is, conceptually, a measure that abstracts from longer-run consequences of current economic activities in that those who estimate it *consciously* do *not* deduct the costs of maintaining the current physical capital stock, let alone the human capital stock. *No* account is taken, that is to say, of "depreciation." No self-respecting private company or homeowner would draw conclusions as to successful performance without taking depreciation into account. Indeed our tax laws frequently invite us to err on the conservative side when doing so. Why do we not then take depreciation into account and record the *net* national product in our growth statistics and international comparisons? The conventional and simple answer is that it is far too difficult. It is worth noting that the same answer is usually offered whenever questions are asked about improved measurement of the distribution of income within nations, the same nations that routinely measure their GNP on a quarterly basis.

There can be little doubt that the data on depreciation *are* at present very weak. To generate such data would, certainly, in our present state of knowledge, require large numbers of fairly arbitrary assumptions. But anyone with more than superficial knowledge of the methodology of national income accounting knows that such assumptions and conventions abound already. Thirty years ago Kuznets asked, for instance, whether it would not be better to *deduct* such expenditures as commuter transport, police services, and national defence from the national product (gross or net) rather than adding them in. (Among other places he discusses such arbitrary choices in measurement in his masterful *Modern Economic Growth*, pp. 20–26). The treatment of household services and a host of other arbitrarily treated items also continue to delight first year economics students around the world. In the early 1950s, the first national income estimates for Nigeria attempted to recognize some purported elements of its culture by estimating the annual number of marriages, multiplying them by the average bride price, and adding the product to the GNP—thereby treating women, for GNP purposes, as consumer durables (Prest and Stewart, 1953). Surely the question must be, again, "what are we trying to measure?"

Secondly, and probably ultimately more important, how we measure development, and, particularly, in the current context, how we treat depreciation, is profoundly based upon our value judgments. Our conventional GNP measure reduces all goods and services to a common money numeraire, established by using market prices (or the nearest possible equivalent). But relative prices are themselves highly variable across countries and over time; and they are also dependent, in part, on government policy. In the discussions over the appropriate treatment of distributional considerations it is generally recognized that prices will themselves alter when income distribution changes; a more equitable distribution will raise the relative price of food and lower that of Cadillacs, other things being equal in the short to medium term. The employment of market prices thus carries with it the implicit value judgment not only that prices are appropriate measures of social "value," but also that the current distribution of income is acceptable, both fairly strong and arbitrary assumptions.

Our twentieth-century market-oriented materialist culture is obviously not the only conceivable way in which human beings may organize themselves or pursue their own welfare. Some social scientists—evidently not usually economists—have repeatedly called attention to these value differences over the years. In the traditional culture of many North American native peoples, for instance, there is a conception of man-in-nature and the need for "sustainability" which appears fundamentally at variance with traditional economistic approaches. Land and resources, in some cultures, are to be left in the state in which they are found. The interests of future generations—of the rest of nature as well as of humanity—are to be respected as a matter of *highest* priority. It is not therefore possible to rationalize the "mining" of the environment via an interest rate at which the interests of future generations are discounted to the present. In effect, the *first* claim upon current income is the need to make up for depreciation. (More about the interest rate below.)

It seems to me that our new concern for "sustainability" requires that we look again at the measurement of depreciation and net national product (and net capital formation) (Bartelmus, 1987). If reputable scientists believe that we are now running down our assets—polluting the water and atmosphere, using up nonrenewable resources, reducing forest cover to a degree that engenders soil erosion and desertification—we should surely be accounting for it in our measures of developmental performance. It seems particularly perverse to record as extra income (gross) the expenditures on the inputs we devote to trying to offset some of these effects, as our current conventions require us to do. When depreciation is fully accounted for—and deducted from our gross measures of production—we are likely to find ourselves, if I read the Brundtland Commission correctly, doing much less well than we thought, particularly so in many of the developing countries. The high measured growth rates of the 1960s may have been, to a significant degree, illusory and the current setbacks in sub-Saharan Africa and Latin America are probably much more serious than previously thought.

Our new knowledge of the longer-run implications of nutritional deficiency will, I am afraid, generate even more depressing conclusions. When we *both* treat depreciation appropriately *and* take better account of the distribution of net income gains, we are likely to find the developing world, overall, to have been barely holding its own in the best cases, and moving significantly backward in all too many others. Quite possibly, we shall be seen to be moving backward at the global level as well.

The world's apparent new concern for sustainability and the environment raises further questions for traditional techniques of economic analysis, particularly development project analysis. The context in which development economists previously commonly encountered the notion of "sustainable" economic growth, ironically, was in that of traditional IMF programs. Conservative fiscal and monetary policies are the only ones, the IMF usually intones, that are "sustainable." The government of Peru in recent years, for instance, over IMF opposition, expanded demand (and reduced its external debt service payments), thereby immediately achieving rapid growth in employment and income. But few expected these gains to last. "Sustainability" is a central element in IMF objectives for the member countries it advises.

"Sustainability" *is* basically a conservative concept. And environmentalists, like the IMF, have long been seen by policymakers and thinkers in the developing countries as too cautious and insensitive to human development imperatives. Developmentalists and politicians, in developing countries, have often been prepared to take more risks. And rationales have been constructed for the realization of such gains as can be realised in the short run, much more generally, on the view that the long run is, after all, only a series of short runs. If the World Bank now adds environmental objectives and sustainability to its list of conditions on its loans, will this necessarily be good for human welfare in the short run in the developing countries?

An interesting paper in a recent issue of *World Development* notes that economists, in particular, have devoted relatively little attention to "sustainability." They are inherently suspicious of absolute objectives—specializing as they do in the logic of trade-offs. In particular, their benefit-cost methodology does not offer any premium for policies or projects that provide a "sustainable" income as opposed to those creating high income in the early years and less thereafter. "Economic principles tend to suggest that the 'mining,' depletion, or elimination of living resources is justifiable from an economic point of view and that unsustainable productive activities may be economically rational" (Tisdell, 1988, p. 381). The reason for this is that economic methodology assesses the value of contributions to future income (whether positive or negative) by discounting them to the present at some agreed (national) interest rate that is intended to represent the "social rate of discount." There has been no shortage of discussions of the selection of an appropriate rate for discounting the future. Yet, though it is crucially important to economic decision making, we do not have a good "fix" on what it should be in different times and places. (In practice, development agencies frequently just lick a finger, hold it to the wind, and declare it to be 10%.)

At a discount (interest) rate of 10%, the present value of a dollar's worth of costs incurred thirty years from now is less than 6¢. Who will act in anticipation of effects thirty years hence when they use such a calculus of benefits and costs? Who will worry about effects that are sixty years away? And how many years does it take to obtain returns from the crucial environmental investments upon which the future viability may depend? When investments at last appear profitable will it already be too late? These are matters of development policy with which the World Bank, newly concerned, and the research community have scarcely begun to wrestle. (See Leslie, 1987, for a forester's perspective on these issues.)

In a world increasingly concerned with the longer-term consequences of current decisions and with the possibility of "irreversibilities" and "threshold effects" in the environment, this methodology—with its implied discounting of the future at rates that are in dispute but are nowhere seen as zero—may be, at least for some purposes, profoundly wrong. Societies making their decisions on the basis of maintaining resources for their children in the same form in which they were received, and implicitly using zero rates of discounting the future, however "economically irrational," may be those that survive. It is noteworthy that Marxist economic practices have traditionally been ridiculed because of their inability to factor in this cost of capital, or "waiting," in their project analysis. Indeed so have early Christian and Islamic doctrines.

The ethics of intergenerational transfer are even more dubious than the economics of intertemporal comparisons. As the Brundtland Commission puts it, there may be "profits on the balance sheets of our generation, but our children will inherit the losses. We borrow environmental capital from future generations with no intention or prospect of repaying. . . . We act as we do because we can get away with it; future generations do not vote; they have no political or financial power; they cannot challenge our decisions" (p. 8). Rawls also noted the fundamental justice issue raised by such decisions (1971).

The author of the paper to which I referred earlier suggests that the risk of a system's collapse under stress-catastrophe must be factored into policymakers' calculations more effectively. Natural resource systems are especially prone to such irreversibilities, going well beyond the hysteresis effects, now fashionable to model in some other branches of economics, to the actual blocking of returns to previous potential equilibria. Developing countries may be ready to take greater risks in their pursuit of rapid development. On the other hand their poorest inhabitants cannot afford to take even minimal chances of unexpected losses and they and their children will bear the brunt of systemic deterioration or collapse; they may therefore be highly risk-averse. At a minimum, I believe, we need to take account of his conclusion:

> Despite continuing differences between economists and ecologists on the desirability of sustainable productive systems and the desirability of sustainable development, it would seem unwise for economists and others undertaking social cost-benefit analysis of projects for LDCs to ignore ecological considerations and spillovers. Indeed the claims in the traditional economic manuals for project evaluation in LDCs that such matters are likely to be unimportant is a serious shortcoming. The ecological consequences of many projects and developments in LDCs have been far from minor" (pp. 381–382).

CONCLUSIONS

This address has no conclusion. I have attempted to highlight some of the areas of our greatest conventional foolishness and some of our greatest areas of ignorance en route to whatever kind of global transformation and development we may be seeking. Frankly, I still see much ignorance about the key requirements for economic growth and development. Even within the context of current efforts at growth-oriented structural adjustment, we simply do not know enough about many of the issues: for instance, the implications for gender distribution of income (and therefore also for child welfare) of changing production structure (notably the shift towards export activity); the relative stability characteristics of Islamic financial systems (on the face of it, the international debt crisis would almost certainly not have arisen in an Islamic system); the potential for export expansion as the escape route for more than a handful of developing countries; the potential for a renewed socialism or other collective forms in the Third World after their many recent apparent setbacks; or the crucial requirements for technical progress.

It is for this conference to seek to generate greater wisdom and to begin to overcome at least a few of these and other areas of ignorance. Knowing so many of the participants as I do, I have every expectation that it will do both. Thank you very much for the opportunity of kicking it off in this way.

REFERENCES

Adelman, I., and Morris, C. T. *Society, Politics and Economic Development*. Baltimore: The Johns Hopkins University Press, 1967.

Bartelmus, Peter. "Accounting for Sustainable Development," Department of International Economic and Social Affairs, United Nations, Working Paper No. 8, November 1987.

Baster, Nancy (ed.). "Special Issue on Development Indicators." *Journal of Development Studies*, 8, 3 (April 1972).

Bhagwati, Jagdish. "Outward Orientation: Trade Issues." In Vittorio Corbo, Morris Goldstein, and Mohsin Khan (eds.), *Growth-Oriented Adjustment Programs*, Washington, D.C.: International Monetary Fund and World Bank, 1987.

Cornia, G. A., Richard Jolly, and Frances Stewart (eds.). *Adjustment with a Human Face*. Oxford: Clarendon Press, 1987.

Diaz-Alejandro, Carlos F. "Goodbye Financial Repression, Hello Financial Crash," *Journal of Development Economics*, 19, 1–2 (September–October 1985).

Economic Council of Canada. *Venturing Forth, an Assessment of the Canada–U.S. Trade Agreement*. Ottawa, 1988.

Feinberg, Richard et al. *Between Two Worlds: The World Bank's Next Decade*. Washington, D.C.: Overseas Development Council, 1986.

Khan, Mohsin S., and Malcolm D. Knight. "Fund-Supported Adjustment Programs and Economic Growth." *IMF Occasional Paper* 41, November 1985.

Krugman, Paul. "Is Free Trade Passé?" *Journal of Economic Perspectives*. American Economic Association, 1, 2 (Fall 1987).

Kuznets, Simon. *Modern Economic Growth: Rate, Structure and Spread*. New Haven: Yale University Press, 1966.

Landau, Daniel, "Government and Economic Growth in the Less Developed Countries: An Empirical Study for 1960–1980." *Economic Development and Cultural Change*, 35, 11 (October 1986): 35–75.

Leslie, A. J. "A Second Look at the Economics of Natural Management Systems in Tropical Mixed Forests." *Unasilva*, 39, 1 (1987).

Michalopoulos, Constantine. "World Bank Programs for Adjustment and Growth." In Vittorio Corbo, Morris Goldstein, and Mohsin Khan (eds.), *Growth-Oriented Adjustment Programs*, Washington, D.C.: International Monetary Fund and the World Bank, 1987.

Moran, Theodore H. "Overview: The Future of Foreign Direct Investment in the Third World." In T. H. Moran et al., *Investing in Development: New Roles for Private Capital?* Washington, D.C.: Overseas Development Council, 1986.

Morris, Morris D. *Measuring the Condition of the World's Poor: The Physical Quality of Life Index*. Washington, D.C.: Overseas Development Council, 1978.

Prest, A. R., and Stewart, I. G. *The National Income of Nigeria, 1950–51*, London: H.M.S.O., Colonial Research Studies No. 11, 1953.

Ram, Rati. "Government Size and Economic Growth: A New Framework and Some Evidence from Cross-Section and Time-Series Data." *American Economic Review*, 76, 1 (March 1986).

Rawls, J. *A Theory of Justice*. Cambridge, Mass.: Harvard University Press, 1971.

Rossi, Nicola. "Government Spending, the Real Interest Rate, and the Behavior of Liquidity-Constrained Consumers in Developing Countries." *IMF Staff Papers*, 35, 1 (March 1988): 104–140.

Sachs, Jeffrey D. "Trade and Exchange Rate Policies in Growth-Oriented Adjustment Programs." In Vittorio Corbo, Morris Goldstein, and Mohsin Khan (eds.). *Growth-Oriented Adjustment Programs*, Washington, D.C.: International Monetary Fund and the World Bank, 1987, pp. 291–325.

Seers, Dudley. "The Meaning of Development." *International Development Review*, 11, 4 (1969).

―――. "What Are We Trying to Measure." *Journal of Development Studies*, 8, 3 (April 1972).

Taylor, Lance. *Varieties of Stabilization Experience*. Oxford: Clarendon Press, 1988.

Tisdell, Clem. "Sustainable Development: Differing Perspectives of Ecologists and Economists, and Relevance to LDCs." *World Development*, 16, 3 (March 1988): 373–384.

4

Toward a Nonethnocentric Theory of Development: Alternative Conceptions from the Third World

Howard J. Wiarda

*[The Ayatullah] Khomeini has blown apart the comfortable
myth that as the Third World industrializes, it will also
adopt Western values.*

Time *(7 January 1980)*

A revolution of far-reaching breadth and meaning is presently sweeping the Third World, and we in the West are only partially and incompletely aware of it. This revolution carries immense implications not only for the Third World and our relations with it but also, more generally, for the social sciences and the way we comprehend and come to grips with Third World change.

We are all aware of the new social and economic forces of modernization sweeping the Third World and perhaps to a somewhat lesser extent of the political and value changes also occurring, including anti-Americanism and anticolonialism. What has received less attention is the way these changes are now finding parallel expression in a rejection of the basic developmental models and paradigms originating in the West, both Marxian and non-Marxian varieties, and a corresponding assertion of non-Western, nonethnocentric, and indigenous ones.[1]

The ongoing Iranian Revolution may not be typical, but it is illustrative. At the popular level, awareness of the profound changes occurring in

From *Journal of Developing Areas*, 17 (July 1983), pp. 433–452. Copyright © 1984 by Western Illinois University.

Iran has been warped and obscured by events surrounding the revolution and the 1979 seizure of the American hostages, by the discomfort those in the more pluralist societies of the West feel toward the Islamic fundamentalists' assertion that there is a single right way and a wrong way to do everything, and by the general "ugliness" (at least as portrayed on our TV screens) of some of the revolution's leaders. Even scholars and others more sympathetic to such radical transformations, in Iran and elsewhere, have tended to focus on the changes occurring in their one area or country of specialization and have not analyzed the more general phenomenon or placed it in a broader, global perspective.[2] Alternatively, they have preferred to see the Iranian Revolution and the coming to power of its ayatullah as an isolated event, readily subject to ridicule and agreed-upon moral outrage and therefore not representing a serious challenge to established Western values and social science understandings.

The proposition argued here, however, is that the rejection of the Western (that is, northwest European and United States) model of development, in its several varieties, is now widespread throughout the Third World, and that there are many new and exciting efforts on the part of intellectuals and political elites throughout these areas to assert new and indigenous models of development. Furthermore, these efforts represent serious and fundamental challenges to many cherished social science assumptions and understandings and even to the presumption of a universal social science of development. Thus, we underestimate or continue to disregard such changes at the risk of both perpetuating our malcomprehension of the Third World areas and retaining a social science of development that is parochial and ethnocentric rather than accurate and comprehensive.[3]

The Iranian Revolution, with its assertion of Islamic fundamentalism and of a distinctively Islamic social science (or model) of development, is in fact but one illustration of a far more general Third World phenomenon. There are common themes in the reexaminations presently under way by many Third World leaders: of Indian caste associations and their role in modernization; of African tribalism not as a traditional institution that is necessarily dysfunctional and therefore to be discarded into the ashcans of history but as a base upon which to build new kinds of societies; of Latin American organicism, corporatism, populism, and new forms of bureaucratic-authoritarianism; of family and interpersonal solidarities in Japan; of the overlaps of Confucian and Maoist conceptions in China. These themes relate to the hostility toward and often the inappropriateness of the Western developmental models in non-Western or only partially Western areas, the nationalistic and often quite realistic assertion of local and indigenous ones, and the questioning of some basic notions regarding the universality of the social sciences. They relate also to the realization that there are not just one or two (First and Second World) paths to development but many and diverse ones, and that the dichotomies between traditional and modern represent not real but false choices for societies where the blending and fusion of these is both likely and more widespread than the necessary or automatic replacement of the former by the latter.[4]

These themes are controversial and provocative, and not all the dimensions and issues can be dealt with here. Rather, my purposes are to present the critique Third World areas are now directing at the Western and, we often presume, universal developmental model; to examine the alternatives they themselves are now in the process of formulating; to assess the problems and difficulties in these alternative formulations; and to offer some conclusions regarding the issue of particularism versus universalism in the social sciences.

THE THIRD WORLD CRITIQUE OF THE WESTERN DEVELOPMENTAL MODEL

> In all frankness, much of our self-inflicted disaster has its intellectual roots in our social sciences faculties.
>
> West Indian economist Courtney N. Blackman,
> in "Science, Development, and Being Ourselves,"
> Caribbean Studies Newsletter (Winter 1980)

The Third World critique of the Western model and pattern of development as inappropriate and irrelevant, or partially so, to their circumstances and conditions is widespread and growing. There has long been a powerful strain of anti-Westernism (as well as anticolonialism) on the part of Third World intellectuals, but now that sentiment is stronger and well nigh universal. The recent trends differ from the earlier critiques of Western modernization theory in that the attacks have become far more pervasive, they are shared more generally by the society as a whole, they have taken on global rather than simply area- or country-specific connotations, and the criticisms are no longer solely negative but are now accompanied by an assertion of other, alternative, often indigenous approaches. Moreover the debate is no longer just a scholarly one between competing social science development models; rather, it has powerful policy implications as well.

One should not overstate the case. As yet, the critiques one reads are frequently as inchoate and uncertain as the concept of the Third World itself. They tend sometimes to be partial and incomplete, fragmented and unsystematic, long on rhetoric but short on reality, often as nationalistic and parochial as the very Western theories they seek to replace. Yet one cannot but be impressed by the growing strength of these critiques, the increasing acceptance and receptivity of them by Third World leaders, and the dawning realization of common themes, criticisms, and problems encountered with the Western model across diverse continents, nations, and cultural traditions.

The criticism centers, to begin with, on the bias and ethnocentrism perceived in the Western model and on its inapplicability to societies with quite different traditions, histories, societies, and cultural patterns.[5] For societies cast in quite different traditions from the Judeo-Christian one, lacking the sociopolitical precepts of Greece, Rome, and the Bible, without the same experiences of feudalism and capitalism, the argument is that the Western model has only limited relevance.[6] Western political theory is faulted for its almost entirely European focus and its complete lack of attention to other intellectual traditions; political sociology in Durkheim, Comte, Weber, or Parsons is shown to be based almost exclusively on the European transition from "agraria" to "industria" and its accompanying sociopolitical effects, which have proved somewhat less than universal[7]; and political economy, in both its Marxian and non-Marxian variants, is criticized for the exclusively European and hence less-than-universal origins of its major precepts: philosophical constructs derived (especially in Marx) from Germany, a conception of sociopolitical change derived chiefly from the French tradition, and an understanding of industrialization and its effects stemming chiefly from the English experience. Even our celebrated "liberal arts education" (basically Western European) has come in for criticism as constituting not an experience of universal relevance but merely the first area studies program.[8] These criticisms of the narrowness and parochialism of our major social science traditions and concepts, as grounded essentially on the singular experience of Western Europe and without appreciation of or applicability to the rest of the world, are both sweeping and, with proper qualification, persuasive.

Third World intellectuals have begun to argue secondly that the timing, sequence, and stages of development in the West may not necessarily be replicable in their own areas. Again, this argument is not new, but its sophisticated expression by so many Third World leaders is. For example, Western political sociology generally asserts, based on the European experience, that bureaucratization and urbanization accompanied and were products of industrialization; in Latin America and elsewhere, however, many Third World scholars are arguing that the phenomena of preindustrial urbanization and bureaucratization would seem to require different kinds of analyses.[9] With regard to timing, it seems obvious that countries developing and modernizing in the late twentieth century should face different kinds of problems from those that developed in the nineteenth; because their developmental response must necessarily be different, there seems to be no necessary reason why the former should merely palely and retardedly repeat the experience of the latter.[10] In terms of stages, the European experience would lead us to believe that capitalism must necessarily replace feudalism; in much of the Third World, however, feudalism in accord with the classic French case seems never to have existed,[11] capitalism exists in forms (populist, patrimonialist, etatist) that hardly existed in the West, and rather than capitalism definitely *replacing* feudalism, it seems more likely that the two will continue to exist side by side. The timing, sequences, and stages of development in most Third World nations are sufficiently different, indeed, that virtually all our Western precepts require fundamental reinterpretation when applied there: the so-called demographic transition, the role of the emerging middle classes, military behavior and professionalization, the role of peasants and workers, the presumption of greater pluralism as societies develop, notions of differentiation and rationalization, and so on.[12]

Not only are the timing, sequences, and stages of Third World development likely to be quite different, but the international context is entirely altered as well. In the nineteenth century, countries like Britain, Japan, and the United States were able to develop relatively autonomously; for today's Third World nations, that is no longer possible. To cite only a handful of many possible illustrations, these nations are often caught up in Cold War struggles over which they have no control and in which they are cast as mere pawns; they are absolutely dependent on outside capital, technology, and markets for their products[13]; they are part of an international community and of a web of international military, diplomatic, political, commercial, cultural, communications, and other ties from which they cannot divorce themselves; moreover, many of them are entirely dependent for their continued development on external energy sources and thus are the victims of skyrocketing prices that they can ill afford to pay and that have wreaked havoc with their national economies. In these and other ways it seems clear the international context of development is entirely different from that of a century to a century and a half ago.

A fourth area of difference perceived by leaders from the Third World relates to the role of traditional institutions. Western political sociology largely assumes that such traditional institutions as tribes, castes, clans, patrimonialist authority, and historic corporate units must either yield and give way (the liberal tradition) under the impact of modernization or be overwhelmed (the revolutionary tradition) by it. Nevertheless, we have learned that in much of the Third World so-called traditional institutions have, first of all, proved remarkably resilient, persistent, and long-lasting; rather than fading or being crushed under the impact of change, they have instead proved flexible, accommodative, and adaptive, bending to the currents of modernization but not being replaced by them.[14] Second, these traditional institutions have often served as filters of the modernization process, accepting what was useful and what they themselves could absorb in modernity while rejecting the rest. Third, we have learned that such traditional institutions as India's caste associations, African tribalism, and Latin American corporatism can often be transformed into agents of modernization, bridging some wrenching transitions and even serving as the base for new and more revered forms of indigenous development.[15] Indeed one of

the more interesting illustrations of this process is the way a new generation of African leaders, rather than rejecting tribalism as traditional and to
be discarded, as the *geist* of Western political sociology would have them
do, are now reexamining tribalism's persistent presence as an indigenous,
realistic, and perhaps viable base on which to construct a new kind of
authentic African society.[16]

Fifth, Third World intellectuals are beginning to argue that the
Eurocentrism of the major development models has skewed, biased, and
distorted their own and the outside world's understanding of Third World
societies and has made them into something of a laughingstock, the butt of
cruel, ethnic, and sometimes racial gibes. For example, the Western bias had
led scholars, those from the West and sometimes those from the Third
World, to study and overemphasize such presumably modernizing institutions as trade unions and political parties; yet in many Third World countries these institutions may not count for very much, and their absence or
weakness often leads these societies to be labeled underdeveloped or dysfunctional. At the same time, institutions that Western political sociology
has proclaimed traditional and hence inevitably fated to die or disappear,
such as patronage networks, clan groups, religious institutions and movements, extended families and the like, have been woefully understudied
and represent some immense gaps in our knowledge concerning these societies; consequently, there exist some fundamental misinterpretations of
them.[17]

Meanwhile, these nations actually do modernize and develop, in their
terms if not always in ours—that is, through coups and barracks revolts
that contribute to an expanding circulation of elites, through larger patronage and spoils systems now transferred to the national level, through assistance from abroad that is often employed not entirely inappropriately in
ways other than those intended, and through elaborated corporate group,
family, clan, and/or tribal networks. Yet the actual dynamics of change and
modernization in these nations have often been made the stuff of opéra
bouffe in *New York Times* headlines or *New Yorker* cartoons or have led to
appalled and holier-than-thou attitudes on the part of Westerners who
would still like to remake the Third World in accord with Judeo-Christian
morality and Anglo-American legal and political precepts. The excessive
attention to some institutions that our ofttimes wishful sociology would elevate to a higher plane than they deserve, the neglect of others, and our ethnocentrism and general ignorance as to how Third World societies do in
fact develop has perpetuated our woeful misunderstanding and inadequate
comprehension of them.[18] Indeed it is one of the greater ironies, and a result
of what we might call our cultural or social-scientific imperialism, that for a
long time Third World intellectuals bought, or were sold, the same essentially Western categories as the Westernizers themselves had internalized,
and that their understanding of their own societies therefore was often no
greater than our own. That condition is now changing very rapidly.[19]

The Western development perspective, furthermore, has recently been subjected to an additional criticism: that it is part of the Western ideological and intellectual offensive to keep the Third World within the Western orbit.[20] This is perhaps the most widespread of the criticisms of the Western development model current in the Third World. Western modernization and development theory is thus seen as still another imperialist Cold War strategy aimed at tying Third World nations into a Western and liberal (that is, United States) development pattern, of keeping them within our sphere of influence, and of denying them the possibilities of alternative developmental patterns. Of course it should be said that not all of those who fashioned the early and influential development literature had such manifest Cold War or New Mandarin goals in mind. Some clearly did,[21] but among others the development literature was popular chiefly because it corresponded to cherished notions about ourselves (that we are a liberal, democratic, pluralist, socially just, and modern nation) and to the belief that the developing nations could emulate us if they worked hard and recast themselves in accord with the American or Western way. This strategy, one would have to admit, was remarkably successful from the late 1950s, when the first development literature began to appear, until the early 1970s. Since that time, however, development has been increasingly tarred with the imperialist brush and discredited throughout the Third World, and hence a whole new generation of young Third World leaders and intellectuals no longer accepts the Western developmentalist concepts and perspectives and is searching for possible alternatives.[22]

Finally, and perhaps most harmful in terms of the long-term development of the Third World, is the damage that has been inflicted on their own institutions because of the Western biases. "Development" is no mere intellectual construct nor is it benignly neutral. There are consequences, often negative, in following a Western-oriented development strategy. I will not discuss here the damage inflicted on countries such as the Congo, Angola, Guatemala, or the Dominican Republic by Cold War rivalries or by such agencies as the International Monetary Fund, whose financial advice to Third World nations has often been ruinous. Instead what concerns us here is the role development has had in undermining such viable institutions as extended family networks, patronage ties, clan and tribal loyalties, corporate group linkages, churches and religious movements, historic authority relations, and the like. By undermining and often eliminating these traditional institutions before any more modern ones were created, development helped destroy some of the only agencies in many Third World nations that might have enabled them to make a genuine transition to real modernity. The destruction, in the name of modernization, of such traditional institutions throughout the Third World may well be one of the most important legacies that development left behind, and it will powerfully affect our future relations with them. For by our actions and our patronizing, condescending, and ethnocentric efforts to promote development among the

LDCs, we may have denied them the possibility of real development while at the same time destroying the very indigenous and at one time viable institutions they are now attempting, perhaps futilely and too late, to resurrect.[23]

The Third World critique of the Western development model as biased, ethnocentric, and often damaging is thus strong, sweeping, and, in its essentials, difficult to refute. Although many of the arguments are not new and though not all Third World critiques are as coherent, global, and organized as presented here, the criticisms are spreading and becoming global, the common elements are being analyzed, and they are increasingly informed by solid facts and argument. It remains for us to examine what the Third World offers in place of the Western schema.

THE ASSERTION OF INDIGENOUS THIRD WORLD DEVELOPMENT MODELS

> *The problem with us Africans is that we've not been educated to appreciate our art and culture. So many of us have been influenced by the British system of education. I went through this system here not knowing enough about my own country. It was almost as if what we natives did wasn't important enough to be studied. I knew all about British history and British art, but about Ghana and Africa nothing.*
>
> Ghanaian art historian and intellectual Nana Apt,
> quoted in New York Times, 13 September 1980, p. 16

The purpose of this section is to provide a sense of the kinds and varieties of new development models emerging from the Third World. Space constraints rule out any detailed treatment here; our survey and *tour* provide only a hint and surface gloss of the new ideas, concepts, and theories.[24] Nevertheless, even in a brief passage it is possible to convey some of the main themes from each of the major areas, to show their common currents, and to begin to analyze the larger patterns. More detailed treatment is reserved for a planned book-length study.[25]

In his influential work *Beyond Marxism: Towards an Alternative Perspective,* Indian political theorist Vrajenda Raj Mehta argues that neither liberal democracy nor communism are appropriate frameworks for Indian development. He attributes their inadequacy to their unidimensional views of man and society. The liberal-democratic view that man is a consumer of utilities and producer of goods serves to legitimize a selfish, atomistic, egoistic society. Communism, he says, reduces all human dimensions to one, the economic, and transforms all human activity into one, state activity, which erodes all choice and destroys life's diversities.[26]

Mehta further argues for a multidimensional conception of man and society incorporating (1) the objective, external, rational; (2) the subjective, internal, intuitive; (3) the ethical, normative, harmonious; and (4) the spiritual and fiduciary. For the development of man's multidimensional personality, society must be structured as an "oceanic circle," an integral-pluralist system of wholes within wholes. The four social wholes of Mehta's well-organized society consist of "those devoted to the pursuit of knowledge, those who run the administration and protect the community from external aggression, those who manage the exchange of services or goods, and those who attend to manual and elementary tasks" (p. 54). Mehta claims that such an integralist-pluralist order will overcome the atomistic limitations of liberal democracy and the economic and bureaucratic collectivism of communism. The logic of "developing wholes" means that each sector of society must have autonomy or *swaraj* within an overall system of harmony and oceanic circles. Emphasizing both the autonomy of the several societal sectors and their integration within a larger whole, Mehta calls this essentially Indian-organic-corporatist system "integral pluralism":

> Integral pluralism insists that the development of society has to be the development of the whole society. The whole is not one, but itself consists of various wholes, of economics and politics, ethics, and religion, as also of different types of individuals. The relationship of each of them to each other is in the nature of oceanic circles (p. 60).

Particularly interesting for our purposes are Mehta's attempts to ground his theory in the reality of Indian culture, history, and civilization. "Each national community," he says, "has its own law of development, its own way to fulfill itself." "The broken mosaic of Indian society," he goes on, "cannot be recreated in the image of the West—India must find its own strategy of development and nation-building suited to its own peculiar conditions" (p. 92). Instead of being dazzled by the national progress of the West and futilely trying to emulate its development model, India should define its goals and choose its means "separately in terms of its own resources and the role it wants to play on the world scene." Rejecting the thesis of a single and universal pattern of development, Mehta advocates an indigenous process of change attuned to the needs of individual societies: "A welcome process of social change in all societies is a process towards increasing self-awareness in terms of certain normatively defined goals in each case, and that the direction of the process and the definition of ends is largely defined by the society's own distinct history and way of life" (p. 104).

Mehta's theory of integral pluralism is a bold and erudite exposition of a model of indigenous development for India. Although he draws some of his ideas eclectically from the West, the specific sources of inspiration for his model are Indian: the Vedic seers, the *Mahabharata*, Tagore, and Gandhi. In contemporary India the model derives particular support from nationalists and from those who advocate the Gandhian model of development, which emphasizes a decentralized economy based on small industries, a reorientation of production in terms of criteria besides prosperity only, a possible decentralized defense industry, and hence a particularly Indian route to development.

Mehta believes that the form of liberal democracy derived from England, the colonial power, is inappropriate and unworkable in the Indian context. Political events in India in recent years would seem to provide abundant though still incomplete evidence for that argument. But neither is communism in accord with India's traditions, he argues. Mehta states that the crisis in Indian politics is due to the fact the constitution and political system are not based on what he calls the "hidden springs" or the underlying institutional and cultural heritage of Indian society. That is why, he writes, there are presently disillusionment, institutional atrophy, spreading chaos, and a concomitant widespread desire to adopt the Gandhian model. Accordingly, the successful ruler and developer in the Indian context

> will be the one who will not only have an idea of the system of international stratification and the position of the dominant powers in it, but also the one who will weave into a holistic view the fact that his society once had a glorious civilization which, due to certain structural defects and rigidities, gave way to conquerors from the outside; he will be conscious of the continuity amidst all the shifts in the historical scene, of the underlying unity amongst a panorama of immense and baffling diversities (p. 115).

No claim is made here that Mehta's book captures the essence of contemporary Indian thinking or that it is necessarily representative of the newer currents emanating from Indian intellectuals or public opinion.[27] It is, nevertheless, illustrative of the kind of thinking and writing now beginning to emerge, and there is no doubt that its clarion call for a nationalistic and indigenous model of development has struck in his country an immensely responsive chord. Moreover, it corresponds closely to other observed phenomena in contemporary India: the increased repudiation of English and Western influences, the rising tide of Indian nationalism, the revival of various religious movements and the corresponding criticisms of Western secularism and pluralism, the justifications for authoritarian rule and of integral and harmonious development, and the reinterpretation of caste associations no longer as traditional institutions that must be destroyed but as indigenous agencies capable themselves of modernization and of serving as transitional bridges of development. These deep-rooted trends help make Mehta's book, and the voluminous writings of numerous other scholars and popularizers, worthy of serious attention.[28]

The new and often parallel currents stirring the Islamic world have received far more popular attention than have those in India. There can be no doubt that a major religious revival is sweeping the world of Islam,[29] but our understanding of the forces at work has been obscured, biased, and retarded by events in Iran and by general Western hostility to them. It is relatively easy in the Iranian case to express our appalled indignation at the summary trials and executions, the brutal treatment of the hostages, and the sometimes wild fulminations of an aging ayatullah; but by doing so we may miss some of the deeper permanent, and more important aspects of the changes under way.[30]

Two major features of the Islamic revival command special attention here. Both are also present in the Indian case. One is the criticism of the Western models, either liberal or communist, as inappropriate and undesirable in the Islamic context. The widespread sentiment in favor of rejecting Western values and the Western developmental model has again been obscured in the popular media by their focusing only on the sometimes ludicrous comments of Iran's religious leaders that the Western model is sinful and satanic. That focus makes it easy to satirize, parody, and dismiss what is, in fact, a widespread criticism and which, coming from other Islamic mouths and pens—in, for instance, Saudi Arabia and Pakistan—is quite realistic and telling. The argument is that the excessive individualism of the liberal model and the excessive statism of the communist one are both inappropriate in the Islamic context: they violate its customs and traditions by importing a system without strong indigenous roots, and they are positively damaging in terms of the Islamic world's own preferred values and institutions.[31]

The second aspect commanding attention, complementary to the first, is the effort on the part of the Iranians and others, once the Western influences were excised or repudiated, to reconstruct society and polity on the bases of indigenous and Islamic concepts and institutions. Once more, what is in fact a serious process has frequently been made ludicrous in the media where only the comic-opera and the most brutal aspects have received attention. But surely the efforts to reforge the links between the state and society that had been largely destroyed by the shah, to lay stress on the family, the local community, a corporate group life and solidarity, and the leader who provides both direction and moral values—in contrast to the alienation and mass society that are among the more visible results of the Western pattern of development—are serious and therefore must command our attention. Important too are the efforts at religious revival and the attempts to reconstruct law, society, and behavior in accord with religious and moral principles, to rejoin politics and ethics in ways that in the West have been nearly irrevocably broken since Machiavelli. Rather than reject such developments out of hand, which further postpones our understanding of them, Westerners must begin to take Islamic society on its own terms, not from the point of view of automatic rejection or a haughty sense of superiority, but with empathy and understanding. Indeed one of the more fascinating aspects that has emerged from this Islamic revival is not only a set of new, innovative, and indigenous institutions but a whole, distinctive Islamic social science of development to go with it.[32]

In Africa the institution around which the discussion revolves is tribalism. Tribalism is one of those traditional institutions, like India's caste associations or Islamic fundamentalism, that was supposed to decline or disappear as modernization went forward. The sentiment that tribalism was to be consigned to the dustbins of history was so deeply ingrained that African leaders themselves were often made to feel ashamed of their own background and origins. Tribalism had to be repressed and denied and the nation-state or the single-party mass-mobilizing system elevated to an artificial importance, which in fact it did not have.[33] When tribalism refused to die, it was rebaptized under the rubric of ethnicity and ethnic conflict, which somehow made it seem more modern.

There are still Westerners and Africans alike who would deny the existence of tribalism and would seek to stamp it out, but among other Africans there is a new and refreshing realism about tribalism, even some interesting albeit not as yet overly successful efforts to reconstruct African society using tribalism as a base. These attempts include new variations on the federal principle, new forms of consociationalism, a corporately based communalism as in Tanzania, or the African authenticity of Zaire. Whatever the precise name and form, these newer approaches to tribalism would seem to be both more realistic and more interesting than the past denial of or wishful thinking about it.

At a minimum, the tribe often gives people what little they have in rural Africa: a patch of land for their huts and maize, leadership, order, and coherence. The tribe often has its own police force, which offers a measure of security. In countries sometimes without effective national welfare or social security, tribal authority and tradition help provide for the old and sick. Tribal ties and solidarities in the cities also help provide jobs, patronage, and positions within the army or bureaucracy. Parties and interest associations are often organized along tribal lines. In the absence of strong states and national political structures, the tribe may be an effective intermediary association providing services and brokering relations between the individual, family, or clan and the national government. Hence while tribalism may weaken over time, it surely will not disappear, and there is a growing and realistic recognition on the part of African leaders that tribalism is part of Africa. Many will find this new realism refreshing and the effort to refashion African polities and social structures in accord with its own indigenous traditions exciting and innovative.[34]

The case of Latin America is somewhat different since it is an area that we think of as already Western.[35] Properly qualified (taking into account Latin America's large indigenous populations, the periodic efforts to resurrect and glorify its Indian past, or the efforts of nations such as Mexico to ground their nationalism in part upon their mestizoness—the new "cosmic race"), this assertion is valid; one must also remember, however, that Latin America is an offshoot or historical fragment of a special time and of a special part of the West, Iberia circa 1500,[36] whose own conformity to the Western model has been and in many ways still is somewhat less than 100 percent.[37] With this in mind, Latin America may be looked on as something of a mixed case, Western and Third World at the same time.

In various writings I have sought to wrestle with this issue of where and in what ways Latin America conforms to the Western pattern and where it is distinctive.[38] In the context of this paper, however, what is striking are the remarkable parallels between the newer currents in Latin America and in other Third World areas. First, there is a growing nationalistic rejection of the United States–favored route to development, a rejection that has even stronger historical roots than in other Third World areas and that found expression as early as the nineteenth century in fears and hostility toward the "colossus of the north" and in the widespread acceptance of the arguments of Jose E. Rodo, who contrasted the spiritualism, Catholicism, personalism, and humanism of Latin America (Ariel) with the crassness, materialism, secularism, pragmatism, and utilitarianism of the United States (Caliban).[39]

Second, and the reverse side of this coin, is the effort to identify what is distinctive in Latin America's own past and present and to determine whether these characteristics can be used to erect a separate Latin American political sociology of development. Such a formulation would emphasize Latin America's persistent corporatism and organic statism, its neomercantilist and state-capitalist economic structures, its personalism and kinship patterns, its Catholicism and the institutions and behavioral patterns of Catholic political culture, its patrimonialism and unabashed patriarchalism, its patron-client networks now extended to the national political level, its distinctive patterns and arenas of state-society relations, and its historic relations of dependency (particularly in recent times) vis-à-vis the United States.[40] There are, as we shall see in the next section, problems with these formulations, not the least of which is that not all Latin Americans accept them or wish to accept them, still preferring to see themselves in terms of and to cast their lot with the Western model. Nevertheless the parallels with other Third World areas are striking, and the attempts by Latin Americans to fashion their own indigenous model and social science of development must command our attention.

Analogous developments in other areas also merit serious study, though here only passing mention can be made of them. In China, for example, the combination of Marxist and Confucian elements in Mao's thought provided not only a new and fascinating synthesis but also some of the key ingredients in the distinctively Chinese model of development.[41]

Japan has achieved phenomenal economic growth rates by borrowing, copying, or synthesizing the technology and organizational models of the West and adapting these to historic and preferred Japanese forms, structures, and ways of doing things.[42] In Poland and elsewhere in Eastern Europe, Marxism is being adapted to local and home-grown institutions such as Catholicism and nationalism. In the Soviet Union there is of course a Marxist socialist state, but no one would disagree it is also a *Russian* Marxist state (however ambiguous and open to disagreement may be its precise meaning).[43] Finally, in Western Europe itself, in whose development patterns the Western model obviously originated there is both a new questioning of what the Western model consists of and whether even the nations of Western Europe conform to it, as well as a rethinking of whether that Western model is in fact applicable to the rest of the world.[44]

These various national and regional traditions need to be examined in detail and the arguments more fully amplified. What seems clear even from this brief survey, however, is that there is a growing rejection of the Western model as irrelevant and inappropriate in areas and nations where the traditions and institutions are quite different and that there exists a growing search for indigenous national institutions and models, based on local traditions instead of those imported from or imposed by the West. These trends seem now to cut across and transcend national and cultural boundaries.

PROBLEM AREAS AND DILEMMAS

> *The notion of a bright new world made up of young*
> *emerging nations is a fairy tale.*
>
> V. S. Naipaul, Among the Believers

There can be no doubt that the idea of a native, indigenous model and social science of development, reflecting and deeply rooted in local practices and institutions rather than imported and surface ones, is enormously attractive. Social scientists need to analyze this rather than merely celebrate it, however, and when that is done numerous problems arise.

First, the search for indigenous models of development may prove to be more romantic and nostalgic than realistic.[45] In some areas and nations (several of the Central American countries, for example), indigenous institutions may well prove weak or nonexistent, incapable of serving as the base for national development. They may, as with the Western model, reflect the preferences of intellectuals rather than those of the general population—or they may reflect the nostalgic longing for a past that no longer exists and cannot be recreated. Such indigenous institutions may have been destroyed in whole or in part by the colonial powers or discredited by the earlier generation of Western-oriented local elites. There may not be an institutional foundation based on indigenous institutions and practices on which to build and hence, for many Third World nations, no light of whatever sort at the end of the development tunnel. The Western model seems not to have worked well, but an indigenous one may not work out either if it reflects the politics of romance and nostalgia rather than the politics of reality.[46]

Second, there are class, partisan, and other biases often implicit in a political strategy that seeks to fashion a model of development based upon indigenous institutions. Such a strategy may serve (though it need not necessarily do so) as a means to defend an existing status quo or to restore a status quo ante, both nationally and internationally. It may serve to justify an existing class, caste, leadership group, or clan remaining in power. It may be manipulated for partisan or personal advantage. For example, in Francisco Franco's efforts to restore and maintain traditional historic Spanish institutions and practices, it was clear that only his rather narrow and particular interpretation of what that special tradition was would be allowed and that other currents and possibilities within that tradition would be suppressed.[47]

Third, the actual practice of regimes that have followed an indigenous development strategy has not produced very many successes. Even on its own terms, it is hard to call the Iranian Revolution, so far, a success. The Mexican Revolution that was once trumpeted as providing an indigenous third way is acknowledged to have sold out, run its course, or died.[48] There has been a lot of talk about African authenticity in recent years, but in countries such as Togo or Zaire the application of the concept has served mainly to shore up corrupt and despotic regimes. Even in Tanzania, which has been widely cited as an example of a serious attempt to build an original African development model, there are immense difficulties accompanying this experiment and a notable lack of enthusiasm on the part of both the peasants who are presumably its prime beneficiaries and the government officials charged with implementing it.[49]

Fourth, it may be that in the present circumstances such indigenous developmental models are no longer possible. The time when a nation could maintain itself in isolation and could develop autonomously and on its own terms may well have passed. All of the Third World is now affected by what Lucian Pye once called the "world culture"—not only styles in dress and music (largely Western) but in social and political systems as well.[50] They are also caught up in what Immanuel Wallerstein called the "world system"—factors such as trade patterns, economic dependency relationships, world market prices, oil requirements, and so on, which have major effects on them but over which they have no control.[51] Additionally, whether one speaks of Afghanistan, El Salvador, or numerous other Third World nations, they are often involved in Cold War and other international political conflicts that cast them as pawns in the global arena and often affect in major ways their internal development as well. All these conditions make it virtually impossible that the outside world would not impinge on any effort at indigenous development, if not destroying it then certainly requiring compromise in numerous areas.[52]

Not only does the outside world impose itself but, fifth, indigenous elites and intellectuals are not all convinced that they wish to follow such a native path. For them, traditional and indigenous institutions are symbols not necessarily of pride and nationalism but of backwardness and underdevelopment. Or they may have mixed feelings that breed confusion, irresolution, and lack of direction. Not all African leaders by any means are convinced that tribalism can serve as a new basis of political organization; hence in Kenya and elsewhere concerted efforts are under way not to build it up but to snuff it out. Indian intellectuals, especially from the lower castes, do not as yet seem ready to accept the arguments concerning the modernizing role the castes may play. Not all Iranian intellectuals accept the virtues of a theocratic state led by the Ayatullah or, even if they are believers in Islamic fundamentalism, are agreed on what precise institutional form that should take.

Latin America is an especially interesting area in this regard, for while most of its intellectuals share varying degrees of antipathy to the United States model and the U.S.-favored development route and want to have a hand in fashioning a nationalistic and Latin American one, they are also terribly uncomfortable with the implications of that position. That new route would imply acceptance of a political system built in some degree upon the principles of corporatism, hierarchy, authoritarianism, and organic-statism—none of which are popular or fashionable in the more democratic nations and salons of the modern world, into which Latin America and its intellectuals, historically plagued by a sense of inferiority and backwardness, also wish to be accepted. Hence they have ambivalent feelings regarding indigenous models and prefer theories of dependency or international stratification that conveniently and more comfortably place the blame on external instead of internal forces.[53]

Sixth and finally, emphasis must be placed on the sheer diversity of these nations and areas and hence the immense difficulties of achieving a consensus on any development strategy, whether indigenous or otherwise. At some levels of analysis, Latin America (and Iberia) may be thought of as part of a single culture area, but it must also be kept in mind that Paraguay is quite different from Argentina, Brazil and Peru from Chile, Nicaragua from Mexico—and that all are at different levels of development. Hence different strategies and models of modernization, even if they could be conceptualized within certain common parameters, would have to be designed for each country of the area.[54] In the Islamic world the same qualifications would have to be introduced; it obviously also makes a major difference if we are talking of the Sunni, the Shiite, or other traditions and combinations of them.[55] A similar case exists in Africa: some observers feel that Islam is the only organized cultural and ideological force capable of offering a coherent and continentwide alternative to the heretofore dominant Western model. This point of view, however, ignores the still-strong Christian and Western influences, the fact that only a small minority of African states are essentially Muslim (that is, at least 75 percent Islamic), the continuing influence of traditional beliefs, and the fact that parts of Africa have no strong cultural identity of any sort. All of these and many other diversities and differentiations would have to be taken into account in creating for each of these areas an indigenous model, or models, of development. Nor should one underestimate the sheer confusion, uncertainty, and chaos surrounding these issues in many Third World nations. For the Third World as a whole and for its component geographic regions and distinct cultural areas, there is too much diversity to be subsumed under any one single theory or set of concepts.

CONCLUSION: TOWARD A NONETHNOCENTRIC THEORY OF DEVELOPMENT

> *The aspiration for something different, better, more truly*
> *indigenous than Western systems of development and yet*
> *as socially and materially effective is palpable everywhere.*
> *"Our own way" is the persistent theme; but it is far more*
> *often advanced as a creed than as a plan.*
>
> Flora Lewis, The New York Times, *31 December 1979*

In numerous areas, the West and the Western model of development intimately associated with its earlier progress seem to be in decline. Western Europe suffers from various malaises of uncertain and often obscure origins, the United States and many of its institutions seem to be in decline, NATO and the Western Alliance are in disarray, and the global system of American hegemony and dominance is being undermined. With this Spenglerian "Decline of the West"[56] has also come a new questioning of and challenge to the development model that was a part of the nearly 500-year-long Western era of domination. It is not just the model itself that is now being challenged, however, but the larger, preeminently Western, and for that reason parochial and ethnocentric, philosophical and intellectual tradition that went with it. What we in the West, because our entire life-spans and those of our intellectual forebears were entirely encompassed within this time frame, assumed to be a universal set of norms and processes by which societies developed and modernized, and of which the West was presumably the leader and model, has now been demonstrated to be somewhat less than that.

With the decline of Western hegemony and the pretension to universalism of the intellectual constructs that are part and parcel of it, and concomitantly with the rise and new assertiveness of various non-Western and Third World areas, has also come the demand for local, indigenous models of development. The critique of the Western model as particularistic, parochial, Eurocentric, considerably less than universal, and hopelessly biased, as not only perpetuating our lack of understanding regarding these areas but also of wreaking downright harm upon them, seems devastating, persuasive, and perhaps unchallengeable. The question is no longer whether the Western model applies or whether it is salvageable but what is the precise nature of the models that have risen to take its place and whether these new models are functional and viable in terms of the Third World areas from which they are emerging.

These issues would seem to represent the next great frontier in the social sciences.[57] Shorn of its romantic and nostalgic aspects, unfettered by the class or partisan biases that sometimes surround it, incorporating both national currents and international ones, taking account of practical realities and not just intellectual constructs, cognizant of both the mixed sentiments of the local elites and the diversities of the societies studied—or at least recognizing these when they do occur—the notion of a nonethnocentric theory of development is now on the front burner. The study of such local, indigenous, native cultural traditions and models, Samuel P. Huntington has said, may well be the wave of the future for the social sciences.[58]

We need now for the first time to begin to take non-Western areas and their ofttimes peculiar institutions seriously, in their own context and traditions rather than from the slanted perspective of the Western social sciences. We need, hence, to reexamine virtually all of our Western social science notions of development. A serious mistake made by Western scholars, for example, is to assume that as people become modernized and educated, they also become Westernized. In fact in much of the Middle East, urbanization and the growth of a literate middle class are prime causes in the growth of interest in Islam. The examples could easily be multiplied. Hence, we need to see local indigenous institutions not necessarily as dysfunctional or doomed to history's ashcans but frequently as viable and necessary in the society we are studying, as filters and winnowers of the modernization process, as agencies of transition between traditional and modern, and as means for reconciling and blending the global with the indigenous, the nationalist with the international. Such an undertaking implies both greater empathy on our part and greater modesty in terms of the claims made for the universalism of the Western examples.

The implications of such a coming to grips with indigenous institutions and of nonethnocentric theories and concepts of development are enormous.[59] Three major areas of impact may be noted here. The first has to do with the Third World and non-Western nations themselves: their efforts to overcome historical inferiority complexes, their reconceived possibilities for development, the new-found importance of their traditional institutions, the rediscovery of many and complex routes to development, their new sense of pride and accomplishment, and so on. It will take some time before the Third World is able to articulate and mold these diverse concepts into viable and realistic development models; the translation of concepts like authenticity into concrete political institutions, educational policies, health programs, and the like is liable to take even longer. Nevertheless, we cannot doubt the reality or growth of such new interpretations, outlooks, perspectives, and syntheses—as between Marxism and an indigenous development tradition, for example, or in the form of a homegrown type of democracy, or as an updated and modernized Islam.

Second, the arguments presented here have immense implications for the social sciences. Not only must we reexamine a host of essentially Western social science assumptions but we must also be prepared to accept an Islamic social science of development, an African social science of development, a Latin American social science of development, and so on—and to strike some new balances between what is particular in the development process and what does in fact conform to more universal patterns. In exploring such indigenous models, we will need to fashion a dynamic theory of change as well as to examine a variety of normative orientations[60]; we will need also to distinguish between a theory of development that comes from many sources and different theories of development for different regions. In the process the rather tired, even moribund, study of development itself, in all its dimensions, is likely to be revived.

Third, there are major implications for policy. In the past three decades not only have virtually all our intellectual concepts and models with regard to developing nations been based upon the Western experience, but virtually all our assistance programs, developmental recommendations, and foreign policy presumptions have been grounded on these same conceptual tools.[61] Hence the approach here suggested is likely to upset many cherished social science notions and, if considered seriously, will necessitate a fundamental set of foreign policy reconsiderations as well.

NOTES

1. P. T. Bauer, *Dissent on Development* (Cambridge: Harvard University Press, 1976); David E. Schmitt, ed., *Dynamics of the Third World* (Cambridge, Mass.: Winthrop, 1974); Frank Tachau, ed., *The Developing Nations: What Path to Modernization?* (New York: Dodd, Mead, 1972); W. A. Beling and G. O. Totten, eds., *The Developing Nations: Quest for a Model* (New York: Van Nostrand, 1970); Robert E. Gamer, *The Developing Nations* (Boston: Allyn and Bacon, 1976);

Lyman Tower Sargent, *Contemporary Political Ideologies* (Homewood, Ill.: Dorsey, 1981); Paul E. Sigmund, ed., *The Ideologies of the Developing Nations* (New York: Praeger, 1972); John Kenneth Galbraith, *The Voice of the Poor* (Cambridge: Harvard University Press, 1982); and Howard J. Wiarda, ed., *New Directions in Comparative Politics* (Boulder: Westview, 1985).

2. For example, Edward Said, *Orientalism* (New York: Pantheon, 1978); Howard J. Wiarda, ed., *Politics and Social Change in Latin America: The Distinct Tradition*, 2d ed. rev. (Amherst: University of Massachusetts Press, 1982).

3. These arguments are expanded in Howard J. Wiarda, "The Ethnocentrism of the Social Sciences: Implications for Research and Policy," *The Review of Politics*, 42 (April 1981): 163–97. It might be noted that an editor's mistake resulted in the mistitling of this paper in the published version.

4. For some parallel arguments see Reinhard Bendix, "Tradition and Modernity Reconsidered," *Comparative Studies in Society and History*, 9 (April 1967): 292–346, reprinted in his *Embattled Reason* (New York: Oxford University Press, 1970); also Joseph R. Gusfield, "Tradition and Modernity: Misplaced Polarities in the Study of Social Change," *American Journal of Sociology*, 72 (January 1967): 351–62.

5. This and other criticisms will not be new to many students of political development. What is new is the widespread articulation of such views within the Third World. Moreover, this critique of the Western model needs to be presented as a prelude to the discussion of indigenous models that follows. For some earlier critiques of the Western development model see Wiarda, "Ethnocentrism"; Bendix, "Tradition and Modernity"; Dean C. Tipps, "Modernization Theory and the Comparative Studies of Society: A Critical Perspective," *Comparative Studies of Society and History*, 15 (March 1973): 199–226; C. D. Hah and J. Schneider, "A Critique of Current Theories of Political Development and Modernization," *Social Research*, 35 (Spring 1968): 130–58. See also the statements on the different meanings of democracy by Costa Rican President Luis Alberto Monge and Nigerian President Alhaji Shehu Shagari at the Conference on Free Elections, Department of State, Washington, DC, November 4–6, 1982; also R. William Liddle, "Comparative Political Science and the Third World," mimeographed (Columbus: Ohio State University, Department of Political Science).

6. An excellent treatment of these themes is Claudio Veliz, *The Centralist Tradition in Latin America* (Princeton, N.J.: Princeton University Press, 1980); also Clifford Geertz, *Negara: The Theatre State in Nineteenth Century Bali* (Princeton, N.J.: Princeton University Press, 1980), in which he shows that the culture and the theater are the substance, not just superstructure.

7. Especially relevant is the general critique of the Western sociological bias in T. O. Wilkinson, "Family Structure and Industrialization in Japan," *American Sociological Review*, 27 (October 1962): 678–82; also Alberto Guerreiro Ramos, "Modernization: Toward a Possibility Model," in *Developing Nations*, W. A. Beling and H. Totten, eds., pp. 21–59; and Gusfield, "Tradition and Modernity."

8. William P. Glade, "Problems of Research in Latin American Studies," in *New Directions in Language and Area Studies* (Milwaukee: University of Wisconsin at Milwaukee for the Consortium of Latin American Studies Programs, 1979), pp. 81–101.

9. Veliz, *The Centralist Tradition*.

10. For a general statement, Leonard S. Binder et al., eds., *Crises and Sequences in Political Development* (Princeton, N.J.: Princeton University Press, 1971).

11. See the classic statement by Marc Bloch, *Feudal Society* (Chicago: University of Chicago Press, 1961).

12. Daniel Bell, *The Coming of Post-Industrial Society* (New York: Basic Books, 1973). On May 26, 1981, in a personal conversation, Professor Bell asserted that by a quite different route he had also "come to similar conclusions regarding the inadequacies of many social science concepts since they derive almost exclusively from a particular Western tradition." Much of the new social science literature emanating from Latin America since the 1960s makes many of the same arguments.

13. The dependency literature is extensive; among the best statements is Fernando Henrique Cardoso and Enzo Faletto, *Dependency and Development in Latin America* (Berkeley: University of California Press, 1978).

14. For a general discussion, S. N. Eisenstadt, "Post-Traditional Societies and the Continuity and Reconstruction of Tradition," *Daedalus*, 102 (Winter 1973): 1–27; and idem, *Modernization: Protest and Change* (Englewood Cliffs, N.J.: Prentice-Hall, 1966).

15. Lloyd I. Rudolph and Susanne Hoeber Rudolph, *The Modernity of Tradition* (Chicago: University of Chicago Press, 1967).

16. The case of Tanzania is especially interesting in this regard.

17. The arguments are detailed in Wiarda, "Ethnocentrism."

18. A more complete discussion with regard to one region is in Howard J. Wiarda, ed., *The Continuing Struggle for Democracy in Latin America* (Boulder, Colo.: Westview Press, 1980).

19. G. A. D. Soares, "Latin American Studies in the United States," *Latin American Research Review*, 11 (1976); and Howard J. Wiarda, "Latin American Intellectuals and the 'Myth' of Underdevelopment" [presentation made at the Seventh National Meeting of the Latin American Studies Association, Houston, November 2–5, 1977, and published in Wiarda, *Corporatism and National Development in Latin America* (Boulder, Colo.: Westview, 1981), pp. 236–38].

20. Susanne J. Bodenheimer, *The Ideology of Developmentalism: The American Paradigm-Surrogate for Latin American Studies* (Beverly Hills, Calif.: Sage, 1971); Teresa Hayter, *Aid as Imperialism* (Baltimore, Md.: Penguin, 1971); Ronald H. Chilcote, *Theories of Comparative Politics: The Search for a Paradigm* (Boulder, Colo.: Westview Press, 1981); Hah and Schneider, "Critique."

21. In a faculty seminar I chaired in 1980–81 on "New Directions in Comparative Politics" at the Center for International Affairs, Harvard University, several of whose members were part of the original and highly influential SSRC Committee on Comparative Politics, it was striking to note in the occasional seminar remarks by these members how strongly the anticommunist ideology of that time pervaded the SSRC Committee's assumptions. One of our seminar members, himself part of the original SSRC Committee, flatly stated that the purpose of this group was to formulate a noncommunist theory of change and thus to provide a non-Marxian alternative for the developing nations. Gabriel A. Almond's now virtually forgotten *The Appeals of Communism* (Princeton, N.J.: Princeton University Press, 1954) was especially important in helping shape this

sentiment. In a volume that grows out of this seminar (*New Directions in Comparative Politics*, forthcoming), I have sought to explain the context and biases undergirding the early development literature.

22. Selig S. Harrison, *The Widening Gulf: Asian Nationalism and American Policy* (New York: Free Press, 1978). My critique of the development paradigm is contained in "Is Latin America Democratic and Does It Want to Be? The Crisis and Quest of Democracy in the Hemisphere," in *The Continuing Struggle*, H. J. Wiarda, ed., pp. 3–24.

23. Samuel P. Huntington, *Political Order in Changing Societies* (New Haven: Yale University Press, 1968); and Wiarda, "Ethnocentrism."

24. See also Sigmund, *Ideologies*. Especially striking are the differences between the old and new editions of this study, and the differences in Sigmund's own thinking as contained in his introductions.

25. Tentatively entitled *Third World Conceptions of Development* and also growing out of the Harvard seminar on "New Directions in Comparative Politics."

26. Vrajenda Raj Mehta, *Beyond Marxism: Towards an Alternative Perspective* (New Delhi: Manohar Publications, 1978), p. 12. I am grateful to my colleague Thomas Pantham for bringing this work and the debate that swirls about it to my attention. Subsequent page references to Mehta will be in parentheses in the text. A parallel volume from Latin America is Jose Arico, *Marx e a America Latina* (Rio de Janeiro: Paz e Terra, 1982).

27. For a critique see Thomas Pantham, "Integral Pluralism: A Political Theory for India?" *India Quarterly* (July–December 1980): 396–405.

28. For another outstanding Indian contribution to the theory of development see Rajni Kothari, *Footsteps into the Future* (New York: Free Press, 1975).

29. G. H. Jansen, *Militant Islam* (New York: Harper and Row, 1980), as well as the special series by Sir Willie Morris in the *Christian Science Monitor*, August–September 1980, and that by Flora Lewis in *New York Times*, December 1979.

30. An especially good statement is by Harvard anthropologist Mary Catherine Bateson, "Iran's Misunderstood Revolution," *New York Times*, February 20, 1979, p. 14.

31. Jansen, *Militant Islam*; Said, *Orientalism*; Barry Rubin, *Paved with Good Intentions* (New York: Oxford University Press, 1980); Shahrough Akhavi, *Religion and Politics in Contemporary Iran* (Albany: State University of New York Press, 1980); Ali Masalehdan, "Values and Political Development in Iran" (Ph.D. diss., University of Massachusetts at Amherst, 1981); and Michael Fischer, *Iran: From Religious Dispute to Revolution* (Cambridge, Mass.: Harvard University Press, 1980). See also the discussion led by Fischer on "Iran: Is It an Example of Populist Neo-Traditionalism?" Joint Seminar on Political Development (JOSPOD), Cambridge, Mass., minutes of the meeting of October 15, 1980.

32. Anwar Syed, *Pakistan: Islam and the Dialectics of National Solidarity* (NY: Praeger, 1982). The implications of Syed's discussion are considerably broader than the case he discusses.

33. David Apter, *Ghana in Transition* (New York: Atheneum, 1967), and Ruth Schachter Morgenthau, "Single Party Systems in West Africa," *American Political Science Review*, 55 (June 1961) have both helped to popularize (and, to a degree, romanticize) the notion of the viability of African single party systems. Henry L.

Bretton, *Power and Politics in Africa* (Chicago: Aldine, 1973) helped to explode those myths.

34. My understanding of these currents in Africa has been enriched by various exchanges with and the seminar presentations of Africanist Naomi Chazan, a colleague in both Jerusalem and Cambridge; and by the writings of Swiss sociologist Pierre Pradervand, *Family Planning Programmes in Africa* (Paris: Organization for Economic Cooperation and Development, 1970); and idem, "Africa—The Fragile Giant," a series of articles in the *Christian Science Monitor*, December 1980. See also Crawford Young, *The Politics of Cultural Pluralism* (Madison: University of Wisconsin Press, 1976).

35. For a partial and inconclusive exchange on this theme see the comments of Susan Bourque, Samuel P. Huntington, Merilee Grindle, Brian Smith, and me in a JOSPOD seminar on "Neo-Traditionalism in Latin America," in minutes of the meeting of November 19, 1980.

36. Louis Hartz et al., *The Founding of New Societies* (New York: Harcourt, Brace, 1964).

37. Howard J. Wiarda, "Spain and Portugal," in *Western European Party Systems*, Peter Merkl, ed., (New York: Free Press, 1980), pp. 298–328; and idem, "Does Europe Still Stop at the Pyrenees, or Does Latin America Begin There? Iberia, Latin America, and the Second Enlargement of the European Community," in *The Impact of an Enlarged European Community on Latin America*, Georges D. Landau and G. Harvey Summ, eds. (forthcoming); also published under the same title as Occasional Paper no. 2 (Washington: American Enterprise Institute for Public Policy Research, January 1982).

38. Wiarda, *Politics and Social Change, Corporatism and Development; The Continuing Struggle*, and (earlier) "Toward a Framework for the Study of Political Change in the Iberic-Latin Tradition: The Corporative Model," *World Politics*, 25 (January 1973): 206–35.

39. Jose E. Rodo, *Ariel* (Montevideo: Dornaleche y Reyes, 1900); an English translation by F. J. Stimson was published under the same title (Boston: Houghton-Mifflin, 1922).

40. Among others, Veliz, *The Centralist Tradition;* Glen Dealy, *The Public Man: An Interpretation of Latin America and Other Catholic Countries* (Amherst: University of Massachusetts Press, 1977); Leopoldo Zea, *The Latin American Mind* (Norman: University of Oklahoma Press, 1963); Octavio Paz, *The Labyrinth of Solitude* (New York: Grove Press, 1961); Richard M. Morse, "The Heritage of Latin America," in *The Founding*, L. Hartz, ed.

41. H. G. Creel, *Chinese Thought: From Confucius to Mao Tse-tung* (Chicago: University of Chicago Press, 1963); Stuart H. Schram, *The Political Thought of Mao Tse-tung* (New York: Praeger, 1976).

42. T. O. Wilkinson, *The Urbanization of Japanese Labor* (Amherst: University of Massachusetts Press, 1965); Ezra F. Vogel, *Japan as No. 1* (Cambridge: Harvard University Press, 1979); and Peter Berger, "Secularity—West and East" (paper presented at the American Enterprise Institute Public Policy Week, Washington, D.C., December 6–9, 1982).

43. For example, Stanley Rothman and George W. Breslauer, *Soviet Politics and Society* (St. Paul, Minn.: West, 1978); Archie Brown and Jack Gray, eds., *Political Culture and Political Change in Communist States* (New York: Holmes and Meier,

1978); Jerry F. Hough and Merle Fainsod, *How the Soviet Union Is Governed* (Cambridge: Harvard University Press, 1979).

44. See, for instance, Raymond Grew, ed., *Crises of Political Development in Europe and the United States* (Princeton, N.J.: Princeton University Press, 1978); and Charles Tilly, ed., *The Formation of Nation States in Western Europe* (Princeton, N.J.: Princeton University Press, 1975).

45. This is one of the criticisms leveled in Pantham, "Integral Pluralism?" against Mehta's *Beyond Marxism*.

46. Pradervand, "Africa."

47. Pantham, "Integral Pluralism"; and idem, "Political Culture, Political Structure, and Underdevelopment in India," *Indian Journal of Political Science*, 41 (September 1980): 432–56; also Wiarda, *Corporatism and National Development*.

48. Susan Eckstein, *The Poverty of Revolution: The State and the Urban Poor in Mexico* (Princeton, N.J.: Princeton University Press, 1977); Kenneth F. Johnson, *Mexican Democracy: A Critical View* (Boston: Allyn and Bacon, 1971); Octavio Paz, *The Other Mexico* (New York: Grove Press, 1972).

49. Pradervand, "Africa."

50. Lycian Pye, *Aspects of Political Development* (Boston: Little, Brown, 1966).

51. Immanuel Wallerstein, *The Modern World-System* (New York: Academic Press, 1976).

52. Unless of course a nation is willing to withdraw entirely and consciously into isolation, but as Cambodia illustrates, that strategy may not work very well either.

53. These issues are addressed in the Introduction to the Portuguese language version of Wiarda, *Corporatism and National Development*, published as *O Modelo Corporativo na America Latina e a Latinoamericanizacao dos Estados Unidos* (Rio de Janeiro: Ed. Vozes, 1983). For an example of such ambivalence see Norbert Lechner, ed., *Estado y Política en América Latina* (Mexico City: Siglo Veintiuno Editores, 1981); also Carlos Franco, *Del Marxismo Eurocéntrico al Marxismo Latinoamericano* (Lima: Centro de Estudios para el Desarrollo y la Participación, 1981).

54. For a country-by-country analysis combined with a common set of theoretical concepts see Howard J. Wiarda and Harvey F. Kline, *Latin American Politics and Development* (Boston: Houghton-Mifflin, 1979).

55. Masalehdan, *Values and Political Development in Iran*.

56. Oswald Spengler, *The Decline of the West* (New York: Knopf, 1932); and much recent literature.

57. See my research agenda as set forth in the edited volumes *New Directions in Comparative Politics* and *Third World Conceptions of Development*.

58. In a personal conversation with the author, December 1979.

59. The research perspectives suggested here and the implications of these as set forth in the concluding paragraphs are explored in greater detail in Wiarda, "Ethnocentrism"; *Politics and Social Change, The Continuing Struggle for Democracy*; and *Corporatism and National Development*.

60. I have attempted to formulate such a theory in "Toward a Framework for the Study of Political Change in the Iberic-Latin Tradition," and in *Corporatism and National Development*.

61. For example, our community development, family planning, agrarian reform, military assistance, labor, economic development, and numerous other foreign aid programs have all been based on the "Western" (i.e., United States and northwest Europe) model, which is one key reason, I would argue, that few of them have worked or produced their anticipated consequences. On this see Robert A. Packenham, *Liberal America and the Third World: Political Development Ideas in Foreign Aid and Social Science* (Princeton, N.J.: Princeton University Press, 1973).

PART TWO

ECONOMIC DEVELOPMENT AND UNDERDEVELOPMENT IN HISTORICAL PERSPECTIVE

The essence of economic development is rapid and discontinuous change in institutions and in economic relations, so it is impossible to construct a rigorous and determinate model of that process. Any student of development must be willing to settle for less. Elegance and rigor are important attributes of economic theory, but they take second place to relevance and applicability. The more rigorous the model, the higher its degree of technical success may be, but the greater its inability to explain economic development. Such a model necessarily omits too many of the most significant variables in economic development, so an inquiry into the origin of economic development and underdevelopment ought not to commence with a highly generalized and abstract model. If a rigorous and determinate model cannot be utilized to study the process of economic development, a less rigorous but more richly textured approach that accounts for the most important socioeconomic variables must be constructed. For this we must turn to history.

One of the greatest weaknesses of mainstream economic theorists is their lack of understanding of the process of development in the West between the seventeenth and twentieth centuries. The development of capitalism in the West was faced with the need for change in the social structure so that the progress-oriented middle class could become the leaders of society. This change often involved a violent struggle for supremacy between the old social order and the emerging new one. The English Revolution of 1640, ending with the Supremacy of Parliament Act in 1688, replaced the feudal lords with the landed gentry and the urban middle class as the dominant classes in England, thus preparing the way for later economic change. The French Revolution of 1789 replaced the old aristocracy with the new middle class, while the absence of such social change was a major factor in the economic stagnation of Spain after the seventeenth century.

This change in social structure enabled the productive use of the social surplus. The social surplus may be viewed as a residual, that part of society's total product remaining after basic consumption needs are met. How a society chooses to use this net product of its labor—squandering it in luxury consumption and military adventure or adding to the country's capital stock—conditions the pattern of development. Of critical importance is who controls the surplus. Are decisions made to favor elites or is the social surplus used to develop society for the good of all?

Because the Western capitalist model forms the core of many Third World development strategies, it is important to have a clear sense of the dynamics of early capitalism and how they compare with development demands today. Dudley Dillard's article outlines the crucial elements in the historical development of capitalism in the West. As Dillard points out in the first reading in this part, "Productive use of the 'social surplus' was the special virtue that enabled capitalism to outstrip all prior economic systems."

In "On the Political Economy of Backwardness," Paul Baran argues the virtual impossibility of capitalist development in the Third World. Focusing on the class relations among the masses, internal elites, and foreign investors, he highlights the contradiction between imperialism, the process of industrialization, and the general economic development of poor nations. For Baran continuous capitalist development is implausible for the Third World because of the power configuration between foreign and domestic decision makers and the people. Capitalism entered most underdeveloped countries the "Prussian Way"—not through the growth of small, competitive enterprise, but through the transfer from abroad of advanced, monopolistic business. Thus capitalist development in these countries was not accompanied by the rise of a strong, property-owning middle class and by the overthrow of landlord domination of society. Instead, an accommodation was reached between the newly arrived monopolistic business and the socially and politically entrenched agrarian aristocracy. Korea and Taiwan are exceptions, but they prove the rule.

As a result, there was neither vigorous competition between enterprises striving for increased output nor accumulation of the social surplus in the hands of entrepreneurs who would be forced by the competitive system to reinvest in the expansion and modernization of their businesses. As a result production was well below the potential level, agriculture continued on a semifeudal basis, and waste and irrationality in industry was protected by monopoly, high tariffs, and other devices.

For these and other reasons the actual social surplus was much lower than the potential social surplus. A large share of the potential social surplus was used by aristocratic landlords on excess consumption and the maintenance of unproductive laborers. In addition, a large share of the actual social surplus was taken by owners for commercial operations promising large and quick profits or for the accumulation of investments or bank accounts abroad as a hedge against domestic social and political hazards. Furthermore, in order to obtain social status and the benefits and privileges necessary for the operation of a business, they emulated the dominant aristocracy in its mode of living. The actual social surplus was further reduced by the substantial quantity of resources used to maintain elaborate and inefficient bureaucratic and military establishments.

Andre Gunder Frank, in "The Development of Underdevelopment," shows that stagnation in the periphery was generated by the same historical process as successful capitalist development. Instead of focusing on relations between classes, Frank concentrates on the nation-state and the incorporation of Latin America and other periphery economies into the world capitalist order. Hierarchical relations between the First and Third World prevented the effective possibility of sustained, dynamic capitalist development for the periphery. Integration into the global economy was achieved through an intermediate metropolis-satellite chain, in which the surplus generated at each stage was successively drawn to the center. The most underdeveloped regions are therefore those with the strongest ties in the past; the strongest developing economies are those which, usually through some crisis, had looser colonial ties.

David Ruccio and Lawrence H. Simon provide an overview of two other analyses of underdevelopment which stem from Marxist analysis. Marxists take issue with the external orientation of Frank and dependency theorists in their explanation of underdevelopment. They concentrate, instead, on the internal development of the means of production and the social relations that characterize them. Marxists argue that periods of stagnation and imbalance are inherent in the processes of capitalist development and that the Third World is indeed successfully pursuing the capitalist growth path.

The section concludes with two historical studies of the processes of development or underdevelopment. Lucile Brockway documents the formative influence of Britain's Kew Gardens on world agricultural production. Through theft and deception Britain and other European countries were able to establish the productive base of their colonial empires, dividing the world into metropolis and satellite in Frank's terms. The Brockway story has a contemporary ring as ethnobotanists scour the world to preserve biological specimens which are threatened by economic expansion; in the process they may provide the basis for future agricultural development.

A fascinating historical case study of modernization without development follows. E. Bradford Burns's study of El Salvador provides a striking example of how the rapid and profound modernization of a once-neglected outpost of the Spanish empire was accompanied by increasing impoverishment of the majority of the inhabitants. It again has a contemporary ring, for it provides keen insight into the Salvadorian civil war that has continued from 1979 into the 1990s. Burns's treatment of the Escuela Militar should seem current, given the central role of its personnel in the 1989 murder of the six Jesuits, their housekeeper, and her daughter.

5

Capitalism

Dudley Dillard

Capitalism [is] a term used to denote the economic system that has been dominant in the Western world since the breakup of feudalism. Fundamental to any system called capitalist are the relations between private owners of nonpersonal means of production (land, mines, industrial plants, etc., collectively known as capital) and free but capital-less workers, who sell their labour services to employers. Under capitalism, decisions concerning production are made by private businessmen operating for private profit. Labourers are free in the sense that they cannot legally be compelled to work for the owners of the means of production. However, since labourers do not possess the means of production required for self-employment, they must, of economic necessity, offer their services on some terms to employers who do control the means of production. The resulting wage bargains determine the proportion in which the total product of society will be shared between the class of labourers and the class of capitalist entrepreneurs.

· · · · · ·

HISTORICAL DEVELOPMENT

1.   Origins of Capitalism

Although the continuous development of capitalism as a system dates only from the 16th century, antecedents of capitalist institutions existed in the ancient world, and flourishing pockets of capitalism were present during the later middle ages. One strategic external force contributing to the breakup of medieval economic institutions was the growing volume of long-distance trade between capitalist centres, carried on with capitalist techniques in a capitalist spirit. Specialized industries grew up to serve

Reprinted from *Encyclopaedia Britannica*, pp. 839–842, by permission of the publisher and the author. Copyright © *Encyclopaedia Britannica*, 1972.

long-distance trade, and the resulting commercial and industrial towns gradually exerted pressures which weakened the internal structure of agriculture based on serfdom, the hallmark of the feudal regime. Changes in trade, industry, and agriculture were taking place simultaneously and interacting with one another in highly complex actual relations, but it was chiefly long-distance trade which set in motion changes that spread throughout the medieval economy and finally transformed it into a new type of economic society.

Flanders in the 13th century and Florence in the 14th century were two capitalist pockets of special interest. Their histories shed light on the conditions that were essential to the development of capitalism in England. The great enterprise of late medieval and early modern Europe was the woolen industry, and most of the business arrangements that later characterized capitalism developed in connection with long-distance trade in wool and cloth.

In Flanders revolutionary conflict raged between plebeian craftsmen and patrician merchant-manufacturers. The workers succeeded in destroying the concentration of economic and political power in the hands of cloth magnates, only to be crushed in turn by a violent counterrevolution that destroyed the woolen industry and brought ruin to both groups. A similar performance was repeated in Florence, which became one of the great industrial cities of Europe during the 14th century. Restless, revolutionary urban workers overthrew the ruling hierarchy of merchants, manufacturers, and bankers, and were in turn crushed in a bloody counterrevolution. Thus both Flanders and Florence failed to perpetuate their great industries because they failed to solve the social problem arising from conflicting claims of small numbers of rich capitalists and large numbers of poor workers.

2.   Early Capitalism (1500–1750)

By the end of the middle ages the English cloth industry had become the greatest in Europe. Because of the domestic availability of raw wool and the innovation of simple mechanical fulling mills, the English cloth industry had established itself in certain rural areas where it avoided the violent social strife that had destroyed the urban industries of Flanders and Florence. Although it was subject to many problems and difficulties, the English rural cloth industry continued to grow at a rapid rate during the 16th, 17th and 18th centuries. Hence, it was the woolen industry that spearheaded capitalism as a social and economic system and rooted it for the first time in English soil.

Productive use of the "social surplus" was the special virtue that enabled capitalism to outstrip all prior economic systems. Instead of building pyramids and cathedrals, those in command of the social surplus chose to invest in ships, warehouses, raw materials, finished goods, and other material forms of wealth. The social surplus was thus converted into enlarged productive capacity. Among the historical events and circumstances that significantly influenced capital formation in western Europe in the early stage of capitalist development, three merit special attention: (1) religious sanction for hard work and frugality; (2) the impact of precious metals from the new world on the relative shares of income going to wages, profits, and rents; and (3) the role of national states in fostering and directly providing capital formation in the form of general-purpose capital goods.

Capitalist spirit   The economic ethics taught by medieval Catholicism presented obstacles to capitalist ideology and development. Hostility to material wealth carried forward the teachings of the Christian fathers against mammonism. Saint Jerome said, "A rich man is either a thief or the son of a thief." Saint Augustine felt that trade was bad because it turned men away from the search for God. Down through the middle ages commerce and banking were viewed, at best, as necessary evils. Moneylending was for a time confined to non-Christians because it was considered unworthy of Christians. Interest on loans was unlawful under the anti-usury laws of both church and secular authorities. Speculation and profiteering violated the central medieval economic doctrine of just price.

Expansion of commerce in the later middle ages stirred controversies and led to attempts to reconcile theological doctrines with economic realities. In Venice, Florence, Augsburg, and Antwerp—all Catholic cities—capitalists violated the spirit and circumvented the letter of the prohibitions against interest. On the eve of the Protestant Reformation capitalists, who still laboured under the shadow of the sin of avarice, had by their deeds become indispensable to lay rulers and to large numbers of people who were dependent upon them for employment.

The Protestant Reformation of the 16th and 17th centuries developed alongside economic changes which resulted in the spread of capitalism in northern Europe, especially in the Netherlands and England. This chronological and geographical correlation between the new religion and economic development has led to the suggestion that Protestantism had causal significance for the rise of modern capitalism. Without in any sense being the "cause" of capitalism, which already existed on a wide and expanding horizon, the Protestant ethic proved a bracing stimulant to the new economic order. Doctrinal revision or interpretation seemed not only to exonerate capitalists from the sin of avarice but even to give divine sanction to their way of life. In the ordinary conduct of life, a new type of worldly asceticism emerged, one that meant hard work, frugality, sobriety, and efficiency in one's calling in the marketplace similar to that of the monastery. Applied in the environment of expanding trade and industry, the Protestant creed taught that accumulated wealth should be used to produce more wealth.

Acceptance of the Protestant ethic also eased the way to systematic organization of free labour. By definition, free labourers could not be compelled by force to work in the service of others. Moreover, the use of force would have violated the freedom of one's calling. Psychological compulsion arising from religious belief was the answer to the paradox. Every occupation was said to be noble in God's eyes. For those with limited talents, Christian conscience demanded unstinting labour even at low wages in the service of God—and, incidentally, of employers. It was an easy step to justify economic inequality because it would hasten the accumulation of wealth by placing it under the guardianship of the most virtuous (who were, incidentally, the wealthiest) and remove temptation from weaker persons who could not withstand the allurements associated with wealth. After all, it did not much matter who held legal title to wealth, for it was not for enjoyment. The rich like the poor were to live frugally all the days of their lives. Thus the capitalist system found a justification that was intended to make inequality tolerable to the working classes.

The price revolution   Meanwhile treasure from the new world had a profound impact on European capitalism, on economic classes, and on the distribution of income in Europe. Gold and silver from the mines of Mexico, Peru, and Bolivia increased Europe's supply of precious metals sevenfold and raised prices two- or threefold between 1540 and 1640. The significance of the increased supply of money lay not so much in the rise in prices as in its effect on the social and economic classes of Europe. Landlords, the older ruling class, suffered because money rents failed to rise as rapidly as the cost of living. The more aggressive landlords raised rents and introduced capitalistic practices into agriculture. In England the enclosure movement, which developed with ever increasing momentum and vigour during the 17th and 18th centuries, encouraged sheep raising to supply wool to the expanding woolen industry. Among labourers, money wages failed to keep pace with the cost of living, causing real wages to fall during the price revolution. The chief beneficiaries of this century-long inflation were capitalists, including merchants, manufacturers, and other employers. High prices and low wages resulted in profit inflation, which in turn contributed to larger savings and capital accumulation. Profit inflation and wage deflation created a more unequal distribution of income. Wage earners got less and capitalists got more of the total product than they would have received in the absence of inflation. Had the new increments of wealth gone to wage earners instead of to capitalists, most of it would have been consumed rather than invested, and hence the working classes of the 16th century would have eaten better, but the future would have inherited less accumulated wealth.

Mercantilism   Early capitalism (1500–1750) also witnessed in western Europe the rise of strong national states pursuing mercantilist policies.

Critics have tended to identify mercantilism with amassing silver and gold by having a so-called favourable balance of exports over imports in trading relations with other nations and communities, but the positive contribution and historic significance of mercantilism lay in the creation of conditions necessary for rapid and cumulative economic change in the countries of western Europe. At the end of the middle ages western Europe stood about where many underdeveloped countries stand in the 20th century. In under-developed economies the difficult task of statesmanship is to get under way a cumulative process of economic development, for once a certain momentum is attained, further advances appear to follow more or less automatically. Achieving such sustained growth requires virtually a social revolution.

Power must be transferred from reactionary to progressive classes; new energies must be released, often by uprooting the old order; the prevailing religious outlook may constitute a barrier to material advancement. A new social and political framework must be created within which cumulative economic change can take place.

Among the tasks which private capitalists were either unable or unwilling to perform were the creation of a domestic market free of tolls and other barriers to trade within the nation's borders; a uniform monetary system; a legal code appropriate to capitalistic progress; a skilled and disciplined labour force; safeguards against internal violence; national defense against attack; sufficient literacy and education among business classes to use credit instruments, contracts and other documents required of a commercial civilization; basic facilities for communication and transportation and harbour installations. A strong government and an adequate supply of economic resources were required to create most of these conditions, which constitute the "social overhead capital" needed in a productive economy. Because the returns from them, however great, cannot be narrowly channeled for private gain, such investments must normally be made by the government and must be paid for out of public revenues.

Preoccupation with productive use of the social surplus led mercantilist commentators to advocate low wages and long hours for labour. Consumption in excess of bare subsistence was viewed as a tax on progress and therefore contrary to the national interest. Mercantilist society was not a welfare state; it could not afford to be. Luxury consumption was condemned as a dissipation of the social surplus. Restrictions on imports were directed especially at luxury consumption.

Opportunities for profitable private investment multiplied rapidly as mercantilist policy succeeded in providing the basic social overhead capital. Rather paradoxically, it was because the state had made such an important contribution to economic development that the ideology of laissez-faire could later crystallise. When that occurred, dedication to capital accumulation remained a basic principle of capitalism, but the shift from public to private initiative marked the passage from the early state of capitalism and the beginning of the next stage, the classical period.

3.   Classical Capitalism (1750–1914)

In England, beginning in the 18th century, the focus of capitalist development shifted from commerce to industry. The Industrial Revolution may be defined as the period of transition from a dominance of commercial over industrial capital to a dominance of industrial over commercial capital. Preparation for this shift began long before the invention of the flying shuttle, the water frame and the steam engine, but the technological changes of the 18th century made the transition dramatically evident.

The rural and household character of the English textile industry continued only as long as the amount of fixed capital required for efficient production remained relatively small. Changes in technology and organization shifted industry again to urban centres in the course of the Industrial Revolution, although not to the old commercial urban centres. Two or three centuries of steady capital accumulation began to pay off handsomely in the 18th century. Now it became feasible to make practical use of technical knowledge which had been accumulating over the centuries. Capitalism became a powerful promoter of technological change because the accumulation of capital made possible the use of inventions which poorer societies could not have afforded. Inventors and innovators like James Watt found business partners who were able to finance their inventions through lean years of experimentation and discouragement to ultimate commercial success. Aggressive entrepreneurs like Richard Arkwright found capital to finance the factory type of organization required for the utilization of new machines. Wealthy societies had existed before capitalism, but none had managed their wealth in a manner that enabled them to take advantage of the more efficient methods of production which an increasing mastery over nature made physically possible.

Adam Smith's great *Inquiry Into the Nature and Causes of the Wealth of Nations* (1776) expressed the ideology of classical capitalism. Smith recommended dismantling the state bureaucracy and leaving economic decisions to the free play of self-regulating market forces. While Smith recognized the faults of businessmen, he contended they could do little harm in a world of freely competitive enterprise. In Smith's opinion, private profit and public welfare would become reconciled through impersonal forces of market competition. After the French Revolution and the Napoleonic wars had swept the remnants of feudalism into oblivion and rapidly undermined mercantilist fetters, Smith's policies were put into practice. Laissez-faire policies of 19th-century political liberalism included free trade, sound money (the gold standard), balanced budgets, minimum poor relief—in brief, the principle of leaving individuals to themselves and of trusting that their unregulated interactions would produce socially desirable results. No new conceptions of society arose immediately to challenge seriously what had become, in fact, a capitalist civilization.

This system, though well-defined and logically coherent, must be understood as a system of tendencies only. The heritage of the past and other obstructions prevented any full realization of the principles except in a few cases of which the English free trade movement, crystallised by the repeal of the Corn Laws in 1846, is the most important. Such as they were, however, both tendencies and realizations bear the unmistakable stamp of the businessman's interests and still more the businessman's type of mind. Moreover, it was not only policy but the philosophy of national and individual life, the scheme of cultural values, that bore that stamp. Its materialistic utilitarianism, its naive confidence in progress of a certain type, its actual achievements in the field of pure and applied science, the temper of its artistic creations, may all be traced to the spirit of rationalism that emanates from the businessman's office. For much of the time and in many countries the businessman did not rule politically. But even noncapitalist rulers espoused his interests and adopted his views. They were what they had not been before, his agents.

More definitely than in any other historical epoch these developments can be explained by purely economic causes. It was the success of capitalist enterprise that raised the bourgeoisie to its position of temporary ascendancy. Economic success produced political power, which in turn produced policies congenial to the capitalist process. Thus the English industrialists obtained free trade, and free trade in turn was a major factor in a period of unprecedented economic expansion.

The partition of Africa and the carving out of spheres of influence in Asia by European powers in the decades preceding World War I led critics of capitalism to develop, on a Marxist basis, a theory of economic imperialism. According to this doctrine, competition among capitalist firms tends to eliminate all but a small number of giant concerns. Because of the inadequate purchasing power of the masses, these concerns find themselves unable to use the productive capacity they have built. They are, therefore, driven to invade foreign markets and to exclude foreign products from their own markets through protective tariffs. This situation produces aggressive colonial and foreign policies and "imperialist" wars, which the proletariat, if organized, turn into civil wars for socialist revolution. Like other doctrines of such sweeping character, this theory of imperialism is probably not capable of either exact proof or disproof. Three points, however, may be recorded in its favour; first, it does attempt what no other theory has attempted, namely, to subject the whole of the economic, political, and cultural patterns of the epoch that began during the long depression (1873–96) to comprehensive analysis by means of a clear-cut plan; second, on the surface at least, it seems to be confirmed by some of the outstanding manifestations of this pattern and some of the greatest events of this epoch; third, whatever may be wrong with its interpretations, it certainly starts from a fact that is beyond challenge—the capitalist tendency toward industrial combination and the emergence of giant firms. Though cartels and trusts antedate the epoch, at least so far as the United States is concerned, the role of what is popularly called "big business" has increased so much as to constitute one of the outstanding characteristics of recent capitalism.

4.   The Later Phase (Since 1914)

World War I marked a turning point in the development of capitalism in general and of European capitalism in particular. The period since 1914 has witnessed a reversal of the public attitude toward capitalism and of almost all the tendencies of the liberal epoch which preceded the war. In the pre-war decades, European capitalism exercised vigorous leadership in the international economic community. World markets expanded, the gold standard became almost universal, Europe served as the world's banker, Africa became a European colony, Asia was divided into spheres of influence under the domination of European powers, and Europe remained the centre of a growing volume of international trade.

After World War I, however, these trends were reversed. International markets shrank, the gold standard was abandoned in favour of managed national currencies, banking hegemony passed from Europe to the United States, African and Asian peoples began successful revolts against European colonialism, and trade barriers multiplied. Western Europe as an entity declined, and in eastern Europe capitalism began to disintegrate. The Russian Revolution, a result of the war, uprooted over a vast area not only the basic capitalist institution of private property in the means of production, but the class structure, the traditional forms of government, and the established religion. Moreover, the juggernaut unleashed by the Russian Revolution was destined to challenge the historic superiority of capitalist organization as a system of production within less than half a century. Meanwhile, the inner structure of West European economies was tending away from the traditional forms of capitalism. Above all, laissez-faire, the accepted policy of the 19th century, was discredited by the war and post-war experience.

Statesmen and businessmen in capitalist nations were slow to appreciate the turn of events precipitated by World War I and consequently they misdirected their efforts during the 1920s by seeking a "return to prewar normalcy." Among major capitalist countries, the United Kingdom failed conspicuously to achieve prosperity at any time during the interwar period. Other capitalist nations enjoyed a brief prosperity in the 1920s only to be confronted in the 1930s with the great depression, which rocked the capitalist system to its foundations. Laissez-faire received a crushing blow from President Franklin D. Roosevelt's New Deal in the United States. The gold standard collapsed completely. Free trade was abandoned in its classic home, Great Britain. Even the classical principle of sound finance, the annually balanced governmental budget, gave way in both practice and theory to planned deficits during periods of depressed economic activity. Retreat from the free market philosophy was nearly complete in Mussolini's Italy and Hitler's Germany. When World War II opened in 1939, the future of capitalism looked bleak indeed. This trend seemed confirmed at the end of the war when the British Labour party won a decisive victory at the polls and proceeded to nationalize basic industries, including coal, transportation, communication, public utilities, and the Bank of England. Yet a judgment that capitalism had at last run its course would have been premature. Capitalist enterprise managed to survive in Great Britain, the United States, western Germany, Japan, and other nations [with a] remarkable show of vitality in the postwar world.

6

On the Political Economy of Backwardness

Paul A. Baran

I

The capitalist mode of production and the social and political order concomitant with it provided, during the latter part of the eighteenth century, and still more during the entire nineteenth century, a framework for a continuous and, in spite of cyclical disturbances and setbacks, momentous expansion of productivity and material welfare. The relevant facts are well known and call for no elaboration. Yet this material (and cultural) progress was not only spotty in time but most unevenly distributed in space. It was confined to the Western world, and did not affect even all of this territorially and demographically relatively small sector of the inhabited globe.

· · · · · ·

Tardy and skimpy as the benefits of capitalism may have been with respect to the lower classes even in most of the leading industrial countries, they were all but negligible in the less privileged parts of the world. There productivity remained low, and rapid increases in population pushed living standards from bad to worse. The dreams of the prophets of capitalist harmony remained on paper. Capital either did not move from countries where its marginal productivity was low to countries where it could be expected to be high, or if it did, it moved there mainly in order to extract profits from backward countries that frequently accounted for a lion's share of the increments in total output caused by the original investments. Where an increase in the aggregate national product of an underdeveloped country took place, the existing distribution of income prevented this increment from raising the living standards of the broad masses of the population.

Reprinted from *The Manchester School* (January 1952), pp. 66–84, by permission of the publisher.

Like all general statements, this one is obviously open to criticism based on particular cases. There were, no doubt, colonies and dependencies where the populations profited from inflow of foreign capital. These benefits, however, were few and far between, while exploitation and stagnation were the prevailing rule.

But if Western capitalism failed to improve materially the lot of the peoples inhabiting most backward areas, it accomplished something that profoundly affected the social and political conditions in underdeveloped countries. It introduced there, with amazing rapidity, all the economic and social tensions inherent in the capitalist order. It effectively disrupted whatever was left of the "feudal" coherence of the backward societies. It substituted market contracts for such paternalistic relationships as still survived from century to century. It reoriented the partly or wholly self-sufficient economies of agricultural countries toward the production of marketable commodities. It linked their economic fate with the vagaries of the world market and connected it with the fever curve of international price movements.

A *complete* substitution of capitalist market rationality for the rigidities of feudal or semifeudal servitude would have represented, in spite of all the pains of transition, an important step in the direction of progress. Yet all that happened was that the age-old exploitation of the population of underdeveloped countries by their domestic overlords was freed of the mitigating constraints inherited from the feudal transition. This superimposition of business mores over ancient oppression by landed gentries resulted in compounded exploitation, more outrageous corruption, and more glaring injustice.

Nor is this by any means the end of the story. Such export of capital and capitalism as has taken place had not only far-reaching implications of a social nature. It was accompanied by important physical and technical processes. Modern machines and products of advanced industries reached the poverty-stricken backyards of the world. To be sure most, if not all, of these machines worked for their foreign owners—or at least were believed by the population to be working for no one else—and the new refined appurtenances of the good life belonged to foreign businessmen and their domestic counterparts. The bonanza that was capitalism, the fullness of things that was modern industrial civilization, were crowding the display windows—they were protected by barbed wire from the anxious grip of the starving and desperate man in the street.

But they have drastically changed his outlook. Broadening and deepening his economic horizon, they aroused aspirations, envies, and hopes. Young intellectuals filled with zeal and patriotic devotion traveled from the underdeveloped lands to Berlin and London, to Paris and New York, and returned home with the "message of the possible."

Fascinated by the advances and accomplishments observed in the centers of modern industry, they developed and propagandized the image of what could be attained in their home countries under a more rational economic and social order. The dissatisfaction with the stagnation (or at best, barely perceptible growth) that ripened gradually under the still-calm political and social surface was given an articulate expression. This dissatisfaction was not nurtured by a comparison of reality with a vision of a socialist society. It found sufficient fuel in the confrontation of what was actually happening with what could be accomplished under capitalist institutions of the Western type.

II

The establishment of such institutions was, however, beyond the reach of the tiny middle classes of most backward areas. The inherited backwardness and poverty of their countries never gave them an opportunity to gather the economic strength, the insight, and the self-confidence needed for the assumption of a leading role in society. For centuries under feudal rule they themselves assimilated the political, moral, and cultural values of the dominating class.

While in advanced countries, such as France or Great Britain, the economically ascending middle classes developed at an early stage a new rational world outlook, which they proudly opposed to the medieval obscurantism of the feudal age, the poor, fledgling bourgeoisie of the underdeveloped countries sought nothing but accommodation to the prevailing order. Living in societies based on privilege, they strove for a share in the existing sinecures. They made political and economic deals with their domestic feudal overlords or with powerful foreign investors, and what industry and commerce developed in backward areas in the course of the last hundred years was rapidly moulded in the straitjacket of monopoly—the plutocratic partner of the aristocratic rulers. What resulted was an economic and political amalgam combining the worst features of both worlds—feudalism and capitalism—and blocking effectively all possibilities of economic growth.

It is quite conceivable that a "conservative" exit from this impasse might have been found in the course of time. A younger generation of enterprising and enlightened businessmen and intellectuals allied with moderate leaders of workers and peasants—a "Young Turk" movement of some sort—might have succeeded in breaking the deadlock, in loosening the hide-bound social and political structure of their countries and in creating the institutional arrangements indispensable for a measure of social and economic progress.

Yet in our rapid age history accorded no time for such a gradual transition. Popular pressures for an amelioration of economic and social conditions, or at least for some perceptible movement in that direction, steadily gained in intensity. To be sure, the growing restiveness of the underprivileged was not directed against the ephemeral principles of a hardly yet existing capitalist order. Its objects were parasitic feudal overlords appropriating large slices of the national product and wasting them on extravagant living; a government machinery protecting and abetting the dominant interests; wealthy businessmen reaping immense profits and not utilizing them for productive purposes; last but not least, foreign colonizers extracting or believed to be extracting vast gains from their "developmental" operations.

This popular movement had thus essentially bourgeois, democratic, anti-feudal, anti-imperialist tenets. It found outlets in agrarian egalitarianism; it incorporated "muckraker" elements denouncing monopoly; it strove for national independence and freedom from foreign exploitation.

For the native capitalist middle classes to assume the leadership of these popular forces and to direct them into the channels of bourgeois democracy—as has happened in Western Europe—they had to identify themselves with the common man. They had to break away from the political, economic, and ideological leadership of the feudal crust and the monopolists allied with it; and they had to demonstrate to the nation as a whole that they had the knowledge, the courage, and the determination to undertake and to carry to victorious conclusion the struggle for economic and social improvement.

In hardly any underdeveloped country were the middle classes capable of living up to this historical challenge. Some of the reasons for this portentous failure, reasons connected with the internal make-up of the business class itself, were briefly mentioned above. Of equal importance was, however, an "outside" factor. It was the spectacular growth of the international labor movement in Europe that offered the popular forces in backward areas ideological and political leadership that was denied to them by the native bourgeoisie. It pushed the goals and targets of the popular movements far beyond their original limited objectives.

This liaison of labor radicalism and populist revolt painted on the wall the imminent danger of a social revolution. Whether this danger was real or imaginary matters very little. What was essential is that the awareness of this threat effectively determined political and social action. It destroyed whatever chances there were of the capitalist classes joining and leading the popular anti-feudal, anti-monopolist movement. By instilling a mortal fear of expropriation and extinction in the minds of *all* property-owning groups the rise of socialist radicalism, and in particular the Bolshevik Revolution in Russia, tended to drive all more or less privileged, more or less well-to-do elements in the society into one "counterrevolutionary" coalition. Whatever differences and antagonisms existed between large and small landowners, between monopolistic and competitive business, between liberal bourgeois and reactionary feudal overlords, between domestic and foreign interests, were largely submerged on all important occasions by the over-riding *common* interest in staving off socialism.

The possibility of solving the economic and political deadlock prevailing in the underdeveloped countries on lines of a progressive capitalism all but disappeared. Entering the alliance with all other segments of the ruling class, the capitalist middle classes yielded one strategic position after another. Afraid that a quarrel with the landed gentry might be exploited by the radical populist movement, the middle classes abandoned all progressive attitudes in agrarian matters. Afraid that a conflict with the church and the military might weaken the political authority of the government, the middle classes moved away from all liberal and pacifist currents. Afraid that hostility toward foreign interests might deprive them of foreign support in a case of a revolutionary emergency, the native capitalists deserted their previous anti-imperialist, nationalist platforms.

The peculiar mechanisms of political interaction characteristic of all underdeveloped (and perhaps not only underdeveloped) countries thus operated at full speed. The aboriginal failure of the middle classes to provide inspiration and leadership to the popular masses pushed those masses into the camp of socialist radicalism. The growth of radicalism pushed the middle classes into an alliance with the aristocratic and monopolistic reaction. This alliance, cemented by common interest and common fear, pushed the populist forces still further along the road of radicalism and revolt. The outcome was a polarization of society with very little left between the poles. By permitting this polarization to develop, by abandoning the common man and resigning the task of reorganizing society on new, progressive lines, the capitalist middle classes threw away their historical chance of assuming effective control over the destinies of their nations, and of directing the gathering popular storm against the fortresses of feudalism and reaction. Its blazing fire turned thus against the entirety of existing economic and social institutions.

III

The economic and political order maintained by the ruling coalition of owning classes finds itself invariably at odds with all the urgent needs of the underdeveloped countries. Neither the social fabric that it embodies nor the institutions that rest upon it are conducive to progressive economic development. The only way to provide for economic growth and to prevent a continuous deterioration of living standards (apart from mass emigration unacceptable to other countries) is to assure a steady increase of total output—at least large enough to offset the rapid growth of population.

An obvious source of such an increase is the utilization of available unutilized or underutilized resources. A large part of this reservoir of dormant productive potentialities is the vast multitude of entirely unemployed or ineffectively employed manpower. There is no way of employing it usefully in agriculture, where the marginal productivity of labor tends to zero. They could be provided with opportunities for productive work only by transfer to industrial pursuits. For this to be feasible large investments in industrial plant and facilities have to be undertaken. Under prevailing conditions such investments are not forthcoming for a number of important and interrelated reasons.

With a very uneven distribution of a very small aggregate income (and wealth), large individual incomes exceeding what could be regarded as "reasonable" requirements for current consumption accrue as a rule to a relatively small group of high-income receivers. Many of them are large landowners maintaining a feudal style of life with large outlays on housing, servants, travel, and other luxuries. Their "requirements for consumption" are so high that there is only little room for savings. Only relatively insignificant amounts are left to be spent on improvements of agricultural estates.

Other members of the "upper crust" receiving incomes markedly surpassing "reasonable" levels of consumption are wealthy businessmen. For social reasons briefly mentioned above, their consumption too is very much larger than it would have been were they brought up in the puritan tradition of a bourgeois civilization. Their drive to accumulate and to expand their enterprises is continuously counteracted by the urgent desire to imitate in their living habits the socially dominant "old families," to prove by their conspicuous outlays on the amenities of rich life that they are socially (and therefore also politically) not inferior to their aristocratic partners in the ruling coalition.

But if this tendency curtails the volume of savings that could have been amassed by the urban high-income receivers, their will to reinvest their funds in productive enterprises is effectively curbed by a strong reluctance to damage their carefully erected monopolistic market positions through creation of additional productive capacity, and by absence of suitable investment opportunities—paradoxical as this may sound with reference to underdeveloped countries.

The deficiency of investment opportunities stems to a large extent from the structure and the limitations of the existing effective demand. With very low living standards the bulk of the aggregate money income of the population is spent on food and relatively primitive items of clothing and household necessities. These are available at low prices, and investment of large funds in plant and facilities that could produce this type of commodities more cheaply rarely promises attractive returns. Nor does it appear profitable to develop major enterprises the output of which would cater to the requirements of the rich. Large as their individual purchases of various luxuries may be, their aggregate spending on each of them is not sufficient to support the development of an elaborate luxury industry—in particular since the "snob" character of prevailing tastes renders only imported luxury articles true marks of social distinction.

Finally, the limited demand for investment goods precludes the building up of a machinery or equipment industry. Such mass consumption goods as are lacking, and such quantities of luxury goods as are purchased by the well-to-do, as well as the comparatively small quantities of investment goods needed by industry, are thus imported from abroad in exchange for domestic agricultural products and raw materials.

This leaves the expansion of exportable raw materials output as a major outlet for investment activities. There the possibilities are greatly influenced, however, by the technology of the production of most raw materials as well as by the nature of the markets to be served. Many raw materials, in particular oil, metals, certain industrial crops, have to be produced on a large scale if costs are to be kept low and satisfactory returns assured. Large-scale production, however, calls for large investments, so large indeed as to exceed the potentialities of the native capitalists in backward countries. Production of raw materials for a distant market entails, moreover, much larger risks than those encountered in domestic business. The difficulty of foreseeing accurately such things as receptiveness of the world markets, prices obtainable in competition with other countries, volume of output in other parts of the world, etc., sharply reduces the interest of native capitalists in these lines of business. They become to a predominant extent the domain of foreigners who, financially stronger, have at the same time much closer contacts with foreign outlets of their products.

The shortage of investible funds and the lack of investment opportunities represent two aspects of the same problem. A great number of investment projects, unprofitable under prevailing conditions, could be most promising in a general environment of economic expansion.

In backward areas a new industrial venture must frequently, if not always, break virgin ground. It has no functioning economic system to draw upon. It has to organize with its own efforts not only the productive process *within* its own confines, it must provide in addition for all the necessary *outside* arrangements essential to its operations. It does not enjoy the benefits of "external economies."

There can be no doubt that the absence of external economies, the inadequacy of the economic milieu in underdeveloped countries, constituted everywhere an important deterrent to investment in industrial projects. There is no way of rapidly bridging the gap. Large-scale investment is predicated upon large-scale investment. Roads, electric power stations, railroads, and houses have to be built *before* businessmen find it profitable to erect factories, to invest their funds in new industrial enterprises.

Yet investing in road building, financing construction of canals and power stations, organizing large housing projects, etc., transcend by far the financial and mental horizon of capitalists in underdeveloped countries. Not only are their financial resources too small for such ambitious projects, but their background and habits militate against entering commitments of this type. Brought up in the tradition of merchandizing and manufacturing consumers' goods—as is characteristic of an early phase of capitalist development—businessmen in underdeveloped countries are accustomed to rapid turnover, large but short-term risks, and correspondingly high rates of profit. Sinking funds in enterprises where profitability could manifest itself only in the course of many years is a largely unknown and unattractive departure. The difference between social and private rationality that exists in any market and profit-determined economy is thus particularly striking in underdeveloped countries.

. . . . . .

But could not the required increase in total output be attained by better utilization of land—another unutilized or inadequately utilized productive factor?

There is usually no land that is both fit for agricultural purposes and at the same time readily accessible. Such terrain as could be cultivated but is actually not being tilled would usually require considerable investment before becoming suitable for settlement. In underdeveloped countries such outlays for agricultural purposes are just as unattractive to private interests as they are for industrial purposes.

On the other hand, more adequate employment of land that is already used in agriculture runs into considerable difficulties. Very few improvements that would be necessary in order to increase productivity can be carried out within the narrow confines of small-peasant holdings. Not only are the peasants in underdeveloped countries utterly unable to pay for such innovations, but the size of their lots offers no justification for their introduction.

Owners of large estates are in a sense in no better position. With limited savings at their disposal they do not have the funds to finance expensive improvements in their enterprises, nor do such projects appear profitable in view of the high prices of imported equipment in relation to prices of agricultural produce and wages of agricultural labor.

Approached thus via agriculture, an expansion of total output would also seem to be attainable only through the development of industry. Only through increase of industrial productivity could agricultural machinery, fertilizers, electric power, etc., be brought within the reach of the agricultural producer. Only through an increased demand for labor could agricultural wages be raised and a stimulus provided for a modernization of the agricultural economy. Only through the growth of industrial production could agricultural labor displaced by the machine be absorbed in productive employment.

Monopolistic market structures, shortage of savings, lack of external economies, the divergence of social and private rationalities do not exhaust, however, the list of obstacles blocking the way of privately organized industrial expansion in underdeveloped countries. Those obstacles have to be considered against the background of the general feeling of uncertainty prevailing in all backward areas. The coalition of the owning classes formed under pressure of fear, and held together by the real or imagined danger of social upheavals, provokes continuously more or less threatening rumblings under the outwardly calm political surface. The social and political tensions to which that coalition is a political response are not liquidated by the prevailing system; they are only repressed. Normal and quiet as the daily routine frequently appears, the more enlightened and understanding members of the ruling groups in underdeveloped countries sense the inherent instability of the political and social order. Occasional outbursts of popular dissatisfaction assuming the form of peasant uprisings, violent strikes, or local guerrilla warfare serve from time to time as grim reminders of the latent crisis.

In such a climate there is no will to invest on the part of monied people; in such a climate there is no enthusiasm for long-term projects; in such a climate the motto of all participants in the privileges offered by society is *carpe diem.*

IV

Could not, however, an appropriate policy on the part of the governments involved change the political climate and facilitate economic growth? In our time, when faith in the manipulative omnipotence of the State has all but displaced analysis of its social structure and understanding of its political and economic functions, the tendency is obviously to answer these questions in the affirmative.

Looking at the matter purely mechanically, it would appear indeed that much could be done by a well-advised regime in an underdeveloped country to provide for a relatively rapid increase of total output, accompanied by an improvement of the living standards of the population. There are a number of measures that the government could take in an effort to overcome backwardness. A fiscal policy could be adopted that by means of capital levies and a highly progressive tax system would syphon off all surplus purchasing power, and in this way eliminate nonessential consumption. The savings thus enforced could be channelled by the government into productive investment. Power stations, railroads, highways, irrigation systems, and soil improvements could be organized by the State with a view to creating an economic environment conducive to the growth of productivity. Technical schools on various levels could be set up by the public authority to furnish industrial training to young people as well as to adult workers and the unemployed. A system of scholarships could be introduced rendering acquisition of skills accessible to low-income strata.

Wherever private capital refrains from undertaking certain industrial projects, or wherever monopolistic controls block the necessary expansion of plant and facilities in particular industries, the government could step in and make the requisite investments. Where developmental possibilities that are rewarding in the long run appear unprofitable during the initial period of gestation and learning, and are therefore beyond the horizon of private businessmen, the government could undertake to shoulder the short-run losses.

In addition an entire arsenal of "preventive" devices is at the disposal of the authorities. Inflationary pressures resulting from developmental activities (private and public) could be reduced or even eliminated, if outlays on investment projects could be offset by a corresponding and simultaneous contraction of spending elsewhere in the economic system. What this would call for is a taxation policy that would effectively remove from the income stream amounts sufficient to neutralize the investment-caused expansion of aggregate money income.

In the interim, and as a supplement, speculation in scarce goods and excessive profiteering in essential commodities could be suppressed by rigorous price controls. An equitable distribution of mass consumption goods in short supply could be assured by rationing. Diversion of resources in high demand to luxury purposes could be prevented by allocation and priority schemes. Strict supervision of transactions involving foreign exchanges could render capital flight, expenditure of limited foreign funds on luxury imports, pleasure trips abroad, and the like, impossible.

What the combination of these measures would accomplish is a radical change in the structure of effective demand in the underdeveloped country, and a reallocation of productive resources to satisfy society's need for economic development. By curtailing consumption of the higher-income groups, the amounts of savings available for investment purposes could be markedly increased. The squandering of limited supplies of foreign exchange on capital flight, or on importation of redundant foreign goods and services, could be prevented, and the foreign funds thus saved could be used for the acquisition of foreign-made machinery needed for economic development. The reluctance of private interests to engage in enterprises that are socially necessary, but may not promise rich returns in the short run, would be prevented from determining the economic life of the backward country.

The mere listing of the steps that would have to be undertaken, in order to assure an expansion of output and income in an underdeveloped country, reveals the utter implausibility of the view that they could be carried out by the governments existing in most underdeveloped countries. The reason for this inability is only to a negligible extent the nonexistence of the competent and honest civil service needed for the administration of the program. A symptom itself of the political and social marasmus prevailing in underdeveloped countries, this lack cannot be remedied without attacking the underlying causes. Nor does it touch anything near the roots of the matter to lament the lack of satisfactory tax policies in backward countries, or to deplore the absence of tax "morale" and "discipline" among the civic virtues of their populations.

The crucial fact rendering the realization of a developmental program illusory is the political and social structure of the government in power. . . . Set up to guard and to abet the existing property rights and privileges, it cannot become the architect of a policy calculated to destroy the privileges standing in the way of economic progress and to place the property and the incomes derived from it at the service of society as a whole.

Nor is there much to be said for the "intermediate" position which, granting the essential incompatibility of a well-conceived and vigorously executed developmental program with the political and social institutions prevailing in most underdeveloped countries, insists that at least *some* of the requisite measures could be carried out by the existing political authorities. This school of thought overlooks entirely the weakness, if not the complete absence, of social and political forces that could induce the necessary concessions on the part of the ruling coalition. By background and political upbringing, too myopic and self-interested to permit the slightest encroachments upon their inherited positions and cherished privileges, the upper classes in underdeveloped countries resist doggedly all pressures in that direction. Every time such pressures grow in strength they succeed in cementing anew the alliance of all conservative elements, by decrying all attempts at reform as assaults on the very foundations of society.

Even if measures like progressive taxation, capital levies, and foreign exchange controls could be enforced by the corrupt officials operating in the demoralized business communities of underdeveloped countries, such enforcement would to a large extent defeat its original purpose. Where businessmen do not invest, unless in expectation of lavish profits, a taxation system succeeding in confiscating large parts of these profits is bound to kill private investment. Where doing business or operating landed estates is attractive mainly because it permits luxurious living, foreign exchange controls preventing the importation of luxury goods are bound to blight enterprise. Where the only stimulus to hard work on the part of intellectuals, technicians, and civil servants is the chance of partaking in the privileges of the ruling class, a policy aiming at the reduction of inequality of social status and income is bound to smother effort.

The injection of planning into a society living in the twilight between feudalism and capitalism cannot but result in additional corruption, larger and more artful evasions of the law, and more brazen abuses of authority.

V

There would seem to be no exit from the impasse. The ruling coalition of interests does not abdicate of its own volition, nor does it change its character in response to incantation. Although its individual members occasionally leave the sinking ship physically or financially (or in both ways), the property-owning classes as a whole are as a rule grimly determined to hold fast to their political and economic entrenchments.

If the threat of social upheaval assumes dangerous proportions, they tighten their grip on political life and move rapidly in the direction of unbridled reaction and military dictatorship. Making use of favourable international opportunities and of ideological and social affinities to ruling groups in other countries, they solicit foreign economic and sometimes military aid in their efforts to stave off the impending disaster.

Such aid is likely to be given to them by foreign governments regarding them as an evil less to be feared than the social revolution that would sweep them out of power. This attitude of their friends and protectors abroad is no less shortsighted than their own.

The adjustment of the social and political conditions in underdeveloped countries to the urgent needs of economic development can be postponed; it cannot be indefinitely avoided. In the past, it could have been delayed by decades or even centuries. In our age it is a matter of years. Bolstering the political system of power existing in backward countries by providing it with military support may temporarily block the eruption of the volcano; it cannot stop the subterranean gathering of explosive forces.

Economic help in the form of loans and grants given to the governments of backward countries, to enable them to promote a measure of economic progress, is no substitute for the domestic changes that are mandatory if economic development is to be attained.

Such help, in fact, may actually do more harm than good. Possibly permitting the importation of some foreign-made machinery and equipment for government or business sponsored investment projects, but not accompanied by any of the steps that are needed to assure healthy economic growth, foreign assistance thus supplied may set off an inflationary spiral increasing and aggravating the existing social and economic tensions in underdeveloped countries.

If, as is frequently the case, these loans or grants from abroad are tied to the fulfillment of certain conditions on the part of the receiving country regarding their use, the resulting investment may be directed in such channels as to conform more to the interests of the lending than to those of the borrowing country. Where economic advice as a form of "technical assistance" is supplied to the underdeveloped country, and its acceptance is made a prerequisite to eligibility for financial aid, this advice often pushes the governments of underdeveloped countries toward policies, ideologically or otherwise attractive to the foreign experts dispensing economic counsel, but not necessarily conducive to economic development of the "benefitted" countries. Nationalism and xenophobia are thus strengthened in backward areas—additional fuel for political restiveness.

For backward countries to enter the road of economic growth and social progress, the political framework of their existence has to be drastically revamped. The alliance between feudal landlords, industrial royalists, and the capitalist middle classes has to be broken. The keepers of the past cannot be the builders of the future. Such progressive and enterprising elements as exist in backward societies have to obtain the possibility of leading their countries in the direction of economic and social growth.

What France, Britain, and America have accomplished through their own revolutions has to be attained in backward countries by a combined effort of popular forces, enlightened government, and unselfish foreign help. This combined effort must sweep away the holdover institutions of a defunct age, must change the political and social climate in the underdeveloped countries, and must imbue their nations with a new spirit of enterprise and freedom.

Should it prove too late in the historical process for the bourgeoisie to rise to its responsibilities in backward areas, should the long experience of servitude and accommodation to the feudal past have reduced the forces of progressive capitalism to impotence, the backward countries of the world will inevitably turn to economic planning and social collectivism. If the capitalist world outlook of economic and social progress, propelled by enlightened self-interest, should prove unable to triumph over the conservatism of inherited positions and traditional privileges, if the capitalist promise of advance and reward to the efficient, the industrious, the able, should not displace the feudal assurance of security and power to the well-bred, the well-connected, and the conformist—a new social ethos will become the spirit and guide of a new age. It will be the ethos of the collective effort, the creed of the predominance of the interests of society over the interests of selected few.

The transition may be abrupt and painful. The land not given to the peasants legally may be taken by them forcibly. High incomes not confiscated through taxation may be eliminated by outright expropriation. Corrupt officials not retired in orderly fashion may be removed by violent action.

Which way the historical wheel will turn and in which way the crisis in the backward countries will find its final solution will depend in the main on whether the capitalist middle classes in the backward areas, and the rulers of the advanced industrial nations of the world, overcome their fear and myopia. Or are they too spellbound by their narrowly conceived selfish interests, too blinded by their hatred of progress, grown so senile in these latter days of the capitalist age, as to commit suicide out of fear of death?

7

The Development
of Underdevelopment

Andre Gunder Frank

I

We cannot hope to formulate adequate development theory and policy for
the majority of the world's population who suffer from underdevelopment
without first learning how their past economic and social history gave rise
to their present underdevelopment. Yet most historians study only the
developed metropolitan countries and pay scant attention to the colonial
and underdeveloped lands. For this reason most of our theoretical categories and guides to development policy have been distilled exclusively
from the historical experience of the European and North American
advanced capitalist nations.

Since the historical experience of the colonial and underdeveloped
countries has demonstrably been quite different, available theory therefore
fails to reflect the past of the underdeveloped part of the world entirely,
and reflects the past of the world as a whole only in part. More important,
our ignorance of the underdeveloped countries' history leads us to assume
that their past and indeed their present resembles earlier stages of the history of the now developed countries. This ignorance and this assumption lead
us into serious misconceptions about contemporary underdevelopment and
development. Further, most studies of development and underdevelopment fail to take account of the economic and other relations between the
metropolis and its economic colonies throughout the history of the world-
wide expansion and development of the mercantilist and capitalist system.
Consequently, most of our theory fails to explain the structure and development of the capitalist system as a whole and to account for its simultaneous

generation of underdevelopment in some of its parts and of economic development in others.

It is generally held that economic development occurs in a succession of capitalist stages and that today's underdeveloped countries are still in a stage, sometimes depicted as an original stage of history, through which the now developed countries passed long ago. Yet even a modest acquaintance with history shows that underdevelopment is not original or traditional and that neither the past nor the present of the underdeveloped countries resembles in any important respect the past of the now developed countries. The now developed countries were never *under*developed, though they may have been *un*developed. It is also widely believed that the contemporary underdevelopment of a country can be understood as the product or reflection solely of its own economic, political, social, and cultural characteristics or structure. Yet historical research demonstrates that contemporary underdevelopment is in large part the historical product of past and continuing economic and other relations between the satellite underdeveloped and the now developed metropolitan countries. Furthermore, these relations are an essential part of the structure and development of the capitalist system on a world scale as a whole. A related and also largely erroneous view is that the development of these underdeveloped countries and, within them of their most underdeveloped domestic areas, must and will be generated or stimulated by diffusing capital, institutions, values, etc., to them from the international and national capitalist metropoles. Historical perspective based on the underdeveloped countries' past experience suggests that on the contrary in the underdeveloped countries economic development can now occur only independently of most of these relations of diffusion.

Evident inequalities of income and differences in culture have led many observers to see "dual" societies and economies in the underdeveloped countries. Each of the two parts is supposed to have a history of its own, a structure, and a contemporary dynamic largely independent of the other. Supposedly, only one part of the economy and society has been importantly affected by intimate economic relations with the "outside" capitalist world; and that part, it is held, became modern, capitalist, and relatively developed precisely because of this contact. The other part is widely regarded as variously isolated, subsistence-based, feudal, or precapitalist, and therefore more underdeveloped.

I believe on the contrary that the entire "dual society" thesis is false and that the policy recommendations to which it leads will, if acted upon, serve only to intensify and perpetuate the very conditions of underdevelopment they are supposedly designed to remedy.

A mounting body of evidence suggests, and I am confident that future historical research will confirm, that the expansion of the capitalist system over the past centuries effectively and entirely penetrated even the apparently most isolated sectors of the underdeveloped world. Therefore, the economic, political, social, and cultural institutions and relations we now observe there are the products of the historical development of the capitalist system no less than are the seemingly more modern or capitalist features of the national metropoles of these underdeveloped countries. Analogously to the relations between development and underdevelopment on the international level, the contemporary underdeveloped institutions of the so-called backward or feudal domestic areas of an underdeveloped country are no less the product of the single historical process of capitalist development than are the so-called capitalist institutions of the supposedly more progressive areas. In this paper I should like to sketch the kinds of evidence which support this thesis and at the same time indicate lines along which further study and research could fruitfully proceed.

II

The secretary general of the Latin American Center of Research in the Social Sciences writes in that center's journal: "The privileged position of the city has its origin in the colonial period. It was founded by the Conqueror to serve the same ends that it still serves today; to incorporate the indigenous population into the economy brought and developed by that Conqueror and his descendants. The regional city was an instrument of conquest and is still today an instrument of domination."[1] The Instituto Nacional Indigenista (National Indian Institute) of Mexico confirms this observation when it notes that "the mestizo population, in fact, always lives in a city, a center of an intercultural region, which acts as the metropolis of a zone of indigenous population and which maintains with the underdeveloped communities an intimate relation which links the center with the satellite communities."[2] The institute goes on to point out that "between the mestizos who live in the nuclear city of the region and the Indians who live in the peasant hinterland there is in reality a closer economic and social interdependence than might at first glance appear" and that the provincial metropoles "by being centers of intercourse are also centers of exploitation."[3]

Thus these metropolis-satellite relations are not limited to the imperial or international level but penetrate and structure the very economic, political, and social life of the Latin American colonies and countries. Just as the colonial and national capital and its export sector become the satellite of the Iberian (and later of other) metropoles of the world economic system, this satellite immediately becomes a colonial and then a national metropolis with respect to the productive sectors and population of the interior. Furthermore, the provincial capitals, which thus are themselves satellites of the national metropolis—and through the latter of the world metropolis— are in turn provincial centers around which their own local satellites orbit.

Thus, a whole chain of constellations of metropoles and satellites relates all parts of the whole system from its metropolitan center in Europe or the United States to the farthest outpost in the Latin American countryside.

When we examine this metropolis-satellite structure, we find that each of the satellites, including now-underdeveloped Spain and Portugal, serves as an instrument to suck capital or economic surplus out of its own satellites and to channel part of this surplus to the world metropolis of which all are satellites. Moreover, each national and local metropolis serves to impose and maintain the monopolistic structure and exploitative relationship of this system (as the Instituto Nacional Indigenista of Mexico calls it) as long as it serves the interest of the metropoles which take advantage of this global, national, and local structure to promote their own development and the enrichment of their ruling classes.

These are the principal and still surviving structural characteristics which were implanted in Latin America by the Conquest. Beyond examining the establishment of this colonial structure in its historical context, the proposed approach calls for study of the development—and underdevelopment—of these metropoles and satellites of Latin America throughout the following and still continuing historical process. In this way we can understand why there were and still are tendencies in the Latin American and world capitalist structure which seem to lead to the development of the metropolis and the underdevelopment of the satellite and why, particularly, the satellized national, regional, and local metropoles in Latin America find that their economic development is at best a limited or underdeveloped development.

III

That present underdevelopment of Latin America is the result of its centuries-long participation in the process of world capitalist development, I believe I have shown in my case studies of the economic and social histories of Chile and Brazil.[4] My study of Chilean history suggests that the Conquest not only incorporated this country fully into the expansion and development of the world mercantile and later industrial capitalist system but that it also introduced the monopolistic metropolis-satellite structure and development of capitalism into the Chilean domestic economy and society itself. This structure then penetrated and permeated all of Chile very quickly. Since that time and in the course of world and Chilean history during the epochs of colonialism, free trade, imperialism, and the present, Chile has become increasingly marked by the economic, social, and political structure of satellite underdevelopment. This development of underdevelopment continues today, both in Chile's still increasing satellization by the world metropolis and through the ever more acute polarization of Chile's domestic economy.

The history of Brazil is perhaps the clearest case of both national and regional development of underdevelopment. The expansion of the world economy since the beginning of the sixteenth century successively converted the Northeast, the Minas Gerais interior, the North, and the Center-South (Rio de Janeiro, São Paulo, and Paraná) into export economies and incorporated them into the structure and development of the world capitalist system. Each of these regions experienced what may have appeared as economic development during the period of its respective golden age. But it was a satellite development which was neither self-generating nor self-perpetuating. As the market or the productivity of the first three regions declined, foreign and domestic economic interest in them waned; and they were left to develop the underdevelopment they live today. In the fourth region, the coffee economy experienced a similar though not yet quite as serious fate (though the development of a synthetic coffee substitute promises to deal it a mortal blow in the not too distant future). All of this historical evidence contradicts the generally accepted theses that Latin America suffers from a dual society or from the survival of feudal institutions and that these are important obstacles to its economic development.

IV

During the First World War, however, and even more during the Great Depression and the Second World War, São Paulo began to build up an industrial establishment which is the largest in Latin America today. The question arises whether this industrial development did or can break Brazil out of the cycle of satellite development and underdevelopment which has characterized its other regions and national history within the capitalist system so far. I believe that the answer is no. Domestically the evidence so far is fairly clear. The development of industry in São Paulo has not brought greater riches to the other regions of Brazil. Instead, it converted them into internal colonial satellites, decapitalized them further, and consolidated or even deepened their underdevelopment. There is little evidence to suggest that this process is likely to be reversed in the foreseeable future except insofar as the provincial poor migrate and become the poor of the metropolitan cities. Externally, the evidence is that although the initial development of São Paulo's industry was relatively autonomous it is being increasingly satellized by the world capitalist metropolis and its future development possibilities are increasingly restricted.[5] This development, my studies lead me to believe, also appears destined to limited or underdeveloped development as long as it takes place in the present economic, political, and social framework.

We must conclude, in short, that underdevelopment is not due to the survival of archaic institutions and the existence of capital shortage in regions that have remained isolated from the stream of world history. On the contrary, underdevelopment was and still is generated by the very same historical process which also generated economic development: the development of capitalism itself. This view, I am glad to say, is gaining adherents among students of Latin America and is proving its worth in shedding new light on the problems of the area and in affording a better perspective for the formulation of theory and policy.[6]

V

The same historical and structural approach can also lead to better development theory and policy by generating a series of hypotheses about development and underdevelopment such as those I am testing in my current research. The hypotheses are derived from the empirical observation and theoretical assumption that within this world-embracing metropolis-satellite structure the metropoles tend to develop and the satellites to underdevelop. The first hypothesis has already been mentioned above: that in contrast to the development of the world metropolis which is no one's satellite, the development of the national and other subordinate metropoles is limited by their satellite status. It is perhaps more difficult to test this hypothesis than the following ones because part of its confirmation depends on the test of the other hypotheses. Nonetheless, this hypothesis appears to be generally confirmed by the nonautonomous and unsatisfactory economic and especially industrial development of Latin America's national metropoles, as documented in the studies already cited. The most important and at the same time most confirmatory examples are the metropolitan regions of Buenos Aires and São Paulo whose growth only began in the nineteenth century, was therefore largely untrammelled by any colonial heritage, but was and remains a satellite development largely dependent on the outside metropolis, first of Britain and then of the United States.

A second hypothesis is that the satellites experience their greatest economic development and especially their most classically capitalist industrial development if and when their ties to their metropolis are weakest. This hypothesis is almost diametrically opposed to the generally accepted thesis that development in the underdeveloped countries follows from the greatest degree of contact with and diffusion from the metropolitan developed countries. This hypothesis seems to be confirmed by two kinds of relative isolation that Latin America has experienced in the course of its history. One is the temporary isolation caused by the crises of war or depression in the world metropolis. Apart from minor ones, five periods of such major crises stand out and seem to confirm the hypothesis. These are: the European (and especially Spanish) Depression of the seventeenth century, the Napoleonic Wars, the First World War, the Depression of the 1930s, and the Second World War. It is clearly established and generally recognized that the most important recent industrial development—especially of

Argentina, Brazil, and Mexico, but also of other countries such as Chile—has taken place precisely during the periods of the two World Wars and the intervening Depression. Thanks to the consequent loosening of trade and investment ties during these periods, the satellites initiated marked autonomous industrialization and growth. Historical research demonstrates that the same thing happened in Latin America during Europe's seventeenth-century depression. Manufacturing grew in the Latin American countries, and several of them such as Chile became exporters of manufactured goods. The Napoleonic Wars gave rise to independence movements in Latin America, and these should perhaps also be interpreted as confirming the development hypothesis in part.

The other kind of isolation which tends to confirm the second hypothesis is the geographic and economic isolation of regions which at one time were relatively weakly tied to and poorly integrated into the mercantilist and capitalist system. My preliminary research suggests that in Latin America it was these regions which initiated and experienced the most promising self-generating economic development of the classical industrial capitalist type. The most important regional cases probably are Tucumán and Asunción, as well as other cities such as Mendoza and Rosario, in the interior of Argentina and Paraguay during the end of the eighteenth and the beginning of the nineteenth centuries. Seventeenth- and eighteenth-century São Paulo, long before coffee was grown there, is another example. Perhaps Antioquia in Colombia and Puebla and Querétaro in Mexico are other examples. In its own way, Chile was also an example since, before the sea route around the Horn was opened, this country was relatively isolated at the end of the long voyage from Europe via Panama. All of these regions became manufacturing centers and even exporters, usually of textiles, during the periods preceding their effective incorporation as satellites into the colonial, national, and world capitalist system.

Internationally, of course, the classic case of industrialization through nonparticipation as a satellite in the capitalist world system is obviously that of Japan after the Meiji Restoration. Why, one may ask, was resource-poor but unsatellized Japan able to industrialize so quickly at the end of the century while resource-rich Latin American countries and Russia were not able to do so and the latter was easily beaten by Japan in the War of 1904 after the same forty years of development efforts? The second hypothesis suggests that the fundamental reason is that Japan was not satellized either during the Tokugawa or Meiji period and therefore did not have its development structurally limited as did the countries which were so satellized.

VI

A corollary of the second hypothesis is that when the metropolis recovers from its crisis and reestablishes the trade and investment ties which fully reincorporate the satellites into the system, or when the metropolis expands to incorporate previously isolated regions into the worldwide system, the previous development and industrialization of these regions is choked off or channelled into directions which are not self-perpetuating and promising. This happened after each of the five crises cited above. The renewed expansion of trade and the spread of economic liberalism in the eighteenth and nineteenth centuries choked off and reversed the manufacturing development which Latin America had experienced during the seventeenth century, and in some places at the beginning of the nineteenth. After the First World War, the new national industry of Brazil suffered serious consequences from American economic invasion. The increase in the growth rate of Gross National Product and particularly of industrialization throughout Latin America was again reversed and industry became increasingly satellized after the Second World War and especially after the post–Korean War recovery and expansion of the metropolis. Far from having become more developed since then, industrial sectors of Brazil and most conspicuously of Argentina have become structurally more and more underdeveloped and less and less able to generate continued industrialization and/or sustain development of the economy. This process, from which India also suffers, is reflected in a whole gamut of balance of payments, inflationary, and other economic and political difficulties, and promises to yield to no solution short of far-reaching structural change.

Our hypothesis suggests that fundamentally the same process occurred even more dramatically with the incorporation into the system of previously unsatellized regions. The expansion of Buenos Aires as a satellite of Great Britain and the introduction of free trade in the interest of the ruling groups of both metropoles destroyed the manufacturing and much of the remainder of the economic base of the previously relatively prosperous interior almost entirely. Manufacturing was destroyed by foreign competition, lands were taken and concentrated into latifundia by the rapaciously growing export economy, intraregional distribution of income became much more unequal, and the previously developing regions became simple satellites of Buenos Aires and through it of London. The provincial centers did not yield to satellization without a struggle. This metropolis-satellite conflict was much of the cause of the long political and armed struggle between the Unitarists in Buenos Aires and the Federalists in the provinces, and it may be said to have been the sole important cause of the War of the Triple Alliance in which Buenos Aires, Montevideo, and Rio de Janeiro, encouraged and helped by London, destroyed not only the autonomously developing economy of Paraguay but killed off nearly all of its population which was unwilling to give in. Though this is no doubt the most spectacular example which tends to confirm the hypothesis, I believe that historical research on the satellization of previously relatively independent yeoman-farming and incipient manufacturing regions such as the Caribbean islands will confirm it further.[7] These regions did not have a chance against the forces of expanding and developing capitalism, and their own development had to be sacrificed to that of others. The economy and industry of Argentina, Brazil, and other countries which have experienced the effects of metropolitan recovery since the Second World War are today suffering much the same fate, if fortunately still in lesser degree.

VII

A third major hypothesis derived from the metropolis-satellite structure is that the regions which are the most underdeveloped and feudal-seeming today are the ones which had the closest ties to the metropolis in the past. They are the regions which were the greatest exporters of primary products to and the biggest sources of capital for the world metropolis and which were abandoned by the metropolis when for one reason or another business fell off. This hypothesis also contradicts the generally held thesis that the source of a region's underdevelopment is its isolation and its precapitalist institutions.

This hypothesis seems to be amply confirmed by the former super-satellite development and present ultra-underdevelopment of the once sugar-exporting West Indies, northeastern Brazil, the ex-mining districts of Minas Gerais in Brazil, highland Peru, and Bolivia, and the central Mexican states of Guanajuato, Zacatecas, and others whose names were made world famous centuries ago by their silver. There surely are no major regions in Latin America which are today more cursed by underdevelopment and poverty; yet all of these regions, like Bengal in India, once provided the life blood of mercantile and industrial capitalist development—in the metropolis. These regions' participation in the development of the world capitalist system gave them, already in their golden age, the typical structure of underdevelopment of a capitalist export economy. When the market for their sugar or the wealth of their mines disappeared and the metropolis abandoned them to their own devices, the already existing economic, political, and social structure of these regions prohibited autonomous generation of economic development and left them no alternative but to turn in upon themselves and to degenerate into the ultra-underdevelopment we find there today.

VIII

These considerations suggest two further and related hypotheses. One is that the latifundium, irrespective of whether it appears as a plantation or a hacienda today, was typically born as a commercial enterprise which created for itself the institutions which permitted it to respond to increased demand in the world or national market by expanding the amount of its land, capital, and labor and to increase the supply of its products. The fifth hypothesis is that the latifundia which appear isolated, subsistence-based, and semi-feudal today saw the demand for their products or their productive capacity decline and that they are to be found principally in the above-named former agricultural and mining export regions whose economic activity declined in general. These two hypotheses run counter to the notions of most people, and even to the opinions of some historians and other students of the subject, according to whom the historical roots and socioeconomic causes of Latin American latifundia and agrarian institutions are to be found in the transfer of feudal institutions from Europe and/or in economic depression.

The evidence to test these hypotheses is not open to easy general inspection and requires detailed analyses of many cases. Nonetheless, some important confirmatory evidence is available. The growth of the latifundium in nineteenth-century Argentina and Cuba is a clear case in support of the fourth hypothesis and can in no way be attributed to the transfer of feudal institutions during colonial times. The same is evidently the case of the postrevolutionary and contemporary resurgence of latifundia particularly in the north of Mexico, which produce for the American market, and of similar ones on the coast of Peru and the new coffee regions of Brazil. The conversion of previously yeoman-farming Caribbean islands, such as Barbados, into sugar-exporting economies at various times between the seventeenth and twentieth centuries and the resulting rise of the latifundia in these islands would seem to confirm the fourth hypothesis as well. In Chile, the rise of the latifundium and the creation of the institutions of servitude which later came to be called feudal occurred in the eighteenth century and have been conclusively shown to be the result of and response to the opening of a market for Chilean wheat in Lima.[8] Even the growth and consolidation of the latifundium in seventeenth-century Mexico—which most expert students have attributed to a depression of the economy caused by the decline of mining and a shortage of Indian labor and to a consequent turning in upon itself and ruralization of the economy—occurred at a time when urban population and demand were growing, food shortages became acute, food prices skyrocketed, and the profitability of other economic activities such as mining and foreign trade declined.[9] All of these and other factors rendered hacienda agriculture more profitable. Thus, even this case would seem to confirm the hypothesis that the growth of the latifundium and its feudal-seeming conditions of servitude in Latin America has always been and still is the commercial response to increased demand and that it does not represent the transfer or survival of alien institutions that have remained beyond the reach of capitalist development. The emergence of latifundia, which today really are more or less (though not entirely) isolated, might then be attributed to the causes advanced in the fifth hypothesis—i.e., the decline of previously profitable agricultural enterprises whose capital was, and whose currently produced economic surplus still is, transferred elsewhere by owners and merchants who frequently are the same persons or families. Testing this hypothesis requires still more detailed analysis, some of which I have undertaken in a study on Brazilian agriculture.[10]

IX

All of these hypotheses and studies suggest that the global extension and unity of the capitalist system, its monopoly structure and uneven development throughout its history, and the resulting persistence of commercial rather than industrial capitalism in the underdeveloped world (including its most industrially advanced countries) deserve much more attention in the study of economic development and cultural change than they have hitherto received. Though science and truth know no national boundaries, it is probably new generations of scientists from the underdeveloped countries themselves who most need to, and best can, devote the necessary attention to these problems and clarify the process of underdevelopment and development. It is their people who in the last analysis face the task of changing this no longer acceptable process and eliminating this miserable reality.

They will not be able to accomplish these goals by importing sterile stereotypes from the metropolis which do not correspond to their satellite economic reality and do not respond to their liberating political needs. To change their reality they must understand it. For this reason, I hope that better confirmation of these hypotheses and further pursuit of the proposed historical, holistic, and structural approach may help the peoples of the underdeveloped countries to understand the causes and eliminate the reality of their development of underdevelopment and their underdevelopment of development.

NOTES

1. *América Latina*, 6, 4 (October–December 1963): p. 8.
2. Instituto Nacional Indigenista, *Los Centros Coordinadores Indigenistas*, Mexico, 1962, p. 34.
3. Ibid., pp. 33–34, 88.
4. "Capitalist Development and Underdevelopment in Chile" and "Capitalist Development and Underdevelopment in Brazil" in *Capitalism and Underdevelopment in Latin America* (New York: Monthly Review Press, 1967).
5. Also see, "The Growth and Decline of Import Substitution," *Economic Bulletin for Latin America*, New York, 9, 1, March 1964; and Celso Furtado, *Dialectica do Desenvolvimiento* (Rio de Janeiro: Fundo de Cultura, 1964).
6. Others who use a similar approach, though their ideologies do not permit them to derive the logically following conclusions, are Aníbal Pinto S.C., *Chile: Un*

Caso de Desarrollo Frustrado (Santiago: Editorial Universitaria, 1957); Celso Furtado, *A Formącao Económica do Brasil* (Rio de Janeiro: Fundo de Cultura, 1959) (recently translated into English and published under the title *The Economic Growth of Brazil* by the University of California Press); and Caio Prado Junior, *Historia Económica do Brasil,* 7th ed., (São Paulo: Editora Brasiliense, 1962).

7. See for instance Ramón Guerra y Sánchez, *Azúcar y Población en las Antillas,* 2d ed., (Havana, 1942), also published as *Sugar and Society in the Caribbean* (New Haven: Yale University Press, 1964).

8. Mario Góngora, *Origen de los "inquilinos" de Chile central,* (Santiago Editorial Universitaria, 1960); Jean Borde and Mario Góngora, *Evolución de la propiedad rural en el Valle del Puango* (Santiago: Instituto de Sociología de la Universidad de Chile); Sergio Sepúlveda, *El trigo chileno en el mercado mundial,* (Santiago Editorial Universitaria, 1959).

9. Woodrow Borah makes depression the centerpiece of his explanation in "New Spain's Century of Depression," *Ibero-Americana,* Berkeley, 35, 1951. François Chevalier speaks of turning in upon itself in the most authoritative study of the subject, "La formación de los grandes latifundios en México," *Problemas Agrícolas e Industriales de México,* 8, 1, 1956 (translated from the French and recently published by the University of California Press). The data which provide the basis for my contrary interpretation are supplied by these authors themselves. This problem is discussed in my "Con qué modo de producción convierte la gallina maíz en huevos de oro?" *El Gallo Ilustrado,* Suplemento de *El Día,* Mexico, nos. 175 and 179, October 31 and November 28, 1965; and it is further analyzed in a study of Mexican agriculture under preparation by the author.

10. "Capitalism and the Myth of Feudalism in Brazilian Agriculture," in *Capitalism and Underdevelopment in Latin America,* cited in note 4 above.

8

Perspectives on Underdevelopment: Frank, the Modes of Production School, and Amin

David F. Ruccio and Lawrence H. Simon

I. INTRODUCTION

The past four hundred years have witnessed the growth and global expansion of capitalism. At least since Adam Smith, bourgeois theorists of capitalism have triumphantly heralded this expansion as progressive and unilinear, limited only by the emergence in the twentieth century of socialist regimes. Insofar as there remain in the world today differences in levels of development and national wealth, these can be best overcome, according to orthodox theory, through the further growth of capitalism. The job of neoclassical development economics is to chart this path of growth for the so-called less-developed countries (LDCs).

The view from the left is very different. Where bourgeois theorists see a story of triumph and progress, radical theorists see one of domination and exploitation in both imperialist and neocolonialist modes on the one hand and struggles for independence on the other. Radicals are unanimous in rejecting the orthodox view as theoretically false and politically inadequate.

From afar, this radical approach might be thought to be a unified theoretical position that can be fairly easily differentiated from its orthodox opposite. To some degree this is true. But the left has also generated in the past two decades complex theoretical debates and opposing positions.

Manuscript prepared for this volume. We would like to thank Charles Wilber, Kenneth Jameson, Vaughn McKim, and Rhoda Halperin for their helpful comments on an earlier draft of this material. The research on this article was supported in part by a grant from the Institute for Scholarship in the Liberal Arts of the University of Notre Dame.

Radical theorists differ, that is, concerning basic issues in their story. Is the development of capitalism a necessary, if unfortunate, step in the path of development for any country? Are the economic structures that have developed in the various nations that were formerly colonies best characterized as capitalist? If so, is it capitalism in the same form as developed in Europe and North America, or a new and indigenous form of capitalism? If not, then how should the economies of the LDCs be characterized?

While most radical analyses accept the existence of a world capitalism system, they differ on how to understand the basic dynamic of this system and on how to describe the relations between the more- and less-developed nations within this system. Again, while most, but not all, radical analyses question whether the present economic structures of LDCs will allow development, they differ as to how to characterize the barriers preventing growth. Radical interpretations also disagree as to how much is to be accepted from the theories of Marx and the Marxist tradition. The spectrum runs from what might be considered orthodox Marxist theories of development to theories that, while acknowledging the importance of Marx, in effect reject nearly all of his important claims about the status and development of the colonial world.

In this essay, we analyze three of the theories that have emerged as contending positions on the left. These three—Dependency Theory as formulated by Andre Gunder Frank, the Modes of Production school, and the theory of Samir Amin—by no means exhaust the radical perspective. This article, then, is not a survey of radical theories of development.[1] Rather, we hope that by looking in depth at three of the alternative views, the issues around which much of the debates have revolved will be clarified.

The three positions that we have chosen are not only major contenders in the debate, but they are related in important ways both historically and conceptually. Theories arise at least partly in reaction to other existing theories that are judged inadequate by those seeking a new departure. The new theory takes up and recasts the challenge of the old one and is best understood in light of this challenge. A theory, then, has at least two tasks: a negative or critical one of arguing against its predecessors, and a positive or constructive one of providing an alternative account of the issues in dispute and of raising new questions. To understand a theory, then, requires placing it in the narrative of the debates in which it arose and developed.

The three theories we have selected have this relationship. Frank's work can be taken as the beginning of the modern debate on the left concerning development.[2] The Modes of Production school arises in direct response to what were seen as inadequacies in Frank's theory of underdevelopment. Amin's work represents an attempt to incorporate and synthesize into an encompassing theory of the world capitalist system various of the theoretical insights of Dependency Theory, the Modes of Production position, and more orthodox Marxist treatments.

Section three provides an analysis of the Modes of Production school. We analyze this position in terms of three distinguishable approaches: the articulation of modes of production, the colonial or peripheral modes of production, and the internationalization of capital. The focus of the discussion is not only on the basic claims of the three approaches, but also on the interrelations and differences among them. We also situate the overall Modes of Production position in the context of the general debate by analyzing the background and motivation for its emergence. In the fifth section, Amin's theory is presented. We end this section with a brief discussion of a recent reply by Amin to his critics in which points of contact and disagreement between his theory and the others we discuss are further clarified.[3]

II. FRANK AND DEPENDENCY THEORY

Andre Gunder Frank is generally credited as the father of Dependency Theory.[4] *Capitalism and Underdevelopment in Latin America,* written in the early sixties and published in English in 1967, was the first important statement of the theory.[5] While Frank certainly had predecessors, as he readily acknowledges, his book can still be used to mark the opening salvo in the debate over Dependency Theory, in part because this book continues to be very influential and is widely cited by both exponents and critics of Dependency Theory. To understand the structure of Frank's argument, however, it is necessary to keep in mind its antecedents, both the positions Frank criticized and the authors upon whom he relied in formulating his own position.

Frank's work grew out of a reaction to both orthodox neoclassical work on development and the views of certain traditional orthodox Marxists, in particular, those prevalent among the Communist Parties in Latin America. According to Frank, both of these opposing positions shared in certain important regards theoretical theses that were faulty. Positively, Frank's views were influenced by the structuralist theory of Prebisch and others in Latin America and by the work of the so-called neo-Marxists, especially that of Paul Baran.[6] In fact, in the theoretical configuration of development economics Dependency Theory is perhaps best located on the continuum somewhere between orthodox structuralist theory and Marxism.

A central thesis shared, according to Frank, by both neoclassical and orthodox Marxist theories of development, and of which he was critical, was that capitalism was a normal and necessary stage of development. This conception of capitalism was part of a more general view of development as occurring through a series of stages. In addition, according to Frank, both of these positions accepted a general dualistic view of so-called Third World societies. Of course, these theses were expressed by each position in very different theoretical language and supported by antithetical theoretical arguments. And, needless to say, the implications each drew from these theses could not be more different. For the neoclassical, capitalism was the end of development, while for the Marxist, it was a necessary, if regrettable, stage to be transcended by socialism. But both agreed that any (nonsocialist) country that needed to develop had to do so within the framework of capitalism, and moreover, that the operations of the capitalist system (of course, conceived differently by the two positions) would lead to higher levels of development in the normal course of things.

In particular, Dependency Theory was defined against the prevailing neoclassical position.[7] That view starts from the assumption that the economies of all countries can be arranged on a scale from least to most developed (from backward to advanced, or from low-income to high-income, modified perhaps by the degree of oil reserves). Development is taken to be a unilinear process, and all nations have undergone and will continue to undergo essentially the same process. Presumably, according to this approach, at some point in the past all countries were at a stage of economic development that would now be considered undeveloped. For reasons generally taken to be extraneous to the theory, at some point certain countries began to develop economically, while others lagged behind or failed to develop at all. Different levels of development reflect different starting points and different growth rates. The presently undeveloped countries, then, have yet to undergo this process, and they should see their future in the past course of the presently more developed countries.

Neoclassical theory typically understands the condition of less-developed countries in terms of what is called a dualistic economy. According to the theory of dualism, an economy of an undeveloped nation has two sectors, one traditional and one relatively modern and developed. The two sectors are taken to be largely independent of each other. They may be linked during the transition to modern growth, however, in that the traditional sector may provide labor and an agricultural surplus to the modern sector. The modern sector, moreover, is intertwined in the world capitalist market, while the traditional sector is in effect precapitalist and more or less untouched by capitalist market relations. The dynamic of growth is due to trade and general economic activity, so the process of development of the whole economy is seen to involve the modernization or transformation of the traditional sector so as to bring it into the sphere of the market and thus expose it to the possibilities of trade and development offered by the free market.

Frank's original formulation of Dependency Theory begins with a rejection of two of the central theses of this neoclassical dualism. First, Frank rejects the dualist model of the economies of the undeveloped nations in which there are two sectors, only one of which, the more developed, is capitalist. Rather, according to Frank, during the era of European capitalist expansion, most areas, even the geographically remote, were incorporated within the network of capitalist relations. As a result, all parts of the economies of undeveloped nations should be seen to be within the web of capitalism. Not to see them as part of the capitalist system is necessarily to misunderstand their nature and operation.

The second thesis of dualism that Frank rejects is that the present condition of the undeveloped countries is similar to some original, predevelopment stage of the presently developed nations. Rather, Frank asserts, despite certain surface similarities (noncomplexity, nonindustrialization, and/or poverty) between the present condition of the undeveloped nations and the reconstructed past of the now developed nations, neither the colonial past nor the present of the undeveloped nations resembles in any important respect the past of the developed nations. If we accept the assumption, which Frank seems to accept, that at some point in the past prior to the emergence and expansion of capitalism all countries were more or less the same developmentally (that is, that there was some kind of "original stage" the exact nature of which is never specified by Frank), then it follows that the present condition of the undeveloped nations is not original, primal, or traditional; rather, this state is itself a product of the historical development of capitalism on a world scale.

This point has two important implications. First, there is no single universal trajectory for development that is followed by all nations, for obviously the discrepancy between the more- and less-developed nations today is a result of at least two different developmental paths. Second, if we call the original, predevelopment stage one of undevelopment, then it is no longer correct to refer to the present condition of the less-developed nations today as undeveloped, since their present condition is itself a product of a historical, developmental sequence. Thus, Frank introduces a new term, "underdeveloped," to characterize the condition of the presently less-developed countries: "The now developed countries were never *under*developed, though they may have been *un*developed."[8]

Underdevelopment is a condition that characterizes the entire economy of a country, regardless of the different levels of sectoral development. It is a condition, moreover, that characterizes all the presently developing nations. This suggests (although by no means entails) that underdevelopment cannot be explained simply in terms of factors internal to the social and economic histories of the underdeveloped nations, for it seems highly unlikely that the histories of so many nations in different parts of the world with different initial conditions would have been such as to have led to the same outcome. Rather, what is suggested is that there is some common, external causal factor. The theoretical task that Frank undertakes is to identify this factor and incorporate it into a theory that explains the nature and development of underdevelopment.

To accomplish this task, Frank constructs a theoretical model that claims to show how the present condition of underdeveloped countries came about historically and is maintained today. This model employs certain theoretical concepts and posits the existence of certain entities or processes. The concepts are theoretical in the sense that their full meaning can be grasped only in the context of their role in the theoretical model. The posited entities or processes are theoretical in a somewhat different sense. First, their natures can be explained fully only in relation to the model and the theoretical concepts it uses. Second, they cannot be perceived or picked out independently of the theoretical model. They are observable, that is, only through the "lens" of the model. At the same time, the explanatory acceptability of the theoretical model depends, at least in part, on the acceptability of the theoretical concepts. As we shall see below, much of the critical reaction to Frank and, indeed, much of the debate concerning Dependency Theory revolves around the acceptability of various theoretical concepts and their utilization in explanations of development.

The key concept in this model is dependency, hence Dependency Theory. This concept is used to pick out and characterize the object of study, namely, the present condition of developing nations. That is, an initial distinction is assumed between developed and developing countries. What are initially identified as developing countries are supposedly picked out through a comparison with the developed countries in terms of certain indices, for instance, an index of wealth, as to both its level and its distribution. The so-called developing nations, Frank then suggests, are better considered as *under*developed rather than *un*developed in order to distinguish states of development historically produced from those that can be considered in some sense "original" conditions. These underdeveloped nations are then characterized as participating in a relation of dependency. It is because of their dependency relationship, which is to be elaborated in the model, that these countries are underdeveloped. That is, dependency causes underdevelopment.

Dependency relations, in Frank's view, require two parties, one dominant and the other dependent. For Frank, the central dependency relationship exists between the various countries of the developed world and those that are underdeveloped. Historically, the relationship was between a colony and the imperial power that conquered it. Today, it is more a matter of an underdeveloped country and those developed countries with which it has primary economic relations. Various names have been given to the parties to these relationships: metropolis/satellite, core/periphery, or center/periphery.

The metropolis-satellite relationship, to use the terms preferred by Frank, is one of dependency because of two features. First, the development of the satellite is dependent on the development of the metropolis, that is, on forces external to the satellite's economy and society. The suggestion in the model is that it is an asymmetrical relationship, with the development of the metropolis being for the most part independent, that is, determined by factors largely internal to the metropolitan economy and society. Thus, dependency in the first instance is a relation of unequal power. The metropolis has power over the course of development in the satellite, but not vice versa. It should be noted that this power need not be consciously realized or exercised, but might be (and generally is) the unintended result of structural relations and operations.

Frank sees the determining relationship as one-sided. Especially in his early work, he does not pay much attention to the reciprocal influence of the satellite on the metropolis. He has, that is to say, an insufficiently dialectical understanding of the dependency relation. To say that the metropolis exercises greater power in the sense that Frank stipulates need not commit one to the denial that there is a sense in which the metropolis is also dependent on the satellite. The key to the relationship is control. The metropolis exercises greater power in that it has greater control within the relationship, in the way that a slavemaster who has control of slaves exercises greater power over those slaves, even while he or she may be very dependent on the slaves and, in general, on the master-slave relationship to reproduce him or herself as slavemaster.

The dependent development of the satellite is such as to disadvantage it further and exacerbate certain problems it experiences such as poverty and distorted development. The loss for the underdeveloped nation is twofold. Not only is it not in control of its own development, but it does not materially benefit from the relation of dependency. It is worth making this second point because a more sophisticated version of neoclassical theory might argue that developing countries do at times enter into dependency relations with developed nations due to certain types of market asymmetries, but that this dependency (here seen as just loss of control in some respects or to some degree) benefits the developing countries because it fosters development per se. It is this latter point that Frank denies. Dependency, for Frank, is a relation of exploitation, and, like "exploitation," "dependency" has a definite negative normative force as well as a descriptive role in Frank's theory.[9] It is also worth pointing out that the object of benefit or harm for Frank is the nation-state as such, rather than, for instance, classes. Frank does discuss the fact that certain classes, local ruling classes, can and do benefit, in the short term at least, from underdevelopment, but this benefit is understood against the backdrop of the harm done to the nation as a whole.

While the locus of dependency relationships in Frank's model is the nation-state and relations between nations, the scope of the theory is properly the world capitalist system. Nations are taken to be component parts of this system. To understand the development of underdevelopment in a particular country, it is necessary to place that country's history in the context of this larger system. It is important, according to Frank, to see capitalism as a world system and to understand its central structures. To fail to do so might well lead one to misidentify both the important structures within the underdeveloped countries and to misunderstand the nature of the dependency relation. Dependency, as we shall see, is explained in terms of its function within the larger system, and the theoretical model used in the explanation must, obviously, correctly characterize the system if the explanation is to be successful. A complete explanation of underdevelopment, then, would require nothing less than a full account of the origin, nature, and development of capitalism.[10]

By specifying that the scope of his theory is the world *capitalist* system, Frank has in effect raised the issue of the definition of "capitalism" that he is using. As various commentators have noted, Frank does not explicitly define "capitalism."[11] Nevertheless, given any number of remarks that he makes, it is a fairly straightforward task to discern how he uses the term. As we have said, Frank takes capitalism to be a world system, one that has existed since at least the sixteenth century. It has gone through three stages: mercantilist, industrial, and financial capitalism. What has remained constant through all the stages is a certain kind of exchange relationship characteristic of metropolis-satellite relations. If the periphery has been capitalist since the first European incursions, and if what has remained constant across the various stages is the nature of the exchange relations, then capitalism must be defined in terms of this relation.[12] Laclau fills out this definition attributed to Frank in the following way: Frank understands by capitalism "a) a system of production for the market, in which b) profit constitutes the motive of production, and c) this profit is realized for the benefit of someone other than the direct producer, who is thereby dispossessed of it."[13]

If capitalism is defined in terms of market exchange relations of a certain kind, we should specify more exactly what kind they are. As we have seen, according to Laclau's interpretation of Frank, the essential capitalist relation is a market exchange whereby profit is realized for the benefit of someone other than the direct producer. We have also seen that dependency relations in general for Frank involve power relations where one party is disadvantaged to the gain of the other. Third, we have noted that for Frank, the dependency relations that generate underdevelopment must be understood in terms of the capitalist world system. Putting these points together, we can conclude that, for Frank, the essential capitalist relation is a dependency relation and thus a relation of power. In other words, capitalism in the first instance is to be regarded as a system of power, power exercised through a particular form of relation, namely, a market exchange relation.

In what sense are capitalist market exchange relations relations of power? According to Frank, dependency relations in general and metropolis-satellite relations within capitalism in particular are best characterized as monopolistic and extractive. The metropolis exerts monopolistic control over economic and trade relations in the periphery. Monopoly domination within a market is, of course, a position of power. This position of power allows the metropolis to extract an economic surplus from the satellite. The appropriation of this surplus and its accumulation in and under the control of the metropolis is the central factor that deprives the underdeveloped nation of the ability to control its own growth and that thus leaves it dependent. The monopolistic, extractive relation was initially established by force of arms, but once it is in place, subsequent development perpetuates it through the structures of dependency and underdevelopment.

Two points should be noted about the monopolistic-extractive nature of the metropolis-satellite relation. The first is that any theory that attempts to conceptualize economic exchanges in what Frank considers the underdeveloped nations in terms of equivalent market exchanges necessarily, from his point of view, distorts the nature of what transpires. The outstanding theoretical issue is, of course, how to verify the existence of monopolistic market distortions and the "exploitative" transfer of surplus. This is a fundamental point of contention between neoclassical theories and Dependency Theory. In general, where a neoclassical theorist would see a free market and mutual advantage, Frank sees a structure of monopolistic relations and surplus transfer.

The second point to note is that Frank's concept of economic surplus is taken more or less directly from the work of Paul Baran. Frank appears to believe that Baran's concept is the same as that used by Marx in his analysis of "the surplus value created by producers and its appropriation by capitalists."[14] Many commentators have pointed out, however, that according to Marx's theory, the extraction of surplus takes place within the capital-wage labor relation within production, while for Frank, the extraction is a function of exchange relations in the market. The two concepts are, therefore, not the same. One difference to be noted in this context is that Marx emphasizes that for the purposes of his model he is assuming that market relations are exchanges of equivalents, while, as we have seen, Frank takes them to be monopolistic power relations involving the exchange of nonequivalents.

In our discussion of dependency relations thus far we have focused on the form of the relation of metropolis to satellite at the level of nation-states. This relation is the primary one within Frank's model. However, the nation-nation relation is not the only form of a metropolis-satellite relation for Frank. Rather, there is a chain of such relationships, all of which manifest the same form or structure. At the pinnacle of this chain is the nation-nation relationship of metropolis-satellite. But within the satellite itself, the structurally identical relationship is repeated on lower and increasingly local levels of the economy. The theoretical model, then, can be seen as a series of steps, each connection from step to lower step reiterating the same structural relations.

One last feature of Frank's theoretical model needs to be mentioned. The model has definite implications for the type of political developments and, in particular, for the nature of the class structure that one can expect to accompany the development of economic underdevelopment. It is necessary for Frank to speak to the issue of political development in order to provide some mechanism to account for how the policy of underdevelopment, as he calls it, is put into effect and maintained, especially after an underdeveloped colony achieves de jure independence, thus making the option to use the open coercion of an imperial power less available.[15]

Within the model, classes are understood in the first instance in terms of structural positions within a system of power relations. At each point in the metropolis-satellite chain, the structure of the chain creates certain objective interests, most important, the interest in controlling the monopoly relationship at that point in the chain so as to be able to benefit from the extractive power available at that position. The group that coheres around that interest is in effect the ruling class of that area, region, or nation. Since the ruling class at each point in the structure is dependent on the entire structure remaining more or less the same, so that the monopoly relationships can be maintained, each ruling class in effect bolsters every other ruling class. All ruling classes thus have an interest in perpetuating the development of underdevelopment, for that is precisely the structure that allows them to satisfy their interests as they find them.

III. THE MODES OF PRODUCTION SCHOOL

The debate concerning Dependency Theory entered a new stage with the emergence of the Modes of Production (MOP) school. The various approaches encompassed by this rubric represent both a criticism of the early forms of Dependency Theory, chiefly as represented by the writings of Frank (and, later, Wallerstein), and an extension of the basic problematic of Dependency Theory. The focus of the explanation of the persistence of underdevelopment is shifted by the MOP theorists away from what they understand to be the excessive emphasis in traditional Dependency Theory on a global scheme that exaggerates the role of external relations and markets. Instead, while not denying the importance of macro phenomena, relations between nations, and flows of commodities, they have focused on developing the concept of mode of production in an attempt to construct an alternative understanding of the phenomenon of underdevelopment. Despite the shift of focus, the object of investigation remains the specific forms of development of what is taken to be the periphery of the world economy. Moreover, the concepts of dependency and underdevelopment, although defined differently, are not themselves challenged. In this sense, the MOP school represents not a break from but, rather, an alternative formulation and extension of Dependency Theory itself.

Within the MOP school, three basic approaches can be distinguished. The "articulation of MOP" approach, as it has been termed, tends to explain the phenomenon of underdevelopment in terms of the relationships among and between the capitalist and other, noncapitalist modes of production existing within underdeveloped economies.[16] A second related approach, that of the "colonial or peripheral MOP," has sought to develop a set of concepts of modes of production that are specific to the colonial experiences and peripheral status of the developing countries.[17] According to this group of theorists, the concepts of modes of production that should be used to analyze the societies of the periphery are fundamentally different from those that have been used to investigate the countries of the center. Finally, there are MOP theorists who focus on what they call the "internationalization of capital" or the laws of motion of the capitalist mode of production.[18] In this view, international development (including development within specific nations) is analyzed in terms of the presumed dominance of the capitalist mode of production in the world economy. Each one of these approaches has staked out a different position in the dependency theory debate. The starting point in all cases is a concept of mode of production; however, they represent three alternative ways of constructing a theoretical model in terms of which an explanation of the past and present economic and social structures of developing countries can be generated.

Background

Although the work of many of the MOP theorists has been relatively well documented,[19] the theoretical sources of this attempt to analyze development by using concepts of modes of production are less well known. There are five major points that should be briefly elaborated. First, the various efforts to construct a theory centered on concepts of modes of production grew out of attempts to provide a link between Frank's relatively global model of metropolis-satellite relations and the ethnographic detail that emerged from detailed, especially anthropological, studies of developing countries. Many researchers found it difficult to relate the wealth of empirical detail generated in the course of field work to the overarching logic of patterns of surplus transfer between the core and periphery of the world economy that form the focus of Frank's model.[20] The concepts and conceptual strategies of a group of French anthropologists who analyzed African underdevelopment in terms of modes of production represented one attempt to bridge this gap between existing theory and empirical research.[21]

A second factor that gave rise to the proliferation of MOP approaches to development was the reaction against Frank's seeing "capitalism everywhere," that is, that commodity flows or markets were present and such markets were sufficient to characterize the society in question as capitalist. Laclau's *New Left Review* article is the *locus classicus* of this criticism of Frank's work.[22] Frank was accused of making all of the underdeveloped countries' social structures capitalist, from the sixteenth century onward, because he mistakenly identified markets or trade relations with capitalism. Laclau's alternative was to emphasize the primacy of the conditions of production over those of exchange.

To this end, Laclau proceeded to define a concept of mode of production as a combination of four factors: the pattern of ownership of the means of production, the form of appropriation of what he called an economic surplus, the degree of the division of labor, and the level of development of the forces of production.[23] In addition, Laclau distinguishes between a "mode of production" and an "economic system" to take account of the participation of *precapitalist modes of production* in a world *capitalist economic system*. An economic system is generally defined by Laclau as an articulated (or combined) set of different modes of production. In particular, the world capitalist system is not conceived to be a uniform production system, that is, a system with one exclusive mode of production. Rather, it is conceived to be an economic system in which both capitalist and noncapitalist modes of production coexist and which is characterized by the predominance of the capitalist mode of production. According to Laclau, Marxist theorists should attempt to understand underdeveloped countries in terms of the system of relations—the articulation—between the capitalist and other, noncapitalist modes of production, rather than in terms of Frank's homogeneous capitalist relations.

Third, the use of the concept of mode of production in Laclau's critique of Frank and as the basis of an alternative framework of analysis that displaces Frank's focus on commodity flows was itself predicated on a return to the work of Marx through the writings of Althusser and Balibar.[24] These two French theorists had taken up the project of reformulating the basic concepts of historical materialism. Among their primary concerns was to combat what they considered to be various non-Marxist forms of "essentialism" within the Marxist theoretical tradition.[25] In particular, the explanation of social phenomena in terms of an essential human nature or an economic determinism was criticized. Their effort to formulate a concept of mode of production, along with the concept of overdetermination, and to produce a nonessentialist Marxist social theory was central to the emergence of the concept of mode of production as an object of theoretical attention.

A fourth source of the MOP school was the reexamination of Marx's own analysis of the so-called original accumulation of capital and the transition from feudalism to capitalism. Marx's account of the emergence and development of some of the economic, political, and cultural conditions of capitalism in a noncapitalist, feudal setting is filtered through the Dobb-Sweezy "transition debate" to become an additional component of the MOP analysis of the transition to capitalism in developing countries.[26] The relevance of the transition debate is twofold. First, the MOP analysis of underdevelopment is concerned with the emergence, or lack thereof, of the capitalist mode of production in the developing countries and hence, implicitly or explicitly, with a comparison with the European experience. Second, once the idea of transition (e.g., to the capitalist mode of production) is analyzed, the combined existence of different, capitalist and noncapitalist modes of production during the period of transition becomes an object of theoretical attention.

Finally, the work of Hindess and Hirst deserves brief mention.[27] Although not explicitly addressed to the question of developing countries, theirs is arguably the most sophisticated attempt to construct a set of concepts of noncapitalist modes of production. Their analyses of primitive communal, ancient, slave, and feudal modes of production were particularly instructive. However, their subsequent rejection, based on both methodological and epistemological considerations, of the concept of mode of production has received much less attention in the MOP literature.[28]

These are some of the historical and theoretical conditions, among others, out of which the MOP school emerged and to which it has responded over time. We turn now to a brief summary of the three approaches that have used the concept MOP as their entry-point into the analysis of dependency and underdevelopment.

Articulation of Modes of Production

Laclau's critique of Frank announced the beginning of a Marxian reconceptualization of dependency theory based on the articulation of modes of production. Taking the concept of modes of production as their starting point, articulation of MOP theorists have sought to analyze the relations among and between the various possible capitalist and noncapitalist modes of production. The overriding objective has been, following Laclau, to produce a general theory of the articulation of modes of production within a capitalist economic system. The central focus of the articulation of MOP theorists is, in particular, the system of relations between the capitalist mode of production and the set of preexisting noncapitalist modes of production in the developing countries. A principal methodological concern in understanding this approach, then, is the constitution and use of the central concepts of mode of production and articulation within their theoretical model.

How can different capitalist and noncapitalist modes of production be combined or articulated in a single social formation within the context of ultimate capitalist development? In general, three alternative forms or models might be used to answer this question. The two salient variables of these models are the form of interaction and the degree of dominance by one mode of production over the others. One possibility is that the various modes of production are seen to exist alongside but essentially independent of one another. This position has traditionally been called "dualism" and Frank's original rejection of it is shared by the articulation of MOP theorists.

A second answer is that the various modes of production in any particular society are interrelated under the dominance of one of these modes of production. One mode of production, for example, capitalism, would be understood to dominate the others in the sense of determining the nature of their existence—their reproduction over time, any changes they may undergo, and their eventual demise. A third possible model holds that the modes of production are combined in such a way that there is, in general, no dominant mode of production. Thus, there would be no general outcome of the articulation of modes of production in the sense of one mode necessarily "winning out" over all others. The only way to understand the particular outcome of articulation, for instance, capitalist development, would be in terms of the analysis of the specific factors involved in the concrete combination of modes of production in any particular society.

It is necessary, then, to understand the notion of articulation in this light. "Articulation," as it is used to analyze the combined presence of different capitalist and noncapitalist modes of production during the course of transition to capitalism, takes on the dual meaning of "joining together" and "giving expression to."[29] Modes of production are conceived to be articulated in a social formation such that (a) the development of each mode of production is closely connected with, in the sense of being both dependent on and/or determined by, the other modes of production; and (b) the way that one mode of production is manifested or expressed cannot be analyzed independently of how others are manifested.

The articulation of MOP approach, then, is meant to provide a conceptual framework to analyze the interrelations between capitalist and noncapitalist modes of production as they manifest themselves in peripheral societies. The particular concern is to map out the development of capitalism from entry to hegemony where it was imposed initially from the outside. The central dynamic is the development of capitalism, understood in terms of the laws (or tendencies) governing its development and involving certain "needs" that come to be met by the noncapitalist modes of production—for instance, a need for a large pool of landless laborers. The development of the noncapitalist modes of production is explained in terms of their ability to satisfy the needs of capitalism. In turn, the development of the capitalist mode of production is understood to be enabled or hindered in terms of the ability of the noncapitalist modes of production to satisfy capitalism's posited needs.

Whether or not the stress is on the changing nature of capitalist expansion, the general conclusion of the articulation of MOP theorists is that the development of capitalism on a world scale involves, first, the creation and maintenance and, then, the breakdown of noncapitalist modes of production. However, at the same time that noncapitalist forms of production are understood to be dominated and at least tendentially supplanted by capitalism, an additional conclusion of the work of the articulation of MOP theorists is that the full, nondistorted development of the capitalist mode of production in the underdeveloped countries is itself blocked by its dependent relation to capitalism in the developed nations.

To appreciate the appearance and further elaboration of the articulation of MOP approach, it is helpful to note the critical tension that exists between this approach and other frameworks of analysis. The articulation of MOP position in some ways agrees with, and at the same time is quite critical of, other frameworks in regard to certain key points. It has already been stated above that this approach was in part a response to Frank's original formulation of Dependency Theory in which peripheral societies were characterized as capitalist from the time they were first inserted into what he termed the capitalist world economy. In contrast to Frank's seeing capitalism everywhere, the articulation of MOP theorists have focused on the continued existence of various noncapitalist modes of production and their articulation with the capitalist mode of production. However, they have also taken a page from Frank's book by insisting that the capitalist mode of production was originally introduced from outside the periphery and that it continues to take its dynamic from the capitalist mode of production in the center. In this sense, the articulation of capitalist and noncapitalist modes of production in the developing countries is a different formulation of the original notion of dependency. As Foster-Carter has stated it, "the 'history of capital itself' *continues* to be 'written outside such social formations'."[30]

The articulation of MOP approach also shares with Frank and the remainder of the Dependency Theory school a criticism of the orthodox "dualist" conception of the developing countries. Arrighi, for example, has analyzed what orthodox economists understand to be the labor surplus economy (for instance, the Lewis model) as a *product* of capitalist development, not as some original state.[31] However, his criticism is distanced from that of Frank in the sense that Arrighi reconceptualizes what others consider to be dualism as a structured combination of capitalism *and* noncapitalism, as an articulated combination of modes of production.

Not surprisingly, a traditional interpretation of the Marxist theory of development has also been the object of criticism in the work of the articulation of MOP theorists. Two aspects of this critique deserve at least brief mention. First, many of the articulation of MOP theorists have argued against the notion of a necessary or inevitable succession of modes of production.[32] Thus, they react against the mechanistic-deterministic tendency often found in some traditional Marxist analyses that hold that there is a unique path of development for all countries. Articulation of MOP theorists maintain that the transition to capitalism in peripheral societies has noncapitalist origins different from those involved in the transition in Western Europe. This means that there is no single succession of stages of development in all countries.[33]

The criticism of traditional Marxist theories of development made by the articulation of MOP theorists often has a second aspect. The question here is whether the transition to capitalism in peripheral societies is fundamentally distinct from the transitions that have occurred elsewhere, especially in Western Europe. The traditional Marxist answer is taken to be that there is no fundamental distinction to be drawn here. The articulation of MOP theorists, on the other hand, argue that something different has been occurring in the peripheral transition to the capitalist mode of production. In particular, the development of capitalism in the periphery is seen as an *uneven* process taking place over an *extended* period of time. As we mentioned above in relation to Rey, the assumption here is that the European transition was, in contrast, relatively smooth and rapid. This attempt to analyze peripheral capitalist development as unlike the supposedly smooth, short development of capitalism in Western Europe is then used by Rey to argue that violence and other aspects of formal colonialism are inherent in the development of the capitalist mode of production in the periphery.

While critics of the articulation of MOP approach can agree that the development of capitalism in the peripheral countries is uneven and prolonged, they can also point out that it is evident that the transition to capitalism during, say, the period 1100–1850 in Western Europe was neither smooth nor of short duration. In support of their position, these critics can point out that the work of historians as diverse as Dobb and Pirenne has demonstrated the extended, often violent nature of the Western European transition to capitalism.[34] Therefore, without denying that there are certainly differences between the transitions to capitalism in the so-called core and periphery countries, critics of the articulation of MOP approach can maintain that it is probably mistaken to attempt to distinguish these transitions on the basis of their relative unevenness or the length of time over which they have been occurring.

In summary, the articulation of MOP theorists construct their understanding of the developing countries in terms of a system of relations between capitalist and noncapitalist modes of production. In particular, the concepts of dependency and underdevelopment are taken over from Dependency Theory and reinterpreted as the persistence of noncapitalist modes of production and the less than full development of the capitalist mode of production in that context. The articulation of MOP approach differs from specifically Frank-like interpretations of Dependency Theory, then, because of the focus on the relationship between capitalism and noncapitalism within the periphery. However, it still takes as given the notion, shared by Dependency Theory, that there are fundamentally different schemes of development that define a core and periphery of a world economy.

Peripheral Modes of Production

A second approach within the MOP school criticizes the specific set of concepts of modes of production that the articulation of MOP theorists have tended to use in their analyses. This alternative approach has sought to specify the concepts of "peripheral modes of production" or "colonial modes of production," a set of *sui generis* modes of production that are said to correspond better than the "classical" concepts of capitalist and noncapitalist modes of production to the conditions of underdevelopment and dependency in the peripheral countries of the world economy.

The modes of production picked out by these new concepts are considered to be qualitatively distinct from those that are used to analyze the development of capitalism in Western Europe and elsewhere. The operative assumption is that the forms of development in the core and periphery are fundamentally different and that different concepts must be used to understand these different forms of development. According to the peripheral MOP theorists, the fact that colonialism changed the precolonial pattern of development—in particular, the precolonial modes of production—in the colonized countries means that what is required is a separate set of concepts of modes of production with which to analyze their colonial and postcolonial experiences. This argument is best summarized by C. F. S. Cardoso:

> The specificity of internal colonial structures and of their historical genesis implies the inadequacy of such categories as "feudalism" to explain them. What is required is the elaboration of a theory of *colonial modes of production,* starting with the notion that such structures are *specific and dependent.*[35]

Here, then, the concept of mode of production is modified by the notion of dependency to produce a framework of analysis based on a set of concepts of peripheral or colonial modes of production. The presupposition seems to be that a mode of production that is affected to some more or less significant degrees by conditions external to the social formation where that mode of production is located is fundamentally different from an "independent" mode of production. For example, according to this approach, the existence of slavery in Brazil during the colonial period would make it a different mode of production, by virtue of its colonial ties with Portugal, from the slave mode of production of ancient Rome. Thus, despite what might at first appear as important similarities between the two cases, different concepts are needed in each case to conduct a proper analysis. This presumption that external influences serve as the criterion for a separate set of concepts of peripheral modes of production is also the origin of the well-known Alavi-Banaji–et al. debate on India.[36]

This attempt to draw a sharp distinction between peripheral and classical modes of production does make it quite evident, however, that the focus of this form of analysis is on the external relations of domination that shape and otherwise determine what are conceived to be the subordinate modes of production of the peripheral countries. In this regard, then, the work of the peripheral MOP theorists is continuous with the earlier work of Frank. They agree with Frank that the dependency condition of the developing world is a result of the domination of economic forces (for the most part) outside the developing countries themselves. Where they differ from Frank is over how best to analyze the internal structures of dependency, whether, for instance, underdevelopment should be analyzed in terms of capitalist relations or whether it should be seen as the result of the logic of development of a different, peripheral mode of production.

Internationalization of Capital

The third major approach to the MOP analysis of dependency and underdevelopment focuses on the internationalization of capital as part of a world system that is to be understood in terms of the laws of motion of the capitalist mode of production. In many ways, Frank's most recent works on "world accumulation" reflect this new focus.[37] Attention is shifted away from the articulation between capitalist and noncapitalist modes of production and away from the specification of specific peripheral modes of production to an analysis of the structure and logic of development of the capitalist mode of production itself. According to the internationalization of capital theorists, the other two MOP approaches do not pay sufficient attention to the "real" dynamic determining world development, i.e., the capitalist mode of production. This mode of analysis presumes the dominance of the capitalist mode of production within the international economy; that is, it implies that the fundamental structure of the world economy is that of the capitalist mode of production and that the logic of world development reflects the laws governing that mode of production. In this way, the internationalization of the capitalist mode of production becomes the new demiurge, propelling the world economy forward and driving a larger and larger wedge between core and periphery.

This focus on the structure and effects of the capitalist mode of production on a world scale may be seen as either a critique or an extension of the two other MOP approaches surveyed in previous sections. It represents a critique to the extent that noncapitalist and peripheral modes of production are replaced by a single global capitalist mode of production. For example, units of production that would be analyzed as feudal or peripheral in the other MOP frameworks would be placed inside a single process of capitalist accumulation by the internationalization of capital theorists. On the other hand, it represents an extension insofar as some theorists argue that the historical period when the other modes of production approaches were applicable has passed. There may have been and probably were either noncapitalist or peripheral modes of production at one time in the developing countries, so they might argue, but these modes of production have been supplanted by a single capitalist mode of production on a world scale. Interpreted thusly, the various MOP approaches would represent a historical sequence at the level of theory that corresponds to the stages of development of the world economy.

However understood, whether as a break from or an extension of the other MOP frameworks, the basic unit of analysis of the internationalization of capital approach is the structure and movement of the capitalist mode of production. Partly in response to the debate between theoretical approaches that argued over the predominance of circulation (Frank) versus that of production (Laclau), the internationalization of capital theorists have defined capitalism in terms of a particular interpretation of Marx's three circuits of commodity-capital, money-capital, and productive-capital. In other words, capitalist production is conceived of as a *unity* of production and circulation. The focus is, in particular, on the global nature of these circuits as they transcend the confines of the nation-state. The symbol of this global process of accumulation is, of course, the transnational or multinational corporation. These corporations embody the logic of the third stage of the international expansion of the capitalist mode of production, intertwining the various parts of the world economy into a single entity and subordinating these parts to the needs of capitalist accumulation.

While they all focus on the internationalization of the various circuits of capital, and therefore of the capitalist mode of production itself, the various internationalization of capital theorists reach different conclusions concerning the continued existence of dependency and underdevelopment. Basically, as exemplified in the preceding example, the positions are two. On the one hand, it is argued that the new international division of labor produced by the internationalization of the capitalist mode of production serves to perpetuate conditions of underdevelopment and the dependency of the peripheral countries on the core countries (where the multinational corporations are based).[38] Underdevelopment and dependency are no longer associated with the persistence of noncapitalist modes of productions, as they are with the articulation of MOP theorists, or with the dependent status of developing countries, as in the peripheral MOP approach; they are effects internal to the capitalist mode of production itself.

On the other hand, the analyses of, for example, Cypher and, even more so, Warren argue that underdevelopment is associated only with the continued existence of noncapitalist modes of production and that these are entirely supplanted by the expansion of the capitalist mode of production.[39] The expansion of the capitalist mode of production on a world scale, particularly within what others would term the periphery, induces a process of unqualified capitalist development. Here the break with the conclusions of Frank and other theorists of the "development of underdevelopment" or "dependent development" is virtually complete.

Even many of those who assume the first position and choose to retain terms such as "dependency" and "underdevelopment" tend to analyze the development of so-called Third World countries solely in terms of the logic of expansion of the capitalist mode of production. A typical statement is the following:

> International markets and economic power structures are increasingly determining the individual decisions made in ever more isolated parts of national economies, even when "noncapitalist" productive groups are involved, such as peasant producers in many Third World economies.[40]

Two factors appear to be lost here. Any dynamic inherent in the particular economic structure, capitalist or otherwise, of a developing country is overlooked in favor of international forces. Second, noncapitalist modes of production recede into the background or disappear completely; thus, we are faced with the collapse of the notion of articulation and an ironic return to Frank's original position, this time in terms of "seeing the capitalist mode of production everywhere."

IV. AMIN

The various conceptualizations of dependency and underdevelopment analyzed in previous sections are synthesized and recast as a distinct version of Dependency Theory in the work of Samir Amin. Basically, Amin combines notions of the world capitalist system, the articulation of modes of production, and the internationalization of capital with a theory of unequal exchange. The result is a theory of development in which the core and periphery are conceived as complementary opposites within a world capitalist social formation. This relation between core and periphery promotes capitalist development in the former while blocking the same path of development in the latter. This conception of dichotomous economic development serves, in turn, as the basis of what Amin considers to be the central political contradiction of the world capitalist system.

Amin begins his theory of development with the presumption of a world capitalist system that is divided into two fundamentally distinct parts—a core and a periphery—that are functionally related. In a manner obviously consistent with Frank's approach, he argues that "the structures of the periphery are shaped so as to meet the needs of accumulation at the center, that is, provided that the development of the center engenders and maintains the underdevelopment of the periphery."[41]

Going beyond Frank, however, Amin realizes the importance of providing a more detailed analysis of the internal structures of the countries of the periphery. Amin shares with the articulation of modes of production theorists a structural explanation of the underdevelopment of the periphery in terms of the system of relations between the capitalist and various noncapitalist modes of production. In general, for Amin, "social formations are . . . concrete, organized structures that are marked by a dominant mode of production and the articulation around this of a complex of modes of production that are subordinate to it."[42]

The particular social formations of the world capitalist economy are analyzed in terms of the dominance of the capitalist mode of production and the subordinate existence of various noncapitalist modes of production. Finally, Amin follows the internationalization of capital theorists in analyzing the various parts of his world economy in terms of the globalization of the capitalist mode of production.

> The predominance of the capitalist mode of production is also expressed on another plane. It constitutes a world system in which all formations, central and peripheral alike, are arranged in a single system, organized and hierarchical.[43]

These three notions (world capitalist system, articulation of modes of production, and internationalization of the capitalist modes of production) are combined, as we show below, with a theory of unequal exchange to constitute Amin's particular theory of blocked development in the periphery.

Amin's work is characterized, then, by this synthesis of other Dependency Theory approaches to produce an alternative model of dependency and underdevelopment. His work is also characterized by the importance it places on history. This focus on history is thematic in at least two senses. First, much of Amin's published work—in fact, some would argue, the best of that work—consists of historical writing. His accounts of the different paths to capitalism in the social formations of the periphery, especially in Africa, are among the best available.[44] Second, Amin conceives of history as providing the "correct perspective" for carrying out the analysis of the developing countries. The terms of his own particular analysis are said to correspond to a perspective that emerges from the history of the developing countries.[45] Theories that have been generated from perspectives that represent the histories of the core countries—in particular, neoclassical and traditional Marxist theories of development—do not correspond, according to Amin, to the reality of the developing countries.

The central element of Amin's model of the world economy is the relationship between the two groups of core and periphery countries as complementary opposites. These two poles are created by the history of capitalist expansion from the core. According to Amin, a core and periphery exist at all of the three stages into which he periodizes capitalist development: mercantilist, premonopoly/competitive, and monopoly/imperialist capitalism. However, the dichotomy becomes "hardened" in the third, imperialist stage: From that point on, no country of the periphery or semiperiphery is capable of joining the core.

The reason for this hardening of the core and periphery is that Amin considers these two parts of the world economy to be governed by fundamentally different laws of development. The contrast is between *autocentric* and *extraverted* accumulation. "I maintain that the dynamic of the core is autonomous, that the periphery adjusts to it, and that the functions the periphery fulfills differ from one stage to another."[46]

Amin is quite specific in stating that autocentric accumulation does not mean autarchy. Rather, autocentric development is a result of the dynamic of development originating in the core itself. The nature of development in the core is such that it determines its own development as well as that of the periphery. The key relation making for a pattern of autocentric accumulation in the center is the balance between increases in productivity and wages.[47] This results in an expansion of the internal market and the balanced development of industries specialized in the production of both producer and consumer goods (or, in Amin's terminology, Departments I and II). This balance between changes in productivity and wages in the center is also supported by surplus transfers from the periphery on the basis of unequal exchange.

The periphery, on the other hand, is barred from achieving such a balance. Its pattern of accumulation is characterized as extraverted, deformed, and dependent. The pattern of accumulation is fundamentally different in the periphery where the coexistence of capitalist and noncapitalist modes of production means that there is no necessary relation between the levels of productivity and wages. Increases in productivity, even in the "modern" export sector, are not translated into corresponding improvements in wages because of the existence of a Lewis-like surplus labor force. The sources of this "surplus labor" are those parts of the economy in which noncapitalist relations are still strong. This imbalance between productivity and wages leaves the domestic market "limited and distorted," so that the key result is a link between production in the export sector and luxury goods consumption.

According to Amin, the peripheral economy is considered to be "disarticulated."[48] It should be emphasized that this concept of disarticulation is quite different from what it might mean for the articulation of modes of production theorists. "Articulation" and "disarticulation" in Amin's sense refer to the economic conditions that give rise to a balance or imbalance between changes in productivity and wages. The result of disarticulation, then, is that the possibility of autocentric accumulation in the periphery is blocked.

The key mechanism in Amin's model whereby the two patterns of autocentric and dependent development are reproduced is the process of unequal exchange between core and periphery. Amin takes over and subsequently modifies Emmanuel's original theory of unequal exchange.[49] Emmanuel takes as given and bases his analysis on differences in real wages between center and periphery. Amin argues that the essential condition for unequal exchange is not merely wage differentials, but rather that these real wage differences are larger than productivity differences. The result, however, is the same as that in Emmanuel's model: The prices (of production) at which the goods of the center and periphery exchange are such that a surplus is transferred to the former from the latter. This surplus transfer means that there is an external drain on internally generated investment funds and the reproduction of a limited internal market. These results then serve to reproduce the general conditions of accumulation that, in turn, give rise to the wage-productivity differentials that are the basis of unequal exchange.

Amin's theory of unequal exchange, like that of Emmanuel and others, has elicited comments and criticisms from many quarters.[50] The most damaging criticism to his general model of the unidirectional transfer of a surplus from the periphery to the core concerns the real wage-productivity disparity between center and periphery. According to Amin, this transfer of surplus requires that production in the periphery be based on a higher rate of exploitation than that in the center. Amin's own equations bear this out. If this is so, critics respond, why is it the case, assuming as Amin does the full mobility of capital, that all production in the core is not transferred to the periphery? Amin's answer is twofold. First, capitalists respond to different profit rates, not to different rates of exploitation. And since Amin's model of unequal exchange assumes the existence of a single, general rate of profit across all industries, there is no apparent reason for capital to be shifted from the core to the periphery. Second, Amin has argued that the absence of a large domestic market in the periphery keeps industry in the core countries. This second response is less than satisfactory because there is no reason that the location of production must coincide with the location of the final market. His own assumption of the existence of international exchange shows this.

His first answer, concerning the difference between profitability and exploitation, is also beset with difficulties. On the one hand, Marx's theory of prices of production and a general rate of profit, which Amin says that he adopts, was part of Marx's attempt to analyze the dynamic nature of capitalist competition.[51] Marx used the concept of price of production as a *hypothetical equilibrium* to illustrate the ceaseless *movement* in the direction of the formation of a general rate of profit. Flows of capital between industries in response to unequal rates of profit so change the conditions of profitability that the hypothetical general rate of profit itself changes. This general rate of profit can be thought of as a shifting equilibrium, an elusive goal that is never reached. Its only purpose in volume 3 of *Capital* is to illustrate the dynamics of capitalist competition by momentarily abstracting from that movement. On the other hand, even assuming a general rate of profit *across* industries does not mean that the rate of profit is equal *within* each industry. The existence of a range of "efficiencies" among firms that make up each industry at any point in time implies that there will be a similar range of profit rates among those firms.[52] The competitive dynamic that forces less efficient producers within an industry to innovate, e.g., by moving to a location where rates of exploitation are supposed to be higher (in the periphery, according to Amin), is not brought to a standstill even if a general rate of profit is imposed across industries.

In general, then, the existence at a point in time of a set of prices does not ensure that the underlying conditions that give rise to those prices will be reproduced over time. In fact, the opposite conclusion is more likely, namely, that the existence of unequal prices of production will cause movements of capital within and between industries so that the conditions of profitability within those industries are changed. The nature of these changes in the conditions of profitability cannot, of course, be predetermined. However, there is no reason, even on the basis of Amin's assumptions, for such capital movements to unilaterally promote capitalist development in one set of countries (the core) and prevent such development in another group of countries (the periphery). Unequal capitalist development in both core and periphery, rather than the "development of underdevelopment," would be the more likely result.

Amin's model of the world capitalist economy starts with a fundamental distinction between core and peripheral patterns of accumulation. This relation of complementary opposites is reproduced over time by the mechanism of unequal exchange. The result, then, of Amin's economic analysis is that the development of capitalism on a world scale is radically dichotomized: While continuing apace in the core countries, the development of capitalism is substantially blocked in the peripheral countries. This underdevelopment means, for Amin, that noncapitalist modes of production continue to exist in the periphery and that the peripheral capitalist mode of production cannot serve as the basis for a process of autocentric development.

It should be relatively clear from our and other summaries of Amin's work that both the starting point and end point of Amin's analysis of the world capitalist system is the fundamental dichotomy between the modes of accumulation in the core and in the periphery. Distinct processes of accumulation are posited at the beginning of his analysis and reproduced over time, through the mechanism of unequal exchange, so that the fundamental differences between these complementary opposite forms of development are present in his conclusions. In addition, the fundamental political contradiction of the world system—between the capitalists of the center and the superexploited workers of the periphery—corresponds exactly to this economic distinction between core and periphery.

The key mechanism that is both cause and effect of this dichotomy, unequal exchange, has been called into question above. Our point is not the substantive one that unequal exchange cannot or does not take place in international trade. Rather, our criticism indicates that the existence of unequal exchange, and the accompanying flows of profits among enterprises within and between industries, cannot ensure the reproduction of the two fundamentally distinct patterns of accumulation that are presumed in Amin's analysis. In addition, it is only the presumption of this essential economic dichotomy between core and periphery that allows Amin to make the fundamental political conflict of the world system that between capitalists located in the core countries and workers located in the periphery. To so reduce the political dynamic within the world system, if such a system can be presumed at all, serves only to "forget about" the other conflicts and contradictions that emerge in the course of world development.

V.   CONCLUSION

There is a wide variety of theories that serve as alternatives to orthodox, neoclassical approaches to development. We have presented three of those theories in this chapter: the Dependency Theory of Frank (and, by extension, Wallerstein), the Modes of Production school, and the approach elaborated by Amin.

All three theoretical approaches are explicitly put forward as dependency and/or Marxian alternatives to bourgeois development theory. Using different concepts, they arrive at conclusions in stark contrast to those put forward by bourgeois economists and other social scientists. Where bourgeois theorists see the development of capitalism as propelling a process of modernization from traditional or backward forms of economic and social organization to modern growth and development, the radical theorists see imperialist domination and exploitation. Thus, these radicals "see" a different reality in the currently less-developed or underdeveloped countries. The difference in the very names used to designate these "poor" countries by the alternative approaches—less-developed vs. dependent and/or underdeveloped—betray these different realities.

Orthodox and radical theorists arrive at different conclusions because their analyses of development start in different places; they have different conceptual "entry-points." Orthodox theorists tend to focus on individual decision-making and begin their analysis with a particular model of human behavior. In neoclassical theory, capitalist economic growth and development are understood in terms of individual utilities or preferences. Prices, the distribution of income, and all other economic phenomena are derived from this utility model of behavior. Individual utilities, taken as given within the model, are considered the principal factor determining the economic forces leading to development. From this perspective, the development of capitalism is generally understood to bring about an increase in individual freedom. This greater freedom, in turn, is seen to help guarantee the accumulation of wealth and social modernization by providing the incentives for rational market behavior. This is true for all countries in which capitalism takes root.

The radical approaches arrive at different conclusions because they start with different concepts. In the case of Frank (and Wallerstein), the circulation of commodities serves as the conceptual entry-point for the analysis of world capitalist development. Laclau and his followers begin with concepts of modes of production to describe and analyze development in the core and periphery of the world economy. Different and unequal national units within a world capitalist social formation is the starting point for Amin's theory of development. Many radicals have attempted to use all three standpoints, by synthesizing concepts of commodity and capital flows, modes of production, and the world capitalist system into a single framework of analysis. Thus, radical approaches tend to replace the model of human behavior of orthodox theory with one of a variety of different concepts (or a combination of them).

It is natural, then, that capitalist development will look very different to these radical theorists in comparison with the bourgeois outlook. Where the orthodox theorists see freedom, the radicals see unequal power relations. The orthodox notion of economic growth for all countries becomes, in radical theories, economic growth for some countries at the expense of growth for all the others. The orthodox theory of a unilinear process of development from traditional to modern societies is similarly challenged by radical theorists: Development occurs in the center while underdevelopment or dependent development occurs in the periphery. In this sense, capitalism is the problem, not the solution.

These radical theories are certainly alternatives to the orthodox approach to development, both in terms of their conceptual entry-points and the conclusions they generate about the process of development. However, they share with their orthodox opposite one crucial element: They tend to reduce the analysis of development to one decisive factor. That is, just as the neoclassical conception of development explains all social phenomena in terms of a particular model of human behavior (psychological utility), the radical theories we have presented tend to explain development in terms of international commodity circulation, the mode of production, or the world capitalist social formation, respectively. The result is that quite different theories end up agreeing on the methodological point that the rest of society can be explained in terms of one essential factor. What they disagree about, then, is what the factor is.

The difficulty with all such approaches is that they attempt to reduce the explanation of a complex and diffuse phenomenon—world development in the past four hundred years—to an ultimately determining factor. One can be justifiably wary of whether any theory of this sort can provide an entirely convincing account.

Orthodox and radical approaches also share another key aspect. They are both directly and indirectly connected to political agendas. Radical theorists tend to be more up-front about their political interests. Orthodox theorists, concerned to claim the mantle of science, tend to shy away from stating explicitly the political dimensions and implications of their approach. Nonetheless, we should recognize that such contrasting theories of development will lead to significantly different consequences for the actual course of development.

NOTES

1. For three recent attempts to survey this literature, see Anthony Brewer, *Marxist Theories of Imperialism: A Critical Survey* (London: Routledge & Kegan Paul, 1980); Gabriel Palma, "Dependency: A Formal Theory of Underdevelopment or a Methodology for the Analysis of Concrete Situations of Underdevelopment?," *World Development*, 6 (July–August 1978): 881–924; and Keith Griffin and John Gurley, "Radical Analyses of Imperialism, the Third World, and the Transition to Socialism: A Survey Article," *Journal of Economic Literature*, 23 (September 1985): 1089–1143.

2. What might be called the classic debate took place in the first decades of this century and largely involved issues of how to interpret and extend Marx's theory to the questions of imperialism and the colonial world. The major figures included Lenin, Luxemburg, Bukharin, and Hilferding. The works listed in footnote 1 all discuss this material. Paul Baran's *The Political Economy of Growth* (New York: Monthly Review Press, 1957) preceded Frank's work by a decade and was very influential in setting the stages for the modern debate.

3. For discussions of a more critical nature focusing in particular on methodological issues, see two essays by the authors, "A Methodological Analysis of Dependency Theory: Explanation in Andre Gunder Frank" and "Methodological Aspects of a Marxian Approach to Development: An Analysis of the Modes of Production School," both in *World Development*, 14 (February 1986): 195–209 and 211–222. Some of the material in the present article has been adopted from these two essays.

4. Fernando Henrique Cardoso, it should perhaps be noted, differs somewhat from this view. See his "The Consumption of Dependency Theory in the United States," *Latin American Research Review*, 12 (1977): 7–24.

5. Andre Gunder Frank, *Capitalism and Underdevelopment in Latin America: Historical Studies of Chile and Brazil* (New York and London: Monthly Review Press, 1967, rev. ed. 1969). Frank's other major works include: *Latin America: Underdevelopment or Revolution* (New York and London: Monthly Review Press,

1969); *Lumpenbourgeoisie: Lumpendevelopment: Dependence, Class, and Politics in Latin America* (New York and London: Monthly Review Press, 1972); *World Accumulation, 1492–1978* (New York and London: Monthly Review Press, 1978); *Dependent Accumulation and Underdevelopment* (New York and London: Monthly Review Press, 1979); and *Critique and Anti-Critique: Essays on Dependence and Reformism* (New York: Praeger, 1984).

6. For a discussion of the structuralist position, see Kenneth P. Jameson, "Latin American Structuralism: A Methodological Perspective," *World Development*, 14 (February 1986): 223–232.

7. For example, Walt W. Rostow, *The Stages of Economic Growth* (Cambridge: Cambridge University Press, 1960). For a recent restatement of this orthodox approach, see Bruce Herrick and Charles P. Kindleberger, *Economic Development*, 4th ed. (New York: McGraw-Hill, 1983).

8. Ibid. (emphasis in the original); see also *Capitalism and Underdevelopment*, pp. 3–6.

9. It should be noted that not all Dependency Theorists would agree with this last point. For instance, dos Santos defines "dependence" in the following way: "Dependence is a conditioning situation in which the economies of one group of countries are conditioned by the development and expansion of others. A relationship of interdependence between two or more economies and the world trading system becomes a dependent relationship when some countries can expand through self-impulsion while others, being in a dependent position, can only expand as a reflection of the dominant countries, which may have *positive or negative* effects on their immediate development." (emphasis added) [T. dos Santos, "The Structure of Dependence," *American Economic Review*, Papers and Proceedings 40 (May 1970): 231–236.] The trouble with this definition is that if in fact the dependency relation has positive effects on the development of the dependent country, then it is hard to see how the theory can serve the critical function that Frank, at least, wants to give it. Three possible replies to this point are (1) that the positive effects are *immediate* and not long-term, and that the long-term effects of dependent development are and must be negative; (2) that even if there are positive effects on development, as long as the dependent country is dominated from without and does not control its own development, there is a violation of national autonomy, if not sovereignty, and this is to be criticized; and (3) that the theory is not meant to be critical, but only descriptive. The problems with these replies are that the first makes it unclear why the short-term positive effects should ever be mentioned; the second reply, if it is intended to support a critical theory, requires an additional argument to the effect that the loss of autonomy is worse than the gain in economic development, and this would be a controversial claim; and the third reply is not accurate, at least in relation to Frank. This entire problem can be sidetracked by building the normative dimension into the concept of dependence from the beginning. Sanjaya Lall also makes the point that "dependence" as used by the Dependency Theory school has a definite normative dimension, namely, that the future development of the dependent economy is adversely affected by its being dependent. See Sanjaya Lall, "Is 'Dependence' a Useful Concept in Analysing Underdevelopment?" *World Development*, 3 (November and December 1975): 799–800. For an additional discussion and critique of Frank's

use of the concept of dependence, see Brewer, *Marxist Theories of Imperialism*, pp. 164 and 177–180.

10. It should be noted that while Frank's view requires a complete account of the origins and development of capitalism, and he acknowledges as much, his early work only gestured at such an account. In more recent work, however, he has attempted to develop more fully this side of his project. See especially, *Dependent Accumulation and Underdevelopment* and *World Accumulation 1492–1789*. It should also be mentioned that Immanuel Wallerstein shares Frank's view of capitalism as a world system and more or less agrees with Frank's understanding of what capitalism is and how it works. Wallerstein's work has, of course, concentrated on the historical development of the capitalist world system, and in many ways the projects and perspectives of Frank and Wallerstein complement each other. Thus many of the points we make about Frank could easily be adapted to fit Wallerstein's work. See Wallerstein, *The Modern World System: Capitalist Agriculture and the Origins of the European World—Economy in the Sixteenth Century* (New York: Academic Press, 1974) and *The Capitalist World Economy* (Cambridge and Paris: Cambridge University Press and Editions de la Maison des Sciences de l'Homme, 1979).

11. See for instance Ernesto Laclau, "Feudalism and Capitalism in Latin America," *New Left Review*, no. 67 (May–June 1971), p. 24; and Brewer, *Marxist Theories of Imperialism*, p. 160.

12. Brewer makes this point in *Marxist Theories of Imperialism*, p. 160.

13. Laclau, "Feudalism and Capitalism in Latin America," pp. 24–25.

14. This point is made by Laclau, ibid., p. 22, and Brewer, *Marxist Theories of Imperialism*, p. 160. This criticism is one to which Frank tries to respond in his later work; see *Dependent Accumulation and Underdevelopment*, p. xii.

15. See *Lumpenbourgeoisie: Lumpendevelopment*, p. 13.

16. The individuals whose work exemplifies the articulation of MOP approach include Laclau, Rey, Arrighi, and Bradby. The most comprehensive surveys of this approach are Aidan Foster-Carter, "The Modes of Production Controversy," *New Left Review*, no. 107 (1978), pp. 47–77, and John G. Taylor, *From Modernization to Modes of Production: A Critique of the Sociologies of Development and Underdevelopment* (London: Macmillan Press, 1979).

17. C. F. S. Cardoso, Banaji, and Alavi are among those who have developed this particular interpretation of MOP analysis. See Foster-Carter, "Modes of Production Controversy," pp. 63–64, and Brewer, *Marxist Theories of Imperialism*, pp. 268–272.

18. The work of Palloix, Cypher, Warren, and Barkin is representative. Unfortunately, the tendency is to submerge this approach within a more comprehensive MOP school of thought; see, e.g., James M. Cypher, "The Internationalization of Capital and the Transformation of Social Formations: A Critique of the Monthly Review School," *Review of Radical Political Economics*, 11 (Winter 1979): 33–49. Our brief survey is an attempt to demonstrate the specificity of this internationalization of capital interpretation of Dependency Theory.

19. For example, in the surveys by Foster-Carter, Taylor, and Brewer.

20. Palma is one who has commented on the problem of "operationalizing" the concepts of Frank's formulation of Dependency Theory; see his "Dependency."

21. The most famous are Rey, Meillasoux, and Terray.

22. Laclau, "Feudalism and Capitalism in Latin America," pp. 19–37.

23. Ibid., p. 33.

24. Many of the MOP theorists have acknowledged their intellectual debt to the work of Althusser and Balibar. A central text in this tradition is Louis Althusser and Etienne Balibar, *Reading Capital* (London: New Left Books, 1975).

25. Essentialism is defined by Althusser and Balibar as a form of analysis in which the relations among social processes are understood in terms of essence—phenomenon relations. It is more or less synonymous with reductionism and determinism. According to Althusser and Balibar, the two most common forms of essentialism in the Marxist theoretical tradition are economic determinism and theoretical humanism. In both cases, an essence (the economy or human nature) serves to ultimately determine all other aspects of society (politics, culture, etc.) as the phenomenal forms of that essence. See, in particular, Louis Althusser, *For Marx* (New York: Vintage, 1970). This critique of essentialism and the project of formulating a nonessentialist interpretation of Marxist theory has been extended more recently by Stephen Resnick and Richard Wolff, "Marxist Epistemology: The Critique of Economic Determinism," *Social Text*, no. 6 (Fall 1982): 31–72.

26. The debate was initiated by the publication of Maurice Dobb, *Studies in the Development of Capitalism* (New York: International Publishers, 1947). The actual debate between Dobb and Paul Sweezy in *Science and Society*, along with other contributions, was published as *The Transition from Feudalism to Capitalism*.

27. Barry Hindess and Paul Hirst, *Pre-Capitalist Modes of Production* (London: Routledge & Kegan Paul, 1975).

28. Barry Hindess and Paul Hirst, *Modes of Production and Social Formation: An Auto-Critique of "Pre-Capitalist Modes of Production"* (Atlantic Highlands, N.J.: Humanities Press, 1977).

29. Cf. the discussion by Foster-Carter, "Modes of Production Controversy," p. 53.

30. "Modes of Production Controversy," p. 23.

31. Giovanni Arrighi, "Labour Supplies in Historical Perspective: A Study of the Proletarianization of the African Peasantry in Rhodesia," *Journal of Development Studies*, 3 (1970): 197–234.

32. Conceptions of historical development based on more or less inevitable successions of MOP are criticized by Umberto Melotti, *Marx y el Tercer Mundo* (Buenos Aires: Amorrotu, 1974).

33. Certainly many of Marx's oft-quoted summary statements on historical development can be interpreted as laying out an inevitable succession of stages; one example is the following: "In broad outline, Asiatic, ancient, feudal and modern bourgeois modes of production can be designated as epochs marking progress in the economic development of society" [Karl Marx, "Preface," *A Contribution to the Critique of Political Economy* (New York: International Publishers, 1970), p. 21]. However, Marx himself made clear that his objective was not to present "an historic–philosophic theory of the general path every people is fated to tread" [Karl Marx and Friedrich Engels, *Basic Writings on Politics and Philosophy*, Lewis S. Feuer, ed. (Garden City, NY: Doubleday, 1959), p. 440]. Stalin's interpretation, to take one example, is exactly such a "philosophy of history"; see his "Anarchism or Socialism?" and "Dialectical Materialism" in J. V. Stalin, *Works*, vol. 1 (1901–1907) (Moscow: Foreign Languages Publishing House, 1952).

34. Dobb, *Studies in the Development of Capitalism,* and Henri Pirenne, *Economic and Social History of Medieval Europe* (New York: Harcourt, Brace, and World, 1937).
35. Ciro Flamarion Santana Cardoso, "Severo Martinez Pelaez y el Caracter del Regimen Colonial," in Carlos Sempat Assadourian et al., *Modos de Producción en America Latina* (Córdoba, Argentina: Ediciones Pasado y Presente, 1974), p. 86 (our translation).
36. Hamza Alavi, "India and the Colonial Mode of Production," in *Socialist Register* (London: Merlin Press, 1975), pp. 160–197, and Jairus Banaji, "For a Theory of Colonial Modes of Production," *Economic and Political Weekly* (Bombay) 7 (December 1972); see, also, the discussion by Brewer, *Marxist Theories of Imperialism,* pp. 270–272.
37. For example, *World Accumulation, 1492–1789* and *Accumulation, Dependence, and Underdevelopment.*
38. See, e.g., Folker Frobel, Jurgen Heinrichs, and Otto Kreye, *The New International Division of Labour: Structural Unemployment in Industrialised Countries and Industrialisation in Developing Countries* (Cambridge: Cambridge University Press, 1981).
39. Cypher, "Internationalization of Capital," and Bill Warren, *Imperialism: Pioneer of Capitalism* (London: New Left Books, 1980).
40. "Internationalization of Capital," p. 158.
41. Samir Amin, *Unequal Development: An Essay on the Social Formations of Peripheral Capitalism,* trans. Brian Pearce (New York: Monthly Review Press, 1976), p. 104.
42. Ibid., p. 16.
43. Ibid., p. 22.
44. For example, *L'Economie du Maghreb,* 2 vols. (Paris: Editions de Minuit, 1966); *Le Developpment du Capitalisme en Cote d'Ivoire* (Paris: Editions de Minuit, 1967); *L'Afrique de l'Ouest Bloquee* (Paris: Editions de Minuit, 1971); and *Neo-Colonialism in West Africa,* trans. Francis McDonagh (New York: Monthly Review Press, 1973).
45. This point concerning the epistemological status of history in Amin's work, as well as the more general analysis of this section, shares much with the more extensive critical analysis of Amin's theory of development by Joseph Medley, "Economic Growth and Development: A Critique of Samir Amin's Conception of Capital Accumulation and Development," unpublished Ph.D. dissertation, University of Massachusetts–Amherst (May 1981).
46. Samir Amin, "Crisis, Nationalism, and Socialism," in Samir Amin, Giovanni Arrighi, Andre Gunder Frank, and Immanuel Wallerstein, *Dynamics of Global Crisis* (New York: Monthly Review Press, 1982), pp. 168–169.
47. This model of autocentric and, below, of extraverted development is presented by Amin in summary form in "Accumulation and Development: A Theoretical Model," *Review of African Political Economy,* no. 1 (1974): 9–26, and explored at length in *Accumulation on a World Scale,* 2 vols. (New York: Monthly Review Press, 1975).
48. Similar concepts of "social articulation" and "social disarticulation" are used by Alain de Janvry (with Elisabeth Sadoulet), "Social Articulation as a Condition for Equitable Growth," *Journal of Development Economics,* 13 (1983): 275–303.
49. Arghiri Emmanuel, *Unequal Exchange: A Study of the Imperialism of Trade,* Brian Pearce, trans. (New York: Monthly Review Press, 1972).

50. See, e.g., the comments by Charles Bettelheim published as Appendices I and III to Emmanuel, *Unequal Exchange,* and the recent survey article by David Evans, "A Critical Assessment of Some Neo-Marxian Trade Theories," *Journal of Development Studies,* 20 (January 1984): 202–226.

51. This interpretation of Marx's theory of value is presented at length by Bruce Roberts, "Value Categories and Marxian Method: A Different View of Value-Price Transformation," unpublished Ph.D. dissertation, University of Massachusetts–Amherst (September 1981).

52. Richard D. Wolff, "Marxian Crisis Theory: Structure and Implications," *Review of Radical Political Economics,* 10 (Spring 1978): 50.

9

Plant Imperialism

Lucile Brockway

"The greatest service which can be rendered to any country is to add a useful plant to its culture," wrote Thomas Jefferson. The movement of plants by human agency has affected the course of history. New staples have prevented famines, as when New World maize and sweet potato were introduced into China in the sixteenth century; they have supported population explosions, as when the Andean white potato spread throughout northern Europe in the eighteenth and nineteenth centuries and fed the workers in the burgeoning industrial cities. New plantation crops have helped to make some nations rich and others poorer, when a local plant–based industry was undermined by a plant transfer.

Seeds have been one of the most precious and easily transported cultural artefacts. They have been exchanged in local and long distance trade, have prompted voyages of discovery, and have been carried thousands of miles by migrating peoples. Only one hundred years ago, the "Turkey red" strain of hard winter wheat, a basic bread wheat, was brought to the United States by German Mennonite immigrants from the Russian Crimea, who carried the seeds in earthenware jars across the Atlantic to their new home in Kansas.

The archaeologist, Kent Flannery, suggests that transhumant bands of food collectors were instrumental in domesticating the first grains in the Middle East over ten thousand years ago by the simple process of carrying them from a niche that was hard to reach, such as the talus slope below a limestone cliff, and planting them in one that was more accessible, such as the disturbed soil around their camp on a stream terrace. In the new niche, the pressures of natural selection were relaxed and human selection was applied. This principle underlies all successful plant transfers. In a new environment selected and shaped by humans, the plant's natural enemies are left behind, and human attention tries to ward off new ones.

From *History Today*, 33 (July 1983), pp. 31–36. Copyright © *History Today*, 4 Wood Street, London EC2U 7JB.

Natural plant monopolies have been short-lived. Being small and easily concealed, like diamonds or gold, seeds have often been smuggled. Until very recently, plant hunters and their sponsors, whether national governments, botanic gardens, commercial nurseries, or pharmaceutical houses, have treated plants as part of nature's bounty, theirs for the taking. Yet any plant worth taking has already been identified and put to use in a local ecosystem. Modern ethnobotanists are more ready than old-time plant hunters to acknowledge the scientific value of local lore, to consult with local experts, and to make suitable arrangements with local or national institutions. It is now generally agreed that rare plants, like minerals, are part of the natural resources of the country in which they are discovered, and are not to be removed without permission and recompense, perhaps merely an exchange of scientific information, perhaps a joint development of the resource. The concept of "ownership" of plants is intimately tied to the rise of the nation-state, to the idea of territorial sovereignty and to respect for the rights of weak and underdeveloped societies.

But in the eighteenth and nineteenth centuries botany was an ally of the expanding European empires. Botanists sailed on the great exploratory voyages of Captain Cook and his successors, collecting plants in the name of science and for the benefit of the mother country. Sir Joseph Banks, amateur botanist, president of the Royal Society, privy councillor to the King, who had sailed as a young man on Cook's first voyage and had participated in the discovery of Botany Bay, was influential in promoting the settlement of Australia to fill the need for a British naval base in the Far East during the Anglo-French struggle for India. Banks had noted the tall pines and wild flax on Norfolk Island and envisaged an Australian colony where settlers would grow provisions and make masts, spars, and sails. Botanists went with the earliest expeditions up the Niger, the Limpopo, the Zambezi. A botanist ran border surveys in the Himalayas and returned with a collection of nearly 7,000 plants. A botanist in the employ of the British East India Company learned the secrets of tea cultivation, and shipped out 2,000 tea plants and 17,000 tea seeds to start the tea industry in India.

"Well-ripened seeds of rarities will always be acceptable. Simply address Hooker at Kew," wrote the director of Kew Gardens in his annual report of 1851. Under William J. Hooker's direction Kew Gardens became a depôt for the exchange of plants within the Empire, receiving seeds from its collectors, propagating them in Kew greenhouses, and sending those plants with economic possibilities to colonies with suitable climates. Cork oaks were sent to the Punjab, ipecac, mahogany, and papyrus to India, West Indian pineapples to the Straits Settlements, tea plants to Jamaica, an improved strain of tobacco to Natal. Plant transfer is as old as the practice of agriculture, but it had never before been undertaken on such a scale.

Victorian botanists were so imbued with the imperialist ethos of the times that in some instances of plant transfer they failed to respect the rights of independent states with whom their government had diplomatic relations, and they gave little thought to the loss sustained by the country of origin. Historians of Kew Gardens never discuss in print the subterfuges and downright illegalities practiced by the Kew collectors in the transfers of cinchona from the Andean republics of Colombia, Ecuador, Peru, and Bolivia in the 1860s, and rubber from Brazil in 1876. They speak only of the humanitarian aspect of the one—quinine from cinchona to treat malaria—and the economic triumph of the other—the great rubber plantations of India, Ceylon, and Malaya. "Many countries owe a great debt, now rarely acknowledged, to those industrious men of Kew who gave their work and often their lives to foster the trade which began their economic development," says Ronald King, Secretary of the Royal Botanic Gardens, the latest in a long line of Kew's praise-singers.

In trying to list those countries that can be said to owe a debt to the Kew collectors, however, it soon appears that they are mostly former British colonies—India, Malaysia, Sri Lanka (Ceylon), Kenya, Zimbabwe (Rhodesia). The rubber plantations of Java, Sumatra, and Borneo, now in the Republic of Indonesia, and of Laos and Vietnam, formerly French Indo-China, were all started from descendants of the rubber seeds which the British removed from Brazil, using grafting, planting, and tapping methods developed by British and Dutch botanists in the colonial botanic gardens. This seed transfer and others like it were undertaken primarily to provide the mother countries of northwestern Europe with tropical commodities produced under their administrative, financial, and judicial control.

In the early days of European expansion, the movement of plantation crops was from the Old World to the New, when the plant riches of the East were carried to the new found lands. On his second voyage, in 1494, Columbus brought sugar cane cuttings to Hispaniola, along with citrus fruits, grape vines, olives, melons, onions, and radishes. Although many of these plants failed in the climate of the Antilles, this was the first step in a two-way transfer of useful plants which A. J. Crosby, Jr., has aptly called "the Columbian exchange." European settlers brought wheat for their daily bread, and New World corn, manioc, peanuts, and sweet potatoes were carried eastward to become the dietary staples of subsistence farmers in many parts of Africa, Asia, and Oceania. But it was the luxuries derived from tropical plants—the nonessential foodstuffs that made a pleasurable addition to the diet, the dyes, and the fibres that had hitherto been available only through trade with the Arabs—that excited the imagination of European traders and governments, and fostered the plantation system in the new tropical colonies.

Sugar cane, originally domesticated in Southeast Asia, was transferred by Arab traders and farmers to Syria and Egypt, and by the tenth century to the islands of the Mediterranean. By the fourteenth century Venetians had learned its culture and the plantation system from the Arabs whom they had displaced. Spaniards and Portuguese carried plantation sugar to the Atlantic Islands (Madeira, the Canaries, the Azores), thence to the Caribbean and Brazil. In 1640 sugar arrived on Barbados, and with it the slave trade and 150 years of prosperity for the West Indian planters, the merchants at home, and the home governments.

The Arabs domesticated coffee, a tree native to the Ethiopian highlands, and introduced it to India, where the Dutch found it and planted it on Ceylon in 1659 and on Java in 1696. One coffee plant from Java reached the Amsterdam Botanic Garden in 1706 and from this one tree most of the coffee plantations of the New World are descended. Seeds from this tree were sent to Surinam (Dutch Guiana) in about 1715; coffee trees went from Surinam to French Guiana and, in 1727, to Brazil, where a great coffee industry was founded that lasts to this day. In the nineteenth century both coffee and cocoa, a native American plant, were taken to the West African colonies to be grown on plantations and by small farmers. Ghana, especially, became dependent on its cocoa exports for foreign exchange and has suffered recently from a drop in the price of cocoa.

Nineteen-year-old Eliza Lucas was responsible for the introduction of indigo to the American mainland. Plants of the genus *Indigofera* have been grown since at least 2000 BC in India to produce a blue dye. Northern Europe did not use indigo in textile dyeing until the seventeenth century when the British and Dutch East India Companies imported it and displaced the woad producers. In the eighteenth century, the French planted indigo in the French Antilles and exported the processed dye cakes, but the process was a closely held secret. A governor of nearby British Antigua, Colonel George Lucas, sent indigo seeds to his daughter, who managed his three South Carolina plantations in his absence. Although the overseer who was sent with the seeds deliberately spoiled the first batches of dye out of loyalty to his home island and fear of ruining its trade, Governor Lucas sent a black slave from one of the French islands, and with his help Eliza Lucas succeeded in mastering the process. In 1744 she sent a sample of six pounds of indigo cakes to London, and distributed the rest of the seeds of the 1744 crop to her neighbours. Three years later, South Carolina sent 135,000 pounds of indigo cakes to London. Parliament voted a bounty on indigo processed in British territories. A French embargo, making exportation of indigo seeds a capital crime, came too late to save their monopoly.

In 1770, Pierre Poivre, Intendant of Île de France (Mauritius), an island in the Indian Ocean on the sea route to India and Indonesia, sent expeditions to the uncharted coasts of the Moluccas to bring back cloves and nutmeg, which he planted in the island's Jardin Royal de Pamplemousses. As a young man Poivre had made a voyage to China and Indochina, was wounded, and lost an arm in Batavia. His enforced stay on Java gave him an opportunity to study the spice trade, which the Dutch had successfully monopolised since the seventeenth century. They regulated production to maintain artificially high prices and kept all foreigners out of their spice islands. In 1755 Poivre had smuggled pepper and cinnamon to Île de France and was ennobled by his king. Britain took the island from the French in the Napoleonic Wars, sent cloves to Zanzibar and Pemba off the East African coast, and nutmeg to Grenada in the West Indies. Grenada is now called "the Spice Island," instead of the Moluccas.

Many important plant sources changed hands through the vagaries of European politics. In 1796 Britain took Ceylon from the Dutch and gained access to the cinnamon monopoly. In the seventeenth century she had acquired Bombay, with its pepper trade, as part of the dowry of Catherine of Braganza, the Portuguese princess who married Charles II. Plants followed the flag, as the European powers fought among themselves for control of Asia, and later Africa.

The situation was quite different when Europeans decided in the nineteenth century that they wanted certain plants native to areas of Latin America which by that time were postcolonial, independent nation-states. Europeans could not bring in their armies, or steal plants from each other. Diplomatic pressure was tried, or subterfuge, or both, as in case of cinchona.

Cinchona's only natural habitat is on the eastern slopes of the Andes, where the bark was collected by forest-dwelling Indians working for absentee land owners. When European observers like the famous naturalist Alexander von Humboldt saw the Indians cutting down whole trees to strip bark, they were convinced that this "wasteful harvesting practice" would kill the industry. In point of fact, the barkless trunks would have been eaten by insects, whereas in six years new shoots sprouting from the roots were ready for cutting. The cinchona transfer is one of the most intrigue-filled tales in plant history, with both the British and the Dutch trying to get seeds out of the Andean republics, and later vying for control of the Asian-based trade. The Andean republics, newly liberated from Spain and plagued by counterrevolution, were too weak to protect their infant cinchona bark industry.

Charles Hasskarl, director of the Dutch Buitenzorg Gardens on Java, penetrated the Caravaya region of Peru and Bolivia in 1854 under an assumed name. Clements Markham, leader of the British expedition in 1860, fled with his seeds from irate local authorities across southern Peru, avoiding the towns, with only a compass to guide him. Richard Spruce, a renowned explorer and botanist who had worked his way up the Amazon headwaters to Ecuador before being hired as a Kew Gardens cinchona collector, set up camp in a remote mountain valley, collected 100,000 dried seeds, and grew over 600 cinchona seedlings. He successfully transported them by raft down to the coast, but these endeavours cost him his health and he never walked again. These efforts, however, yielded few living plants, except for Spruce's "red cinchonas," which supplied the stock for thousands of cinchona trees planted in the hilly areas of India and Ceylon. Ironically, this "red bark" of commerce proved to be inferior in quinine content to the Ledger varieties grown by the Dutch on Java from seeds purchased in 1865 from an English trader, whose Aymara servant smuggled them out of Bolivia, was imprisoned for his treason, and died from prison hardships.

In addition to this piece of luck as regards species, the Dutch program of intensive care of the cinchona trees gave them a further advantage over the British planters, and by the 1890s a cartel of Dutch quinine processors had control of the market. Many British planters in India and Ceylon switched to tea. The market for South American wild bark had already dwindled to near zero, from a high point of nine million kilos of bark in 1881 before plantation bark had come on the market in quantity.

But those who contend that the British cinchona coup turned out to be a costly fiasco miss the point. The British government did not undertake the cinchona transfer for the benefit of planters, but because it wanted to protect the health of its troops and civil administrators in India, where British rule had been severely shaken by the Sepoy Mutiny of 1857. And this was accomplished: British-made quinine and quinidine were reserved for the representatives of the British *raj*, and Britain's grip on India was made more secure by an influx of soldiers and civil servants who no longer feared "the deadly climate."

The much-vaunted program to sell government-made "totaquine," a less refined and cheaper antimalarial derived from cinchona bark, 'at every post office in Bengal' was never pursued with vigour and was soon allowed to lapse. European quinine processors made big profits from plantation-grown cinchona bark in South Asia. Quinine became a more and more expensive drug, mostly beyond the purse of the indigenous peoples of malarial areas, but useful to their Western masters, and expecially to Western armies. In the First World War the Allies faced a shortage of quinine, since the neutral Netherlands sold bark and quinine to Germany. A representative of Howard & Sons, the British quinine processing firm, negotiated an agreement to pool Allied resources and to get access to the Java bark. He also "saved" the output of British cinchona estates from going to the India office, hence to the Indian public. In 1942 when the worst combined famine and malaria epidemic hit India and Ceylon, taking over two million lives, the British would not release quinine stockpiled in India to the civilian population. The cinchona plantations of Java were at that time in the hands of the Japanese and constituted one of the great prizes of their conquest of Southeast Asia. The United States, also desperately in need of quinine for its military forces in the South Pacific, instituted a successful crash program to rehabilitate the wild cinchona of the Andes. In two and a half years 18,000 tons of cinchona bark were harvested for processing in the United States.

Quinine was also essential to the British, French, and Germans in their "scramble for Africa," where appalling death rates had confined Europeans to the coast until quinine prophylaxis was adopted. It seems no coincidence that the New Imperialism of the late nineteenth century represented a European expansion into parts of the world where malaria was hyperendemic.

In the post–Second World War era, synthetic drugs largely replaced quinine in the Western world, but there was still a market for the drug. In 1959 a new cartel of Dutch, German, French, and British quinine processing companies was formed to control every aspect of the production and distribution of the world's supply of quinine, with reserved geographic markets for each firm and a uniform system of pricing. The main objective of this cartel was to eliminate competition, both among themselves and from outsiders, in bidding for the huge United States stockpile of bulk quinine, surplus war material then being put on the market. Members of the cartel agreed not to buy quinine from the Bandoeng factory in the Republic of Indonesia, a legacy from Dutch colonial days and the largest non-European processor of cinchona bark. By restricting its market, the cartel also gained access to Javanese cinchona bark which would otherwise have gone to the Bandoeng factory.

The celebrated rubber transfer occurred in 1876 when Henry Wickham, an English adventurer in the employ of Kew Gardens and the India Office, made off with a boatload of about 70,000 Hevea rubber seeds. Wickham hoodwinked the Brazilian customs officer, telling him that he had a cargo of "exceedingly delicate botanical specimens specially designated for delivery to Her Britannic Majesty's own Royal Gardens of Kew." The precious seeds were soon planted in Kew's greenhouses, and in a few months 1,900 rubber seedlings were en route to the Peradeniya Gardens in Ceylon. Seeds from Ceylon were sent to the Singapore Gardens, where Henry Ridley, a Kew-trained botanist, worked out the wound response method of tapping. He was called "Mad Ridley" or "Rubber Ridley" for his pains, but in 1895 he finally persuaded a few British planters in Malaya to try the new crop.

At the turn of the century 98 percent of the world's rubber came from Brazil. By 1919 the Brazilian rubber industry was dead. Singapore was thereafter the rubber capital of the world. In the 1930s, before the end of the colonial era, 75 percent of the world's rubber, by that time a vital strategic resource in both peace and war, came from British-owned plantations. Indentured Chinese labourers opened up the forests in Malaya; impoverished Tamils from India came across the straits to Malaya and Ceylon to work rubber and got caught up in debt peonage. The old agrarian empires of Asia supplied a docile and inexhaustible labour force.

In the early 1870s when Kew Gardens and the India Office first began trying to get rubber seeds out of Brazil (the first three attempts were failures because the seeds did not germinate), the wild rubber trade did not suffer from the cartel conditions that developed later. Britain had no conceivable reason of national security for invading Brazil's sovereignty by the surreptitious removal of one of its natural resources, merely an economic incentive, and in the preautomotive era, not a very strong one at that. Yet because the motorised West has depended heavily in this century on rubber emanating from Asian plantations, the rubber seed transfer, when it is remembered, is generally treated as an admirable exploit. Wickham's deceit of Brazilian authorities is not mentioned.

After the rubber coup of 1876 Kew Gardens did not undertake any organised expedition in contravention of laws prohibiting the exportation of Latin American plants, nor has any subsequent plant removal had the economic and political importance of rubber. But Britain still urged her consular officials to send home specimens of protected plants and reports on their propagation and processing, and Kew Gardens continued to seek such plants for study and to print such trade secrets in the name of science.

A case in point is sisal, a hard fibre suitable for making twine and rope. Sisal is obtained from the leaves of agave species native to the dry areas of Central America. The fibre was known and used by the Mayan Indians. In the 1830s commercial production was begun on the great *haciendas* of northern Yucatan. The Indian labour force was attached to the *haciendas* by debt peonage, easily enforced because Ladino appropriation of the water holes made independent village life impossible. After 1875, when grain production was intensified on the American plains, the Argentine pampas, and in eastern Europe to feed the growing urban populations of both North Atlantic seaboards, sisal was in great demand as a binder twine for wheat sheaves. The sisal plantations of Yucatan became vast agricultural factories, with American capital supplying machines to strip the fibre from the waste pulp, and railroads to take the sisal to the ports. Yucatan, once Mexico's poorest state, became its richest, and Mérida a glittering city.

Kew's interest was aroused. It was thought that sisal would do very well in the Bahamas and the other drier islands of the West Indies, which were languishing in postsugar, pretourist doldrums, as well as in Fiji, Mauritius, and perhaps India. But Mexico would not export its plants, nor give away its trade secrets. In 1890, however, the British consul in Vera Cruz obliged by sending Kew two lots of sisal plants, many of which were "dead on arrival," to quote a Kew report. Specimens were sent to the botanic gardens of Antigua, Fiji, and Singapore. In 1892 Kew published, in its *Bulletin of Miscellaneous Information*, a series of articles describing in detail the production and processing of Mexican sisal. Kew had done its part, according to its charter, in "aiding the Mother Country in everything that is useful in the vegetable Kingdom."

But the British plans miscarried. Scientific information travels easily to peoples culturally prepared to receive it. A German agronomist working for the German East Africa Company read the *Kew Bulletin* articles and found there, in a report of the director of the Trinidad garden, the name of a sisal bulbil supplier in Florida, where sisal plants had grown wild since 1840. Dr. Henry Perrine, former United States consul in Campeche, Mexico, had received from Congress in 1836 a grant of land on Biscayne Bay on which he intended to establish a botanic garden of exotic plants. While waiting for the Seminole War to be over, he settled with his family and his plants on Indian Key. Among the plants he brought from Mexico were figs, indigo, mulberry, tamarinds, mangoes (all originally from the East), and agaves. He had been given permission to take the agaves out of Yucatan in appreciation of his personal services to the community of Campeche during a cholera epidemic. In 1840 Dr. Perrine was killed in an Indian raid and his abandoned plants spread to the mainland.

A sisal industry never developed in Florida, but descendants of Perrine's sisal plants furnished the start of a thriving industry in East Africa, where German colonists adopted modern methods of planting, harvesting, and processing sisal, using a labour force of native tribesmen coerced into labour by land alienation and head-tax payments. Kenya, just to the north, started a similar industry from purchases of German bulbils, before a 1908 German embargo on their sale. Britain acquired German East Africa under the terms of the Versailles Treaty in 1919, and with the colony (then Tanganyika, now Tanzania) its sisal industry. Between the world wars, Java had huge sisal plantations. By the 1960s Mexico's share of the world's hard fibre trade had dropped to 12 percent; Manila hemp accounted for 13 percent; most of the rest was East African sisal. Another Latin American plant-based industry had been undermined in favour of European colonies in the Eastern hemisphere.

The white settlers in the East African highlands also grew coffee, tea, and maize for export to Europe. The agricultural value of the East African colonies rested entirely on introduced plants. The political repercussions of this imposed agricultural system are still reverberating today. But their contribution to the prosperity of the Empire was minor in comparison to that of the South Asian colonies, especially Malaya with its rubber, and Ceylon with rubber and tea. Java under the Dutch was the richest jewel in any colonial crown, with its plantations of rubber, cinchona, coffee, tea, sisal, and tobacco.

The partnership between colonising governments and botanic gardens in the transfer and scientific development of useful plants was mutually beneficial. State subsidy supported the science of botany, pure and applied. Botanic gardens repaid the national investment many times over, in the form of new plantation crops and improved yields. Tropical monoculture under European direction wrested an enormous bounty from the earth, but it also produced political and ecological imbalances with which the modern world must struggle.

FOR FURTHER READING

The Columbian Exchange by Alfred W. Crosby, Jr. (Greenwood Press, Westport, Conn.) is a delightful short work on the two-way seed transfers between the Old and New Worlds. A good introduction to the important food and fibre cultivars is *Plants and Civilization* by Herbert G. Baker (Wadsworth, Calif.) or *Seeds and Civilization* by Charles B. Heiser, Jr. (Freeman, San Francisco, Calif.). Clements Markham (John Murray, 1860 and John Murray, 1882) and Henry Wickham (Kegan Paul, 1908) have published accounts of their efforts and adventures as Kew collectors in Latin America; the journal of the great botanist Richard Spruce, edited by Alfred Russel Wallace, was published posthumously (Macmillan, 1908). The role of botanic gardens in seed transfer and development is treated in *Science and Colonial Expansion* by Lucile H. Brockway (Academic Press, 1979).

10

The Modernization of Underdevelopment: El Salvador, 1858–1931

E. Bradford Burns

"What most strikes me on arriving from Europe is the absence of all extreme poverty," Mrs. Henry Grant Foote observed approvingly of El Salvador in the mid-nineteenth century.[1] The British diplomat's wife concluded that Southern Europe and the major cities of England suffered far worse poverty and human misery than the diminutive—and other observers would add "backward"—Central American republic. These first impressions of the country, to which Queen Victoria's government had posted Mrs. Foote's husband in 1853, were also her conclusions strengthened by eight years of residence there.

Her memoir revealed at least one explanation for the satisfactory quality of life: people enjoyed access to land. The large Indian population still possessed a part of its communal lands, ranked by Mrs. Foote as among the "most fertile" areas of El Salvador.[2] Those who chose not to live in the communities, she noted, "generally have their own little piece of land and a house on it."[3] The outskirts of the capital, San Salvador, seemed almost Edenic in her prose: "The environs of the city are very beautiful, being one mass of luxuriant orange and mango trees, bending beneath their load of fruit, and the cottages of the poor people are remarkably neat and clean, each surrounded by its own beautiful shrubbery of fruit trees."[4] These observations buttressed her conclusion of the ready availability of food. The simple society excluded sharp distinctions between rich and poor. The Englishwoman praised the practical modesty among the upper class, although its humility sometimes bemused her. At one point she chuckled: "One custom struck us as very peculiar in this state. Everyone, from

From *Journal of Developing Areas*, no. 18 (April 1984), pp. 293–316. Copyright © 1984 by Western Illinois University.

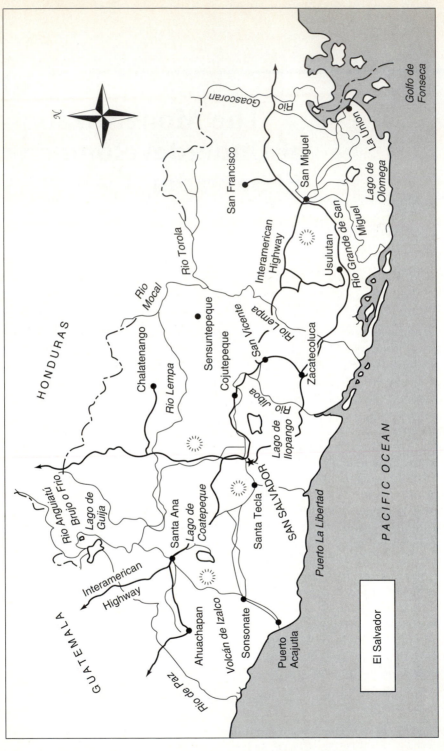

FIGURE 1 **El Salvador.**

162

President downwards keeps a shop, and no one objects to appear behind his counter and sell you a reel of cotton, the wives and daughters officiating in the same capacity."[5] She left an incomplete although suggestive portrait of the new nation, characterizing life as bucolic, devoid of social and economic extremes.

Around the middle of the century, a small group of foreign travelers and diplomats, among them John Baily, E. G. Squier, Carl Scherzer, and G. F. Von Tempsky, visited El Salvador.[6] Their accounts corroborated Mrs. Foote's. Although those visitors considered the small nation to be overcrowded even then, they agreed that most of the population owned land, either individually or collectively. The large hacienda existed but did not monopolize the rural economy. Squier noted, "There is little public and unclaimed land in the state, and few large tracts held by single individuals."[7] He contrasted that aspect of land tenure favorably with the experience of other nations he knew. The Indians, who at midcentury comprised at least a quarter of the population, worked either their communal lands or individual plots. A large number of them exclusively inhabited a Pacific coastal area of 50 by 20 miles between the ports of La Libertad and Acajutla, "retaining habits but little changed from what they were at the period of conquest," according to Squier.[8] All the travelers lauded the generosity of nature and spoke of the abundance of food. Von Tempsky recalled that the Indian village, Chinameca, he visited in 1855 was "well supplied with the necessaries of life."[9] Particularly impressed with the region of Sonsonate, Scherzer lauded the abundance, variety, and low price of food.[10] None mentioned either malnutrition or starvation.

The largely subsistence economy produced rather leisurely for the world market. Indigo, traditionally a principal export, earned $700,000 of $1,200,000 from foreign sales in 1851. Minerals, balsams, skins, rice, sugar, cotton, and cacao accounted for much of the rest.

Even though the foreign visitors waxed eloquent about some idyllic aspects of life as they lived and perceived it in El Salvador, not one pretended that the isolated nation was a rustic paradise. Problems existed. The visitors lamented the disease and political turmoil. Still, even if life did not mirror the ideal, a socioeconomic pattern that benefited many had emerged in the long colonial period and much briefer national period: food was produced in sufficient quantity to feed the population, the economy was varied, little emphasis fell on the export sector, the land was reasonably well distributed, the foreign debt was low, and the absence of the extremes of poverty and wealth spoke of a vague degree of equality. Having endured for some time, however, by the 1850s such characteristics were about to disappear. The El Salvador those foreigners observed was on the threshold of change and a rather rapid and dramatic change at that.

Over the course of three centuries, Spain had implanted its political, economic, social, and cultural institutions in its vast American empire with varying degrees of effectiveness. Those regions nearest the viceregal capitals or well integrated into imperial trade patterns bore the most vivid testimony to their successful implantation. Consequently, no matter what great distances might have separated Lima from Mexico City, the gold mines of Colombia from the silver mines of Bolivia, or the sugar plantations of Cuba from the cacao estates of Venezuela, similarities in economic and political structures outweighed inevitable local variations. Historiographic studies tend to dwell on the relative changelessness and continuity of some of those institutions over half a millenium. The institutions surrounding the use of land and labor are two useful examples; the concentration and authoritarian exercise of political power is another. Still, the metropolitan institutions did not fully penetrate every part of Spanish America. To the degree they did not, those regions remained marginal to international trade and isolated from the primary preoccupations of the crown. Fusing Iberian, Indian, and African cultures and institutions, such regions remained nominally subordinate to a distant monarch but for practical purposes more responsive to local conditions.

More regional diversity existed in Spanish America during the period when the colonies obtained their independence, 1808–1824, than there would be at the end of the century. The reasons for the rapid homogenization during the nineteenth century are not difficult to find. Many of the elites in all the newly independent governments had embraced or would embrace the ideas that sprang from the European Enlightenment. They admired French culture, while they looked to England for their economic vigor. As the nineteenth century waxed, their collective desire grew to create in the New World a replica of Europe north of the Pyrenees. To emulate the "progress" the elites believed characteristic of their model nations, they needed capital. They obtained it through loans, investments, and trade, all three of which linked them ever more closely to North Atlantic capitalism. Marvelous advances in communication and transportation facilitated the growing conformity forged by common goals and trade patterns. One major consequence was that as the new nations neared the first centenary of their independence, the institutional patterns of Latin America reflected a more striking similarity than they had after more than three centuries of Iberian domination. To achieve conformity required certain areas and nations, those that once had been marginal to Spanish interests and thus most superficially incorporated into European commercial patterns, to change dramatically. A predominately export-oriented economy linked to international capitalism became the dynamo propelling that profound, rapid change. In certain cases, radical transformation—almost revolutionary in some instances—challenged the stereotypes of "changelessness" and "continuity" often applied to the entire area.

One of the new nations, El Salvador, provides a striking example of the rapid and profound change of a once-neglected outpost of the Spanish empire. Further, its experience with progress or modernization accompanied by the increasing impoverishment of the majority of the inhabitants illustrates how a Latin American nation could modernize without developing.[11]

Spanish institutions had imperfectly penetrated El Salvador. Throughout the colonial period that small area bore a closer resemblance to its Indian past than to any of the bustling centers of colonial Spanish America. Like the other Central Americans, the Salvadorans remained geographically isolated and largely self-sufficient. As Adriaan C. van Oss convincingly argued, the Central Americans had "turned their backs on the coasts and thereby on intensive commerce with the motherland."[12] Yet, within the short span of three decades, roughly between 1860 and 1890, El Salvador acquired the economic, political, and social institutions characterizing the rest of Latin America. These included a dynamic and modernizing export sector based on monoculture and the predominance of the large estate producing for foreign trade; a subservient, impoverished, landless rural labor force; concentration of economic and political power within the hands of the principal planters who exercised it from a single dominant city, the capital, which, if it fell short of duplicating its urban model, Paris, nonetheless contained districts reflecting the architectural influence of nineteenth-century Europe; and a political understanding and tolerance between an increasingly professional military and politicoeconomic elites. In a number of fundamental aspects, El Salvador became nearly indistinguishable from the other Spanish-speaking nations. The process by which that formerly isolated and singular state acquired institutions characteristic of the rest of Spanish America as well as the consequences of that process merit study.

For three centuries Central America formed part of the Spanish empire before it fell briefly under Mexican rule. A shaky confederation, the United Provinces of Central America, emerged in 1824 but crumbled under political rivalries a decade and a half later. In 1839, some of the leading citizens of San Salvador declared the independence of El Salvador, although the vision of a greater Central American fatherland remained constant in El Salvador. Promulgating a constitution in 1841, the Salvadorans embarked on a tempestuous political journey. The population of the new republic, estimated in 1855 to be 394,000, consisted largely of Indians and mestizos with a small minority of whites, blacks, and mulattoes (see Table 1). Most of the population lived in the countryside.

The economic structures characteristic of the long colonial past remained intact during the first half of the nineteenth century. El Salvador continued to export in small quantities marginal products of limited demand. The Spanish mercantilist legacy rested lightly on the region because of its isolation and economic insignificance. The land-use patterns accommodated both Spanish and Indian practices. The Indian villages held

TABLE 1   **Estimates of the Population
of El Salvador, 1821–1930**

Year	Population
1821	250,000
1855	394,000
1878	554,000
1882	612,943
1892	703,500
1900	783,433
1910	986,537
1920	1,178,665
1930	1,353,170

SOURCE: Jeffry   Royle   Gibson,   "A
Demographic Analysis of Urbanization:
Evolution of a System of Cities in Honduras,
El Salvador, and Costa Rica," Ph.D. diss.,
Cornell University, 1970, p. 80.

the land they needed; the traditional Indian communities survived. The haciendas, the large estates owned by Spaniards and their descendants, also existed. In the early nineteenth century, there were approximately 440 haciendas averaging close to 2,000 acres each.[13] They accounted for one-third of the land area. The Indian communities produced food for local consumption. So did the haciendas, but they also grew the principal export crops, foremost of which was indigo.

Indigo production required both a regular and a seasonal labor force. The haciendas drew their workers from neighboring Indian communities. They also slowly but steadily encroached on Indian lands. The control of the political institutions of the new republic by a small merchant and planter class complemented those trends. The new national elite fully understood the importance to their own prosperity of controlling land and labor. No longer did a distant Spanish crown thwart them. For the time being, however, certain other realities inhibited their economic expansion. The frequent wars in Central America, a scarcity of capital and credit, a disruption of trade routes and patterns, and the lack of any products in high demand in foreign markets caused a general economic decline throughout much of the first half of the nineteenth century. Those political and economic realities enforced a kind of balance between the Indian communities and the haciendas. Both seemed to provide satisfactory, if very modest, lifestyles. Such was the El Salvador described by Foote, Squier, Von Tempsky, Scherzer, and Baily.

After 1858, new socioeconomic patterns took shape. Greater political stability and closer contact with the North Atlantic nations, principally the

United States, France, and Great Britain, partially explain the emergence of the new patterns. Very importantly, the elite found a new crop, coffee, that the country could grow and profitably sell abroad. More than anything else, concentration on the growth and export of that single crop altered old institutions. Before the end of the century, the new coffee estates became the base of economic production, political power, and social organization. The coffee planters emerged as the powerful economic, political, and social elite.

Instrumental in initiating the challenge to the old system, President Gerardo Barrios (1858–1863) directed the fledgling nation's first steps toward modernization and change. A trip through Europe in the early 1850s had influenced him profoundly. In one letter back to El Salvador, he proclaimed his mission: "I urgently needed this trip to correct my ideas and to be useful to my country. . . . I will return to preach to my fellow countrymen what we Central Americans are and what we can become."[14] He did. He informed the legislative assembly in 1860 that he intended to "regenerate" the nation.[15]

In a pattern already becoming familiar throughout Latin America, those who would "regenerate" their society advocated rather uncritically the models provided by the leading capitalist nations of the North Atlantic. Their agrarian, industrial, and technological advances awed the Latin American elites. Those nations seemed to have found the sure road to "progress," a gloriously nineteenth-century notion for which the current social science concept "modernization" is synonymous. In the minds of the elites, "to progress" came to mean to re-create the European model in Latin America. Carried to its extreme, it even signified the encouragement of European immigration to replace the Indian and African peoples of the New World. Within a broad Latin American perspective, Barrios was by no means unique in either his discovery of Europe or his hope of recreating his nation in its image. Within the narrow confines of bucolic El Salvador, however, he seemed to be something of a visionary ready to deny the past in order to participate in an alluring if uncertain future.

Barrios characterized the nation he governed as one that was "backward," "destitute," and "misgoverned," and into which he believed he introduced "progress."[16] Both a military commander and the owner of a medium-sized estate, the president represented the nascent middle class in his lifestyle, outlook, and aspirations. His government vaguely encompassed a liberalism characteristic of later nineteenth-century Salvadoran politics. He favored individual liberties, opposed dictatorial rule, and sought to end the neofeudalism dominating the countryside. He succeeded in accelerating a rural shift from neofeudalism to neocapitalism. In a not unfamiliar pattern in nineteenth-century Latin America, however, liberty during the Barrios years—as thereafter—smiled exclusively on the elites, and authoritarian rule remained the practice despite rhetoric to the contrary.

A devoted francophile, President Barrios incorporated Liberal and Positivist ideas into his policies to turn his country from its Iberian and Indian past to a closer approximation of a rapidly changing Western Europe. In 1860, the first program he announced for his government included these five goals: promotion of agriculture, industry, and commerce; introduction into El Salvador of the progress that distinguished other nations; encouragement of immigration; reform of the educational system in accordance with the latest European ideas; and construction of roads and ports to facilitate international communication and transportation. Such goals typified the modernizers of nineteenth-century Latin America. Soon after the announcement of his program, the president promulgated the nation's first civil code and a new educational plan, both of which inevitably drew on the latest European models. In true Positivist fashion, Barrios believed the government should play a direct role in encouraging exports.[17] The most immediate results of his policies were to facilitate the growth of capitalism and to promote foreign commerce. Indeed, exports doubled between 1860 and 1862.[18]

Barrios appreciated the incipient agrarian and commercial changes already under way in El Salvador. In 1853, steamship service had been inaugurated between El Salvador and California. Six years later, the government began to pay a subsidy to the Pacific Mail Steamship Company to service the Salvadoran ports. As one immediate consequence, sugar and rum exports rose, a trend Barrios applauded. United States diplomats stationed in San Salvador also spoke enthusiastically about the rising export trade facilitated by the steamships.[19] President Barrios not only encouraged the growth of crops with an international demand but favored land and labor laws complementary to such agrarian enterprise.

Understanding the importance of coffee on the world market and the suitability of El Salvador's rich volcanic soil to produce it, the president promoted its production.[20] Farmers had first started to grow small amounts of coffee for local consumption in the eighteenth century. Governmental encouragement of its production dated from 1846, without noticeable results. Barrios assumed a vigorous role in its promotion in order both to diversify exports and to increase national income. Under his direction, coffee exports had their modest beginnings. In his presidential address to the legislative assembly on January 29, 1862, he emphasized the impetus his government gave coffee, predicting (incorrectly) that within two years El Salvador would be the major coffee producer in Central America.[21]

In the decades after Barrios (really even including the Conservative government of Francisco Duenas, 1863–1871),[22] the Liberals articulated a program of goals focusing on the modernization of the transportation and communication infrastructures, the expansion of coffee exports, the adoption of European models, and the strengthening of governmental power. Never loath to use force to implement their program, they extended their authority from the presidential palace to the most remote hamlet.

The relatively complex process of coffee production engendered a series of crises in the traditional neo-Hispanic and neo-Indian institutions that had adequately served a society whose economy leisurely grew indigo and food crops.[23] The eventual triumph of coffee, a kind of victory of modern capitalism, necessitated new institutional arrangements.

Coffee production differed significantly from indigo, traditionally the primary export. The indigo plant grew without need of a great deal of care or investment. Within a year, the farmer could harvest it, although the amount of pigment increased if harvest could be delayed two or even three years. Indigo production required a small permanent work force supplemented during the harvesting and processing, both of which were relatively uncomplicated. Coffee could be grown under a variety of conditions on lands ranging from a small plot or a few acres to vast extensions of land. Small coffee planters seemed to flourish in some parts of Latin America. Colombia provided a useful example. In El Salvador, however, the growing and most especially the processing of coffee took place on medium-sized and large estates. Care, conservation, and fertilizing of the land and preparation of the coffee, including drying, processing, and sacking, required considerable capital and a large permanent work force generously augmented during the harvest season. Coffee planters waited three to five years for the first harvest. They required considerably more capital, patience, and skill than the producers of indigo. Those requirements severely limited the number of coffee growers but particularly the number of processors. Handsome profits, however, reimbursed the few who met the requirements.

The lure of a lucrative market prompted those planters who could bear the financial burden to expand their estates, which grew at the expense of communal landholdings and small landowners. The shift in landowning patterns fundamentally altered the lifestyle of the majority. The governments enthusiastically encouraged this change: they facilitated the concentration of land into fewer and fewer hands. Thus, in the decades between 1860 and 1890, the landholding patterns came to resemble the commercial capitalistic models characteristic of plantation economies elsewhere in the world. The first step was to label the Indian communal lands as retrograde, antiprogressive. They stood accused of the heinous crime of delaying or even preventing modernization. In short, they preserved the "backward" past. President Barrios initiated the legal attack on the *ejidos*, landholding communities, and the *tierras communales*, municipally owned and worked lands. His policies forced part of those lands onto the market, just as ambitious entrepreneurs sought more acres for coffee trees.

An official governmental land survey in 1879 revealed that only a quarter of the land still belonged to the villages.[24] The government of President Rafael Zaldivar (1876–1885) promptly oversaw the disposal of those remaining lands. Zaldivar proudly wore the modernizing mantle of Barrios, demonstrating his admiration for his predecessor by erecting an imposing mausoleum for him. An editorial in the *Diario Oficial* in early 1880 summarized the official attitude toward the communal lands, revealing once again the ideological continuity of the governments after 1858:

> On the one hand, we see virgin fertile lands that are calling for the application of capital and labor to reap the wealth that is promised; while on the other, we see the majority of the inhabitants of our villages content to grow crops of maize and beans that will never raise this miserable people above their sorry position. They will remain in the same wretched state they endured in colonial times. . . . The government is determined to transform the Republic, to make each one of the villages, yesterday sad and miserable, into lively centers of work, wealth, and comfort.[25]

Action followed. In early 1881, the government abolished the tierras communales. With far-reaching consequences, the decree denounced ancient practices to declare unequivocally the economic policy in vogue for some decades dramatically enforced after 1881: "The existence of lands under the ownership of *Communidades* impedes agricultural development, obstructs the circulation of wealth, and weakens family bonds and the independence of the individual. Their existence is contrary to the economic and social principles that the Republic has accepted." A year later, a law dissolved the ejidos for the same reason: they were "an obstacle to our agricultural development [and] contrary to our economic principles."[26] The communidades and ejidos bore the blame, according to official thinking, of thwarting "progress," meaning, of course, the expansion of coffee culture. In both cases, the lands were divided among community members. Such actions disoriented the Indian and folk populations, which had little concept of private ownership of land. Quite the contrary, they identified the community and the land as one: the land existed for the commonweal of the group. The community cared for the land in an almost religious fashion. Cooperation rather than competition governed the economic behavior of those populations. In the government's judgment, the Indians and rural folk obviously were not prepared to contribute to El Salvador's capitalist future.

Once the communal lands were distributed into small plots, the coffee planters set about acquiring the land. Experience proved that it was easier to befuddle and buy out the new, small landowner than the well-entrenched and tradition-oriented community.[27] The emerging rural class system, increasingly characterized by a small group of wealthy coffee planters and processors on the one hand and a large body of ill-paid laborers on the other, contrasted sharply with the more equalitarian structures of rural El Salvador prior to 1860.

Export patterns altered radically during the same decades. From the colonial period into the early 1880s, El Salvador had enjoyed varied agrarian production and export: maize, indigo, tobacco, sugar, cacao, coffee, cotton, and tropical fruits. The midcentury invention of synthetic dyes doomed the most important of those exports, indigo. Coffee more than made up for its demise. The export statistics tell the tale. In 1860, coffee composed but 1 percent of the exports; in 1865, 8 percent; and in 1870, 17 percent. In 1875, for the first time, the value of coffee exports exceeded indigo exports, quite a change from 1865 when the value of indigo exports amounted to 15 times that of coffee. Table 2 indicates the changing nature of El Salvador's exports during the critical 1864–1875 period. In 1879, coffee accounted for 48.5 percent of the total value of all exports. By 1910, it accounted for $4,661,440 of exports totaling $5,696,706. Indigo by then earned only $107,936 on the world markets. During the decade of the 1880s, El Salvador became virtually a monoagricultural exporting nation, its economic prosperity largely dependent on the purchase of coffee by three or four nations, which, in turn, supplied investments, technology, and manufactured goods in quantities commensurate with the profits from coffee sales.

The domination of the national economy by coffee obviously affected the rural folk, the overwhelming majority of the population. The expanding coffee estates continued to dispossess vast numbers of them of their lands. They, then, depended on the coffee plantations for work and, to the relief of the coffee planters, formed a sizable pool of unemployed and underemployed who could be hired at meager wages. At the same time, the increasingly unstable position of larger numbers of the rural population created discontent and unrest among them. The rural poor protested their deteriorating situation. Major uprisings occurred in 1872, 1875, 1880, 1885, and 1898. The planter-dominated governments addressed the problem of maintaining order not only to assure tranquillity but just as importantly to ensure a docile and plentiful labor supply. Threatening fines, arrests, and punishments, the Vagrancy Laws of 1881 required the populace to work. The Agrarian Law of 1907 further regulated the rural working class, while it authorized the organization of a rural constabulary to provide the physical protection the landowners' demanded. Agricultural judges—in a fashion somewhat reminiscent of the Spanish *repartimiento* system—made certain that the labor force was available when and where the planters needed it. The new rural police enforced the judges' decisions, intimidated the workers, protected the planters, and guaranteed the type of rural order the planters believed essential to their prosperity. They already had closely identified national well-being with their own.

TABLE 2 **Value of Exports, 1854–1875**
(In Silver Pesos)

Year	Total Value of Exports	Value of Indigo Exports	Percentage of Exports	Value of Coffee Exports	Percentage of Exports	Value of All Other Exports	Percentage of Exports
1864	—	1,129,105	—	80,105	—	—	—
1865	2,765,260	1,357,400	49.0	138,263	1.5	1,369,597	49.5
1866	2,463,437	1,548,000	64.3	197,075	8.1	682,362	27.6
1867	3,056,388	1,979,850	64.7	275,075	9.1	801,463	26.2
1868	3,521,020	2,131,500	60.5	528,153	15.0	861,367	24.5
1869	3,906,100	2,447,550	62.7	507,793	13.0	950,767	24.8
1870	3,902,041	2,619,749	67.1	663,347	17.0	618,945	15.9
1871	3,896,588	2,308,317	59.2	662,420	17.0	925,851	23.8
1872	3,763,838	2,786,574	74.0	489,299	13.0	487,965	13.0
1873	3,521,096	1,808,037	51.2	1,056,329	30.0	662,730	18.8
1874	3,949,858	1,721,378	43.5	1,342,952	34.0	885,528	22.5
1875	5,070,172	1,160,700	22.9	1,673,157	33.0	2,236,351	44.1

SOURCE: Rafael Menjívar, *Acumulación Originaria y Desarrollo del Capitalismo en El Salvador* (San José, Costa Rica: Editorial Universitaria Centroamérica, 1980), p. 35.

By the end of the century, coffee had transformed El Salvador. The landowning structures, the land-use patterns, and the relationship of the workers to the land were radically different. Whereas in 1858, there existed a reasonable balance between large estates, small landholdings, and ejidos, by 1890, the large estate dominated. The increasing accumulation of capital in a few hands strengthened the coffee estate, improved coffee processing, and further facilitated coffee exportation.

A tiny but significant group of capitalists appeared by the end of the century. Foreign immigrants, who invariably married into the leading Salvadoran families, played a disproportionately important role among them. They skillfully combined their wider knowledge of North Atlantic capitalism with local needs. A small number of Salvadoran capitalists from both the upper and middle classes and the local representatives of British capitalists joined them. Some of them controlled the processing and/or export sectors of the coffee industry, highly lucrative and strategic enterprises. Their interests obviously intertwined with those of the coffee planters.

Political stability accompanied economic growth and change. Begining with the government of Barrios in 1858 and ending with that of General Antonio Gutierrez in 1898, the chiefs-of-state stayed in office longer then their predecessors. In that 39-year time span, 7 presidents governed for an average of 5.7 years each, more than double the time the chiefs-of-state between 1839 and 1858 had served. Five of the presidents had military backgrounds. Force dislodged each president from office. The administration of Tomás Regalado, 1898–1903, marked a transition. General Regalado came to power through force, regularized his position through election, served the constitutional four-year term, and then stepped down from the presidency at the end of that term.[28]

The coffee elites had codified the political rules for their domination in the Constitution of 1886. It remained in force until 1939, the longest lived of El Salvador's many constitutions. Suppressing communal landownership, it emphasized the inviolability of private property. Within the classic framework of nineteenth-century liberalism, the document valued the individual over the collective. It enfranchised literate male adults, a minority in a land where illiteracy prevailed. Characterized as authoritarian and elitist, it served the planters handsomely during the half-century it was in force, defining the political boundaries of the "modern" state they sought to create.[29] It contributed significantly to the new political stability.

Increasing political stability, rising exports and income, economic growth, and a careful attention to the servicing of foreign debts nominated El Salvador as a candidate for foreign loans used to purchase a wide variety of consumer items the coffee class fancied, to introduce foreign technology, and to modernize the economy. Not unnaturally, a government in the service of the planters favored investment in and modernization of the infrastructure servicing the coffee industry. Renovation of two important ports, La Libertad and Acajutla, was completed in the 1860s. The first bank opened its doors in 1872, and they multiplied in number during the decade of the 1880s. The republic entered the railroad era in 1882 with the opening of a modest 12-mile line between Sonsonate, a departmental capital and one of the principal commercial centers, and Acajutla. The line facilitated the export of the varied local products, among which coffee was rapidly becoming the most important. English loans in 1889 promoted the expansion of an incipient railroad system that also fell under English administration.

British investments accompanied loans and together they assured Britain's economic preeminence. Besides railroads, mining attracted British capital. In 1888, the English established the Divisadero Gold and Silver Mining Company and the following year, the Butters Salvador Mines. The British began to enter the banking business in El Salvador in 1893.

The coffee interests also appreciated the importance of a modern capital, the symbol of their prosperity, as tribute to their "progressive" inclinations, and the focal point of their political authority. By the end of the century larger numbers of the richest families were building comfortable, in some cases even palatial, homes in the capital. They broke some of their immediate ties with the countryside and the provincial cities to become a more national elite centered in San Salvador.

A sleepy capital of 25,000 in 1860, San Salvador boasted of no pretentions. A visitor in the mid-1880s remembered: "There is very little architectural taste shown in the construction of the dwellings or of the public buildings . . . the streets are dull and unattractive. . . . The public buildings are of insignificant appearance."[30] It compared unfavorably with the cities of similar size in Latin America. Sensitive to that reality, the newly prosperous coffee elites resolved to renovate the capital, expunging the somnolent past in favor of the envisioned vigor of the future. The city took on new airs as the center of a booming economy. By 1910, the population numbered more than 32,000. The central streets had all been paved and electricity illuminated the city. An excellent drainage system ensured the good health of the inhabitants. A series of new buildings, among them a commodious headquarters for the governmental ministries, a cathedral, and a market, added to the modernity. The elites boasted of attractive homes in the capital. The new and beautiful Avenida de la Independencia combined with ample parks and plazas to provide grace and spaciousness to the city. The modern, still somewhat quiet capital made a favorable impression on visitors. Above all else it spoke of—and symbolized—the prosperity that coffee afforded the nation.[31]

The very restricted democracy fostered by the Constitution of 1886 functioned smoothly in the early decades of the twentieth century. From

1903 to 1931, each president was elected in the approved fashion—selected by his predecessor and ratified by a limited electorate—and served for the constitutional mandate of four years. The politicians respected the doctrine of "no reelection." Peaceful selection and rotation of presidents contrasted sharply with the violence characteristic of the change of governments in the nineteenth century. The preponderance of civilian presidents was also unique. Of the eight men elected to the presidency during the 1903–1931 period, only one was a military officer, General Fernando Figueroa (1907–1911).

The prosperity and power of the coffee planters reached their culmination during the years 1913–1929, an economic and political period referred to as the Melendez-Quiñonez dynasty because of the two related families that held the presidency. Those families ranked among the largest coffee producers. When an assassin felled President Manuel Enrique Araujo in 1913, Vice-President Carlos Melendez assumed the presidency as the constitution provided and then won the presidency in his own right during the elections the following year. In 1919, his brother, Jorge Melendez, succeeded him for four years, followed by his brother-in-law, Alfonso Quiñonez Molina, for another quadrennial. This tightly knit family political dynasty demonstrated the ease incumbent presidents enjoyed in manipulating elections to select their successors. It further illustrated the increasingly narrow political base of the coffee planters. Indeed, fewer and fewer men controlled the thriving coffee industry, particularly the processing and export. During the dynasty, perhaps more than at any other period, those linked to coffee exports were able to monopolize both economic and political power. One obviously enhanced the other. Wealth conferred the prestige that facilitated political manipulation. In turn, their control of the government complemented their economic interests. During those years, the planters successfully held the small but aggressive urban middle class at bay, repressed or manipulated the impoverished majority—both the rural masses and the growing urban working class—and neutralized the military, from whose ranks had arisen so many of the nineteenth-century presidents.

The actual exercise of political power by the coffee class forged a unique chapter in Salvadoran history: prolonged civilian rule. When General Figueroa, a constitutionally elected president, left the presidential palace in 1911, civilian politicians occupied it for the succeeding two decades, a remarkable record, never equaled before or since. Of course the economic strength, political influence, and social domination of the coffee elites had been a reality since the last decades of the nineteenth century. From the beginning of their rise to economic and political power in the 1860s and 1870s they had enjoyed amiable relations with the military. The planters counted on the military to support a political system complementary to coffee exports. Economic prosperity, after all, facilitated the modernization and professionalization of the army. The easy shift from military to civilian presidents manifested the harmonious relations between the planters and the officers.

The army had won its laurels on the battlefield. Nearly a century of international struggles—the frequent wars against Guatemala, Honduras, Nicaragua, and assorted foreign filibusters—and of civil wars created a strong and reasonably efficient army, perhaps the best in Central America. A prudent government pampered the military. A military academy to train officers functioned sporadically. In 1900, the third such school, the Escuela Politécnica Militar, opened, only to be closed in 1927. Five years later the government inaugurated the Escuela Militar, still functioning. Thus, for most of the years of the twentieth century, a professional academy existed. In 1909, the government contracted with Chile for a military mission to improve the training of officers. The Escuela Politécnica Militar and the Escuela Militar provided a reasonable-to-good education for the cadets and fostered the corporate interests of an officer class. Increasingly the academy drew its cadets from the urban middle and lower middle classes, two groups enthusiastically advocating the modernization of the country.[32] While the officers' concept of modernization tended to parallel that of the planters, it also emphasized the need for up-to-date military training and equipment, manifested a growing faith in industrialization, and responded to the vague but powerful force of nationalism.

In 1910, the government reported that its army consisted of an impressive 78 staff officers, 512 officers, and 15,554 troops on active duty (a figure that seems to be inflated).[33] Percy F. Martin, in his exhaustive study of El Salvador in 1911, reported: "The Government . . . have [sic] devoted the closest care and attention to the question of military instruction, and the system at present in force is the outcome of the intelligent study of similar systems in force in other countries, and the adaptation of the best features existing in each. A very high esprit de corps exists among the Salvadoran troops, and, for the most part, they enter upon their schooling and training with both zeal and interest."[34] The government favored the officers with good pay, rapid promotion, and a host of benefits. Martin marveled at the comforts provided by one of the officers' clubs: "For the use of officers there exists a very agreeable Club, at which they can procure their full meals and all kinds of light refreshments at moderate prices: while the usual amusements such as drafts, cards, billiards, etc., are provided for them. So comfortable is this Club made that officers, as a rule, find very little inducement to visit the larger towns in search of their amusements."[35] A contented military was the logical corollary to planter prosperity.

The further solidification of the corporate interests of the military was encouraged by the establishment in 1919 of a periodical for and about the military and in 1922 of a mutual aid society, the *Círculo Militar*. More than an economic association, it encouraged the moral, physical, and intellectual

TABLE 3   **Coffee Production, 1924–1935**

Year	Pounds
1924–1925	95,020,000
1925–1926	101,413,000
1926–1927	66,139,000
1927–1928	149,474,000
1928–1929	134,042,000
1929–1930	143,301,000
1930–1931	165,347,000
1931–1932	105,822,000
1932–1933	141,096,000
1933–1934	127,869,000
1934–1935	130,073,000

SOURCE: Edelberto Torres Rivas, *Interpretación del Desarrollo Social Centroamericano* (San José, Costa Rica: Editorial Universitaria Centroamérica, 1973), pp. 284–85.

improvement of its members. One knowledgeable visitor to Central America in 1928 claimed that El Salvador had the best-trained army in the region.[36]

Peace and order at home combined with increasing demands for coffee ensured a heady prosperity for the planters and their government. With the exception of an occasional poor year, usually due to adverse weather, production moved upward after 1926 toward an annual harvest of 130,000,000–140,000,000 pounds, as Table 3 illustrates. After 1904, El Salvador produced at least one-third of Central America's coffee, its closest competitors being first Guatemala and second Costa Rica. After 1924, Salvadoran production surpassed that of Guatemala to hold first place in quantity (and many would add quality) in Central America. The elites and the government became increasingly dependent on income from coffee production.

A significant change in El Salvador's international trade pattern also took place. In the nineteenth century, El Salvador sold much of its exports to the United States and bought most of its imports from Europe. In the twentieth century, that triangular pattern became increasingly bilateral due to a closer trade relationship with the United States, which bought more Salvadoran exports than any other nation and began to furnish most of its imports as well.

Growing U.S. investments in El Salvador further linked the two nations economically. Prior to the opening of the twentieth century, U.S. investments had been practically nonexistent. In 1908, they totaled a modest $1.8 million, but they rose rapidly thereafter: $6.6 in 1914; $12.8 in 1919; and $24.8 in 1929. While these sums were insignificant in terms of total U.S.

investments abroad, which in Latin America alone accounted for over $1.6 billion by the end of 1914, they represented a sizable proportion of the foreign investments in El Salvador by 1929. United States investors consequently began to exert influence over the Salvadoran economy. The pro-U.S. attitudes of the presidents of the Melendez-Quiñonez dynasty greatly facilitated the penetration of North American interests into El Salvador, while World War I reduced the British presence.[37]

The coffee planters and their allies exuded confidence. Coffee prices, land devoted to coffee production, coffee exports, and coffee income all rose impressively after 1920. At no time from 1922 through 1935 did coffee represent less than 88 percent of the total value of exports. During three of those years, 1926, 1931, and 1934, it accounted for 95 percent. The amount of land producing coffee increased from 170,000 acres in the early 1920s to 262,000 acres in the early 1930s. Meanwhile, coffee growing and processing concentrated in ever fewer hands with no more than 350 growers controlling the industry by the mid-1920s. The largest enjoyed annual incomes of $200,000.[38]

Ruling from their comfortable and modern capital, the planters and their allies were creating an impressive infrastructure of roads, railroads, and ports as well as a telegraphic and telephone communication network. The plantations, the government, and the army were efficiently run. In their own terms, the elites were highly successful. Still, they nurtured visions of further change. Some fretted over the dependence on coffee for prosperity and talked of the need to diversify agriculture. A few experimented with cotton as an alternate export. Others spoke in terms of industrialization, and limited amounts of capital did support an incipient manufacturing sector. The elites even discussed the extension of democratization and the inclusion of the lower classes in the political process. It was the talk of a contented minority that wanted to perfect their political and economic systems. Benefiting from the great changes wrought by transforming a largely peasant and subsistence economy into a plantation and export economy, the coffee elites assumed that their own prosperity reflected the well-being of the nation they governed.

While the shift to coffee culture may have created an aura of progress around the plantation homes and the privileged areas of the capital, it proved increasingly detrimental to the quality of life of the majority. One U.S. observer contrasted the lifestyles of the classes in 1931:

> There is practically no middle class between the very rich and the very poor. From the people with whom I talked, I learned that roughly ninety percent of the wealth of the country is held by about half of one percent of the population. Thirty or forty families own nearly everything in the country. They live in almost regal splendor with many attendants,

send their children to Europe or the United States to be educated, and spend money lavishly (on themselves). The rest of the population has practically nothing. These poor people work for a few cents a day and exist as best they can.[39]

This grim observation was by no means novel. After a tour of Central America in 1912, Charles Domville-Fife concluded that "there are more comparatively poor people in this country [El Salvador] than there are in some of the larger states."[40] An academic study of the 1919–1935 period speaks of "recurrent food shortages" and "economic desperation" among the masses in a period of high living costs and low wages.[41] The cost of basic foods skyrocketed between 1922 and 1926: corn prices, 100 percent; beans, 225 percent; and rice, 300 percent. The importation of those foods, once negligible, became significant in 1929.[42]

An analysis of the class structure in 1930 suggests the concentration of wealth: it categorized 0.2 percent of the population as upper class.[43] An accelerating rate of population increase accentuated the problems of poverty. The population reached 1,443,000 by 1930. The vast majority was rural. Yet, only 8.2 percent could be classified as landowners.[44]

The very changes that facilitated the concentration of land into fewer hands also precipitated the social and economic disintegration of the lifestyle of the overwhelming majority of the Salvadorans. The changes squeezed off the land those who grew food for their own consumption and sold their surpluses in local marketplaces. The relative ease of access to land—hence, food—depicted by the five travelers in the 1850s was no longer accurate after 1900. The dispossessed depended on seasonal plantation jobs. Some began to trickle into the towns and capital propelled by rural poverty and the search for urban jobs, which either did not exist or for which they were unprepared. The extent of the new social and economic disequilibrium was not immediately appreciated. Impressive economic growth masked for a time the weakness of the increasingly narrow, inflexible, and dependent economy.

As is true in such overly dependent economies, events in distant marketplaces would reveal local weaknesses. By the end of the 1920s, the capitalist world teetered on the edge of a major economic collapse whose reverberations would shake not only the economic but also the political foundations of El Salvador.

With his term of office nearing an end in 1927, President Quiñonez picked his own brother-in-law, Pio Romero Bosque, to succeed him, a choice with significant consequences. Don Pio, as Salvadorans invariably refer to him, turned out to be more liberal, less conventional, and highly unpredictable in comparison with his three predecessors of the Melendez-Quiñonez dynasty. He entered office riding high on the wave of coffee prosperity, but the international financial crisis that began in 1929–1930 soon tossed his government into a trough of economic troubles, testing all his skills in navigating the ship of state.

The dynamic sector of the economy suffered the vicissitudes common to nations dependent on the export of a single product. In an indictment before the Legislative Assembly, Minister of Finance José Esperanza Suay pointed out the cause of the nation's economic plight: "The coffee crisis that this year [1929] has alarmed everyone clearly indicates the dangers for our national economy of monoculture, the domination coffee asserts over agrarian production."[45] El Salvador may have been an efficient coffee producer, but it was not the only one. In fact, exporters were beginning to outnumber importers. The economic prosperity of at least ten Latin American nations, of which Brazil was by far the most important, also depended on coffee sales. At the same time, a few African areas were producing coffee for export. Demand fell while supplies remained constant or even increased in some instances. Consequently the price dropped drastically. In 1928, El Salvador sold its coffee for $15.75 per hundred kilograms—in 1932, for $5.97. The financial consequences for El Salvador can readily be perceived in an economy in which coffee constituted 90 percent of the exports and 80 percent of the national income. Not surprisingly therefore, government revenues plummeted 50 percent between 1928 and 1932. El Salvador witnessed the highest index of rural unemployment in Central America. Small coffee growers suffered severely. Their loss of land through bankruptcy and foreclosure—an estimated 28 percent of the coffee holdings—augmented the estates of the large landowners. The problems revealed a modernized but underdeveloped economy, one that readily responded to foreign whims but failed to serve Salvadoran needs.

The planters' reaction to the mounting problems exacerbated the nation's economic woes. They increased the amount of land devoted to coffee in an effort to make up for falling prices. The consequences of that trend were as obvious as they were disastrous: the economy depended more than ever on coffee, more peasants lost their land, rural unemployment rose, and food production for internal consumption declined.[46]

President Romero Bosque tried valiantly to ride out the economic storm. Politically he fared better. Practicing the liberal ideology he preached, he permitted the full play of those liberties authorized by the Constitution of 1886 but hitherto suppressed. His administrative talent and his unimpeachable honesty impressed his fellow countrymen. He determined to make honest men of politicians. He turned on his less-than-scrupulous predecessors and even sent Quiñonez into exile. Those actions heightened his popularity despite the economic crisis.

To the amazement of all and the consternation of the professional politicians, Don Pio decided to hold an honest presidential election in 1931. Contrary to all previous political practices, the president advanced no candidate. It was indeed a historical first. Since no political parties existed, a few hastily organized to take advantage of the unprecedented opportunity to electioneer.

The six new parties represented the interests of the working, professional, middle, and planter classes and thereby reflected the social changes overtaking El Salvador.[47] A small but vocal urban working class had emerged in the 1920s, flexing its muscle in several important strikes. The presidents of the dynasty flirted occasionally with that potential source of political power. Their policies gyrated from wooing the workers to repressing them. In 1925, some workers and intellectuals, with the assistance of communist leaders from Guatemala, founded the Communist party of El Salvador. In the excitement of preparation for the 1931 election, a Labor party also emerged. It nominated Arturo Araujo, who enjoyed a genuinely popular following. The candidate sought to distance himself from his more radical supporters, the foremost of whom, Agustín Farabundo Martí, was busy organizing rural labor, an activity guaranteed to disturb landlords and arouse the suspicion of the military.

To avoid any of the international influences among the Labor party members, most notably of communism, Araujo turned to the ideas of Alberto Masferrer to enhance his party's program. An intellectual, philosopher, and writer, Masferrer dominated Salvadoran letters.[48] The strongest voice of the newly invigorated nationalism in El Salvador, he criticized the institutions that had been shaped by the coffee class and called for greater social justice. In Patria, the prestigious and lively newspaper he founded on April 27, 1928, Masferrer protested against the presence of foreign companies, the lack of decent housing, and the high cost of living. He advocated industrialization and the protection of national resources from foreign exploitation. He denounced those "who have the souls of a checkbook and the conscience of an account ledger," those who kept "the people in misery, who kill by hunger thousands of persons, and who cause more than half the workers to die due to lack of food, shelter, or rest before they reach the age of thirty."[49] Both the extreme left and right verbally assaulted Masferrer. The right labeled him a dangerous Bolshevik, criminal agitator, and subversive. The left attacked him as a demagogue, traitor, and right-wing socialist.

For his campaign, Araujo adopted Masferrer's program of *vitalismo*, the "vital minimum" that the philosopher defined as "the sure and constant satisfaction of our basic needs."[50] Thus, Araujo campaigned for the nine major points advocated by vitalismo, among them: hygenic, honest, and fairly remunerated work; medical care, potable water, and decent sanitation; a varied, adequate, and nutritious diet; decent housing; sufficient clothing; expedient and honest justice; education; and rest and recreation. Within the context of Salvadoran society in late 1930 and early 1931, Araujo ventilated some "revolutionary" views. Vitalismo, he declared, would be financed by transferring funds from the military budget to social expenditures. One can but speculate about the reaction to such a proposition within the confines of those comfortable officers' clubs.

Masferrer himself held some unconventional ideas about the role of the military within Salvadoran society. That fully one-sixth of the national budget went to the army in 1929 disturbed him. It was not productive investment; it did not contribute to national development. "For a country that no longer fights wars, our army is extraordinarily expensive. . . . And, if there are no longer any wars to fight, why should the state maintain such a burdensome institution?" he asked.[51] The army could serve much more useful national goals if it added to its traditional roles of protection from foreign invaders and the maintenance of internal order those of building and maintaining roads, providing water to the villages, improving the health of the inhabitants through sanitation campaigns, protecting the forests, and helping the population in times of natural disaster.

Araujo also heeded Masferrer's call for land reform. The philosopher advocated the nationalization of the land and its redistribution.[52] He classified the landowning system as well as the relations between the landlords and rural workers as "feudal": "The lord in this case is the landowner, he who gives and takes, he who permits the worker to reside on his lands or expels whoever does not obey or please him."[53] Araujo planned to have the government buy the land from the rich and redistribute it to the poor.

With its platform firmly buttressed by the ideas of Masferrer, the Labor party aroused the enthusiasm of large numbers of people who viewed its program as the means to solve the deepening economic difficulties and to create a more just society. For his running mate, Araujo chose a military man, General Maximiliano Hernandez Martinez. The general had borne the presidential standard of the small National Republican party before he joined forces with Araujo. First as a presidential candidate and later as a vice-presidential candidate, Martinez appealed to the popular classes on social issues.

Honoring his promises, Don Pio remained impartial during the selection of presidential candidates and the campaign. The elections took place in early January 1931. Araujo won. He confronted an impossible task. Somehow he had to reconcile the vast differences among the Labor party, the coffee planters, the military, and the newly emergent middle class. He had to accomplish his miracle in the midst of the worst—and what would be the longest—economic crisis in modern Salvadoran history. The problems cried for bold action; an irresolute president proved to be incapable of acting. He ignored the "vital minimum" program that he had supported during the campaign. His inaction confounded and then alienated his followers. Frustrations mounted daily; unrest resulted.

On December 2, 1931, the military responded to the crises precipitated by economic collapse and political unrest. The soldiers turned out of office the first and thus far only freely elected president, who fled the country after less than one year in office. The military coup was the first in 33 years—since November 1898, when General Tomás Regalado seized power—and the first staged by professional army officers who did not come from the dominant socioeconomic class.[54] Three days later the military junta turned power over to the constitutional vice-president, General Hernandez Martinez, who also had served as minister of war.[55] His exact role in the coup d'etat still remains unexplained. Invested with power, he governed energetically for the next 13 years, a record of political longevity in El Salvador.

Most sectors of society greeted the military seizure of power with relief. It had become painfully apparent to all that President Araujo, immobilized by the economic debacle and the inability of the national institutions to respond to new demands, could not govern. The majority thought the young officers who carried out his overthrow would be able to resolve the crises threatening to destroy the nation. Rightly or wrongly, the populace put trust and hope in those officers. The Marxist student newspaper *Estrella Roja* congratulated the military on the coup d'etat. It reiterated the belief that the incompetence of Araujo "imposed a moral obligation on the military to remove him from office." The newspaper quickly pointed out, however, that the coup itself could resolve few of the nation's fundamental problems:

> Pardon our skepticism. We do not believe that the coup will end the Salvadoran crisis which is far more transcendental than a mere change of government. The crisis has deeper roots than the incapacity of Don Arturo. It results from the domination of a capitalist class that owns all the land and means of production and has dedicated itself to coffee monoculture.[56]

Although no profound institutional changes were forthcoming, Araujo's downfall represented something more than "a mere change of government." It initiated new alliances and a sharing of power. In short, it ended the coffee planters' monopoly of economic and political power.

The economic collapse alone had not triggered the coup. The causes of the political change also included the growing social, economic, and political complexities engendered by incipient industrialization and growing urbanization, more intensive nationalism, the roles played by immigrants, an urban proletariat, an expanding middle class, and professional military officers in an increasingly varied society, improved transportation and communication, and efforts to diversify the economy. Further, any explanation of the coup must take into account the inability of President Araujo to govern, an unfortunate reality in the country's first democratic experiment,

TABLE 4   **Populations of the Five Largest Cities, 1930**

City	Population
San Salvador	89,385
Santa Ana	39,825
Santa Tecla	20,049
San Miguel	17,330
Sonsonate	15,260

SOURCE: Gibson, "A Demographic Analysis of Urbanization," p. 338.

which may have revealed as much about institutional structures as it did about the chief executive.

The demands on the government varied, and while some could be reconciled, others could not. The rural folk looked to the communal past for a solution to their plight. They wanted the government to return land to them. The planter elites obviously favored the present land distribution and the export economy from which they had extracted so many benefits for such a long period. The expanding middle class and the professional military thought in nationalistic terms that included a reduction in the level of dependency, a wider sharing of social benefits, and industrialization. Their solutions to the crises lay in the cities. Urban growth had been slow, and, as Table 4 shows, the populations of the five largest cities remained relatively small. Urban dwellers accounted for only 15 percent of the population. Yet, they provided many of the leaders advocating innovations.

The events of 1931 brought to a close a dynamic period in the history of El Salvador during which the coffee planters had gained economic and political ascendancy to dominate the nation. Stresses during the preceding decade demonstrated the increasing difficulty the coffee planters experienced in governing the nation. The brief political experiment under Don Pio and Don Arturo had been sufficient to prove that a functioning, pluralistic democracy would not work to the planters' best advantage. They lost their political monopoly. The coup in 1931 signified that they would not regain it. They understood by then that they would benefit most from an authoritarian government managed by the military and complementary to some of the goals of the middle class, which wanted access to the national institutions and upward mobility. Those groups worked out a suitable arrangement to the exclusion of the rural masses and the urban working class. They divided the tasks of government after December 5, 1931: the military exercised political power, while the landowners, in alliance with sympathetic bankers, merchants, exporters, and segments of the urban middle class, controlled the economy. Each respected the other. General Martinez succeeded in reestablishing oligarchical control, although he could not return the nation to the status quo ante 1931. El Salvador was entering a new phase of history.

During the 1858–1931 period, El Salvador reshaped its institutions in order better to export coffee; modernization had taken place, producing some of the advantages its advocates had predicted. There were more and better roads, a modest railroad system, efficient ports, and a capital city with sections boasting all the amenities of its European or U.S. counterparts. Almost everything connected with the export of coffee and the lifestyles of the elites seemed up to date, indistinguishable from what one might find in the capitals of the major industrial nations. Impressive growth had taken place. The statistics measuring population, coffee production, and foreign investments had risen impressively, and, until 1929, so had national income. An observer could conclude that certain aspects of national life had progressed in the course of seven decades, that the "progressive" El Salvador of 1931 differed considerably from the "backward" nation Barrios had resolved to "regenerate" in 1858.

National life was different, but not always in a positive way. Quite another legacy of growth and progress was the nation's acute dependence on the export of a single product, coffee, for its prosperity. Monoculture and plantations were some of the results, and they dominated the economy. The efficient production of coffee did not extend to foodstuffs. The countryside fed the population less adequately than before. By the end of the 1920s, El Salvador began to import food, not because the land could not feed the people—the hoary excuse of overpopulation has been disproven—but rather because the planters used it to grow export crops.[57] On several levels, the nation had lost control of its own economy. By 1931, El Salvador confronted a series of political and economic crises, the consequences of the type of modernization its governments had imposed.

The perceptive observations of two commentators, widely spaced in time, reveal the basic difference separating the El Salvador of the end of the 1850s from that of the end of the 1920s. Mrs. Foote had lived among a well-fed population. Large estates, small farms, and communal lands coexisted. The relatively varied export sector had played a significant but not the dominant role in the economy. The critical eye of Alberto Masferrer viewed quite a different situation. He assessed the state of Salvadoran society in 1928 in this way:

> There are no longer crises; instead, there are chronic illnesses and endemic hunger. . . . El Salvador no longer has wild fruits and vegetables that once everyone could harvest, nor even cultivated fruits that once were inexpensive. . . . Today there are the coffee estates and they grow only coffee. . . . Where there is now a voracious estate that consumes hundreds and hundreds of acres, before there were two hundred small farmers whose plots produced corn, rice, beans, fruits, and veg-

etables. Now the highlands support only coffee estates and the lowlands cattle ranches. The cornfields are disappearing. And where will the corn come from? The coffee planter is not going to grow it because his profits are greater growing coffee. If he harvests enough coffee and it sells for a good price, he can import corn and it will cost him less than if he sacrifices coffee trees in order to grow it. . . . Who will grow corn and where? . . . Any nation that cannot assure the production and regulate the price of the most vital crop, the daily food of the people, has no right to regard itself as sovereign. . . . Such has become the case of our nation.[58]

In vivid contrast to Mrs. Foote's earlier observations, Masferrer saw a hungry population with limited access to the use of land, a population whose basic need for food was subordinated to the demands of an export-oriented economy. The "progress" charted by the Salvadoran elites had failed to benefit the overwhelming majority of the citizens.[59] Prosperity for a few cost the well-being of the many.

The contrasts between Foote's and Masferrer's observations suggest that little or no development had taken place, if one measures development by a rising quality of life index and the maximum use of resources, natural and human, for the well-being of the majority. Thus, the contrasts provoke serious questions about the wisdom of the type of modernization and economic growth El Salvador pursued after 1858, since neither addressed the needs of the majority of the Salvadorans. Rather, they left a legacy of poverty, dependency, and class conflict that succeeding generations of generals, politicians, and planters have not been able to resolve.

NOTES

1. Mrs. H. G. Foote, *Recollections of Central America and the West Coast of Africa* (London: Newby, 1869), p. 101.
2. Ibid., p. 84.
3. Ibid., p. 61.
4. Ibid., pp. 54–55.
5. Ibid., p. 60.
6. John Baily, *Central America: Describing Each of the States of Guatemala, Honduras, Salvador, Nicaragua, and Costa Rica* (London: Saunders, 1850); E. G. Squier, *Notes on Central America, Particularly the States of Honduras and Salvador* (New York: Harper, 1855); Carl Scherzer, *Travels in the Free States of Central America: Nicaragua, Honduras, and San Salvador*, 2 vols. (London: Longman, 1857); G. F. Von Tempsky, *Mitla: A Narrative of Incidents and Personal Adventures on a Journey in Mexico, Guatemala, and Salvador in the Years 1853–1855* (London: Longman, 1858). In a much later and certainly more scholarly study, David Browning tends to confirm the main theses of these more impressionistic travelers: *El Salvador: Landscape and Society* (Oxford: Oxford University Press, 1971).

7. Squier, *Notes on Central America*, p. 326.

8. Ibid., p. 331.

9. Von Tempsky, *Mitla*, p. 424.

10. Scherzer, *Travels in the Free States*, vol. 2, pp. 148, 195–96.

11. For a series of useful case studies of the effects of the penetration of international capitalism upon the local economies during the nineteenth century, see Roberto Cortes Conde, *The First States of Modernization in Spanish America* (New York: Harper, 1974).

12. Adriaan C. van Oss, "El Régimen Autosuficiente de España en Centro América," *Mesoamérica* (Guatemala) 3 (June 1982): 68.

13. Browning, *El Salvador*, pp. 85, 87.

14. Letter of General Gerardo Barrios, Rome, November 21, 1853, printed in the *Revista del Departamento de Historia y Hemeroteca Nacional* (San Salvador) 11 (March 1939): 42.

15. That speech is printed in Joaquin Parada Aparicio, *Discursos Médico-Historicos Salvadoreños* (San Salvador: Editorial Ungo, 1942), p. 222.

16. Address to the General Assembly, January 29, 1862, printed in Italo Lopez Vallecillos, *Gerardo Barrios y su Tiempo*, vol. 2 (San Salvador: Ministerio de Educación, 1967), p. 219.

17. Gary G. Kuhn, "El Positivismo de Gerardo Barrios," *Revista del Pensamiento Centroamericano* (Managua), 36 (July–December 1981): 88. For a more general statement on Positivism in El Salvador see Patricia A. Andrews, "El Liberalismo en El Salvador a Finales del Siglo XIX," ibid., pp. 89–93.

18. Kuhn, "El Positivismo," p. 87.

19. ". . . the commerce of the Central American States has wonderfully increased, and especially within fifteen years and since the establishment of the line of steamers from Panama. This has introduced and established regularity, certainty, and dispatch in their communication with the rest of the world. It has organized and maintained a mail service and secured a rapid, sure, and safe mode of commercial intercourse and exchange. In the interests which are thus growing up into importance, [sic] and wealth and commanding influence will be found the means of counteracting the unfortunate results of their political systems, and those interests must soon be powerful and widespread enough to be able to finally put down the political system which retards or hinders their development. . . . Since the establishment of the Panama Company's Steamers, the Revenues from the Custom House in . . . Salvador have more than quadrupled. The foreign commerce of all the Republics, which, previous thereto, was in the hands of a few who could afford to import cargoes around Cape Horn, has been opened to all. . . . The growth of California and the States on the Pacific has opened new courses for their trade" (James R. Partridge to Secretary of State, April 22, 1865, Diplomatic Dispatches from U.S. Ministers to Central America, General Records of the Department of State, National Archives of the United States of America). "The Republic of Salvador, though territorially much the smallest of the five Central American States, is *first* in the amount of exports and only *second* in population. It has three seaports on the Pacific, La Unión, La Libertad, and Acajutla, at all of which the Panama Railroad Steamers stop twice a month, up and down, and at which American vessels land and receive freight and passengers. In the other Central American States these steamers land only at one port" (A. S. Williams to Secretary of State, March 27, 1867, ibid.).

20. Lopez Vallecillos, *Gerardo Barrios,* pp. 127–28, 216–18.

21. Ibid., pp. 216–17.

22. This interpretation of the Duenas administration rests on the assessments of Derek N. Kerr, "La Edad de Oro del Café en El Salvador, 1863–1885," *Mesoamérica* (Guatemala) 3 (June 1982): 4, 7, as well as on the diplomatic dispatches of A. S. Williams. In particular, see his dispatches of January 12 and February 8, 1969, to the U.S. Secretary of State, Diplomatic Dispatches from U.S. Ministers to Central America, General Records of the Department of State, National Archives of the United States of America.

23. For an understanding of the negative effect the introduction of coffee culture had on the peasantry of Costa Rica and Guatemala, see Mitchell A. Seligson, *Peasants of Costa Rica and the Development of Agrarian Capitalism* (Madison: University of Wisconsin Press, 1980); and David J. McCreery, "Coffee and Class: The Structure of Development in Liberal Guatemala," *Hispanic American Historical Review,* 56 (August 1976): 438–60.

24. Browning, *El Salvador,* p. 190.

25. Ibid., p. 173.

26. The quotations from the Law for Extinction of Communal Lands, February 26, 1881, and the Law for the Extinction of Public Lands, March 2, 1882, are found in William H. Durham, *Scarcity and Survival in Central America: Ecological Origins of the Soccer War* (Stanford, Calif.: Stanford University Press, 1979), p. 42.

27. This trend was almost universal throughout Latin America. For the general discussion consult E. Bradford Burns, *The Poverty of Progress: Latin America in the Nineteenth Century* (Berkeley and Los Angeles: University of California Press, 1980), particularly pp. 132–54. For specific discussions of El Salvador see Browning, *El Salvador,* particularly pp. 146, 147, 167, 173, 175, and 214; Alastair White, *El Salvador* (Boulder, Colo.: Westview, 1982), p. 93; and Rafael Menjivar, *Acumulación Originaria y Desarrollo del Capitalismo en El Salvador* (San José, Costa Rica: Editorial Universitaria Centroamericana, 1980), pp. 123–27.

28. Jorge Larde y Larín, *Guía Histórica de El Salvador* (San Salvador: Ministerio de Cultura, 1958), pp. 32–43.

29. Rafael Guidos Vejar, *El Ascenso del Militarismo en El Salvador* (San Salvador: UCA/Editores 1980), p. 65.

30. William Eleroy Curtis, *The Capitals of Spanish America* (New York: Harper, 1888), 180–81.

31. Percy F. Martin, *Salvador in the XXth Century* (London: Arnold, 1911), pp. 256–75.

32. The role of the military in El Salvador, 1858–1931, and the relations between civilian politicians and military officers adhere in general terms to the broad observations made by Edwin Lieuwen concerning the behavioral pattern of the military throughout Latin America in the nineteenth and early twentieth centuries. See his *Arms and Politics in Latin America* (New York: Praeger, 1961), pp. 17–35. Vejar provides the details and some general conclusions for the study of the Salvadoran military in the nineteenth and early twentieth centuries in *El Ascenso del Militarismo.*

33. Martin, *Salvador,* p. 86.

34. Ibid., p. 87.

35. Ibid., p. 88.

36. Arthur J. Ruhl, *The Central American* (New York: Scribner's, 1928), p. 174.
37. Rafael Menjivar covers the topic and statistics of growing U.S. investments in *Acumulación Originaria*, pp. 55–81.
38. The statistical data in this paragraph are drawn largely from Everett A. Wilson, "The Crisis of National Integration in El Salvador, 1919–1935" (Ph.D. diss., Stanford University, 1969), pp. 108–41.
39. Major A. R. Harris, U.S. Military Attache to Central America, December 22, 1931, National Archives of the United States, R. G. 59, File 816.00/828, as quoted in Thomas P. Anderson, *Matanza: El Salvador's Communist Revolt of 1932* (Lincoln: University of Nebraska Press, 1971), pp. 83–4.
40. Charles W. Domville-Fife, *Guatemala and the States of Central America* (London: Francis Griffiths, 1913), pp. 285–86.
41. Wilson, "Crisis of National Integration," pp. 29, 115, 128.
42. Ibid., pp. 126–27; Durham, *Scarcity and Survival*, p. 36.
43. Alejandro R. Marroquín, "Estudio Sobre la Crísis de los Años Treinta en El Salvador," *Anuario de Estudios Centroamericanos*, 3 (1977): 118.
44. Ibid.
45. Quoted in ibid., p. 121.
46. Vejar, *Ascenso del Militarismo*, pp. 102, 100.
47. These parties were the Partido Evolución Nacional (National Evolution party), representing the most conservative and economically powerful groups; the Partido Zaratista (party of Alberto Gomez Zarate), grouping together the urban supporters of Zarate who favored the policies of the "Dynasty"; the Partido Constitucional (Constitutional party), sharing much of the conservative philosophy of the National Evolution party and appealing largely to the same groups; the Partido Fraternal Progresista (Progressive Fraternal party), directed by a general and enjoying military support, appealed to the rural workers in a paternalistic way; Partido Nacional Republicano (National Republican party), also directed by a general, Maximiliano Hernandez Martinez, and uniting professionals, students, workers, and some coffee growers; and the Partido Laborista (Labor party), appealing to the urban and rural workers as well as to smaller farmers. Ibid., pp. 113–14.
48. Hugo Lindo, "El Año de Alberto Masferrer," *Inter-American Review of Bibliography*, 29 (July–September, 1969): 263–77. His biographers tend to be uncritical. One, Matilde Elena Lopez, characterized him as Central America's "broadest thinker," one of the "most illustrious men of the continent," and a "revolutionary." *Masferrer: Alto Pensador de Centroamérica: Ensayo Biográfico* (Guatemala City: Editorial del Ministerio de Educación, 1954), p. 9.
49. Quoted in Marroquin, "Estudio Sobre la Crisis," p. 144.
50. Alberto Masferrer, *Patria* (San Salvador: Editorial Universitaria, 1960), p. 83. The first edition of *El Minimum Vital* appeared in 1929. This essay draws on Masferrer's newspaper discussions of his idea and on the definitive textual edition: *Minimum Vital y Otras Obras de Carácter Sociológico* (Guatamela City: Ediciones del Gobierno, 1950), pp. 179–210.
51. Masferrer, *Patria*, p. 219.
52. Ibid., 189–90.
53. Quoted in Marroquín, "Estudio Sobre la Crisis," p. 145.
54. Vejar, *Ascenso del Militarismo*, p. 12.

55. There is no doubt that Maximiliano Hernandez Martinez is a controversial figure in Salvadoran historiography, generally denounced as an "eccentric"—if not
"insane"—dictator. Two scholars of twentieth-century Salvadoran history,
Everett A. Wilson and Robert V. Elam, suggest that some revisionist assessments of Martinez may be in order. Wilson concludes, "There are several indications that Martinez, in spite of the notorious eccentricity and brutality of his
long regime, presided over significant national reconstruction in the early
1930's" ("Crisis of National Integration," p. 233). Elam emphasizes, "Perhaps no
president in this nation's history began with a broader base of support than that
enjoyed by Maximiliano Hernandez Martinez in 1932" ["Appeal to Arms: The
Army and Politics in El Salvador, 1931–1964" (Ph.D. diss., University of New
Mexico, 1968), p. 45].
56. Vejar, *Ascenso del Militarismo,* p. 131.
57. A major theme of William H. Durham, *Scarcity and Survival in Central America,* is
that if Salvadorans would make more efficient use of their land, they would be
able to feed themselves well.
58. Masferrer, *Patria,* pp. 179–82.
59. The Salvadoran situation amply illustrates the theme of the impoverishment of
the majority as Latin America "progressed" or "modernized" in the nineteenth
century set forth in Burns, *The Poverty of Progress.* For an economist's view of
that theme, consult Robert E. Gamer, *The Developing Nations: A Comparative
Perspective* (Boston: Allyn and Bacon, 1976). Another useful economic analysis,
but with a contemporary emphasis, is: David Felix, "Income Distribution and
the Quality of Life in Latin America: Patterns, Trends, and Policy Implications,"
Latin American Research Review, 18, 2 (1983): 3–34.

PART THREE

DEVELOPMENT, DEMOCRACY, AND CONTEMPORARY INTERNATIONAL INSTITUTIONS

Eastern Europe was the focus of much of the earliest Western writing on issues of economic development. Its level of development notably lagged the remainder of Europe, and the experiences of both Europe and of the Soviet Union seemed to provide guidance in solving its problems. A classic article by Paul N. Rosenstein-Rodan appeared in 1943 and set out the need for a "big push" of state-led, across-the-board industrialization, a theme elaborated by Kurt Mandelbaum in 1945.

After following the Soviet model of development, the Eastern European countries have reappeared as the newest less developed countries, and so are again at the center of the development debate. Their 1989 revolutions have removed them from the Soviet bloc and opened them to the development models of Europe and the United States, and to greater ties with the Western economic system. They have begun to receive foreign assistance from individual govern-ments and international institutions, have become a subject of studies such as the World Bank's *World Development Report, 1990,* and have begun to reorient their economies, often dramatically. The model with most support is free market liberalization and openness to the international economy (see Lipton and Sachs, 1990), the model described in Part One as "conventional foolishness" by Gerald Helleiner.

The short-run effects were made familiar by the experience of Latin America with the model during the 1980s: rising unemployment, dramatic reductions in wages and standards of living, by an estimated 30 percent in Poland (Sachs and Lipton,

1990), all accompanied by reductions in social services to their people. The economy of East Germany completely collapsed and had to be absorbed by West Germany. On the other side, inflation has generally stabilized and exports have risen as liberalization has been undertaken. The whole process has been cushioned by inflows of foreign resources and reschedulings of debt payments as the Western countries and Japan attempt to aid and guide the process. These wrenching short-run dislocations are dismissed as the costs necessary for acceleration of development in the long run, a long run which had yet to arrive in Latin America after a decade of implementing the model.

Nonetheless, the development problem and development thinking have come full circle, back to where Eastern Europe plays a central role in both. The most significant effect of Eastern Europe on development thinking may well be in the political realm, however, in the political economy of development. For as Andre Gunder Frank observes in his article, the events in Eastern Europe indicate that "The role of participatory social movements in social transformation requires reappraisal." Those broad-based movements in Eastern Europe, many with an ethnic element, many incorporating a direct challenge to the nation as well as the state, and none based on political parties, may represent the form in which new challenges to nondemocratic rule are exerted. Indeed, these themes relate directly to Wiarda's article of Part One. Their effect has been dramatic, and its direction is unpredictable. Indeed, events have moved so rapidly in Eastern Europe and the former East Germany that some of the specifics in the Gunder Frank article (1990) have already been overtaken by events. Nonetheless, the centrality of decentralized democratic movements has continued, for example, the Slovak challenge to the Czechoslovak central government or the renewal of popular demonstrations in Leipzig, but now against the unified German government.

The movements in Eastern Europe grew out of economic as well as political failure, an experience shared with much of the developing world in the 1980s. Gunder Frank remains skeptical, however, about the ability of the countries of Eastern Europe to solve these problems, and expects the earlier polarizations to be replaced by new economic and social divisions, now mediated by the market.

Samir Amin, treated by Ruccio and Simon in Chapter 8, restated his position as these changes were unfolding (Amin, 1987). He again called attention to the effect of capitalist expansion (accumulation on a world scale) on developing countries, on the periphery which now must include Eastern Europe. The relative equality of the core countries came at the cost of increasing inequalities and polarizations in the periphery as the latter's interdependence with the world economy grew. Oppressive states of "modernized dictatorships" were the result in the periphery. Amin reiterated that the key to changing the situation was popular national revolutions, much as occurred in Eastern Europe. However, his model of economic change following the revolution was to "delink" from the international economy in order to chart a more independent course consistent with national goals, an approach successfully taken by India and China during most of the 1970s and 1980s. In Amin's eyes, such an approach would avoid the tremendous dislocations currently occurring in Eastern Europe as well as provide greater likelihood of future success in development. His position should be remembered as events in Eastern Europe unfold.

The next two articles, Bob Devlin's on the Latin American debt situation and Richard Feinberg's on the negative transfer from international organizations to Latin America, analyze the workings of the financial side of the international economic system. Since the Mexican debt default in 1982, the international financial system has failed to contribute to the development efforts of most of Latin America, the Caribbean and Africa, and many other countries throughout the world. Devlin describes the debt situation in Latin America and the role played by banks and governments. He then details the deterioration in economic performance in Latin America, exacerbated by the resource transfer from those countries through the debt overhang, a transfer of $179 *billion* between 1982 and 1988. Devlin attributes this sorry outcome to halfhearted international public policy, and he details the steps that have been taken and which might become available to confront this continuing problem. He is cautiously optimistic that the international financial system can adjust and begin to make a positive contribution to Latin American development.

Feinberg's analysis parallels Devlin's. He points out that the major official financial institutions dealing with Latin American—the World Bank, the International Monetary Fund, and the Inter-American Development Bank—have all begun to extract more funds from Latin America in debt repayment than they are lending to the area. This is a direct reversal of the desired direction of resource flow and certainly is compounding Latin America's economic problems. Feinberg, like Devlin, rejects the view that this is a systemic problem and suggests steps to ensure that resources flow *to* Latin America rather than *from* the area. Nonetheless, both articles raise fundamental questions about the benefits to Third World countries of integrating into the international financial system.

Implicit in all of these articles is a critique of the reigning model of integration into the world economy, particularly through an export promotion strategy. This particular question will be taken up by Hamilton in Chapter 21. Let us summarize one other study of export promotion here, however, by Berberoglu (1987). He examined six countries with very advanced industrial sectors: Argentina, the Philippines, Brazil, Mexico, South Korea and Taiwan. Berberoglu found that an export-led strategy in these countries simply facilitated the exploitation of wage-labor on a world scale (a point made as well by Standing in Chapter 19). In the six countries examined, export-led growth was accompanied by the rise of an authoritarian state, the persistence of inflation, low wages, a large number of work accidents, and a skewed income distribution. For example, South Korea has the world's highest rate of industrial accidents. The resistance of organized labor in all of the countries to government policy, seen most clearly in strikes and mass demonstrations, is also evidence of the strategy's failure. This explains why the candidate of the Workers' Party of Brazil, Lula, was only narrowly defeated in the presidential elections of 1989.

In summary, each of the articles provides a perspective on the two crucial issues for the political economy of development during the 1990s: democracy and participation in the domestic economies, and the relation of individual economies to the international economic system.

REFERENCES

Amin, Samir. "Democracy and National Strategy in the Periphery." *Third World Quarterly*, 9, 4 (1987).

Berberoglu, Berch. "The Contradictions of Export-oriented Development in the Third World." *Social and Economic Studies*, 36, 4 (1987).

Lipton, David, and Jeffrey Sachs. "Creating a Market Economy in Eastern Europe: The Case of Poland." *Brookings Papers on Economic Activity* (1990):1.

Mandelbaum, Kurt. *Industrialization of Backward Areas.* Oxford: Basil Blackwell, 1945.

Rosenstein-Rodan, Paul N. "Problems of Industrialization of Eastern and South-Eastern Europe." *Economic Journal*, 53 (June–September, 1943): 202–211.

Sachs, Jeffrey, and David Lipton. "Poland's Economic Reform." *Foreign Affairs*, 69, 3 (Summer 1990).

11

Revolution in Eastern Europe: Lessons for Democratic Social Movements (and Socialists?)

Andre Gunder Frank

The course and speed of events in Eastern Europe, which have surprised everyone (including their protagonists), call for an agonising reappraisal of widely held theories and deeply felt ideologies of socialism, of the nature of democracy and social democracy, and of the role of social movements in both. Moreover, both the economic causes and consequences of these sociopolitical processes merit more attention than has been usual in the euphoric reception of the 1989 revolution. Their analysis offers at least a dozen important lessons, which are explored below. Hopefully, they can embolden us all to face, and act, in the future.

The role of participatory social movements in social transformation requires reappraisal. It was, in initiating and carrying these events, perhaps greater than ever before. My previous writings about social movements referred to those in the East as pluri-class based, but said little more than that they are growing massively and rapidly. Pluri-class participation in social movements seems to have continued in the East, while in the West participants are drawn predominantly from the middle class (especially the intelligentsia), and in the South social movements include these but are pre-dominantly popular/working-class based.[1] Leadership of the social move-ments in the East has also been drawn from the intelligentsia, but participa-tion seems also to have included people from other middle-class backgrounds, as well as masses of working-class people. As elsewhere,

Note : The author is grateful for comments on the first draft to Michael Ellman (especially on economics and history), to Marta Fuentes (on economics and social movements), and to Kim Hunter for editorial help beyond the call of duty.

From *Third World Quarterly*, 12, 2 (April 1990), pp. 36–52.

women have participated more massively and in more important positions in these new social movements. This social composition of the movements may also help account for their less hierarchical and more anti-authoritarian character than in the traditional institutions whose power and legitimacy they challenged. This class and gender composition of the social movements, and their participation beyond all expectations in social transformation in Eastern Europe and parts of the USSR, now demands further analysis.

The peaceful character of the momentous social movements and political transformations in 1989 in Eastern Europe merits special attention. The movements themselves were deliberately peaceful, and little or no force of arms was used to repress them—except in Romania,[2] where armed repression by the Securitate was successfully countered by the army, which took the people's side in a (largely spontaneous?) uprising. Not only the role of the army, but also the spontaneity and suddenness of this popular uprising in Romania, should be distinguished from social movements elsewhere in Eastern Europe. These had much longer, deeper, and more organisational roots in the churches of East Germany, in Carta 77 in Czechoslovakia, in a multitude of peace and environmental movements in Hungary and, of course, in Solidarity and the Catholic Church in Poland. Bulgaria, perhaps, was between these and Romania. In the Russian parts of the USSR social movements and a multiplicity of "clubs" have also been playing major roles in promoting *perestroika* and *glasnost*. Indeed, to permit "his" *perestroika* and *glasnost* to progress, the general secretary of the Communist Party, Mikhail Gorbachev, has had to appeal, over the heads of his own party, to social movement mobilisation of people both outside and inside the party. The efficacy of all these different kinds of peaceful social movements in promoting social transformation requires reevaluation.

The demand for democracy was and remains so far-reaching and deep as to expand the meaning of democracy itself. We must advance beyond parliamentary political and state economic democracy to include "civil democracy" in civil society. That is, democratic participation and demands include, but also extend far beyond, the institutional confines of parliamentary political democracy and of economic democracy, for example, to the rejection of the corruption and privileges of the *nomenclatura*. Street-level and local democratic participation and participatory democracy expresses itself through a myriad of other institutional (church, for example), more or less organisational, and even spontaneous and rapidly changing forms. Our understanding of democracy, therefore, also requires revision and extension.

The role of party politics is downgraded, at least relatively, by these peaceful social movements and their demands for democracy. Many movements and their members reject and/or redefine exclusive or principal reliance on party politics. Not only do they mobilise and organise people and their demands through other forms, the movements are also conscious-ly and explicitly antiparty. Of course, they stand in particular against the communist parties, but they also reject (becoming) any other party. Several social movements rejected transforming themselves into political parties after achieving their immediate goals of liberation. At a national activist meeting of Neues Forum in East Germany 80 percent of those present were against transforming the movement into a party for the coming national elections. Czechoslovakia's Civic Forum has a "loose organisation" with "no master plan, no bylaws, and its strategy is not drafted by paid consul-tants."[3] A founder of the Left Alternative in Hungary declares that it is "a theoretical tendency, not a party. On the contrary it is an anti-party organi-sation from the base of the society."[4]

However, the movements' memberships include people who were, or still are, in parties (even the Communist Party), and the movements expect some of their members to become active in new parties—but as individuals. The organisational independence of the movements, *qua* movements, was fought for too hard and is too precious to be easily sacrificed to party politi-cal demands and exigencies. On the contrary, the movements are very con-scious of the contribution they must, and can only, make to democracy as social movements, and not as, or at least in addition to, political parties.

Nationalism and ethnicity were also factors in all of the social move-ments in Eastern Europe. Nationalism (if only anti-Russian) and ethnic issues helped mobilise people into these social movements and then to define some of their demands. In the Baltic republics of the USSR, national-ism is perhaps the major force in the social movements and one which forms their demands. Other ethnic, national, and religious differences and demands are mobilising people against Soviet power and against each other in ethnic/nationalist (social?) movements in the Transcaucasian and Central Asian regions of the USSR. Of course, each of these movements is as different from the other as each ethnicity and nation, and their circum-stances are unique. Moreover, the ethnic and nationalist demands of the moment are very much influenced by each group's more or less privileged class and geopolitical–economic position of dominance or subordination and by recent changes in these. Many of the more nationalist and ethnically based movements include, or even prioritise, demands for national state power. These demands also distinguish them from other social movements, which do not aspire to state power.

The problem of state power poses a difficult and partly novel challenge to the social movements and their relationship to political parties and to the state. The revolutions of 1989 were made by largely peaceful social move-ments that sought and achieved the downfall of governments and the crumbling of state power—which they mostly did not want to replace themselves. In the face of political state power vacuums, East European social movements have found themselves "obliged" to (re)organise to exercise state power. Lech Walesa declared that the greatest error Solidarity ever made was to assume government in Poland, but also that "it had no choice." Neues Forum in East Germany and Civic Forum in Czechoslovakia resist becoming parties, but cannot avoid intervention in rebuilding and running the state. Some of the social movements' membership must adopt a sort of double militancy, one in the movement and another in a political party. For example the leading Czech dissident, Vaclav Havel, became state president.

Indeed, the most urgent political problem after "liberation" is widely presented as what to do about the state. Worries abound (at home and abroad) that the state has crumbled in East Germany, has [crumbled] in Romania and—God forbid!—threatens to do so in a USSR that is armed to the teeth with nuclear weapons. Who will be "responsible" for managing the nuclear button in the no-longer-responsible superpower; who, even, will keep "public order" on the streets of East Berlin and Bucharest? The fear for stability is expressed abroad (for East Berlin "four-power" control has been proposed as a "solution," whilst all that is offered to Moscow is a prayer for Gorbachev). At home, however, the dilemma presents itself in more practical terms: if "we" do not act to assume positions of power, or at least to support our allies who have or want some, then others will so act and/or support our enemies. Thus, liberation or not, the "liberating" social movements are obliged more to conform to existing state institutions than to reform them. The hope for greater civil democracy lies in new social movements replacing those that succumb to existing institutions and their own institutionalisation by them.

The institutionalisation of movements into parties and state power is nothing new, of course. Many political parties started as social movements, and some ended up managing, even becoming indistinguishable from, state power. The now sixty-year-long all-powerful Mexican Partido Revolucionario Institucional (PRI) even incorporates this transition into its name. Indeed, some communist parties in Eastern Europe, the USSR, and elsewhere could be said to have begun life as a social movement (albeit more of the "old," petit-bourgeois led, "working class" kind). Even so, they or their "leader" unwittingly assumed the position, *"l'état c'est mois."*

The conflict between *fundi* (fundamentalist movement goals and procedures) and *realo* (realist party organisation and state power compromises), which is splitting the Green Movement/Party in West Germany, is also built into the external (and perhaps internal) circumstances of the social movements in Eastern Europe. Thus, economic, political, and other exigencies may propel the social movements in Eastern Europe in the direction of state power, towards compromises of principle and the political cost of failure, in the face of impossible economic and other odds. In Poland Solidarity now has to push bitter IMF medicine down its members' throats and administer shock treatment to the body public. Nationalist (and some ethnic) movements, however, often aspire to "independent" national–ethnic state power, or seek to share it in amalgamation with their ethnically homogeneous neighbour state. Hardly any seem to consider their own weakness in the face of the same economic crisis that is the motor of their movements.

The economic crisis, which has been expanding and deepening in Eastern Europe and the USSR, contributed materially to the desire and ability of these movements to mobilise so many people for such far-reaching political ends. The late 1970s and the 1980s is now called "the period of stagnation" in the USSR. It generated an accelerating economic crisis and an absolute deterioration of living standards in most of Eastern Europe, as well as in Latin America, Africa, and other parts of the world.[5] Significantly, especially in Eastern Europe, this period also spelled an important deterioration and retrocession in its standards of living and ability to compete, compared with Western Europe and even to the newly industrialising countries (NICs) in East Asia. Moreover, the course and mismanagement of the economic crisis generated shifts in positions of dominance, privilege, dependency, or exploitation among countries, sectors, and different social (including gender and ethnic) groups within the USSR and Eastern Europe. All of these economic changes and pressures generated or fuelled social discontent, demands, and mobilisation, which express themselves through enlivened social (and ethnic–nationalist) movements. It is well known that economically based resentment is fed by the loss of "accustomed," absolute standards of living—as a whole or in particular items and by related relative shifts in economic welfare among population groups. Most economic crises are polarising, further enriching the better off and further impoverishing those who were already worse off, especially women.

This change may also generate resentment and mobilisation in both groups. The less privileged mobilise to defend their livelihood against the "system" and those who benefit from it. Such underprivileged ethnic groups include Turks in Bulgaria, Hungarians in Romania, Gypsies and others in Hungary, Albanians in Serbia, Serbians in Yugoslavia, Bohemians in Czechoslovakia, Azerbaijanis, and a host of others in the Soviet Union, who among other problems, have recently been plagued by massive unemployment.

However, the more privileged also develop resentments against the "system," which obliges the richer to "carry" or "subsidise" their "good-for-nothing," "lazy," poorer neighbours. Moreover, these more privileged groups see even greener pastures for themselves on the other side of the border between socialism and capitalism. These include many Russians, Armenians, and others in the USSR, especially the Estonians, Latvians, and Lithuanians. They also include Slovenians and, to a lesser extent, Croatians in Yugoslavia. They include, of course, many Germans in the former GDR, whose eyes (and feet!) turned toward the economic magnet in the West.

Whatever their current degree of privilege, thousands of "ethnic Germans" in the USSR, Poland, and Romania have suddenly discovered an age-old feeling of Germanity and a desire to partake of the German miracle in the federal republic. The population at large (beyond its particular(ist) ethnic, national, and other groups) also mobilises, or at least is more readily mobilisable in support of demands based on increasing economic resentment. These demands are easily politicised to extend to and be expressed by the participatory exercise of economic, political, and civil democracy—not to mention the ethnic and nationalist demands into which they can also be easily reformulated. These recently augmented, economically based resentments are indisputably a major factor in generating (and accounting for) widespread popular mobilisation through the movements in Eastern Europe and the USSR.

However, strategic and political changes prepared new world and regional political circumstances, which also helped the social movements initiate, proceed with, and succeed (so far) in their social mobilisation and political demands. Particularly important in Eastern Europe was the abrogation of the Brezhnev doctrine. Perhaps Gorbachev turned the Brezhnev doctrine on its head to exert pressure for political and economic change in Eastern Europe. For instance, the Hungarian foreign minister reportedly consulted the Soviet ambassador and received his approval before opening the border with Austria, which unlocked the floodgates from East Germany. During his visit to East Germany Gorbachev literally planted the kiss of death on the cheek of Erich Honecker and then signalled that armed repression of the 9 October rally in Leipzig would be unacceptable. Some reports have it that he even threatened to place locally stationed Soviet troops between the demonstrators and any threatened attack by the East German state.

In the USSR itself, of course, *perestroika* and *glasnost* have paved the way for the mobilisation of the movements; these, in turn, are both a necessary mobilising factor to promote *perestroika* and *glasnost,* and a threat to the same should they get out of hand. Poland and China have already demonstrated that economic restructuring is subject to severely limited political reform, though possibly counterproductive without it. The Hungarian example has demonstrated that they can and must go hand in hand, at least so far. Perhaps also considering the experience abroad, Gorbachev has clarified that *glasnost* is a *sine qua non* of successful *perestroika* in the USSR. Successful *perestroika* is a *sine qua non* for the USSR maintaining any kind of power, let alone a superpower status in the competitive world political economy. Perhaps paradoxically, therefore, political abrogation of the Brezhnev doctrine and some "liberation" of the USSR from its economic burdens in Eastern Europe are also political–economic imperatives for the maintenance of strategic security and the promotion of economic development in the USSR today.

In short, these political and strategic changes are an important contributory factor to the mobilisation and success of these social movements. Moreover, the world economic crisis and its particular manifestations in the USSR and Eastern Europe are contributing factors, both directly, through their generation of economically based resentments, and indirectly, through the economic imperatives they pose for the political changes. Of course, the importance of these economic, political, and strategic circumstances invites further elucidation.

The euphoria of democratic success and the honeymoon of liberation has relegated all these economic processes and polarising problems to the last baggage car of the popular express train. Its locomotive seems to run on political steam alone and it is fuelled or even pushed along by the social movements themselves. The press, in particular (and all the more so in the West), has depicted almost the whole process as a jubilant joy ride to freedom and democracy. But, whilst social change of this nature can be a euphoric process, the economic structure and process and its problems are not transformed by political euphoria alone.

The bitter reality of worsening economic privation impresses itself daily upon the population in Poland and much of Yugoslavia. The situation is less harsh, but also bites in Hungary, Czechoslovakia, Bulgaria, and east Germany, and worsens by the day in the USSR. Romania enjoys a temporary respite from the ravages of food exporting, but such problems will soon follow. Few people in these countries may know, or care to calculate, the importance of the economic reality underlying and guiding the directions of this political train. It is like the railway tracks and points, as well as the roadbed underlying them: it directs or at least limits the movement of the train.

In Poland already (and threatening elsewhere), it is as if the bulky economic baggage is moving relentlessly forward through the train, displacing more and more of the social movement passengers along the way. As a result, the anger of the passengers is increasingly displaced from political oppression to economic privation. The passengers' anger is also diverted against each other, against the more privileged passengers and cars to the fore (and by them against those in the back who are only "useless weight" to pull along), and by almost all the passengers and crew against the locomotive, the station masters, and perhaps the whole railroad system. Of course, every passenger will insist on using the newly won democracy and the associated social movements to have his/her say on these matters of vital concern, and rightly so. Many passengers may soon wish to lend new (social movement) support to some populist, novice driver who promises final deliverance, especially from unwanted fellow passengers. The Serbian leader Milosevic and his support already offers a sufficiently terrifying example. Ethnic and national(ist) cars may well soon be detached from the train in Yugoslavia, the USSR, and perhaps elsewhere. The forward cars in the Baltics, in Slovenia, and in east Germany may find looser or firmer attachment to other more Westerly directed locomotives. What (if any) alternative political–economic tracks—or sidings, more likely—may be available to the more rear cars is harder to say.

Thus, the very social movements that first served as vehicles of liberation could threaten the political–democratic processes they had launched themselves. Indeed, in the throes of economic and political crisis, derivative or other social movements could become vehicles of ethnic, nationalist, and class strife and rivalries—with unforeseeable consequences, which could include dictatorial populist backlashes against the newly won democracy.

A historical comparison of the revolutions and their social (but not nationalist) movements of 1789, 1848, 1917, 1968, and 1989, and some comparative reflections on the place and role of Russia, may be in order. This can put the revolution of 1989 into some kind of historical context, in place of a conclusion to this review of an ongoing process in Eastern Europe and the USSR. The 1789 revolution was initially peaceful, but it turned violent and to counterrevolution after taking state power. It was a "bourgeois" revolution to pave the way for capitalist development, but it was not antifeudal. (In the aftermath, on the winning side of the Napoleonic Wars and at Vienna, Russia became a European power.) The revolutions of 1848 were a combination of peaceful and violent assaults on state power, but all of them were violently repressed and condemned to failure. Thus, these revolutions did not immediately impose liberal bourgeois principles over conservative ones, although many of their policies were eventually adopted, but with little thanks to social movements led by the working class. (Russia again lost influence in Central Europe in the face of German unification and economic development. After losing the Crimean War, Tsar Alexander II freed the serfs and introduced his own *perestroika* and *glasnost* with some, but insufficient, results.)

The 1917 revolution began peacefully in February, then resorted to more force to pass state power from the tsars to the Kerenski government. In October–November 1917 the initial aim was to exercise a peaceful threat to influence the existing government, but the revolutionary process accelerated into an armed assault on state power. It proved successful, but led to civil war and the subsequent power of the Soviet Communist Party. Working class (social) movements failed everywhere in postwar Europe; even in Russia workers were a tiny percentage of the revolutionary forces, one which was further reduced by their decimation in the civil war. (During World War I, Lenin had made a separate peace at Brest–Litovsk and forfeited Soviet Russia's share of the spoils. However, as conqueror on the winning side of World War II and at Yalta and Potsdam, Soviet Russia assumed and was awarded a dominant role in Central—now "Eastern"—Europe and then world superpower status.)

The 1968 "revolutions" were largely peaceful social movements, often repressed by force of arms, even though none aspired to or seriously threatened state power. A particular distinguishing feature of the "new" social movements was that they were not working-class led or based. On the contrary, 1968 represents the acknowledgement that social movements must reach and appeal far beyond the "traditional," industrial working class and its communist party and/or unionised leadership. The Prague Spring, if it be included among 1968 "movements," contemplated a peaceful transfer of power within the existing state apparatus, but was reversed through military invasion by the Soviet army. The 1968 Tet offensive in Vietnam was, of course, another matter. (Soviet power was challenged here and there, but survived.)

The revolutions of 1989 started peacefully as widespread and deepgoing social movements. They succeeded, quicker and more than even their protagonists expected, in putting civil democracy in civil society to work to achieve political liberation. Finally, the domino theory, which was feared on previous occasions but remained inoperative, worked this time—albeit rather unexpectedly. It did so in part because the social movements suffered no armed repression, either domestic or foreign (except in the more "independent" Romania, where, however, the army turned to support and save the popular uprising). The mild resistance by the regimes, of course, was conditioned by changes in circumstance and policy in the USSR. Their collapse, in some cases, in the face of these movements almost saw the destruction of the state power and institutions that "guarantee public order," so much so that even commentators in the West took alarm. Perhaps this alarm reflects the failure—or let's hope it is only a delay—to appreciate the momentous de facto reformulation and extension of the democratic process when, to paraphrase Abraham Lincoln, it is extended "by, of and for the people" beyond parliamentary political democracy to civil democracy in civil society.

At the same time the economic structures and processes underlying these sociopolitical transformations have not received the attention that their importance merits. However, the hard knocks of economic life still threaten to divert, albeit hopefully not to revert, these social movements and political processes in dangerous directions. If, like 1789, 1989 will go down in history as a year of revolution, what portends for 1990 and its decade—analogous to the 1790s? Whether some kinds of counterrevolutionary Thermidors may still be in the offing (and when) we would not like now to foresee. [Beginning with military failure in Afghanistan (another Crimean War?), the "imperial" reach of the USSR is under effective political challenge due principally to economic failure, and the "Union" may effectively break up. Russia, whether still "soviet" or not, may thereby be relatively weakened but perhaps absolutely revitalised and strengthened.[6]]

Actually existing socialism has undergone an important transformation because of these events and requires reconsideration. To account for these events and transformations, the prime determining factor has been the failure of actually existing (non) socialism in Eastern Europe and the USSR to compete economically with the West. It is well known that the centrally planned economies achieved relative success through forced absolute growth. Heavy industry and, in some countries, large scale industrial agriculture boomed. Social services were provided and assured, but not individual services. It has become equally apparent that these inflexible economies were unable to promote intensive growth. It was precisely during the recent technological revolution, particularly computerisation in the West and in the East Asian NICs that the centralised economies of the USSR and Eastern Europe were unable to keep pace. On the contrary, they lost ground both absolutely and relatively. This was the most determinant starting point of the social movements and revolutions. As an economic failure, moreover, "socialism" has proved to be no match for nationalism. First in Yugoslavia, Hungary, and (above all) Poland, then in the Baltics, Transcaucasus, Central Asia, the Ukraine, and elsewhere in Eastern Europe, nationalism challenged the political economic order and demanded democratic self-determination. With economic success neither these social and nationalist movements nor this (kind of) demand for democracy would have developed, much less this move to marketise the economies.

Such observations about Eastern Europe, however, require a brief, parenthetical, comparative glance at other parts of the world. It is noteworthy that economies throughout Africa, most of Latin America, and parts of Asia have recently suffered the same competitive failure, manifested in disastrously declining absolute living standards and relative marginalisation from the world economy. Many of them have suffered even more than most economies in Eastern Europe. Perhaps Poland, Romania, Bolivia, Argentina (maybe Burma), and much of Africa top the sad list of greatest decline. Social movements have also developed in many of the other countries outside Eastern Europe, yet in none of them with similar results, or such far-reaching goals. In Africa the considerable *volte-face* in political–economic orientation, away from socialisation and the East to support of ethnic and national independence at home, has been achieved without dramatic change. The return to political democracy in Latin America was only marginally carried by the many social movements, despite some of their claims to the contrary. The most dramatic process of democratisation, in Argentina, was far less the result of the human rights movements (the Madres de la Plaza de Mayo, and others) than it was of the defeat of Argentine military forces by those of Britain, with military aid from the USA and the political support of the whole Western world. In Burma the social movement was repressed by force of arms. So it was to one degree or another in many other countries, from Chile, to Mexico, Jamaica, Gabon, and Sri Lanka. In any of these countries social movements with the force and threat of those in Eastern Europe would have been drenched in blood.

Of similar significance is the fact that in none of these other countries has there been a serious attempt to replace the obviously failing economic system by another, radically different one, let alone to replace the failure of capitalism by socialism. On the contrary, in terms of economic organisation there has been a move to the right, to marketisation (privatisation) every-where. Moreover, the failure of "socialism" in Eastern Europe can only accelerate marketisation elsewhere, no matter how socially costly runaway capitalism has already proved. None of the new democratic regimes in Latin America propose to reform, let alone to turn back, export-led growth (be it absolute growth as in Chile or absolute decline as in Argentina): the democratic opening is itself under threat from the repressive economic measures that democratic governments are obliged (not least by the inter-vention of the IMF) to impose on their populations.

Indeed, Iran has been the only notable exception to all these experi-ences. The armed-to-the-teeth regime of the Shah disintegrated, as its Winter Palace was stormed and taken by an unarmed peaceful crowd, the spearhead of a deep-going social movement. However, the movement was led by the exiled fundamentalist leader, Ayatollah Khomeini, who returned in triumph and channelled this religion-led social movement into the con-struction of a Shiite Islamic theocratic state. It renounced and denounced Soviet communist and US imperialist satans equally and, at enormous sac-rifice to its population, fought a ten-year war against its Sunni Islamic neighbours in Iraq. (Both financed the war by their sales of oil on the world market.)

Thus, the failure of socialist, but also of many capitalist and mixed, economies is marked above all by their inability to compete adequately on the world market. Of course, this has always been the case; it is in the "nature" of any competition that only few can win and many must lose. This process of selection operates largely irrespective of the capitalist or socialist "system" that they use to compete, which is at best a contributory factor in the inevitable selection of winners and losers. Therefore, the eco-nomic failure and loss of "socialism" per se is relative to both the success and also the failure of "capitalism" to compete in the same ("capitalist") world market. The replacement of one "system" by the other is no guaran-tee that any economy will then compete more successfully; most will con-tinue to lose the race.

The move away from "socialism" to the greater marketisation of East European economies and their further integration into world competition comes on the heels of recently increased and still-growing economic weak-ness. Therefore, they pose great economic and political dangers, not the least of further economic failure and of popular political disillusionment and backlash.

The economic crisis in Eastern Europe and the USSR is almost certain to deepen further in the short run. Both deepening crisis and market response will result in greater shortages, new unemployment, rampant inflation, and disruption to the welfare state. All of these—particularly the latter—will increase the already disproportionate burden on women and children. In the USSR Gorbachev was ill advised by Abel Aganbegyan to push for *perestroika* and acceleration of growth in the economy at the same time. The result has been an economic (and political) disaster: restructuring temporarily reduces growth, instead of increasing it, and the simultaneous attempt to accelerate threw an additional spanner into the works.

In Eastern Europe, too, economic restructuring is bound to involve transitional economic dislocation in different degrees and forms. It will be the most absolutely severe in Poland, as well as in the south and east of Yugoslavia and the USSR, which have the weakest and most recently weakened economies. Romania was also weakened, especially by Ceaucescu's policy of exporting all to pay off the debt. Ceasing to export so much food can offer temporary relief and some resurrection of agriculture, but not of industry. East Germany faced the prospects of immediate *ausverkauf* to the West Germans who already came to buy subsidised consumer goods at 10 or 20:1 exchange rates between Western and Eastern marks. East Germany, which had long been a de facto silent member of the EC through its privileged access to the West German market, also had the earliest prospects of full integration in the EC. However, the weakening of the state in East Germany and its dependent confederation with or even integration into the West German state left east Germany with scarce political–economic bargaining power in Germany, the EC, and Europe. Czech and Hungarian state power may offer more competitive bargaining power and benefits to (parts of) their populations. Everywhere, however, the first steps toward productive integration are likely to be the sale of East European productive assets to West European firms and others, some of whom will engage in asset-stripping instead of real investment. In Eastern Europe itself few have the money to successfully outbid foreigners for "privatised" assets. Only some small enterprises could be run as "cooperatives," in reality firms that must also compete in the market.

The political–economic move to marketisation and privatisation, whether "capitalist" or "socialist," which is engendered by the social movements in Eastern Europe, can at best replace one economic and social polarisation by another. The corruption and privilege derived from communist party rule can be largely (but not entirely) eliminated, but marketisation and privatisation engender another, more automatic, economic and social polarisation of income and position between the genders, among class, ethnic groups, and regions. A minority will float to the surface of a, perhaps first, ebbing and then rising tide; the majority will sink even further below the surface. This polarisation is likely to progress ethnically, nationally, and internationally. Therefore, it will further exacerbate ethnic and national tensions, conflicts, and movements within and among states. The more competitively privileged regions and peoples are likely to improve their positions further, perhaps by closer economic and political relations or even integration with neighbours to the west and north. Underprivileged minorities here, and underprivileged majorities in unintegrated places, are likely to become increasingly marginalised. The dream of joining Western Europe may, thus, be realised only for the few. At best, some parts of the East may become another southern Europe, albeit at the cost to both of competing with each other. (Fears have already been raised in the south of Europe.) However, many in Eastern Europe—and perhaps in the southeastern parts of the USSR—face the real threat of Latin Americanisation, a fate which has already befallen Poland. East European countries face domestic inflation and foreign devaluation, and then currency reform, perhaps by shock treatment. The social costs are certain, but the economic successes are not, as repeated failures in Argentina and Brazil have recently demonstrated. In some cases, particularly in the USSR, even economic Africanisation (or at least Mideasternisation) and political Lebanonisation is a serious threat. In the short run, any breakup of the Second World will permit some of its members to join the (capitalist) First World, but most will be relegated to the (also capitalist) Third World.

The question arises of a possible, different socialism for the future. How and what would it come to be? An oft-posed issue, at least by some who consider themselves socialists, is whether the USSR and Eastern Europe (indeed any other place) has been socialist at all. Since their answer is a resounding "no," they also argue that the long-standing failures and critiques of actually existing socialism, which finally gave rise to the revolutions of 1989, were not really of socialism, but of Stalinism or some other aberration of, or imposter for, true socialism. The ideological implication of this argument is, of course, that these failures do not compromise the true socialist cause and do not oblige real socialists to undertake an agonising reappraisal. Real socialists, then, need only insist more than ever on their own critiques of actually existing (non)socialism to differentiate "us" (goodies) from "them" (baddies). The "practical" implication of this "theory" is that, experience notwithstanding, true socialism is still around the corner— or at least down the road.

However, the real practicality and even theoretical coherence of this, perhaps well-meaning, argument clashes with all world social–political–economic reality. To begin with, if ever there was an argument that only preaches to the already (auto)converted, then this is it. It could not possibly convert those who have already experienced actually existing socialism, even if it were really nonsocialism: those amongst them who reject most of the previously existing (non)socialism are likely to continue to reject any potential "real" socialism. Indeed, many of them are likely to put their faith in the magic of the market and some, alas, in far-right politics. On the other hand, those who now lose the benefits of their previous experience will only yearn for the "good old days" of order and stability and the (non)socialist *ancien régime*. Among these, those who had little and now lose even that will recall their modest benefits and ask for renewed order, if not of the old "communist" variety, then perhaps of a new "fascist" one. Only those who received much from the old party may now, under a new democratic socialist guise, try to hang on to as much of it as possible. The social democratic argument will also lack appeal for those elsewhere who never wanted themselves or anyone else to experience "socialism" or "communism," of whatever kind. Therefore, it is wholly unrealistic to think that the damage of the whole experience to the idea of socialism, of democratic or whatever kind, can simply be wished away by latter-day professions of one's own purity against others' former sins.

Second, however anti-Stalinist the subjective intent of this argument, its objective consequence is to stick to the guns of the Stalinist theory of socialism in one country (or even smaller community). Beyond disregarding the first problem and that of transition to this socialism in theory and praxis, this argument clashes with the same practical reality of having to compete in practice the whole world over. Yet the inability to do so was the fundamental failure and undoing of the Stalinist system, socialist or otherwise. Whatever the kind of socialism, capitalism, mixed economy, Islamic political economy, or other system that people may "choose," they cannot escape worldwide competition; it is a fact of life. Cooperation as an "alternative" is all very well, so long as it is more competitive.

Third, the (only?) alternative interpretation of "real" socialism is "world" socialism. Beyond its unreality for any foreseeable future, it is difficult to imagine what this might ever mean. What would distinguish this world socialism from world capitalism, so long as competition reigns as a fact of life in the future as it has for millennia in the past?

What of the chances for social democracy, if not democratic socialism? One time "socialists" in the West and the East, including Mikhail Gorbachev himself, have found new appreciation for and interest in social democracy as the *desideratum*, which best combines both "socialism" and "democracy." They, again including Gorbachev, look to Sweden, and sometimes to Austria, as the model for Eastern Europe and even for the USSR. In the architectural design for the new Common European Home, many socialists and social democrats would further provide for social democratic, if not democratic socialist, influences emanating from the East into the West. Thus, the whole of Europe would become another Sweden writ large. As Gandhi answered when he was asked what he thought of European civilisation, "It would be a good idea." Unfortunately, these good ideas take little account of some hard realities.

Thus, even disregarding the USSR, which is hardly realistic, the prospects for early Swedenisation in Eastern Europe are not very bright. On the contrary, it will take much effort by all, including Western Europe and even the USA and Japan, only to lay some—indeed, even to protect already existing—economic (social democratic) foundations for political social democracy in Eastern Europe. It is at best uncertain whether, and how much, a West German/European Marshall Plan would promote social democracy in Eastern Europe. Nor is it certain that such an enterprise would advance the progressive version of social democracy (with small or large "s" and "d") and defeat conservative politics and parties in the West. Investment in good business (but not in unprofitable social investments) in the East could easily spell more polarisation in the West as well. Really "new" social movements, East and West, could develop both to reflect and to propel such accelerated polarisation.

Thus, socialists are indeed obliged by the hard facts of life to rethink socialism, if they insist on sticking to their socialist ideology at all. We would not pretend to do this rethinking here and now, let alone do it alone. To be realistic, however, any such socialism would have not only to take account of competition, but to rewrite the rules of the (competitive) game under which it takes place. Gender, class, national, ethnic, religious, community, as well as economic, political, social, cultural, ideological, and other interest groups and family or individual interrelations would have to have new participatory social (movement) expressions and institutional protection of and guarantees for the mutual respect of their democratic expression and for the peaceful resolution of their conflicts of interest beyond anything hitherto known. Realistically, the prospects for any such "democratic socialism," or otherwise, are still dim. Indeed, all the evidence is that things will, and will have to, get worse before they get better. However, things may get so much worse and so rapidly so that mankind may face a common economic–ecological and/or military–political and, therefore sociocultural, crisis of such alarming proportions and absolute threat to physical survival, that we will finally be moved to get ourselves together.

NOTES

1. M. Fuentes and A. G. Frank, "Ten Theses on Social Movements," *World Development,* 17 (February 2, 1989); A. G. Frank and M. Fuentes, "Social Movements in Recent World History," in S. Amin, G. Arrighi, A. G. Frank, and I. Wallerstein, *Transforming the Revolution: Social Movements in the World System* (New York: Monthly Review Press, 1990).
2. As this article goes to press Soviet troops occupy the streets of Baku, the capital of Azerbaijan.
3. *New York Times/International Herald Tribune,* December 7, 1989.
4. *International Viewpoint,* December 11, 1989, p. 13.
5. A. G. Frank and M. Fuentes, "Nine Theses on Social Movements," *Economic and Political Weekly,* 22, 35 (August 29, 1987).
6. On the variety of social movements and their nineteenth- and twentieth-century history, see S. Amin et al., *Transforming the Revolution.*

12

Options for Tackling the External Debt Problem

Robert Devlin

I. THE CURRENT SITUATION

1. Searching for Progress

Looking to the North, one sees the OECD economies out of recession, and indeed enjoying one of the longest periods of noninflationary economic expansion in their modern history.[1] A highly decentralized international lender-of-last-resort facility (composed of the IMF, World Bank, Bank for International Settlements, OECD central banks, treasuries, export credit agencies, and the private banks themselves) has proved its effectiveness in averting the destabilizing defaults in Latin America that threatened to emerge from the systemic payments crisis of that region.[2] Thus, in the middle of the worst financial crisis since the 1930s, private banks have generally performed remarkably well. For example, throughout the crisis years of 1982–1986 the international earnings of United States banks remained buoyant, and indeed their overall growth of net income accelerated as these institutions diversified into new profit opportunities at home (Table 1). Negative earnings manifested themselves only in 1987, on account of the first large-scale allocation of reserves against possible losses on the Latin American portfolio.[3] The industry, however, rebounded in the first half of 1988, reporting a strong recovery of earnings.[4]

Moreover, behind this strong earnings performance an impressive "growth-oriented adjustment" of the banks' loan portfolio in Latin America is under way. Again the United States banks are illustrative: by March 1988, they had reduced their absolute exposure in the region by 12% with respect

From *CEPAL Review*, 37 (April 1989), pp. 27–34.

TABLE 1   **United States Banking: Selected Indicators**
(Percentage of Total Average Assets)

	1980	1981	1982	1983	1984	1985	1986	1987
Net interest revenue	2.8	2.8	3.1	3.3	3.4	3.6	3.6	3.4
Money centre banks	2.4	2.4	2.8	2.9	3.1	3.2	3.2	2.9
Regional banks	3.4	3.3	3.4	3.7	3.9	4.1	4.0	3.0
Net income	0.62	0.59	0.59	0.67	0.65	0.66	0.67	−0.31
Money centre banks	0.51	0.52	0.54	0.64	0.60	0.69	0.70	−0.65
Regional banks	0.76	0.67	0.66	0.69	0.70	0.64	0.65	0.01
International earnings	—	—	—	—	—	—	—	—
Money centre banks	0.27	0.30	0.32	0.29	0.27	0.26	0.22	−1.33
Regional banks	—	—	—	—	—	—	—	—

SOURCE: ECLAC, on the basis of data in Thomas Hanley et al., *A Review of Bank Performance* (various editions), New York: Salomon Brothers.

to June 1982 (Table 2), while doubling their primary capital, all of which enabled them to cut in half their Latin American loan-to-capital ratio, from a precarious 124% to a much more manageable 58% (Table 3). United States money centre banks now have 25–30% of their LDC portfolio backed by loan loss reserves, while many United States regional and continental European banks have a corresponding coverage of 50% or more (Table 4).[5] In sum, the international management of the payments difficulties in Latin America has helped the bankers to convert a situation which was originally, for them, a severe "crisis" into something more akin to a "problem." Indeed, the success of the bankers' adjustment is reflected in signs of complacency in financial circles about the Latin American situation: in the view of some experts, a refusal to pay by any one of the major debtors—Brazil, Mexico, Argentina, or Venezuela—would not now create undue stress in the world banking system.[6]

The creditors' diagnosis of the problem in Latin America is also certainly more realistic now than it was at the outset. Gone are the rosy scenarios about a short-term liquidity crisis; most creditors now recognize that the problem in Latin America is structural, because time-consuming internal economic and social transformations are needed in most debtor countries to competitively produce and sell the tradeable goods required to generate foreign exchange for normal servicing of the debt. Likewise, there is now recognition that protracted belt tightening in the debtor countries is counterproductive: in order to politically legitimize necessary reforms and to raise the mass of domestic savings available for investment and debt service, countries clearly must achieve a sustained expansion of their economies.

The more realistic diagnosis has also led to more realistic responses. Some banks, recognizing that the "time" implicit in the restructuring pro-

TABLE 2 Exposure of United States Banks in Latin America

| | MILLIONS OF DOLLARS | | | | | | | | | ANNUAL GROWTH RATES (TOTAL EXPOSURE) | | |
| | JUNE 1982 | | | DECEMBER 1987 | | | MARCH 1988 | | | 1986 | 1987 | March 88/June 82 |
	Top 9	Rest	Total	Top 9	Rest	Total	Top 9	Rest	Total			
Latin America	48,714	33,368	82,082	49,757	24,720	74,477	49,015	23,116	72,311	−3.0	−5.4	−11.9
Oil-exporting countries	23,567	17,285	40,852	20,699	12,446	33,145	20,066	11,621	31,867	−6.0	−6.7	−22.0
Bolivia	231	137	368	39	24	63	38	20	58	−13.6	−29.2	−84.2
Ecuador	1,257	910	2,167	1,137	650	1,787	1,119	586	1,705	3.1	−11.4	−21.3
Mexico	13,602	11,619	25,221	13,396	9,002	22,398	12,848	8,240	21,088	−3.7	−4.9	−16.4
Peru	1,330	1,017	2,347	441	400	841	390	392	782	−23.3	−27.4	−66.7
Venezuela	7,147	3,602	10,749	5,686	2,370	8,056	5,671	2,383	8,054	−10.8	−7.8	−25.1
Non-oil-exporting countries	25,147	16,083	41,230	29,058	12,274	41,332	28,949	11,495	40,444	−0.3	−4.2	−1.9
Argentina	5,595	3,212	8,807	6,709	2,521	9,230	6,766	2,452	9,281	3.5	2.0	4.7
Brazil	12,336	8,179	20,515	15,763	6,507	22,270	15,754	5,986	21,740	0.2	−5.7	6.0
Colombia	2,075	961	3,036	1,398	675	2,073	1,350	700	2,050	−15.0	−3.8	−32.5
Costa Rica	221	259	480	178	139	317	176	133	309	−5.2	−20.6	−25.6
Chile	3,314	2,761	6,075	3,907	1,964	5,871	3,841	1,778	5,619	0.1	−6.1	−7.5
El Salvador	53	16	69	8	41	49	6	46	52	12.2	−10.9	−24.6
Guatemala	96	53	149	29	19	48	29	12	41	−32.4	4.3	−72.5
Honduras	139	64	203	42	64	106	36	68	104	−9.3	—	−48.8
Nicaragua	257	168	425	13	30	43	13	28	41	−26.7	−34.8	−90.3
Paraguay	299	28	327	60	17	77	58	12	70	−37.4	−28.0	−78.6
Dominican Republic	338	108	446	263	80	343	263	82	345	−6.6	−14.0	−22.6
Uruguay	424	274	698	688	217	905	657	198	855	0.8	1.8	22.5

SOURCE: ECLAC, on the basis of United States Federal Financial Institutions Examination Council, *Statistical Release*, various numbers.

TABLE 3   **United States Banking: Latin American Exposure as a Percentage of Primary Capital**

	JUNE 1982			MARCH 1988		
	Top 9	Rest	Total	Top 9	Rest	Total
Latin America	180.0	85.4	124.0	96.7	31.8	57.7
Oil-exporters	87.1	44.2	61.8	40.2	16.1	25.7
Non-oil-exporters	93.0	41.2	62.2	56.5	15.7	32.0
Memo item:						
Primary capital[a]	27.1	39.1	66.2	51.5	77.7	129.1

[a]Billions of dollars.

SOURCE: ECLAC, on the basis of data from the United States Federal Financial Institutions Examination Council, *Statistical Release*, various numbers.

cess erodes some of the present value of the income stream of their assets in Latin America, began in 1987 to more aggressively adjust downward the valuation of their loans in the region.[7] Moreover, the devaluation of assets has sometimes resulted in relief for the debtors as banks now show an increasing willingness to accept formal debt reduction schemes through direct or indirect participation in debt-equity swaps,[8] the purchase of below market interest rate exit bonds,[9] the conversion of debt into bonds at a discount,[10] direct buybacks,[11] etc.

The new diagnosis likewise has induced better responses from the multilateral lenders. The recognition of the structural problem has brought the World Bank from the background of the international debt strategy to the centre of the playing field.[12] Meanwhile, the IMF has accommodated to the new realities by extending its adjustment programs to up to four years, lengthening the period of review of its performance criteria to six months, as well as creating a new expanded contingency financing facility.

Turning South, one finds that the crisis has coincided with some positive changes in Latin America. There are today thirteen democratic governments in the region compared to only four in the late 1970s.[13] On the economic front, the severity of the crisis in Latin America has certainly broken the back of the dogmatism sometimes attached to import substitution development strategies and so-called inward-looking development. Indeed, one senses the emergence of a new pragmatism in the formulation of development policy. While eschewing some of the more simplistic prescriptions for economic liberalization emanating from the North, the achievement of international competitiveness is now a central preoccupation of the authorities of the region. Most countries are manifestly eager to learn the art of producing and selling for highly competitive international markets. The popular notion of the State as the handmaiden of development also has

TABLE 4   **United States Banking: Reserves Set Aside on LDC Portfolio**
(Millions of Dollars)

	RESERVING 1987			Total Estimated Reserves	Percentage of LDC Portfolio
	II Quarter	IV Quarter	Total		
Money centre banks					
Bankers Trust	700	—	700	1,000	25
Chase Manhattan	1,600	—	1,600	2,000	25
Chemical Bank	1,100	—	1,100	1,360	25
Citicorp	3,000	—	3,000	3,325	25
Manufacturers Hanover	1,700	—	1,700	1,787	25
J.P. Morgan and Co.	850	—	850	1,330	25
Republic N.Y. Corp.	100	10	110	200	40
Bank of Boston Corp.	300	200	500	430[a]	55[a]
First Chicago	780	240	1,020	1,132	39
Selected regional banks					
Bank of New England	97	100	197	192[a]	75[a]
Midlantic Corp.	30	25	55	54[a]	63[a]
Mellon Bank	290	180	470	621[a]	45[a]
Banc One Corp.	53	—	53	7	67
NBD Bancorp.	54	—	54	106	50
Sovran Financial	—	—	—	44	45
First Union Corp.	25	—	25	28	49
First Republic Bank	275	—	275	350	26
Bank America Corp.	1,100	—	1,100	2,004	20
First Interstate	500	180	680	612[a]	54[a]
Security Pacific	558	350	908	980[a]	54[a]
Wells Fargo	550	39	589	850[a]	50[a]
First Wachovia Corp.	50	31	81	55	60

[a]Medium- and long-term loans.

SOURCE: ECLAC, on the basis of data in Thomas Hanley and others, *A Review of Bank Performance: 1988 Edition,* New York, Salomon Brothers, 1988.

undergone reassessment; there is a general awareness that government resources are inefficiently deployed and that private initiative offers more potential for development.[14]

Good intentions obviously are not enough. However, while Latin America's efforts to alter the direction of its development policy and restore creditworthiness do not warrant unreserved applause, it would be equally unfair to ignore the great adjustments that have actually been undertaken and the sacrifices they have involved. Between 1982 and 1988 the region transferred US$179 billion to its creditor countries.[15] Moreover, that outward net transfer of resources from Latin America was policy-induced, for it was made possible only because the region rapidly converted a longstanding trade deficit—averaging nearly US$2 billion per annum in 1978–1981—into a massive trade surplus that averaged US$26 billion per annum in 1982–1988. The trade surpluses, in turn, could not have come about without exchange rate devaluations, adjustments of domestic interest rates, fiscal correction (including the selling off of State enterprises), compression of real wages, etc.[16] Also, the domestic effort must be evaluated in the light of an unhelpful external environment. Aside from protectionism, exports have been hindered by historically low average unit prices, which have caused the value of exports to expand by only a small fraction of the recorded growth of export volume (Table 5).

2.   Itemizing the Setbacks

While there have been signs of progress on some fronts, there have also been setbacks of major importance. In the last six years, the North has lost export markets,[17] and hence jobs and GNP growth, due to a reduced capacity to import in Latin America. OECD firms with direct investments in Latin America have not been able to escape the crisis; their profitability has fallen and corporate uncertainties in Latin America are certainly up.[18] United States banks, which are those with the greatest exposure in Latin America, have lost ground in the international race for dominance of financial markets: expansion into a world of financial liberalization is a capital-intensive endeavour, and the time and resources United States banks must allocate to propping up their slumping Latin American portfolio has clearly put them at a competitive disadvantage. Moreover, although it is difficult to prove definite links, it is also suspected that the increased supply of illicit drugs from Latin America is at least partially linked to shortages of foreign exchange in the region.

The North may also have suffered a serious erosion of the value of its "goodwill" in Latin America. On the one hand, creditors have repeatedly failed to keep their promises of new financing for the debtors; most recently the Baker Plan's 1985 commitment to mobilize US$20 billion of new bank finance and US$9 billion of official loans over three years has remained unfulfilled. Multilateral net disbursements to the region have declined rather than increased, while private bank loans have been few and far between, and heavily concentrated in the hands of only a lucky few within the so-called Baker 15 (Tables 6 and 7). Meanwhile, the IMF's credibility has been further tarnished over the last few years because its programs continue to be associated with economic recession; this has caused more countries to distance themselves from the Fund exactly when in principle the need for its guidance is greater than ever (Table 8). The 1988 Toronto Summit's priority attention to Africa's debt problem, contrasting with the continued inertia on the Latin American front, was also not very helpful.[19] Finally, the United States administration's often unconstructive approach to the Inter-

TABLE 5   **Latin America: Exports of Goods**
(Index, 1980 = 100)

	VALUE ANNUAL AVERAGES			VOLUME ANNUAL AVERAGES			VARIATION[a]	
	1978–1981	1982–1987	1988[b]	1978–1981	1982–1987	1988[b]	VALUE	Volume
Latin America	85	99	115	96	126	156		52.7
Oil-exporters								
Bolivia	82	95	87	95	125	152		50.5
Ecuador	86	70	56	99	74	69		(73.7)
Mexico	87	95	89	102	128	159		35.7
Peru	81	131	134	93	181	228		65.2
Venezuela	81	75	68	98	94	71		(180.5)
	82	70	54	104	85	106		(79.8)
Non-oil-exporters								
Argentina	88	103	139	98	127	159		57.8
Brazil	97	94	94	114	124	131		—
Colombia	89	119	166	95	144	197		65.3
Costa Rica	86	103	150	95	114	174		99.0
Chile	95	97	120	107	114	121		32.3
El Salvador	79	87	146	93	130	158		23.1
Guatemala	88	66	59	96	79	78		(141.2)
Haiti	84	71	73	91	83	83		(176.1)
Honduras	76	93	83	85	112	82		70.4
Nicaragua	89	92	115	95	96	106		309.1
Panama	123	76	48	144	87	45		(102.3)
Paraguay	—	—	—	—	—	—		—
Dominican Republic	96	136	251	93	132	239		99.5
Uruguay	96	80	85	103	103	107		—
	89	102	130	97	121	130		59.1

[a]Variation between annual average of 1978–1981 and 1982–1987. Numbers in parentheses refer to cases where both value and volume declined over the two periods.
[b]1988 data estimate from ECLAC, *Preliminary Overview of the Latin American Economy* (LC/G.1536), Santiago, Chile, January 1989, table 8.
SOURCE: Calculated from data of ECLAC Division of Statistics and Quantitative Analysis.

TABLE 6   **15 Baker Plan Countries: Medium-Term Bank Credits, 1986–1988**[a]
(Millions of Dollars)

	1986	1987	January–August 1988
Total	483	10,004	6,250
Argentina	17	2,100	—
Bolivia	—	—	—
Brazil	—	—	5,200
Chile	—	—[a]	—
Colombia	201	87	1,000
Cote d'Ivoire	—	—	—
Ecuador	220	32;(300)[b]	—
Mexico	—	7,700	—
Morocco	—	25	50
Nigeria	—	—	—
Peru	—	—	—
Philippines	—	—	—
Uruguay	45	—	—
Venezuela	—	30	—
Yugoslavia	—	20	—

[a]In a rescheduling in 1987 Chile secured a "retiming" of its interest payments which saved the country about US$450 million in 1988.
[b]Cancelled.

SOURCE: OECD, *Financial Statistics Monthly*, various numbers, Paris, and ECLAC, Economic Development Division.

TABLE 7   **IMF, World Bank, and IDB: Net Transfers to Latin America**
(Billions of Dollars)

	1980	1981	1982	1983	1984	1985	1986	1987
1. Net disbursements	2.3	2.7	4.0	8.8	7.4	5.3	4.4	2.1
IMF	−0.1	0.1	1.2	5.7	3.3	1.5	0.2	−0.5
World Bank	1.2	1.3	1.4	1.7	2.1	1.9	2.7	1.6
IDB	1.2	1.3	1.4	1.4	2.0	1.9	1.5	1.0
2. Interest charges	1.0	1.2	1.3	1.7	2.2	2.7	3.6	4.0
IMF	0.1	0.1	0.1	0.3	0.6	0.9	0.9	0.8
World Bank	0.6	0.7	0.8	0.9	1.0	1.1	1.7	2.1
IDB	0.3	0.4	0.4	0.5	0.6	0.7	1.0	1.1
3. Net transfers (1–2)[a]	1.1	1.5	2.8	7.2	5.2	2.6	0.7	−1.9
IMF	−0.2	—	1.2	5.4	2.7	0.6	−0.8	−1.3
World Bank	0.5	0.6	0.6	0.8	1.1	0.8	1.0	−0.5
IDB	0.8	0.9	1.0	1.0	1.4	1.2	0.5	−0.1

[a]May not sum properly due to rounding.

SOURCE: Calculated from data provided by SELA.

TABLE 8   **Latin America: Participation in Multilateral Adjustment Programs**

	IMF		WORLD BANK	
	1982–1983	1987	1982–1983	1987
Total	13	6	1	9
Oil-exporters	3	2	—	3
Bolivia	—	x	—	x
Ecuador	x	—	—	x
Mexico	x	x	—	x
Peru	x	—	—	—
Venezuela	—	—	—	—
Non-oil-exporters	10	4	1	6
Argentina	x	x[a]	—	x
Brazil	x	—[b]	x	x
Colombia	—	—	—	x
Costa Rica	x	x	—	x
Chile	x	x	—	x
El Salvador	—	—	—	—
Guatemala	x	—	—	—
Haiti	x	—	—	—
Honduras	x	—	—	—
Nicaragua	—	—	—	—
Panama	x	—	—	—
Paraguay	—	—	—	—
Dominican Republic	x	—	—	—
Uruguay	x	x	—	x

[a]"Out," at least transitorily in 1988.
[b]"In" in 1988.
SOURCE: ECLAC, Economic Development Division, based on the respective institution's data.

American Development Bank's problems has been a severe source of contention in hemispheric relations.

The setbacks for Latin America since the outbreak of the crisis have been very dramatic. Who would have imagined back in 1982 that by 1988 Latin America's per capita gross domestic product would be nearly 7% below the 1980 figure?[20] While domestic savings have been higher than ever before, since 1982 the region's domestic investment—vital to any serious campaign to make Latin America's goods and services more internationally competitive—has been 22% below the average annual level recorded in 1978–1981 (Table 9). On a per capita basis the investment performance has been even worse: in 1987 such outlays were the highest of the six years of the crisis, yet even so per capita investment in that year was the lowest since 1971![21] Inflation has increased spectacularly in Latin America; the

TABLE 9   **Gross Domestic Savings and Investment in Latin America**[a]

	SAVINGS INDEX 1980 = 100		INVESTMENT INDEX 1980 = 100	
	1978–1981	1982–1987	1978–1981	1982–1987
Latin America	96	107	94	73
Oil-exporters	—	—	—	—
Bolivia	91	57	129	64
Ecuador	92	114	93	74
Mexico	94	113	92	69
Peru	95	79	89	80
Venezuela	107	83	117	74
Non-oil-exporters	—	—	—	—
Argentina	112	104	88	51
Brazil	90	110	91	78
Colombia	97	113	99	110
Costa Rica	103	184	85	70
Chile	82	122	90	57
El Salvador	85	74	134	85
Guatemala	94	98	117	77
Haiti	91	150	96	107
Honduras	101	83	98	63
Nicaragua	—	—	93	134
Panama	80	100	94	86
Paraguay	83	69	93	85
Dominican Republic	107	151	92	95
Uruguay	123	155	91	50

[a]Market prices and 1980 dollars.

SOURCE: Calculated from data of ECLAC, Division of Statistics and Quantitative Analysis.

regional average was nearly 500% in 1988, with rates reaching three digits for two countries (Argentina and Brazil) and four digits for another two (Nicaragua and Peru). Real wages have for the most part been depressed, while official unemployment is disturbingly high.[22] Although the social repercussions of the crisis are hard to quantify, there are studies which suggest an important deterioration on many fronts and confirm what the casual observer senses when visiting almost any Latin American capital city.[23]

Finally, the evolution of the debt burden indicators has not been entirely encouraging. After seven years of costly adjustments the region's debt-to-export ratio in 1988 (339%) was 60% higher than in 1980. On the other hand, the interest/exports ratio had fallen to 28% by 1988, and although that was still extremely burdensome, it was nevertheless the lowest level recorded since 1981 (Table 10).

TABLE 10 **Latin America: External Debt**

	DEBT[a]	DEBT/EXPORTS		DEBT/GDP		INTEREST/EXPORTS		ARREARS	
	1988[b]	1981	1988[b]	1981	1988	1981	1988[b]	1987	Sept. 1988
Latin America	401.4	247	339	46	53	28	28	x	x
Oil-exporters	159.2	220	343	—	—	23	28	x	x
Bolivia	3.9	348	595	—	—	35	35	x	x
Ecuador	105	202	388	51	80	23	33	x	x
Mexico	96.7	259	339	52	62	29	29	—	—
Peru	16.2	239	442	45	70	24	22	x	x
Venezuela	31.9	160	290	56	49	13	26	—	—
Non-oil-exporters	242.1	273	337	—	—	34	28	x	x
Argentina	56.8	329	541	55	81	36	40	x	x
Brazil	114.6	313	321	39	42	40	30	—	—
Colombia	15.9	199	218	24	33	22	21	x	—
Costa Rica	4.1	229	260	90	108	28	20	—	x
Chile	19.1	311	236	73	74	39	23	x	—
Cuba	(5.7)[c]	—	—	—	—	—	—	—	—
El Salvador	1.9	174	185	—	—	8	10	x	x
Guatemala	2.8	96	225	—	—	8	13	—	x
Haiti	0.8	155	276	—	—	3	7	x	x
Honduras	3.2	180	290	—	—	14	14	—	x
Nicaragua	6.7	464	2 068	—	—	37	103	x	x
Panama	4.2	92	—	—	—	—	—	x	x
Paraguay	2.2	171	324	—	—	15	12	—	x
Dominican Republic	3.8	168	220	—	—	19	13	x	x
Uruguay	6.1	183	354	51	97	13	23	x	—

[a]Billions of dollars.
[b]ECLAC, *Preliminary Overview of the Latin American Economy, 1988* (LC/G.1536), Santiago, Chile, January 1989.
[c]Excluded from totals. Represents debt with so-called market countries in 1987.
SOURCE: ECLAC, Economic Development Division.

II. WHY THE SKEWED DISTRIBUTION OF COSTS BETWEEN CREDITORS AND DEBTORS?

The review of the situation since 1982 suggests some improvements, but also points to serious setbacks for the creditor and debtor countries alike. Yet the review also highlights a distribution of benefits and costs that is clearly skewed against the debtor countries. In effect, thanks to a growth-oriented adjustment, private banks now only have a problem in Latin America; the countries of the region, in contrast, have a development crisis of ever deepening proportions. Why?

Impatient creditors often point to: (i) bad economic policies in the debtor countries, coupled with their excessive debt accumulation in the 1970s; and (ii) an unwillingness in the 1980s to make and persist with the hard economic decisions needed to turn the Latin American economies around. Moreover, there often exists by implication the notion that if creditors provide comprehensive relief for the debtors this will raise moral hazard, as well as giving rise to a tendency to abuse the degrees of freedom won thanks to the relaxation of the efforts to restructure the region's economies and make them more competitive internationally.

The debtors, on the other hand, tend to focus on the harsh external environment and the weight of the outward transfer of resources.[24] The argument is by now well developed. Expenditure switching policies normally take a great deal of time to work their way through the economies, especially in structurally uncompetitive ones. Thus, the large trade surplus needed to effectively service debts at high real rates of interest can be achieved in the short term only with a disproportionate amount of import compression and domestic economic recession. Moreover, since it is inherently difficult for developing countries to quickly raise domestic savings (especially during an economic slowdown), the outward transfer of resources tends to have its counterpart in reduced investment and social expenditure, which is counterproductive, because it hampers economic restructuring and future capacity to service debts. Furthermore, the changing of relative prices for the purpose of making an external transfer tends to aggravate inflationary pressures. This situation is complicated by the fact that debt servicing is largely the responsibility of the public sector, giving rise to an internal budgetary transfer problem. As demonstrated even in the United States, tax and public expenditure decisions belong in extremely delicate political terrain. If there is no broad domestic political consensus to accept a decisive increase in taxes and a lowering of public expenditure to accommodate the transfer, the State must mobilize the necessary resources through an inflationary tax. This is a risky strategy that can easily degenerate into hyperinflation.[25]

As in most polarizing issues, the truth probably lies in between the extremes of the arguments of the two groups. To overcome the development crisis and put Latin American debtors back on track, adequate and sustained internal effort is unquestionably a necessary first step in a successful restructuring process. Thus far the internal efforts have been of varying intensity and duration in the region, but such efforts have certainly been made. As mentioned earlier, domestic policy has induced a transfer of resources to the creditor countries of US$179 billion, or more than 4% of GDP per annum. To illustrate the magnitude of the transfer, suffice it to recall that this exceeds the outward net transfer forced on defeated Germany under the 1919 Treaty of Versailles (2.5%) and defeated France under the 1871 Treaty of Frankfurt (2.3%).[26] The debtors also deserve some patience from the creditor countries: to turn around a development strategy that worked reasonably well for 50-odd years is much more than a six-year project.[27] In addition, the economic transformation is being attempted simultaneously with a fragile transition to political democracy. A peripatetic course might be a likely feature of any process of economic transformation built on a very weak and emerging institutional framework.

Moreover, it is always difficult to isolate the contribution made to economic recovery by domestic efforts from the effects of the external environment. If that environment had been clearly supportive of the debtors' efforts to adjust and restructure, one could more comfortably point an accusing finger at lack of serious domestic effort. But in most respects the external environment has been extremely unsupportive of Latin America's adjustment policies. Of critical importance in this regard is the fact that the region's adjustment process has been badly underfinanced from the outset of the crisis.[28] Indeed, whether it be the formula of 7% annual expansion of bank lending that emerged in 1982, or the Baker Plan's 2 1/2% per annum formula, financing volumes have not satisfied the modest targets that the creditors have variously committed themselves to.[29] Underfinancing for the debtors translates into overtransferring of resources to creditors. The transfer problem is therefore a real one that has undermined the efficiency of the debtor countries' policies for adjustment and restructuring.

III. THE MOST CONSPICUOUS WEAK LINK: HALF-HEARTED INTERNATIONAL PUBLIC POLICY

A systemic debt crisis is a collective problem. In these circumstances, negative externalities emanating from the private market are notoriously indiscriminating, drawing into the problem prudent and imprudent lenders/borrowers alike, and even passing serious costs onto those not even remotely involved in the problem.[30] Moreover, rational individual responses to the situation can be very damaging to the collective good and escalate the costs for all. Hence the need for public intervention in the marketplace, first, to stabilize private expectations, and second to assist in restructuring the market agents (borrowers, lenders, or both) in a way that is functional to the renewed solvency of the system and to global recovery with minimum social disruption. Given the opportunities for "free riding" when externalities exist, and its adverse effects on the efficiency of any institutional arrangement, effective public solutions often are to varying degrees coercive in nature.[31] All these principles are usually put into practice when severe financial strain emerges in the domestic markets of the creditor countries.[32]

The international debt crisis that emerged in 1982 has in fact been subject to international public management.[33] Yet, the effectiveness of the latter as an instrument in the promotion of global prosperity and development in an interdependent world has been severely limited. This is because the international debt management strategy has not evolved much beyond a lender-of-last-resort function designed to keep the Northern banking system stable. Indeed, with time it has become increasingly obvious that it is the sporadic threat of a destabilizing default, rather than the sustained requirements of financing economic restructuring in the debtor country, that brings forth new credits. The faster the banks have strengthened their balance sheets, the tighter external financing has become. Meanwhile, however, official lenders have not been given the means to pick up the slack; indeed, they are aggravating the problem as the net flow of resources from these institutions has now turned negative (Table 7).

The latest phase of the international debt strategy—the so-called Market Menu Approach—does not rectify the situation. To the extent that it represents a public policy initiative at all, it repeats the basic flaw of the earlier stages: the day to day mechanics of a supposedly multilateral debt management program remain biased toward the narrow objective of securing an orderly adjustment of private financial portfolios in the North.

The initial phase of the debt management strategy was characterized by a "holding action" designed to enable the international financial system to avoid accounting losses via commercially priced reschedulings and new money packages. Now, the latest phase is primarily oriented to the gradual adjustment of the banks' asset values and enhanced risk diversification through schemes involving debt swaps and securitization. As for the macroeconomic issue of finance to support economic reforms, investment, growth, and restored creditworthiness in the debtor countries, it largely remains a passive residual to this process. It is in this sense that the Market Menu is basically a private creditors' menu.

As ECLAC has shown in a recent study, from the perspective of the debtors' macroeconomic needs the Market Menu may list some interesting "appetizers," but the "main entrées" simply are not there.[34] The market-based approach of the menu relies on the principle of voluntary responses from the individual creditors, with little more than moral support from their governments. However, conventional market financing is procyclical in nature and therefore new capital will be unlikely to flow spontaneously to Latin America in a macroeconomically significant volume as long as potential creditors see big discounts of 50% or more on existing debt.

As for the new and more exotic instruments designed around portfolio adjustments, their natural development will be only gradual. It is well known that private markets operate at the margin and each new instrument must start small even under favourable circumstances.[35] In Latin America advance is further slowed by complex free rider and international legal, tax, and accounting problems in the market, as well as many institutional investors' lack of familiarity with the region. There are also demand constraints in Latin America as questions of sovereignty and monetary control limit the potential expansion of some of the creditors' preferred instruments in the Market Menu.[36]

Another consideration is that the bulk of the proposed debt reduction instruments in the menu act on the principal. Since countries are not amortizing debt anyway, the immediate impact of the transaction on the balance of payments is indirect, in the form of reduced interest payments; hence relief will be marginal until the cumulative scope of the reduction of the principal becomes very large.[37] The menu also has the serious drawback that voluntary market transactions are effected only sporadically, making it difficult to predict the timing of conversions, their distribution among the different countries, the amount of relief for the balance of payments, and the effectiveness of the conversion with respect to the support of a domestic program for economic reform and restructuring.

In sum, when left to their own devices, private markets naturally unwind from a large debt overhang only slowly. The amount of debt swapped and converted at a discount into other types of assets will undoubtedly rise markedly in the years ahead.[38] Yet for the immediate future the Market Menu Approach—at least as currently formulated—will only chip away at the corners of the region's problems because it does not address the urgent central macroeconomic issue of today: how to finance in a sustained and predictable way the economic reforms and new investments that Latin America will need to initiate growth now and begin to restore its capacity to service foreign debts. From the standpoint of a collective economic problem and collective solutions, the Market Menu Approach therefore clearly represents unambitious public policy. Indeed, in some essential ways the market menu seems to have thrust us back to the 1930s, when debtor countries and private creditors groped inefficiently for 20 years for a way to unwind from the debt overhang of that period.[39]

IV.   WHERE DO WE GO FROM HERE?

The Latin American debt problem should be viewed in its proper context, as a collective international problem: at a time when private sources of credit for Latin America have collapsed, the reliance on voluntary private "micro" responses from the menu to resolve a systemic macroeconomic financial problem promises to delay the adjustment of both debtor and creditor countries and raise costs for the international community as a whole. The systemic aspects of the problem give theoretical and practical support to the idea that there is a need for more aggressive production of international public goods designed to accelerate the adjustment of debtor and creditor countries alike, as well as to ensure that costs are distributed in such a way that they can be paid for out of future growth of the global economic system.

The reason why the proposal for a multilateral debt conversion facility has repeatedly appeared in the debate about debt, and will not go away despite rather heated rejections by the leaders of the international debt strategy, is that it is the most complete expression of the systemic nature of the debt problem in the Western Hemisphere and the social efficacy of a collective solution.[40] Obviously, many of the details of such a complex facility, as well as auxiliary regulatory, accounting, and tax measures, need to be refined, but the basic thrust of the proposed initiative—an orderly and macroeconomically significant reduction of the present value of debt in return for orderly adjustment of economic policy—is in the best spirit of good public economic policymaking in an interdependent world. As an interim step to negotiating such a complex facility, one could envision—under the auspices of IMF-approved exchange restrictions within the context of an official standby program—an immediate temporary freezing of interest payments (with forced capitalization of the difference) at levels consistent with specified targets of investment and growth in the debtor economies.

A less ambitious public policy could consist simply of the approval of ad hoc public guarantees on bank loans and market debt reduction instruments, coupled with supportive modification of tax and accounting rules for the banks. This could grant the credit enhancement needed to bring a volume of conversions and buybacks sufficient to generate rapid and significant balance-of-payments financing for the debtor countries. Bolivia's recent debt buyback at 11 cents on the dollar is a good example of how ambitious intervention by the international public sector can bring about a quick and substantial reduction of the debt overhang.

Ad hoc guarantees, while more effective than the hands-off approach of the current Market Menu, are not without their drawbacks, however. On the one hand, the distribution of relief among countries may be arbitrarily based on political factors, while the timing of that relief remains uncertain. On the other, since ad hoc arrangements tackle free rider problems and other negative externalities only in a piecemeal fashion, their cumulative cost over the medium term could be actually more than a full-fledged debt reduction facility today.

Should Latin America promote these and other collective international initiatives? Certainly yes. Should Latin America bank its future development on the imminent emergence of comprehensive public initiatives?

Probably not. Collective solutions for a large number of individual economic agents are notoriously difficult to organize when customs, traditions, legal standards, strategies, and economic circumstances differ. To act collectively, there must be a common sense of extreme stress. This sense of stress existed in Northern financial circles in 1982 when virtually all national banking systems were vulnerable to defaults in Latin America; this explains the amazingly quick and extraordinarily tight global coordination among the creditors to avoid default in the early years of the crisis.[41] However, as the banks' vulnerability to default has receded, and as interest in Latin America's markets has become increasingly overshadowed by developments in vibrant Asia, as well as in the emerging new Common Market of Europe and the free trade area of North America, even that limited coordination has broken down into an extremely muddled approach, where each creditor is now increasingly set free to cut its own deal. Indeed, in most respects the so-called Market Menu legitimizes the serious de facto breakdown in coordination among creditors and their governments and multilateral agencies.[42]

Collective solutions also typically have immediate costs, whereas the benefits are spread out more gradually. Serious financial and external adjustment problems limit the United States' ability to respond to difficulties in the hemisphere with new money, at least on the scale that we had become accustomed to in the 1950s and 1960s. Meanwhile, it remains to be seen to what degree Japan and Europe will be willing to fill the financial void in the region, and whether this can be done without creating serious conflict over the traditional distribution of political spheres of influence.

New public initiatives therefore could be very slow in emerging, or else they could be of insufficient scale to tackle the development crisis in the region. But this does not mean that the Market Menu is the only game in town. Indeed, the debtors have gradually developed their own menu of options which includes various types of moratoria on debt service payments. Notwithstanding recent developments in Brazil, more than half of the countries in Latin America are now deploying this latter approach (Table 10). It is also important to remember that most of the recent debt restructurings carried out under the official Market Menu have evolved out of concessions by the creditors, designed to either coax a country out of a moratorium, or prevent it from entering one.[43] Moreover, these agreements can represent more than a temporary respite from a threat of future moratorium only to the degree that they adequately address the underlying capacity to pay of the debtor. So far, only the recent Bolivian agreement would unequivocally fall into this category.

The debtors' menu of options should not be underestimated. In the past an organized formal or informal threat to impose full or partial limits on payments has proven difficult partly because of the lack of internal consensus on what to do about the outward net transfer of resources. It is possible to observe, however, a series of interesting shifts in political alliances in a number of important debtor countries which suggest that that consensus may now be emerging in more countries as we move into the seventh year of the development crisis of the region.

In addition, the debtor countries will gradually learn the secrets of how to sustain growth in a state of full or partial moratorium. Most earlier limits on payments evolved out of the force of events, set off by a poor domestic economic policy, or were mistakenly conceived as an end in and of itself, which only served to stimulate self-defeating populism. Now, however, there are signs of greater sophistication. Perhaps because of some recent bad experiences, more countries seem to realize that, in order to be a successful instrument for economic recovery, a temporary moratorium must evolve out of a coherent economic program designed to vigorously correct internal and external disequilibria. Furthermore, the limit on payments must be partial and conciliatory in nature, with lines of communication to the creditors kept open and constructive proposals offered to them for resolving the problem in a context compatible with an explicit growth-oriented economic reform program of the debtor country. To the extent that debt service is forcibly rechannelled into a coherent and sustainable economic program and gratuitous conflict is avoided, the country enhances the possibility of eventually winning a more realistic settlement on the outstanding debt.

V.   CONCLUSIONS

We have seen that the outward transfer of resources from Latin America hinders adjustment, growth, and economic restructuring through its aggravation of either the foreign exchange constraint, the savings/fiscal constraint, or both. In the absence of systematic payment guarantees from the creditor governments, the voluntary market options in the Menu Approach promise to reduce that transfer burden only gradually over a long haul and with a high degree of uncertainty regarding the amount and timing of relief, as well as its distribution among the debtors. In the meantime, the external finance requirements for supporting macroeconomic programs of growth and restructuring remain unsatisfied. It is thus no surprise that there are very few countries in Latin America which have so far been able to sustain a process of adequate growth with price stability.

An international strategy for growth and reconstruction which benefits only a few problem debtors is clearly a half-hearted international public policy. Yet, it could be unproductive for the debtor countries of Latin America to sit back and wait for the creditor governments to rescue them from their plight with more ambitious international public initiatives. We have seen that collective solutions to a systemic problem emerge more out of a sense of urgency than a sense of good will. As long as the Northern financial systems can successfully adjust to the debt overhang with minimum public assistance, and as long as the economic problems of the region do not provoke open manifestations of political radicalization in the debtor countries, it will be difficult for a comprehensive public policy response to emerge from the heterogeneous bloc of creditor countries. Clearly, then, the solution to Latin America's crisis of debt and development must, more than ever, come from "inside" the region. This approach is moreover aided today by the serious cracks and disputes that have been developing in the creditors' negotiating bloc, coupled with the lessening importance of the Latin American portfolio in the global economy, because this state of affairs affords more freedom to the debtor countries regarding the formulation of policies designed to lower the outward transfer of resources.

Countries undoubtedly will want to approach the reduction of this transfer in different ways. A minority of countries will find it appropriate to work entirely within the official framework of the Market Menu Approach, periodically rescheduling debts on commercial terms, seeking involuntary loans, and participating in debt reduction schemes voluntarily sanctioned by the creditors. Other countries, however, will decide, or be forced by events, to limit the transfer through a partial or total stoppage of payments. In some cases the limit (or threat of a limit) on debt service will be a very transitory bargaining tactic designed to achieve more favourable conditions within the officially sanctioned debt management scheme, but in others it will be a longer-term policy stance designed to force the creditors to share in the costs of a medium-term program of economic growth and restructuring.[44] A prolonged partial or full moratorium will, of course, drive down secondary market prices of the debt to the floor and thereby give the countries more leverage in establishing the pace and discounted terms of eventual debt settlements.[45]

As for cooperation among the debtor countries of the region, past experience suggests that this can be only of very limited scope in view of the heterogeneous conditions of the borrowers. However, as the common stress of the development crisis intensifies, the barriers standing in the way of regional cooperation may be overcome, bringing forth more effective joint initiatives to reduce the net outward transfer of resources.

In sum, the classic market mechanism for resolving a debt overhang—default—was temporarily suspended by the unprecedented international debt management strategy of the early 1980s. However, as we move through the seventh year of the region's debt servicing difficulties, some of the classic market dynamics of the 1930s seem to be taking hold. Private credit markets have failed and do not discriminate well among the debtors, while new credit is withheld regardless of the countries' economic policies and capacity to pay. Just as in the 1930s, some countries in Latin America are normally servicing their foreign debt without much refinancing, but most are not. Trading of debt paper has accelerated, and secondary market prices reflect large discounts. Some of the debtors' economies manage to overcome the external constraints, while others do not. This is clearly a very unsatisfactory solution to the debt overhang, with unnecessary costs for debtors and creditors alike. However, it is the only realistic option until there is more far-sighted political leadership in the creditor countries.

NOTES

1. During 1983–1988 growth of GNP in the industrialized countries averaged 3.5% per annum. Given the voters' preference for continuity in the political leadership of the North, this rate of growth would seem to be satisfactory. However, as Sidney Dell remarked to the author, the performance is not satisfactory when viewed from the needs of an interdependent world: OECD economic growth has been highly volatile, uncertain as to its sustainability, and has imparted relatively little buoyancy to the debtor's terms of trade. The growth rate is calculated from data in IMF, *World Economic Outlook,* advance copy (Washington, D.C.: IMF September 25, 1988), p. 71.
2. For an analysis of these international facilities see Philip Wellons, *Passing the Buck* (Boston: Harvard Business School Press, 1987), chap. 7. For an analysis of how these facilities were applied during the Latin American crisis see ECLAC, *External Debt in Latin America* (Boulder, Colo.: Lynne Rienner Publishers, 1985), chap. 3, and ECLAC, *The Evolution of the External Debt Problem in Latin America and the Caribbean,* Estudios e Informes de la CEPAL series, no. 72 (LC/G.1487/Rev.1–P), Santiago, Chile, 1988, United Nations publication, sales no.: E.88.II.G.10, chap. 1.
3. The increase in loan loss reserves was induced by actions of Citibank, which raised reserves by US$3 billion in the second quarter of 1987. For competitive reasons, most other United States banks with Latin American exposure copied Citibank to one degree or another. Consequently, United States banks reported US$11 billion in losses in the second quarter, which represented the industry's worst performance since the 1930s. See ECLAC, "Economic Survey of the United States of America," Washington Office, August 24, 1988, p. 29, published later as *Economic Survey of the United States, 1987* (LC/G.1477; LC/WAS/L.3/Rev.1), Santiago, Chile, February 1989.
4. See Thomas Hanley et al., *Developing Country Exposures—Have Investors Recognized the Degree of Progress Made by Money Center Banks?* (New York: Salomon Brothers, July 21, 1988), p. 2.
5. For the situation of European banks, see Gunner Wiegand, *Western Europe and the Latin American Debt Crisis,* working paper no. 12, Madrid, 1988, p. 20.
6. *Daily Telegraph* (UK), "Time to Break the Cycle of Third World Debt," August 30, 1988.
7. At the beginning of 1988 this process further intensified. In April–June 1988 the largest United States banks had loan charge-offs of US$0.9 billion, up from US$0.6 billion in the first quarter of the year. See T. Hanley and others, op. cit., p. 2.

8. Debt/equity swaps in Argentina, Brazil, Chile, and Mexico totalled US$5 billion in 1987. Peter Truell, "Cutting Losses," *Wall Street Journal*, September 23, 1988, supplement, p. 10 R.

9. In the 1988 debt rescheduling of Brazil roughly 100 banks subscribed to exit bonds amounting to about US$1 billion. The bonds carried a 6% interest rate for 25 years.

10. Early in 1988 Mexico converted US$3.67 billion of commercial bank debt into US$2.56 billion of bonds, which represented a 30% discount. The bonds had a single 20-year maturity and carried an interest rate of 1.63% over LIBOR. The principal of the bond was secured by the government's purchase of a 20-year United States Treasury zero-coupon bond for an amount equivalent to the outstanding Mexican government bonds.

11. In March 1988 Bolivia arranged to buy back US$318 million of its public commercial bank debt—nearly 50% of the total with these lenders—at a price of 11 cents on the dollar. The resources for the buyback arrangement came from OECD countries. The operation was facilitated by the establishment of a special escrow account in the IMF for the depositing of OECD contributions. Meanwhile, in mid-1988 Chile negotiated with its banks an arrangement to use up to US$500 million of its international reserves to buy back bank debt at a discount. In November 1988 Chile bought back US$299 of bank debt at 56 cents on the dollar.

12. The most recent manifestation of this was the willingness of the World Bank to sponsor a restructuring loan for the government of Argentina even though the Argentine economic authorities could not reach prior terms with the IMF for a standby agreement. See Stephen Fidler, "World Bank Agrees Argentine Loan," *Financial Times*, September 26, 1988.

13. The four democratic governments in the 1970s were Colombia, Costa Rica, the Dominican Republic, and Venezuela. It should be added that Ecuador's democratic institutions were restored in April 1979.

14. Commercial bankers recognize the emergence of this new consensus in the region. See, for instance, John Reed, "New Money in New Ways," *International Economy* (October/November 1987): 50.

15. See ECLAC, *Preliminary Overview of the Latin American Economy, 1988* (LC/G.1536), Santiago, Chile, January 3, 1989, table 15.

16. For a detailed analysis of the process of adjustment in Latin America, see Andrés Bianchi, Robert Devlin, and Joseph Ramos, "El Proceso de Ajuste en la América Latina," *El Trimestre Económico*, 44, 216 (October/December 1987).

17. One study has shown that by 1985 United States exports to Latin America were 28% below levels recorded in 1981 and 47% below the potential export level. The latter is defined as maintenance of a constant export share vis-à-vis GDP. See Joint Economic Committee, United States Congress, "Trade Deficits, Foreign Debt and Sagging Growth," Washington, D.C., September 1986, table 6.

18. For example, rates of return on United States direct investment in Latin America declined from an average of 17% in 1980–1981 to 6% in 1982–1985. See United Nations Centre on Transnational Corporations, *Transnational Corporations in World Development: Trends and Prospects* (ST/CTC/89), New York, 1988, United Nations publication, sales no. 88.II.A.7, p. 82.

19. The scheme for African debtors allows creditor governments to write off one-third of the debts, or cut interest rates by half or 3.5 percentage points, or lengthen the amortization period to 25 years. The plan has been criticized as not being radical enough for these problem debtors. See *Financial Times*, "Africa's Debt Burden," September 30, 1988, p. 18.
20. ECLAC, *Preliminary Overview*, op. cit., table 3.
21. ECLAC, Division of Statistics and Quantitative Analysis.
22. Data from ECLAC, *Preliminary Overview*, op. cit.
23. World Bank, "Poverty in Latin America: The Impact of Depression," Washington, D.C., 1986.
24. For a more complete analysis see ECLAC, *Restrictions on Sustained Development in Latin America and the Caribbean and the Requisites for Overcoming Them* (LC/G.1488(SES.22/3)/Rev. 1), Santiago, Chile, February 9, 1988. The study that helped to shift the analytical focus of the debt debate to the question of the transfer problem is Helmut Reisen and Axel Van Trotsenberg, *The Budgetary and Transfer Problem*, Paris, Organization for Economic Co-operation and Development (OECD), 1988.
25. An analysis of the complex relationship between debt service and inflation can be found in Rudiger Dornbusch, "Debt, Inflation and Growth: The Case of Argentina," Washington, D.C., International Monetary Fund, February 16, 1988.
26. See Bianchi, Devlin and Ramos, op. cit., p. 891.
27. The per capita GDP in Latin America grew by a respectable 3% per annum over 1950–1980.
28. Ground has focussed on this issue. Conventional criteria suggest that the transitory components of external shocks should be financed. However, according to Ground's estimates, the external finance made available to Latin America over 1982–1985 covered only 37%, 25%, 36%, and 16% of the respective transitory components of the adverse external shocks in that period. See Richard Ground, "The origin and magnitude of the recessionary adjustment in Latin America," *CEPAL Review*, no. 30 (LC/G.1441), Santiago, Chile, December 1986, p. 72.
29. When the crisis first broke out, private banks, in conjunction with the IMF, committed themselves to an annual expansion of 7% in their credit exposure in the region. The actual expansion in the first round of reschedulings came closer to 6% and fell dramatically thereafter. Then, in September 1985, Secretary Baker of the United States Treasury established a new target for bank credit expansion of $2^1/2$% per annum for 3 years. This goal was not fulfilled; indeed, the response of the banks was to begin a sustained reduction of their exposure in the region. Moreover, the slack was not picked up by multilateral and bilateral lenders.
30. Colombia is a good illustration of this problem: with a debt-to-export ratio of only a little over 2:1 and a debt-to-GDP ratio of 34%, it has had tremendous difficulty securing fresh credit from the private banks.
31. Detailed analysis of the problems of collective action and public goods can be found in James Buchanan, *The Demand and Supply of Public Goods* (Chicago: Rand McNally and Co., 1968), chap. 5.
32. The collective nature of the problem even manifests itself in isolated payments crises of individual firms. Because of this, bankruptcy laws often impose collec-

tive solutions upon a firm's creditors. See Thomas Jackson, *The Logic and Limits of Bankruptcy Law* (Cambridge, Mass.: Harvard University Press, 1986).

33. By now the nature of the coordinated policies of the IMF, OECD Central Banks, and Treasuries with the creditor banks and debtor governments is so well known that it is not necessary to summarize it here. If desired, however, details may be found in ECLAC, *External Debt in Latin America*, op.cit., pp. 47–86.

34. ECLAC, *The Evolution*, op. cit., chapter 11.

35. See Mahesh Kotecha, "Repackaging Third World Debt," *Standard and Poor's International Credit Week,* August 1987, p. 9; and Kenneth Telljohann, "Analytical Framework," *Prospects for Securitization of Less Developed Country Loan* (New York: Salomon Brothers, June 1987), p. 11.

36. "Negative side effects" are particularly complex in the popular debt-equity swaps. See Group of Thirty, *Finance for Developing Countries,* New York, 1987.

37. As an illustration, the original goal of the Mexican-Morgan Guaranty bond operation of early 1988 was to convert US$20 billion of debt. If this goal had been attained at an average (rather optimistic) discount of 40%, something of the order of US$350 million of net interest payments would have been saved. While this type of operation had many merits, including the banks' formal recognition of market discounts, its significance as a vehicle for macroeconomic financing is less apparent in view of the US$7 billion interest burden with the private lenders. In any event, as mentioned in note 10, the banks' reception to the plan was less enthusiastic than had originally been hoped for. A detailed analysis of the Mexican bond offer can be found in Kenneth Telljohann and Richard Buckholz, *The Mexican Bond Exchange Offer* (New York, Salomon Brothers, January 1988).

38. The volume of secondary market trading in 1987 is estimated to have been about US$12 billion. Some expect that figure to rise to US$25 billion in 1988. To put these figures in perspective it must be remembered that they include considerable double counting and therefore do not mirror actual debt conversions. The figures also are still small relative to the estimated US$300–350 billion of problem LDC debt in the international commercial banking system. See Richard Lawrence, "Banker Proposes Solution to Argentina, Brazilian Debt," *Journal of Commerce,* September 28, 1988; and Eugenio Lahera, *La Conversión de la Deuda Externa: Antecedentes, Evolución y Pérspectivas* (LC/R.614), UNDP/ECLAC Project "Finance for Development," Santiago, Chile, ECLAC, September 1987.

39. For a good review of the portfolio adjustments of debtors and creditors in the 1930s and 1940s, see Marilyn Skiles, *Latin American International Loan Defaults in the 1930s: Lessons for the 1980s?*, Federal Reserve Bank of New York, research paper no. 8812, April 1988.

40. In the contemporary debate early proposals were made by Peter Kenen and Richard Weinert. Kenen proposed conversion at a discount, while Weinert proposed conversion at par with below-market interest rates, on the grounds that this would spread the banks' losses over time. See Peter Kenen, "A Bailout for the Banks," *The New York Times,* March 1983 and Richard Weinert, "Banks and Bankruptcy," *Foreign Policy.* no. 50, Second Quarter, 1983, pp. 128–149. Kenen has recently updated and expanded his proposal. See Peter Kenen, "A Proposal for Reducing the Debt Burden of Developing Countries," Princeton, N.J., Princeton University, March 1987. Other people proposing a global debt conver-

sion facility are: John La Falce, "Third World Debt Crises: The Urgent Need to Confront Reality," *Congressional Record*, Washington, D.C., 133, 34, (March 5, 1987); Don Pease, "A Congressional Plan to Solve the Debt Problem," *International Economy* (March/April 1988): 98–105; James Robinson, "A Comprehensive Agenda for LDC Debt and World Trade Growth," London, American Express Bank, March 1988; Percy Mistry, "Third World Debt," May 1987; and Arjun Sengupta, "A Proposal for a Debt Adjustment Facility," Washington, D.C., IMF, March 8, 1988.

41. The coordination was so good that Latin Americans began to perceive the formation of a creditors' cartel. See OAS, "Desarrollo Integral y Democracia en América Latina y el Caribe: Ideas y Agenda para la Acción," Washington, D.C., September 28, 1987, p. 23.

42. The breakdown of the cartel reflects itself in the growing disputes among all parties in the creditor bloc about how to share responsibilities in the management of the debt issue. Serious public disagreements have broken out among the private banks, between the banks, their governments, and the multilateral lenders, among the creditor governments, between the creditor governments and multilateral lenders, and even between the World Bank and IMF (over the recent World Bank loan program in Argentina, mentioned in note 12). For an analysis of the breakdown of the creditor coordination, see ECLAC, *The Evolution,* op. cit.

43. This manifested itself clearly during the fourth round of reschedulings. See ECLAC, *Economic Survey of Latin America and the Caribbean, 1987: Advance Summary* (LC/G.1511), Santiago, Chile, pp. 42–60.

44. There are various ways a moratorium can be established. For some techniques that draw partially on the experience of the 1930s, see ECLAC, ibid.

45. Again, this is what happened in the 1930s. Indeed, some countries stopped debt service to accumulate resources for a buyback of debt at very low market prices. See M. Skiles, op. cit.

13

Defunding Latin America: Reverse Transfers by the Multilateral Lending Agencies

Richard E. Feinberg

The international financial institutions (IFIs) must address two key issues as they confront the debt and development problems of Latin America. Both issues centre on the urgent need to reduce the transfer of resources (approximately $20 billion each year) from Latin America to the international financial system[1]: first, whether the IFIs can reverse the disturbing trend of joining the commercial banks as net financial drains on the capital-short region; and second, what role they should play in reducing the persistent transfer of financial resources from Latin America to private lenders.

Both these issues are central to the basic agenda of the International Monetary Fund (IMF), the World Bank,[2] and the Inter-American Development Bank (IDB). These institutions were established in part to transfer capital from North to South (for the IMF such transfers are "temporary," until a balance-of-payments problem has been resolved), and to catalyse the movement of private capital to profitable investments in developing nations. The challenge facing the IFIs in the 1990s is to fulfil these aims in the face of new and difficult circumstances.

TRENDS IN IFI RESOURCE TRANSFERS

The transfer of wealth from North to South makes sense on both economic and moral grounds. The rates of return should be higher in capital-poor nations, but private investors may hesitate to commit their capital because of perceptions of high risk: therefore public institutions must step in. At the

An earlier version of this article was presented at a conference at the Jerome Levy Economics Institute in October 1988. From *Third World Quarterly*, 11, 3 (July 1989), pp. 71–84.

same time, raising living standards in the Third World is a humanitarian act, which generally serves the commercial and security interests of the USA by widening markets for US products, strengthening market mechanisms, and promoting political moderation. These statements are uncontroversial and explain why the IFIs have generally enjoyed bipartisan backing.

But the IFIs are no longer serving this basic purpose. In 1987, for the first time, all three IFIs drained more money out of Latin America than they put in. The combined net resource transfer (NRT)—disbursements minus principal and interest repayments—was a negative $2.5 billion (Table 1). The IMF received nearly $2 billion in net transfers, the World Bank $800 million, and the IDB just $100 million. Most important, this reverse capital transfer is not a momentary blip, but rather the result of underlying trends that, if not altered, will produce similar outcomes into the 1990s. Under current policies, and even assuming the approval of capital injections and subsequent substantial increases in annual loan commitments by the World Bank and the IDB, the negative net resource transfer will persist at least throughout 1991 (Table 1).

1987 was a turning point in financial relations between the IFIs and Latin America. From being a significant source of financial resources, the multilateral lending agencies became a net drain on the region's balance of payments. Earlier in the decade, in the wake of the debt crisis and the halt in private lending, the IFIs sharply increased their disbursements, causing the combined NRT to leap from under $3 billion in 1982 to over $13 billion during 1983 and 1984. All three institutions contributed to this effort to pump funds into the region. In 1986, however, the IMF began to show a negative NRT, which pushed the combined effort down to under $1 billion.

TABLE 1   **The IFIs Net Resource Transfer to Latin America, 1980–91 ($ Billions)**

	1980	1981	1982	1983	1984	1985	1986	1987	1988[a]	1989[b]	1990[b]	1991[b]
IMF	−0.2	−0.3	1.7	6.4	3.0	0.4	−1.0	−2.0	−0.6	−0.6	—	—
IBRD	0.6	0.5	0.6	0.8	1.1	0.8	1.3	−0.5	−0.8	−1.0	−1.5	−2.0
IDB	0.6	0.6	0.7	0.7	1.2	0.9	0.5	−0.1	−0.5	−0.3	−0.2	0.2
Total[d]	0.9	0.8	2.9	7.9	5.3	2.1	0.8	−2.5	−1.9	−1.9	−1.7[c]	−1.8[c]

[a]Estimates.
[b] Projections.
[c]Excludes the IMF.
[d]Totals may not add due to rounding.

SOURCE: For the IMF, *World Economic Outlook,* April 1988 and September 1988, and *International Financial Statistics,* July 1988; for the World Bank, *World Debt Tables (1987–88),* and by communication; for the IDB, Annual Report 1986, and by communication; and author's calculations. World Bank estimates include the recent GCI. IDB estimates assume agreement on the seventh replenishment, commitment levels of $4 billion in 1989 and $6 billion in 1990 and 1991, and traditional disbursement schedules.

In 1987 all three IFIs turned in a negative performance, which was repeated in 1988.

The main causes of this negative trend are the same for all three institutions: amortisation and interest charges on outstanding debt shot up from a combined $2 billion in 1980 to $10 billion in 1987 (Table 2). For example, as a result of loans made earlier in the decade to Latin America, annual repayments to the IMF jumped from around $200 million in 1982–84 to $1.9 billion in 1986, and to $3.3 billion in 1987 (Table 2). Charges (including interest and commitment fees), which were nominal in the early 1980s, reached $1 billion per annum from 1985–87. (The IMF periodically adjusts its interest charges, which floated around 7 percent in 1986, but fell to around 6 percent by 1988.) These charges will decline as loans are amortised, but of course the amortisation payments greatly exceed the interest savings.

World Bank principal repayments have been rising at an accelerating rate during the 1980s, from $398 million in 1980 to $2.3 billion in 1987 (Table 2). Under current Bank policy assumptions, repayment requirements will reach $3.8 billion by 1991. Interest payments have also increased, reflecting the Bank's decision to adjust its rates (fixed at 7.6 percent as of September 1988) in order to cover the cost of funds and the growth of the region's outstanding disbursed debt from $7.7 billion in 1980 to $18.7 billion in 1986.

Similarly, IDB repayments have risen from $260 million in 1980 to $712 million in 1987, and are projected to reach $1.5 billion in 1991 (Table 2). Interest and other charges have risen from $330 million to $1.1 billion.

For all three agencies, disbursements have not kept pace with repayments. After the surge in lending in 1983–84, IMF disbursements have actu-

TABLE 2   **The Rapid Rise in Latin American Debt Service to the IFIs ($ Billions)**

	1980	1981	1982	1983	1984	1985	1986	1987
IMF								
Amortisation	0.5	0.3	0.2	0.2	0.2	0.4	1.9	3.3
Interest	0.1	0.1	0.2	0.5	0.8	1.1	1.1	1.1
World Bank								
Amortisation	0.4	0.5	0.7	0.8	1.1	1.2	1.8	2.3
Interest	0.6	0.7	0.7	0.8	1.0	1.1	1.7	2.0
IDB								
Amortisation	0.3	0.3	0.3	0.3	0.4	0.4	0.6	0.7
Interest	0.3	0.4	0.4	0.5	0.6	0.7	1.0	1.1
Total	2.2	2.3	2.5	3.1	4.1	4.9	8.1	10.5

SOURCE: For the IMF, *World Economic Outlook*, April 1988 and September 1988, and *International Financial Statistics*, July 1988; for the World Bank, *World Debt Tables (1987–88)* and by communication; for the IDB: Annual Report 1986 and by communication; and author's calculations. World Bank estimates include the recent GCI. IDB estimates assume agreement on the seventh replenishment, commitment levels of $4 billion in 1989 and $6 billion in 1990 and 1991, and traditional disbursement schedules.

ally declined. Reflecting a stagnation in commitment levels, IDB disbursements are lower today than in 1984. In contrast, the World Bank more than doubled its disbursements from 1981/82–1986/87, but the increase was still insufficient to compensate for the rise in repayments and interest. Even with the general capital increase (GCI), the World Bank's NRT will remain negative if the Bank adheres to its stated intentions of increasing commitment levels by only 10 percent per annum over the next five or six years—to about $20 billion in the early 1990s.

Theoretically, a net positive inflow could be a sign of success for the IFIs. For the IMF, it could signal that member states had successfully restored equilibrium to their balance of payments. For the development agencies, it could mean that borrowers had reached that stage of rapid, sustained growth where they are ready to graduate from dependency on official finance and are capable of relying on private capital markets for their external financial needs. Alas, neither is a true picture of Latin America today. The region's external accounts are under severe strain and Latin America has lost access to private capital markets.

At some point, lenders inevitably experience net reflows. The inflection point is reached more quickly when interest rates are high, as they have been during the 1980s. But this emergence of a negative NRT vis-à-vis the IFIs comes at a most inopportune time for Latin America. Public capital is needed to offset the sudden and dramatic withdrawal of private lenders and investors. A positive public inflow is particularly critical at a time when many Latin American nations are attempting ambitious adjustment programs that require high rates of investment. Monies are needed for the modern plants and equipment whose output will be competitive on world markets. The IFIs themselves are strong advocates of this investment-intensive adjustment strategy. However, the negative NRT undermines the very policies that they advocate and threatens to frustrate the region's efforts at structural adjustment.

IMPROVING IFI PERFORMANCE

There are two basic ways to correct the financial performance of the IFIs: increasing the disbursement rate and altering the amortisation schedule. It would not be advisable for the IFIs to lower their interest charges significantly unless their cost of funds falls; on the contrary, the IFI need an income stream sufficient to compensate for the rising volume of loans on nonaccrual status. I shall first consider the disbursement options open to each institution.

The International Monetary Fund

The IMF has considerable resources to lend to Latin America as it is by no means facing a liquidity crisis.[3] It holds over $40 billion in unused loanable hard currencies, about $40 billion in gold valued at current market prices, and lines of credit from several capital-surplus nations. In addition, the IMF could seek to activate the General Arrangements to Borrow (GAB), a pool of funds that industrial countries can make available to the IMF to support major debtor nations, among other functions. Alternatively, the IMF Board could decide to create more of its own money, or Special Drawing Rights (SDRs), as most members have advocated, and industrial countries could agree to provide a disproportionate share of the SDR issue for developing nations. While such generosity would be financially equivalent to a loan or grant, it could be engineered outside normal national budgetary processes and therefore be less taxing politically for the governments of industrialised countries.

The IMF maintains that it does not have this kind of leeway—that it needs to husband its liquidity to cover potential borrowings by industrialised countries. However, no industrialised country has borrowed from the IMF for over a decade. In reality such nations, when in need of finance, have alternatives to the IMF, including the greatly expanded private capital markets and swap arrangements among their own central banks.

The IMF management wants an increase of 100 percent in its basic resources or quotas, equal to about SDR $90 billion. It wanted action in 1988, but the US government preferred to wait until the World Bank's capital increase passed through Congress. The IMF argues that its resources need to be doubled to keep pace with the growth in international capital markets and world trade, and to be able to increase lending levels to developing nations. This case would be more persuasive if the IMF were making better use of its existing resources and capabilities.[4]

The World Bank

The approval of a $75 billion GCI in 1988 gives the World Bank the means to increase disbursements sharply. The Bank also has a vehicle for rapid disbursement—its structural adjustment loans (SALs), which provide balance-of-payments support for agreed reforms.

Structural adjustment loans can include broad macroeconomic variables, or can focus more narrowly on particular sectors. Sector loans, which have been more common in Latin America, typically pursue such reforms as trade liberalisation, reorganisation of state-owned enterprises, reform of financial markets, and agricultural taxation and pricing policies. Structural adjustment loans account for about one quarter of Bank lending. The apparent ceiling of $500 million per loan is arbitrary, and reflects political pressures coming from the Bank's executive directors rather than a calculation of what is needed to make the program work economically. The Bank's ability to persuade countries to undertake politically risky reforms would also be enhanced if it could put up more money. There is no good reason why strong adjustment programs, which require massive investment and sustained political support, should not receive more substantial external assistance.

The Inter-American Development Bank

The IDB's search for new capital resources was stalled for two years by its conflict with the Reagan administration, and by an inability to disburse all of its existing resources because recipient governments cannot provide the necessary counterpart funds. In the hope of attaining a $20–25 billion increase in lending capacity that would permit a near doubling of loan commitments, the IDB management has already acceded to US demands that 20–25 percent of resources be used for policy-based lending and that hand-picked US personnel be placed in key policy positions. The major Latin American nations drew the line, however, at the US insistence that it be given a virtual veto power over individual loans. The US position revealed unwarranted insecurity and distrust—it already enjoys substantial power to block loans. Moreover, the IDB had acceded to the USA's main substantive demands, and many Latin American governments are now ready and willing to undertake structural reforms. A complex compromise on voting procedures was finally hammered out in March 1989, and the IDB secured a $26.5 billion capital increase.

The IDB's other major financial problem stems from the inability of financially strapped recipient governments to provide the required counterpart funds. The result is $10 billion in committed but undisbursed project loans. These funds could be put to use through temporary relaxation of counterpart requirements and the initiation of policy-based loans, which would not be tied to specific investment projects and therefore would require no counterpart funds.

Amortisation Schedules

All three institutions have resisted participation in the Paris Club, where official, bilateral debts are rescheduled in order to protect their preferred creditor positions. This posture, however, does not rule out alternative approaches to grappling with the problem of rising repayments. For example, the IMF has lengthened the repayment period for the more ambitious stand-bys ("extended fund facilities") from 5–7 years to 5–10 years. It could strengthen this reform initiative by introducing contingency clauses that would allow for slower repayments in the event of adverse shocks, just as current agreements call for accelerated repayments in the event of good fortune. Furthermore, the IMF could transform past stand-by arrangements retroactively into extended arrangements, thereby stretching out amortisation schedules.[5]

Recognising the mounting repayment problem, the World Bank temporarily extended the grace period on new loans to middle-income countries from 3 to 5 years, and approved an annuity scheme for low-income borrowers (those with per capita incomes below $836 in 1986) that will reduce repayment burdens in the earlier years of a loan. The World Bank could go further by significantly lengthening grace periods on existing as well as new loans. Such retroactive terms adjustment would be justifiable on several grounds. First, borrowers' economic conditions have deteriorated sharply, creating circumstances not envisioned when loan agreements were originally structured. Second, the IFIs are finding that structural adjustment programs often take longer to yield results than was anticipated when the programs began. Third, the external payments crisis facing debtor nations warrants adjustment by all creditors. The simple doubling of the current five-year grace period by the World Bank would immediately affect repayment on the $8 billion in disbursements made to Latin America from 1980–84, and would eventually delay amortisation on the $16 billion in disbursements made from 1985–88. The result would be an annual saving for Latin America of about $700 million in 1990, rising to $1.7 billion by 1993. These reforms would, however, cause the Bank to hit the lending ceilings fixed by the recent GCI before 1998, as currently anticipated.

The fear at the Bank that such retroactive terms adjustment might injure its credit rating is unwarranted. If implemented as a final, unilateral action, it would not pull the Bank into the troublesome reschedulings that bilateral and private creditors are enmeshed in. Moreover, the World Bank's credit rating on private markets is more a function of the guarantees of the major industrialised-country governments than of the quality of the Bank's portfolio.[6]

The New Vision

In sum, there are plenty of options available to enable the IFIs once again to provide resources for Latin America. Rather than the projected negative NRT of approximately $3 billion, the IFIs could manage a positive NRT of some $5–6 billion by around 1991 (Table 3). Most significantly, this transformation could be accomplished without additional resources beyond the proposed IDB replenishment, although a quota increase for the IMF would make it easier for the monetary authority to boost lending while maintaining large liquid reserves.

The IMF could achieve an increase in disbursements of about $2 billion by either permitting greater access to its existing resources or by issuing SDRs; it could raise this sum by another $2 billion through a quota increase. The World Bank could increase disbursements by $2 billion, doubling the size of those structural adjustment loans likely to be signed under existing policies, and reducing repayments by $1.1 billion through the retroactive

TABLE 3   **Potential IFI Expansion to Latin America, circa 1991 ($ Billions)**

		NET RESOURCE TRANSFER	
	Increase in Disbursements	Current Policy	Potential Flows
IMF	2.0 (existing resources or SDRs)		
	2.0 (quota increase)		
Subtotal	4.0	−1	3
World Bank	2.0 [doubling structural adjustment loan (SAL) size]		
	1.1 (retroactive terms adjustment)		
Subtotal	3.1	−2	1.1
IDB	1.2 (replenishment plus SALs)		
	0.5 (counterpart funds relaxation)		
Subtotal	1.7	0.2	1.9
Total	$8.8	−$2.8	$6.0

SOURCE: Table 1 and author's estimates.

terms adjustment discussed above. The IDB could double its annual commitments to $6 billion, and devote one-quarter of this sum to fast-disbursing policy-based loans through the contemplated seventh replenishment; within two years, this faster pay-out rate could increase disbursements by an estimated $1.2 billion. Faster utilisation of the IDB's pipeline—clogged up by the counterpart funds requirement—could inject an additional $500 million. This $8–9 billion improvement in the IFIs' combined net resource transfer would equal more than 40 percent of the average annual resource drain that Latin America experienced from 1985–87.

Individual loans, of course, would still be made on a country-by-country basis, conditioned upon the design and implementation of necessary stabilisation and strong structural adjustment programs. The international agencies have both a moral and financial right to condition their loans on the adoption of policies that will improve the welfare—and the future repayment capacity—of borrowing nations. Importantly, the offer of more resources would increase the power of the IFIs to promote such reforms, as well as the ability of borrowers to sustain reform programs. The provision of more resources would also help to catalyse private capital flows to Latin America.[7]

PRIVATE FINANCIAL MARKETS

The heart of the resource transfer problem lies in the private credit markets. By lending heavily in the 1970s and early 1980s, and then closing the credit windows after 1982 when global interest rates rose and loans became due, the banks first provided strongly positive, and then demanded strongly negative, resource transfers. The volume of resources involved—in both positive and negative phases—far surpasses the activities of the IFIs. In Latin America, net disbursements to the private credit markets alone swung from an annual average of positive $42 billion in 1980–81 to a negative $3 billion in 1986–87.[8]

The Bretton Woods agencies have always viewed themselves as catalysts of private capital flows. In the short term, IMF and World Bank programs often seek to gather associated private flows to help finance stabilisation programs and supplement development efforts. In the longer term, by promoting successful stabilisation efforts and more vigorous growth, they strive to promote additional private investment.

The debt crisis and the closely related resource transfer problem have heightened IFI attention to the private credit markets. Although the IFI have only recently begun explicitly to use the resource transfer terminology, as soon as the debt crisis struck in 1982 they began to seek ways to reduce effectively the NRT from the debtor nations to the commercial banks. In particular, the IMF pressed commercial banks to cover a portion of interest payments falling due by participating in new money packages. More recently, the IFIs have begun to entertain methods for slicing the negative NRT by reducing the stock of outstanding private debt and therefore debt service.

As the debt and development malaise has persisted, the IFIs' interest in stemming the NRT to the private markets has grown. They are alarmed at the economic decline of their clients, annoyed that their own capital is "roundtripping" to service the assets of other creditors, and fearful that their own rising exposures are becoming increasingly jeopardised. Particularly at the World Bank, many staff express fatigue at playing handmaiden to dispirited private banks.

New Lending

The IFIs have tried hard to catalyse new commercial bank lending through a variety of mechanisms. The IMF has sometimes conditioned its stand-bys on modest amounts of new lending by the commercial banks. This "concerted lending" generated $32 billion in private commitments in 1983–84, accounting for the bulk of new private lending to the major debtor nations.[9] More recently, however, its persuasive powers have waned. Private bank commitments tied to IMF programs declined to $2.2 billion in 1985 and to negligible amounts in 1987, with the exception of one big money package for Mexico, and to zero throughout the first three-quarters of 1987, except for a $2 billion commitment to Argentina. While predictions of the death of new money packages have proved to be premature, as the 1988 $5.2 billion commercial bank commitment to Brazil suggests, it is increasingly difficult for the IMF to convince banks to increase their exposure in heavily indebted nations.

The World Bank is now tentatively trying to step into the breach. With the support of the US Treasury, the Bank has used its guarantee authority sparingly based on two premises: that private banks should bear some of the risk; and that the Bank might as well make the loan itself since guarantees are billed 100 percent against Bank lending capacity. It is a matter of debate as to whether the Bank's Articles of Agreement would have to be amended for a system to be adopted in which only a fraction of contingent liabilities are charged against total lending amounts.

The World Bank's efforts to draw in private capital through traditional cofinancing arrangements have largely failed, and it is now trying to persuade private creditors to participate in financial packages tied to economic reform programs. It is arguing that the medium-term nature of its programs offers comfort to banks beyond that gained by association with 12–18 month IMF stand-bys. In 1985 the commercial banks agreed to cofinance policy-based loans to Colombia and Chile, and more recently have agreed to participate in joint IMF–World Bank concerted lending packages to Mexico and Brazil, with some commercial bank disbursements contingent upon compliance with World Bank sector agreements. Nevertheless, most World Bank sector loans continue to be unaccompanied by private financing. The World Bank has yet to establish the mechanisms and procedures for ensuring that the commercial banks make significant contributions to most Bank-backed reform programs.

Debt Service Reduction

In the light of the reluctance of commercial banks to increase their exposure, attention is increasingly turning to the option of reducing debt service. The World Bank has been anxious to play a role in pioneering debt service reduction schemes, as has been IMF Managing Director Michel Camdessus, but the Reagan administration was a decisive restraint. The Bush administration, however, has made an about turn, and in March 1989 urged the World Bank and the IMF to use the financial and guarantee authorities to support debt reduction. Understandably, both institutions would shy away from any grand debt conversion scheme which left them, directly or indirectly, holding $100 billion or more of Third World debt. As an alternative, the IFIs might participate in approaches such as these:

Buybacks   The IMF has already facilitated the Bolivian buyback of about half its commercial debts by administrating funds provided by bilateral donors that were then used to purchase bank debts at 11 cents on the dollar. The IFIs might initiate a similar program of their own, whereby they provide a portion of the financing for deep-discount buybacks that would increase a member nation's development prospects. For smaller debtors whose liabilities are selling on secondary markets at a small fraction of their face value, buybacks could significantly reduce scheduled debt service.

Guarantees-for-asset swaps   The IFIs could provide partial or full guarantees for financial instruments issued by debtor nations that would buy back at a discount old debts owed to commercial banks. The problem with this option is that guarantees of the full stream of interest payments would eat deeply into IFI resources, while simple guarantees on the principal loan provide a weak inducement for the banks, as indicated by the disappointing response in early 1988 to the Mexican bond offer.

Interest guarantees   Guarantees of interest could take two forms. The IFIs could guarantee interest payments on new instruments that the debtors swapped at a discount for old debts. Alternatively, without altering the stock of debt, the IFIs could guarantee renegotiated, below-market interest payments for either the entire maturity or for 2–3 years on a rolling basis. If two years of 4.5 percent interest payments were covered on $250 billion in commercial bank debts owed by the highly indebted developing nations, the guarantee ceiling would be $22.5 billion. Any of these mechanisms to reduce debt service could be tied to IFI-approved reform programs that should, over the longer term, increase the value of the banks' remaining exposure. At the same time, so long as the mechanisms were to reduce significantly the immediate NRT to the commercial banks, they could be advanced as "burdensharing" rather than a "bank bailout."

NET RESOURCE TRANSFER REDUCTION

As the central conceptual framework for a new attack on the debt problem, the IFIs could adopt a strategy of "net resource transfer reduction." The World Bank and the IMF could set country targets for new lending and debt restructuring that would leave enough capital in each developing country to permit adequate investment and growth. Reversing the current approach, debt strategy would be subordinate to growth objectives.

To implement this strategy, the IFIs would require the firm support of key member governments. But it is in the interests of the industrial countries to restore growth to Latin America, to reopen export markets, and to help stabilise the region's democratic institutions. While an NRT reduction strategy might cause short-term pain among some banks, it also promises to increase the value of the banks' remaining assets.

It could be argued that the proposed strategy simply postpones the problem by piling new debts on old ones. Of course, to the extent that the negative NRT is slashed through debt reduction, the stock of debt would diminish. But even where new loans are made, it is to be hoped that the combination of enhanced capital availability and policy reform will improve national debt service capacity in the medium term. As a result of fiscal reform and export growth, Latin America could be in a stronger position to manage its debts and repay loans by the mid-1990s.

An NRT reduction strategy would require that debtors be treated on a strictly case-by-case approach. Some nations, such as Colombia and South Korea, have strong enough export performance and actual or prospective access to private capital markets to be able to meet interest obligations fully and reach growth targets. Other nations require an alleviation of debt service. Correspondingly, for some nations relief can be temporary, while for others more permanent debt reduction arrangements will be necessary.

Under this strategy, each creditor could choose for itself whether it wished to provide new monies or receive less debt service, negotiating with each debtor the exact choice of financial instruments. A formula such as the present discounted value of each creditor's contribution could be used to measure rough equivalence. Whereas it is unreasonable to expect commercial banks to become a source of net capital in the foreseeable future, they would be called upon to reduce their receipt of net financial resources. At the same time, the IFIs would generally be expected to sustain positive transfers to nations undertaking reform programs, at least until they resume growth.

A variation on this approach would be to establish the politically attractive and simple objective of a zero NRT for Latin America. If the current negative NRT is about $20 billion, the IFIs and the commercial banks could divide this burden roughly between them. The IFIs would make their contribution of $8–10 billion by transforming the projected $3 billion drain into a positive $6 billion net flow. The banks would reduce their net intake by about $10–12 billion through country-by-country combinations of new lending and debt service reduction. The contribution of the IFIs would in effect be recycled to cover payments to the commercial banks. However it would now occur in the context of a more equal burdensharing and a new strategy supportive of the ultimate objectives of the international financial institutions: the growth of developing nations within a stable and expanding international economic system.

NOTES

1. UN Economic Commission for Latin America and the Caribbean. *Economic Survey of Latin America and the Caribbean, 1987: Advance Summary.* April 1988, table 16, p. 45.
2. The term World Bank will be used here as synonymous with the International Bank for Reconstruction and Development (IBRD), the hard-loan window of the World Bank Group, also composed of the soft-loan International Development Association (IDA), which does little business in Latin America, and the International Finance Corporation (IFC), which promotes private investment.
3. For a fuller discussion, see R. E. Feinberg and F. Bacha, "When Supply and Demand Don't Intersect: Latin America and the Bretton Woods Institutions in the 1980s," *Development and Change*, 19 (1988).

4. In March 1989, US Secretary of the Treasury Nicholas Brady indicated that the USA would relax its opposition to a quota increase if the IMF made a greater contribution to the alleviation of the Third World debt problem.

5. I am indebted to Jacques J. Polak for suggesting this idea.

6. This point is forcefully argued in C. Blitzer, "Financing the World Bank," in R. E. Feinberg, ed., *Between Two Worlds: The World Bank's Next Decade* (Washington D.C.: Overseas Development Council/Transaction Books, 1986), pp. 135–60.

7. The important issues of policy reform and "conditionality" are addressed in R. E. Feinberg, "The Changing Relationship between the World Bank and the International Monetary Fund," *International Organization*, 42, 3 (Summer 1988).

8. International Monetary Fund, *World Economic Outlook* (Washington D.C.: IMF, 1988), table A41, p. 163.

9. International Monetary Fund, *International Capital Markets: Developments and Prospects* (Washington D.C.: IMF, January 1988), table 24, p. 76.

PART FOUR

AGRICULTURE IN DEVELOPMENT

Development economists have always assigned the agriculture sector a central role in the development process, but our understanding of that role has evolved with time. Early development theorists emphasized industrialization, though they counted on agriculture to provide the necessary output of food and raw materials, along with the labor force that would gradually be absorbed by industry. Later thinking moved agriculture more to the forefront of the development process; the hopes for technical change in agriculture and the "green revolution" suggested that agriculture could be the dynamo for growth—and there were clear gains in this regard. Processed agricultural products were important contributors to the export-led growth pattern of countries, such as Taiwan, which were able to attain notable increases in per capita GNP. Chile's recent rapid growth has been largely through agricultural exports.

Agriculture continues to be important in virtually all developing countries, and so it will continue to play a central role in any development process. According to the World Bank's *World Development Report, 1990,* 33 percent of total production in low-income countries originates in agriculture, and 14 percent of production in lower-middle-income countries is from agriculture. The rural population still bulks large in most countries, e.g., 80 percent in Kenya, 77 percent in India, and 59 percent in Guatemala.

Changes in individual countries and in the world economy suggest a further rethinking of agriculture in development, and the articles in this section represent that effort.

Gene Ellis's "Two Tales of a City" (Addis Ababa in Ethiopia) is a cautionary tale in many ways, illustrating the fragile balance between human activity and nature by focusing on the urban eucalyptus forest of Addis. Ellis combines historical information with new satellite observations of the urban forest to document a 33

247

percent decline in the forest in a period of three years after new
policies were implemented in 1974. The result has been ecological
disruption, forcing the use of much less appropriate fuels and
requiring the exploitation of more distant sources of fuelwood.

Parallel examples could be found in many countries under
many different types of governments, and the yearly publication of
the Worldwatch Institute, *The State of the World*, provides ample
documentation of the many environmental threats. Ellis's tale
reemphasizes Helleiner's earlier point, that any development can
succeed only if it is "sustainable," if the environment can
accommodate the changes. This must be a starting point in any view
of the role of agriculture in development.

Another dimension of agriculture in developing countries is the
variety of its forms, often within a given country. The early vision of
an agriculture based upon midsized "family farms" is the exception
rather than the rule, and the development challenge is greater as a
result. Subsistence agriculture coexists with highly capitalized
corporate agriculture, and production may be sold in local village
markets or in the highly integrated world agricultural markets. The
remaining articles in the section provide an understanding of this
variety and the linkages among the different levels.

Joseph Stiglitz employs a modification of the standard
neoclassical model to explain the persistence of a rudimentary (and
"inefficient") form of organizing agricultural production,
sharecropping. Stiglitz's "new development economics" is an
attempt to generalize across all countries in the mode of early
development thinkers. He assumes rational individual behavior and
competition but modifies that familiar model by assuming that
information is costly, and therefore less than perfect, and that
institutions adapt to reflect these costs. The modified model allows
him to describe or explain sharecropping, cost-sharing between
sharecropper and landlord, the dual role of landlord and credit
provider, and some elements of technical change. The article is
especially provocative in the challenge it presents to other theories of
the peasant; Stiglitz attempts to set out the criteria by which a choice
could be made among the competing theories. We should note that
the explanation for the situation of peasants provided by historical
studies such as Burns's history of underdevelopment in El Salvador
is dismissed because it is only one case study.

Schejtman adopts one of those other stances: that the persistence
of the peasantry in the face of the onslaught of development can best
be understood by treating the peasant economy as a specific form of
organizing production. Peasants are not irrational, as the pure
neoclassical model would seem to imply; rather, they make a

complex set of decisions that cannot be captured in the simple utility maximization assumption. The key consideration, which raises all the issues of gender in development and of the treatment of children, is that the family is the production unit for the peasantry and it is both a production and a consumption unit. This explains a series of other aspects of peasant behavior, the use of labor, the partial integration with the market economy, and the stance toward risk and technical change. And it ultimately sets the peasants apart from commercialized agriculture. Schejtman in no way idealizes this form of production, which generally results in peasants getting paid less for their products and for their labor. However, his treatment helps us understand how and why the peasant economy has maintained itself in Latin America as well as most other areas of the developing world. The peasantry does not exist in isolation, however, and there are a large number of factors that affect its continuation. He examines them according to whether they encourage the breakup of the peasant economy, its recovery, or finally its persistence.

These considerations are a good bridge to the last article, which returns our focus to that of Part Three, the effect of the international economy on the process of development, specifically on agriculture and on food.

Byerlee concentrates on international trade in one staple commodity, wheat, which has a peculiar importance in agriculture trade. There are eighty-four developing countries which do not produce wheat, so wheat exports are dominated by developed countries; even so, wheat imports by developing countries doubled during the 1970s. The impact was often quite great, affecting domestic food production, resulting in notable changes in consumption patterns, and often leading to balance-of-payments pressures and overprotected domestic processing industries, though the effects vary across the world. For example, the East Asian economies have been quite careful that the increase in wheat consumption was not primarily from imports and that it did not result in a protected domestic processing industry. Byerlee documents the important role that wheat has played in the entire agricultural system, and particularly in international agricultural trade. In listing the various factors that have influenced this process he places primary emphasis on the role of government policies, and finds that the main beneficiaries have been middle-class consumers of low-priced wheat products.

The combination of the articles in Part Four provides an up-to-date overview of the agricultural sector in development. Each national economy has an agricultural sector which is quite varied and complex and which remains an important element of the development process. Not even the newly industrializing countries (NICs) are exceptions. And the subsistence or peasant sector continues to absorb large portions of the population in many countries. However, the internationalization of agriculture has a profound impact in all countries, and it has been anything but purely beneficial to their development efforts.

REFERENCES

The World Bank, *The World Development Report, 1990* (New York: Oxford University Press, 1990).

Worldwatch Institute, *The State of the World, 1990* (New York: Worldwatch Institute, 1990).

14

In Search of a Development Paradigm: Two Tales of a City

Gene Ellis
University of Denver

One of the most pressing problems confronting development planners in Africa is how to increase local supplies of fuelwood. As explained in a donor-commissioned report at the beginning of the current decade:

1. Not nearly enough trees are being planted to meet future rural and urban needs: during the next 20 years, "annual fuelwood planting will need to increase by about 15 times over current levels," and even this assumes optimistically that "up to a fourth of future fuelwood demand will be met by conservation or . . . alternative fuels." In fact, negligible resources are being devoted to establishing new "plantations of any significant size."[1]

2. African governments cannot be expected to meet these needs because they "will obviously not have the funds from their own resources to pay for programs of this size."[2]

3. In many countries, "the necessary national cadres of foresters and/or extension agents simply do not exist . . . transportation and other logistic support is often lacking."[3]

4. Most governmental efforts to regulate access to land on which fuelwood is being grown have been ineffective, and to make matters worse the local inhabitants have often been alienated from forestry staff who have been placed in policing rôles, making cooperation in other initiatives less likely.

This study was aided by a Faculty Research Grant from the University of Denver, and was discussed at the Workshop on Energy, Forestry, and Environment held by the U.S. Agency for International Development Bureau for Africa, Nairobi, December 6–11, 1981. From *The Journal of Modern African Studies*, 26, 4 (1988), pp. 677–83. Reprinted with the permission of Cambridge University Press.

5. The costs of creating fuelwood projects have been high and variable: "Sahel (CILSS) is using an illustrated average of $725 per hectare for village woodlots based on recent field experience . . . The World Bank's proposed five-year planting averages $765/hectare in East Africa and over $850/hectare in West Africa."[4]

The above-cited document noted that although a large-scale multi-purpose reafforestation project in Algeria had reported costs of only about $300/hectare, a field study had revealed that as much as $1,080 was required for labour alone, while the overall costs per hectare of reafforestation had been estimated to be as high as $1,600 by the World Food Program.[5] It is small wonder that two American experts, asked separately which donor-supported forestry projects would be able to pay for themselves in the market-place if unsubsidised, both answered tersely, "None."

The almost universal conclusion seems to be that drawn by Frances Gulick in 1980, namely "that there must be massive fuelwood planting programs."[6] But in a situation where governments are without adequate resources, where skilled personnel are not available, where donors are increasingly constrained, and where marginal costs are high and rising, is not a strategy based on "more of the same" doomed to failure? Given the sheer magnitude of what needs to be done and the inadequacy of the public efforts which can be mounted, resources must be mobilised on a wider scale. Hence the search for responses which can and will be replicated by the process of what might be called "contagion."[7]

THE FIRST TALE: THE DEVELOPMENT OF THE ADDIS ABABA FOREST

Traditionally, the Imperial Court of Ethiopia had been a "moving capital," slowly transversing the Highlands, subjugating and taxing peoples and resources as it went.[8] However, having been influenced greatly by foreigners who hoped that it might be feasible to construct a railway that would "open up" the interior—not least by providing a suitable location for their missions—Emperor Menelik decided towards the close of the nineteenth century to create a permanent headquarters for his government and administration at Finfini, to be known as Addis Ababa, or "New Flower." The rapid build-up of facilities and population put extreme pressure on local forest supplies, and hence the inhabitants were ordered not to cut or burn down trees without permission, and to replant any areas that were so cleared.

The laws went unheeded and unenforced, and it was reported that travellers approaching Addis Ababa at the turn of the century had to do without wood for several days, so scarce was the supply.

After a few Europeans had brought in as many as 26 varieties of eucalyptus, Menelik threw his support behind their introduction by distributing seedlings at nominal prices, and by exempting any lands so planted from taxation. By 1899 a writer noted that the owners of small holdings were growing eucalyptus in hopes of high profits, and that many houses and roads were rapidly becoming surrounded by these trees. Indeed, such was the latter's popularity that when in 1913 the newly created Ministry of Agriculture ordered that these woodlands should be uprooted in the belief that eucalyptus dried up water supplies, the proclamation went unheeded.

The shortage of fuelwood had been eased by the 1920s, and by the Italian invasion in 1936 the Addis Ababa forest was estimated to cover not less than 4,000 hectares. Aerial photography showed that this had increased to 7,900 hectares in 1957, and to 10,400 hectares in 1964, roughly keeping pace with the growth of the population.

What are the main lessons that can be learnt from this successful indigenous enterprise?

1. The creation of the eucalyptus forest was an example of that ideal type of donor-assisted scheme in which those involved concentrate on "teaching how to fish" rather than on supplying the needy with food.

2. Although the external assistance was limited, it appears to have been a necessary ingredient. The eucalyptus seedlings were all exotic to Ethiopia, the costs of transportation were high relative to any expectation of private returns, the growth and organisation of the forest took several decades, and there were few if any chances of being able to create a monopoly of output that would be profitable enough to repay the total outlay.[9]

3. There were no long-term governmental inputs, unlike many modern forestry projects. Indeed, by the 1960s, eucalyptus was still considered to be a "plantation" tree and hence neglected by the Forestry Research Institute.[10]

4. The countryside remained denuded while the urban forest expanded. Jane Jacobs presents a convincing case that cities developed agriculture first, and exported it later to rural areas.[11] Certainly, in Ethiopia the information and techniques from abroad arrived first in Addis Ababa, where the location of the forest minimised transport and energy costs, and where the inhabitants then provided the demand. In addition, the counterproductive defects of the traditional land-tenure system were avoided.[12]

5. The lack of professional advice proved to be no disadvantage, and may have been a blessing in disguise. Despite the validity of certain scientific criticisms—for example, the stems were "neither pruned nor stripped of leaves,"[13] with the seedlings having been planted at a far higher density than would have been recommended by a "text-

book forester"—the crude techniques proved to be enduring and economic. The explanation, of course, is that research conducted by experimental stations might seek to discover, for example, "optimal" watering rates for maximum growth according to the perceived standards of particular disciplines, whereas these might have little or no relation to what can best be done by peasants, given their circumstances and constraints.

6. The "running costs" of the forest were minimal. No expensive supervisors were needed (as thought necessary for a proposed F.A.O./U.N.D.P. project), and there were few transportation expenses. Many women were prepared to walk daily as far as 14 kilometres to purchase fuel from the wood-cutters and retail it in the city. Because of the forest's location, all parts of the trees (including twigs, leaves, and stems) were utilised. Of that which was trucked, the bulk was informally transported on top of contracted loads. It is doubtful if planners would have dared to devise a development project that required the bulk of forest products to be carried to the market on the backs of both animals and people, but this mode of carriage resulted in large-scale employment, and enabled bundles of wood to compete in the market with alternative fuels.

7. Lastly, the continuing viability of this early twentieth-century industry must be emphasised. It endured throughout an enemy invasion, and despite benign neglect by the Ethiopian authorities, in one of the poorest and least literate economies in the world.

Given that there will never be enough external assistance to fund all the reafforestation that is needed, whether in state plantations or in village woodlots, and given the limitations of indigenous governments as regards expertise, administrative and managerial talent, and especially finance, then the focus of the efforts of donors must be to complement and draw out the resources of the private sector, and not to compete with highly subsidised, nonreplicable efforts.

A SECOND, CAUTIONARY TALE: NEVER TROUBLE TROUBLE TILL TROUBLE TROUBLES YOU

In late 1974, the Imperial Government was overthrown by a coup d'état, and the following year the revolutionary leaders began implementing a program of extensive rural reforms, making "land to the tiller" for the first time a reality in Ethiopia. At about the same time, the new régime nationalised not only urban property but also woodlands and forests. This led to a great reduction in the number of seedlings that were being grown along the Awash river, so that far fewer were transported and transplanted to plots near the capital. In addition, the inhabitants were given strong incentives to cut down and market as many trees as possible before adequate policing powers to enforce the proclamation could be institutionalised.

The short-term impact of these changes was estimated by examining two high-level "photographs" of the eucalyptus forest of Addis Ababa that were taken on January 31, 1973 and February 11, 1976 by means of the "Landsat" remote sensing technology (Figure 1). In order to quantify the loss that had taken place, a grid containing 7,200 squares was established, and after these had been studied it became clear that the postrevolutionary photograph contained 32.8 percent fewer "dots," each representing approximately one acre or 0.4 hectare of eucalyptus forest-cover.[14] Although it seems indisputable that the forest did in fact recede (and by approximately this order) over the three-year period, it is open to debate what caused the losses. However, during several months in late 1975, Allan Hoben of Boston University and I were involved in an attempt to assess the effectiveness of the land reforms, and both the conversations by day and the sound of axes by night made us very aware of the negative reactions to the changes that had taken place in the system of incentives.

Of course, other influences were also at work, notably the severe transportation bottlenecks in the early stages of the revolution that diminished the flow of charcoal into Addis Ababa, thereby increasing the demand for locally produced fuelwood and the rate of exploitation. In addition, it must be admitted that the need to replant eucalyptus is reduced by the fact that it regularly "coppices"—i.e., sprouts from the severed stumps. It is nevertheless clear that there was a dramatic decrease in the Addis Ababa forest between the observations, and it seems certain that this can be attributed to the changed incentives.

❀   ❀   ❀

The presence of an extremely modest "external aid" project by foreign embassies in Addis Ababa at the turn of the century led to the introduction of eucalyptus into Ethiopia and to the beginnings of the forest that grew with the population over the years, and which supplied a major portion of the city's energy needs. Although aid was probably necessary for the creation of the forest, no long-term governmental inputs were required, in neither research nor support services. The point to emphasise is that the incentives provided by the urban market were sufficiently attractive to enable the efforts of large numbers of individuals to be organised productively by small profit-making entrepreneurs.

Throughout most of the continent it is *not* a case of "if it works, don't fix it," or that there is a "natural" system which will provide adequate incentives, because the energy sector in Africa can scarcely be described as "working." In the Ethiopian case, fuelwood shortages did not readily give rise to rural forestry, given the constraints of the land-tenure system. The

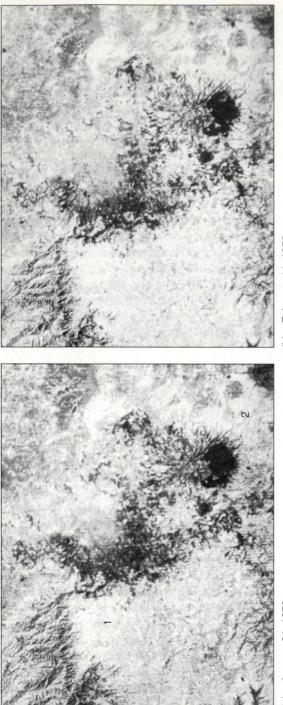

(a)   January 31, 1973

(b)   February 11, 1976

FIGURE 1   These photos were taken on January 31, 1973, and February 11, 1976. The dark crescent around Addis Ababa (1) is forested mountain slopes. Further south (2) is another mountain planted with eucalyptus. A large blow-up was used to divide the city into a grid from which forest losses could be determined. The photo with the largest forest is, of course, the "before" of 1973; that with the smallest, 1976.

conclusions to be reached are rather that a forest must be designed which can reproduce itself, and that interventions likely to affect either the direct or indirect incentives should be examined carefully since they may have a devastating impact.

POSTSCRIPT

And how are things today, some 13 years after the nationalisation of trees? A recent report of the Ethiopian National Energy Authority summarises the present position.[15]

1. Despite the efforts of the government, 85 percent or more of the biomass fuels consumed in Addis Ababa have been supplied, transported, and marketed by small-scale entrepreneurs, most of whose activities are "illegal" in the sense that they have originated in the unauthorised cutting of trees.[16]

2. Whereas "fuels" such as canvas, rubber, and leather scraps were only used "years ago" in such small-scale industrial undertakings as brick-making, they are now burnt in households as well. As the report notes, this raises real health considerations: "their use at all demonstrates the delicate balance between supply and demand in Addis Ababa," and is a "real negative trend factor."[17] In addition, dung is increasingly used as a fuel in the city, as it has been for many years in the countryside.[18]

3. The price of wood fuel has risen sharply in Addis Ababa from an estimated Ethiopian $38.79 per metric ton in 1975 (the year of the revolution), to E.$101.92 in 1980, and to E.$250 in 1988. Although some of this increase has been caused by inflation (basic grain prices rose over this period by a factor of 4 or more), and some represents the increasing demand of the growing population, it is also evident (given the other indicators) that the supply constraints have become acute, and that the ready elasticity noted in the earlier city forest system has been lost.[19]

4. The private production of wood has been replaced by about 200 square kilometers of eucalyptus plantations around Addis Ababa that are managed by peasant associations. Unfortunately, their "enforcement activities . . . are not consistent in any way or place," with resulting uneven incentives, as well as uncertainties and disruptions in supply. The report calls attention also to the problems caused by the short growing rotations of 2–3 years, since 5–7 are needed if there is to be a proper maturation cycle. In addition, the illegal nature of much of the cutting, and the "nonconservation" orientation of legal harvesting (due to inadequate incentives offered by

the present system of public ownership), are helping to cause excessive rates of stump mortality. Increasingly, roots are being sold in the urban market as firewood.[20]

5. The government has endeavoured to replace the private vendors of firewood, charcoal, and construction poles in Addis Ababa with as many as 31 biomass fuel depots that are "primarily a wholesale operation working under price-controlled conditions." The "in-forest" price for a 40-kilogram sack of charcoal is so low (E.$3.50), as against what it will fetch in the market (E.$21.29), that only very poor quality fuel is sold to the depots. Although the latter appear "to be reasonably managed and to have a grasp of the magnitude of the problems in Addis Ababa," the time taken between harvesting and transporting trees was so excessive that the depots sometimes received logs that had rotted and hence deteriorated in value.[21]

In summary, it is clear that the changes in the mid-1970s are still having a profound effect today, and that the government has not been able to create alternative incentives that will sustain a viable fuelwood-supplying forest. More importantly, in light of the limited resources at their command, the authorities have not yet devised a system which is "contagious" as regards the required behaviour of producers. Supply has not kept pace with demand, prices have risen, rotation times have been cut, and poor fuel substitutes with significant social costs (dung, rubber scraps) have been introduced. The crisis may have reached dangerous proportions:

> The 1986–87 price surge should be viewed as an indicator of just how fragile and volatile the fuelwood supply is. . . . Any supply disruption will likely lead to an immediate pricing reaction from the private sector, and spontaneous social turmoil could result. *Interventions will have to be well thought out and very carefully implemented* to not cause unnecessary perturbations.[22]

NOTES

1. Frances A. Gulick, "Suggested Approaches for CADA Initiatives in Fuelwood Production," U.S. A.I.D./Africa, Washington, D.C., October 18, 1980, p. iii, citing the World Bank's Renewable Energy Task Force survey of needs in 10 countries (Central African Republic, Chad, Ethiopia, Gabon, Mali, Rwanda, Somalia, Tanzania, Uganda, and Burkina Faso, then known as Upper Volta), where fuelwood accounts for 90 percent or more of all energy consumed.
2. Ibid., p. iv.
3. Ibid., p. 14. According to James W. Howe and Frances A. Gulick, "Firewood and Other Renewable Energies in Africa: A Progress Report on the Problem and the Response," Overseas Development Council, March 31, 1980, p. 21: "A recent case history from a Kougougou (Upper Volta) regional development project,

assisted by FAO/UNDP funds, illustrates the fact that, without manpower, transport, and gasoline, foresters, however well motivated, cannot be expected to service and supervise even small-scale planting programs successfully."

4. Gulick, op. cit., p. 12.

5. Fred Weber, "A Reforestation Project in Algeria: What It May Mean to Future Forestry and Conservation Activities in Sub-Saharan Africa," US AID/Africa, February 12, 1981. In Brazil, where the government had chosen to create plantations rather then follow the path of community forestry, the public subsidy alone ranged from $1,235 to $2,025 per hectare, thereby giving this plantation project "the dubious distinction of being one of the most costly man-made forests in the world," according to "The Socio-Economic Context of Fuelwood Use in Small Rural Communities," US AID Evaluation Special Study No. 1, August 1980, p. 113.

6. Gulick, op. cit., p. 13.

7. The term "contagion" refers to the spread of technologies by emulation alone, and was first used in this sense, as far as I know, by William Gross, then head of Volunteers for International Technical Assistance.

8. The information in this section is based on the following: Richard Pankhurst, *Economic History of Ethiopia, 1800–1935* (Addis Ababa, 1968), pp. 247, 705, and 707; the National Academy of Science's Ethiopian case-study, *Firewood Crops: Shrub and Tree Species for Energy* (Washington, D.C., 1981); Ronald J. Horvath, "Addis Ababa's Eucalyptus Forest," in *The Journal of Ethiopian Studies* (Addis Ababa), 6 (1968): 13–19; and from limited observations during fieldwork in 1970–1 and 1975.

9. There is evidence that all developed countries, whether socialist or capitalist, have found it necessary to provide public funds for agricultural research and development; apart from the fact that the initial costs are so high, the flow of information cannot readily be privatised to create sufficient incentives. For a discussion of the dilemma which the production and utilisation of knowledge creates for private enterprise, see Harry G. Johnson, "The Efficiency and Welfare Implications of the International Corporation," in Charles P. Kindleberger, ed., *The International Corporation: A Symposium* (Cambridge, Mass., 1970), pp. 35–56.

10. Horvath, loc. cit., p. 17.

11. Jane Jacobs, *The Economy of Cities* (New York, 1970), chap. 1.

12. See Allan Hoben, *Land Tenure among the Amhara of Ethiopia: The Dynamics of Cognatic Descent* (Chicago and London, 1973), and Dan Franz Bauer, *Household and Society in Ethiopia* (East Lansing, 1977), for an examination of several land-tenure systems and their impact on innovation.

13. *Firewood Crops*, p. 180.

14. For a description of the technology and uses of remote sensing, see Barry N. Haack, "Landsat: A Tool for Development," in *World Development* (Oxford), 10, 10, 1982, pp. 899–909. My thanks go to the Regional Remote Sensing Facility in Nairobi, which provided the photographs.

15. Ethiopian National Energy Authority, "Biomass Fuels Supply and Marketing Review. Interim Report on Biomass Fuels Production, End-Use Efficiency, and Sales Mechanisms," Addis Ababa, April 1988, written by Robert A. Chronowski, under the direction of Lemma Eshetu of ENEA. Although the authors clearly note that their findings are less than statistically robust because of the logistical

difficulties encountered during the three-week survey, I have taken the view that the reported evidence is worth summarising.

16. Ibid., p. 1.
17. Ibid., p. 26.
18. Ibid., p. 15.
19. Ibid., p. 9. The price series upon which the data are based were taken from the World Bank and from the CEPPE. Addis Household Fuel Survey, Addis Ababa, 1986.
20. Ethiopian National Energy Authority, op. cit., pp. 3 and 13–14.
21. Ibid., pp. 3 and 10.
22. Ibid., p. 6, my emphasis.

15
The New Development Economics

Joseph E. Stiglitz

1. INTRODUCTION

For the past 15 years, I have been attempting to construct a consistent view of less developed economies and the development process, to identify in what ways they are similar and in what ways (and why) they are different from more developed economies.[1] I cannot present even a summary of these views here. What I have been asked to do is to present one piece of that perspective, that relating to the organization of the rural sector, and to explain why I (or someone else) should "believe" these theories, or at least, why they are more plausible than several widely discussed alternative theories.

There are five central tenets of my approach:

1. Individuals (including peasants in the rural sectors of LDCs) are rational, that is, they act in a (reasonably) consistent manner, one which adapts to changes in circumstances.

2. Information is costly. This has numerous important implications: individuals do not acquire perfect information, and hence their behavior may differ markedly from what it would have been if they had perfect information. When individuals engage in a trade (buying labor services, extending credit, renting land or bullocks), there is imperfect information concerning the items to be traded; thus, transactions which would be desirable in the presence of perfect information may not occur. Similarly, certain contracts, e.g., performing certain services at a certain standard, may not be feasible,

I am indebted to A. Braverman and R. Sah for helpful discussions. Financial support from the National Science Foundation is gratefully acknowledged. Reprinted with permission from *World Development*, 14, 2 (1986), pp. 257–65. Copyright © 1986 by Pergamon Press, Ltd.

especially if it is costly to ascertain, *ex post*, whether or how well those services have been performed.

3. Institutions adapt to reflect these information (and other transaction) costs. Thus, institutions are not to be taken as exogenous, but are endogenous, and changes in the environment may lead, with a lag, to changes in institutional structure.

4. The fact that individuals are rational and that institutions are adaptable does not, however, imply that the economy is (Pareto) efficient. The efficiency of market economies obtains only under the peculiar set of circumstances explored by Arrow and Debreu. These include a complete set of markets and perfect information, assumptions which, if questionable in more developed economies, are clearly irrelevant in LDCs. With imperfect information and incomplete markets, the economy is almost always constrained Pareto inefficient, i.e., there exists a set of taxes and subsidies which can make everyone better off (see Greenwald and Stiglitz, forthcoming).

5. This implies that there is a *potential* role for the government. That is, the government could effect a Pareto improvement if (i) it had sufficient knowledge of the structure of the economy; (ii) those responsible for implementing government policy had at least as much information as those in the private sector; (iii) those responsible for designing and implementing government policy had the incentives to direct policies to effect Pareto improvements, rather than, for instance, to redistribute income (either from the poor to the rich or vice versa, or from everyone else, to themselves), often at considerable loss to national output. Informational problems, including incentive problems, are no less important in the public sector than in the private; the fact that we have studied them well in the latter does not mean that they are not present in the former. The consequence of these remarks is to make us cautious in recommending particular government actions as remedies for certain observed deficiencies in the market.

2. THE BASIC OUTLINES OF THE THEORY OF RURAL ORGANIZATION

In this section, I wish to outline what the general approach presented above says about the economic organization of the rural sector. There are a wide variety of institutional arrangements observed in different LDCs. One set that has been of longstanding interest to economists is sharecropping. Earlier views of sharecropping held that it was an inefficient form of economic organization: the worker received less than the value of his marginal product, and thus he had insufficient incentives to exert effort. The question was, how could such a seemingly inefficient form of economic organization have survived for so long (and why should it be such a prevalent form of economic organization at so many different places at different times?). For those who believe in even a modicum of economic rationality, some explanation had to be found.

One explanation that comes to mind is that peasants are more risk averse than landlords: if workers rented the land from the landlords, they would have to bear all of the risk. Though workers' risk aversion is undoubtedly of importance, it cannot be the entire explanation: there are alternative (and perhaps more effective) risk-sharing arrangements. In particular, in the wage system, the landlord bears all of the risk, the worker none. Any degree of risk sharing between the landlord and the worker can be attained by the worker dividing his time between working as a wage-laborer and working on his own or rented land.[2]

The other central part of the explanation of sharecropping is that it provides an effective incentive system in the presence of costly supervision. Since in a wage system, the worker's compensation is not directly related to his output, the landlord must spend resources to ensure that the worker actually works. In a sharecropping system, since the worker's pay depends directly on his output, he has some incentives to work. The incentives may not be as strong as they would if he owned the land (since he receives, say, only half the product); but that is not the relevant alternative. Sharecropping thus represents a compromise between the rental system, in which incentives are "correct" but all the risk is borne by the worker, and the wage system, in which the landlord who is in a better position to bear risk, bears all the risk but in which effort can only be sustained through expenditures on supervision. This new view (Stiglitz, April 1974) turns the traditional criticism of sharecropping on its head: it is precisely because of its incentive properties, relative to the relevant alternative, the wage system, that the sharecropping system is employed.

The contention that the rental system provides correct incentives is, however, not quite correct. The rental system provides correct incentives for effort decisions. But tenants make many decisions other than those involving effort; they make decisions concerning the choice of technique, the use of fertilizer, the timing of harvest, etc. These decisions affect the riskiness of the outcomes. For instance, many of the high-yielding seed varieties have a higher mean output, but a greater sensitivity to rainfall. Whenever there is a finite probability of default (that is, the tenant not paying the promised rent), then tenants may not have, with the rental system, the correct incentives with respect to these decisions. Of course, with unlimited liability, the worker could be made to bear all of the costs. But since the tenant might be unable to pay his rent even if he had undertaken all of the "right" decisions, and since it is often difficult to ascertain whether the individual took "unnecessary" risks, most societies are reluctant to grant unlimited liability, or to use extreme measures like debtor prisons, to ensure that individuals do not take unnecessary risks.[3] Hence, in effect, part of the costs of risk taking by the tenant is borne by the landlord.[4] With sharecropping, both the landlord and the tenant face the same risks.[5]

Thus, sharecropping can be viewed as an institution which has developed in response to (1) risk aversion on the part of workers; (2) the limited ability (or desire) to force the tenant to pay back rents when he is clearly unable to do so; and (3) the limited ability to monitor the actions of the tenant (or the high costs of doing so).

The general theory has been extended in a number of directions, only three of which I can discuss here: cost sharing, interlinkage, and technical change.

In many situations, there are other important inputs besides labor and land, such as bullocks or fertilizer. How should these inputs be paid for? Clearly, if the worker pays all of the costs, but receives only a fraction of the benefits, he will have an insufficient incentive to supply these other inputs. Cost sharing is a proposed remedy. If the worker receives 50% of the output, and pays 50% of the cost, it would appear that he has the correct incentives: both benefits and costs have been cut in half.[6]

But in fact, though cost shares equal to output shares are common, they are far from universal. How do we explain these deviations from what seems both a simple, reasonable rule, and a rule which ensures economic efficiency? To find the answer, we again return to our general theoretical framework, which focuses on the role of imperfect information. First, it is clear that the landlord may want the tenant to supply more fertilizer than he would with a 50–50 rule, if increasing the fertilizer increases the marginal product of labor, and thus induces the worker to work harder. Remember, the central problem of the landlord is that he cannot directly control the actions of his worker; he must induce them to work hard. The reason that sharecropping was employed was to provide these additional incentives.

But if a cost-sharing arrangement can be implemented, it means that the expenditures can be monitored; and if the expenditures can be monitored, there is no necessity for engaging in cost sharing; rather the terms of the contract could simply specify the levels of various inputs. But workers typically have more information about current circumstances than the landlord (in the fashionable technical jargon, we say there is an asymmetry of information). A contract which specifies the level of inputs cannot adapt to the changing circumstances. Cost-sharing contracts provide the ability and incentives for these adaptations, and thus are more efficient contracts than contracts which simply specified the level of inputs.[7]

Another aspect of economic organization in many LDCs is the interlinkage of markets: the landlord may also supply credit (and he may also supply food and inputs). How can we explain this interlinkage? Some have claimed that it is simply another way that landlords exploit their workers.

We shall comment later on these alternative explanations. For now, we simply note that our general theory can explain the prevalence of interlinkage (both under competitive and noncompetitive circumstances). We have repeatedly noted the problem of the landlord in inducing the worker both to work hard and to make the "correct" decisions from his point of view (with respect to choice of technique, etc.). Exactly analogous problems arise with respect to lenders. Their concern is that the borrower will default on the loan. The probability of a default depends in part on the actions taken by the borrower. The actions of the tenant-borrower thus affect both the lender and the landlord. Note too that the terms of the contract with the landlord will affect the lender, and vice versa: if the landlord can, for instance, reduce the probability of default by supplying more fertilizer, the lender is better off. The actions of the borrower (both with respect to effort and the choice of technique) may be affected by the individual's indebtedness, so that the landlord's (expected) income may be affected by the amount (and terms) of indebtedness. There appear to be clear and possibly significant externalities between the actions of the landlord and the actions of the lender. Whenever there are such externalities, a natural market solution is to internalize the externality, and that is precisely what the interlinkage of markets does.[8]

Thus, interlinkage is motivated by the desire for economic efficiency, not necessarily by the desire for further exploitation of the worker.

Interlinkage has, in turn, been linked to the incentives landlords have for resisting profitable innovations. Bhaduri[9] has argued, for instance, that landlords-cum-creditors may resist innovations, because innovations reduce the demand for credit, and thus the income which they receive in their capacity as creditors. Braverman and Stiglitz[10] have shown that there is no presumption that innovations result in a reduction in the demand for credit. Credit is used to smooth income across periods, and under quite plausible conditions, innovations may either increase or decrease the aggregate demand for credit. But they argue further that what happens to the demand for credit is beside the point.

The central question is simply whether the innovation moves the economically relevant utilities possibilities schedule outward or inward. The utilities possibilities schedule gives the maximum level of (expected) utility to one group (the landlord) given the level of (expected) utility of the other (the workers). The economically relevant utilities possibilities curve takes into account the information problems which have been the center of our discussion thus far, for instance, the fact that with sharecropping, individuals' incentives are different from what they would be with costless monitoring. The utilities possibilities schedule with costless monitoring might move one way, the economically relevant utilities possibilities schedule the other. Thus, for instance, there are innovations which, at each level of input, increase the output, but which, at the same time, exacerbate the incentives-monitoring problem. Such innovations would not be socially desirable. Landlords would resist such innovations, as well they should, though from an "engineering" point of view, such innovations might look desirable.

The consequences of interlinkage for the adoption of innovations, within this perspective, are ambiguous. There are innovations which would be adopted with interlinkage, but would not without it, and conversely; but the effect of the innovation on the demand for credit does not seem to play a central role.

Though the landlord correctly worries about the incentive-monitoring consequences of an innovation, one should not jump to the conclusions either that the landlords collectively make decisions which maximize their own welfare, or that the landlord always makes the socially efficient decision. The landlord, within a competitive environment, will adopt an innovation if at current prices (terms of contracts, etc.) it is profitable for him to do so. Of course, when all the landlords adopt the innovation, prices (terms of contracts) will change, and they may change in such a way that landlords are adversely affected.[11] In a competitive environment landlords cannot resist innovations simply because it is disadvantageous to them to do so. (By contrast, if they are in a "monopoly" position, they will not wish to resist such innovations, since presumably they will be able to capture all the surplus associated with the innovation.)

But just as the market allocation is not constrained Pareto efficient (even assuming a perfectly competitive economy) whenever there are problems of moral hazard, so too the market decisions concerning innovation are not constrained Pareto efficient. (We use the term constrained Pareto efficient to remind us that we are accounting for the limitations on information; we have not assumed the government has any information other than that possessed by private individuals.) Though in principle there exist government interventions which (accounting for the costs of information) could make everyone better off, whether such Pareto improving interventions are likely to emerge from the political process remains a moot question.

3.   ALTERNATIVE THEORIES

In this section, I wish to present in summary form what I view to be the major competing approaches to understanding the organization of economic activity in the rural sector.

In many respects, I see my view as lying between other more extreme views. In one, the peasant is viewed as rational, working in an environment with reasonably complete information and complete and competitive markets. In this view, then, the differences between LDCs and more developed countries lies not so much in the difference between sophisticated, maximizing farmers and uneducated rule-bound peasants as it does in differences in the economic environments, the goods produced by these economies, their endowments, and how their endowments are used to produce goods. In this view, sharecropping is a rational response to the problems of risk sharing; but there is less concern about the incentive problems than I have expressed; with perfect information and perfect enforceability of contracts, the sharecropping contract can enforce the desired level of labor supply and the choice of technique which is efficient. These theories have had little to say about some of the other phenomena which I have discussed: interlinkage, technical change, cost sharing. Interlinkage might be explained in terms of the advantages in transactions costs, but if transactions costs were central, one should only have observed simple cost-sharing rules (with cost share equalling output share).

By contrast, there are those who view the peasant as irrational, with his behavior dictated by customs and institutions which may have served a useful function at some previous time but no longer do so. This approach (which I shall refer to, somewhat loosely, as the institutional-historical approach) may attempt to describe the kinds of LDCs in which there is sharecropping, interlinkage, or cost sharing. It may attempt to relate current practices to earlier practices. In particular, the institutional-historical approach may identify particular historical events which lead to the establishment of the sharecropping system, or the development of the credit system. But this leaves largely unanswered the question of why so many LDCs developed similar institutional structures, or why in some countries cost shares equal output shares, while in others the two differ. More fundamentally, a theory must explain how earlier practices developed; and to provide an explanation of these, one has to have recourse to one of the other theories. Thus, by itself, the institutional-historical approach is incomplete.

Still a third view emphasizes the departures from competitiveness in the rural sector, and the consequent ability of the landlords to exploit the workers. In some cases, workers are tied to their land; legal constraints may put the landlord in a position to exploit the worker. But in the absence of these legal constraints, one has to explain how the landlords exercise their allegedly coercive powers. In many LDCs there is a well-developed labor market. Many landlords need laborers at harvest time and at planting time. The worker chooses for whom he will work. It is important to recognize that the exploitation hypothesis fails to explain the mechanisms by which, in situations where there are many landlords, they exercise their exploitative power.[12] More generally, it fails to explain variations in the degree of exploitation over time and across countries. The fact that wages are low is not necessarily evidence of exploitation: the competitive market will yield low wages when the value of the marginal product of labor is low.

The exploitation hypothesis also fails to explain the detailed structure of rural organization: why cost shares are the way they are, or why (or how) landlords who can exploit their workers use the credit market to gain further exploitative capacity.

There may be some grain of truth in all these approaches. Important instances of currently dysfunctional institutions and customs can clearly be identified. Institutional structures clearly do not adapt instantaneously to changed circumstances. Yet, as social scientists, our objective is to identify the systematical components, the regularities of social behavior, to look for general principles underlying a variety of phenomena. It is useful to describe the institutions found in the rural sector of LDCs, but description is not enough.

Therefore, I view the rationality hypothesis as a convenient starting point, a simple and general principle with which to understand economic behavior. Important instances of departures from rationality may well be observed. As social scientists, our objective is to look for *systematic* departures. Some systematic departures have been noted, for instance in the work of Tversky, in individuals' judgments of probabilities, particularly of small probability events; but as Binswanger's 1978 study has noted, departures from the theory appear less important in "important" decisions than in less important decisions. Many of the seeming departures from "rationality" that have been noted can be interpreted as "rational" decision-making in the presence of imperfect information.

I also view the competitiveness hypothesis as a convenient starting point.[13] Many of the central phenomena of interest can be explained without recourse to the exploitation hypothesis. Some degree of imperfect competition is not inconsistent with the imperfect information paradigm: the imperfect information paradigm provides part of the explanation for the absence of perfect competition; it can help identify situations where the landlords may be in a better position to exploit the workers. Moreover, to the extent that imperfect information limits the extent to which even a monopoly landlord can extract surplus from his workers, the imperfect information paradigm can provide insights into how he can increase his monopoly profits. The theory of interlinkage we have developed can thus be applied to the behavior of a monopolist landlord.

There is one other approach that has received some attention that is, in fact, closely related to the one I have advocated: the transactions cost approach, which attempts to explicate economic relations by focusing on transactions costs. Information costs are an important part of transactions costs (though information problems arise in other contexts as well). My reservations concerning the transactions cost approach lie in its lack of specificity: while the information paradigm provides a well-defined structure which allows one to derive clear propositions concerning, for instance, the design of contracts, the transactions cost paradigm does not. Thus, the transactions cost approach might provide some insight into why cost sharing is employed, but not into the terms of the cost-sharing agreement. The transactions cost paradigm might say that economies of scope provide an explanation for why the landlord also supplies credit, but it does not provide insights into when the landlord-cum-creditor would subsidize credit, or when he would "tax" it. Moreover, while the information paradigm identifies parameters which affect the magnitude of the externalities between landlords and creditors, and thus enables, in principle, the identification of circumstances under which interlinkage is more likely to be observed, the transactions cost paradigm can do little more than to say that there are circumstances in which the diseconomies of scope exceed the economies, and in these circumstances there will not be interlinkage.

4.   CRITERIA FOR EVALUATING ALTERNATIVE THEORIES

In the previous section, I discussed briefly some of the major competing hypotheses. In this section, I wish to outline a set of criteria for evaluating a theory, and to apply these criteria to these alternative theories. No novelty is claimed for the criteria; no attempt is made to provide a general epistemological theory.[14] These are presented more in the spirit of a "working man's" criteria.

We can divide the criteria into two groups: internal and external. The internal criteria include[15]:

1. *Internal consistency:* Are the axioms (underlying assumptions) mutually consistent, and do the conclusions follow from these assumptions?
2. *Simplicity:* In general, the fewer the assumptions required to explain the given phenomena, the better.
3. *Completeness:* The assumptions of the model should be as "primitive" as possible. Thus, in macroeconomics, a theory which explains unemployment in terms of wage rigidities is, in this sense, incomplete: it leaves open the question of why wages are rigid.

The external criteria include:

1. *Verifiability* (or falsifiability): The theory should have at least some implications which are verifiable or falsifiable, in principle; that is, it should at least be possible to design thought experiments under which some of the implications of the theory could be rejected.
2. *External consistency:* Are *all* the implications of the model consistent with observations? Note that among the (obvious and direct) implications of the model are those that directly follow from the assumptions; thus, if an assumption itself can be falsified, the model will not possess the property of external consistency. Friedman's contention that a theory should be judged only by the validity of its conclusions is, in this view, wrong. Theories whose assumptions

seem unreasonable, i.e., whose assumptions themselves can be falsified or whose assumptions have other implications which seem
unacceptable (i.e., can be falsified) should be rejected. *Some* of the
implications of many "bad" theories may be correct; indeed, probably no theory that has received any attention has *all* of its implications inconsistent with (at least some interpretations of) the data.
But a good theory should have no implication which is inconsistent
with observations.

3. *External completeness:* The theory should have something to say
   about as many regularities that have been observed in the area of
   study as possible. Thus, a theory which explains both why there is
   sharecropping as well as the determinants of the shares is better
   than a theory which simply explains why there is sharecropping.
   This is closely related to the criteria of:

4. *Specificity:* A good theory should make as many specific predictions
   concerning particular phenomena as possible.

5. *Predictive power:* A good theory should not only be consistent with
   regularities which have already been noted, but also suggest new
   regularities which have not yet been noted.

6. *Generality:* The same general hypotheses should be able to explain
   phenomena in widely different contexts.

I now want to review the performance of the alternative theories in
terms of these basic criteria. The imperfect information paradigm does well,
I would argue, on all of the criteria. The work in this area has been marked
by an attempt to state clearly the assumptions, and to derive its conclusions
from the assumptions: it does well on the criterion of internal consistency.
Similarly, it does well on the other two internal criteria: the assumptions are
simple and are reasonably primitive. Though in most work, the information
technology is taken as given, in some ongoing research (see, e.g.,
Braverman-Stiglitz, forthcoming), even this is taken to be endogenously
determined. The theory provides specific predictions which are verifiable,
and indeed has something to say about virtually every aspect of rural economic organization. It makes predictions concerning a variety of regularities that should be found in LDCs, but unfortunately, these have not been
subjected to rigorous testing. At the same time, there is no well-agreed
upon regularity that seems inconsistent with the theory.

One of its most attractive properties, however, is that the information
paradigm provides a general framework which is applicable to both developed and less developed economies. The concerns about effort and choice
of technique which are central to sharecropping reappear, in somewhat
modified form, in the analysis of labor and capital markets in more developed countries. It shares this property with the "rational peasant, with per-

fect markets and complete information" paradigm. But the latter theory fails to provide a good account of the differences between developed and less developed economies.

But my major objection to the rational peasant model with full information and complete markets (as with the corresponding theories of developed economies) is that it is inconsistent with many observations and it fails to provide explanations of others.

It does not explain why sharecropping is employed (with perfect information, there are a variety of equivalent contractual forms; if sharecropping were employed, the contract would specify the amount of labor to be supplied).

It fails to explain cost sharing, and in particular why cost shares should differ from output shares.

It assumes that there is a complete set of risk markets; it is clear that individuals cannot purchase insurance against many important risks and that this has important consequences for their behavior.

In most small villages, it is not reasonable to assume that if a landlord offered a rupee less to his wage laborers, he would obtain no workers. In many situations, there appear to be workers who are willing to work at the going wage, but fail to obtain employment: there appears to be involuntary unemployment, a phenomenon which seems inconsistent with the classical competitive models.

This theory can be adapted to make it at least seem to explain the phenomena under study and to make it seem less inconsistent with the facts[16]: indeed, our imperfect information paradigm can be thought of as one such adaptation. But we would argue that it is a fundamental alteration, one which affects our views of economic relations under a wide variety of circumstances. When a theory provides predictions which are inconsistent with the facts in a wide variety of circumstances, and when it fails to provide explanations of important regularities, what is needed is not an ad hoc modification of the model on a case-by-case basis, but rather a basic reformulation: the imperfect information paradigm provides such a reformulation.

The transactions cost approach represents another attempt to modify the basic theory in a consistent way. As we have commented above, information costs are a particular form of transaction costs, and I find many aspects of the transactions cost approach attractive.[17] But the theory fails on several of the critical external criteria: to the extent that the theory relies on unobservable transaction costs, it often seems to fail the test of falsifiability; just as the present set of economic relations is justified by current (unobservable) transaction costs, changes in the nature of economic relations are "explained" by reference to similarly unobservable changes in transaction costs. The theory also fails the test of specificity of predictions and of external completeness: as we noted, while it may provide an explanation for why sharecropping is employed, it cannot explain the nature of the cost-sharing arrangements and has little to say about other items of the share-cropping contract.

By contrast, the exploitation theory fails on both the internal and external criteria for judging theories. There is not a clearly stated set of primitive assumptions from which the conclusions logically follow. For instance, if the structure of economic relations is determined by the attempt of landlords to exploit their workers, what determines the limits on their capacities to do so? The theory fails to explain why sharecropping provides a better method of exploitation than other forms of contractual arrangements; it fails to explain why cost sharing enhances the ability of the landlord to exploit his workers. It fails to explain the circumstances under which cost shares would exceed output shares. And it fails to explain why providing credit enhances the ability of the landlord to exploit the peasant. When there are many landlords in a community, it fails to explain how they can act collusively together. The experience with cartels in other areas is that it is hard to maintain collusive arrangements voluntarily when the number of participants becomes more than a few. If this is true here, then the theory only provides an explanation of the structure of economic relations within communities with a limited number of landlords; if this is not true in LDCs, why?

To the extent that the theory relies on the notion of power which cannot be independently quantified, the theory is not falsifiable: one can always account for differences in the terms of the contract over time or geographically in terms of differences in power.[18] To the extent that the theory fails to provide answers to these questions, it is seriously incomplete.

5. CONCLUSIONS

The theory of rural organization which is based on rational peasants in environments in which information is imperfect and costly provides a simple explanation for a wide variety of phenomena in LDCs. It represents an important application of a more general paradigm, what I have referred loosely to as the "Imperfect Information Paradigm" which has been useful in explaining phenomena under a wide variety of settings, under competition, oligopoly, and monopoly, in labor markets, capital markets, insurance markets, and product markets. The richness of social phenomena is such as to make it unreasonable to expect any theory to explain all of the observed variations in institutions and behavior. But a theory should at least be able to explain the important regularities. Here, we are concerned with explaining sharecropping, both its widespread use, and the form it takes; it should explain cost sharing, with cost shares frequently differing from output shares, and the interlinkage of credit and land markets. This our theory does, and the competing theories fail to do. There is a rich set of further predictions emanating from our theory which have yet to be tested. Whether, when these tests are performed, the theory will still stand, or whether it will have to be modified, or abandoned, remains to be seen.

NOTES

1. For two surveys of certain aspects of this work, see Stiglitz (1982b, 1985).
2. See Stiglitz (April 1974).
3. Indeed, such extreme measures may have deleterious incentive effects, discouraging risk taking.
4. See Johnson (1950); Allen (1985).
5. This aspect of sharecropping has been emphasized by Johnson (1950), and by Braverman and Stiglitz (1982a). See also Stiglitz and Weiss (1981).
6. See Heady (1947).
7. See Braverman and Stiglitz (1982b).
8. See Braverman and Stiglitz (1982a). This problem is discussed in the more general information theoretic literature under the rubric of the multiple principle-agent problem. The externalities which we have discussed here arise in virtually all moral hazard problems. See Arnott and Stiglitz (1984).
9. See Bhaduri (1973).
10. Braverman and Stiglitz (forthcoming).
11. If the innovation, at the current prices, increases the demand for workers enough, then the terms of the contracts may shift sufficiently in workers' favor to make landlords worse off. This is analogous to what, in more simple contexts, is referred to as a Pigou land-saving innovation.
12. Note that recent advances in repeated games have shown how collusive outcomes can be attained even in noncooperative settings. Thus, landlords in rural economies where mobility is limited and in which there are only a few landlords in any community may well act collusively. The circumstances in which these noncooperative collusive arrangements work well has, however, not been well studied.
13. Indeed, with limited labor mobility, in small villages the labor markets are unlikely to be perfectly competitive; at the same time, the landlord is far from a labor monopolist. The real world is probably better described by a model of "monopolistic competition" than either of the polar models, monopoly or perfect competition.
14. Similarly, this is not the place to provide an evaluation of alternative theories (e.g., the theories of Karl Popper).
15. This list is not meant to be exhaustive. An important criterion in other contexts is *robustness*; the conclusions of the theory should not be sensitive to small perturbations in the assumptions.
16. When the theory gets complicated by these ad hoc modifications it loses the property of simplicity, which was originally one of its main virtues.
17. It is sometimes suggested that, once transactions costs are accounted for, equilibrium with rational peasants will have all the standard efficiency properties that economies with no transactions costs have. This is another example where the conclusion does not follow logically from the assumptions; the conclusion is

arrived at by reasoning by analogy. Transactions costs (including information costs) are "like" other production costs. Why, once these are appropriately accounted for, should not the economy still be efficient?

Unfortunately, it turns out that, in general, economies with imperfect information (or incomplete markets) are not constrained Pareto efficient (where the term "constrained" Pareto efficient simply reminds us that we have appropriately taken into account the transactions costs (information imperfection, incomplete markets). (See Greenwald and Stiglitz, forthcoming.) The formalization of Adam Smith's invisible hand conjecture is one of the great achievements of modern economic theory; the Fundamental theorem of economics, like any other theorem, depends on the assumptions. The assumptions concerning perfect information, no transactions costs, and complete markets are not innocuous assumptions, but are central to the validity of the result. Information costs may, in some respects, be like other costs of production, but the differences are sufficiently important to invalidate the Fundamental Theorem of Welfare Economics.
18. Thus, "power" is to the exploitation theory what transactions cost is to the transactions cost model.

REFERENCES

Allen, F. "The Fixed Nature of Sharecropping Contracts." *Journal of Public Economics* (March 1985): 30–48.

Arnott, R., and J. E. Stiglitz. "Equilibrium in Competitive Insurance Markets." Mimeo. (Princeton University, 1984).

Bhaduri, A. "Agricultural Backwardness under Semifeudalism." *Economic Journal* (1973).

Binswanger, H. P. "Attitudes Towards Risk: Experimental Measurement Evidence in Rural India." *American Journal of Agricultural Economics*, 62, 3 (August 1980): 395–407.

Binswanger, H. P. "Attitudes Towards Risk: Implications and Psychological Theories of an Experiment in Rural India." Yale University Economic Growth Center DP 286 (1978b).

Braverman, A., and J. E. Stiglitz. "Sharecropping and the Interlinking of Agrarian Markets." *American Economic Review*, 72, 4 (September 1982a): 695–715.

Braverman, A., and J. E. Stiglitz. "Moral hazard, incentive flexibility and risk: Cost sharing arrangements under sharecropping," Princeton University, Econometric Research Center Memorandum No. 298 (1982b).

Braverman, A., and J. E. Stiglitz. "Cost Sharing Arrangements under Sharecropping: Moral Hazard, Incentive Flexibility and Risk." Mimeo. (Princeton University, 1985).

Braverman, A., and J. E. Stiglitz. "Landlords, Tenants and Technological Innovations." *Journal of Development Economics* (forthcoming).

Greenwald, B., and J. E. Stiglitz, "Externalities in Economies with Imperfect Information and Incomplete Markets." *Quarterly Journal of Economics* (forthcoming).

Heady, E. "Economics of Farm Leasing System." *Journal of Farm Economics* (August 1947).

Johnson, D. Gale "Resource Allocation under Share Contracts." *Journal of Public Economics* (April 1950): 111–23.

Newbery, D., and J. E. Stiglitz. "Sharecropping, Risk Sharing, and the Importance of Imperfect Information," paper presented to a conference in Mexico City, March 1976, and published in Ja. A. Roumasset et al., eds., *Risk, Uncertainty and Development* (SEARCA, A/D/C, 1979), pp. 311–41.

Newbery, D., and J. E. Stiglitz. *The Theory of Commodity Price Stabilization* (Oxford University Press, 1981).

Newbery, D., and J. E. Stiglitz. "The Choice of Techniques and the Optimality of Market Equilibrium with Rational Expectations." *Journal of Political Economy*, 90, 2 (April 1982): 223–46.

Stiglitz, J. E. "Rural-Urban Migration, Surplus Labor and the Relationship between Urban and Rural Wages." *East African Economic Review*, 1–2 (December 1969): 1–27.

Stiglitz, J. E. "Alternate Theories of Wage Determination and Unemployment in LDCs: The Labor Turnover Model." *Quarterly Journal of Economics*, 87 (May 1974): 194–227.

Stiglitz, J. E. "Incentives and Risk Sharing in Sharecropping." *Review of Economic Studies*, 41 (April 1974): 219–55.

Stiglitz, J. E. "The Efficiency Wage Hypothesis, Surplus Labor and the Distribution of Income in LDCs." *Oxford Economic Papers*, 28, 2 (July 1976): 185–207.

Stiglitz, J. E. "Some Further Remarks on Cost-Benefit Analysis." In H. Schwartz and R. Berney, eds., *Social and Economic Dimensions of Project Evaluation* (IDB, 1977); Proceedings of the Symposium on Cost-Benefit Analysis, IDB, Washington, D.C., March 1973, pp. 253–82.

Stiglitz, J. E. "Alternative Theories of Wage Determination and Unemployment: The Efficiency Wage Model." In Gersovitz et al., eds., *The Theory and Experience of Economic Development: Essays in Honor of Sir W. Arthur Lewis* (London: George Allen & Unwin, 1982a), pp. 78–106.

Stiglitz, J. E. "Structure of Labor Markets and Shadow Prices in LDCs." Presented at World Bank Conference, February 1976, in R. Sabot, ed., *Migration and the Labor Market in Developing Countries* (Boulder, Colo.: Westview Press 1982b), pp. 13–64.

Stiglitz, J. E. "The Wage-Productivity Hypothesis: Its Economic Consequences and Policy Implications." Paper presented to the American Economic Association, 1982.

Stiglitz, J. E. "Economics of Information and the Theory of Economic Development." *Revista de Econometria* (forthcoming).

Stiglitz, J. E., and A. Weiss. "Credit Rationing in Markets with Imperfect Information." *American Economic Review*, 71, 3 (June 1981): 393–410.

Tversky, A. "Intransitivity of Preferences." *Psychological Review*, 76 (1969): 31–48.

16

The Peasant Economy: Internal Logic, Articulation, and Persistence

Alexander Schejtman

INTRODUCTION

Until very recently, studies on economic development, agrarian structure, and the agricultural economy in Latin America, whatever the school of theory to which their authors subscribed, failed to perceive peasant agriculture as a specific and distinct form of organization of production.

Under the approaches derived, to a greater or lesser extent, from nineteenth-century liberalism and the Ricardian school of political economy, the peasantry was a sociocultural remnant of the past—whether termed feudal, precapitalist, or traditional—destined to disappear fairly rapidly as a result of the growth of commercial agriculture and manufacturing; for that reason, it merited no more consideration as a form of production than that involved in analysis of the mechanisms which encourage or hinder its "modernization."

For neoclassical economists, the peasant family unit did not constitute a specific object of analysis as distinct from the agricultural enterprise (or, for these purposes, from any other production unit), since as far as the behaviour of the producer was concerned, the differences they observed could all be attributed to different scales of production and differences in the relative availability of factors. For that reason, decisions concerning what, how, and how much to produce were considered to be governed, in both cases, by the tendency for the ratio between the marginal productivity and the price of each of the "factors" used to become uniform; in other words, the allocation of resources was governed by a single type of operating logic.

From *CEPAL Review*, no. 11 (August 1980), pp. 115–134.

The persistence of the peasantry—or, more precisely, the fact that the substantial fall in numbers forecast by political economy seems unlikely to occur within a time scale of significance for social analysis and for the formulation of development strategies—as well as the inability of neoclassical analysis to account for a number of salient features of the behaviour of the peasant producer,[1] have led in the past decade to the emergence of an extensive literature devoted to reexamining the terms in which the peasant question has traditionally been tackled in economic analysis.

Two landmarks may be observed in this process of reexamination. First, a number of critiques have been made since the mid-1960s of the dualist propositions of various schools of thought, both those founded on the traditional-modern dichotomy and those drawn up in terms of the dichotomy between feudalism and capitalism. Second, a tendency has emerged to analyse the peasant economy as a *sui generis* form of organizing production, based on the "rediscovery" of the writings of the so-called Russian populists of the 1920s, and particularly those of A. V. Chayanov and his Organization of Production school.[2]

The criticism of dualism was a factor in the abandonment of the view of peripheral societies as split into two sectors: the traditional, precapitalist, semifeudal or feudal sector, regarded as a relic of a colonial past, and the modern, dynamic or capitalist sector, whose task was to "absorb" and transform the former in its image and likeness.

In opposition to this approach there arose the view that both sectors had been formed by a single historical process, and that they were articulated within a global whole of which both formed an integral part, each accounting for the other. This involved abandonment of the idea of backwardness, and implicit or explicit acceptance of the possibility that peasant forms might persist or even be created as part of a dynamic of capitalist development.

The second of the landmarks mentioned earlier—the study of peasant economy, which is also the fundamental purpose of this article—represents an effort to study an important part of the peripheral economies which, having been described as "traditional," had suffered from neglect in analysis or had simply been assimilated to a single allegedly universal rationality corresponding to that of the "maximizer" of the neoclassical type.

The central part of the present article falls within the context of this latter objective. It constitutes an attempt to combine in a single formulation the contributions of various writers to describing the peasant economy, in an effort to demonstrate both the theoretical legitimacy and the empirical importance of this conceptualization in the formulation of development strategies for countries with a substantial peasant sector.

In addition to analysing the peasant economy as a specific form of organizing production—the principal purpose of the article—we shall in the second part sketch the contrast between the main features of peasant agriculture and those characteristic of commercial or capitalist agriculture. The article concludes with a few considerations on the nature of the insertion or articulation of peasant agriculture within the economy as a whole.

I.   THE SPECIFIC CHARACTERISTICS OF THE PEASANT ECONOMY

The concept of the peasant economy encompasses that sector of domestic agricultural activity in which family-type units engaged in the process of production with the aim of ensuring, from one cycle to another, the reproduction of their living and working conditions, or, to put it another way, the reproduction of the producers and the unit of production itself. Achieving this objective means generating, firstly, the means of subsistence (biological and cultural) of all members of the family, active or not, and secondly—over and above those needs—a fund designed to pay for the replacement of the means of production used in the production cycle and to deal with the various eventualities which may affect the existence of the family group (illness, expenses for formal occasions, and so on).

The operating logic applied to the productive resources available, in other words the logic which governs the decisions concerning what, how, and how much to produce and what to do with the product obtained, falls within the framework of the objectives described above, and gives the peasant economy its own rationality which is distinct from that of commercial agriculture. The latter, in contrast, decides what, how, and how much to produce in such a way as to maximize rates of profit and accumulation. In this regard, then, we would appear to be faced with two specific and distinct forms of social organization of production.[3]

If one postulated the existence of a universal rationality as regards criteria for the allocation of resources, and if one considered that differences in behaviour between the various types of unit should be attributed exclusively to differences of scale and of resource availability, one would have to classify as purely "irrational" a number of basic, recurrent, and empirically observable phenomena in areas where the peasant economy prevails.

By way of illustration we might mention some of these phenomena, which point to the existence of a specific peasant rationality different from the commercial rationality.

An evaluation of the economic results achieved by peasant units over one or more cycles, using conventional "factor cost" concepts, will show in the vast majority of cases that these units systematically incur losses. In other words, when the costs of this type of unit are evaluated, using market prices to impute land rent, current wages to estimate the cost of family labour used, and market prices to impute the value of inputs which are not purchased in the market, with monetary costs actually incurred being added to this total, and when in valuing the product the goods sold are added to those consumed on the spot, valued at market prices, the difference between the value of the product and the cost thus calculated is very often negative. This type of result, which would seem to suggest that "half of mankind is today engaged in productive activity which registers a continuous deficit, is, nevertheless, a sort of *reductio ad absurdum*"[4] and constitutes "an instructive example not of the stupidity or philanthropy of peasants, but of the mistakenness of the belief that there is only one economic rationality in all places and at all times."[5]

The ability of peasant units to sell their livestock at prices which would in many cases signify losses (even with respect to his current costs) for an efficient commercial producer further testifies to the existence of two different ways of valuing resources and products in the two types of economy.

Another phenomenon of this type may be observed in the readiness of the peasant tenant to pay rents (in cash or in kind) which are generally higher than those prevailing in capitalist forms of letting, without any noneconomic pressure necessarily being applied. In neoclassical terms, one might say that the peasant is prepared to pay as land rent more than the estimated value of the "marginal product of the land" or, in the case of purchases of land, to pay for it more than the value of the expected rent, discounted at the internal rate of return on capital which encourages an entrepreneur to invest.[6]

Similarly revealing is the presence in some areas of peasant units which, while possessing productive resources in similar quantities or proportions, cultivate their land with different levels of intensity.[7] This would appear to reveal inefficient or irrational practices on the part of some of these producers, who would seem to have rejected voluntarily an economic "optimum" of the neoclassical type. The same judgment would apply to situations of multiple cropping (or multiple activity), or where staple products occur exclusively despite the possibility of increasing the product through specialization or through inclusion of commercial products involving speculation or risk.

The examples given above are far from exceptional in areas of peasant agriculture, and by no means exhaust the number of empirical observations suggesting the existence of a type of rationality which is distinct from the commercial rationality and is determined by factors of a historical and structural nature, both within and outside the units of production, which will be examined below in some detail.

1.   The Family-Based Nature of the Production Unit

The peasant unit is at the same time a unit of production and a unit of consumption where household activity is inseparable from production activity. In this unit, decisions relating to consumption are inseparable from those which relate to production, and when production is embarked upon little or no use is made of (net) wage labour. This characteristic, which provides an

explanation for many others, has been recognized as being of central importance by all writers who have dealt with the subject of the peasant economy; they have even pointed out that, in many cases, the nuclear or extended nature of the family is an integral part of a production strategy for
survival.

As early as 1913 studies may be found which highlight the phenomenon mentioned above and define peasant units as "consumer-labour
enterprises, with the consumer needs of the family as their aim and the
labour force of the family as their means, with no or very little use of wage
labour."[8] T. Shanin, one of the classics of rural sociology, regards the peasant unit as "characterized by a nearly total integration of the peasant family's life and its farming enterprise. The family provides the work team for
the farm, while the farm's activities are geared mainly to production of the
basic consumption needs of the family plus the enforced dues to the holders of political and economic power."[9] J. Tepicht shares this view: "in our
model the grounding in the family signifies a symbiosis between the agricultural enterprise *(ferme)* and the household economy *(ménage)*."[10]
Chayanov states that "in the family economic unit, which makes no use of
hired labour, the composition and size of the family is one of the main factors in the organization of the peasant economic unit."[11]

The division of labour within the family unit is effected on the basis of
differences of age and sex, and is frequently governed by custom as regards
men's work and women's work. The implications of this attitude to work
are analysed below.[12]

2.   The Irrevocable Commitment to the Family Labour Force

The entrepreneur can regulate the labour force in his unit of production at
will—if we leave aside legal restrictions—as the market dictates. In contrast, the head of the family in a peasant unit takes as his starting point the
family labour force available and has to find productive employment for all
its members. S. H. Franklin, in an important study on the European peasantry,[13] highlights this commitment as the central feature of the peasant unit:

> The head of the peasant unit *(chef d'entreprise)* lacks the freedom of
> action (of the capitalist entrepreneur) to regulate the labour force. His
> labour force is made up of his relations ("kith and kin") . . . and engag-
> ing and dismissing them in accordance with the dictates of some exter-
> nal regulatory mechanism would be at once inhuman, impractical and
> irrational. Inhuman because only in exceptional circumstances is it pos-
> sible to find alternative job opportunities. Impractical because the mem-
> bers of his labour force, as members of the family, have a right to a
> share in the ownership of the means of production . . . Irrational
> because the objectives of the undertaking are first and foremost
> genealogical, and only secondarily economic, since the task of the *"chef"*

is to maximize the labour input rather than profit or any other indicator of efficiency.[14]

Figure 1 clearly shows the implications of this feature, as well as others which will be referred to later, but which Franklin seems to have missed.

The shaded areas in the graph include sets of observations on the intensity of labour (hours per year per hectare) for units of different area with different numbers of standard labour units.[15] The ranges should be read as follows: the (shaded) upper set includes observations on units covering less than 10 hectares; the next on units of between 10 and 20 hectares, and so on until the last, which includes observations on units covering more than 50 hectares.

It may be noted that what Franklin calls the "labour commitment of the *chef d'enterprise*" is reflected in the fact that, for a given range of areas, there is a tendency to raise the number of working days per hectare as the number of labour units increases. In contrast, what is not given sufficient prominence by Franklin is that for each level of size and number of labour units there is a whole range of labour intensities per hectare which tends to be broader as the size of the unit declines. This, as we shall see below, suggests that among the units in a single area category and with the same number of labour units, the number of consumers per labour unit may vary.

FIGURE 1

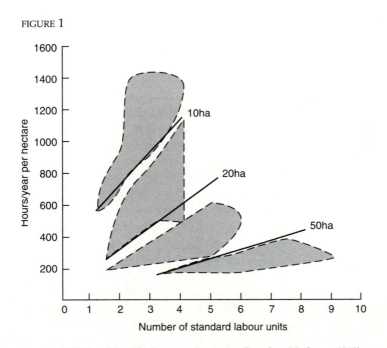

SOURCE: S. H. Franklin, *The European Peasantry* (London: Methuen, 1969), p. 17, where he cites the results of a field study by Van Deeren (1964).

3.   Labour Intensity and Chayanov's Law

The intensity with which factors are used—given a certain availability of factors and a certain technological level—is determined by the degree to which requirements for the reproduction of the family and the unit of production, including debts or undertakings to third parties, are met.

Generally, and all other things being equal, there will be a tendency to intensify labour as the ratio of dependents to labour units rises. In other words, for equal resources (land and means of production), the number of working days per hectare will tend to rise with the ratio between consumers who have to be supported and family labour available. On the other hand, if the amount of land available increases, the number of working days per hectare will tend to fall, all other things being equal. In this regard, it may be said that within the technology range characteristic of the peasant economy, the dominant form of substitution is between land and labour (operating in both directions), in contrast to commercial agriculture, where the dominant substitution is that which tends to occur between capital and labour and between capital and land.[16]

The "rules" for intensification mentioned above can be represented more clearly using a simplified graphic model (Figure 2)[17] where resources (land, means of production, labour force, and so on) and technology are of a given magnitude and are common to all the family units represented, with variations only in the number of the consumers which each unit must support. These consumers are represented in terms of an "average consumer," in standard consumer units (Uc) into which the different age and sex groups of the family members have been converted. This variable (Uc) is represented in the graph as a downward projection of the horizontal axis. The horizontal axis proper (Uc) indicates the available family labour, standardized and expressed in man-hours per year.

If we assume that available working days are greater than $\overline{OY}$, which is the point of greatest intensity (or the point where the marginal product of labour, measured in terms of grain, would become zero), the minimum point of intensity (man-hours per year per unit of area) will depend on Uc, increasing in the same direction as Uc. For Uc = 4, the hours of labour will be $\overline{OX}$; for Uc = 5 they will rise to $\overline{OZ}$, and so on up to $\overline{OY}$ for Uc = 9, where the minimum intensity required and the maximum intensity possible will coincide.

In this case (Uc = 9), the product required to satisfy consumption by this unit is equal to $\overline{OC}$, which is the maximum possible in the light of the land, means of production, and technology available. For all the other cases (Uc ≤ 8) the minimum acceptable intensity would be determined, in the sense, for example, that a family with Uc = 4 has to perform at least $\overline{OX}$ working days; but beyond this point, and up to $\overline{OY}$, determination of the specific level of intensity—what Chayanov calls the "self-exploitation of the labour force"—would be established on the basis of the ratio between the

FIGURE 2

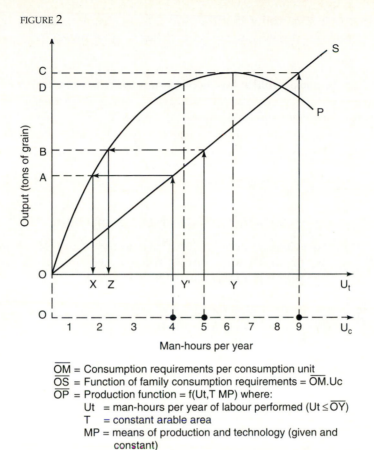

$\overline{OM}$ = Consumption requirements per consumption unit
$\overline{OS}$ = Function of family consumption requirements = $\overline{OM}$.Uc
$\overline{OP}$ = Production function = f(Ut,T MP) where:
    Ut   = man-hours per year of labour performed (Ut $\leq \overline{OY}$)
    T   = constant arable area
    MP = means of production and technology (given and
             constant)

SOURCE: A. Schejtman, "Elementos para una Teoría de la Economía Campesina: Pequeños Propietarios y Campesinos de Hacienda," *El Trimestre Económico*, XLII(2), 166, Mexico City, April–June 1975.

satisfaction of needs which exceed minimum needs and the shortage of additional labour required to meet them.[18] It is unnecessary to point out that when resources are insufficient (Uc > 9 in the example), not only will the intensity used be the maximum possible, but in addition it will be necessary to seek additional employment in order to secure an income which will ensure the reproduction of the family and the unit of production, or else face its deterioration or break-up.[19]

Since in general the situation of peasant units is at or near the point of maximum intensity, the margin for subjective considerations regarding the marginal utility of products and the marginal disutility of effort, which are of central importance in Chayanov's argument, is narrow enough to be irrelevant in practice and to permit determination of the level in terms which lead one to consider that the peasant unit tends to seek to raise its income as much as possible, regardless of the effort involved[20]:

> In contrast to the capitalist, who does not commit funds if he is not assured of a rate of profit at least in proportion to them, and also in contrast to the wage earner, who for each hour of overtime will demand as much as, or more than, he demands for ordinary working hours, the 'personnel' of a family farm are prepared to contribute additional labour to raise their overall income, which [given the operation of the law of diminishing returns—A.S.] will be remunerated at a lower price, reducing the average value of their collective 'pay.'[21]

4. The Partially Market-Oriented Nature of Peasant Output

Peasant economy ceases to be a "natural" economy, or one of on-the-spot consumption, or self-sufficiency, from the moment when a varying proportion of the material requirements for its reproduction, whether inputs or final consumption goods, must be acquired in the market, using money. For this purpose, the family unit is forced to join the market for goods and services as a supplier of products and/or of labour power.

However, in contrast to a United States farmer or any other kind of family undertaking of a commercial nature, the family unit generally comes to market in its capacity as a producer of use values (to use the classical terminology) and not of products which have been defined a priori as commodities, unless elements of external compulsion so dictate. In other words, the decision concerning what to produce is not based on the marketability of the product, but on its role in supporting the family and the production unit.

Frequently, even the manner of selling what has been produced reflects this feature of the peasant economy. Thus, when the product or products sold are the same as those which feature in the basic diet (maize, beans, wheat, and so on), the peasant does not, at the time of the harvest, identify how much will be sent to market and how much will be consumed on the spot, but takes out for sale small parts of what has been harvested as the need arises for purchases and payments. Only on an *ex post* basis is it possible to reconstruct how much has been sold and distinguish it from what has been consumed on the spot. Only the presence of external constraints—either of an ecological nature (such as the fact that cultivation of basic grains is impossible)[22] or of a socioeconomic nature (such as the existence of land earmarked by law for a specific purpose)—or the existence of advances or borrowings which give the creditor power to make decisions concerning the crops will prevent the full expression of the partially market-oriented nature of peasant output.

Obviously, the more the peasant unit depends on purchased inputs and goods for its reproduction, the greater (other things being equal) will be the role which market considerations play in decisions on what and how to produce.

It may be deduced from the above that we do not subscribe to the characterization of the peasant economy as a "simple mercantile economy" adopted by various writers,[23] since, although we agree that the aim of this type of economy is to reproduce its component units, we feel that the internal operating logic is not a purely market-oriented logic, such as that which would be applied by a Western farmer or craftsman. At the same time, to quote Tepicht, in the context of the theory from which the description "simple mercantile economy" has been taken, the latter "is but the embryo of the capitalist economy," while the "historical vocation" of the peasant economy appears to be very different from this role, in so far as this type of economy persists not only in many formations of a capitalist type but even in those of a socialist type, as will be emphasized below.[24]

5.   The Indivisibility of the Family Income

At the beginning of the article it was pointed out that when evaluating the results of the economic activity of peasant units, conventional economic analyses "discovered" deficit situations in most cases. This was the result of applying to such units accounting categories identical to those applied to commercial agriculture, where rent, wages, and profit are an objective reality. For this purpose, the analyses imputed market values to the effort made by the peasant and his family within their own unit, conferring on him the dual character of entrepreneur and wage earner and thus creating a schizoid being who, if he pays himself the current wage in his capacity as a wage earner, is guilty of irrational or philanthropic behaviour as an entrepreneur, since he not only fails to secure the average profit but suffers systematic losses in the "capital" advanced; if, on the other hand, the average profit is imputed to him as remuneration for his entrepreneurial activities, he is cheating himself as a wage earner, by failing to allocate himself even a reproduction wage.

In contrast to this fiction, which we feel throws no light on the motivations of the peasant as a producer, the important categories are those which have an objective existence or which are capable of being objectified on the basis of the concrete behaviour of the units.

In this regard, the result (and the aim) of the economic activity of the family unit is the total family income (gross or net, in cash and in kind) derived from the joint efforts of its members, in which it is not possible to separate the part of the product attributable to rent from that attributable to wages or profits.[25]

6.   The Nontransferable Nature of a Portion of Family Labour

One of the special features of the peasant unit is that it makes use of labour power which would not be in a position to create value in other production contexts. We refer to the work of children, old people, and women and to the unsystematic use of the spare time of the head of the family and his adult children of working age. This is one of the reasons for the ability of the family unit to bring products to the market at prices markedly lower than those required to stimulate commercial production.

According to Tepicht, peasant labour "is composed of at least two *qualitatively different* parts, both because of the nature of the forces it uses (some transferable to other economic sectors and others not), and because of the natural character of its products and the labour remuneration which is concealed in the prices at which they can be sold."[26] In other words, "what the peasant unit is in a position to produce with marginal forces in exchange for a marginal payment requires a completely different estimate by society (the market) if one considers the labour force required for this type of output."[27]

This is so much so that even in countries with centrally planned economies one may observe that, in collective units, the ratio between payments per working day devoted to livestock raising and payments per working day devoted to crop farming is greater than 1, whereas the implicit ratio (as indicated by the prices of the products concerned) in the peasant units is substantially less than 1.[28]

This ability to make use of the marginal labour force (that is to say, to convert it into products) may also be extended to land in the sense that areas which are marginal for commercial agriculture because of their extremely low productive potential—in other words, areas which are not even regarded as resources by commercial agriculture—can nevertheless support the peasant family, since the family regards any element which is capable of contributing to a net increase in the family income as a resource for as long as its reproduction requirements remain unsatisfied and there exists a margin within which its labour can productively be intensified.

A. Warman refers very lucidly to this phenomenon:

> The peasant family in a capitalist society is first and foremost a unit which produces using unpaid labour. The labour of children and women, which is the object of very limited circulation as a commodity in capitalist Mexico, is one of the most important components of the peasant product. Women and children contribute thousands of working days which are invested in the independent production of peasants, in addition to performing work which is not strictly productive but which reduces outgoings and makes it possible to continue living with incomes which in statistical terms would be not just insufficient, but downright ridiculous.[29]

Elsewhere he writes that

> Looking after livestock demands more energy than it yields, but this energy is distributed over a longer period and in units of low intensity

which can be entrusted to people who cannot fully participate in labour during the critical period because they have little physical energy (such as children or old people) or who carry out other occupations at the same time (such as women). Owning livestock proves to be rational: it is like borrowing energy which is paid back with interest, but in instalments which can be paid by those without a full-time occupation in farming.[30]

7. The Special Type of Risk Internalization

For an entrepreneur, at least in theoretical terms, the risk or uncertainty which attaches to the profits that can be derived from alternative applications of his capital are viewed in the decision-making process as probability functions which prompt him to seek at least a degree of proportionality between profit and risk. In the case of the peasant, his vulnerability to the effects of an adverse result is so extreme that, following Lipton,[31] it seems appropriate to take the view that his behaviour as a producer is guided by a kind of "survival algorithm" which leads him to avoid risks despite the potential profits which would arise if he accepted them. Lipton states that, while a well-off American farmer may prefer a 50% probability of obtaining US$5,000 or US$10,000 to the certainty of obtaining US$7,000, an Indian farmer who is offered a choice between a 50% probability of X rupees or 1,000 rupees and the certainty of 700 rupees per year, with which he can barely feed his family, cannot put X much below 700.[32]

The way peasant units thus internalize risk and uncertainty is another of the reasons that help to explain the persistence of cropping methods which, though they generate lower incomes, lessen the variability of the expected values of output. These considerations also explain why peasants will not consider growing certain crops which produce a higher yield per unit area, but which are subject to substantial variations in prices or involve a complex marketing mechanism.[33]

8. Labour-Intensive Technology

The need to take maximum advantage of the most abundant resource (the labour commitment referred to in the previous paragraph) and the existence of unfavourable terms of trade for peasant products in the overall or local market give rise to a tendency to reduce the purchase of inputs and means of production to the lowest possible level. As a result, the intensity of means of production per worker, or of purchased inputs per unit of product or per working day, are generally well below those of commercial or capitalist agriculture. In this regard, the decision on what to produce seems to be guided by the criterion of maximizing labour power per unit of product generated and/or minimizing purchased or hired inputs and means of production.

9.   Membership of a Landgroup

In contrast to an agricultural enterprise, the peasant unit cannot be viewed as a unit separate from other similar units, but always appears as part of a larger grouping of units with which it shares a common territorial base[34]: what A. Pearse defines as the landgroup, which consists of "a group of families forming part of a larger society and living in permanent interdependence interaction, and propinquity by virtue of a system of arrangements between them for the occupation and productive use of a single land area and the physical resources it contains, from which they gain their livelihood."[35] J. Tepicht, for his part, calls this social context the "protective shell of the family economy."[36]

The very reproduction of the peasant family unit depends in many cases on the complex system of nonmarket exchanges conducted with a greater or lesser degree of reciprocity within the landgroup. Even the survival or decline of the family units frequently depends on the degree of cohesion which the landgroup maintains in the face of limitations on its scope for survival, generally arising from the development of commercial agriculture.

In fact, as is emphasized below, the penetration and development of market relations progressively weaken the role of the landgroup in the cycle of social reproduction of the family units, with the result that this reproduction occurs on an increasingly individual basis, which is unquestionably less secure.

Despite the crucial importance which the landgroup has had and continues to have in accounting for the persistence of the peasantry, and despite the importance it should have when any rural development strategy based on the peasantry is being drawn up, there has very often been a tendency to restrict analysis of the peasant economy to analysis of the family unit. A. Warman, in contrast, emphasizes that "it is obvious that the family cannot remain in a position to produce without capital and without opportunities to accumulate and cannot subsist without reserves or savings, in an environment dominated by capitalist relationships, without the support of a larger grouping which furnishes conditions of stability in this contradictory situation. In the case of Mexico, the larger grouping takes the form of the agrarian community, in which one may observe on a broader and more complex, though still partial, scale the production relations of the peasant economy."[37]

10.   Commercial Agriculture: Principal Contrasts

By way of concluding this first chapter it seems appropriate to outline the principal features of commercial agriculture so that we can contrast them, albeit in general terms, with those which have been highlighted as being characteristic of the peasant economy.

A description of this sector does not call for a very detailed conceptual effort, since—given the level of abstraction in this chapter—its principal features are only too well known; reference has already been made to some of them when contrasting them with those of the peasant economy. Accordingly, it will be sufficient to point out that in commercial units there is a clear separation between capital and labour power, and that as a result profit, wages, and even land rent are categories which are the objective expression of relations between owners of means of production, landowners, and sellers of labour power.

Kinship relations are completely divorced from production relations; in other words, what we have called the commitment to the labour force does not exist.

The relations between units are regulated by universal market laws in which there is no place for exchanges based on reciprocity, or, to put it another way, on considerations of community and kinship.

Production is exclusively market-oriented (though for some crops a margin is left to allow for internal consumption or use as inputs within the unit), in the sense that decisions on what and how to produce are completely unrelated to what the producers and their families consume.

Considerations of risk and uncertainty arise strictly in terms of probabilities, in the sense that they are internalized in the decision-making process as ratios between magnitudes of profit expected and probabilities associated with each magnitude.

The principal aim of production, and accordingly the criterion used to determine what to produce, how much, how, and for what purpose, is to secure at least average profit, which is destined for accumulation (and, of course, consumption by the entrepreneurs).

The contrast between the two forms of social organization of production referred to is represented diagramatically in Table 1.

II. ARTICULATION AND BREAK-UP OF PEASANT AGRICULTURE

So far we have restricted ourselves to analysing the rules which govern the internal operation of the peasant economy, and the differences which emerge from a comparison with those applying to commercial agriculture. We will now consider the way in which these characteristics influence the position of the peasant economy in the national society of which it is part.

1. The Concept of Articulation

We consider the concept of articulation of different forms of social organization of production—the peasant and the capitalist forms—to be of central importance in classifying the phenomena which we wish to examine.

TABLE 1

	Peasant Agriculture	Commercial Agriculture
Purpose of production	Reproduction of the producers and the production unit	Maximization of the rate of profit and capital accumulation
Origin of the labour force	Basically the family and, on occasion, reciprocated loans from other units; exceptionally, marginal quantities of wage labour	Wage labour
Commitment of the head to the labour force	Absolute	Nonexistent, apart from legal requirements
Technology	Very labour-intensive; low intensity of "capital" and of purchased inputs	Greater capital intensity per labour unit and higher proportion of purchased inputs in the value of the final product
Destination of the product and origin of inputs	The market, in part	The market
Criterion for intensification of labour	Maximum total product, even at the cost of a fall in the average product — Limit: nil marginal product	Marginal productivity $\geq$ wage
Risk and uncertainty	Assessment not based on probabilities; "survival algorithm"	Internalization based on probabilities, in the search for rates of profit proportional to risk
Nature of the labour force	Makes use of nontransferable or marginal labour	Uses only transferable labour on the basis of skills
Components of net income or product	Indivisible family product or income, realized partially in kind	Wage, rent, and profit, exclusively in the form of money

By articulation we mean the relationships (or system of relationships) which link the sectors in question one with another and with the rest of the economy, forming an integrated whole (the economic system) whose structure and dynamics are determined by (and in turn determine) the structure and dynamics of the parts.[38]

Articulation takes the form of exchanges of goods and services (or values) between sectors: exchanges which are characterized by their asymmetry[39] (or lack of equivalence), and which lead to transfer of surpluses from the peasant sector to the rest of the economy, as a result of a form of integration in which the peasant economy sector is subordinated to the remaining elements in the structure (capitalist agriculture and the urban-industrial complex).[40]

Although this articulation is expressed or becomes visible at the level of the market relations between sectors—in the markets for products, inputs, labour, and even land—the terms of this exchange, or its asymmetrical nature, cannot be explained at this level, but originate in differences at the level of the process of production, i.e., the level of the forms of production or differences in the operating logic specific to each of the sectors.

We shall first consider the main forms of articulation, and then examine how the nature of each form may be "explained," in the final analysis, in terms of differences in the process of production.

2. Articulation in the Market for Products

An initial form of articulation, or, to express it differently, of exploitation of peasant agriculture, is that which arises in the market for products to which the peasant comes to sell part of his output and to buy inputs and final goods which he requires for his reproduction. There the terms of trade, or the relative prices of what he buys and what he sells, are and always have been systematically unfavourable to him. Regardless of the fact that the terms of trade may record improvements in a specific period and with respect to a base year, there is a sort of "primordial" undervaluation of peasant products which is inherent in the very structure of relative prices (as between peasant production and capitalist production), formed over generations, on which the reproduction of the economy as a whole is crucially dependent because of the well-known relationship between food prices, wage levels, and the rate of profit.[41]

Although the extent of inequality in exchange—in other words, the magnitude of the surplus transferred from the peasant sector to the rest of society through the above-mentioned mechanism—can rise or fall depending on the greater or lesser bargaining power (social power in the market) which each party can exert in the market relationship, its origin lies in the internal logic of production in each sector, and not in the market relationships, although this is where it is expressed.

The "secret" which makes unequal exchange possible is to be found in the readiness of peasant agriculture to produce at prices lower than those which a capitalist producer would require in order to do so in the same conditions, since while it is sufficient for the former to meet the requirements for the reproduction of the labour force employed and the fund for the replacement of the means of production used, the latter sector requires in addition a profit which is at least equal to the average profit in the economy.

If, to simplify, we assume that the labour force employed in the two cases is the same, that the cost of its reproduction is covered by wages, that the inputs purchased are the same in both cases, and that the peasant's replacement fund is equal to the entrepreneur's depreciation, the difference in the prices at which each will be prepared to produce will be the average profit, if they pay the same rent, or the profit plus land rent if both own the land.[42]

> The small peasant landowner behaves neither like the owner of property nor like the capitalist entrepreneur. As a matter of principle he is obliged to produce regardless of conditions on the market, or he will fail to survive. Immediately he *contents himself with the equivalent of a wage,* without raising the question of rent, or even the question of profit. The small peasant behaves exactly like a wage-paid piece-worker.[43]

This is precisely why peasant agriculture may be found in areas (marginal lands) and in lines of products where capitalist undertakings would be uneconomic.

This is the phenomenon which lies at the very foundation of the formation of the price systems, and particularly of the historical process of formation of relative prices between agriculture and industry, which have made possible a systematic transfer of surpluses from the peasantry to other sectors through the medium of exchange.

This situation does not apply only to the peripheral countries, since it arises in any economy (capitalist or socialist) where there is a substantial sector involving family producers, even the "farmer" type, whose product—to quote G. J. Johnson, referring to the United States—is supplied to society at "bargain prices": "A cynic might even say that the family farm is an institution which operates in order to encourage the families of farmers to provide quantities of labour and capital at rates of return which are substantially lower than the norm in order to supply the economy as a whole with agricultural products at bargain or sale prices."[44] This is why over long periods the rise in agricultural productivity in many developed countries has not been accompanied by proportional increases in the incomes of farmers, in contrast to what happens in the remainder of the economy.[45]

This asymmetry exerts pressure for the intensification of family agriculture, which, in the "farmer" type, usually takes the form of overinvestment and, in the peripheral peasant type, that of more intensive self-exploitation of family labour.[46]

State subsidies, either provided directly through the medium of low prices for inputs and products and credit at low interest rates, or implicitly through the financing of infrastructure for which the beneficiaries are not charged, represent no more than a form of partially compensatory recognition of this phenomenon.[47]

3. Articulation in the Labour Market

Another area where articulation is expressed is the labour market, particularly, though not exclusively, the market for agricultural day-labourers, who can be engaged by the commercial sector at wages lower than their cost of survival or reproduction.

If no peasant economy sector existed, the wage bill would have to be sufficient at least to guarantee the sustenance and reproduction of the labour employed, in other words the sustenance, over time, of the labour force required by the process of accumulation and growth. If an average rate of profit prevailed in both sectors (agriculture and industry), this would lead to higher agricultural prices, with the consequent chain reaction on wages, profits, and accumulation.

The fact that a substantial proportion of the labour force employed in commercial agriculture (and even in urban-industrial activities) originates from or is more or less directly linked with the peasant economy, and that its conditions for reproduction are in part generated in the peasant economy, permits a reduction of the wage bill by means of the dual mechanism whereby wages paid per day worked are lower than in other sectors, while payment is made only for days actually worked, however low this number may be, regardless of the fact that this may by no means cover the annual subsistence of the worker himself, and still less that of his family. The viability of capitalist agriculture is frequently due to the fact that it is possible to pay wages lower than the reproduction cost of the labour, especially in areas where the differential land rent (in the Ricardian sense) is very low or nonexistent.[48]

Temporary rural migrations from areas of peasant agriculture to areas of commercial agriculture merely confirm this interdependence.

Similarly, in the case of the sale of labour power, the possibility of a nonequivalent exchange—in other words, the possibility of paying less than the reproduction cost of the labour employed—is a phenomenon which, although it is expressed in the labour market, and although it may appear to depend exclusively on the bargaining power between the parties, has its origin in the conditions of production and reproduction of the peasant economy.

The above is connected not only with the fact that subsistence is assured in part by the peasant economy itself, but also with the fact that the amount of labour power supplied by the peasants, as well as the wage levels they are prepared to accept, are determined by the production conditions characterizing the unit to which they belong. In this regard, the further the peasant is from obtaining the level of income (in cash and in kind) required for reproduction in his own unit, the greater will be the number of days he is prepared to work in exchange for a wage, and the higher the level of intensity with which he is working his plot of land, the lower will be the wage necessary to attract him away from it, in accordance with the phenomenon of diminishing returns.

The diagram (Figure 3), which is of course an oversimplification of real conditions, helps to clarify the above: Here we are comparing two production units (A and B), whose average and marginal product curves (AP' and BQ', AP and BQ), in this example indicate greater availability of land in unit B. Let us assume that magnitude OC× OM is equal to the net reproduction income. Unit A, with the maximum possible intensity (in other words, using OP working days and with nil marginal productivity), does not achieve the reproduction income, since OC×OP < OC×OM. It will therefore be sufficient to offer a wage equal to OS (= RT) so that the peasant will work away from the plot for at least PR working days (assuming

FIGURE 3

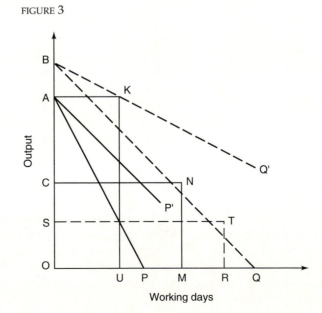

that the family labour available is greater than OR) so as to ensure that $(OC \cdot OP) + (PR \cdot RT) = (OC \cdot OM)$. In contrast, the peasant on unit B, who can achieve the reproduction income on his own plot $(OC \cdot OM = UK \cdot OU)$ by working OU days, will not be prepared to sell labour power unless the wage offered is greater than UK.

The two articulation mechanisms described (product market and labour market), though significantly different in form, nevertheless have a common basis: the peasant unit's capacity and readiness (for structural, not philanthropic reason) to undervalue its working time with respect to the patterns established by the rules of operation of the capitalist sector, either as labour power proper, or as labour power materialized in the products which it places on the market.

This capacity is the source both of the peasantry's strength, in the sense of a force working for its persistence, and of its weakness, in the sense of a force working for its break-up.

4.   Break-up, Recovery, and Persistence

As was pointed out in the introduction, all the schools of thought which derive from liberalism (liberals proper, rationalists, positivists, marxists, and so on) postulated the transitional nature of the peasantry, which was regarded as a segment of society doomed to disappear—some of its members converted into *bourgeois*, the rest converted into proletarians—as a result of the vigour of capitalist development. Peasantries in specific societies were considered cultural and/or social relics from former times.

Although it is true that the relative importance of the peasant sector, as a segment of the population, has been declining, nevertheless in the peripheral countries the peasantry remains one of the largest groups, since it rarely accounts for less than a third of the working population. If this is a mere transitory phase, it must be recognized that the transition has been very lengthy. What is more, in some societies the influences working for its disappearance have been checked, to some extent, by others which are not only preventing its disappearance but even, in specific areas and circumstances, creating peasant forms of organization of production where they did not exist previously.

From the political and economic policy viewpoint, and bearing in mind the above considerations, it seems more sensible to abandon the assumption of transitoriness and take the view that for the foreseeable future (and for a period relevant in terms of policy formulation) the peasantry will persist. Consequently, it is necessary to undertake an analysis of the forces working to ensure its persistence, and those fostering its break-up, so that they can be taken into account in the formulation of development strategies and policies designed to ensure that the peasant sector plays a role commensurate with its potential.

In the discussion below, break-up of the peasant form will be understood to mean the process which leads to the progressive narrowing down
of options which would permit the family unit to survive using its own
resources: in other words, loss of the ability to generate a volume of output
which is equivalent to the fund for family consumption and the fund for the
replacement of inputs and means of production.

Recovery will be understood to mean those processes which reverse
the above-mentioned trend, as well as those which lead to the creation of
peasant units in areas where they did not exist before.

In general terms, the forces working in favour of the persistence, recovery, or break-up of the peasant sector act on, and have their basis in, the
basic network of relations between and within sectors (between the peasant
and the rest of society), which we have defined as a form of articulation
which subordinates the peasant form to the national economy and society,
and whose principal features have already been described. In other words,
these forces help to intensify, redefine, or restrain the elements of asymmetrical symbiosis of a structural nature which have been encompassed here
under the concept of articulation through subordination. In this sense these
forces can be viewed as superstructural elements, which affect and are
affected by the structure defined as articulation.

For descriptive purposes, these forces may be grouped on the basis of
their origin, and a distinction may be drawn between those which stem
from the State and its policies; those generated by the action of the intermediary persons or institutions, or brokers, that represent a link between the
peasantry and the rest of the economy; those generated by the conscious
actions of the commercial sector; and those which derive from the dynamics
of demographic and ecological factors.

1. Action by the State. Since the State is an expression of the correlation
   of social forces at each moment in time, its action cannot fail to be a
   blend of contradictory forces, even if the resultant of these forces is
   the maintenance of the conditions of reproduction of the social
   whole and, consequently, the maintenance of the type of articulation
   to which we have been referring.

   In general, policies which involve subsidies to the peasant sector,[49] such as credit at preferential rates, support prices, the establishment of minimum wages (especially if compliance is monitored),
   and so on, are actions which tend to limit or check the break-up of
   the peasant unit by making possible terms of trade, in various areas,
   better than those which would be achieved in free market conditions.

   Agrarian reform and new settlement are also, at least in theory,
   policies which impede the break-up of peasant units, and even
   encourage their creation through the subdivision of larger geo-

graphical units and the development of complementary legislation and action to protect the units created.

In contrast to the above-mentioned actions, public investment in irrigation, or in improving communications and prospects for the export of produce, has frequently led to increased imposition on the resources of the peasant sector—both directly, through appropriation of the areas in question by commercial agriculture, and indirectly, through accentuation of the (asymmetrical) trade relations in the process of reproduction of the peasant economy—and have thereby increased its vulnerability.

2. Action by intermediary elements. Here we are referring to the various types of mechanism for intermediation which link the peasantry to the rest of the economy and permit the extraction of surpluses at the level of relations of distribution and exchange. In general, these intermediary persons and/or institutions make use both of the possibilities opened up by the specific operating logic of the peasant economy and of those derived from the lesser bargaining power of units from the sector and the intermediaries' monopoly (sometimes on a very small scale) of the channels through which this sector is linked to society as a whole.

The functions of the intermediary elements have been classified by A. Warman as follows:

a. Material adaptation of products, involving a sort of scaling down of what reaches the peasant sector as a product, and a scaling up of what leaves the peasant sector for the rest of the economy;

b. "Conversion of symbols," involving "translation" into the peasant language of the external norms of trade and accounting, in other words, converting units of weight, quality standards, and so on into generally accepted terms;

c. The physical movement of the products which enter or leave the peasant economy from and to the external world;

d. The mobilization of finance by means of which the peasant can be more fully integrated in the market for consumer goods or inputs, to a greater extent than would be possible if he sold his products or labour power himself.

These types of function make it possible to extend market relations in the process of reproduction of the peasant economy and to integrate it in the rest of the national (and international) economy. In order to fulfil this function, the intermediary element "is located between two modes of production, handles two types of language, two types of social relationship and economic rationality, and guides the flow of capital towards the dominant mode. He himself obtains a profit from all his acts, equally when he converts weights into kilos and when he lends money for the sowing of onions. . . .

His success depends on his flexibility and diversification, on his being able to sell seven different things and accept a chicken in payment."[50] Each of the functions described involves the appropriation of surpluses, and in this regard contributes to the break-up of the peasantry; however, to the extent that the persistence and reproduction of the peasantry depend on exchange through the medium of trade, the intermediary elements contribute to its survival, although they exact a high price.

3. **Action by enterprises responsible for processing and intermediation.** Although strictly speaking this phenomenon should be included among the structural components of articulation, we have decided to highlight it separately since it is a recent tendency in the organization of agricultural production. We refer to the phenomenon of the contracts commonly drawn up between large agro-industrial or agri-business enterprises and the peasants of specific regions.

   These contracts reflect a tendency on the part of capital to abandon direct control of land and the processes of primary production and replace them by financial and commercial control of a huge network of small and medium-sized "independent" producers, either by creating a sort of peasantry economically attached to them or by "attaching" a preexisting group of peasants, who can be induced to work on advantageous conditions which—for the reasons already indicated—business agriculture would not accept. This is particularly true in situations where the process of break-up of the peasantry can be halted only by exploring avenues for labour intensification which involve the partial or total abandonment of traditional farming patterns and their replacement by market-oriented patterns with high unit values.

4. **The dynamics of demographic and ecological factors.** Natural growth in the peasant population, which is appreciably greater than the expansion of the already inadequate capacity of the remaining sectors to absorb that growth productively, is reflected in increasing pressure on land, or, to put it another way, a deterioration in the land/man ratio, not only in the sense of an arithmetical fall but in the no less important sense of a decline in the productive potential of the existing land.

   In general, this is a force which contributes to the break-up of the peasantry, since fragmentation—which is the result of the subdivision of plots as a consequence of population growth—is an inescapable sign of a rise in the fragility or vulnerability of the peasant economy and a prelude to its disappearance.

   The existence of possibilities of working outside the plot can help to defer the impact of this tendency through "subsidization" of the continued existence of the unit with incomes obtained outside it. Within the peasant segment, the above-mentioned forces give rise to a process of differentiation or polarization, in which a minority of the units not only succeed in preventing break-up but even turn the intensification in market-oriented relations to their account and achieve a certain amount of accumulation.

Another section achieves a sort of equilibrium between the various forces and succeeds in maintaining its conditions of reproduction over time with a greater or lesser degree of security.

For the majority, however, the dynamics of break-up—which takes the form of a progressive loss of their ability to support themselves—are inexorable and can be alleviated only by the possibility, which is not always available, for the producer or the members of his family to obtain incomes from outside the plot.

In socioeconomic analysis of the peasant sector, and in the diagnoses which precede the formulation of a strategy for its development, it is of crucial importance to recognize the type of heterogeneity to which the processes of differentiation indicated here can lead.

In other words, we may, for the purposes of description, stratify the peasant segment as a function of the magnitude of a specific variable within a continuum (land, output, and so on). The important distinction is whether or not internal conditions exist for the support of the production unit and/or the landgroup.

This criterion can be used to distinguish at least three important categories within the peasant agriculture sector:

a. The infrasubsistence segment, or "poor peasant" segment, made up of those units which need incomes from outside the plot in order to attain a minimum subsistence income. This appears to be the segment recording fastest relative growth in Latin America[51];

b. The stationary, "simple reproduction" or "average peasant" segment, made up of that part of the peasantry whose product is sufficient to cover the fund for family consumption and the fund for the replacement of inputs and means of production, from one cycle to another;

c. The surplus-producing or "rich" peasant segment, made up of those units which, with their resources, more or less systematically generate a surplus over and above what is required for the reproduction of the family and the production unit, although they cannot always convert it into accumulation. Whether or not this stratum will lose its peasant status—in other words, whether or not it will become involved in a process of accumulation founded on the systematic engagement of nonfamily labour on a substantial scale—will depend on conditions which it is beyond the scope of this paper to analyse.

NOTES

1. Reference is made to several of these features in section I.1.

2. The impact of Chayanov's writings on Western literature made itself felt surprisingly late, even though one of his articles, containing the most important part of his contribution to theory, was published in 1931 by the University of Minnesota Press in a group of papers edited by P. Sorokin, C. Zimmerman, and C. Galpin (A. V. Chayanov, "The Socioeconomic Nature of Peasant Farm Economy," in *A Systematic Source Book in Rural Sociology*). Nevertheless, neither anthropologists nor economists seem to have become aware of Chayanov's importance until the mid-1960s. Eric Wolf, who quotes the text mentioned above, was one of the first to take up the essence of Chayanov's argument, in his book *Peasants* (New Jersey: Prentice-Hall, 1966) (pp. 14 and 15). In the same year, D. Thorner, B. Kerblay, and R. E. F. Smith published—in addition to a biographical analysis of the writer and an assessment of his contributions to theory—two of his most important works [see A. V. Chayanov, *The Theory of Peasant Economy* (Illinois: Richard D. Irwin, Inc., 1966)]. It was after the publication of this book that Chayanov's work became widely known both in the English-speaking world and in Latin America.

3. We shall speak here of forms of organization of production (or, more briefly, forms) in order to avoid a debate on whether or not the peasant economy is a mode of production in the sense in which the term is used in historical materialism. Although such a debate might be of importance as regards some of its theoretical implications, it is not germane to the purposes of the present article, which are limited to showing that what is involved is a form of production which is different from the commercial form and is governed by its own rules. Those interested in the debate can consult, for example: R. Bartra, *Estructura Agraria y Clases Sociales en México* (Mexico City: Ed. Era, 1974), who considers peasant agriculture as a simple market mode. This view is shared by M. Coello, "La Pequeña Producción Campesina y la Ley de Chayanov," *Historia y Sociedad*, no. 8, Mexico City, 1975. J. Tepicht, *Marxisme et Agriculture: Le Paysan Polonais* (Paris: A. Colin, 1973), pp. 13–46, regards it as being a mode in its own right. A. Warman adopts a similar position in . . . *Y Venimos a Contradecir* (Mexico City: La Casa Chata, 1976), chap. 6.

   Among the critics of the "mode of production" approach, see H. Bernstein, "Concept for the Analysis of Contemporary Peasantries" (mimeo, to be published shortly in M. J. Mbiling and C. K. Omari, *Peasant Production in Tanzania*, University of Dar es Salaam) or, following a different argument, G. Esteva's article "La Economía Campesina Moderna" (photocopy supplied by the author), 1979. In P. Vilar, "La economía campesina," *Historia y Sociedad*, no. 15, Mexico City, 1977, we find a notable critique of the validity of the concept of the peasant economy. The *Journal of Peasant Studies* (*JPS*), London, has published a large number of articles on the subject of the peasant mode (or form); see, for example: J. Ennew, P. Hirst, and K. Tribe, "'Peasantry' as an Economic Category", *JPS*, 4, 4 (July 1977); M. Harrison, "The Peasant Mode of Production in the Work of A. V. Chayanov," *JPS*, 4, 4 (July 1977); D. E. Goodman, "Rural Structure, Surplus Mobilization, and Modes of Production in a Peripheral Region: The Brazilian North-East," *JPS*, 5, 1 (October 1977); and C. D. Scott, "Peasants, Proletarianization and the Articulation of Modes of Production:

The Case of Sugar-cane Cutters in Northern Peru, 1940–1969," *JPS*, 3, 3 (April 1976).

4. W. Kula, *Théorie économique du système féodal,* quoted by R. Bartra, op. cit., 1973, p. 36.

5. J. Tepicht, op. cit., 1973, p. 36.

6. A. Schejtman, "Elementos para una Teoría de la Economía Campesina: Pequeños Propietarios y Campesinos de Hacienda," *El Trimestre Económico,* XLII(2), 166, Mexico City, April–June 1975; republished in *Economía Campesina* (Lima: DESCO, 1979).

7. In areas where the amount of land is very limited, this phenomenon may not be manifested very clearly. However, when the peasant unit faces no major limitations on its choice of desirable scales (as in the humid tropics, or in areas with extensive stretches of previously unfarmed land which has not yet been appropriated by large landowners), differences of scale may be observed which cannot be explained in terms of the availability of other complementary resources (labour force, tools, and so on) but must be attributed to objectives different from those which enter into the definition of economic "optima."

8. T. Shanin, "A Russian Peasant Household at the Turn of the Century," in T. Shanin, ed., *Peasants and Peasant Societies* (Harmondsworth, Middx.: Penguin, 1971), p. 30, quoting a Russian encyclopaedia published in 1913.

9. Ibid.

10. Tepicht illustrates this by citing a region of Algeria (Zeribe) where a study of "the joint property type" (of the old extended families) indicates an almost complete absence of "mixed" situations of joint production activity and separate kitchens, or vice versa. Either the couples join together in work in the fields and at the table, or they separate and become modernized both in the fields and at the table (even if they live under the same roof). Op. cit., pp. 23–24.

11. Chayanov, 1974, op. cit. Chayanov even comes to see in the family structure (size, ages, sexes) the principal element of economic differentiation; we do not share this view, as is indicated below at the beginning of the section on differentiation.

12. The great flexibility which may be observed in this symbiosis between the undertaking and the family is illustrated by A. Warman with reference to the Zapata period: "as access to the land controlled by the *hacienda* became more difficult, the extended family gained strength as the most efficient unit for securing an independent supply of maize and raising wage incomes to cover subsistence for the peasants. It was the only form of organization which made it possible to survive and maintain the men in fighting condition." Op. cit., 1977, p. 307.

13. S. H. Franklin, *The European Peasantry* (London: Methuen, 1969).

14. The expression "maximize the labour input" is ambiguous; strictly one should speak of maximizing the input of *productive* labour, that is, labour which generates increases in net income, and not labour in general.

15. We assume that "standard labour units," which is the variable used by Franklin, implies that the various categories of worker in the unit have been reduced to a homogeneous unit, using criteria which are unfortunately not clear.

16. J. Tepicht, op cit., pp. 24 and 26.

17. Taken from A. Schejtman, op. cit.

18. A. V. Chayanov, op. cit., 1974, p. 84.

19. A. Warman (op. cit., 1976, p. 326) sets out this "law" as follows: "Once subsistence requirements have been met, the peasant stops producing. Firstly, the diminishing returns from the more intensive activity mean that any additional income over the subsistence minimum demands a disproportionate increase in activity. Secondly, incorporation in the capitalist market means that any rise in income leads to a rise in the transfer of surpluses." Warman also introduces the problem of subordination, to which we shall refer below.

20. J. Tepicht, op. cit., p. 41.

21. Ibid., p. 35.

22. An interesting example of an ecological constraint is furnished by certain forms of co-ownership of livestock observed in the Mexican humid tropics, where, as a result of the fact that the peasants find it impossible to continue with agriculture based on felling, clearing, and burning—because the pressure of numbers on the land does not permit renewal of the plant cover required for this practice—a system of co-ownership has arisen between private stock raisers and *ejidatarios*, whereby the former concentrate on fattening and the latter on breeding. The cattle belong to the stock raiser, and the *ejidatarios* are entitled to half the calves (normally the females) and to the milk, in exchange for the use of their pastures and their care of the livestock under the co-ownership agreement. In these circumstances, the milk, which is sold or is made into cheese for sale, comes to play part of the role of maize, and the female calves the role which livestock normally plays in peasant agriculture: a savings fund and an illusory form of accumulation.

23. See note 3 for author references. The term "simple" is used by these writers to describe a situation where there is neither accumulation of surpluses nor any increase in the production capacity of the units over time.

24. J. Tepicht, op. cit., p. 18.

25. See A. V. Chayanov, 1966, op. cit., pp. 2–5, and J. Tepicht, op. cit., p. 36. Perhaps the only virtue of the fiction referred to above is to show that peasant units are prepared to supply their products at prices below those which a capitalist producer would demand in order to pay current wages and rents and obtain at least the average profit. However, the reasons why this occurs are totally obscured by this form of evaluation or calculation. R. Bartra, in his study on Mexican agrarian structure (Bartra, op. cit., pp. 58–66), makes use of the categories of wage, rent, and profit in the manner indicated.

26. J. Tepicht, op. cit., pp. 39–40.

27. Ibid., p. 38.

28. Ibid., pp. 36–37.

29. A. Warman, op. cit., p. 310.

30. Ibid., p. 298.

31. M. Lipton, "The Theory of the Optimizing Peasant," *Journal of Development Studies*, IV (April 1968): 327–51.

32. Ibid., p. 345.

33. An intuitive approach, corroborated by some empirical evidence, indicates a certain correlation between the value (and degree of liquidity) of the assets the peasant owns and his ability to take risks, either by adding crops and/or techniques which, although more profitable, are also more risky than the traditional ones, or by specializing in some of the traditional crops instead of maintaining the pattern of a larger number of crops occupying small areas, which is charac-

teristic of the poor peasant. In this regard, livestock destined for breeding, the principal form of saving, fulfils the function of insurance against poor harvests or the adverse result of a risk taken, so that those who possess most livestock are most prepared to introduce innovations in cropping patterns or methods. A. Schejtman, *Hacienda and Peasant Economy*, degree thesis, University of Oxford, 1970, chap. 4.

34. We have avoided the term "rural or local community" which is used so frequently in the literature, since it implicitly contains the idea that the group in question shares common interest, which is not always the case, and raises "an empirical problem which should not be introduced into the definition" of these groupings. D. Lehman, *On the Theory of Peasant Economy* (photocopy provided by the author), p. 15; and H. Mendras, quoted by J. Tepicht, op. cit., p. 22.

35. A. Pearse, *The Latin American Peasant* (London: Frank Cass, 1975), p. 51. This is identical to the concept used by Warman in *Los Campesinos: Hijos Predilectos del Régimen* (Mexico City: Nuestro Tiempo, 1972), p. 145, when he speaks of a "group which shares a common territorial base."

36. J. Tepicht, op. cit., p. 20.

37. A. Warman, op. cit., 1976, p. 314; see also p. 325.

38. This concept is used by many writers in a sense very close to that given it in this paragraph. Examples are J. Bengoa, "Economía Campesina y Acumulación Capitalista," *Economía Campesina*, op. cit., pp. 251–86; R. Bartra, op. cit., pp. 79–87; A. Warman, op. cit., pp. 324–37; G. Oliver, *Hacia una Fundamentación Analítica para una Nueva Estrategia de Desarollo Rural* (photocopy) (Mexico City: CIDER, 1977), pp. 176–99.

39. The term "asymmetry" was used by Warman (op. cit., 1976, p. 325), in a sense similar to that which we are using here, in order to contrast (symmetrical) relationships within the peasant community with those which arise between that community and the rest of society. "In the peasant mode of production the internal relationships are oriented towards symmetry, towards reciprocity, in order to make it possible to ensure the subsistence of the families, the smallest efficient units in the grouping. The community is the context through which flow the relationships of reciprocity which play the role of redistributing resources, flexibly transmitting the use of the means which make agricultural production, the basic activity of this mode, possible. Among the different peasant communities the symmetrical relationship is realized through the direct exchange of complementary goods by the producers themselves. In order for the resources to be exchanged symmetrically, they must be under the independent command and control of the peasants, whether or not they are formally recognized as their possessions." We shall see below when analysing the phenomenon of peasant differentiation, how the loss of independent control over their conditions of reproduction leads to the emergence of asymmetrical relationships even within the landgroup.

40. In order to define this form of articulation, some writers have adopted the term "subsumption," which encompasses the concepts of integration and subordination (G. Esteva, op. cit., p. 4).

41. J. Tepicht, "Economia Contadina e Teoria Marxista," *Critica marxista*, no. 1, Rome, 1967, p. 76.

42. Land rent (imputed or actually paid) will have to be added to profit if we compare a peasant landowner with an entrepreneur landowner, since while the for-

mer would be prepared to overlook the value of this rent, or (to express it more clearly) to view it as an integral part of his total "reproduction" income, the latter will demand a return equivalent to that on his other capital.

43. K. Vergópoulos, "Capitalismo Disforme," in S. Amin and K. Vergópoulos, *La Cuestión Campesina y el Capitalismo* (Mexico City: Nuestro Tiempo, 1975), p. 165. Chayanov made exactly the same observation: ". . . we take the motivation of the peasant's economic activity not as that of an entrepreneur who as a result of investment of his capital receives the difference between gross income and production overheads, but rather as the motivation of the worker on a peculiar piece-rate system which allows him alone to determine the time and intensity of his work." Op. cit., 1966, p. 42.

44. Quoted by J. Tepicht, op. cit., 1967, p. 74.

45. "As an example one might cite the case of French agriculture after the last world war. Denis Cespède has shown very clearly the transfers of agricultural values to the benefit of the industrial sector. Between 1946 and 1962, agricultural productivity rose from 100 to 272, while nonagricultural productivity rose from 100 to 189.2. Nevertheless, over the same period the per capita income of the active population rose from 100 to 167.8 for agriculture, while for the nonagricultural sectors it increased from 100 to 205.4. Let us note in passing that starting in 1937 a similar situation arose in the United States, where average annual growth in the productivity of agricultural labour substantially exceeded that of industrial labour: 3.8% compared with 1.4% for the years 1937–1948, and 6.2% against 3% for 1948–1953." K. Vergópoulos, op. cit., p. 169.

46. See G. J. Johnson, "The Modern Family Farm and Its Problems," in *Economic Problems of Agriculture in Industrial Societies* (London: Macmillan, 1969).

47. In order to gain a vivid idea of what would be involved if this asymmetry were to be completely corrected, one need simply observe what happened in the urban-industrial world when the oil-producing countries decided to cease subsidizing the energy which they were selling to the industrialized countries at prices lower than production costs in absolute terms. Oil, like land, is a nonrenewable resource (though this applies in a more relative sense to the latter), and can command absolute rent. The fact that, in agriculture, this rent has declined, and even disappeared in many cases, is no more than the result of the subordination of agriculture to the requirements of urban-industrial development.

48. We make this qualification because in areas with high differential rents which can be appropriated by the entrepreneur landowner, he is in a position to secure extraordinary profits which enable him to compensate both for the unfavorable price relations and for the payment of wages equivalent to the reproduction cost of the labour.

49. We are using the term "subsidies" in the sense that the prices or values involved are more favourable to the peasantry than those to which they would be subjected in the market without State intervention. In no case are they subsidies in the sense of a return of the impositions arising from the structural relations which are expressed in the price system.

50. A. Warman, op. cit., 1976, p. 332.

51. It need barely be noted that rural workers who are landless or, rather, who are not attached to a family unit which possesses land, are not regarded as peasants in the sense in which this term has been used here.

17

The Political Economy of Third World Food Imports: The Case of Wheat

Derek Byerlee
CIMMYT, Islamabad, Pakistan

INTRODUCTION

Much attention has been focused on the increase in food imports by Third World countries during the last decade. This increase is usually equated with a growing gap between food production and consumption in developing countries. Yet projections, whether based on simple projection methods or more formal econometric models, have consistently underestimated imports by developing countries. For example, FAO and USDA forecasts of wheat imports by developing countries for 1985 (made in 1977–78) had already been exceeded by 20%–25% in 1981.[1]

This paper takes a new look at trends in food imports by developing countries. It focuses on wheat imports in the context of the wider food policy, institutional, and external trade environment in which these imports occur. It departs substantially from the traditional econometric approaches, which emphasize regional aggregates, to analyze evidence at the country level, where national food policies are made. An analysis across countries interpreted in the light of national and international policies provides fresh insights into the political economy of rapidly increasing wheat imports.

Wheat has special significance in the analysis of food policy and food imports in the Third World. First, cereals constitute the bulk of Third World

I am grateful to Robert Tripp and Jim Longmire for comments on an earlier draft of this paper. Views expressed in this paper are not necessarily those of CIMMYT. *Economic Development and Cultural Change*, 35, 2 (January 1987), pp. 307–328. Copyright © 1987 by The University of Chicago.

food imports, and, among cereals, wheat is by far the dominant food grain import. In 1980, wheat accounted for an estimated 86% of food grain imports by Third World countries.[2] Since the postwar years, when Europe was the major wheat buyer in international markets, wheat imports have been increasingly destined for the Third World (including China), which now accounts for two-thirds of total world wheat imports. In particular, in the last decade, wheat imports by developing countries have expanded extremely rapidly, doubling from 1970 to 1981. Second, unlike rice, world wheat *exports* are dominated by developed countries, which produced about two-thirds of the world's wheat and accounted for about 95% of total exports in 1979–81. Third, a significant group of 84 developing countries lying in the tropical belt between 23 degrees south latitude and 23 degrees north latitude currently do not produce wheat. Hence, there is a basic inconsistency between the traditional food staple (i.e., rice, coarse grains, or roots and tubers) and the importation of wheat, a nontraditional staple with little immediate prospects for local production. Finally, wheat—more than any other cereal staple—usually undergoes a greater degree of commercial processing before being consumed. This means that transportation, processing, and marketing costs make up a larger proportion of final consumer prices (over 80% for bread), and consumer prices are more sensitive to the influence of policy interventions and market distortions at each stage of the process.

This paper begins by summarizing recent patterns in wheat consumption and imports in the Third World. A framework is then developed to explain these trends in light of both national food policies and policies of the exporting countries. The framework is applied in a cross-country analysis of wheat imports and policy interventions. The evidence on biases in national and international food policies in favor of wheat products is developed in some detail, and policy measures to arrest growing dependence on food imports are discussed.

RECENT TRENDS IN CONSUMPTION AND IMPORTS

During the last 2 decades, wheat has shown a remarkably rapid and widespread increase in its contribution to diets in the Third World. Data from FAO indicate that, in all major regions, wheat consumption has increased more than any other food staple in both a relative and absolute sense (see Table 1). Consumption of rice has also increased but to a much smaller extent than that for wheat. To a large extent increased wheat consumption reflects a widespread substitution for so called inferior food staples—coarse grains and roots and tubers—whose per capita consumption has declined (Table 1). These trends in consumption patterns have accelerated during the 1970s, when wheat consumption in the Third World grew at an annual rate of 5.4%. An estimated 80% of the

TABLE 1   **Aggregate Changes in Consumption of Food Staples, by Region (%)**

	Staple Food Calories Provided by Wheat, 1975–77	ANNUAL GROWTH RATE IN PER CAPITA AVAILABILITY OF STAPLE FOODS FOR HUMAN CONSUMPTION, 1961–77			
		Wheat	Rice	Coarse Grains	Roots and Tubers
1. Countries where wheat is the traditional food staple[a]	72	1.3	2.0	−1.2	−.1
2. Large mixed-cereal economies (India, China, Mexico)	28	2.8	.4	−.7	−2.1
3. Tropical belt of countries where wheat is not a traditional staple[b]	15	2.7	.8	−.6	−.5

[a]Includes countries from Morocco to Pakistan and the Southern Cone of Latin America.
[b]Includes countries lying between 23 degrees north latitude and 23 degrees south latitude.
SOURCE: Calculated from FAO, *Food Balance Sheets* (Rome: FAO, 1981).

increase in world wheat consumption in this period occurred in the developing world.[3]

Although these changing consumption patterns were general across countries, there is a sharp division between countries in the extent to which increased wheat consumption was supplied by domestic production or by imports. For the largest wheat producers (China, India, Pakistan, and Turkey), rapid increases in domestic production have supported increased consumption and in some cases allowed for import substitution. For all other regions, increased consumption has largely been met by imports (Table 2). This includes those regions where wheat is a traditional food but import dependence is high (e.g., over 100 kilograms per capita of wheat is imported by countries of North Africa) and the tropical zone, where wheat consumption is much lower but almost all wheat is imported (e.g., Southeast Asia and sub-Saharan Africa).[4] Many countries in the tropical belt now have per capita wheat imports (and consumption) of 30–50 kilograms per year.

In summary, in 1978–80 there was a total of 65 developing countries consuming over 100,000 tons of wheat annually. Forty-six of these countries were less than 50% self-sufficient in wheat and 26 (i.e., those in the tropical belt) did not produce wheat (i.e., less than 20,000 hectares). Wheat import dependence has increased in almost all Third World countries (except the four largest producers) to reach high levels by the 1980s.

TABLE 2   **Relationship between Wheat Consumption, Production, and Imports in Major Developing Country Regions**

	Wheat Consumption per Capita, 1978–80 (kg)	Wheat Imports per Capita, 1978–80 (kg)	Increase in Wheat Consumption per Capita, 1961–65 1978–80 (kg)	Increased Consumption Supplied by Imports (%)	Growth Rate 1961–65 to 1978–80 (% year) Wheat Consumption per Capita	Wheat Production per Capita
Eastern and Southern Africa	16	8	4.1	66	1.8	0
Western Africa	13	13	8.6	100	6.6	[a]
North Africa	184	118	54.0	90	2.2	−1.6
Middle East (except Turkey)	167	54	39.0	51	1.2	0
South Asia	52	4	16.2	0[b]	2.3	4.0
Southeast Asia	13	13	7.4	100	5.3	[a]
East Asia	69	12	32.8	17	4.0	4.1
Mexico, Central America	50	27	13.1	70	1.9	−.2
Andes	38	35	4.5	100[c]	.8	−6.2
Southern Cone (except Argentina)	67	38	16.3	59	3.3	1.3
All developing countries[d]	61	14	20.0	26	2.5	2.4

[a]Non-wheat-producing regions.
[b]Production increased faster than consumption so that imports decreased.
[c]Production decreased so that imports increased to maintain per capita consumption.
[d]Includes Argentina and Turkey.

SOURCE: Calculated from FAO Tapes of Production and Trade Statistics.

A FRAMEWORK FOR ANALYZING THE DYNAMICS OF WHEAT IMPORTS

Figure 1 is a schematic representation of the complex of factors underlying the dynamics of wheat consumption and imports in the Third World. Both domestic and international actors operate to influence wheat consumption. On the domestic side, the main actors are *(a)* producers; *(b)* consumers; and *(c)* local grain-transport, storage, and processing industries. The main international actors are private and public agencies involved in the world wheat trade. In some cases, such as grain shipment and processing, international and domestic actors may be closely linked.

It is hypothesized that "natural" market forces operating on both the demand and supply sides tend to promote wheat consumption. With increasing incomes, consumer preferences are expected to favor wheat, especially in countries where wheat is not a traditional staple and consumers seek to diversify diets. The world supply of wheat and world market prices are also expected to be favorable to consumption of wheat prod-

FIGURE 1   **Major influences on wheat consumption and imports in the Third World.**

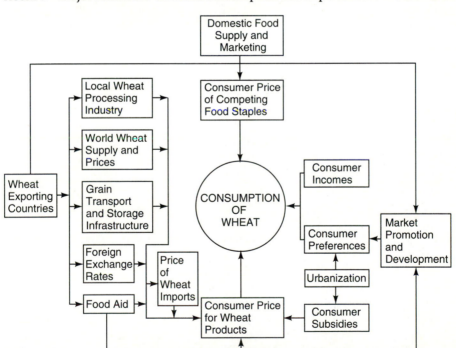

ucts because of rapid technological change in some major wheat-producing countries (e.g., the United States, India, and China).

A central thesis of this paper is that governments, in both importing and exporting countries, have been key actors, whose interventions in wheat markets have consistently reinforced market phenomena and rapidly accelerated the substitution of wheat products for traditional staples. Government interventions on the domestic side are shown toward the right-hand side of Figure 1. These include *(a)* interventions in production of wheat and competing food staples; *(b)* investments, taxes and subsidies, and controls on the marketing and processing of wheat, both domestic and imported; *(c)* explicit consumer subsidies on wheat products; and *(d)* influences on consumers' preferences through market promotion and development. Interventions by governments of both the importing and exporting countries also influence the price of *imported* wheat, including *(a)* trade and exchange rate policies of both importers and exporters, *(b)* subsidies and credit facilities for wheat exports, *(c)* the provision of food aid (largely wheat), and *(d)* marketing and promotion policies by private and public agencies of exporting countries.

Finally, it is hypothesized that a number of influential interest groups have been important in biasing policy interventions toward wheat consumption and imports. These include the influence of middle-income urban consumers in food policy decisions, the vested interests and market power of the wheat-processing sector, and the linkages of this sector with exporting interests in developed countries, such as grain exporters or milling and shipping industries. Interest groups in exporting countries have also succeeded in distorting the policies of these countries toward wheat exports to the Third World. To a large extent, all of these interest groups reinforce each other in promoting wheat consumption.

Clearly, a comprehensive analysis of all of these factors and their linkages is beyond the scope of this paper. My focus is largely on the domestic policy environment with somewhat less attention to the international environment.

THE DOMESTIC POLICY ENVIRONMENT AND WHEAT CONSUMPTION

The Urban Bias of Wheat Consumption

Increased wheat consumption in the developing world has to a large extent occurred in urban areas. This is less so in the traditional wheat-consuming countries of the Middle East/North Africa, but even in that region there is a tendency to switch from coarse grains (such as barley) to wheat with migration to urban areas. Table 3 shows wheat consumption by rural and urban areas in three groups of countries. In countries where wheat consumption is relatively low, consumption is more strongly biased to urban areas. Furthermore, for this group of countries, wheat consumption is biased toward middle- and upper-income groups. Typically, the richest 25% of households have a per capita consumption of wheat twice that of the poorest 25%.[5] Income elasticities of demand in these countries generally range from 0.5 to 1.0 and are higher than for any other cereal staple. This underlines the important effect of incomes on wheat consumption and its substitution for other cereals.

TABLE 3   **Consumption of Wheat Products in Rural and Urban Areas in Selected Countries**

Country or Region	Year	Annual per Capita Consumption of Wheat Products (kg/year)	
		Rural Areas	Urban Areas
High wheat consumption (>100 kg/capita/year):			
India, Punjab State	1974–75	130	117
Egypt	1974–75	109	178
Pakistan	1982	150	100
Intermediate wheat consumption (30–100 kg/capita/year):			
Peru	1972–73	28	43
Sri Lanka	1981	26	57
India, Bihar State	1974–75	39	57
Sudan	1982	25	84
Low wheat consumption (<30 kg/capita/year):			
Brazil	1975	9	29
Indonesia, Java	1980	3	32
Philippines	1975–79	5	18
Kenya	1974–75	10	30
India, Andhra Pradesh State	1974–75	2	9

SOURCE: Government of India, *National Sample Survey: 28th Round, Oct. 73–June 74* (New Delhi: Department of Statistics, 1977); H. Alderman, J. von Braun, and S. A. Sakr, *Egypt's Food Subsidy and Rationing System: A Description*, Research Report no. 34 (Washington, D.C.: IFPRI, 1982); P. A. Cornelisse and S. N. H. Naqvi, *The Anatomy of the Wheat Market in Pakistan* (Islamabad and Rotterdam: Pakistan Institute for Development Economics and Erasumus University, 1984); Fundação Instituto Brasileiro de Geografia e Estatistica, *Estudo Nacional da Despesa Familiar* (Rio de Janeiro, 1978); P. Lizardo de las Casas Maya, "A Theoretical and Applied Approach to the Formulation of Alternative Agricultural Sector Policies" (Ph.D. diss., Iowa State University, 1977); D. I. Steinberg et al., *Sri Lanka: The Impact of PL480 Title I Food Assistance*, AID Impact Evaluation no. 39 (Washington, D.C.: USAID, 1982); D. Franklin, M. P. Demousin, and M. W. Harrell, *Consumption Effects of Agricultural Policies: Bread Prices in the Sudan* (Raleigh, N.C.: Sigma One Corp., 1982); S. L. Magiera, *The Role of Wheat in the Indonesian Food Sector*, Foreign Agricultural Economics Report no. 170 (Washington, D.C.: USDA, 1981); M. E. C. Bennagen, "Staple Food Consumption in the Philippines," Working Paper no. 5 (Washington, D.C.: IFPRI, 1982); N. Shah and K. Frohberg, "Food Consumption Patterns—Rural and Urban Kenya," Working Paper (Vienna: IIASA, 1980); FAO, *Review of Food Consumption Surveys*, vol. 2, *Africa, Latin America, Near East, Far East* (Rome, 1977).

There is considerable evidence that wheat is preferred as a convenience food. In urban areas, there is a strong tendency to switch to processed products, which require less preparation and reduce costs of cooking fuel. The data for Egypt (Table 4) vividly show these trends. There is also some evidence that women's participation in the labor force increases bread consumption.[6]

Biases in Consumer Pricing Policy toward Wheat Imports

A major factor in increased wheat consumption in urban areas has been the widespread intervention by governments in food marketing, resulting in reduced prices of wheat products to urban consumers. The most common and direct intervention has been to subsidize wheat flour or bread to consumers. In the traditional wheat-consuming countries of the Middle East/North Africa, these subsidies often represent 50% or more of the total cost of providing flour (based on imported wheat) to consumers or bakers (Table 5). Subsidies also occur in most of the mixed cereal economies of South and East Asia (e.g., China and India), although they are often lower (20%–30%) and in India are targeted to low-income consumers through ration shops. Wheat-producing countries of Latin America, such as Mexico and Brazil, also had high subsidy levels (see Table 5). Even a number of non-wheat-producing countries—such as Sri Lanka, Cuba, and the Ivory Coast—have had substantial consumer subsidies on wheat products. Overall, over half of the 56 countries for which data were available had consumer subsidies on wheat products. In most cases, these subsidies are specific to wheat. Rice is also subsidized in a number of countries, whereas subsidies on maize and other coarse grains exist in only a handful of countries (e.g., Mexico).

In a few countries (e.g., Pakistan, Egypt, and Mexico in some years), low consumer prices for wheat products result from policies that reduce

TABLE 4   **Composition of Retail Purchases of Wheat and Wheat Products by Rural and Urban Areas, Egypt (%)**

Wheat Product	1954–55		1974–75	
	Rural	Urban	Rural	Urban
Grain[a]	75	9	49	4
Flour	17	23	33	14
Bread	7	68	18	81
Total	100	100	100	100

[a]Includes consumption of home-grown grain.

SOURCE: H. Alderman, J. von Braun, and S. A. Sakr, *Egypt's Food Subsidy and Rationing System: A Description*, Research Report no. 34 (Washington, D.C.: International Food Policy Research Institute, 1982).

TABLE 5   **Classification of Countries according to Level of Consumer Subsidy on Wheat Products, 1980–81**

	High Subsidy (>40%)	Moderate Subsidy (10%–40%)	No Significant Subsidy	Significant Tax on Wheat Products (>20%)
Sub-Saharan Africa	2	6	3	1
Middle East/North Africa	9	4	—	—
Far East, wheat-producing	1	3	—	—
Far East, non-wheat-producing	—	2	6	3
Latin America	4	4	6	2
All countries for which data available	16	19	15	6

NOTE: Column entries are number of countries and are based on subsidies on imported wheat. In most cases, subsidies on domestically produced wheat are somewhat higher.

SOURCE: D. Byerlee, *The Increasing Role of Wheat Consumption and Imports in the Developing World,* CIMMYT Economics Paper no. 5/83 (El Batan, Mexico: CIMMYT, 1983).

producer prices for wheat below world prices, although in almost all these cases direct government subsidies have played a more important role than low farm prices (see Table 6). Aside from these countries, there is little evidence in favor of the conventional wisdom that governments have maintained low producer prices in order to favor urban consumer-interest groups.[7]

TABLE 6   **Classification of Countries by Nominal Protection Coefficients for Producers and Consumers, Early 1980s (% of Countries)**

	NPC FOR CONSUMERS			
	<.85	.85–1.15	>1.15	Total
NPC for producers:				
<.85	31	11	0	42
.85–1.15	12	11	0	23
>1.15	19	0	15	34
Total	62	23	15	100

NOTE : The NPC (Nominal Protection Coefficient) is the ratio of domestic prices (converted at the official exchange rate) to world prices adjusted by marketing and transport costs. Adjusted NPCs, calculated at shadow exchange rates by correcting for differential domestic and international inflation, indicated a lower percentage of countries subsidizing producers (i.e., 23% of countries with NPC > 1.15).

SOURCE: D. Byerlee and G. Sain, "Food Pricing Policy in Developing Countries: Bias against Agriculture or for Urban Consumers?" *American Journal of Agricultural Economics,* 68 (1986), pp. 961–969.

Trade and exchange-rate policies also often favor low wheat prices to consumers, relative to competing staples. Because wheat is regarded as an industrial input (i.e., to the milling industry), explicit or implicit tariffs for wheat are typically kept low. Meanwhile, other staple foods are protected either by tariffs (in the case of cereals) or by high international transport costs (for roots and tubers). At the same time, many countries, especially in sub-Saharan Africa, have maintained overvalued exchange rates, which have reduced the cost of wheat imports relative to domestically produced staples. A number of countries have also recently established two-tiered exchange rates under which wheat is invariably classified as an "essential" item and imported at the cheaper rate (e.g., Ecuador).

The effect of these various policy interventions on prices of wheat products have been threefold. First, the absolute price of wheat products to consumers is often low. Table 7 shows the distribution of bread prices in wheat-importing countries in relation to a "world" price based on imported wheat in economies such as Panama and Hong Kong with relatively free markets. For most countries, especially the major wheat importers of the Middle East/North Africa and Mexico and Brazil, consumer bread prices are low; for many, bread prices are less than one-half of world prices. Second, the price of wheat products is often low in relation to competing food staples. I have estimated that, for consumer prices based on imported grains, the ratio of the price of wheat flour to rice should be slightly less than 1.0 in a free-trading country. For wheat flour to maize, the price ratio should be close to 2.0.[8] In many countries of sub-Saharan Africa and Latin America where coarse grains are an important staple (e.g., Ivory Coast, Ghana, Nigeria, Egypt, Sudan, Ecuador, and Brazil), wheat flour based on

TABLE 7 **Distribution of Bread Prices by Developing Country Region, 1980–81 (No. of Countries)**

	Low Prices (<US$.60/kg)	"Normal" Prices[a] (US$.60–1.00/kg)	High Prices (>US$1.00/kg)
Sub-Saharan Africa	7	10	5
Middle East/North Africa	11	—	—
South Asia	4	1	—
Southeast and East Asia	—	3	5
Latin America	6	6	5
Total	28	20	15

NOTE: Based on conversion at the official exchange rate. Overvalued exchange rates reduced real prices further in a number of countries, especially in sub-Saharan Africa.
[a]"Normal" bread prices are based on prices in importing countries with relatively free trade policies. In Hong Kong, Panama, and Singapore, bread prices were approximately US$.80/kg. A 25% variation in this price has been selected to allow for differences in local processing costs.
SOURCE: Calculated from data reported in ILO, *Bulletin of Labour Statistics* (various issues), supplemented and edited by the author.

imported wheat was cheaper than the locally produced coarse grain staple in 1980–81. Likewise in East Asia (e.g., Korea and Japan), wheat flour was much cheaper than rice (the local staple) because of high protection to domestic rice production. However, in some rice-producing countries, the price of wheat products relative to rice was high due to high tariffs on imported wheat (e.g., Colombia) and/or subsidies or export taxes on rice (e.g., Thailand). No country for which data are available had high wheat flour prices relative to maize (i.e., a ratio of 2:1 or above). Third, policy interventions in favor of wheat have resulted in declining *real* consumer prices for wheat products, both absolutely and relatively, over a wide array of countries (Tables 8 and 9). The major exception once again has been in the rice economies of Southeast Asia, where real bread prices have increased significantly. In relatively "free market" economies, such as Hong Kong, real bread prices changed little in the 1970s.

There is ample evidence that wheat consumption is sensitive to prices, especially in countries where wheat is not a traditional staple. Estimated price elasticities in these countries usually exceed −0.5 (absolutely) with relatively high cross-price elasticities with respect to rice.[9] Declining real prices of wheat products may explain half or more of the rapid increase in per capita wheat consumption in many countries during the 1970s.[10]

Although the evidence on biases in consumer pricing policy across countries is overwhelming, the consequences of this bias and the reasons for its existence have not been sufficiently analyzed. Several factors appear to converge in favor of wheat. In a number of wheat-producing countries, such as Mexico, India, and China, distinct surplus wheat-producing regions exist where government grain-procurement agencies find it convenient to purchase urban food requirements. Hence it is relatively easy to control procurement prices. Rapid technological change and relatively stable yields in the largely irrigated wheat environments of these countries have also facilitated the growing importance of wheat in government procurement strategies. In wheat-importing countries, the fact that wheat is readily available in world markets and usually passes through a small number of mills makes it relatively easy to control prices.[11]

Perhaps more important, urban populations—particularly middle- and upper-income groups who consume much of the imported wheat—are an important political power base capable of influencing policy. In almost all countries, wheat subsidies have been captured largely by urban populations and in many cases by the middle- and upper-income urban groups. For example, Alvarez estimated that before Peru eliminated food subsidies in the late 1970s (60% of which went for wheat), 83% of the subsidies were received by the urban population and 40% by the middle- and upper-income groups of Lima who made up only 10% of the total population.[12] A similar situation prevailed in Brazil and Indonesia.[13] Only in South Asia (India, Sri Lanka, and Bangladesh) has there been an effort to target wheat

TABLE 8   **Classification of Countries by Annual Percentage Change in Real Prices of Bread, 1971–81**

Region	No. of Countries Where Data Available	Annual Change in Real Price of Bread (% of Countries)					
		<−3%	−3%−−1%	−1%−1%	1%−3%	>3%	Total
Sub-Saharan Africa	17	35	18	18	18	12	100
Middle East/North Africa	8	50	38	—	12	—	100
South Asia/Southeast Asia	12	—	8	25	8	58	100
Latin America	16	44	12	—	6	38	100
All developing countries	53	32	17	11	11	28	100
Industrialized countries	13	—	8	31	62	—	100

SOURCE: See Table 7. Consumer prices deflated by the consumer price index from IMF, *International Financial Statistics* (Washington, D.C.: various issues).

TABLE 9   **Changes in Real Prices of Wheat Flour, Rice, and Maize in Selected Countries, 1970s**

		Change in Retail Prices (%)		
City and Country	Period	Wheat Flour	Rice	Maize, Other Coarse Grain
São Paulo, Brazil	1969–79	−46	−1	167
Cali, Colombia	1970–80	7	−3	62
Mexico City, Mexico	1970–80	−48	18	−19[a]
Khartoum, Sudan	1971–81	−44	—	1[b]
Djakarta, Indonesia	1969–79	−22	−8	9
Dakar, Senegal[c]	1970–80	163	−30	10§
Manila, Philippines[c]	1968–78	168	−19	7

NOTE: Annual average consumer prices deflated by the consumer price index.
[a]Maize tortillas.
[b]Sorghum.
[c]Bread subsidies were drastically cut in Senegal, and import protection increased in Philippines in the 1970s.
[d]Millet.
SOURCE: See Table 5.

subsidies to low-income consumers. Many subsidy programs were initiated in 1974–75 to protect consumers from high world wheat prices at that time. Other countries instituted subsidies when wheat food aid was eliminated or reduced.[14] Finally, many governments with strict consumer price controls for flour or bread have been reluctant to raise prices in line with inflation, which has led to rapid real price declines and increasing subsidy levels in countries with high inflation rates (e.g., Mexico and Brazil).

Urban Food Supplies and Wheat Imports

There are also a number of factors operating on the supply side that influence wheat consumption in urban areas. With strong preferences for wheat products, lagging domestic production of staple foods, and poor infrastructure for transporting and marketing domestic food production in urban areas, there has been a natural tendency to import wheat to feed urban consumers, especially in countries where large cities are located on the coast. This is evident in the relatively low year-to-year variability in wheat imports by most countries (Table 10). In most cases, wheat imports have steadily increased with little relationship to domestic cereal production except in some major wheat-producing countries. Also, wheat imports are relatively inelastic with respect to world prices since both consumer and producer prices are usually fixed by government policy and often do not reflect changes in world prices.[15] Rice imports, on the other hand, are more variable and depend on domestic rice production as well as fluctuations in

TABLE 10   **Index of Variability in Wheat and Rice Imports: Selected Wheat-Producing and Non-Wheat-Producing Countries, 1966–80 (%)**

Country	Wheat	Rice
Wheat-producing:		
Syria	54	32
Iran	44	49
Morocco	13	a
Mexico	82	a
Chile	31	62
Non-wheat-producing:		
Ghana	20	16
Indonesia	26	29
Philippines	12	a
Honduras	11	50
Venezuela	12	a

NOTE: Calculated as $I = CV\sqrt{1 - \overline{R}^2}$, where CV is the coefficient of variability and R is the corrected coefficient of determination from a linear time trend regression. The lower the index, I, the less the variability around the trend line.
[a] Not calculated because country is exporter or insignificant importer of that commodity.
SOURCE: See J. D. A. Cuddy and P. A. Della Valle, "Measuring the Instability of Time Series Data," *Oxford Bulletin of Economics and Statistics*, 40 (1978): 79–85.

world rice prices.[16] This strategy of relying on wheat imports to supply urban consumers is most advanced in Latin America, where close to two-thirds of the population now lives in urban areas. In the Andean region, wheat consumption has reached 40 kilograms per capita, over 90% of which is imported and most of which is consumed in urban areas.

Using wheat imports to feed urban consumers is to some extent reinforcing. A marketing, storage, and processing infrastructure has been developed accordingly. Because these investments are usually oriented toward port facilities and located in large coastal cities, they cannot be readily utilized to market domestic food production. In addition, the wheat-processing sector (i.e., milling and baking) is highly wheat specific and cannot be converted to processing domestically produced food because either mills are located at a substantial distance from the wheat-producing region or, more commonly, wheat is not produced locally and is not likely to be, in the near future, in the tropical belt of countries. Indeed, the wheat-processing sector in developing countries is often a powerful interest group able to influence and even control grain-procurement strategies.[17] This sector has grown very rapidly in the last 10–20 years so that the proportion of wheat flour in international wheat trade has declined.[18] The most rapid growth of the milling industry has occurred in the tropical belt, where countries such

TABLE 11   **Examples of Tariff Protection Provided to Wheat-Milling Industry**

		IMPORT DUTY (%)	
	Year	Wheat Grain	Wheat Flour
Republic of Korea	1975	0	30
Philippines	1975	10	30
Kenya	1975	0	40
Sierra Leone	1974	0	167
Guatemala	1975	6	50
Ecuador	1979	0	70
Papua New Guinea	1982	0	Banned
Nigeria	1982	5	15

SOURCE: Data for 1975 are from FAO, *Review of Agricultural Policies* (Rome: FAO, 1976). Other data were collected by the author.

as Nigeria, Sri Lanka, and Indonesia—which were importing most of their wheat as flour in 1970—have recently become self-sufficient in flour production. Nigeria and Indonesia, in fact, have an excess of milling capacity beyond their annual consumption of 1.5–2.0 million tons of wheat. Ironically, the larger flour mills in the world are now located in these non-wheat-producing countries. While there are cost economies in grain versus flour transport, there is little evidence that it is an efficient use of resources to establish a capital- and foreign-exchange-intensive local milling industry in non-wheat-producing countries. This industry usually receives high tariff protection from imported flour (Table 11) and in many cases operates at a high margin relative to mills in developed countries.[19] More important, once established, the industry has a vested interest in continuing wheat imports, even if local production of cereals other than wheat offers the opportunity for import substitution. There are only a few cases in which wheat imports by non-wheat-producing countries have declined, and these have occurred in times of acute foreign exchange crises, such as in Sierra Leone, Guyana, and Ghana in 1982–83.

THE EXTERNAL INFLUENCES

World Wheat Prices and Policies of Exporting Countries

A number of external factors related to world wheat markets and policies of exporting countries have promoted wheat imports and consumption. The simplest of these is the fact that the price of wheat in international markets is significantly lower than the main competing food grain (i.e., rice), is less variable, and has tended to decline over time relative to rice.[20] Nonetheless, the costs of wheat imports are often underestimated since wheat is usually processed using foreign-exchange-intensive milling and baking methods and over one-quarter of the product (i.e., the bran) is used for animal feed.[21]

The lower price of wheat in world markets reflects rapid technological change in wheat-exporting countries as well as agricultural policies of exporting countries. The United States in the 1960s and the EEC in the 1970s have explicitly subsidized wheat exports. It is estimated that EEC export subsidies reduced the world market price of wheat by 11% in the 1970s.[22] In recent years, aggressive credit programs have provided attractive terms for purchase of wheat in world markets.

Food Aid

Food aid has also been a major external influence on wheat imports. Over 80% of cereal food aid is provided in the form of wheat or wheat flour, and this proportion holds for both countries where wheat is a traditional staple and countries where wheat is not a staple. Food aid originated with a specific objective of disposing of the surpluses of exporting countries and developing markets for commercial sales of these products. In the early 1960s, nearly 60% of Third World wheat imports (excluding China) were provided by food aid. In the 1970s, the amount of wheat food aid declined and now averages only 12% of total wheat imports of developing countries. Nonetheless, it remains important to some countries, such as Egypt, Sri Lanka, the Sudan, and Bolivia.

The impact of food aid on food imports and domestic cereal production is complex and country specific, and a full discussion is beyond the scope of this paper.[23] The most direct effect is to lower the real price of wheat imports (often to half or less than half of the price of commercial imports) and, in many cases, to provide wheat free of charge. Recent studies have shown that countries that receive significant amounts of wheat food aid (e.g., Bangladesh, Bolivia, and the Sudan) have higher per capita wheat imports than non-food-aid countries of comparable levels of income and urbanization.[24] Furthermore, current commercial imports of wheat by the tropical countries are positively related to the amount of wheat received as food aid in the past.[25] This long-run effect reflects several factors, such as (a) an established consumer exposure and even preference for wheat products, (b) market promotion activities often associated with food aid programs, (c) institutionalization of low wheat prices to urban consumers, and (d) establishment of a local wheat-processing industry to accommodate food aid imports.

Finally, the possible negative impact of food aid on domestic food production is a subject of continuing controversy. In the Andean region, domestic wheat production declined in response to reduced producer prices for wheat during the 1960s when most wheat was imported as food aid.[26] In other cases, such as Brazil, domestic producer prices for wheat were supported at a level above world prices, and domestic wheat production increased rapidly.[27]

Other External Influences

Wheat-exporting countries have actively promoted bread consumption in many countries. Private as well as public agencies of exporting countries have provided technical advice and training for the establishment of local milling and baking industries and for introducing new wheat products to consumers.[28] In contrast, export promotion efforts for rice and especially maize for food are relatively weak.

Furthermore, the milling and baking industry in many developing countries is owned or closely linked to the grain industry of the exporting countries. This is particularly the case in Latin America and Africa, where flour mills and large bakers or other manufacturing industries based on wheat (e.g., the biscuit industry) are frequently owned by multinational corporations with links to the grain-export business.[29] These industries often consist of one or a few firms that undertake sales and shipment of wheat as well as local processing and can exert considerable pressure on government policy. In some cases, foreign aid agencies of donor countries have actively supported the development of a baking industry.[30]

More recently, a fourth external influence, the International Monetary Fund, has exerted considerable pressure *against* the set of national policies discussed above.[31] With the current debt crisis, countries receiving loans from the IMF have committed themselves to more realistic exchange-rate policies and to elimination of bread subsidies. These policies have led to sharp increases in bread prices in 1982–83 in a number of countries, such as Brazil, Ecuador, and Nigeria. Nonetheless, the effect has been only partial, and growth of wheat consumption may have slowed but has not declined. Furthermore, the political significance of bread prices has recently been demonstrated by widespread protests in Tunisia and Morocco when bread subsidies were reduced in 1984. In both cases, governments reversed their decision to raise bread prices.

IMPLICATIONS FOR FOOD IMPORTS AND FOOD POLICY

The data presented here clearly demonstrate the special place of wheat in national and international food policy decisions. Governments have attempted to control both producer and consumer prices of wheat in almost all Third World countries. Relative to other food staples (except possibly rice), these policy interventions have been to a remarkable extent successful in controlling prices. With controlled producer and consumer prices, wheat imports have been the major instrument of food policy to equate supply and demand. Furthermore, while Third World food imports are often equated with efforts to reduce hunger and the interests of feeding the poor, the evidence of this paper suggests otherwise, especially in countries where wheat is not a traditional staple. Food imports in these countries represent a desire of middle-income urban consumers for a low-cost convenience food.

The size of the policy interventions and the number of countries involved are sufficient to account for much of the growth of food imports to the Third World in the last decade. Consumer subsidies alone account for a large share of wheat imports. Taking the large wheat importers alone (over 500,000 tons annually), the weighted average subsidy on wheat in 1981 was over 50% of consumer prices. Even assuming a relatively inelastic demand (−0.33), wheat imports by this group of countries would be at least one-third lower if market prices prevailed. These countries together make up well over half of commercial wheat imports by the Third World. This, together with wheat imports as food aid (over 6.0 million tons) and subsidized exports by the EEC (14 million tons), which are largely destined to Third World countries, suggests that a significant share of wheat imports by the Third World is accounted for by direct government interventions in wheat markets.

The regions with the strongest prospects for continuing rapid increases in wheat imports are the tropical belt of non-wheat-producing countries in Southeast Asia and sub-Saharan Africa. Here urbanization is still low but increasing rapidly. In sub-Saharan Africa, population growth in 35 major capitals now averages 9% annually.[32] At this rate, not only the marketed food surplus but also the associated marketing, transportation, and storage requirements must double in size every 8 years simply to maintain per capita food consumption in urban areas at current levels. The strategy of turning to imported wheat (reinforced by consumer pricing policies) to meet urban food supplies is likely to continue unless there is a drastic reversal in domestic food production and food policy. In Southeast Asia, pricing policies often lead to relatively high wheat prices, but rapidly rising incomes and urbanization still promote demand for wheat products.

Almost all Third World countries have expressed an objective of reducing food imports. For most countries, food policy measures are available to arrest the trend toward increased reliance on imported wheat. In the wheat-producing countries of the Middle East and North Africa, considerable potential exists for increasing domestic wheat production.[33] Targeting of urban consumer subsidies to the poor would also reduce demand and free resources for development of the domestic food sector.

For the non-wheat-producing countries of the tropics, substitution of wheat imports will require a combination of strategies including (a) increased domestic production of local food staples, (b) development of convenience food based on local staples (e.g., composite flours for bread), and (c) removal of policy-induced price disincentives against consumption of local staples. Sri Lanka, Colombia, and Senegal are examples of countries that reduced or eliminated bread subsidies in the 1970s. They are also among the handful of countries where per capita wheat consumption has declined. At the same time, acceptance of food aid in the form of local cereals will reduce the impact of wheat food aid (other than emergency aid) on consumer habits and slow the development of a wheat-processing industry. Importation of wheat as flour rather than grain would also provide a more temporary nature to wheat imports than the establishment of a local milling industry. The removal of tariff protection on wheat milling is probably sufficient in most countries to arrest the development of this industry.

There is now a renewed emphasis on finding ways to make local staples into acceptable convenience foods for urban consumers. This includes the numerous but not very successful attempts to produce composite flours by mixing local staples and wheat flour for bread making. In most cases, however, the major obstacle is pricing policy that maintains low wheat prices relative to local staples and provides no incentive to substitute for imported wheat.

All of these food policy alternatives to slow the trend in wheat imports are, of course, challenging the very interest groups that have led to the growth of wheat imports in the last 2 decades. Yet there is some hope for optimism, given the policy changes in a number of countries during the economic crisis of 1982–83. International and donor agencies can reinforce these trends through more appropriate food aid policies and more attention to the underlying causes of food imports. In particular, those charged with analyzing the "food gap" will need to pay more attention to variables such as urbanization and consumer price policies in making their projections. This argues for more analysis of food policy at the country level, which can then be built up into aggregate regional and world projections.

NOTES

1. See, e.g., projections in FAO, *Agriculture: Towards 2000* (Rome: FAO, 1979).
2. Imports of rice, the single most important food staple of developing countries, are only about one-sixth of wheat imports and have grown much more slowly. Imports of coarse grains by developing countries have risen rapidly, but almost all were destined to animal feed. See CIMMYT, *World Maize Facts and Trends,* Report no. 1 (El Batan, Mexico: CIMMYT, 1981).
3. D. Byerlee, *The Increasing Role of Wheat Consumption and Imports in the Developing World,* Economics Paper no. 5/83 (El Batan, Mexico: CIMMYT, 1983).
4. Throughout this paper, the term "tropical countries" refers to countries that are entirely or almost entirely within the latitude belt 23 degrees north to 23 degrees south.
5. Byerlee, (note 3 above).
6. D. Franklin, M. P. Demousin, and M. W. Harell, *Consumption Effects of Agricultural Policies: Bread Prices in the Sudan* (Raleigh, N.C.: Sigma One Corp., 1982).
7. This issue is analyzed in detail in D. Byerlee and G. Sain, "Food Pricing Policy in Developing Countries: Bias against Agriculture or for Urban Consumers?" *American Journal of Agricultural Economics,* 68 (1986), pp. 961–969. There is substantial evidence that producer pricing policy is more favorable to producers

than earlier studies had indicated. For earlier evidence, see W. L. Peterson, "International Farm Prices and the Social Cost of Cheap Food Policies," *American Journal of Agricultural Economics*, 61 (1979): 12–21; and E. Lutz and P. L. Scandizzo, "Price Distortions in Developing Countries: A Bias against Agriculture," *European Review of Agricultural Economics*, 7 (1980): 5–27. However, the large size of consumer subsidies relative to government revenues has undoubtedly reduced government investments in promoting domestic food production.

8. Assumes export prices of wheat, rice, and maize of x, 2x, and 0.75x, respectively; international freight and handling 0.3x; marketing margin of 15% of CIF price; milling rate .72; and a 10% markup to represent the mill to retail margin. Margins were based on data from several countries. See Byerlee (note 3) for details.

9. Recent estimates of price elasticities for wheat products are as follows: −0.8 for the Philippines [H. Bouis, "Demand for Cereal Staples in the Philippines," unpublished paper (Washington, D.C.: IFPRI, 1982)]; −0.9 for Brazil [W. Gray, *Food Consumption Parameters for Brazil and Their Application to Food Policy*, Research Report no. 32 (Washington, D.C.: IFPRI, 1982)]; −0.4 for the Sudan (Franklin et al.); −1.8 for Indonesia [S. L. Magiera, *The Role of Wheat in the Indonesian Food Sector*, Foreign Agricultural Economics Report no. 170 (Washington, D.C.: USDA, 1981)]; and −1.1 for Sri Lanka [H. Alderman and C. P. Timmer, "Consumption Parameters for Sri Lankan Food Policy Analysis, *Sri Lankan Journal of Agrarian Studies*, 1 (1980): 1–12].

10. For evidence, see Franklin et al. on the Sudan and Gray on Brazil.

11. C. Hodges and T. Roe, "Government Intervention into the Market for Wheat in Four Low-Income Countries" (paper presented at the meeting of the American Agricultural Economics Society, Logan, Utah, 1982).

12. E. Alvarez, *Política Agraria y Estancamiento de la Agricultura, 1967–77* (Lima: Instituto de Estudios Peruanos, 1980).

13. For Brazil, see Gray. For Indonesia, see A. J. Nyberg, "Food Policy—Import Substitution or Import Dependence" (paper presented to the Third Biennial Meeting of the Agricultural Economics Association of Southeast Asia, Kuala Lumpur, 1979).

14. This is partially supported by a negative correlation of −.46 between current bread prices and wheat food aid per capita received during 1955–75 in a cross-sectional analysis of 39 tropical countries. See Byerlee (note 3 above).

15. Econometric analyses of wheat imports also support this view. See P. C. Abbott, "Modeling International Grain Trade with Government Controlled Markets," *American Journal of Agricultural Economics*, 61 (1979): 22–31; and C. L. Jabara, "Cross-Sectional Analysis of Wheat Import Demand among Middle-Income Developing Countries," *Agricultural Economics Research*, 34 (1982): 34–37.

16. W. P. Falcon and E. A. Monke, "International Trade in Rice," *Food Research Institute Studies*, 17 (1979–80): 176–306.

17. W. J. Carbonell and H. Rothman, "An Implicit Food Policy: Wheat Consumption Changes in Venezuela," *Food Policy*, 2 (1977): 305–17.

18. Wheat flour production increased at an annual rate of 23.4% in Brazil, 7.6% in Indonesia, 11.1% in Kenya, 11.7% in Cuba, 14.4% in Guatemala, and 7.2% in the Philippines between 1975 and 1980. See United Nations, *Monthly Bulletin of Statistics* (various issues).

19. Personal communication with mill operators in Ghana, Indonesia, Senegal, Mexico, and the Dominican Republic suggests that milling margins (ex-mill price of flour in wheat equivalent divided by mill delivery price of wheat) are often of the order of 20%–40% compared with margins close to zero in industrial countries where the value of by-products pays for the milling cost. See also Magiera (note 9 above).

20. R. Barker and R. W. Herdt, *The Asian Rice Economy* (Washington, D.C.: Resources for the Future, 1985); and Falcon and Monke (note 16 above).

21. Flour milling of imported wheat is usually undertaken in large, capital-intensive mills. Baking techniques, however, may range from very small scale, labor-intensive firms to large, capital-intensive industries. See E. Chuta, *Choice of Appropriate Technique in the African Bread Industry with Special Reference to Sierra Leone*, World Employment Program Working Paper (Geneva: International Labor Organization, 1981); and C. B. Baron, ed., *Technology, Employment and Basic Needs in Food Processing in Developing Countries* (New York: Pergamon Press, 1980).

22. V. Koester, *Policy Options for the Grain Economy of the European Community: Implications for Developing Countries*, Research Report no. 35 (Washington, D.C.: IFPRI, 1982).

23. For a recent review of effects of food aid, see C. Stevens, *Food Aid and the Developing World* (London: Croom Helm, 1979).

24. See Byerlee (note 3 above); Abbott (note 15 above); Hodges and Roe (note 11 above).

25. Byerlee (note 3 above).

26. L. Dudley and R. J. Sandilands, "The Side Effects of Foreign Aid: The Case of Public Law 480 Wheat in Colombia," *Economic Development and Cultural Change*, 23 (1975): 325–36; and M. Valderrama, "Effecto de las Exportaciones Norte-americanas de Trigo a Bolivia, Perú, Ecuador y Colombia," *Estudios Rurales Latinoamericanos*, 2 (1979): 173–98.

27. L. Hall, "Evaluating the Effects of PL480 Wheat Imports on Brazil's Grain Sector," *American Journal of Agricultural Economics*, 62 (1980): 19–28.

28. See W. Wilson, "U.S. Wheat Associates: Recipe for Successful Marketing," *Foreign Agriculture*, 20 (1982): 18–19; "U.S. Export Development Programs," *Agriculture Abroad* (August 1981).

29. The large grain-exporting companies, Continental and Bunge, and U.S. flour millers such as General Mills, Pillsbury, and International Multifoods each own and operate flour mills in several Latin American countries. In West Africa, flour mills in Sierra Leone, Liberia, and Nigeria are owned by Seaboard Corporation, a grain-shipping company now linked to Cargill that also owns mills in Guyana and Ecuador. In Francophone countries, mills are owned by a French grain-marketing and milling cooperative. In many countries, such as Indonesia and Nigeria, the state also owns a significant interest in flour mills. See P. Barback and P. Flynn, *Agribusiness in the Americas* (New York: Monthly Review Press, 1980); M. Lajo, "Perú: Monopolio y Vulnerabilidad Almentaria," *Comercio Exterior* (Mexico City), 32 (1982): 84–94; D. Johnson, "International Multifoods Strategy in Venezuela," *Agribusiness Worldwide* (February 1981), pp. 38–42, and "Pillsbury's Involvement with the Saudi Arabian Flour Mills," *Agribusiness Worldwide* (October 1980), pp. 38–43.)

30. L. Freeman, "CIDA, Wheat and Rural Development in Tanzania," *Canadian Journal of African Studies*, 16 (1982): 479–504. USAID involvement in a bakeries project is discussed in "Problems Delay Egyptian Plants," *Milling and Baking News* (Kansas City, Mo.), vol. 63 (October 4, 1983).

31. See D. K. Willis, "The Link between International Aid and Riots in African Streets," *Christian Science Monitor* (April 20–26, 1985).

32. J. Meerman and S. H. Cochrane, "Population Growth and Food Supply in Sub-Saharan Africa," *Finance and Development*, 19 (1982): 12–17.

33. See D. Byerlee and D. L. Winkelmann, *Accelerated Wheat Production in Semi-Arid Areas: Economic and Policy Issues*, Economics Working Paper no. 81/2 (El Batan, Mexico: CIMMYT, 1981).

PART FIVE

INDUSTRY IN DEVELOPMENT

One of the tenets of early development economics emphasized by Sen was the fundamental importance of industrialization in development, and he provided evidence that countries which have industrialized have performed better on many development indicators. The strongest evidence is provided by the newly industrialized countries (NICs), particularly Taiwan and South Korea, but also Singapore, Hong Kong, Brazil, and Mexico.

The one clear lesson of the last forty-five years of development theory and policy is that there are no simple answers. In many countries the industrialization effort reached definite limits by the 1970s when the attempt to substitute for imports was unable to generate enough resources to make the process self-sustaining. Often the enterprises were sustained only by government subsidies, or if they were state-owned enterprises, they became contributors to the fiscal deficit and to increasing inflationary pressures in their national economies.

Even at its best the impact of industry on the domestic economy was not unambiguously positive. It often resulted in a protected sector characterized by high incomes to a few owners and high wages for a small elite labor force. For the most part Third World industries did not generate their own technologies, remaining dependent on international sources of technology, and reducing the dynamism that they transmitted to the domestic economy. Industry still offered the possibilities of backward and forward linkages that were noted long ago by Albert Hirschman (1958), but their effect on the economy was neither uniform nor powerful for most countries.

Finally, the evolution of the international economy has also affected the role of industrialization. Virtually every country in the world has made an effort to industrialize and to sell its industrial products in the world market. Thus international competition has increased substantially. At the same time the control over technology and information has given an advantage to the transnational corporations which are located primarily in the developed world, providing them a formative influence on the entire industrialization process, not always to the benefit of developing countries as a group or of any particular country.

The end result is that we must rethink the role of industry in development and must update it to take account of the contemporary situation. Industry will play an important role in any development process, but not in the manner the early development economists had envisioned. This updating is the task of this section.

Bob Sutcliffe's article clearly reflects this rethinking. His socialist perspective emphasized the need for large-scale industrial production and for a high degree of autarky or independence from the international economy. He found that there have indeed been major strides toward industrialization but that they have not always contributed to improved satisfaction of human needs or to modernisation, implying that a much more tentative stance toward industry may be warranted and that intermediate technologies may play a positive role. His article was first published in 1984, and he criticized both socialist and capitalist economists for overestimating the benefits and underestimating the costs of industrialization. He also pointed to the tendency for socialism to become a euphemism for nationalism and for dictatorship, a warning which presaged the reactions in Eastern Europe and in the republics of the Soviet Union. He concluded that a true development policy must not use the claims of either capitalism or socialism to gloss over the costs that many development policies entail.

Sutcliffe's disavowal of simplistic socialist views of industrialization is followed by the articles of Standing and of Bienen and Waterbury, which cast a similarly negative light on the liberalization, supply-side economics, and privatization approaches to industry that became popular with the free market ideology of the Reagan and Thatcher administrations.

Standing's treatment of global feminization documents both the increased labor force participation of women and the accompanying decrease in the benefits which had traditionally accompanied industrial employment: job security, higher pay, job safety, and the security of insurance programs. His assessment is that the supply-side programs which have encouraged deregulation and cutthroat international competition have created a "cult of insecurity," a view Sutcliffe would share. The effect of development processes on women and on issues of gender has become an important concern of contemporary development economics; Standing's conclusion is that current industrial strategies are eroding their control in very important areas and are increasing women's vulnerability. He suggests a broad-based rethinking of industrial and labor policy to take these trends into account. He also points out that privatization is likely to affect women negatively since they are relatively better off in public enterprises.

The push to privatize state-owned enterprises has been an important component of neoconservative efforts to reduce the role of governments in developing countries. Bienen and Waterbury provide an overview of the many factors entering into this effort. Contrary to the euphoric pronouncements of free enterprise economists who see privatization as the road to development, especially in Eastern Europe, the authors find that "the payoffs for adjustment generated by privatization are relatively small, and there is a high opportunity cost in time and management devoted to the complicated task of preparing public assets for sale." Poland's current problems in operationalizing its program of privatization is proof of their observation.

Nonetheless there is scope in development efforts for privatization: there are state enterprises that are inefficient; there are areas where the private sector has matured and the human resource base has improved, often through government education policies, making greater private activity more feasible; and there are certainly economic areas in which the state should reduce its scope of activity. The fiscal crisis faced by many developing countries will increase the pace of privatization activity when it can relieve fiscal pressures, and it is entirely likely that the new decade will see a contraction of the role of government. It seems to us less likely that this is "the dawn of a new era of unfettered markets and private enterprise" than "one of adjustment in which the state seeks to redefine the instruments and scope of its intervention." These are the issues that the final two articles of this section specifically consider.

Clive Hamilton provides an overview of the Asian development success stories, Taiwan, South Korea, Singapore, and Hong Kong, and also assesses the likelihood of similar changes occurring in eight other countries of South and Southeast Asia. His framework would apply to any other country in the world as well. The ability of a country to follow this pattern of industrialization, and its success in doing so, depend on international conditions, on internal economic conditions and policies, and finally on domestic politics and power relations. The first of these is not likely to be as benign as in the past; the domestic requirements are to increase saving, improve management, and modernize the agricultural sector; and the process is more likely if an industrial capitalist class dominates politics or is at least the major influence on state power. Hamilton makes his analysis specific by examining the prospects of success for the eight countries, finding them poor for Indonesia, the Philippines, Nepal, and Bangladesh, doubtful for India and Pakistan, and favorable for Malaysia and Thailand.

The final article by Helen Shapiro and Lance Taylor is an excellent summary of where thinking on industrialization is today, and a good example of another approach to the "new development economics." They assess the earlier debates on the role of industry and emphasize a central weakness, the nonexistence, or at least the superficial treatment, of the state. Their approach is to draw on a wealth of empirical information from case studies of industry, the state, and development in the belief that "elements of the strategies appropriate to large and small countries are best described through empirical generalizations rather than the abstract model used by neoclassical theory." This methodology differs fundamentally from Stiglitz's "new development economics" of Part Four. They are able to specify seven boundary conditions for successful industrialization and then to make eleven generalizations useful in understanding that process and in developing policies toward industrialization. While, as we might expect, there is no simple answer to the question of the role of industry in development, Shapiro and Taylor conclude that the experience of the last forty years does provide a basis for steps which can improve the contribution of industry to the development process.

As was the case with the agricultural sector, there has been active rethinking of the sectoral dimensions to development, based on the wealth of experience that has been gained. The international context will have a major impact on any national development strategy that is undertaken, and success in establishing a viable set of domestic policies will affect the contribution which industry can make.

REFERENCE

Hirschman, Albert O. *The Strategy of Economic Development*, New Haven: Yale University Press, 1958.

18

Industry and Underdevelopment Reexamined

R. B. Sutcliffe

I

In my book entitled *Industry and Underdevelopment,* written for the most part fifteen years ago, I argued the following positions:

1. That the industrialization of countries was (according both to pure theory and to historical experience) necessary to eliminate human poverty and satisfy human needs with rising standards of living; only a small number of areas or countries could, due to super-generous natural endowments, escape this logic;

2. That up to the present only a privileged few countries had industrialized successfully, and that it did not look from the evidence as if the underdeveloped countries were undergoing the process at all, or at best they were undergoing it at a very slow pace;

3. That successful modern industrialisation in general requires the use of large-scale units of production to take advantage of economies of scale; and also the use of modern technology which usually means relatively capital-intensive techniques. This is one of the advantages of being a latecomer. Nonetheless many qualifications to this were

School of Economics and Politics, Kingston Polytechnic. I am grateful to other contributors to this volume for comments on an earlier draft, especially to the editors, to David Evans, and to Martin Bell; and to Kaighn Smith for help with the numbers. From *Journal of Development Studies,* 21, 1 (October 1984), pp. 121–133. Reprinted by permission from the October 1984 issue of *Journal of Development Studies* published by Frank Cass & Company Ltd., 11 Gainsborough Road, London E11, England. Copyright Frank Cass & Co. Ltd.

made and a cautious welcome was given to certain versions of intermediate technology and forms of technological dualism;

4. That because there was something in the existence of, or policies of,
industrialised countries which prevented the independent industrialisation of the underdeveloped ones, such a process was only possible if these latter could immunise themselves against the damaging effects of contact with the industrialised countries; and this, with
many qualifications, suggested the need for a fairly high degree of
economic autarky which quite possibly could only be achieved
through socialism in the underdeveloped countries; this was combined with a generally positive evaluation of the economic aspects
of the Soviet, and often also the Chinese, model of industrialisation.

These positions, I think, coincide with or overlap a range of positions which
have become a kind of orthodoxy throughout a large part of the development economics profession, especially on the socialist and nationalist left.
This orthodoxy includes various theories which have come to be known
under the collective title of "dependency theory."

All these ideas have been more widely discussed during the period
since I did the reading for my book. Now, on reflection, I find that just
about all of them require at least a good deal of critical modification, and
some of them more of a thoroughgoing revision. In this article I will briefly
explain why, referring to a number of the more controversial and interesting writings on the subject in the last few years. These include: Michael
Lipton's *Why Poor People Stay Poor*; Fritz Schumacher's *Small Is Beautiful*;
Frances Stewart's *Technology and Underdevelopment*; Arghiri Emmanuel's
Intermediate or Underdeveloped Technology?; Gavin Kitching's *Development
and Underdevelopment in Historical Perspective*, and Bill Warren's *Imperialism,
Pioneer of Capitalism*. All of these are works which have in some way managed to have an impact on discussion within the field of development economics by changing the terms of the existing debate. They have all, therefore, forced economists working in the field of development to reexamine
old positions.

II

Gavin Kitching's stimulating book gives a good summary of the traditional
and almost universally accepted argument for industrialisation as a necessary step towards the elimination of human poverty. It is based on the
expanding variety of human needs as material standards rise, and as such it
is incontestable, almost axiomatic. But, more than before, I think it needs
some quite strong qualifications.

The argument is a theoretical one. It assumes that more or less any conceivable evolution of consumption preferences for some distance above the

mere subsistence level of income involves a rising share of industrial goods. In principle, it could be objected, these goods could be supplied for any given population by the production and exchange of other nonindustrial goods and services as long as the levels of productivity and the terms of trade of the nonindustrial sectors allow it. In other words, in principle a nation of bee-keepers, or of bankers, or of masseurs, or of airline pilots could have a high standard of living. And of course nonindustrial workers in industrialised countries often do have a high standard of living. That there should be a whole nation of such people, however, is scarcely possible—it could occur only for small countries extraordinarily well endowed by nature. In any case, for one nation to live like that implies industrialisation somewhere else to provide inputs to the primary production or services. So this whole line of argument is not really one against industrialisation in general, only in some very special places.

Another objection to the standard pro-industrialisation argument is less often made but is, in my view, much more important. The theoretical argument for industrialisation as a route to satisfying human needs does not prove that real historical or present-day industrialisations in fact do supply human needs well. Conceivable ideal industrialisation will satisfy needs; but "actually existing industrialisation" (to adapt a phrase of Rudolph Bahro) may not. And I contend that in most cases it does not.

It is surely a fact that the standard, universally accepted *theoretical* defence of industrialisation has never been the main motive for any actually existing industrialisation. Real-world industrialisations have not been motivated directly by the desire to satisfy human needs in general. In cases where industrialisation has been fostered by state authorities then this has usually been done as a means of increasing the military might of the nation against others, or to augment the power of the ruling group within their own country. Hence a very great part of industrial output during the process of industrialisation has taken the form of goods which in no way meet human needs but rather create the means to destroy or intimidate human beings.

Also, even if the irreducible nature of human tastes dictates a high proportion of industrial output it does not follow that either the total amount of industrial goods which have been produced, or their composition between different products, are consonant with satisfying human needs. In other words some very radically different structure of industrialisation might in principle have met human needs better. No doubt it is reaction against the deficiencies of actually existing industrialisation which has partly fuelled the popular argument for "basic needs" strategies; and some of these are very rejecting of industrialisation in a way that I do not intend to be.

The frequent noncongruence in practice between actual industrial output and the fulfilment of human needs illustrates one way in which important truths can be obscured by economists' excessive concentration on industrialisation as a process in the life of *nations* (the abstract) rather than of *people* (the concrete). Another problem with this national emphasis is geographical. Even in the most industrialised of nations there are areas of economic backwardness where industrialisation and its effects have not penetrated. Usually, of course, in the industrialised countries there are no longer large numbers of people living in "preindustrial conditions" in those areas because the original inhabitants have long since migrated to the more industrialised areas (urbanisation). Historically, too, industrialisation was accompanied by another form of migration—international migration from the slower or nonindustrialising areas to the faster industrialising areas—particularly of course from Europe to North America. This form of migration has—for racist and other reasons—become much more difficult in the modern epoch. Therefore international migration is now largely ruled out as a method of spreading the "benefits" of industrialisation to a wider proportion of the world's population. This is perhaps one reason why it does make some sense to emphasise the polarisation of developed/industrialised and underdeveloped/nonindustrialised areas today as a polarisation of *nations* rather than as one of the forms of intranational polarisation which have been common to all industrialisations.

On the other hand, to see the polarisation between nations as the main and invariable feature of modern economic change can be extremely misleading. It passes over the fact that some industrial growth has taken place in the underdeveloped countries and that important processes of polarisation have been taking place within them; and this is related to patterns of world industrial growth which, because of the growing internationalisation of the capitalist economy, are less comprehensible in terms of nations than they were in the past.

The dependency/national polarisation approach used to be taken to imply that all nations as at present constituted ought, if they want to enrich themselves to European levels, to undergo a parallel process of national industrialisation. At best this argument could only apply to broad *regions* since, although the economies of scale argument is often taken much too far, there are enough technical economies of scale to mean that it is inconsistent for very small nations (of which there are very many in the Third World) both to want to enrich themselves and to want to undergo a complete industrialisation within their own borders. It is almost certain, and no longer widely denied, that some processes of industrialisation which have actually occurred (measured in terms of the composition of GDP and so on) behind high tariff walls have led not to national enrichment but to some national impoverishment. Political decentralisation in general seems to me to be desirable, but not with every decentralised unit aiming to construct an industrial replica of the superstates within its own borders.

The most ardent proponents of rapid industrialisation will often admit that actually existing industrialisations may leave something to be desired in their meeting of human needs; but, they argue, at any event they have created the *potential* for those needs to be met more effectively. This argument is related, I think, to the question of the relative valuation of the consumption of different generations. It tends to value the consumption of future generations highly relative to the present one (and the present one highly relative to past ones). Even in general philosophical terms this balance of interest would be hard to justify to those whose needs are not met today. It can only be defended by arguing that to ignore the interests of the unborn will (by storing up crisis and disaster) in fact cause more long-run suffering for the living than valuing their consumption relatively low. But in any event such decisions are never in the real world taken by society as a whole according to rational philosophical argument. They are taken by ruling classes and elites (often assisted by economists and other intellectuals). And those who are relatively privileged today will be likely to act as if they value the consumption of future generations more than the consumption of present ones (themselves excepted). Those who starve today would no doubt evaluate differently. But by definition they do not have the power.

Of course it can be argued, again theoretically, that it is possible to conceive a rapid industrialisation and the restriction of today's consumption taking place in a much more egalitarian manner than they have in practice. Thus high levels of investment *could* be financed with less poverty and deprivation today. (In general terms this is the argument associated with the left opposition in the Soviet industrialisation debate.) This is correct in theory, but there is no example of it in practice, which suggests that the political conditions for it are at very best extremely difficult to attain and may be altogether unattainable (Skouras, 1977). If the inevitable political concomitants of rapid industrialisation are what has been observed then this is surely an argument if not for less rapid industrialisation then at least against the adventuristic industrialisation targets so beloved of planning bureaucrats and politicians.

To sum up, a theoretical argument for industrialisation based on human need is obviously valid in theory. But it is not proved by existing or past industrialisations. Most people involved in the theoretical discussion can see themselves as beneficiaries of past industrialisations. But more knowledge of the costs paid by the victims of all the capitalist and noncapitalist industrialisations of the past ought to make us very wary of the application of the theoretical argument to industrialisation in the present. Economists should therefore devote more attention to the quality of industrialisations as they affect the lives of living human beings. So far industrialisation has been more historically progressive in theory than in practice.

III

Although I shall not keep alluding to them, the points made in the previous section have some relevance to evaluating the quantitative data on the recent industrialisation of underdeveloped countries. I accept that the available evidence on this suggests a faster rate of industrial growth in the underdeveloped countries than I had expected at the time of writing *Industry and Underdevelopment*.

According to the World Bank statisticians, the aggregate rate of growth of both industrial and manufacturing output have been over 3 percent a year for 34 low-income countries and over 6 percent a year for 59 middle-income countries over the two decades 1960–81 (World Bank, 1983). These rates have been higher than for the industrialised capitalist countries and so the share of the underdeveloped countries in the world's manufacturing output (excluding high-income oil producers and East European planned economies) has risen a little—from 17.6 percent in 1960 to 18.9 percent in 1981[calculated from World Bank (1983)]. Their share of world exports of manufactures rose from 3.9 percent to 8.2 percent in the same period. To view this slightly differently the developing countries' share of the manufactured imports of all industrial countries rose from 5.3 percent in 1962 to 13.1 percent in 1978 (World Bank, 1982). According to the World Bank figures, the share of the GDP of low-income countries arising in the industrial sector rose from 25 percent in 1960 to 34 percent in 1981. For manufacturing the rise was only from 11 to 16 percent. The record is much more modest for this group if India and China are omitted (and it is China which really makes the difference). For the remaining countries the share of industry rose from 12 to only 17 percent; and for manufacturing, from 9 to 10 percent. In the middle-income group the changes were from 30 to 38 percent for industry, and from 20 to 22 percent for manufacturing alone (World Bank, 1983).

As everyone has to acknowledge, the performance of different countries has varied very much. A very high proportion of the aggregate growth, especially of manufactured exports, has been concentrated in a very few countries indeed. These are the ones generally known as the Newly Industrialised Countries (NICs).

Of course, it is a debatable point how much significance should be attached to this qualification. The optimists argue that the NICs are an *example* which any underdeveloped country could have followed with the right policies. They imply that there is no overall problem of markets for potential competitively produced manufactured exports. Some of those who do acknowledge that the potential market is limited argue that the NICs, through good fortune or good policy, did relatively better than other countries, but do not rule out the possibility that the benefit could be more evenly spread if not much greater in the aggregate. Among the more orthodox pessimists, other than those who seek spuriously to deny the success of the NICs, most regard them as *exceptions* to the general failure of the underdeveloped countries to industrialise. There has certainly been some polarisation between the NICs and other developing countries, even though this phenomenon may not be as clear as is often supposed, since there are some near-NICs and not-so-near-NICs.

Despite the NICs there is little evidence that more than a handful of countries have in the last two or three decades been passing through an equivalent process of industrialisation to that which transformed the structure of society and the level of labour productivity in, say, nineteenth-century Europe or twentieth-century Japan.

Such a qualitative structural change is of course hard to measure. But it was some approximation to it which I was trying to achieve by proposing in *Industry and Underdevelopment* a multidimensional definition of an industrialised country. It would be only honest to admit that I started from a preconception about which countries could be regarded as industrialised and which could not. I then looked for a quantitative basis for the presupposed qualitative difference between these two classes of countries. The "test" of industrialisation I arrived at was a three-part one: industrialised countries were defined as those with 25 percent or more of GDP in the industrial sector; with 60 percent of industrial output in manufacturing; and with 10 percent of the population employed in industrial activities. The reasons for this definition are not worth repeating here. I reiterate it because I want to look at the results which would be obtained by applying the same "tests" today (most of the figures used in the book were from the mid-1960s) (Sutcliffe, 1971, pp. 16–26).

Under the definition the countries which were "industrialised" at the time of writing *Industry and Underdevelopment* were the expected countries of Western Europe, Eastern Europe, North America, Japan, and Australasia with the addition of Argentina, Hong Kong, and Malta. No doubt Singapore would have figured in them too had I been able to obtain the appropriate figures. On the borderline were Uruguay, Israel, Yugoslavia, and Portugal.

Since then, according to the latest figures, all the borderline cases have crossed the line and are now industrialised according to these criteria. The only countries to have passed the combined test since then are South Korea and probably Taiwan. An examination of other candidates, including NICs and near-NICs, suggests that most of them are not even approaching the fulfilment of the three criteria of the definition and this is usually because industrial employment is not expanding as a share of the population, though on the first two criteria alone (the sectoral structure of output) many of them would "pass."

I believe that these results call into question some of the optimistic conclusions drawn from the aggregate statistics by writers such as Bill Warren.

A number of other statistical points also tend to deepen my scepticism of the "optimistic" perspective.

First, there remains a vast difference between the level of manufacturing output per head of population in the most retarded of the advanced industrialised countries and even the most statistically industrialised of the underdeveloped ones. So while the definitions based on sectoral shares and the labour force show South Korea to be as industrialised as the UK the difference between the two countries' levels of manufacturing output per head (1978 figures) is between $621 and $2,667. In a number of Third World countries (of which South Korea is an example) real structural change has been taking place which in relation to the patterns followed historically by the presently advanced industrialised countries is "premature."

Part of this may be a statistical illusion due to differences between domestic and world relative prices. But I believe that many countries have in a real sense structurally industrialised at a much lower level of labour productivity than was the case in the advanced countries. Of the NICs only Singapore has a level of manufacturing output per head higher than some industrialised countries; and that is an unfair comparison given that Singapore is a city-state without a hinterland or rural sector. Singapore's statistics can prove very little; other individual cities in the Third World might show similar results if they could be statistically isolated from their hinterlands (for example, São Paulo).

Second, in a number of cases the noted structural shifts in the composition of output are more apparent than real since they result not from a rise in industry so much as a fall in agriculture. In the last 15 years agricultural performance in many underdeveloped countries has been notoriously bad. Out of the World Bank's low-income category 23 out of 33 countries have experienced a decline in food output per head during the 1970s (World Bank, 1982, table 1). This tragic phenomenon produces a pattern of structural change which appears to be the same but in reality differs from that of successfully industrialising countries. "Industrialism" here is a sign not of economic advance but of economic decline.

Third, statistics produced by UNIDO suggest another important phenomenon. In aggregate they show a fairly fast rise in industrial output in underdeveloped countries between 1955 and 1979 (around 7 percent, which squares with the World Bank figure). But they also show (in contrast to the received wisdom) that industrial employment has also grown quite fast (UNIDO, 1982). Putting these two figures together, however, does not amount to a double success story because it implies a low increase in industrial productivity—of less than 2 percent a year. Yet everyone points to evidence of the adoption of high productivity modern techniques in many industries (and this is in fact widely regarded as a problem in itself). If that is really happening then these aggregate figures imply that some of the remarkably high increase in industrial employment has been in occupations which have extremely low levels of labour productivity.

There could be two reasons for this. One is that the product mix of new employment has been towards relatively low productivity industries. But this is unlikely since the UNIDO figures show that the aggregate figures are replicated in virtually all separate industries. So we cannot conclude that the phenomenon has been due to the unbalanced growth of any particular industry. The other possible reason is that the increase in employment has taken place in low productivity techniques. This may be connected with widespread observations that there is in underdeveloped countries a large sector of very primitive small-scale workshops which are very far from modern factory industry. This is seen by various economists as a form of disguised unemployment, or as part of the "informal sector." Again, however, it is hard to believe that this phenomenon, although it surely exists, shows up in aggregate statistics for industrial output and employment since statistics for these kinds of activities are notoriously elusive. If they were included in full then the tendency for slow productivity growth in industry would be even more marked; it may even become productivity decline. While a mystery remains, these speculations suggest once again that not all statistical industrialisation represents economic progress in the normally accepted sense.

The available statistics suggest to me that both extremes in the argument over the industrialisation record of the Third World are wrong: both Warren's optimistic view that industrialisation, the equivalent of the process which transformed the advanced countries, is now taking place quite rapidly in the underdeveloped ones; and the orthodox dependency view that hardly anything significant is happening. The truth seems not to be midway between the two but more complex and ambiguous than either. A form of industrialisation has been taking place in quite a widespread manner. But in many countries it is composed of different elements which are not homogeneous and do not unambiguously represent economic modernisation.

In many countries what seems to be happening is that modern industry is growing at high and rising productivity levels and at the same time small-scale, more primitive industry survives at low, possibly declining productivity levels, but provides a meagre living for a growing share of the people. What may be occurring therefore is a process of internal polarisation, one which is more complex and more extreme than I envisaged when writing *Industry and Underdevelopment* and one which is very different from what took place in the successful industrialisations of the past.

IV

Heated debates have raged over the last ten years or so about the related questions of choice of techniques, economies of scale, urban bias, and so on. On this collection of questions economists have tended to range themselves in two rival camps: those who favour rapid industrial development, extol modern technologies, reject (or ignore) the notion of urban bias, and so on; and those who favour rural development, think urban bias has been significant and damaging, and favour the use of intermediate (or appropriate) technology. Harking back to earlier debates on related subjects Kitching (1982) and Byres (1979) have described parts of this discussion as one between populists and antipopulists, the latter by implication being on the side of historical progress, the former being largely backward-looking.

The socialist tradition in the last century has by and large rejected the kinds of arguments which are today produced by such writers as Schumacher and Lipton. Just as Marx and Engels are supposed to have vanquished the Utopian socialists, Lenin defeated the Narodniks and (dare one add?) Stalin triumphed over Bukharin, so today populists are widely seen by socialists as the remnants of a losing tradition. On the whole I think this was the position adopted in my book, though with some reservations. Today I regard those reservations as much more important. But the debate is one which takes place at so many levels that it is hard to disentangle them into some coherent threads.

Socialist orthodoxies usually contain a strong belief in the idea that the use of the most advanced techniques will maximise the surplus and thereby the rate of development, and that such techniques are becoming increasingly large-scale and capital-intensive. However, despite many obstinate attempts to deny it (such as that recently by Emmanuel [1982]), there is convincing evidence that in many activities less capital-intensive techniques may be surplus-maximising, that not all technical progress implies growing minimum scale of production, and that better directed research can result in more appropriate techniques (Stewart, 1978; Kaplinsky, 1982). Such newly discovered techniques can sometimes not only be economically and technically efficient but can also possess other virtues.

The choice of techniques debate has seldom broken out of a neoclassical mould. It is usually posed as a discussion about maximising output or the rate of growth of output. So far it has not fully incorporated work on technology which sees the choice of technique as much more than a technical, economic choice. From the point of view of the choosers (whether they be capitalists or state bureaucrats) technological choice is often determined by questions of control and discipline of the labour force within the production process. Machine-paced operations may be chosen not for their superiority in terms of technical efficiency but for their ability to enforce labour discipline. From the point of view of the worker the nature of technology can determine much of the character of her or his life. Of course, many labour-intensive technologies are associated with the most inhuman forms of exploitation and wage slavery. But also many capital-intensive technologies, especially of mass, assembly-line production, are associated with the loss of human independence and control by the worker.

If we are to consider industrialisation not from the point of view of the nation-state or other inhuman abstractions but from the point of view of its relationship with real human beings alive, and to be born, then these points are every bit as important as the ones concerned with the maximising of output and growth (which also of course indirectly affect real people's lives). This is why I think that the populists, intermediate technologies, and the like have introduced a crucial set of considerations into the debate on industrialisation.

This does not mean that I agree with all that they say. But I think that it is important for economists to admit that the questions they raise are necessary dimensions to the problems of industrialisation and the choice of technology which are excluded from the usual economists' debate. Unfortunately the reason that they are excluded is that they represent in some form the interests of those who stand to be the victims of the industrialisation process. These are usually the groups in society that do not have an audible voice. When they do, the practical choice of technology becomes a different question. The reason, for example, why the level of productivity in the German motor industry is higher than in the British surely has a lot to do with the ability of British workers' trade unions to defend themselves against the consequences of advanced technologies. And it is hard to imagine that Soviet industrialisation would have occurred in anything like the way it has if the political voices of the working class had not been so completely stifled.

I think that the consequence of this argument is that in political systems which are basically exploitative, be they capitalist or "socialist," the existence of elements of workers' democracy may, by constraining technological choice, slow down the process of industrialisation. But that does not mean that there is a trade-off between democracy and industrialisation, at least not in any simple sense. It is part of the job of economists who are concerned both with democracy and with long-term economic progress to search for ways of transcending this trade-off. One element of this would surely be intermediate technology—not conceived of as a traditional technology designed to preserve traditional ways of life which can be oppressive to those condemned to lead them (especially to women) as more modern forms of tyranny, but rather conceived as modern forms of technology which allow endurable labour processes. This would only make sense in a humane and democratic form of society which hardly exists today anywhere on earth. But that fact does not seem to me to justify economists collaborating in making choices which are rational only in the context of societies in which it is the beneficiaries, and not the victims, of industrialisation who take all the decisions.

There is nevertheless an unsatisfactory aspect to the view of many of the populists and appropriate technologists—their failure to distinguish between different classes of victim in the industrialisation process. Traditional or rural exploiters tend not to be sufficiently distinguished from those whom they exploit today. This can be particularly true of Michael Lipton's (1977) notion of urban bias which elides class distinctions within rural (and urban) society as Terry Byres (1979) quite convincingly argues. On a different plane, it is worth reminding ourselves that a humane concern for the victims of actually existing industrialisation can easily slip into a defence of preindustrial privilege and exploitation, an opposition to radical change of any kind, and a defence of the values and modes of life of villages which are so often especially reactionary and oppressive.

It has often been said that it is necessary to accept (for *whom* to accept we may ask?) the suffering attendant on processes like industrialisation in the interests of material progress which will pave the way for a better life for future generations. If ever this view was justified it no longer is today. Partly this is because the advanced nature of technology means that (at least if research and development work is radically redirected) the potential choices are far wider than they were in the nineteenth century. The resources and technology surely now exist to resolve all the principal material problems of humanity. We live in potential affluence; the potential is unrealised for reasons which are basically political.

V

The main source of unease I have tried to draw attention to is the tendency among economists on various sides of the debates about industrialism to which I have briefly referred, to ignore the problem of the victims. This has been especially evident, I think, in the generally positive evaluation among economists, especially socialists, of the industrialisation of the Soviet Union, a process mainly directed towards increasing the military power under the control of a dictatorial group and one in the course of which millions died or suffered unbelievable torments. Often these things are either passed over; or else there is a rather blithe assumption that somehow all the economic success of the Soviet Union could be repeated without its political aspects. This has generally been the line of those who support the positions of the left opposition on industrialisation during the 1920s debate and after.

I have always believed that in some sense Stalinism held back rather than advanced the development of the Soviet Union by imprisoning the creative human endeavour of the majority of its citizens. But I do not think that means that economically the same process would have been possible in a more humane environment. The kind of nationalist industrialisation which took place in the Soviet Union in some ways required the politics which went with it. A more humane and democratic process could have occurred only in the context of a much more open, less nationalistic and militaristic environment—a fact which supporters of the left opposition then and now have too often forgotten.

The cult of Soviet success has combined with the analysis of dependency theory to produce the notion that the most appropriate road to industrialisation in the Third World today is via a noncapitalist route which would of necessity be relatively autarkic. This was a major theme of *Industry and Underdevelopment* and others have developed it more explicitly. I now believe that it is the wrong way round to look at the relation of socialism and industrialisation. It sees socialism not so much as an end defined in terms of social justice and individual fulfilment, but as a means to effect separation from the international capitalist economy. It becomes a theory of "socialism in one country" in many countries. Socialism is devalued, as it is in practice so often in the real world, into a euphemism for nationalism and perhaps for dictatorship as well. It loses a central element of the nineteenth-century socialist tradition which is its internationalism—the idea that material and political problems in the world as a whole will be resolved only by a combined struggle of the oppressed in the advanced and the backward parts of the world because their exploiters are internationalised. The internationalism of capitalism was seen in that tradition as something to be built on rather than something to be reversed.

However, the reaction of Warren and others to the deficiencies of nationalist socialism seems to me to be equally wrong. Warren and Emmanuel reassert Marx's surely invalidated expectation that capitalism was capable of developing the whole world in the image of the advanced countries and that the working class would then inherit an advanced planet. Just as much as the advocates of the noncapitalist road to industrialisation, such arguments imply a conception of historical progress in which the suffering of victims is seen as inevitable and ultimately justified. Growing inequality can be interpreted as a necessary element in a process of development which would enable the problems of the majority of people to be resolved in the future. Emmanuel argues that:

> if capitalism is hell there exists a still more frightful hell: that of less developed capitalism . . . if [capitalist] development does not *ipso facto* lead to the satisfaction of 'social needs', it nonetheless constitutes, via the political struggles made possible by a certain pluralism inherent in the higher phase of the industrial revolution, a much more favourable framework for a certain satisfaction of these needs than those of past class regimes (Emmanuel, 1982, p. 105).

I think that the experience has substantially invalidated these ideas that capitalist development has created and can still create the material preconditions for socialism which requires merely political struggle at the right moment in history (but not yet!) (Auerbach, 1982). The economic structure of advanced capitalism is inappropriate in very many ways as a material basis for a socialist society. It is inappropriate to a very great extent in terms of the products it produces (armaments, far too many motor cars, planned obsolescent goods, and so on). It is even more inappropriate in terms of the forms of participation in the labour process possible with the favoured technology (over-centralisation, de-skilling, etc.). It is in many ways a totalitarian, alienating experience which does not create, even destroys, the values which could help to build a truly socialist society. Capitalist development has helped to create a view of socialism which is centralised, statist and bureaucratically controlled from above—a necessary measure until the "cultural level of the people" can be raised.

I believe that it is at least possible to contemplate a process of economic development and industrialisation in the poor countries which would have less of these deficiencies of actually existing industrialisation, capitalist or "socialist." Socialist thinking on these questions needs to recapture some of its Utopian traditions.

As a caste development economists have been a very privileged stratum during the years since 1945. We have found it easy to earn very high salaries and live interesting and even exotic working lives. I do not think that this disentitles us from having views about the world. But it does disentitle us from recommending that the material suffering of anyone alive today should be regarded as acceptable in the interests of the abstraction of human progress. It should oblige us to contribute to the search for a more humane road to economic development than the rocky path represented by actually existing industrialisation.

REFERENCES

Auerbach, Paul. "From Menshevism and Post-Revolutionary Adventurism to Stalinism and the New Industrial State." Kingston Polytechnic School of Economics and Politics, *Discussion Paper in Political Economy*, no. 39, 1982.

Byres, T. J. "Of Neo-Populist Pipe-Dreams: Daedalus in the Third World and the Myth of Urban Bias," *Journal of Peasant Studies*, 6, 2 (1979).

Emmanuel, A. *Appropriate or Underdeveloped Technology?* Chichester: John Wiley, 1982.

Kaplinsky, R. "Fractions of Capital and Accumulation in Kenya." Institute of Development Studies, University of Sussex, Brighton, 1982. Mimeo.

Kitching, Gavin. *Development and Underdevelopment in Historical Perspective: Populism, Nationalism and Industrialisation*. London and New York: Methuen, 1982.

Lipton, Michael. *Why Poor People Stay Poor: A Study of Urban Bias in World Development*. London: Temple Smith, 1977.

Schumacher, E. F. *Small is Beautiful: Economics as if People Mattered*. New York: Harper & Row, 1973.

Singh, Ajit. "The 'Basic Needs' Approach to Development *vs.* the New International Economic Order: The Significance of Third World Industrialisation." *World Development*, 7, 6 (1979).

Skouras, Thanos. "The Political Concomitants of Rapid Industrialisation." (Thames Papers in Political Economy), Thames Polytechnic, London, 1977.

Stewart, Frances. *Technology and Underdevelopment*. London: Macmillan, 1978.

Sutcliffe, R. B. *Industry and Underdevelopment*. London: Addison Wesley, 1972.

UNCTAD. "Recent Trends and Developments in Trade in Manufactures and Semi-manufactures of Developing Countries and Territories: 1977 Review." Report by the UNCTAD Secretariat, Geneva, 1978.

UNIDO. *Yearbook of Industrial Statistics*. Vienna: UNIDO, 1982.

Warren, Bill. *Imperialism: Pioneer of Capitalism*. London: Verso, 1980.

World Bank. *World Development Report*. Washington, D.C. : IBRD, 1982.

World Bank. *World Development Report*. Washington, D.C.: IBRD, 1983.

19

Global Feminization through Flexible Labor

Guy Standing
International Labor Organization, Geneva

1. INTRODUCTION

The 1980s might be labeled the decade of labor deregulation. It has also marked a renewed surge of feminization of labor activity. For reasons to be considered, the types of work, labor relations, income, and insecurity associated with "women's work" have been spreading, resulting not only in a notable rise in female labor force participation, but in a fall in men's employment, as well as a transformation—or feminization—of many jobs traditionally held by men. It is no coincidence that this shifting pattern has been closely related to an erosion of labor regulations. There has been *explicit* deregulation, whereby formal regulations have been eroded or abandoned by legislative means, and *implicit* deregulation, whereby remaining regulations have been made less effective through inadequate implementation or systematic bypassing.

To elaborate on this thesis, it is necessary to trace the emergence of the supply-side politico-economic agenda that has dominated policy making in most of the world in the 1980s. This agenda, it will be argued, has led to a series of changes in women's economic roles, increasing their use as workers but weakening their income and employment security in both low-income industrializing and industrialized countries. By focusing on the global spread of flexible labor practices and the supply-side "structural adjustment" development strategy, it will be argued that existing policies—and the data on which they are based—are inadequate, and that specific

Thanks are due to Loretta de Luca, Jo-Ann UnRuh, Caren Grown, and Frances Williams for assistance and comments. From *World Development*, 17, 7 (1989), pp. 1077–1098. Copyright 1989, Pergamon Press.

alternatives offer far more hope of benefiting working women and men in the coming decade.

2. LABOR IMPLICATIONS OF SUPPLY-SIDE ECONOMICS: THE CULT OF INSECURITY

For most of the twentieth century, and particularly after 1945, the dominant development model can be described as "social adjustment," with a redistributive welfare state as the long-term objective. It was to be achieved through a diverse array of labor rights, protective legislation, and other forms of security, and a larger role for the public sector in economic and social policy. In the 1970s that model ran into trouble, first losing its legitimacy and then being displaced from intellectual hegemony by the early 1980s.[1]

In considering the changing economic situation and its effects on women, six developments have been critical. First, whereas previously trade took place between countries or regions with similar costs (or labor rights) and was a fairly small percentage of most countries' Gross National Product (GNP), in the 1970s the global economy became far more open to internationally competitive trade, as various low-income countries became producers of exports and potential exports. A second factor was that by the late 1970s sustained Keynesian demand management had become associated with rising inflation, and internationally had contributed to excessively rapid lending. The result was indebtedness, as deflationary policies were adopted in the industrialized countries in the mid- and late-1970s. A third related factor was that the welfare state became perceived by some as "crowding out" productive investment and by others as ineffectual in redistributing the benefits of growth. A fourth factor was what some have called technological stalemate, whereby labor-saving innovations became more predominant than product innovations, which led to a more intense search for cheap-labor forms of production. The subsequent "technological revolution," associated with microelectronics and satellites, was a fifth eroding factor, since it gave rise to more managerial options and to more intensive international competition, partly because the new technology was so internationally mobile. Finally, the growth of open unemployment accompanying these developments weakened workers' bargaining power and put welfare states under tremendous pressure.

Although one could quibble with these stylized facts, essentially they combined to give intellectual and political legitimacy to an ideology of supply-side economics, where market mechanisms and cost competitiveness were given overwhelming emphasis. This crystallized in a global strategy of "structural adjustment and stabilization," and has been linked to radical changes in labor relations in most parts of the world economy.

This argument does some injustice to nuance in the interest of brevity. But in essence, the supply-side model entails a global strategy of growth based on open economies, with trade liberalization as vital and export-led growth as the only viable development strategy. As such, cost competitiveness is elevated to utmost significance, and from that, labor market regulations become "rigidities," which raise costs and thus harm living standards and employment. An irony is that in the 1980s many of the previous objectives of economic growth, notably a whole set of labor and social rights, became perceived increasingly as costs and rigidities.

A few key features of the supply-side agenda are worth noting. The goal of "rolling back the State" means focusing on rewarding merit and combining fiscal reform with a minimalist rather than "redistributive" welfare state; poverty alleviation and universal social security are no longer priority issues. A consequence of increasing "selectivity" or "targeting" has been that fewer people are entitled to state benefits in industrialized countries. This has given a boost to "additional worker" effects (pushing more women into the labor market), the informal or "black economy," and precarious forms of working, since those without rights to benefits have been obliged to find whatever income-earning work they can. It is scarcely an exaggeration to say that the leaders have become the led; international competition from low-income countries where labor costs and labor rights are least developed has been instrumental in weakening the rights and benefits of those in the lower end of the labor market of many industrialized economies.[2] In effect, within labor markets income security has been eroded, and economically and socially vulnerable groups have been most likely to suffer.

The supply-side economic model rejects neocorporatist State planning and incomes policy, whereas faith in market mechanisms is absolute. One consequence is that the strength of "insiders" in the labor market has also been eroded, notably unionized (male) wage workers. That in turn has strengthened the pressure for labor market deregulation, weakening both employment security legislation and customary practices preserving job security. In country after country, including many developing countries, governments have taken steps to make it easier for employers to dismiss workers or reduce the size of their labor force, as, for example, in the Philippines, where legislation is planned to remove most enterprises from coverage by various labor laws. By such means, they have encouraged a more flexible approach to job structures, making it easier to alter job boundaries and the technical division of labor. This has reduced the job "rights" of existing employees and allowed greater resort to so-called external labor markets. Because the employment, income, and job security of insiders has weakened, employers have been able to substitute lower-cost labor. In many cases, job flexibility also reduces the premiums that employers usually attach to workers' employment continuity and on-the-job experience.

A further aspect of supply-side economics concerns income security directly. Governments have been urged to remove or weaken minimum wage legislation and institutional safeguards, on the grounds that such wages reduce employment. One might question the logic of that argument, but among the likely consequences of a weakening of protective machinery is a growth of very low-wage employment, consisting of jobs paying "individual" rather than "family" wages. Research shows that when low-wage jobs spread, it is women whose employment in them increases. Even in many developing countries where minimum wage legislation was only weakly enforced, it at least set standards and had demonstration effects. Deregulation sanctions and encourages bad practices.

An aspect of the supply-side agenda has been the stabilization and structural adjustment policy packages urged on many developing countries by the International Monetary Fund (IMF), the World Bank, and other international and national donor agencies, largely in the wake of the debt crisis. To assess what is happening and likely to happen to women in the labor market, we must appreciate what this orthodox strategy involves.

First, overwhelming emphasis is put on trade liberalization and the need to orient production to export-led industrialization. This entails cutting subsidies to domestic "nontradeable" production, often including staple food items (with such effects as lengthening women's working day). It has meant macroeconomic deflation to reduce domestic consumption or living standards, so as to shift resources to export industries, again often having adverse effects on low-income women who produce basic consumer goods. The supply-side agenda has meant a focus on cost-cutting international competitiveness, in practice implying a strenuous search for ways of lowering unit labor costs, which of course means that firms will find ways of employing workers prepared or forced to take low-wage jobs. Finally, it has also meant a spread of new production techniques, usually as part of the search for least-cost methods. This, no doubt, has increased the scope for more refined technical divisions of labor. Thus, for such conventional supply-side reasons as improved efficiency and renewed growth, governments have been pressed to remove labor market regulations, cut the public sector, and privatize public enterprises and services, all of which in one way or another have eroded employment security and led to a reduction of employment.

In the context of this global supply-side perspective, corporate management strategy has evolved in clear directions in the past decade. Stimulated by high unemployment, by new technology, by more aggressive international competition (notably from Japan and the newly industrialized countries), by deregulation and the erosion of union strength, and by the desire to overcome the uncertainty induced by the international economic instability, enterprises everywhere are devising means of reducing the fixed costs of labor. There is a global trend to reduced reliance on full-time wage and salary workers earning fixed wages and various fringe benefits. Companies and public sector enterprises in both developed and developing economies are increasingly resorting to casual or temporary workers, to part-timers, to subcontracting, and to contract workers. In the process, they further erode employment and income security.

Particularly in industrialized countries there has been a shift in these directions and from direct to indirect forms of employment, including sub-contracting from larger to smaller units of production, "networking," and a revival of homeworking and other forms of outwork. But these trends have also been occurring in industrializing economies, where until recently it had been presumed that the long-term trend of industrial development would involve a shift from unregulated, informal labor to secure, regular employment. The global pursuit of flexible low-cost labor has encouraged industrial enterprises everywhere to reduce their fixed wage labor force, make payment systems more flexible, and use more contract workers, tem-porary labor, and out-sourcing through use of homeworking or subcon-tracting to small informal enterprises that are not covered by labor or other regulations and that bear the risks and uncertainty of fluctuating business. That is the context in which to assess the changing labor market position of both men and women in many parts of the world.

At the same time, industrial enterprises have been introducing modern technologies that have been associated with changing skill and job struc-tures. The debate over the "de-skilling" or upgrading effects of modern technology is unresolved, but the evidence seems to support two pertinent trends. The use of craft skills learned via apprenticeships and prolonged on-the-job learning has declined; such crafts have traditionally been domi-nated by male "labor aristocracies." Second, there is a trend toward skill polarization, consisting of an elite of technically skilled, high-status special-ist workers possessing higher-level institutional qualifications, coupled with a larger mass of technically semi-skilled production and subsidiary workers requiring minor training typically imparted through "modules of employable skill," that is, by short-term courses of a few weeks or even by on-the-job learning. This polarization places greater reliance on external than on internal labor markets, since more workers are in "static" rather than "progressive" jobs involving little or no prospect of upward mobility, or firm-specific returns to on-the-job continuity. This, of course, weakens one reason traditionally given for discrimination against women: that women have a higher probability of labor turnover. If there were less bene-fit from on-the-job learning and experience, this presumption would not matter, even if true. Indeed, for many monotonous jobs high turnover may have a positive benefit for employers, since maximum efficiency may be reached after only a few months, thereafter plateauing or declining. This is one reason for resorting to temporary employees, for job-rotating, or for collapsing job classifications into more broadly based job clusters such that workers can be shifted from one set of tasks to another from time to time. But this represents a growth of job insecurity to accompany the income and employment insecurity that have marked the growth of more flexible labor markets.

3. GLOBAL FEMINIZATION?

In the 1960s, economists commonly argued that the growth of the modern sector in developing countries contributed to the marginalization of women as workers.[3] But the distinction between "modern" and "traditional" or "formal" and "informal" sectors has become much less clear, if it ever was clear. In various respects, trends discussed in the preceding section represent widespread informalization of labor in most sectors. This may well explain the absolute and relative growth in the use of female labor around the world and a "feminization" of many jobs and activities traditionally dominated by men. Although the concepts and measurements of labor force participation are notorious, the international data strongly suggest that women's participation has been rising while male equivalent participation has been falling (see Tables 1 and 2).

First, outward-oriented development strategies, based on export-led industrialization, have brought a rapid growth of low-wage female employment. Indeed, no country has successfully industrialized or pursued this development strategy without relying on a huge expansion of female labor. And in export processing zones of many industrializing countries it is not uncommon for three-quarters of all workers to be women.

The reasons are well known. Much of the assembling and production line work is semi-skilled and low paid; young women, particularly in the newly industrialized countries (NICs) in Asia, have been socially and economically oppressed for so long that they have low "aspiration wages" and low "efficiency wages."[4] They are prepared to work for low wages for long work weeks, normally without agitating to join unions, and when their productivity declines after a few years of youthful diligence they are replaced by new cohorts.

Typically, in countries that have pursued the export-led industrialization strategy recommended as part of structural adjustment programs, the female labor force participation rate is high and has risen. In such countries the female share of nonagricultural employment has grown (see Tables 3 and 4). And it is likely that the female share of production worker employment is also relatively high and rising. The available figures generally bear this out, even though in some countries, particularly in Latin America, the relationship may have been weakened by the debt-induced recession (see Table 5).

These limited data are still inconclusive, although they scarcely support Boserup's thesis that with industrial development women would be

TABLE 1   Variations in Adult[a] Male and Female Activity Rates in the 1980s

	MEN, ROSE		MEN, FELL		MEN, NO CHANGE	
	Developing	Developed	Developing	Developed	Developing	Developed
WOMEN, ROSE						
	Barbados	Canada	Algeria (−)[b] Costa Rica (−)	Australia (0)	Honduras	Austria
	Chile	South Africa	Ecuador (−)	Finland (−)	Indonesia	Denmark
	Egypt		Israel (−)	France (0)	Mauritius	New Zealand
	Guam		Korea, Rep. (0)	Fed. Rep. of Germany (0)	Pakistan	Sweden
	Jamaica		Kuwait (+)	Greece (+)	Puerto Rico	
	Peru		Netherlands Antilles (0)	Italy (+)	Seychelles	
	Senegal		Singapore (+)	Japan (+)	Sri Lanka	
	Thailand		Trinidad and Tobago (0)	Netherlands (+)	Venezuela	
				Norway (+)		
				Portugal (−)		
				Spain (+)		
				United States (+)		
	22%[c]	10%	25%	60%	22%	20%
WOMEN, FELL						
	Cameroon (−) Argentina (+)	0	Haiti	0	0	0
	6%	5%	3%	0	0	0
WOMEN, NO CHANGE						
	Bolivia	Iceland	Bahrain	Ireland	Hong Kong	0
	Panama		Guatemala		Syrian Arab Rep.	
	Philippines				Zambia	
	8%	5%	6%	5%	8%	0

[a]Age coverage is 15–64 except as follows: 15–49: Cameroon (1985), Syrian Arab Republic (1984); 15–59: Costa Rica, Panama, Seychelles (1985); Sri Lanka (1981), Thailand, Zambia; 16–59: Guam; 16–64: Puerto Rico, Norway, Spain, Sweden; 18–64: Israel (1980); 20–59: Algeria; 20–64: Finland (1980), Italy, Jamaica, South Africa.
[b]Symbols in parentheses indicate net direction of change, male and female combined: (+) Net increase; (−) Net decrease; (0) Zero net change.
[c]Percentage of countries in the category.

SOURCE: ILO, *Yearbook of Labor Statistics* (various years).

TABLE 2   **Variations in Activity Rates[a] (Persons 15–64), 1980s by Percentage
of Countries with Each Type of Change, Total and by Sex**

Population	Type of Change	Developing Countries	Developed Countries
Women	Increased	69	90
	Decreased	8	0
	No change	22	10
	Total	99	100
Men	Increased	36	15
	Decreased	33	65
	No change	31	20
	Total	100	100
Total	Increased	61	65
	Decreased	22	15
	Compensated[b]	8	20
	No change	8	0
	Total	99	100

[a]For national definitions of activity rates and labor force participation, refer to the ILO *Yearbook of Labor Statistics.* For a critique of the relevance of this concept in developing countries, see Standing (1981). Figures have been rounded.
[b]Activity rates of men and women changed in the opposite directions, involving a fall in male and a rise in female activity rates, so that they approximately offset each other.

pushed out of production work. In support of an alternative thesis that trade liberalization and export-led industrialization tend to increase female employment, it has been observed that the female proportion of productive wage workers rose in all countries that had set up large Export Processing Zones—the Dominican Republic, El Salvador, Honduras, Hong Kong, Republic of Korea, Malaysia, Mexico, the Philippines, Puerto Rico, Singapore, Sri Lanka, and Thailand.[5] Productive employment, of course, covers only direct wage earners, and there is growing evidence that, for reasons discussed in the previous section, much of the employment connected with export industries, as well as others, is indirect if not concealed altogether. A very good example comes from a study in Mexico that should be replicated in many more countries. This study showed that production was organized through a complex process of subcontracting, with the labor-intensive, lower-paid, more informal activities being put out to women workers, many of whom were not recorded in the workforce.[6] This is a classic instance of "modern" production relying on what is depicted as "premodern," or informal, labor relations. The pressure to avoid overhead and other indirect labor costs in the quest for competitiveness has surely accentuated such tendencies.

TABLE 3   Percentage Share of Women in Nonagricultural Employment,[a] 1975–87

Country	Source[b]	1975	1980	1985	1986	1987
Africa						
Botswana[c]	(3)	19	24	30	31	n.a.
Egypt[d]	(1)	10	11	16	n.a.	n.a.
Gambia[e]	(3)	10	12	15	15	n.a.
Kenya	(3)	n.a.	17	20	21	21
Malawi	(3)	7	9	16	14	n.a.
Mauritius	(3)	20	26	35	36	36
Niger[c]	(2)	4	4	7	7	n.a.
Swaziland	(3)	22	26	31	31	n.a.
Tanzania[d]	(3)	12	17	17	n.a.	n.a.
Zimbabwe	(3)	13	13	16	n.a.	n.a.
Latin America and the Caribbean						
Barbados[c,f]	(1)	42	43	44	45	45
Bermuda	(3)	n.a.	43	46	47	47
Brazil [c,f]	(1)	33	35	38	39	n.a.
Chile	(1)	n.a.	34	36	36	35
Colombia	(1)	37	39	38	39	40
Costa Rica	(1)	n.a.	30	34	34	35
Cuba	(3)	n.a.	36	41	41	n.a.
Haiti	(4)	66	71	n.a.	n.a.	n.a.
Jamaica	(1)	46	48	48	48	n.a.
Netherlands Antilles[g]	(4)	35	n.a.	37	37	n.a.
Panama[e]	(1)	38	39	40	40	40
Paraguay	(4)	39	35	n.a.	n.a.	n.a.
Peru	(1)	n.a.	n.a.	n.a.	n.a.	40
Puerto Rico	(1)	35	38	39	40	40
Trinidad and Tobago	(1)	28	31	34	34	34
Venezuela	(1)	32	32	32	32	32
Asia and the Pacific						
Bahrain[e,h]	(4)	n.a.	10	11	n.a.	n.a.
Cyprus[c]	(4)	30	33	35	35	36
Hong Kong	(3)	40	39	40	40	41
India	(3)	10	11	12	12	n.a.
Indonesia[c]	(1)	37	34	37	39	n.a.
Israel	(1)	33	37	39	39	40
Jordan[d]	(3)	14	17	23	n.a.	n.a.
Korea, Rep.	(1)	33	35	38	38	39
Malaysia	(1)	n.a.	30	33	34	n.a.
Philippines	(1)	47	46	48	48	47
Singapore	(1)	30	35	36	38	38
Sri Lanka	(3)	18	18	25	28	n.a.
Syrian Arab Rep.[d,e]	(1)	8	9	9	n.a.	n.a.
Thailand	(1)	42	42	44	44	n.a.

[a]Coverage refers to total employed except as follows: Employees—Botswana, Gambia, Kenya, Mauritius, Niger, Swaziland, Tanzania, Zimbabwe, Cuba, India, Jordan, Sri Lanka; All persons engaged—Malawi, Bermuda, Hong Kong. Figures have been rounded.
[b](1) Labor force survey; (2) Social insurance statistics; (3) Establishment surveys; (4) Official estimates.
[c–h] Figures were not available for the years specified, and those of the closest years were given as follows: [c]1975 = 1976; [d]1985 = 1984; [e]1980 = 1979; [f]1980 = 1981; [g]1975 = 1977; [h]1985 = 1982.

SOURCE: ILO, *Yearbook of Labor Statistics* (various years).

TABLE 4   **Percentage[a] of Women among Manufacturing Employees, Developing Countries, 1975–87**

Country	Source[b]	1975	1980	1985	1986	1987
Africa						
Botswana	(3)	n.a.	17	27	24	n.a.
Kenya	(3)	n.a.	9	10	10	10
Mauritius	(3)	49	56	62	59	57
Swaziland	(3)	16	26	27	31	n.a.
Tanzania	(3)	10	9	n.a.	n.a.	n.a.
Zimbabwe	(3)	8	7	7	n.a.	n.a.
Latin America						
Costa Rica	(1)	n.a.	27	30	30	31[c]
Cuba	(3)	n.a.	26	31	31[d]	n.a.
Mexico	(2)	n.a.	21	25	26	n.a.
Panama	(1)	25	n.a.	24	26	n.a.
Puerto Rico	(3)	48	48	49	48	48
Venezuela	(3)	21	24	n.a.	n.a.	n.a.
Asia and the Pacific						
China	(4)	n.a.	40	40	41	41
Hong Kong	(3)	52	50	50	50	50
India	(3)	9	10	10	9	9
Jordan	(3)	12	10	n.a.	n.a.	n.a.
Korea, Rep.	(3)	n.a.	45	42	42	n.a.
Singapore	(1)	41	47	46	47	48
Sri Lanka	(3)	32	31	39	45	n.a.
Thailand	(1)	41	42	45	45	n.a.

[a]Figures have been rounded.
[b](1) Labor force survey; (2) Social insurance statistics; (3) Establishment surveys; (4) Official estimates.
[c]Prior to 1987: including mining.
[d]Prior to 1986: including water.

SOURCE: ILO, *Yearbook of Labor Statistics* (various years).

Other aspects of the structural adjustment strategy have also affected women's employment. Consider three: the pursuit of lower wages (and greater wage differentials and wage flexibility), labor market deregulation, and the cutback of the public sector, through either general public expenditure contractions or privatization.

Not only do women workers receive lower wages in general, but they are more prepared to work for lower "aspiration wages" for well-known reasons. The erosion of minimum wage legislation, or of its implementation, and the sanctioning of a general lowering of wages are likely in themselves to lead to a substitution of women for men, partly because men are less willing to work for sub-family wage rates and partly because they

TABLE 5 **Proportion of Women among Production Workers (All Statuses^a)**
(Percentage, 1970s and Most Recent)

Country	Source^b			Country	Source^b		
Africa				Belize	C	1970	1980
Botswana	C	1981	1984–85		C	10	13
	LFSS	7	23	Costa Rica	C	1973	1987
Cameroon	C	1976	1982		HS	12	20
	OE	12	8	Chile	C	1970	1986
Egypt	LFSS	1975	1984		LFSS	12	15
	LFSS	2	6	Dominican Republic	C	1970	1981
Ghana	C	1970	1984		C	22	14
	C	35	45	Ecuador	C 10%	1974	1982
Morocco	C 10%	1971	1982		C	15	12
	C 5%	16	23	El Salvador	C	1971	1980
Mauritius	C	1972	1983		HS	19	24
	C	6	21	Guatemala	C	1973	1981
Seychelles	C	1971	1981		C	14	12
	OE	10	15	Guyana	LFSS	1977	1980
South Africa	Cs	1970	1985		C	15	9
	C	7	13	Haiti	C	1971	1982
Tunisia	C	1975	1980		Cs	43	32
	LFSS	24	22	Jamaica	LFSS	1976	1986
Latin America and the Caribbean					LFSS	26	23
Bahamas	HS	1970	1980	Mexico	C	1970	1980
	C	11	12		C	24	17
Barbados	HS	1977	1987	Panama	C	1970	1986
	LFSS	22	26		LFSS	11	12
				Paraguay	C 10%	1972	1982
					C	28	18

^aIncludes conventional categories: own-account workers, employees, employers, and unpaid family workers. Figures have been rounded.
^bC = Census; C . . . % = Census: sample tabulation, size specified; Cs = Census: sample tabulation, size not specified; HS = Household survey; LFSS = Labor force sample survey; OE = Official estimates.
SOURCE: ILO, *Yearbook of Labor Statistics* (various years).

would be expected to respond to lower wages by reducing their "effort bargain." So, employers are inclined to hire women more readily. While the promotion of female employment may be desirable, this is surely not the way to achieve it.

As for labor market deregulation, it has affected the economic position of women in various ways. Consider the principle of "equal pay for equal work." As of late 1988, 108 countries had ratified the International Labor Organization's (ILO's) Equal Remuneration Convention No. 100. Among those that have not ratified it are a disproportionate number of countries

TABLE 5   **Proportion of Women among Production Workers (All Statuses[a])**
(Percentage, 1970s and Most Recent) (*continued*)

Country	Source[b]			Country	Source[b]		
Peru	C	1972	1981	Korea, Dem.	C 10%	1970	1976
	C	14	11	People's Rep.	LFSS	24	30
Puerto Rico	LFSS	1975	1988	Korea, Rep.	C	1975	1987
	LFSS	20	24		LFSS	28	31
St.-Pierre and	C	1974	1982	Malaysia	C	1970	1980
Miquelon	C	7	5		C	17	22
Trinidad and Tobago	LFSS	1978	1986	Nepal	C	1971	1976
	LFSS	13	12		HS	9	21
Uruguay	C 12%	1975	1985	Philippines	C	1970	1987
	C	20	18		HS	33	22
Venezuela	C 25%	1971	1987	Singapore	C	1970	1987
	HS	10	10		LFSS	19	29
Virgin Islands	Cs	1970	1980	Sri Lanka	C	1971	1981
(United Kingdom)	C	2	5		C	15	13
Asia and the Pacific				Syrian Arab Republic	LFSS	1970	1984
					LFSS	5	4
Bahrain	C	1971	1981	Thailand	LFSS	1970	1980
	C	0	1		LFSS	29	30
Bangladesh	C	1974	1984				
	C	5	17	**Oceania**			
Brunei	C	1971	1981	Cook Islands	C	1976	1981
	C	3	4		C	22	15
Hong Kong	Cs	1976	1986	Fiji	C	1976	1986
	C	37	33		C	4	10
India	C	1971	1981	French Polynesia	C	1977	1983
	C	12	13		C	8	17
Indonesia	C	1971	1985	Samoa	C	1976	1981
	HS	27	26		C	6	9
Israel	Cs	1972	1987	Tonga	C	1976	1986
	LFSS	12	13		C	5	13
Jordan	OE	1976	1979				
	C	3	1				

that are pursuing an export-led industrialization strategy, especially those with large export processing zones: Hong Kong, the Republic of Korea, Malaysia, Mauritius, Singapore, Sri Lanka, and Thailand. Other countries, like India, have different legal minimum wages for men and women in certain industries, on the official presumption that women do the less arduous work, which is far from the case. Besides such loopholes in official regulations, any informalization of labor relations can be expected to undermine whatever protective effect regulations might have on equal wages. Accordingly, more labor market flexibility implies implicit deregulation, and could be expected to lead to a widening of sexual earnings inequality. The available data, for what they are worth, suggest a more complex story. While the sex differential is relatively great in economies pursuing export-led industrialization, the differential shows signs of narrowing in Korea, unlike other NICs (see Table 6). Not too much should be read into those figures, since money earnings are only part of total compensation; a loss of entitlement to fringe benefits is most closely associated with labor flexibilization.

It is often claimed that regulations designed to protect women workers generously contribute to discrimination against them by employers. This has been reported from countries where, for example, maternity leave benefits are paid mainly or wholly by the employer[7]; the problem is apparently less acute in countries in which the benefits are funded through worker and employer contributions to the social security system.[8] Nevertheless, informalization of employment reduces labor costs in that respect and means that fewer women workers receive such benefits. Legislation targeted at relatively large industrial enterprises stipulating that they must provide crèches has also been cited as deterring the recruitment of women wage workers.[9] Once again, explicit and implicit deregulation may mean more employment of women, but on less favorable terms. Mothers of young children are left to find alternative—and probably costly or inadequate—child care arrangements. Or they may take informal, low-income work that can be combined with childrearing, or drop out of the labor force altogether. In effect, labor deregulation of this kind means transferring labor costs from the firm, or even the State, to the individual workers, most of whom are in the poorer strata of society.

In various countries regulations have long existed to limit the working time of women workers or to prohibit night work, as stipulated by ILO Convention No. 89 of 1948. These regulations have been criticized by supply-side and structural adjustment theorists on the grounds that they reduce employment of the "protected" groups. It is interesting that 62 countries have ratified the Night Work (Women) Convention, but whereas 26 of those did so in the 1950s and 22 did so in the 1960s, only 10 ratified in the 1970s and only 4 in the 1980s; five have denounced it in the past eight years. With the spread of shift work, often done by women, governments have not only moved away from such regulations, but have failed to implement those that exist or have granted exemptions to various industries, often those operating in export zones, as in Malaysia, Mauritius, and Pakistan.[10]

The shift away from large centralized workforces toward more decentralized, flexible systems implies less emphasis on those behavioral characteristics that traditionally have been cited as justification for discrimination against the recruitment of women, such as women's alleged higher absenteeism and labor turnover.[11] Indeed, in the desire to avoid overhead and other nonwage labor costs, the decentralization—including putting out,

TABLE 6 **Female Earnings as a Percentage of Male Earnings in Manufacturing** (Selected Developing Countries)[a]

Country	1975	1976	1977	1978	1979	1980	1981	1982	1983	1984	1985	1986	1987
Africa													
Egypt	68	75	63	92									
Kenya	66	77	56	54	70	63	59	76	80	77	76	73	63
Tanzania	71	79	88	82	82	79	78						
Swaziland		66	78	71	83	81	82	81	61	55	72	73	
Latin America													
El Salvador	90	86	81	82	79	81	86	89	77	84	82		
Netherlands Antilles							51	66	65	67	68	64	
Asia													
Burma	89	82	103	87	89	86	89	91	92	94	99	86	
Cyprus	47	49	50	48	50	50	54	56	55	56	56	56	58
Hong Kong								78	79	81	79	78	76
Jordan				54	60	58	64						
Korea, Rep.	47	49	45	44	44	45	45	45	46	47	47	49	50
Singapore						62	62	63	64	65	63	56	58
Sri Lanka						81	87	82	71	69	72	78	71

[a]Blank spaces indicate no available data. Figures have been rounded.

SOURCE : ILO, *Yearbook of Labor Statistics* (various years).

contract labor, and subcontracting to subsidiary enterprises—typically puts more pressure on workers to cut their labor supply "price." We should, therefore, give more attention to the mechanisms of control that force workers to labor with high intensity for miserably low incomes, an issue discussed more fully in the next section.

What about the implications for skill formation? Both deregulation and "flexibilization" have accelerated the erosion of notions of vocational skill and of job security (traditionally defended by demarcation rules). Within many industries, skill polarization favors the feminization of employment. Traditionally, sexual inequality *within* the labor market has been perpetuated through sexual segregation in entry to specific jobs, covering both the level of recruitment and subsequent promotion. However, if a growing proportion of all "jobs" have no promotion potential—that is, are "static" rather than "progressive"—then one mechanism intensifying sexual inequality is reduced.[12] Moreover, the well-known "overcrowding" explanation of low female earnings—due to women being crowded into a smaller number of sex-typed jobs—may well lose force if the jobs being whittled away are predominantly "male jobs." Of course, this might be offset if male workers proceeded to bump out women from other slots or took the major share of the new jobs. However, the latter seems unlikely to happen. Although much less so in Latin America than in other regions, not only do the data suggest that women are being substituted widely for men in various occupational categories, including manufacturing and production work in countries as diverse as Ghana, Swaziland, Bangladesh, and Costa Rica (see Tables 4 and 5), but there are good reasons to suppose that substitution will continue as a long-term trend.

This is further supported by a remarkable change between the 1970s and 1980s. In the earlier decade, women's unemployment rates rose relative to men's in many more countries than where the reverse occurred. In the 1980s, in the vast majority of both industrialized and developing countries, female unemployment declined relative to male, so that in a substantial number their open unemployment rate became lower than the male equivalent. This marked a tremendous shift.[13]

Some observers attribute substitution to growing labor force attachment of women, some to improvements in schooling or access to training, some even to the beneficent effects of antidiscrimination legislation. But it has almost certainly more to do with the feminization of labor, a desire to have a more disposable (or flexible) labor force, with lower fixed costs, and so on. In other words, for women there will be *less* problem of job entry. As so often, among developing countries the Republic of Korea has been at the forefront of change in this respect; there, 24 of the 30 jobs formerly barred to women have been recently opened to them.

This decrowding process extends to both manual and nonmanual employment. Traditionally, women have comprised a comparatively large

proportion of all professional and technical workers in developing countries, largely because of their prominence in professions such as teaching
and nursing. Traditionally, with development the growing professions
were in industry, where in most parts of the world women have been
underrepresented. However, it seems to be a global trend that enterprises
have been restructuring to erode middle management, following an era
when this category had mushroomed almost everywhere. Now, many mid-
dle-management functions are being delegated either to clerical workers,
most of whom are women (except in some South Asian countries), or to
production workers. Whether one interprets the trend as one of upgrading
or reskilling or simply intensifying clerical work, the long-term trend is
likely to be a further substitution of women for men. It would be a mistake
to think this trend has relevance only for industrialized countries such as
the United States. It is further reason for believing that the importance of
sexual segregation per se in perpetuating sexual inequality in the labor
market will decline. Policy attention should be focused elsewhere.

Before turning to that issue, it is worth reiterating that for manual production jobs, technological and organizational changes have tended to create a jobs polarization, with an elite of technicians (or "crafticians") in spe-
cialist jobs coexisting with a growing mass of semiskilled flexi-workers and
a dwindling number of jobs for technically unskilled workers. This may
increase female industrial employment—because semi-skilled, static jobs
are reserved largely for women—but the disappearance of low-wage jobs at
the bottom may hit the most vulnerable groups of all; impoverished, uneducated women are left to "crowd" into those jobs, pushing down their
wages even further. As a remedial policy, it may be too late or impractical
to stress basic education for such women. Basic education may be part of
the long-term policy answer, but for currently uneducated women forced to
compete for the low-paying, unskilled jobs in industry, minimum wage and
other forms of protective regulations and/or strong trade unions representing their interests are surely essential. Those who wish to see such regulations dismantled need to offer some more viable alternative.

In the more flexible labor markets envisaged for the 1990s, the attendant insecurities will be intensified by a web of dependency relations.
Decentralized or individualized relationships between workers and
employers, or between workers and impersonal enterprises or middle-men,
give much greater scope to exploitative and oppressive forms of control,
including debt bondage, outright coercion, and casual beck-and-call labor
relations. This is where policy will have to focus.

Along with deregulated and decentralized labor in industry, a key
theme of the orthodox structural adjustment strategy is "privatization."
This has severe implications for women. Not only are women's wages and
employment conditions better on average in the public sector than in the
private, but wage differentials between men and women are smaller in the

public sector.[14] There is *prima facie* reason to suppose, therefore, that women's wages will fall absolutely and relatively by virtue of cutbacks in the public sector or as a result of privatization. But the extent of decline will vary. The tendency will be relatively less likely where there is a so-called policy of cutting public expenditure with a human face, so that smaller cuts are made in social programs like health and education, sectors where women public employees are concentrated.

A complicating aspect in assessing the impact of privatization and public expenditure cuts is that the incidence of redundancy may hit women disproportionately hard, especially where they make up a relatively large proportion of less secure, nontenured posts or marginal positions. Careful study of this phenomenon is still required, since we do not know which groups suffer relatively from the direct effect.[15] However, it is interesting to note that the scanty data available do indicate that in many developing and industrialized countries, women not only have accounted for a greater share of public sector than private sector employment—with notable exceptions, such as India—but their share of public employment has, if anything, grown in recent years (see Table 7).

The indirect effects are even harder to unravel. In countries where men have predominated in the public sector, as in most of Africa, they will make up the great majority of redundant workers. Will those men drive women out of small businesses or those few private-sector wage jobs that women have obtained? Ex-public-sector workers often have received large redundancy payments with which they could acquire petty capital and drive out existing businesses, many of which are dominated by women.[16] This tendency may be compounded by the contacts men gained from their long presence in the public sector.

In short, women have good reason to fear the marginalization effects of privatization, at least in Africa. But this is not all. Falling public employment may, as in Peru, lead to more women entering the low-income labor market as "additional workers" because of higher male and female unemployment.[17] If they enter an already crowded sector, one can predict that average incomes will decline, along with the security of participating in such activities.

Finally, stabilization and adjustment strategies have involved deflation of aggregate demand, leading to higher unemployment and more widespread resort to informal survival responses among the poor, particularly in urban areas. Women have long been concentrated in such activities, both as petty traders or "pre-entrepreneurs" and as dependent workers, whether in familial enterprises or as wage workers. In eras of stagnation and recession, these activities will normally become more precarious, and the vulnerable groups will be hit hardest. However, in many countries women are well entrenched in self-employment and in small-scale production and trade. Indeed, although there is little time-series information available, the data suggest that in most countries for which such statistics are available, women have comprised a growing proportion of the self-employed (see Table 8). Whatever else the data might suggest, they do not indicate that women have been squeezed out of own-account activities by recent economic developments. What such activities include, and conceal, is quite another matter, and may represent a deterioration in the labor market position of women in general. Unfortunately, the data are rather unhelpful in this regard, which brings us to a crucial issue for the further understanding of what is happening to women in developing countries, and thus, what policies donors and planners should consider for the near future.

4. DATA PRIORITIES

Much has been made of the "invisibility" of women workers in conventional labor force statistics. It is time that we concentrated on the distortions provided by the available data on women's labor activity. This issue is particularly acute in the context of what appears to be a growing diversity of forms of labor relations.

The basic starting point is that the conventional "work status" classification (used tentatively earlier) is grossly deficient. Too many types of labor relations are compressed into the four statuses: own-account, employer, unpaid family worker, and wage worker. To understand the mechanisms of labor force participation, data are needed on different forms of *control.*

While we cannot go into details here, seven critical aspects of control are insufficiently covered by conventional labor statistics. The first is *control over self,* over one's own labor power; bonded laborers or serfs have no control over their choice of activity, and as we know many women are extremely vulnerable in this respect in many parts of the world. Second, there is *control over labor time.* Many women have no choice over whether they work the number of hours that would suit their particular needs and, as in typical export processing zones, have to accept 60 hour workweeks, drop out of the workforce, or lose a disproportionate part of their income for failing to fulfill the required quota.[18] The number of workers who are in such onerous situations, where, for example, a flexible payment system means that they would forfeit their bonus share of income for failing to work the full, long workweek, is unknown.

Third, there is *control over means of production,* such as land, tools, and spaces in which to work. Women usually have little or no control in that respect, and may have to rent machines or have their labor status determined by others such as middlemen who own equipment. Although some attention has been paid to women's lack of control over means of production and its consequences for incomes and work activity, the full range of control mechanisms should receive far more attention, for they have adverse consequences for equity, efficiency, and economic growth.

TABLE 7 **Female Share of Public Service Employment,**[a] **Selected Developing Countries** (Percent)[b]

Country	1975	1976	1977	1978	1979	1980	1981	1982	1983	1984	1985	1986	1987
Africa													
Benin							15						
Botswana			13			20		35	37		36		
Burkina Faso	16									20			
Burundi							41					38	
Ethiopia								20		22		23	
Kenya	18	18	19	19	18	18	19						
Malawi							12	12	11	12	12		
Morocco									29	28	28	29	
Nigeria			11	11	11	13							
Rwanda									32		33		
Swaziland			27	27	26		25	31	30	32	33	34	
Latin America and the Caribbean													
Barbados							43	45	42				
Bolivia					24	24	24	24					
Brazil							23			24			
Cuba	30	31	30	30	31	33	33	37	38	39	39		
Jamaica					48	50	48	48					
Panama				46	47			41	43	43	43	45	
Trinidad and Tobago								32				34	
Venezuela					41	41	42	43		43	44	45	46

Asia and the Pacific

Bahrain								32	32	31		
Cyprus	20	21	28	29	30	31	32	32	32	33	33	
Hong Kong			21	22	24	23	25	28	28	28	29	29
India							10			11		
Indonesia				23	23	23	24	27	27	29	29	
Kuwait								31		34		
Qatar					11	12	20	19	21	20		
Syrian Arab Republic						20	24					

[a]Public service employment in the total public sector except: Central government—Burundi, Ethiopia, Mali, Rwanda, Kuwait, Bahrain; Government—Botswana, Morocco, Mexico, Trinidad & Tobago; Federal government—Nigeria; Public administration—Brazil.

[b]Blank spaces indicate no available data. Figures have been rounded.

SOURCE: Bahrain: Statistical Abstract, 1985; Barbados: "Labour Force Report," 1975–83; Belize: "1980–81 Population Census of the Commonwealth Caribbean"; Benin: "Revue de Statistique et de Legislation du Travail," July 1984; Bolivia: "Anuario de Estadisticas del Trabajo,: 1982; Botswana: "Statistical Bulletin," regular publication; 1977: Employment Survey 1982; Brazil: "Anuario Estatistico do Brasil," regular publication, 1986; government reply; Burkina Faso: "Annuaire Statistique du Burkina Faso," October 1984; Burundi: Government reply, ILO General Report, JCPS, 3rd Session, 1983; Cuba: "Anuario Estadistico de Cuba," 1986; Cyprus: 1977–82, "Statistical Abstract," 1985 and 1986; 1983–86; "Labour Statistics Bulletin," December 1986; Ethiopia: Government reply; Hong Kong: "Hong Kong Monthly Digest of Statistics," regular publication; India: "Pocket Book of Labour Statistics," regular publication, data supplied to ILO, government reply; Indonesia: Statistical Yearbook of Indonesia, regular publication; Jamaica: "The Labour Force," regular publication; Kenya: "Statistical Abstract," regular publication; Kuwait: Government reply; Malawi: "Reported Employment and Earnings Annual Report," regular publication; Mali: ILO research data; Mexico: "Encuesta Continua Sobre Ocupacion, 2nd Semester 1978"; Montserrat: "9th Statistical Digest," 1984; Morocco: "Annuaire Statistique du Maroc," regular publication; Nigeria: Digest of Statistics, regular publication; Pacific Islands: "Quarterly Bulletin of Statistics," 1980; Panama: "Situacion Social; Estadisticas del Trabajo," regular publication; Paraguay: "Encuesta de Hogares por Muestra: Mano de Obra," 1977; Peru: "Censos Nacionales de Poblacion y de Vivienda," July 1984; Qatar: "Annual Statistical Abstract," regular publication; Reunion: "Economie de la Reunion, Panorama," 1987; Rwanda: Government reply; Swaziland: "Employment and Wages," regular publication; Syrian Arab Rep.: "Statistical Abstract," regular publication; Trinidad and Tobago: "Quarterly Economic Report," regular publication; Venezuela: "Encuesta de Hogares por Muestreo," regular publication.

TABLE 8   **Share of Women in Self-Employment (Nonagricultural Sectors) in Selected Developing Countries**
(Percentage, 1970s and Most Recent)[a]

Country	Source[b]			Country	Source[b]		
Africa				**Asia and the Pacific**			
Ghana	C	1970	1984	Bangladesh	C	1974	1984
	C	73	77		C	3	8
Seychelles	C	1971	1981	Hong Kong	Cs	1976	1986
	OE	23	19		C	16	20
Latin America				India	C	1971	1981
and the Caribbean					C	9	8
				Indonesia[c]	C	1971	1985
Costa Rica	C	1973	1987		HS	24	41
	HS	13	27	Korea, Dem.	C	1970	1976
Chile	C	1970	1986	People's Rep.	LFSS	25	39
	LFSS	28	28	Korea, Rep.	C	1975	1987
Dominican Republic	C	1970	1981		LFSS	29	35
	C	23	27	Kuwait	C	1975	1985
Ecuador	C	1974	1982		C	1	1
	C	25	22	Nepal	C	1971	1976
El Salvador	C	1971	1980		HS	13	31
	HS	48	65	Singapore	C	1970	1987
Guatemala	C	1973	1981		LFSS	13	19
	C	29	25	Sri Lanka	C	1971	1981
Mexico	C	1970	1980		C	12	9
	C	28	33	Thailand	LFSS	1970	1980
Peru	C	1972	1981		LFSS	40	44
	C	31	29	United Arab	C	1975	1980
Puerto Rico	LFSS	1975	1988	Emirates	C	1	1
	LFSS	16	15				
Venezuela	C	1971	1987				
	HS	17	23	**Oceania**			
				Fiji	C	1976	1986
					C	15	23
				French Polynesia	C	1977	1983
					C	31	33
				Samoa	C	1976	1981
					C	30	27

[a]Figures have been rounded.
[b]C = Census; Cs = Census: sample tabulation, size not specified; HS = Household survey; LFSS = Labor force sample survey; OE = Official estimates.
[c]Includes agriculture.

SOURCE: ILO, *Yearbook of Labor Statistics* (various years).

Fourth, there is *control over raw materials*, inputs purposely transformed into output. Many women, in particular, are exploited by monopolist merchants or manufacturers who charge them excessive amounts for their material so that their net income is much less than it may appear from piece payments.

Fifth, there is *control over output*. If a woman carpet maker were allowed or enabled to sell her wares herself, she could often do far better than when she is forced to accept payment for it from relatives, a merchant, or a manufacturer. No decent study of working women should leave out this dimension of the production process.

Sixth, there is *control over proceeds of output*. This usually means control over the income derived from work. Crude earnings data can be far more misleading indices of net disposable income for some groups than for others. In many situations, women workers receive very little net disposable incomes for themselves or for their immediate needs because relatives or intermediaries deduct large parts of it. Thus, if a woman receives only 20 percent of the income from her work because some intermediary takes the remainder, her welfare would scarcely be improved by policy assistance focused on raising her gross income (through training, for instance), since most of her poverty would be "structural." It is for such reasons that policy makers should focus far more on the multiple mechanisms of control.

Seventh, there is *control over labor reproduction*. This too is critical, and refers to the ability to develop and maintain the woman's own "skills" and work capacity. As such, it is not the same as control over one's labor power. In the case of labor reproduction, the concern is primarily with workers' capacity and with education and training. Many impoverished women have so little control over their working lives that their working *capacity* is debilitated by what they are forced to do. They may seem to earn a reasonable income today, but it is earned only by loss of future earning capacity. Although ample anecdotal evidence on this process exists, far more analytical and policy attention should be focused on this aspect of work.[19] That aside, control over labor reproduction concerns the skill development potential of specific activities. Most workers—and the vast majority of women, in particular—are trapped in work activities in which they have no possibility of developing skills. The controls and constraints may consist of the type of work or external mechanisms. In some places, for example, social norms dictate that to remain in the social structure women do the gathering and weeding, sewing, dairying, and animal husbandry; they have no access to other skills. How are such behavioral patterns reproduced? Although the social pressures are crucial, efforts should be made to identify the direct mechanisms. More statistical information is needed on such forms of control.

In sum, if more relevant policies are to be developed and if international donors are to increase their effectiveness, then analyses and data gathering should concentrate not just on the relative "invisibility" of working women, but also on the distortions of conventional data in other, even more crucial respects. Access to and control over means of production are often cited as vital for raising the autonomy and real living standards of women. This is surely correct, but should not lead to neglect of other aspects of the production and distribution process, where access and control are equally important.

5. LABOR VULNERABILITY

If there is an international feminization of labor relations, is there a corresponding growth of vulnerability, precariousness, and insecurity? The notion of vulnerability is complex, and it may be useful to proceed by recognizing that specific groups are vulnerable by sector, by social stratification, and by labor status.[20]

Women are, first, vulnerable to income and employment insecurity by virtue of the *sector* of their involvement, and their relative disadvantage varies by sector. In most low-income countries women in agriculture and rural areas generally are the most desperately affected, particularly on plantations. Outside agriculture, as the data reviewed earlier showed, women comprise a disproportionately large number of employees of small-scale enterprises, precisely where vulnerability to bankruptcy and chronic impoverishment are usually greatest. Often women in those units are unpaid or severely underpaid, a problem made worse by implicit and explicit labor deregulation of small-scale businesses; sex-related income differentials tend to be much greater in small units, perhaps because larger enterprises are affected by formal regulations and social exposure that lessen wage discrimination. This suggests that efforts to promote small-scale enterprises—often in preference to large concerns—are likely to worsen women's economic vulnerability unless countervailing measures are implemented.

Women have been extensively employed by multinational export-oriented enterprises, often in export processing zones. Critics have been vociferous in highlighting the adverse consequences, although other observers point out that conditions are often much worse for women not employed by such multinationals. Anybody who has been into, say, modern electronics factories in Southeast Asia, has to recognize the force of the latter argument. Nevertheless, one must also recognize the forms of vulnerability to which women workers are exposed in such enterprises. First, they are employed largely in semiskilled, static jobs with little or no chance to develop skills or aptitudes that they could use subsequently. They are then vulnerable to a loss of vital social skills and working capacity, because they must work excessively long workweeks and often face exposure to health-sapping working conditions. This problem has been compounded by the overwhelming preference of employers for young single women who are expected and encouraged to leave their jobs after a few years or when they marry. Compared to other workers, their employability declines fairly quickly, making them vulnerable to aging earlier than most people. Have policy makers really addressed the question: what then?

Such industries are also vulnerable to international trade fluctuations and to productive investment and disinvestment decisions taken in another part of the globe. Enterprises may have to lay off production workers with little warning—one more reason that they prefer women.[21]

The other major sectoral dimension is the public-private sector one, since as noted earlier, women workers fare relatively better in public sector enterprises. If privatization schemes are to proceed, international agencies and others must be persuaded to introduce measures that protect the incomes and employment conditions of women workers affected by the change. Too few privatization initiatives have paid attention to the vulnerability of the workers who lose the relative security of public sector employment.

Finally, there are those sectors in which women are vulnerable to "invisibility." In most parts of the world women represent large proportions of the workforce in agricultural small-holdings, in family farms or businesses, and in petty trade, all of which tend to be inadequately recorded or recognized when policies are being devised or reformed. Perhaps in international and national policy debates this invisibility problem is less than used to be the case. But everyone should be wary about the issue becoming passé, for adequate solutions have not yet been found to the conceptual and statistical problems.

Women are also peculiarly vulnerable by virtue of their *social status*, besides their systematic oppression in most cultures of the world. Social stratification takes many forms, some of which relate to "life-cycle" events, some to other stratifying social influences. One common stratifying influence is migrant status. Women make up a majority of migrants in many developing countries, and many of them travel alone in search of work. Too often this aspect has been neglected in women's studies or in donor programs. Women migrants and, most of all, women labor circulants are acutely vulnerable. They tend to gain entry to labor markets only by taking the most precarious jobs and have little prospect of upward mobility. The plight of such women is desperate. In India, for example, it has been widely reported that hard-pressed rural families send wives and daughters to cities to support them through prostitution.[22] And in Thailand thousands of young village girls flock to Bangkok to work as prostitutes until their "charms fade," often in notorious conditions.[23] Other young women enter urban labor markets through domestic employment, for little pay, often unknown to any labor authority or conveniently overlooked. Far more attention should be given to the mechanisms of control used in the migration process and to the kinds of policies that could ameliorate the vulnerability of what are, typically, ill-educated teenagers.

Two other dimensions of social vulnerability deserve even more emphasis than they have received in recent years. Many women, probably the vast majority, are vulnerable to poverty and labor market marginalization by virtue of their dependency status in families. Others, however, are primarily or wholly responsible for their household income and subsistence. They tend to be among the poorest of the poor. In Costa Rica, for example, although only 16 percent of urban households were recorded as being headed by women, more than 37 percent of indigent (the poorest) urban households were female headed.[24] In the Sudan, a quarter of all low-income households were headed by women, half of whom were over 50.[25] In Calcutta, the poorer the household, the more likely it was to be dependent on female earners. Across the world the story is essentially the same: single mothers, widows, and migrant women dependent on their own resources are the most vulnerable of all, not only to poverty, but to exploitation and labor marginalization.

Finally, workers are vulnerable by virtue of their *labor status.* Earlier sections of this paper have depicted the international feminization of labor as closely associated with growing labor flexibility, by which secure, protected well-paid wage employment is once again being displaced by other labor relations. One can predict that when enough data have been generated on these issues, the two trends will be shown to be linked closely. As it is, women are most vulnerable to insecure labor status employment. For instance, they are more likely to be hired as marginal, casual wage workers. In some countries, the introduction, strengthening, or enforcement of minimum wage regulations has led to the substitution of women casual workers for male permanent workers. In Zimbabwe, for example, underpayment persisted through a conversion of permanent to casual, contract or piece-rate workers, since they were not covered by the regulations; this was most likely to happen in small-scale enterprises.[26]

In India, women are also concentrated in casual wage labor, and relatively high female unemployment has been attributed in part to women being able to obtain only short-term casual jobs. Elsewhere, women wage workers are more often than men classified in that peculiar category, "permanent casuals," and thereby unable to acquire legal entitlement to benefits or statutory forms of protection.

Beyond recognized wage labor, evidence is mounting that women are increasingly utilized as "outworkers." Particularly with respect to this heterogeneous category one needs to focus on the diverse mechanisms of control and exploitation (bearing in mind that "control" and "exploitation" are not synonymous). Valuable research projects are in progress on "putting out" industries and other forms of outwork. But so far, few effective strategies to enhance the status and living standards of such workers have been implemented.

Of course, many "self-employed" women are far from the image that the term conventionally implies. At the very least, statistically, own-account workers should be separated from contract or piece-rate outworkers, whose net earnings tend to be minimal, and even negative in slack periods or in periods of illness or family mishaps. These contract workers are the most "flexible" labor force of all, bearing a large share of the risk of business fluctuations. In many countries, the international recession in the 1980s and the adoption of stabilization and structural adjustment policies led enterprises to shift from direct wage employment to such forms of labor.[27] As noted earlier, the renewed growth of such indirect, flexible labor will necessitate a considerable policy reformulation in the near future if the previous international trend toward social protection is to be revived.

6. CONCLUSION

It would be pretentious to pose a full policy and research agenda on the basis of this brief overview. Nevertheless, some leading questions do suggest themselves. First, if the era of labor flexibility persists, will women and men be pushed far more into labor statuses in which they face multiple forms of control? To answer that question, we need to review critically the type of statistics that are collected, and consider alternative concepts that could identify potential points of policy intervention. Second, to what extent are earnings or income data valid measures of women's net disposable income, that is, the cash or other income that they could use for their own needs? Taking account of deductions by intermediaries, including relatives, it is likely that a large and growing proportion of women workers receive much lower net incomes than the scanty data on earnings suggest. Third, whither labor regulations in labor markets characterized by informality and flexible work statuses? If regulations on, for instance, wages, safety, and maternity leave are being eroded or bypassed, how could workers organize to obtain socially desirable benefits, and how could governments assist? Fourth, the same questions arise with respect to social security, especially bearing in mind that even in many industrialized economies a dwindling proportion of women actually are entitled to existing social security.

Fifth, whither antidiscriminatory legislation? Discrimination is a particularly insidious process; even if one form of discrimination is partially tackled, other forms are likely to grow, which is why it needs to be attacked on many fronts at once. It is possible that the sexual segregation of jobs is becoming *relatively* less important, and that career paths and differential access to fringe benefits and bonus payments is becoming relatively more critical.[28]

Sixth, has too much attention been devoted to schooling and training as the avenue to higher incomes, labor market security, and mobility? Besides the likelihood that most forms of labor market inequalities are structural, it is possible that in recruiting for a wide range of jobs, screening devices other than formal schooling are becoming more important, while prior vocational training is scarcely needed for access to most jobs. This is because a more developed technical division of labor and growing emphasis on semiskilled labor must surely diminish the relevance of vocational training. Of course we should not dismiss automatically the need for training policies, but "training" should be put in its proper context—a minor component of any strategy to improve women's economic and labor market status.

Seventh, how could unions protect women in the more flexible labor markets of the 1990s? Unless communal unionism develops in place of craft or industrial unions, protection of vulnerable groups will be partial at best and easily circumvented. Male-dominated trade unions must fully incorporate women and struggle for "women's issues" at least as strongly as for others; otherwise their collective strength will continue to dissipate.

Finally, when will donor agencies and national policy makers turn to that most neglected of groups, older women? Already a majority of the elderly (aged 55 or older) are in developing countries. Their marginalization in almost all respects is a somber specter, too often resulting in premature death, thereby concealing the seriousness of the process. With urbanization and industrialization, kinship support networks are being eroded, yet very few women workers have pension rights; nor do women have employment security or access to retraining or labor market assistance in times of recession or structural adjustment. If this paper made just one plea, it would be that international agencies should devote more resources to assisting older women workers, the growing number who will soon be in that category, and those pushed out of the labor force prematurely—the easily ignored "potential" workers in their 50s and 60s. Given today's flexible, insecure labor processes, and weakened social support systems, the needs of older women have never been greater.

These eight sets of issues are by no means exhaustive, but they do suggest some reordering of priorities. Although women may be gaining economically in some crude senses of that term, the crucial point is that feminization in the sense used here represents pervasive insecurity. Traditionally, women have been relegated predominantly to more precarious and low-income forms of economic activity. The fear now is that their increased economic role reflects a spread of those forms to many more spheres. That is scarcely what should be meant by progress.

NOTES

1. Standing (1988).
2. That is not an argument for cutting exports from industrializing economies, as some might claim.
3. Boserup (1983).
4. The "aspiration wage" is the level at which a person would be prepared to accept employment; the "efficiency wage" is the wage level at which a worker would work with optimum efficiency once in employment. Many people fail to make this distinction.
5. Anker and Hein (1986), p. 95.
6. Beneria and Roldan (1987).
7. For example, di Domenico (1983); Date-Bah (1986).
8. See, for example, Scott (1986).
9. International Center for Research on Women (1980).
10. See, for example, Dror (1984), p. 709.
11. Anker and Hein (1985).
12. Standing (1981).
13. An important caveat here is that the data do not include observations for many African countries. For those which have observations, the trend is in the same direction as that in other regions.
14. See, for example, Papola (1986). During the past decade of adjustment, private-public sector wage differentials have apparently narrowed or disappeared in many countries, particularly for "educated labor."
15. An official US study found that women were disproportionately affected by job cuts in the privatization of federal agency programs. Rein (1985), p. 132.
16. Collier (1988).
17. Scott (1986), especially p. 357.
18. See, for example, Fuentes and Ehrenreich (1983), p. 23.
19. See Standing (1981), chap. 4, for one review of evidence on this issue.
20. A more detailed discussion of these dimensions is presented in Standing (1987).
21. Lim (1985), p. 30. This was a joint UNCTC/ILO study.
22. Pandhe (1976), p. 52.
23. Phongpaichit (1982).
24. Pollack (forthcoming).
25. ILO (1976), p. 70.
26. Shopo and Moyo (1986).
27. See, for example, Penouil and Lachaud (1986), pp. 37–38.
28. Relatively more attention should be paid to the factors that cause women to shift from male-dominated to female-dominated jobs rather than to those that cause initial sex segregation. See, for example, Jacobs (1983).

REFERENCES

Anker, R., and C. Hein. "Why Third-World Urban Employers Usually Prefer Men." *International Labour Review* 124, no. 1 (January–February 1985): 73–90.

Anker, R., and C. Hein, eds. *Sex Inequalities in Urban Employment in the Third World* (London: Macmillan, 1986).

Beneria, L., and M. Roldan. *The Crossroads of Class and Gender: Industrial Homework, Subcontracting and Household Dynamics in Mexico City* (Chicago: University of Chicago Press, 1987).

Boserup, E. *Women's Role in Economic Development* (New York: St. Martin's Press, 1970).

Collier, P. "African Public Sector Retrenchment: An Analytical Survey." WEP Labour Market Analysis Working Paper no. 27 (Geneva: ILO, November 1988).

Date-Bah, E. "Sex Segregation and Discrimination in Accra-Tema: Causes and Consequences." In R. Anker and C. Hein, eds., *Sex Inequalities in Urban Employment in the Third World* (London: Macmillan, 1986), chap. 6, pp. 235–276.

Deshpande, L. K. "Flexibility in the Bombay Labour Market." WEP Labour Market Analysis Working Paper no. 24 (Geneva: ILO, August 1988).

di Domenico, C. M. "Male and Female Factory Workers in Ibadan." In C. Oppong, ed., *Male and Female in West Africa* (London: George, Allen and Unwin, 1983).

Dror, D. M. "Aspects of Labour Law and Relations in Selected Export Processing Zones." *International Labour Review* (November-December, 1984): 709.

Fuentes, A., and B. Ehrenreich. *Women in the Global Factory* (New York: Institute for New Communications, South End Press, 1983).

International Centre for Research on Women. *Keeping Women Out: A Structural Analysis of Women's Employment in Developing Countries* (Washington: USAID, 1980).

International Labour Organisation. *Growth, Employment and Equity: A Comprehensive Strategy for the Sudan.* (Geneva: ILO, 1976).

Jacobs, J. "The Sex Segregation of Occupations and the Career Patterns of Women" (Harvard University, Ph.D. dissertation, May 1983).

Lim, L. *Women Workers in Multinational Enterprises in Developing Countries* (Geneva: ILO, 1985).

Pandhe, M. K., ed. *Bonded Labour in India* (Calcutta: Indian School of Social Sciences, 1976).

Papola, T. S. "Women Workers in the Formal Sector of Lucknow, India." In R. Anker and C. Hein, eds., *Sex Inequalities in Urban Employment in the Third World* (London: Macmillan, 1986), chap. 4, pp. 171–212.

Penouil, M., and J. P. Lachaud. "Le Secteur Informal et la Marché du Travail en Afrique Noire Francophone." World Employment Programme, Working Paper no. 37 (Geneva: ILO, 1986).

Phongpaichit, P. *From Peasant Girls to Bangkok Masseuse* (Geneva: ILO, 1982).

Pollack, M. "Urban Poverty and the Labour Market in Costa Rica." In G. B. Rogers, ed., *Trends in Urban Poverty and Labour Market Access* (Geneva: ILO, forthcoming).

Rein, M. "Women in the Social Welfare Labor Market" (Berlin: Wissenschaftezentrum, Discussion papers 85–18, 1985).

Scott, A. M. "Economic Development and Urban Women's Work: The Case of Lima, Peru." In R. Anker and C. Hein, eds., *Sex Inequalities in Urban Employment in the Third World* (London: Macmillan, 1986), chap. 8, pp. 313–365.

Shopo, J., and S. Moyo. "Vulnerable Segments of the Labour Market in Zimbabwe" (ILO-SATEP, May 1986, mimeo.).

Standing, G. *Labour Force Participation and Development* (Geneva: ILO, 2d ed., 1981).

Standing, G. "A Labour Status Approach to Labour Statistics." World Employment Programme Working Paper no. 139 (Geneva: ILO, August 1983).

Standing, G. "Vulnerable Groups in Labour Processes." WEP Labour Market Analysis Working Paper no. 13 (Geneva: ILO, May 1987).

Standing, G. "European Unemployment, Insecurity and Flexibility: A Social Dividend Solution." WEP Labour Market Analysis Working Paper no. 3 (Geneva, ILO, July 1988).

20

The Political Economy of Privatization in Developing Countries

Henry Bienen and John Waterbury
Princeton University, New Jersey

1. INTRODUCTION

Privatization is, as Starr notes (1988, p. 1101) a "fuzzy concept that evokes sharp political reactions." The term has been used to cover a range of policies from those of governmental disengagement and deregulation to the sale of publicly owned assets (see *inter alia*, Hemming and Mansoor, 1988, p. 1). At its broadest and also at the most symbolic level, privatization represents a countermovement to the growth of government that has characterized much of the post–World War II period in industrial and developing countries. It may mean reducing all forms of state control over resource allocation. In what follows, however, we adhere to a more narrow definition of privatization that refers to the sale or leasing of assets in which the state has a majority interest, and the contracting out of publicly provided services. While often associated with privatization programs, the liquidation of publicly owned assets, the sale of minority shares in what are already private enterprises, the deregulation of private economic activity,

Note: This paper has drawn extensively on the proceedings of a conference on Public Sector Reform and Privatization held at Princeton University, April 22–23, 1988, under the auspices of the Center of International Studies. The conference was part of a project on the same subject funded by the J. Howard Pew Freedom Trust. We are grateful to the J. Howard Pew Freedom Trust for its support. Henry Bienen also expresses his thanks to the Ford Foundation and the Leon Lowenstein Foundation for their support of his research in 1988–89 on the politics of structural adjustment. In addition to our colleagues' contributions, listed in the reference section of this paper, we are grateful for the informed comments and criticisms of Carlos Bazdresch of the Colegio de Mexico and of Mohammed Qasem Ahmed of the University of Jordan.

376

and efforts to make public sector enterprises behave more like private ones are not, strictly speaking, instances of privatization. We realize that these lines cannot always be clearly drawn: a publicly owned bank with a minority equity holding in a private company may effectively control that company; so too private firms, as in the US defense industry, may have the government as their only customer. Our definition is, therefore, of the *ceteris paribus* variety.

Given the size of the public sector in many developing countries, the potential macroeconomic change that privatization might bring about is substantial. The state sector writ large may be the single largest employer. In Egypt, over half of the nonagricultural work force is on the state's payroll. There and in many other African and Middle Eastern countries, the state has operated, de facto, as the employer of last resort for the university educated (Waterbury, 1983, pp. 57–122). The state is often the dominant supplier of health and educational services. Its consumer subsidy programs affect retail prices, while administered prices of intermediate goods affect processed and manufactured products. Control of substantial segments of banking and insurance determines interest rates and insurance premiums. Control of the social security system puts in state hands the fate of pensioners (Jones and Mason, 1982; Aharoni, 1986; Floyd, Gray and Short, 1984; Ramanadham, 1984). The broad scope of state activities has made the state, in many less developed countries (LDCs), the arena in which issues of income distribution and social equity are fought out. It is probably the case that part of the impulse for privatization and reduced state intervention stems from an effort to depoliticize some of these distributional issues.

The fundamental questions are: whether broadly or narrowly defined, how far will the process of privatization go? What will be its scope? What will be the pace and sequence of privatization measures? We argue here that privatization in most developing countries is, in part, a response to the need for fiscal austerity and is designed to reduce deficits generated by state enterprises. Pace and scope, in consequence, will be determined by the process of implementing more broadly gauged programs of structural adjustment and liberalization. Part of the adjustment process will surely entail reform of the public sector, which in the long run may be more consequential than privatization. In this article, however, we shall be mainly concerned with the latter.

Public sector reform and privatization will be determined importantly by the way in which the public sector was built in the first place. There are those who argue, on the basis of fairly compelling evidence, that it matters less how public sectors originate than their present size, composition, and the nature of vested interests attached to them (Jones and Mason, 1982, pp. 19–23). This view minimizes inherited ideological and programmatic constraints. Public sector enterprises are typically founded under the headings listed below. These are not mutually exclusive, and most societies will have enterprises set up according to most or all of these headings, or single enterprises that are designed to meet more than one objective:

- Equity objectives: redistribution of income, job creation, regional development
- Infrastructure development and other "lumpy" investments (e.g., steel, petrochemicals)
- Collection of monopoly rents, especially on minerals
- Filling in for a deficient private sector
- Taking over failed private enterprises
- Countering capitalist monopolies
- Nationalizing foreign or indigenous private enterprise
- Strengthening economic sovereignty, especially vis-à-vis multinational corporations
- Building national strength through the defense sector

We accept with some reservations the proposition of Vernon (1988, pp. 18–19) that privatization today is being driven by a spirit of pragmatic reaction to at least three decades of failed experiments in public enterprise, and that true ideological shifts that question the appropriateness of state intervention in the economy are fairly rare. We need to remember, however, that certain kinds of interventions will be easier to undo than others. State enterprises set up to support or nurture the private sector will be easier to turn over to private buyers than those created because of an ideological bias against private capital and in order to control its "speculative" and "parasitic" tendencies. Even when it is widely recognized that public sector enterprises (PSEs) are grossly inefficient, it does not follow that there will be broad-based support for handing them over to private interests. Bank nationalizations in India in 1969, in Mexico in 1982, and perhaps even in Peru in 1987 were very popular outside of business circles, and reprivatization would be commensurately unpopular. Privatizations that strengthen the indigenous private sector will be more feasible than those that cast aside old concerns for economic sovereignty by selling important assets (steel mills, mines, the national airline) to foreign buyers. Where states have not traditionally emphasized their commitment to redistribute income, as in Taiwan or South Korea, it will be easier to divest even if divestiture eliminates jobs. As we explore below, it may be possible for new regimes or new political coalitions to break with past policies and obligations, but the origins and ideological rationales for state interventionism do play a role in shaping the course of privatization.

To assess the constraints on and possibilities for privatization, one must have a clear picture of the economic sectors that will gain or lose, and of the gains and losses that will be sustained by the constituent elements of dominant political coalitions. Economic sectors and coalition constituents may overlap. We shall pay particular attention to organized labor, the indigenous private sector, managerial and civil service elites, and the armed forces. In examining the interplay of affected interests, we hope to shed some light on the principal differences between developing and industrial nations and on the frequently larger differences within the ranks of the LDCs themselves.

This exercise leads us to a number of conclusions that we substantiate below. First, privatization is probably easier to implement than has been supposed because the equity costs are relatively small compared to those of the broader structural adjustment process. However, it also appears to be the case that the payoffs for adjustment generated by privatization are relatively small, and there is a high opportunity cost in time and management devoted to the complicated task of preparing public assets for sale. Thus we do not expect privatization to profoundly transform public/private balances in most LDCs.

Second, we believe that the impetus for privatization in LDCs has been derived as much from an internal recognition of the failings of public enterprise as it has been imposed by donors and creditors.

Third, while organized opposition to privatization may not be substantial, there may be only a narrow set of actors that actively supports it. This includes a few policy makers, financial managers, and external creditors. It is an open question whether established private sector interests will welcome privatization.

Fourth, depending on the country under scrutiny, reduced state intervention, deregulation, and privatization may be best seen as an attempt to strengthen the state fiscally, both through deficit reduction and by bringing into the formal economy (where they can be taxed) economic activities that had been driven into the parallel economy through overregulation.

Fifth, we expect the process of privatization, or in more general terms the reduction of state intervention in the economy, to be nonlinear and in fact reversible. Particularly if structural adjustment and privatization are based upon export-led growth strategies, the possibilities for the collapse of private enterprises will be great. The state will be left to pick up the pieces.

2. DISTINCTIONS BETWEEN ADVANCED INDUSTRIAL AND DEVELOPING NATIONS

Privatization in LDCs, conceived as a part of the broader process of structural adjustment, will emerge as a policy issue in a predictable sequence in which, initially, efforts are made to reform public enterprise performance, and, when these efforts fail to produce the desired efficiency gains, liquidation and privatization of specific enterprises are contemplated. In some countries, policy makers have concluded that public enterprise is beyond reform (see UNDP, 1988). In others, such as Mexico, the process of improving public enterprise performance goes hand in hand with privatization.

This could be said for advanced industrial economies as well. Are there fundamental differences between developed and developing countries in terms of the context in which privatization is pursued? In a general sense, negative rather than positive incentives have driven the process in LDCs. Reduction of deficits and of rates of inflation have played a determining role, whereas in France and Britain revenue generated from the sale of public assets has been a major consideration. Shedding costly redistributive programs is an important objective in LDCs, even at the expense of alienating traditional sources of political support, while in France and the United Kingdom privatization offers an opportunity to build "popular capitalism" and middle-class electoral support.

True, both sets of countries are concerned with deficit reduction, and it is the case that over the decade 1975–85, central government deficits of industrial and of developing countries together varied within a range of 3–5.6% of GDP. According to Calder (1988), Japan's privatization program was spurred by a rise in the deficit to 6.1% of GNP in 1979. Only toward the end of the period, when the US deficit was significantly reduced, did developing country deficits exceed those of the industrialized nations (*IMF Survey*, January 25, 1988). However, the overall deficits of public sector enterprises were much higher in LDCs, some 4% of GDP in the late 1970s, than in industrialized nations where they averaged 1.75% and were declining (Floyd et al., 1984, pp. 144–45).

The LDCs also typically have large external debts relative to GDP, with heavy servicing requirements. It is crucial that they maintain their creditworthiness and access to external capital. Budget deficit reduction may be the quickest and most direct route to improving public finances and reducing inflation. Inflation reduction will protect efforts to expand exports through currency devaluation, and export expansion may be the measure of international creditworthiness. PSE deficits thus take on a peculiar significance in the adjustment process in LDCs.

An obvious difference between the sets of countries is the relative size of the middle-income strata (here again, variation within the ranks of LDCs is as great as that between developed and developing nations). The narrowness of these strata in most LDCs makes difficult privatization based on the small shareholder and popular capitalism. In contrast, both France and Great Britain, through their privatization programs, have added millions of new investors to their private sectors.

This same narrowness contributes to the "thinness" of capital markets in LDCs. More important in this respect, however, is the fact that in many LDCs private enterprises raise capital through the banking system rather than by directly selling shares on capital markets. Moreover, many closely held groups in Latin America, the Middle East, and South and East Asia prefer to remain private rather than undergo the disclosure that public share offerings would require. That situation is changing as the likes of Koç Holding in Turkey or Tata Industries in India make public share offerings in some of their subsidiaries, but the change is not likely to be rapid.

By and large, we conclude that the stock market is not likely to be a major vehicle for the implementation of privatization in LDCs, but this situation could change fairly quickly. The Bombay Exchange in India and the South Korean stock exchange have expanded prodigiously in the last 15 years. India now has some 10 million shareholders. The volume of trading on the Bombay exchange was about US$2.6 billion in 1986, and in 1987 capital gains taxes yielded about US$170 million (*The Times of India*, February 7, 1986; *India Today*, August 15, 1988, p. 86). The volume of South Korea's exchange is about $200 million per *day*, and there are 500 companies traded on it, capitalized at $45 billion (*The Economist*, June 25, 1988).

Other large, industrializing LDCs present a startlingly different picture. In 1986, there were only about 200,000 investors in the Mexican exchange and only 130 issues were traded. The top 10 traded companies had issued only $830 million in shares. Such market thinness produces enormous volatility: the Mexican exchange index rose 600% in the 13 months prior to October 1987 and then plummeted (*Latin American Monitor*, various issues). In Turkey, over the same period, the index of the Istanbul exchange rose 1000%. There are only 1000 regular traders on the Istanbul exchange, and average monthly volume in 1985 was $850,000. New share offerings in 1986 barely exceeded $10 million (Coşan and Ersel, 1987; *Euromoney*, December 1986). Finally, in Egypt, despite efforts since the middle 1970s to revive the Cairo exchange, the annual traded volume has reached only about $150 million. Over the last six years, $130 million in new issues has been offered to the public, with an estimated $25 million being acquired by noninstitutional buyers (*al-Ahram*, July 18, 1988). To give some sense of orders of magnitude, the book value of Egypt's nonfinancial PSEs in 1986 was about $22 billion. In Nigeria, where 92 companies, valued between $2 and $3 billion, are being considered for privatization, it is virtually out of the question that the local stock exchange could handle the share issues (Lewis, 1988; *South*, October 1988, p. 44).

Like the capital markets, the medium- and large-scale private sectors in LDCs tend to be thin. This was one reason that many LDCs initiated public sector enterprises in the first place. The problem appears to be most acute in Africa and the Middle East, leaving policy makers with three distasteful options: maintenance of the status quo, sales to foreign or local minority interests, or liquidation. In LDCs where the private sector is deeper and more diversified (South Korea, India, Turkey, Mexico, Chile) there may be viable private purchasers of publicly owned assets, but they often will be popularly viewed as oligopolists who should not be allowed to expand their empires through privatization. They may be needed to act as what the French call the *noyau dur* to protect the traded value of the privatized assets, but in the LDCs there is little check on their control from small investors.

In the LDCs, adjustment and privatization are liable to become entangled in deep-seated regional and ethnic conflicts to a degree uncommon in advanced industrial societies. Often private interests that might be able to purchase public assets are drawn from minorities such as the Chinese throughout Southeast Asia, or the Indians and Syro-Lebanese in Africa. Malaysia's public sector was built as a counterweight to Chinese economic predominance and to nurture a native Malay entrepreneurial class. Until that class has taken shape, privatization may look like selling the store to the Chinese. Thus when we look at ruling coalitions and sectoral interests, we must see the extent to which they cut across or overlap with ethnic, regional, and religious interests.

3.   STRUCTURAL ADJUSTMENT AND PRIVATIZATION

There are differences in the timing, sequence, and structure of the expansion of the public sector within and between industrial and developing countries. Similarly, there are and will be differences in the timing, sequence, and structure of privatization reforms. Indeed, the timing and sequencing issues refer not just to the pace and scope of privatization—which industries or services will be sold or eliminated, what kinds of regulations will be conceived—but also to when privatization will itself be undertaken within the gamut of structural adjustment and stabilization reforms.

Stabilization reforms are usually associated with International Monetary Fund (IMF) conditionality programs and refer to currency devaluation, credit contraction, and reducing of public sector deficits. Insofar as selling or eliminating public enterprises may lessen fiscal pressures, privatization measures are discussed as part of stabilization programs. Privatization offers equity to the public as a way of moving toward fiscal balance instead of increasing public debt or, for that matter, increasing taxes. However, privatization and public sector reform are usually discussed under two different headings from that of stabilization: neoconservative transformation and structural adjustment. A "neoconservative transformation" is one in which a political leadership sets out to fundamentally reorganize social and political as well as economic agreements. The aim is to change a pattern of political and social power in a country directly, not slowly and as a byproduct of economic change. Chile under General Pinochet is an example where union activity was restricted, public enterprises sold, and various social programs dismantled (Foxley, 1983). Obviously, the aim in Chile was not to achieve a limited balance-of-payments solution, which is what IMF stabilization programs are designed to accomplish.

Lying between IMF stabilization packages and neoconservative transformations in terms of scope are the structural adjustment programs associated with the World Bank and the Reagan administration's aid policies. Here, loans, investments, and aid are conditioned on the design and implementation of a certain set of reforms. These include: trade liberalization (moving away from licenses and quantitative restrictions on imports, to reducing the scope and size of tariffs); getting domestic prices in line with world market prices; improving revenues by widening tax bases and reforming the administration of taxes; diminishing government deficits by lowering public expenditures, especially subsidies. In the first instance, reducing government deficits is seen as essential to lower inflation and to allow for new domestic and foreign investment.

It is within the category of reduction of government deficits and interference in the economy that privatization is usually seen as part of the package of structural adjustment reforms. Government expenditures can be lowered by cutting the public wage bill. This can be done by lowering real wages by delinking them from inflation. If wages are sticky, public employees can be fired. It may be easier actually to sell public enterprises or completely eliminate them than to fire some workers. Typically, investment is frozen or reduced in PSEs, forcing them to self-finance or driving them to the commercial banking sector, as has occurred in Turkey, India, and Egypt.

Of course, there are other ways to cut public expenditures. Consumer subsidies on goods and services can be reduced or eliminated (Bienen and Gersovitz, 1986). Military spending can be cut. Each of these policy measures provides economic gains and costs to different constituencies. Each carries its own risks for political stability.

Moreover, while the policy packages can be thought of separately for analytical purposes, they are usually interrelated. Privatization of state enterprises is likely to have implications for trade liberalization. The success or failure of one set of measures in economic terms will have implications for the economic utility of other measures. Or, if political resistance to, say, a cut in consumer subsidies of foodstuffs is very great and government must spend more on repression or its legitimacy weakens, there are implications for the successful implementation of other measures. Thus, we need a model of general political economy interactions if we are to understand the implications of privatization measures.

An IMF stabilization program is aimed at changing prices of final goods, intermediate inputs, and factors of production. We can categorize winners and losers from these programs by examining impacts on various groups, for example, agriculture versus industry or import versus export sectors, or on owners of different factors of production. If exporters are growers of a particular crop, e.g., cocoa, they may also be from a particular ethnic group, e.g., Yoruba-speaking people in Nigeria. The political consequences of programs must be seen by taking account of ethnic and regional as well as class and sectoral factors. In the first instance, however, a large body of economic theory allows systematic analysis of the effects of structural adjustment and stabilization programs on the incomes of different owners of factors of productions (Bienen and Gersovitz, 1985).

Privatization of assets might not change relationships between factors of production at all. Of course, if the public sector simply eliminates enterprises rather than selling or giving them to private owners, jobs will be eliminated. These will be the jobs of workers and managers in the firms that are affected. Private owners of remaining firms will benefit because competition will be lessened, and if the public firms received special benefits from access to loans, import licenses, and intermediate goods the benefits to remaining firms may be very great. Labor and managerial costs should be lowered by releasing more people into the remaining market. Of course, the effect on workers and managers who lose jobs will depend on whether factors of production can easily move among firms or sectors of the economy. Factors of production are said to be completely mobile if they always earn the same return regardless of the sector in which they are employed. The costs of reallocating factors among sectors will be lower when the switching is gradual rather than rapid.[1]

We need also to know how sticky are wages in an economy. Are unions strong enough to protect the real wages of workers in firms in the private sector or in public sector enterprises that are not eliminated? If privatization means the elimination of public sector jobs as well as a change in ownership, what will be the impact on fired workers and on those still employed? Even when a change in asset ownership rather than the liquidation of an enterprise occurs, workers and unions often fear that economic efficiency will be sought through elimination of jobs. Indeed, one of the major claims for private rather than public ownership is that featherbedding and payroll padding of workers and managers alike, which occur in the public sector because there is no bottom line and no discipline of the market (Hanke, 1987, p. 49), will be greatly reduced and costs streamlined.

However, there is relatively little consensus on the determinants of the assumed wage and price rigidities that lead to unemployment. Different macroeconomic analysts would stress such factors as price and wage expectations that are slow to adjust, explicit wage contracts with fixed horizons that are not coordinated among employers, implicit contracts between employers and employees that favor layoffs over wage cuts, or mechanisms for job search. No theory of labor markets can predict with confidence the extent and duration of unemployment that would accompany privatization programs (Azariadas and Stiglitz, 1983).

Furthermore, privatization is, as noted, one component of a gamut of structural adjustment programs implemented together or sequentially. Thus, in Mexico, privatization is taking place along with credit contraction, fiscal austerity, and trade liberalization. The employment effects of fiscal austerity and credit contraction may be much greater than those attendant on privatization or liquidation of public enterprises.

To compound the problem, we have poor information on unemployment in developing countries. There are no comparative studies which analyze the characteristics of different countries that suggest how a given degree of austerity leads to more or less unemployment for different periods, much less how privatization affects unemployment.

Without good data on labor markets, it is difficult to give precise answers about who is unemployed and for how long. The same aggregate unemployment rate can be produced by varying numbers of individuals unemployed and lengths of unemployment. Indeed, it is only relatively recently that economists have grouped the unemployed in the United States and the United Kingdom by age, sex, and skill levels (and even here the statistical data are not strong; see Clark and Summers, 1979; Nickell, 1980). Little corresponding evidence is available for less developed countries (Bienen and Gersovitz, 1985, p. 739).

We do know, however, that public sector employment as a share of total modern-sector nonagricultural employment varies by country and by region. Cutting public sector employment is more difficult in those countries where the public sector uses a very high share of total nonagricultural labor. In Africa, public sector workers are 54% of nonagricultural employees compared to corresponding figures for Asia of 36% and for Latin America of 27% (Heller and Tait, 1983). Cutting public sector employment is especially hard in Africa because reemployment of these workers is difficult. This is more true for white collar than for industrial workers.[2]

If workers have been redundant or highly inefficient, they have been paid on the back of someone else, perhaps agricultural producers who have been receiving lower than world market prices for their products, or other producers who have been competing for scarce inputs at a disadvantage. However, decreases in employment of workers who have been productive will have negative effects on the level of output and on short-term growth. This may occur if efficient subcontractors to inefficient public enterprises lose their main customer through liquidation of public enterprises.

Governments that embark on privatization programs may try to sell off either the most or the least productive enterprises. They will have an easier time doing the former, and they simply may have to eliminate enterprises where there are no takers. They may strike bargains with unions in order to secure cooperation for selling some enterprises by promising to maintain wages in others. If the organization of labor is reasonably centralized, and tied to a political party or government body, a fair degree of cooperation may emerge. This describes one major recent liquidation (Fundidora de Monterrey) in Mexico. However, while the central Mexican trade federation has cooperated with government's economic policies, individual unions ceased to give their full support to the ruling party in the 1988 Mexican presidential election.

4.   THE POLITICS OF PRIVATIZATION

The politics of privatization, like those of other reform measures, consist in holding out future gains to the general public as well as to specific beneficiaries, such as private sector capitalists who have competed with the public sector. The gains are weighed against immediate costs to those who lose jobs and influence. The political risk involved is obvious: beneficiaries of the status quo may be able to paralyze the reform process before future beneficiaries of that process can be organized to support it. As we shall see, moving from one constellation of coalitional interests to another provides the major political test, and some regimes may be better suited to manage the transition than others.

A prior question, however, is what factors drive leaders and policy makers to commit themselves to the reform process? Structural adjustment and occasionally privatization may be mandated by the IMF and World Bank or by bilateral donors and commercial banks. There is a general perception in the LDCs that the packages are imposed by the creditors with little sensitivity to local conditions and constraints. Every reform undertaken by Tanzania since the early 1980s has been under donor duress. In Guinea, a 1986 structural adjustment loan from the World Bank was made contingent on a sweeping privatization program. On the other hand, there is good evidence that in Africa and elsewhere the need for reform, if not its actual implementation, has been widely recognized independently of donor pressure (Hyden, 1986; Wilson, 1988).

Algeria, after the fall of international petroleum prices, undertook a reassessment of its entire development strategy and the role of the state in it. Deconcentration of PSEs, begun earlier, is being accelerated; deregulation and encouragement of the private sector has begun; and the greatest symbol of the socialist revolution, the self-managed farm sector, has been reorganized into cooperatives with title to land vested in farm families. Algeria has never lost its good international credit rating, and donor pressure has not been a major factor in the reform process. Similarly, India since 1980 has promoted trade liberalization and deregulation without strong external pressure. Sharad Marathe, an economist by training, was for two decades a senior civil servant in the Ministry of Industry and once Secretary to the Government of India for Industry. Writing in the mid-1980s (1986, p. 262), he reflected on his experience:

> . . . the institutional forms or the operating mechanisms have failed to achieve the results expected from them. Indeed, the time has come when in order to effectively pursue our commitment to the values of

democratic socialism, i.e., growth, liberty, and equality, it is urgently necessary to critically review and reconsider our traditional emphasis on State ownership or monopoly of productive assets, and also the detailed administrative regulation and control over a wide range of economic activity.

We believe Marathe's statement to be typical of a broad range of insider reassessments in the LDCs. For technocrats and perhaps for some political leaders, a commitment to "the magic of the market" has been important. They may be persuaded by the economic logic of privatization. To translate this new awareness into policy constitutes the main political challenge.

The implementation of reform policy, and of privatization within it, will be tempered by:

(a) The origins of the public sector itself
(b) The nature of the state's deficit and fiscal crisis
(c) The nature of coalitions with vested interests in the status quo
(d) The preoccupation of leadership for the control of economic resources and patronage

(a)   Ideological Rationales

On the first point, the role assigned to PSEs within broader ideological frameworks does matter. Countries that have eschewed socialist programs and that have accorded considerable legitimacy to private sector activity can promote a reduced role for the state and privatization on efficiency grounds alone. Some of the newly industrializing countries of Asia, as well as Brazil, the Ivory Coast, and Pakistan (with the exception of the Bhutto period) would fall into this category. By contrast, countries that have emphasized the redistributive role of the state in pursuit of social justice and have criticized the inability of the private sector to serve those goals, will find it difficult to reduce state intervention and to privatize without calling the legitimacy of the regime into question. In this respect one thinks of India, Tanzania, Algeria, or Egypt. Both "liberal" and quasi-socialist regimes may find it difficult to allow foreign private interests to acquire important publicly owned assets.

(b)   Deficits

We noted earlier that PSEs contribute significantly to the overall deficits of many LDCs, even in those that have emphasized efficiency criteria in assessing enterprise performance. At the end of the 1970s, for example, the share of PSEs in Brazil's overall deficit varied between 66 and 76%. In addition, PSEs tend to be highly leveraged, and debt servicing often represents a major part of their operating deficits. Privatization may be seen as a quick fix for deficit reduction, in the sense that once sold, the PSE drops out of public accounts, although it may show up later as a source of corporate tax revenue. Privatization is not a quick fix, however, in the sense that preparing PSEs for privatization can be very time-consuming, and, in trying to attract buyers, may entail the state's absorption of the outstanding debt of the firm. Eliminating expensive charges on the public purse is often more important than the revenue generated by selling the enterprises. There may also be a political window of opportunity, before opposition to privatization solidifies, to sell in haste, generally through undervaluing the assets. In the Sudan in 1972 and in Bangladesh a decade later, military regimes "returned" nationalized assets to the private sector in great haste. We know the details only of the Bangladesh reprivatization (Lorch, 1988), while the Sundanese case is more anecdotal.

It appears often to be the case that the social and economic impacts of other parts of the reform programs will be more severe than those directly attributable to privatization. Hiring and salary freezes, de-indexing wages, cuts in investment budgets and social services, reduction of consumer subsidies, and devaluation are likely to cause immediate hardship far in excess of anything resulting from privatization. Consider that in Mexico between 1981 and 1983, 1.5 million jobs were lost in the formal economy before privatization was even an item on the policy agenda (Carr, 1983, p. 104).

Thus, in one sense privatization may be relatively easy. Organized interests may focus much more on other aspects of the reform package that loom larger in social welfare terms. Most LDCs, however, face shortages of technocrats capable of managing a reform process that is often carried out in an atmosphere of crisis. There are several fires raging at once—deficits, inflation, gross imbalances in external accounts, debt servicing, etc.—and very few firemen. It may take as many hours of technocratic time to prepare a small PSE for privatization as it would to prepare a large international bond offering. The latter might have a far larger payoff in dealing with the crisis than the former. In Turkey, for example, it took a three-month search to find a new general manager for Sümerbank, a large PSE slated for privatization, and to begin what is envisaged as a two-year process of corporate restructuring before privatization. At the same time, Turkey in 1988 and for the next three years must come up with $7 billion or more annually to service its foreign debt. It is not difficult to see where priorities will lie in deploying Turkey's thin line of financial managers. It is in part for this reason that privatization to date in LDCs has consisted largely of the simpler tasks of selling off minority state shares (e.g., Turkey and Mexico) or of outright liquidation.

There may be a strong correlation between extremely poor performance of public enterprises and the degree of political difficulty in getting

rid of them by privatizing. In Africa, a number of studies have documented the poor returns on public enterprises through bureaucratic and political
interference in their operations (Nellis, 1986). Yet it is in Africa where
capital markets are least developed. Privatization is likely to mean, in the
short run, outside Nigeria and a few other countries, foreign ownership or
citizenship ownership which is politically unacceptable because the citizens are of Asian or Middle Eastern extraction or may be indigenous but
from the "wrong" ethnic group, e.g., Kikuyus in Kenya today (Cowan,
1987, p. 15). In Africa, communal problems, in addition to the relative
difficulty of shifting to alternative private sector employment, suggest that
political difficulties will be most severe where public sector harm is
greatest.

(c) Dominant Coalitions and Social Pacts

The third and perhaps most important political constraint lies in the maintenance or transformation of dominant coalitions. One can argue that in
many LDCs state-led, import-substituting industrialization (ISI) produced a
standard coalition consisting of the political elite, frequently the military,
the state managers, organized labor, civil servants and large parts of the
professional middle class closely involved in the programs of an interventionist state. Generally neglected were the small-scale private sector, the
agricultural sector, and the informal sector. In Egypt, India, Turkey,
Mexico, Tanzania, and Algeria, these coalitions have been remarkably stable. With the passage of several decades of ISI, they have also become predictably entrenched. In varying degrees, structural adjustment programs
and privatization threaten, or are perceived to threaten, their material interests. They are variously equipped to resist reform.

   In contrast, those that may benefit from reforms are not well organized,
and incumbent leadership may have great difficulties in reaching out to
them. We would expect, *ceteris paribus,* that reform would stimulate private
enterprise in general, but in particular both rural and urban interests producing for export will gain. They may be numerically strong, but many are
dispersed farmers. Though in aggregate their economic weight may be
great, given the fact that in the ISI coalition they had little political voice,
they will appear a frail reed to lean upon in the reform process.

   In the ISI coalition, organized labor and other lower- and middle-
income groups have been party to social pacts by which these groups trade
political support, or at least docility, for protection of their standard of living and a continued state commitment to redistribution. Advanced industrial nations have had their counterpart to these pacts in what some have
called Keynesian ententes. In the course of the adjustment process, be it the
United Kingdom under Thatcher or Mexico under de la Madrid, various
facets of these pacts are broken by the state.

In many LDCs, the term "social pact" is actually used. When this social pact is being broken, it is described in terms ranging from the technical "de-indexing" or "linking wages to productivity" to "no more iron rice bowl" or "there's no free lunch." In LDCs, the social pact has in fact often consisted in a package of free health and educational services, high levels of consumer subsidies, guaranteed employment, and implicitly indexed wages. The social pact is associated with high levels of consumption in urban areas, high levels of deficit financing, high levels of imports and external borrowing, and with relatively low levels of worker productivity. Successful structural adjustment fundamentally alters the pacts.

Job creation has been and remains a crucial part of the social pacts of many LDCs. It is high population growth rates and the concomitant high rate of growth of new entrants into the work force, not rates of unemployment, that set LDCs off from advanced industrial societies. The general pressure for states to insure high levels of employment is intense, but, as we have noted, deficit reduction may require public hiring freezes and, as in Mexico, substantial reductions in the numbers of those on state payroll. In this respect, privatization may take two forms: (i) to give the private sector the incentives to expand and to create jobs at a rate faster than that of the state; and (ii) to shift public enterprises and services into private hands so that they may rationalize employment, retrain, and redeploy.

The strength of organized labor varies greatly across countries. It has been relatively weak in South Korea, where there is no social pact, and relatively strong in Argentina, where it is credited with blocking many attempts at PSE reform or privatization (*The Economist*, August 6, 1988, p. 57). Often in the ISI coalition, labor is represented by a large peak confederation with whose leadership the regime can make deals. But here too generalizations are dangerous; in Egypt and Mexico such peak organizations have been longstanding members of dominant coalitions and have exercised veto power over government policy (on Egypt, see Bianchi, 1986), while in India the union movement is highly fragmented and corporatist bargains are hard to strike. We may expect, however, that organized labor will be concentrated in the state sector in general (teachers, nurses, accountants, etc.) and in public sector enterprises.

The reform process and privatization are regarded with understandable apprehension by organized labor. In both Japan (Calder, 1988) and the United Kingdom (Suleiman, 1988), privatization has in part aimed at reducing the influence of organized labor, while in Turkey and Chile, military authoritarians stripped unions of some of their legal rights prior to promoting privatization. Few workers can be persuaded to accept the birds-in-the-bush of future employment generation in an expanding private sector over the bird-in-the-hand of secure public employment.

Regimes engaged in structural adjustment can generally sense the limits to which labor can be pushed. As breaking points are approached, they may try to renegotiate social pacts and to associate organized labor with the austerity measures. The Jaruzelski regime in Poland in mid-1988 appears to have been driven to just such an attempt. Brazil, Argentina, and Israel all renegotiated their pacts with labor and the private sector in launching their heterodox shock programs in the mid-1980s. Only Israel's appears to be holding. In December 1987, Mexico drew up a solidarity pact with labor and the private sector in what was dubbed the *chocquecito* (little shock).

It is still the case that in the 1980s labor, organized and unorganized, has experienced absolute declines in standards of living in Turkey, Mexico, and Nigeria among others. These declines have been provoked by the austerity measures associated with deficit reduction, not by privatization. Moreover, labor has been relatively powerless to block them. Still, the defection of a substantial portion of organized labor in Mexico to opposition candidates in the summer elections of 1988 shows that there are potentially high costs to alienating this part of the coalition.

In scores of LDCs, the military has either directly managed economic strategies or has been a crucial partner in dominant coalitions. Whether "liberal" authoritarians as in Brazil, Indonesia, and South Korea, or socialist populists as in Burma, Egypt under Nasser, or Peru under Velasco, they have carved out economic domains under military control. When militaries took over in Asian, African, Middle Eastern, and Latin American countries, they often created their own industrial and trade enterprises in order to provide jobs for ex-soldiers and to have independent sources of funds under their control. In so doing, they generally invoked security concerns (Lissak, 1976; Bianchi, 1984; Crouch, 1978; Bienen and Moore, 1987).

Many PSEs, from factories and trading companies to farms and transportation firms, are controlled by the military, or, as in Turkey, by the officers' pension fund. Some of these economic interests involve public-private partnerships, but the important point is that military establishments in many LDCs find themselves heavily involved in the civilian economy through what is essentially public sector enterprise. Indeed, Argentina's Fabricas Militares, founded in 1941, was charged with achieving industrial self-sufficiency for the country (Baklanoff, 1986, p. 3). Such establishments may not be ardent advocates of privatization. In Chile, standardbearer of neoconservative transformations, the military has retained its control over the copper sector and kept it under public ownership (Sigmund, 1988). In Egypt, when a leasing arrangement between General Motors and the public sector Nasr Automotive fell through, the Military Industrial Organization, with a South Korean partner, came forth with a project to manufacture passenger cars.

Often the managers of public assets themselves are singled out as primary opponents of public sector reform and privatization. The summation of Jones and Mason (1982, p. 19; see also Haggard and Kaufman, 1988, pp. 25–26) is typical:

> Once a public enterprise is in public hands for any significant period of
> time, then there develops a strong inertia (defended by various interest
> groups) that tends to keep it in the public sector regardless of ideology
> or performance.

The evidence for managerial opposition is meager. A better case can be
made for foot-dragging, but even there the evidence is scanty (Waterbury,
1988). One must distinguish between the political appointee foisted off on a
public enterprise and the (more or less) professional manager. The former
will sink or swim according to the strength of his political connections. The
latter to some extent will be judged on performance.

Even in fairly advanced LDC economies, there is not an abundance of
managerial personnel. The professional managers of PSEs, by and large,
have the option to move into the private sector. Their skills in financial and
personnel management, and in production engineering, make them attractive to fledgling and established private firms. More important, because of
the close relationship between public and private enterprise in many LDCs,
these managers provide an insider's knowledge of bureaucratic procedures
and the positioning of crucial policy actors.

Options for exit may not be exercised. In relatively few African countries have public sector managers or civil service administrators left the
public sector willingly to work in private enterprises or to engage full time
in their own entrepreneurial activities. This has occurred in Kenya, Nigeria,
and the Ivory Coast, but rarely elsewhere. In Malaysia, Morocco, Senegal,
and Mexico, the state has encouraged senior civil servants and managers to
move into the private sector by taking over foreign-owned businesses or
contracting out public business to new firms.

Even when the top executives of the Ministries of Finance or the central
banks urge privatization, we should not forget that there are sprawling
middle echelons of civil servants in ministries and agencies whose primary
function is to control and monitor the PSEs. Privatization would cut directly
into their functional *raison d'être*. Top-level civil servants may not have the
same exit options as the managers of public enterprises. We suspect that
civil service elites may have more of an incentive to thwart public sector
autonomy and privatization than the managers of the PSEs themselves,
although this will vary enormously from country to country.

The most substantial private sector interests have had some voice in
many ISI coalitions. In some instances that voice has been very weak (e.g.,
Egypt until the late 1970s, Algeria, Tanzania) and the regime has denied the
private sector political legitimacy. In other countries (Turkey, Mexico,
India, Peru, the Philippines) the private sector has had de facto influence
over policy without a fully legitimate role in formal politics. Whatever the
coalitional arrangement, parts of the private sector have benefited in many
ways from state-led ISI and will not be obvious proponents of undoing the

state enterprise sector nor of shifting to export strategies, although the two need not be linked.

> Import-substituting policies generally begin by protecting final con-
> sumer goods, while allowing the relatively free import of capital goods.
> As ISI continues, however, protection is extended upstream into inter-
> mediate and capital goods industries. In political terms, this broadens
> the coalition of industries supporting protective policies . . . (Haggard
> and Kaufman, 1988, p. 26).

The private sector has been sheltered from foreign competition, supplied with underpriced inputs produced by PSEs, such as chemicals, steel,
fertilizers, yarn, electricity, and fuel. It has been sustained by governmental
and PSE subcontracting and purchasing of supplies and services. There are
many fetters that accompany these benefits—high levels of regulation and
licensing, price controls, crowding out from domestic credit and foreign
exchange markets, and discriminatory tax rates. Exporters frequently have
had to pay above world market prices for inputs. The private sector would
certainly like to see these fetters removed, but it is not clear that it wants to
buy and operate on a competitive basis the public firms that have heretofore been its suppliers and customers. Often the public sector banking system has acted to absorb financial risk for the private sector, rolling over
credits, deferring payments, refinancing failing firms, and occasionally converting private debt to public equity. Reform and privatization may, to
some extent, remove that safety net. Privatization will thus mean not only
the transfer of assets but forcing the existing private sector to become lean
and mean. If to do so entails eliminating jobs and even whole enterprises,
we may see the preconditions for a new cycle of state takeovers.

If our surmise of private sector ambivalence is correct, who will be able
and willing to purchase publicly owned assets? It may be that vast amounts
of local savings are waiting to be tapped if only savers and investors receive
positive returns on their funds when inflation rates are brought down and
governments' policies become predictable. Even if this were true, privatizations in most developing countries, unlike France, Britain, Spain, or even
Portugal and Greece, are unlikely to have electoral payoffs for center-right
coalitions, presuming there will be competitive elections. In short, the economic base for popular capitalism is weak and so too is the payoff in terms
of broad-based political support.

That leaves institutional buyers, both local and foreign. The most eligible domestic actors are likely to be closely held private conglomerates—*gru-
pos, chaebols,* etc.—many of which own their own banks and, along with a
few domestic counterparts, cartelize local markets for a range of products.
There may be considerable political costs entailed in allowing these large
private interests to expand their empires. However, the latter may not be

eager to do so anyway. One reason that local capital markets are so thin is that these groups have not wanted to go public because of the amount of disclosure that could be required. Likewise, if closely held private conglomerates were to bid on the sales of public enterprises, they would have to open their books and operations to public scrutiny. The bait has to be very tempting.[3]

Let us return to the theme of coalitions and social pacts. Social pacts have proved costly not only in terms of economic efficiency but in terms of political credibility as well. For decades, the state took upon itself the role of redistributing income, providing social welfare, and leading the drive for industrialization. In welfare and income terms its efforts have frequently failed, at least as measured against initial promises. Privatization in this light may be seen as a means of relieving the state of some of its social obligations, of removing from the state arena some of the issues of setting wages, providing benefits, determining productivity norms, and generating employment. It asks the private sector, in essence, to share not only in the benefits of state patronage, but also in the risks and social costs of development.

(d)   Maintenance of Power

The fourth major variable shaping the politics of adjustment and privatization is the maintenance of power. Public enterprise is best seen, according to Shepherd (1976, p. xv, as cited in Baklanoff, 1986, p. 4) "as simply an expression of political power, and its ability to serve a distinct or even understandable public interest is primarily a matter of chance." Or, in the words of Lal (1987, p. 277), "The State is then seen as seeking to maximize its own utility (including incomes, perquisites, and power) and not necessarily the welfare of its citizens." Even those leaders who articulate the need to reduce state intervention in the economy and to divest the state of some of its assets may hesitate to move ahead for fear of losing control of crucial political resources. This, for instance, appears to be the dilemma of Turgut Özal, the Turkish Prime Minister, a man devoted to reducing the weight of the Turkish state in the economy, but also a man in need of all the state resources available in order to maintain his narrow electoral majority.

Likewise, Herbst suggests that the public sector expanded in Africa perhaps more from the needs of political leaders for greater authority over their societies than from market failures or ideology, although these are not mutually exclusive (Herbst, 1988; citing Callaghy, 1984). Public enterprises provided political leaders with resources to distribute—jobs, funds, status—and allowed them to regulate a wide range of activities, or at least try to regulate such activities. Regulatory options were not so available because of weak administrative systems, and politicians believed that direct control through enterprises that produced and distributed would allow them to make strategic interventions.

The state has loomed large in the rapid expansion of the industrial sector in Mexico and Brazil. In the past, political power rested not on winning open elections in Mexico but on manipulating a bureaucratic apparatus and dealing with the not insignificant private business sector by providing carrots in the form of access to credit, licenses, and contracts. As Mexico in recent years has moved away from quantitative restrictions to tariffs and has engaged in some privatizations, leaders have partially given up mechanisms and resources they previously had used. They also have moved to more competitive party and electoral systems. How far can this go? If discretionary resource allocation is to be narrowed considerably, then the ruling party, the PRI, will have to base its control on risky elections, as the 1988 Presidential election demonstrated. Now, the PRI leaders are able to make many thousands of appointments to state corporation boards and to service institutions. True, as Schneider argues (1988), patronage support is often unreliable. Elements of both the bureaucratic elite and the private sector elite can withhold support in Mexico. The first can paralyze bureaucratic action and the second can threaten capital flight and disinvestment.

(e) Political Continuity

It has been widely debated whether adjustment and reform are more easily carried out under authoritarian or democratic regimes. Reading the evidence from Rajiv Gandhi's attempts to liberalize and deregulate the Indian economy, Kohli (1989) sees India's democratic system producing paralysis (see also Haggard and Kaufman, 1988, for a summary of the debate). We want to phrase the problem differently. In many instances, the crucial variable may be the degree of continuity or discontinuity in the makeup of the regime and its dominant coalition. Gandhi in India, Mwinyi in Tanzania, Mubarrek in Egypt, Salinas in Mexico, or, for that matter, Gorbachev in the USSR, are all examples of would-be reformers who emerged from and have been integral parts of longstanding coalitions of state and nonstate interests. Among them, only Rajiv Gandhi has operated consistently in a system with competitive elections, but all have to some extent been captives of their coalitions.

By contrast, sharp discontinuities in regimes offer the possibility for far-reaching change. The most dramatic examples are those of Pinochet replacing Allende and launching his neoconservative transformation or, conversely, of the Sandinistas replacing Somoza and launching a socialist transformation. The point is that radical regime change will lead to a radical restructuring of coalitions premised on a redistribution of state assets and the rewriting of public policy. As Bermeo has shown (1988), the collapse of Franco's regime in Spain, and the advent of a democratically elected socialist government under Felipe Gonzalez, has led to the breakup of state interests that had sustained Franco's coalition. Likewise, the Aquino govern-

ment in the Philippines took similar measures to undo Marcos' base of support (Haggard, 1988).

Electoral change, in the absence of regime change, represents an intermediate form of political discontinuity and may lead to significant restructuring of coalitions and changes in policy. Obvious examples include
Seaga's 1980 victory over Manley in Jamaica, Jayawardene's over
Bandanaraike in Sri Lanka, Thatcher's in the United Kingdom, and the two
1980s victories of the Socialists in France. In all these instances, democracy
and broad-based restructuring of the state sector went hand in hand.

In Latin America and in southern and western Europe, privatization
requires new regimes or coalitions of policy makers, relying on different
social groups to bring about public sector reform. In these regions, there are
more organized participants in politics and policy determination than there
are in Africa, where the elite of the state is the critical constituency. Even in
Africa, however, sometimes enough support for policy innovation can be
gathered either because business as usual poses stark outcomes or because
enough people in critical roles are seized of new opportunities.
Paradoxically, policy change may be more easily brought about with fewer
participants in the policy process.

We do not want to offer a monolithic explanation. Many regimes are
capable of reform from within. Civilian leaders like Bourguiba in Tunisia or
Houphouet-Boigny in the Ivory Coast have led their countries through
more than one revamping of economic strategy. Particular leaders can shift
gears significantly, as Rawlings did in Ghana when he adopted a far-reaching stabilization program under IMF auspices or as Didier Ratsiraka has
begun to do in the Malagasy Republic after a decade of nationalizations and
state interventionism. Leaders are capable of abrupt shifts in direction, for
example Lopez Portillo's nationalization of the Mexican banks at the end of
his *sexenio* in 1982. A shift of military leaders can also lead to adoption of
structural adjustment policies, as occurred from Buhari to Babangida in
Nigeria and from Boumedienne to Ben Jdid in Algeria.

The examples given above show that even without sharply discontinuous regime change, adoption of a structural adjustment package is possible.
But it is significant that none of the examples cited involves truly democratic systems, with the problematic exception of Mexico. Innovators can come
to the fore or leaders can change their minds. This may be easier to do in
systems where votes do not count. However, even in nonelectoral systems,
leaders must find enough support or create new bases of support to sustain
privatization policies.

5. CONCLUSION

The idea of selling public enterprises is no longer heresy, even in countries
of quasi-socialist persuasion like India, Tanzania, Algeria, or Senegal. Thus,

determined leaders, aiming to undo the coalitions of predecessors they want to discredit or from whom they want to distance themselves, aided by small groups of technocrats committed to greater economic efficiency, can promote privatization in the midst of a generally indifferent citizenry. The real question is how much time can they devote to the task when other economic issues loom larger on the policy agenda?

In a situation of political risk, and in the context of economic policies that must have a dose of austerity for some time to come, is it likely that privatization measures will significantly reduce state control of the economy or the share of state ownership of GDP in most developing countries? It may be much more likely that other policies of structural adjustment will be used. Trade liberalization can proceed incrementally (and in Mexico it has been a major reform). Cutting certain consumer subsidies can also be done in some countries in a way that does not provoke massive reactions (Bienen and Gersovitz, 1986). Politicians will have to choose among risky options.

The complex of issues constituting the broad parameters of structural adjustment makes it unlikely that the privatization process will be linear. The history of Japan since the late nineteenth century is instructive in this respect, revealing cycles of state expansion and contraction (Calder, 1988). Wilson (1988, p. 27), in exploring three scenarios of public sector expansion and contraction in Africa, suggests that in good economic times states may reassert their control over economies and expand the public sector.

While accepting this possibility, we want to suggest that new forms of economic crisis may produce a reassertion of state interventionism. This is especially so for LDCs that are trying to build adjustment around an export-led growth strategy. The private sector finds itself in double jeopardy: (1) incurring high levels of foreign and domestic debt in order to modernize and compete; and (2) becoming dependent on foreign markets over which it has no control. Chile in 1983 showed what could happen when reprivatized industries, unable to service dollar debts at high interest rates, collapsed and were taken back into the public sector. That may not be an uncommon scenario in the LDCs. In several LDCs, public sector banks hold a large part of private sector domestic debt. If there is widespread default due to high domestic interest rates and shrinking foreign markets, the banks would probably take over the enterprises. Indeed it is not inconceivable that in some LDCs, after an unsuccessful experiment with liberalization and privatization, populists—perhaps in uniform—would reinvoke formulae of state-led growth. Japan witnessed such a period in the 1930s, and Turkey in the 1960s. When one looks at contemporary Sri Lanka, Argentina, the Sudan, or the Philippines it is not difficult to imagine similar outcomes.

For most LDCs for many years to come there will be large public enterprises in utilities, transport, minerals and metals, and defense that embody huge sunk costs and usually large current deficits. In India in 1985, the cumulative deficit of the state electricity boards was as great as that of the rest of the public sector combined. In Nigeria, the national airline loses $8.6 million a month and its debts exceed $450 million. Examples proliferate. Still, the issue of seeking formulae for management autonomy, pricing, financing, and performance assessment for these residual PSEs should be important both domestically and among the donor community. These PSEs continue to contribute to the economic crisis, while the alleviation that privatization might afford is still years away.

It should not need restating that the LDCs contain within them as much variance in economic characteristics as that existing between them and the advanced industrial societies. Even large LDCs reveal such variance. Still, it may be useful to speculate about the future of different regions in terms of structural adjustment and privatization.

In sub-Saharan Africa, the rulers' preoccupation with power maintenance, and the short time horizon that accompanies it, mean that some regimes will go to the brink of economic collapse, or even over it, before remedial measures are taken. Incumbent leaders may persist in business as usual, but business as usual is no longer possible. Thus it is in Africa that one can reasonably expect pronounced regime discontinuity and the possibility of sharply altered development strategies. We do not mean to minimize the commitment to reform in Senegal, the Ivory Coast, Guinea, Ghana, Nigeria, and the Malagasy Republic, but implementation is just beginning.

In Latin America, where—in contrast to Africa—private sectors are old, indigenous, and relatively powerful, we may see them effectively come to dominate the state arena through centrist electoral systems. PSEs would be maintained to service the needs and to absorb risk for the private sector. In the Middle East, Turkey might well follow this path.

In northeast Asia, as Cumings (1984) and Hofheinz and Calder (1982) have persuasively argued, there may be emerging a Japanese-inspired model. It is built on an alliance of mercantilist state agencies with powerful private conglomerates, working together to sustain export-led growth. In some ways, the lines between public and private sectors, or between private interest and public policy, are the least distinct in this region. Because of the relatively low commitment of the state, outside of the People's Republic of China, to social welfare, restructuring public-private balances is not as politically loaded as it is elsewhere in the LDCs. Moreover, this is the only region in which population growth is stabilized or stabilizing and in which economic growth may be constrained by labor shortages rather than oversupply.

Finally, there are the giants scattered across these regions for whom the older ISI models are still viable. Included are India, Brazil, China, and to a lesser extent Mexico, Indonesia, and Nigeria. The size of the domestic resource base and market are the crucial factors here. In these countries, the older formulae and the coalitional interests associated with them are particularly entrenched. Concessions to reform, sometimes major as in the case of Mexico and Nigeria, will be made and a concerted effort to boost exports undertaken. But it may also be in these countries that, as Ernest Wilson has speculated, good economic times will bring about a reassertion of state intervention and an expansion in the public sector.

It is thus an open question whether we are at the dawn of a new era of unfettered markets and private enterprise, or rather at one of adjustment in which the state seeks to redefine the instruments and scope of its interventionism.

NOTES

1. Among the idealized situations with respect to factor mobility that economists often consider are: (1) an economy with the same two factors of production, both of which are perfectly mobile between both sectors; (2) an economy with final goods, each produced using two factors of production, one of which is specific to a particular sector and one of which is common to both sectors and perfectly mobile between them; (3) an economy with two final goods, each of which is produced using two factors of production, all four factors being specific to their particular sectors and hence immobile.
2. There is much variation by sector and by country. The public sector employs over 95% of the mining employees in Ghana and 99% in Zambia, but 33% in Kenya. Manufacturing sectors show a wide dispersion also from 15% public sector in Ghana to almost half in Tanzania and Zambia. See Herbst (1988), table 1, p. 5.
3. As noted earlier, governments may have to make offerings highly tempting. In Turkey, the giant holding company, Sümerbank, has a book value of TL 3 trillion while the value of its state-owned shares is TL 200 billion.

REFERENCES

Aharoni, Y. *The Evolution and Management of State-Owned Enterprises.* Cambridge: Ballinger Publishing Company, 1986.

Azariadas, C., and J. E. Stiglitz. "Implicit Contracts and Fixed Price Equilibrium." *Quarterly Journal of Economics,* 98, Supplement (1983): 1–22.

Bachman, D. "China and Privatization." Paper presented at the Privatization Working Conference, Princeton, N.J.: Princeton University, 1988.

Baklanoff, E. N. "The Dependent 'Entrepreneurial' State, Public Enterprise and External Debt in Latin America." *UFSI Report,* no. 17 (1986).

Berg, E., and M. M. Shirley. "Divestiture in Developing Countries." World Bank Discussion Papers, no. 11. Washington, D.C.: The World Bank, 1987.

Bermeo, N. "The Politics of Public Enterprise in Portugal, Spain and Greece." Paper presented at the Privatization Working Conference, Princeton, N.J.: Princeton University, 1988.

Bianchi, R. "The Corporatization of the Egyptian Labor Movement." *Middle East Journal,* 40, 3 (1986): 429–44.

Bianchi, R. *Interest Groups and Political Development in Turkey.* Princeton, N.J.: Princeton University Press, 1984.

Bienen, Henry, and M. Gersovitz. "Consumer Subsidy Cuts, Violence, and Political Stability." *Comparative Politics,* 19, 1 (October 1986): 25–44.

Bienen, Henry, and M. Gersovitz. "Economic Stabilization, Conditionality and Political Stability." *International Organization,* 39, 4 (1985): 729–654.

Bienen, Henry, and J. Moore. "The Sudan Military Economic Corporation." *Armed Forces and Society,* 13, 4 (Summer 1987): 489–516.

Calder, K. E. "Public Corporations and Privatization in Modern Japan." Paper presented at the Privatization Working Conference, Princeton, N.J.: Princeton University, 1988.

Callaghy, T. *The State-Society Struggle: Zaire in Comparative Perspective.* New York: Columbia University Press, 1984.

Carr, B. "The Mexican Debacle and the Labor Movement." In D. L. Wyman, ed., *Mexico's Economic Crisis: Challenges and Opportunities.* San Diego, Calif.: University of California, 1983, pp. 91–116.

Clark, K. B., and L. H. Summers. "Labor Market Dynamics and Unemployment: A Reconsideration." Brookings Papers on Economic Activity, no. 1. Washington, D.C.: Brookings Institution, 1979, pp. 12–71.

Coşan, F. M., and H. Ersel. "Turkish Financial System: Its Evolution and Performance 1980–1986." *Inflation and Capital Markets.* Presented at the OECD-CMB Conference, Capital Market Board Publications no. 7, Bant, Bolu, Turkey, August 1987, pp. 27–65.

Cowan, L. G. "A Global Overview of Privatization." In S. H. Hanke, ed., *Privatization and Development.* San Francisco, Calif.: Institute for Contemporary Studies, 1987.

Crouch, Harold. *The Army and Politics in Indonesia.* Ithaca, N.Y.: Cornell University Press, 1978.

Cumings, B. "The Origins and Development of the Northeast Asian Political Economy: Industrial Sectors, Product, Cycles, and Political Consequences." *International Organization,* 38, 1 (Winter 1984): 1–39.

de Macedo, J. B. "Banking Competition under Socialism: A Case Study of Portugal." Paper presented at the Privatization Working Conference, Princeton, N.J.: Princeton University, 1988.

Ersel, H., and G. Sak. "The Financial Structure of the Corporations Subject to CMB Supervision: 1979–1984." *Inflation and Capital Markets.* Presented at the OECD-CMB Conference, Capital Market Board Publications no. 7, Bant, Bolu, Turkey, August 1986, pp. 89–109.

Fariborz, G., et al., *Privatization for Development: Strategies and Techniques.* Washington, D.C.: International Management Center, International Law Institute, 1987.

Floyd, R. H., C. Gray, and R. P. Short. *Public Enterprise in Mixed Economies.* Washington, D.C.: International Monetary Fund, 1984.

Foxley, A. *Latin American Experiments in Neo-Conservative Economics.* Berkeley: University of California Press, 1983.

Haggard, S. "The Philippines: Picking up after Marcos." In R. Vernon, ed., *The Promise of Privatization.* New York: Council on Foreign Relations, 1988, pp. 91–121.

Haggard, S., and R. Kaufman. *The Politics of Stabilization and Structural Adjustment.* Prepared for the NBER Project on Developing Country Debt, Cambridge, Mass.: NBER, 1988.

Hanke, S. H., ed. *Privatization and Development.* San Francisco: International Center for Economic Growth, ICS Press, 1987.

Heller, P., and A. Tait. "Government Employment and Pay: Some International Comparisons." *Finance and Development*, 20, 3 (1983): 44–47.

Hemming, R., and A. M. Mansoor. *Privatization and Public Enterprises.* Occasional Paper no. 56, Washington, D.C.: International Monetary Fund, 1988.

Herbst, J. "Power and Privatization in Africa." Paper presented at the Privatization Working Conference, Princeton, N.J.: Princeton University, 1988.

Hofheinz, Roy, and Kent Calder. *The East Asia Edge.* New York: Basic Book, 1982.

Hyden, G. "Business and Development in Sub-Saharan Africa." *UFSI Reports*, no. 25 (1986).

Ikenberry, J. "The International Spread of Privatization Politics: Inducements, Learning and 'Policy Bandwagoning.'" Paper presented at the Privatization Working Conference, Princeton, N.J.: Princeton University, 1988.

Jones, Leroy P., and Edward S. Mason. *Public Enterprise in Less-Developed Countries.* Cambridge: Cambridge University Press, 1982.

Kohli, A. "Politics of Economic Liberalization in India." *World Development*, 17, 3 (1989).

Lal, D. "The Political Economy of Economic Liberalization." *The World Bank Economic Review*, 1, 2 (1987): pp. 273–99.

Leeds, R. S. "Privatization of the National Commercial Bank of Jamaica: A Case Study." Unpublished, September 1987.

Lewis, P. M. "State, Economy and Privatization in Nigeria." Paper presented at the Privatization Working Conference, Princeton, N.J.: Princeton University, 1988.

Lissak, M. *Military Roles in Modernization: Civil-Military Relations in Thailand and Burma.* Beverly Hills, Calif.: Sage Publications, 1976.

Lorch, K. *The Privatization Transaction and Its Longer-Term Effects: A Case Study of the Textile Industry in Bangladesh.* Unpublished. Cambridge, Mass.: Harvard University, Center for Business and Government, 1988.

Marathe, S. *Regulation and Development: India's Policy Experience of Controls over Industry.* New Delhi: Sage, 1986.

Nellis, J. R. *Public Enterprises in Sub-Saharan Africa.* World Bank Discussion Paper no. 1. Washington, D.C.: The World Bank, 1986.

Nickell, S. "A Picture of Male Unemployment in Britain." *Economic Journal*, 90 (1980): 776–94.

Pazos, F. "Import Substitution Policies, Tariffs, and Competition." In J. L. Dietz and S. H. Street, eds., *Latin America's Economic Development.* Boulder, Colo.: Lynne Rienner, 1987, pp. 147–55.

Penati, A. "Macroeconomic Policies to Reduce Inflation: Lessons from the Italian and Turkish Experiences." *Inflation and Capital Markets.* Presented at the OECD-CMB Conference, Capital Market Board Publications no. 7, Bant, Bolu, Turkey, 1987, pp. 387–409.

Ramanadham, V. V. *Public Enterprises and the Developing World.* London: Croom Helm, 1984.

Sappington, D. E. M., and J. Stiglitz. "Privatization, Information and Incentives." NBER Working Paper Series, no. 2196. Cambridge, Mass.: NBER, 1987.

Scheetz, T. "Public Sector Expenditures and Financial Crisis in Chile." *World Development*, 15, 8 (1987): 1053–75.

Schneider, B. R. "The Bureaucratic Political Economies of Brazil and Mexico and the

Prospects for Privatization." Paper presented at the Privatization Working Conference, Princeton, N.J.: Princeton University, 1988.

Shepherd, W. G. *Public Enterprises: Economic Analysis of Theory and Practice.* Lexington, Mass.: D. C. Heath, 1976.

Sigmund, P. "Chile: Privatization, Reprivatization, Hyperprivatization." Paper presented at the Privatization Working Conference, Princeton, N.J.: Princeton University, 1988.

Starr, P. "The Limits of Privatization." In S. H. Hanke, ed., *Prospects for Privatization.* New York: The Academy of Political Science, 1987, pp. 124–37.

Starr, P. "The Meaning of Privatization." *Yale Law and Policy Reviews,* 6 (1988): 1101–36.

Subramanian, A. "Public and Private Sector Choices: The Case of the Indian Fertilizer Industry." Paper presented at the Privatization Working Conference, Princeton, N.J.: Princeton University, 1988.

Suleiman, E. "The Politics of Privatization in Britain and France." Paper presented at the Privatization Working Conference, Princeton, N.J.: Princeton University, 1988.

Tignor, R. L. "African Capitalism: An Historical Overview." Paper presented at the Privatization Working Conference, Princeton, N.J.: Princeton University, 1988.

UNDP. "Sub-regional Meeting on the Role of the Private Sector in Economic Development." Draft report, Lagos, Nigeria: UNDP, May–June 1988.

Vernon, R. *The Promise of Privatization: A Challenge for U.S. Policy.* New York: Council on Foreign Relations, 1988.

Waterbury, J. "The Political Context of Public Sector Reform and Privatization in Egypt, India, Mexico and Turkey." Paper presented at the Privatization Working Conference, Princeton, N.J.: Princeton University, 1988.

Waterbury, J. *The Egypt of Nasser and Sadat: The Political Economy of Two Regimes.* Princeton, N.J.: Princeton University Press, 1983.

Wilson, E. "Privatization in Africa: Domestic Origins, Current Status and Future Scenarios." *Issue: A Journal of Opinion,* 16, 2 (1988): 24–29.

21

Can the Rest of Asia Emulate the NICs?

Clive Hamilton

The high growth rates of the East Asian newly industrialised countries (NICs)—Taiwan, South Korea, Singapore, and Hong Kong—have made the economic performances of many other countries, including advanced ones, appear poor by comparison. Sustained real growth rates of 8 or 9 percent have expanded the limits of the possible well beyond the expectations of the 1950s and 1960s. Never before had countries been transformed so quickly from poor, underdeveloped economies into middle-income, industrial economies. The question naturally arises as to whether other countries can emulate the NICs, or, to pose the question quite differently, whether other countries are likely to adopt the strategies of South Korea and Taiwan in particular. Posing the question in these two ways raises a fundamental issue that will underlie the present discussion, that of whether economic success is principally due to the actions of governments in finding and applying the right policies.

This article focuses on four countries of Southeast Asia—Indonesia, the Philippines, Malaysia, and Thailand—and four countries of South Asia—Nepal, Bangladesh, Pakistan, and India—and discusses their prospects for industrial growth over the next twenty years. While it is possible to analyse current conditions and growth prospects, history is notoriously unpredictable, forever throwing up combinations of circumstances that no one can forsee. The present stage of Philippine history is an excellent example of this difficulty.

It needs to be asked at the outset what it is about the NICs that others want to emulate. The most remarkable aspect of the NICs' performance is

I would like to acknowledge the valuable comments of Sisira Jayasuriya, Hal Hill, Jamie Mackie, and Colin Barlow, all of the Research School of Pacific Studies, Australian National University. The conclusions reached are my own. From *The Third World Quarterly*, 87, 4 1987: 1225–1256.

their sustained high real growth rates of GDP (see Table 1). It is necessary to distinguish fast growth from the more general concept of development, although the two are clearly related. "Development" is taken here to mean the general improvement in human living conditions, including access to more consumption goods, better health care, greater job security, and better working hours and conditions. There are various quantitative indicators of these which are commonly used—per capita income and its distribution, the level of employment, life expectancy, and so on. These indicators of development do not cover the broader social changes that characterise the process. We will ignore development and concentrate on growth, although development does not necessarily follow growth.

Growth itself does not tell us anything about the process through which it occurs. Many forms of economic change involve fast growth. The dominant force behind rapid growth in the countries with which we are concerned here can be defined as the accumulation of industrial capital involving the expansion of investment in productive activity.

Accumulation of industrial capital can occur in various forms. The ownership of capital can be in domestic or foreign hands; the markets

TABLE 1   **Comparing Sizes and Growth Rates**

	Gross Domestic Product $bn		Annual Growth Rate of GDP 1973–84	GDP per Capita $ 1984	Annual Growth Rate of GNP per Capita 1965–84	Share of GDI in GDP 1984
	1965	1984				
South Korea	3	83	7.2	2110	6.6	29
Taiwan	3	57	8.5[a]	2794[b]	6.7[c]	21[d]
Hong Kong	2	30	9.1	6330	6.2	24
Singapore	1	18	8.2	7260	7.8	47
Indonesia	4	80	6.8	540	4.9	21
Philippines	6	33	4.8	660	2.6	18
Malaysia	3	29	7.3	1980	4.5	31
Thailand	4	42	6.8	860	4.2	23
Nepal	1	2	3.1	160	0.2	19
Bangladesh	4	12	5.0	130	0.6	16
Pakistan	5	28	5.6	380	2.5	17
India	46	162	4.1	260	1.6	24

[a]1971–85.
[b]National income per capita.
[c]1966–85 GDP per capita.
[d]Share of gross capital formation.
SOURCE: World Bank, *World Development Report 1986*, Washington D.C.; Taiwan, *Statistical Yearbook 1986*, Taipei.

served by industrial firms may be at home or abroad; ownership may be private or public. We are concerned here with capitalist development that is, the accumulation of capital in private hands. Some countries may have more state or collective enterprises than others, but in the NICs which are being emulated and the countries which are attempting to emulate them, it is private capital that is the principal dynamic force behind economic growth. As will become apparent in the discussion below, growth and development in socialist countries require a different mode of analysis.

It should also be stated at the outset that we are not arguing that industry is the only source of growth. The agricultural, mining, and service sectors are also of central importance. But the developed countries and the NICs have, uniformly, become advanced through the development of industry.[1] Other sectors, especially services and mining, may come to be the most dynamic sectors, but it is industry that leads most countries from underdeveloped to developed status.

What is it about industry that gives it this special status? Three factors can be identified. Firstly, industry takes a leading role partly because of its technological character, in particular its amenability to the investment of capital (mechanisation) and its proneness to technical advance. Secondly, as income rises, consumption preferences shift to industrial products. Thirdly and most importantly, industry has proven to be the principal bearer of capitalist social relations. Capitalism—the relationship between private ownership of the means of production and wage labour—has been and remains the central dynamic force for accumulation, the expansion of the means of production.

The question of the prospects for growth in Asia may be expressed in this form: What are the prospects for the rapid and sustained accumulation of industrial capital? The conditions which permit sustained accumulation are both economic and political. First international economic conditions will be considered, then internal economic conditions and, finally, the amenability of domestic power structures to accumulation.

Notice first, however, that considering the prospects for growth and development in Asia, or in the Third World generally, implies that the conditions facing each country are shared. This inevitably puts a great deal of stress on the importance of international economic conditions in determining the rate of growth. International economic conditions may be very important, especially for a small country, but they may also be irrelevant if the internal conditions are not conducive to growth. These include the internal political conditions, which vary enormously and are particular to each country's history.

Moreover, the question of emulating the NICs often implicitly assumes that the starting position of the rest of Asia is that of the NICs in the 1950s or early 1960s. In fact, circumstances have changed dramatically. Interna-

TABLE 2   **Changes in Economic Structure**

	SHARE OF AGRICULTURE IN GDP		SHARE OF INDUSTRY IN GDP		Growth Rate of Industry	Labour Force in Agriculture (percent)
	1965	1984	1965	1984	1973–84	1980
South Korea	38	14	25	40	10.9	36
Taiwan	24	6	30	46	10.5[a]	20
Hong Kong	2	1	40	22	8.0	2
Singapore	3	1	24	39	8.6	2
Indonesia	59	26	12	40	8.3	57
Philippines	26	25	28	34	5.3	52
Malaysia	30	21	24	35	8.7	42
Thailand	35	20	23	28	8.7	70
Nepal	65	56	11	12	—	93
Bangladesh	53	48	11	12	7.6	75
Pakistan	40	24	20	29	7.6	55
India	47	35	22	27	4.4	70

[a] 1971–85.

SOURCE: World Bank, *World Development Report 1986*, Washington D.C.; Taiwan, *Statistical Yearbook 1986*, Taipei.

tionally, world markets are much tighter; there is increased competition between less developed countries. National economies have also changed very substantially; indicators of structural change in our sample of countries are included in Table 2.

INTERNATIONAL FACTORS

The foremost common factor influencing the growth prospects of developing countries is the growth of the world economy. The growth of markets for exports depends on the general buoyancy of the world economy and changes in levels of protection aimed at products from developing countries. With the rapid growth in world trade over the last twenty-five years, the potential trading opportunities for South and Southeast Asia are greater than they were for the NICs in the early 1960s. Continued growth of South–South trade and the opening of the People's Republic of China to imports provide further opportunities.

While recent increases in protection by some industrial countries have been most detrimental to labour-intensive exports from developing countries, this protectionism is unlikely to be extended, given the political dominance of free trade ideology, and may be wound back. Nevertheless, the region is now crowded with NICs, near-NICs, and aspiring-NICs so that

TABLE 3   **Features of the Trade Regime**

	Share of Exports in GDP 1984	Growth Rate of Exports 1973–84	SHARES IN 1983 EXPORTS OF			Commodity Concentration[b] 1985
			Fuels, Minerals, etc.	Other Primary	Other	
South Korea	37	15.1	3	6	91	26
Taiwan	57	14.4[a]	2	8	90	11
Hong Kong	107	12.9	2	6	92	—
Singapore	—	7.1	31	13	56	32
Indonesia	23	1.4	80	12	8	64[c]
Philippines	21	5.6	13	36	51	14
Malaysia	56	7.5	35	43	22	45[c]
Thailand	24	10.4	6	62	32	26
Nepal	11	—	5	43	52	20
Bangladesh	8	2.9	4	35	61	66
Pakistan	11	7.4	2	34	64	36[c]
India	6	3.3	18	29	53	—

[a]1971–85.
[b]Percentage contribution of three major commodities or items in total merchandise exports.
[c]1984.

SOURCE: World Bank, *World Development Report 1986*, Washington D.C.; Taiwan, *Statistical Yearbook 1986*, Taipei; Column 6—Asian Development Bank, *Key Indicators of Developing Member Countries of ADB*, July 1986.

the competition for markets between exporters has become intense. This is reflected in the attempts by various countries in the region to attract foreign export-producing capital by means of ever more tempting subsidies.

The World Bank[2] predicts a growth rate of per capita GDP in developing countries of between 2.0 and 3.9 percent for the decade 1985–95, with exports growing at a rate of between 3.2 and 7.1 percent. The influence of the growth of the world economy on each country will clearly depend on its degree of integration into world markets. An indication of the degree of integration of our selected countries is the share of exports in GDP which appears in column 1 of Table 3. According to World Bank projections, middle-income oil importers such as Thailand will perform particularly well, especially if they are exporters of manufactures, whereas oil exporters such as Indonesia and Malaysia will find it more difficult in an era of lower oil prices. Low-income Asian countries—including those in South Asia—have quite good prospects despite, or perhaps because of, their low dependence on the world economy. However, it is difficult to see good prospects for the stagnant economies of Nepal and Bangladesh which are barely managing to grow in per capita terms (see column 5 of Table 1).

Those countries which have a high dependence on exports of commodities are likely to have difficulty with the volatility that this dependence imparts to their economies. Sustained growth is based on sustained investment and the latter requires a degree of stability and certainty about the future. Indonesia, Malaysia, and Bangladesh are more likely to suffer (see column 6 of Table 3), although Bangladesh is not heavily dependent on exports. It is not possible to predict changes in prices of primary commodities on world markets.

A few other features of the world economy have changed substantially since the early 1960s when the NICs entered their periods of rapid industrialisation. Firstly, there is much greater international trade in technology. It is now technically easier to set up factories and to introduce new production processes than it was twenty-five years ago, so that the logistical difficulties of establishing a new industry are much reduced. On the other hand, access to some of the more sophisticated technology is much more expensive. Secondly, the growth of international banking now provides much easier access to credit for financing industrial investments. This will be discussed in more detail in the next section, but it is worth noting here that the greater availability of finance is, like technology, offset by its much greater cost.

DOMESTIC ECONOMIC CONDITIONS

Within each country various economic factors contribute to or detract from the overall rate of growth. These factors can be roughly divided into those which contribute to the availability of savings and those which influence the productiveness or efficiency of potential investments. They are not sufficient in themselves to ensure high levels of productive and self-sustaining investment; several political conditions, to be discussed in the next section, are required to ensure that high savings are transformed into productive investments, but the savings and investment criteria can be thought of as necessary conditions.

The principal factors which ensure the availability of savings to investors are a high domestic savings rate, the absence of serious foreign drains on domestic resources through debt burdens, the associated access to foreign credit, and financial institutions sufficiently developed to permit savers and industrial investors to come together. This last factor should not be overemphasised, however, because while the existence of sound institutions can encourage additional savings, in the absence of official institutions, informal lending in kerb markets will always spring up to satisfy the needs of at least some savers and investors. For example, South Korea has long been held up as an example of the problems of financial disintermediation, but in practice, flourishing kerb markets have satisfied most commercial needs.

Some indicators of these principal factors appear in Table 4. The savings rates for the NICs in columns 1 and 2 indicate the levels required for

TABLE 4   **Factors Contributing to the Availability of Savings**

	DOMESTIC SAVINGS RATE		LONG-TERM DEBT SERVICE IN 1984 AS PERCENTAGE OF		Credit Rating[f]	M2/GDP
	1970–81	1982–84	GNP	Exports	1987	1983
South Korea	24	27	6.6	15.8	59.9	38
Taiwan	32	24	—	—	74.5	56[g]
Hong Kong	28[a]	26	—	—	69.3	110[h]
Singapore	29	42	—	—	74.8	73
Indonesia	20	20	5.5	19.0	45.5	21
Philippines	25	20	4.5	17.9	22.1	25
Malaysia	25	29	—	—	57.0	61
Thailand	21	20	5.4	21.5	53.6	48
Nepal	15[b]	9	0.4	3.4	—	29
Bangladesh	9[c]	1	1.3	14.2	19.2	26
Pakistan	13[d]	6	2.8	27.1	30.4	44
India	20[e]	22	1.1	13.8	50.6	42

[a]Savings exclude net current transfers from abroad; elsewhere these are included.
[b]1976–81.
[c]1973–81.
[d]1972–81.
[e]1970–79.
[f]Country credit ratings provided by leading international banks.
[g]1977.
[h]1980.

SOURCE: Columns 1 & 2—World Bank, *World Tables* 3rd edition, Washington D.C.; World Bank, *World Development Reports* 1984–86, Washington D.C.; Taiwan, *Statistics Yearbook 1986*, Taipei. Columns 3 & 4—World Bank, *World Development Report 1986*. Column 5—*Institutional Investor*, March 1987. Column 6—IMF, *International Financial Statistics 1985*.

sustained growth. The Southeast Asian countries more or less satisfy this domestic savings condition, but among the countries of South Asia only India has been able to attain a savings rate of 20 percent. A high level of foreign debt may be indicative of the confidence international lenders have in the growth prospects of the country concerned; more often, high levels of debt have not been covered by a compensatory expansion of productive capacity. In these circumstances, the significance of accumulated debt lies in the drain it represents on resources for potential investment. When export revenues fail to grow the debt provides a very serious strain on the economy. Debt-service ratios for 1984 are recorded in the fourth column of Table 4. Note that these ratios refer to long-term debt only, so that in practice a substantially greater proportion of annual export revenue is being spent on debt servicing. Those countries that have substantial debts and are unlikely to be able to expand export revenues rapidly, such as the Philippines, Indonesia, Thailand, and Pakistan, are likely to experience problems. The credit ratings of column 5 are indicative of the ease with which each country will be able to obtain foreign loans. The Philippines among the Southeast Asian countries will have difficulties, and only India among the South Asian countries will have easy access to foreign funds.

Since the mid-1970s a great literature has burgeoned on the growth-inhibiting effects of financial repression. Too much has been made of this; both South Korea and Taiwan maintained very fast growth for years while their financial systems were severely repressed by tight government control. Informal markets are impossible to suppress, although the high interest rates they charge can deter potentially productive investments, especially by small farmers. This is why governments committed to both high growth and financial regulation always need to provide public loans at low rates to industrial and other ventures. In column 6 of Table 4 we record the ratio of M2 (money and quasi-money) to GDP which provides a rough indication of levels of financial development. It is apparent that only Indonesia and the Philippines among the Southeast Asian countries may run into problems in supplying private savings to investors, while the ratios of Nepal and Bangladesh, though low, are probably adequate for their stages of development.

The conditions that are required to translate a high volume of savings into a high volume of productive investment are in large measure political and will be discussed in the next section. For the present it is important to attempt to get some idea of how productive these investments might be. It is very difficult to determine this in advance even for a single project, but there are some features of the economic environment which are prima facie conducive to greater productiveness of invested resources. One of these is the quality of the workforce. Some indicators of the quality of the workforce for the eight countries under study are provided in Table 5. Note that there is a strong relationship between income levels on the one hand and school enrolments and literacy rates on the other. While causation clearly runs more strongly from income levels to educational levels, countries which start out with higher-quality workforces will, ceteris paribus, have an advantage. India and the Philippines stand out from their groups in this regard.

Notice also that investment in improving the quality of the workforce overall is undermined by rapid population growth (column 3 of Table 5). Nepal, Bangladesh, and Pakistan will find it difficult to raise the quality of labour, while high educational levels in the Philippines will be eroded if population continues to grow at the present rate.

A further dimension of the workforce environment of investments is the level of application of labour, including the number of hours worked. Comparative data on this is patchy.[3] The degree of control by management over the labour force depends on both political factors such as repression of trade unions and economic factors such as the level of unemployment and alternative sources of income. Data on these are notoriously unreliable, but

TABLE 5   **Factors Contributing to the Productiveness of Investments**

	Secondary School Enrollments as Percentage of Age Group 1983	Literacy Rate 1980	Population Growth Rate 1980–2000	Annual Growth Rate of Real Wages in Manu-facturing in the 1970s	Average Monthly Salaries of Industrial Workers US$ 1978
South Korea	89	96	1.4	9.0	312
Taiwan	56[a]	90	1.3[b]	7.2	165
Hong Kong	68	90	1.2	2.4	254
Singapore	69	84	1.0	6.5	198
Indonesia	37	62	1.9	—	130
Philippines	63	83	2.2	−6.6	75
Malaysia	49	60	2.1	1.4	150
Thailand	29	86	1.7	5.9	126
Nepal	22	19	2.6	—	—
Bangladesh	19	26	2.4	1.4	—
Pakistan	16	24	2.6	4.2	—
India	34	36	1.9	2.0	—

[a]Estimate only.
[b]1985 growth rate only.
SOURCE: Column 1—World Bank, *World Development Report 1986;* Taiwan, *Statistical Yearbook 1986.* Column 2—ADB, *Key Indicators 1986.* Column 3—as for column 1. Column 4—ESCAP, *Economic and Social Survey of Asia and the Pacific 1985,* table I.29 (the years of coverage vary; see the source for details); Taiwan, *Statistical Yearbook 1986.* Column 5—Limqueco (1983, p. 291).

it would seem that most of the countries in question provide conditions amenable to stern control over industrial labour, with possible exceptions being provided by the Philippines, Malaysia, and India where trade union movements are relatively strong.

Some of these factors are expressed in the labour costs which industry faces but not always in a direct way. It may be that countries with stern control over labour have higher levels and growth rates of wages. Nevertheless, other things being equal, lower labour costs are important for the productiveness of investments principally in the case of traded goods. Once again reliable comparative data are scarce, particularly as wage rates within a country are not uniformly high or low but vary between markets for different types of labour. However, one can determine in general whether a country's wage levels are appropriate for its level of development and for a given level of reliance on international trade. High wage growth in Pakistan and Thailand may present difficulties, while falling real wages in the Philippines would be favourable to further industrial growth.

A second set of factors influencing the potential productiveness of investments relates to the appropriateness of the technology employed and the efficiency with which machinery and equipment are used. These are management decisions and reflect the quality of management of industrial enterprises. The determinants of the quality of management are probably more difficult to isolate and quantify than the determinants of the quality of labour, but this factor can be of crucial importance. Long experience in a commercial environment is undoubtedly important; industrialists in Korea and Taiwan could draw on their experience in the industries that grew up in the period of Japanese occupation. Exposure to the management practices of foreign companies can help in principle, but many countries have complained of the unwillingness of foreign companies to pass on their managerial skills. Within our group of countries, India and Pakistan, with longer histories of industrial production, have a natural advantage, while the *bumiputra* policies of Malaysia are likely to expand rapidly the cadre of effective managers. Indonesia, per contra, lacks a broad, high-quality management base and will take many years to acquire it.

A further significant factor in creating a favourable economic environment for investments is the development of physical infrastructure. A rough indication of the infrastructural development effort is contained in columns 1 and 2 of Table 6. Among the Southeast Asian countries, Indonesia and Malaysia appear to spend much more of their GDP on economic services than the Philippines and Thailand, while among the South Asian countries, India lags well behind the others possibly because of its relatively well-developed base. In the case of Nepal, and less so Bangladesh, geological instability and the very underdeveloped infrastructural base necessitate the channelling of a great proportion of government spending into building basic transport and power systems.

High levels of military expenditure can be a serious drain on resources which would otherwise be available for productive investments. Indications of levels of military spending appear in the third column of Table 6. In Southeast Asia, the Thai military extract a high price for staying out of government, while in South Asia tension between Pakistan and India imposes serious burdens on their economies.

A final key factor affecting the general efficiency of investments is the influence which tariffs, subsidies, and other measures that affect relative prices have upon resource allocation. Inefficient tariffs, for instance, can direct investments into areas of production which will not be internationally competitive and will therefore require continued protection. On the other hand, judicious use of tariffs can permit the establishment of new industries which may form the backbone of sustained development. The Korean government and Taiwanese authorities were unhesitating in their use of protection to foster local industry. Despite the recent, ideologically motivated clamour for liberalisation, no valid general statement about the merits or demerits of protection as such can be made.

TABLE 6   **Factors Contributing to the Productiveness of Investments**

	Share of Government Expenditure in GDP 1984	Proportion of Government Spending on Economic Services 1972–1984	Share of Defence in Central Government Expenditure 1983
South Korea	17	24	32
Taiwan	14	20	—
Hong Kong	15	22	—
Singapore	34	18	19
Indonesia	23	62[b]	12
Philippines	11	36	14
Malaysia	35	26	—
Thailand	18	19	20
Nepal	19	52	5[e]
Bangladesh	14	51[c]	—
Pakistan	25[a]	32[d]	35
India	15	24[d]	20

[a]1983.
[b]1975–84.
[c]1973–84.
[d]1975–80.
[e]1982.

SOURCE: Column 1—ADB, *Key Indicators 1986*. Column 2—ADB, *Key Indicators 1986*; World Bank, *World Tables*, 3rd edition. Column 3—World Bank, *World Development Report 1986*.

The focus of this article has been on factors which directly influence industrial development rather than the agricultural sector. In fact, sustained urban industrial growth needs to be preceded or accompanied by a transformation of traditional agrarian social structures and production techniques. If this does not occur, the rural sector will impose an intolerable drain on industrial production, on account of:

1. The failure of the farming majority to provide a market for manufactured consumer goods. Even under export-oriented industrialisation, the bulk of demand for industrial output remains domestic;
2. Continuing high agricultural terms of trade resulting in high food prices and thus high wages in the cities;
3. The obligation for governments to divert substantial resources into agriculture without significant productivity increases resulting;
4. The burden of the traditional social relationships rooted in agricultural systems which work against the dynamic social instability that is characteristic of periods of rapid economic change.

Agriculture will provide a sympathetic environment for rapid industrial development if it has been shaken out of its fixed ways and is amenable to penetration by new relationships and technologies. Taiwan and Korea started out after the Second World War with a natural advantage in this regard. Japanese colonialism had thoroughly transformed traditional agrarian social relations and revolutionised methods of agricultural production, the former especially in Korea and the latter especially in Taiwan.[4] Land reform in the 1950s grew out of the rural turmoil left by the Japanese and took the process of agricultural transformation further. Not only did land reform destroy the rural power base of the landlord classes, but owner-cultivation was a means of improving agricultural productivity when combined with sympathetic state policies.

Elsewhere, the development of capitalism in agriculture has been a powerful force in destroying old social relations and the dead weight of custom, as well as providing a means for rapid improvement in productivity. Of the three principal forms of agricultural production relations—landlord-tenant, owner-cultivator, and capitalist—the first has tended to be associated with rural stagnation and political opposition to industrialisation policies, while the last, capitalism, has tended in recent times to be a dynamic force for growth. However, the relevance of the forms of agricultural production relations for industrial development lies not so much in the form or forms which dominate agriculture but in the *transition* from one form to another or others. It is the process of change itself that has been seen to be historically important.

It should be made clear that the sorts of agrarian revolutions we are talking about generally leave a large part of the rural population pauperised and starving for long periods, perhaps several decades. They are the casualties of social and economic transition; capitalist growth generally entails the impoverishment for long periods of large sections of the population.

In Southeast Asia, the Malaysian system of large plantations combined with small cash-crop farming has provided the necessary level of unsettlement in the rural sector. Less than half of Malaysian farmers own land,[5] and wage labour is very prevalent. While share-cropping is also widespread, capitalist farming is the dynamic mode. Indications of the prevalence of tenancy and the development of capitalist agriculture elsewhere can be found in Table 6. It is worth noting that tenancy is not nearly as widespread in South and Southeast Asia as it was in Northeast Asia (Japan, Korea, Taiwan) before the Second World War.[6] On the one hand, this frees South and Southeast Asia from some of the restraints on generalised growth and development imposed by traditional landlord-based agriculture; on the other hand, these countries are less able to benefit from the liberating effects of the overthrow of these traditional systems.

In India and Indonesia tenancy is relatively uncommon while wage-labour in agriculture is widespread. In Indonesia over recent decades, ten-

TABLE 7   **Characteristics of Agriculture**

	Percentage of Holdings Wholly Owned[a]	Percentage of Farms Hiring in Labour[a]	Growth Rate of Agriculture 1972–85	Fertiliser Consumption per Hectare 1983
South Korea	—	—	7.7[b]	3311
Taiwan	—	—	1.5	—
Hong Kong	—	—	—	—
Singapore	—	—	−2.6[b]	7833
Indonesia	74	70	4.0[c]	745
Philippines	58	24	3.8	320
Malaysia	—	—	4.7	1115
Thailand	85[g]	29	4.5[d]	240
Nepal	—	—	1.7[e]	137
Bangladesh	58	45	1.7[f]	596
Pakistan	42	37	3.0	586
India	92	89	2.4[c]	394

[a]Figures are for the years, in order of appearance in the table, 1973, 1971, 1978, 1977, 1972, and 1970–71.
[b]1981–85.
[c]1972–84.
[d]1973–85.
[e]1976–85.
[f]1979–1985.
[g]*South*, September 1986 reports that in some areas 40 percent of farmers were renting all or part of their land.
SOURCE: Columns 1 and 2—Booth and Sundrum (1985), tables 6.6 and 1.7. Column 3—ADB, *Key Indicators 1986*. Column 4—World Bank, *World Development Report 1986*.

ancy has been declining while wage labour has been growing, especially in Java. The technology of the Green Revolution and associated state policies, particularly in India, have strengthened the tendency towards capitalist farming. In India this was given an initial impetus by land reforms in the 1950s. In Thailand, tenancy is fairly uncommon but so is agricultural wage-labour, which suggests a predominance of family farms of sufficient size to provide a living. This helps explain the low level of fertiliser application in Thailand (see column 4 of Table 7). However, wage labour in agriculture has been rising rapidly since the early seventies,[7] suggesting significant change in traditional systems.

In the Philippines, the figures misleadingly indicate a relatively low level of use of wage-labour and a predominance of owner-cultivation. The capitalist plantation sector is more important than the figures suggest. The degree of landlessness and the prevalence of wage-labour have been rising in recent years. The instability of the agricultural sector in recent times, apart from the political difficulties it creates, is likely to stimulate the industrialisation process. Land reform, if it is significant, is likely to raise levels of output, reinvigorate the rural economy, and weaken the power of big landowners who resist the policies and changes necessary for rapid industrial growth. However, significant land reform in the Philippines is very unlikely.

In Bangladesh and Pakistan the use of wage-labour is common and so is tenancy. The situation is similar in Nepal. However, Bangladesh and Pakistan have experienced rises in landlessness (about a third of households were landless in Bangladesh in 1977) and a concomitant rise in the use of wage labour. In Pakistan particularly there has been a significant trend towards tenant evictions and a shift in power to middle-level farmers.[8] In Bangladesh and Nepal the patterns of farm ownership and production are settled and rigid and will not lend themselves easily to the upheavals that inevitably accompany industrial transformation. Where possible, the introduction of Green Revolution technology can help to transform these old patterns, though at the expense of the landless and owners of miniature farms. This has been true in Pakistan where capitalist farming has been replacing tenancy since the 1960s.

DOMESTIC POLITICAL CONDITIONS

The availability of adequate savings and opportunities for productive investment do not ensure that productive investments will actually occur. The transition from adequate savings to productive investment depends on political conditions broadly conceived. It has been argued that growth means that circumstances are favourable for the accumulation of industrial capital. These circumstances are complex products of diverse historical processes and generally involve the absence of political dominance by classes which derive wealth from unproductive, or zero-sum, activities. In order to encourage growth, political power must be in the hands of people at least sympathetic towards industrial development and perhaps under the influence of "growth coalitions"[9] made up of a nascent class of industrialists, technocrats committed to "modernisation," a "progressive" military, and possibly foreign capital. A growth coalition may ride on the back of popular political movements motivated by nationalism or by revolt against old exploitative relationships.

There are various sources of wealth accumulation which limit the scope for industrial accumulation and which lie at the root of low growth and underdevelopment. The traditionally most widespread form of holding wealth in underdeveloped countries is land ownership, and in many countries, as we will see, this remains the source of economic and political power of the ruling elites. It is important to distinguish landlords who derive income from renting out land to tenants, and capitalist farmers who employ wage-labour and gain income from the sale of agricultural products.

The second principal form of unproductive wealth accumulation lies in merchant activities. Commercial or merchant capital derives profit from trade, including international trade, without adding value to goods. Revenue is often derived through some sort of monopoly position and the ability to engage in speculation. While wholesale and retail activities are essential to industrial production and are in these circumstances productive, these services can contribute to overall economic growth only up to a point, a point beyond which they result only in redistribution. Another source of wealth often closely associated with commercial capital is financial capital, which often appears as informal lending and borrowing in both urban and rural areas. While financial capital may, like commercial capital, be subordinated to the needs of industrial capital, the dangers are that usury will become more attractive than productive investment and that the indebtedness of industrial firms may lead to asset stripping by creditors.

A third form of zero-sum activity covers a range of activities that might be summed up as profiteering and corruption, and includes profiteering from government contracts and aid monies. In some countries this form of wealth accumulation is extremely well developed and dominates the business activities of the urban propertied classes especially. It may result in the syphoning-off for consumption purposes of the bulk of the resources available for investment.

The fourth major form of unproductive wealth is represented by foreign capital flows. This may take the form of monies being deposited abroad by local wealthy elites, or it may be in the form of profit-taking by transnational corporations operating within one's borders. It is quite possible for outflows of funds overseas to diminish dramatically the resources available for productive investments at home, just as it is possible for capital inflows to add to domestic productive investments.

The last important drain on potentially productive resources is the state. Bloated, inefficient bureaucracies can soak up huge amounts of revenue, while military spending to maintain unstable or unpopular regimes can absorb vital development resources.

The distinction between productive and unproductive investments corresponds to the distinction between social and private profitability. An investment is socially profitable if it mobilises national resources in a way that expands national output. Such a project may also be privately profitable, but an investment which is privately profitable may not necessarily generate social profits. Private profits in such circumstances result from redistribution rather than efficient resource mobilisation and these investments are unproductive.

The importance of each of the above forms of asset accumulation is that they give control over potentially productive resources to groups which are likely to invest them in unproductive activities such as land ownership for rental purposes, usury, commodity speculation, extravagant consumption, military expansion, and overseas bank accounts. One of the essential thrusts of economic policymaking in the NICs, especially Taiwan and South Korea, was to limit severely, and in some cases to eliminate, opportunities for zero-sum activities. Landlordism was abolished, corruption was largely eliminated, speculation and usury were controlled, and foreign exchange flows were wholly regulated.

The difficulty all of this raises for the prospects of growth is that nascent industrial capital generally lacks the political as well as the economic power to impose on the economy and society the conditions it needs for rapid accumulation. One historically proven method is for industrial capital to accumulate gradually—in favourable economic conditions—until it can gain political power through economic strength. This was the case in Britain. If there is entrenched resistance from the old ruling class the supremacy of industrial capital may be attained through violent revolutions which sweep away the old social forces, such as in France, the USA, and most recently perhaps the Philippines.

In the Third World today, to achieve political power or at least to gain significant power over policy, industrial capital needs an ally. Sometimes, it seeks such an ally in military regimes, which may appear committed to economic development, to breaking the power of the landlords and promoting business. South Korea and Taiwan may seem to provide examples of this though detailed analysis of these situations reveals greater complexity.[10] Often, however, military regimes are aligned with reactionary social forces, especially landlords (such as in Latin America) or they may be wholly committed to their own enrichment and military adventure.

Sometimes, foreign powers see some advantage in encouraging development in their colonies or spheres of influence. They then give support to burgeoning business interests to ensure that they gain political power. This was the case in Singapore, for example.

Workers and peasants may align themselves with business classes under a nationalist banner in order to expel a common foreign enemy or a landlord-dominated or corrupt regime. These sorts of alliances sometimes back-fire on the bourgeois classes since the suitability of political conditions to capitalist hegemony may also make a country suitable for a revolution from below. In addition to the lower classes, intermediate classes including powerful bureaucracies, the police and the petty bourgeoisie, as well as professionals, may be brought together in the cause of nationalism.

The essential political condition for capitalist industrial growth was defined above as the absence of the political dominance of classes which derive wealth from unproductive activities or which are otherwise hostile to industrial development. This implies that the state should be free from the overwhelming, if not the total, influence of these classes—landlords, speculators, money-lenders, the military, and foreign interests inimical to industrial development.

It would be a mistake, however, to believe that the dominance of the state directly by industrial capital will bring about ideal conditions for industrial accumulation. The business class collectively may need protection from itself. Unconstrained, it may well create economic conditions which are comfortable for existing businesses but inimical to continued growth, for example and in particular, through protection from foreign competition. The transition from import-substituting industrialisation to a more open industrial economy needs to occur at a point where domestic business is strong enough to withstand international competition but not so well established as to be able to protect itself indefinitely.[11] Businesses need to be allowed to fail in order for the economy to continue to be efficient. This defines a further political condition necessary for sustained accumulation: economic policy needs to be aimed at economic growth through private accumulation rather than at simply protecting private capital. That is, it is necessary to have a state that is capable of taking hard decisions which are contrary to the interests of sections of the business class.

These carry with them a further implied political condition, namely that the state is both sufficiently strong and sufficiently independent from particular class interests to implement policies that will promote accumulation at the expense of other interests. Four of the most important of these sorts of policies are land reform, suppression of corruption, regulation of finance capital, and the control of labour. State power may be democratically or undemocratically based.

The next task is to apply these general statements to the particular histories and class structures of the eight countries selected for study. The purpose is to look very briefly at the social parameters that determine whether industrial capital can become the dynamic economic force within each country. In such brief reviews many of the subtleties are lost.

Indonesia

In Indonesia, the landlord class, such as it is, has not in recent times held the position of political authority that it has in countries like Malaysia and the Philippines. On the other hand, the Chinese who have dominated business in Indonesia have not been powerful enough in the face of ethnic and class hostilities to form political organisations to dominate the state. Some years after the fall of Sukarno in 1965, a very powerful bureaucratic-military elite emerged and remains the source of political power today.

The political power of the military-bureaucratic elite has been translated into economic power, so that powerful military or ex-military families now form the main focus of wealth accumulation in Indonesia. This wealth accumulation, however, is not based directly on productive activities, but takes the form of "tributes" extracted from the productive and unproductive activities of others. The dominant sources of government wealth have been oil sales, foreign investments, and foreign aid and the spending of this revenue has been the making of fortunes for favoured businessmen and others connected to the government. Generals and important military families take a share of most foreign ventures permitted to operate in the country, and the government allocates lucrative contracts and franchises to favoured families including, and especially, the family of Suharto. Nevertheless, a substantial portion of oil revenues in the boom years did go into building infrastructure and agricultural improvement.

The scale of corruption is unusual: it is so deep-rooted in the present political structure that it almost forms a mode of economic reproduction of its own. But even corruption needs to be based on some form of productive activity, and these are the businesses run by foreign and local, mostly Chinese, companies. The military-bureaucratic elite has largely stayed out of managing and furthering productive activities, relying on its partnership with these business groups. Moreover, this relationship and the continued viability of the regime has required that from time to time the more extreme abuses of political power be controlled, as in the case of the reform of the customs service in 1985.

While corruption has imposed a massive burden on the economy, by the end of the boom years of the 1970s a substantial class of domestic capitalists had emerged,[12] or rather, had been established, since its expansion had been very much a product of the economic activities of the state. This capitalist class has limited political power and is not so much the ally of the state as its prisoner. While the economy was flushed with oil revenue, the government could afford to be serious about building an industrial economy based on indigenous capital accumulation. The drastic decline in oil revenues has demonstrated that the state's commitment to growth and development is constrained. To pursue industrialisation, Indonesia would now need seriously to attack corruption and to expose much of domestic business to the cold winds of international competition as the economy can ill afford to featherbed domestic industry. The close ties between senior members of the government and some key business interests make this unlikely.

The economic self-interest of the ruling group will prevent it from ending the corruption and protection of local business that would be necessary for sustained growth. If we compare the present Indonesian military regime with that of South Korea in the 1950s and 1960s, the striking difference is how little the South Korean officers became directly involved in business and how ruthless they were in suppressing corruption. Both regimes were strong enough to take the necessary measures, but only the South Koreans have been willing to take them.

Philippines

Under Marcos in the Philippines, the principal sources of wealth for the ruling classes were rents and profits from land ownership, including the sugar and coconut plantations, and the profits to be had from corruption, speculation, and government favour. Some of the foreign loans accumulated in the Marcos era were used to finance property deals and to expand personal bank accounts (especially of political friends and relations of the President) rather than to finance productive enterprise. While the ruling class has since the 1950s diversified into industry and commerce, the foundations of the wealth and power of many families remain in the provinces. The Aquino family falls into this category. Nevertheless, within the propertied classes a new group has emerged whose interests are tied directly to industrial accumulation.

The downfall of the Marcos regime was a product, as much as anything else, of the disaffection of major segments of the business class whose interests were being seriously harmed by the economic decline brought on by government mismanagement. But the bourgeois revolution of 1986 was directed much more against the close associates of the former President than at the old oligarchy itself.

The old oligarchy remains very much in place (as do many of the cronies) although there is no doubt that, for the time being, many forms of zero-sum activity associated with the Marcos regime are now more difficult. Rapid industrial development now depends on whether the new government has the political will to weaken drastically the power of the old landed oligarchy while maintaining an independence from the new business class. While land reform is a real possibility, it is going to be neither far-reaching nor confiscatory, so that the mass of workers and peasants will have to pay off the loans made to compensate the landowners. Nor will there be moves to turn landowners into industrial-capitalists, a scheme which had some success in South Korea, Taiwan, and Japan.[13]

Under present conditions, the political power of the old oligarchy, backed by powerful sections of the military, is too strong to permit the unleashing of industrial progress. The government remains heavily under the influence of classes whose interests lie other than in rapid industrial expansion, and is not in a position to take the harsh measures necessary for industrialisation to become the principal economic force.

Malaysia

In Malaysia, plantation wealth was mostly in the hands of foreign companies until taken over by the state in the 1970s. This means that the powerful landlord class that industrial capital has had to contend with elsewhere has been less influential. Nevertheless, landed interests are a significant force within the United Malay National Organisation (UMNO), the dominant political party. The political influence of the landlords is partly neutralised, however, by that of the Malay peasantry, whose welfare is important to the political leadership.

The traditional centres of economic power in Malaysia have been the foreign, especially British, companies based on the plantations, and Chinese businesses engaged in commerce and some industrial processing. While there is no clearly dominant political class, the state has weakened the power of these groups firstly by acquiring ownership of the largest parts of the plantation, mining, and banking sectors, and secondly by giving preference to ethnic Malays over Chinese in encouraging new ventures. The New Economic Policy (NEP) set out explicitly to create a class of Malay capitalists, not so much in place of but complementary to the Chinese businesses. The strategy of state acquisitions followed by divestment to Malays (in the 1990s) could be quite successful. Certainly in South Korea, the government had success in creating a class of indigenous capitalists by handing over state property formerly owned by the Japanese.

Industrial growth will depend largely on the ability of the state to limit zero-sum activities. This may prove difficult. While heavily involved in the economy, the government is firmly committed to seeing private capital as the motor of industrial development. On the other hand, the governing class's commitment to growth is tempered by its need to keep various class interests satisfied, including those of the Malay working and peasant classes. At present the state is required to respond to strong demands from various segments of society and relies to some extent on broad support. This makes it difficult to take severe measures which will cause some to suffer. In the years ahead, the state will become increasingly dominated by the class of wealthy Malays it is now creating. The scope for corruption and nepotism—which is already significant in the NEP—will expand and industrial growth will be more difficult. Nor is there a politically powerful, cohesive, technocratic bureaucracy, as in Thailand, which can act as a counter to sectional interests.

The military is not politically important, but any dramatic decline in economic fortunes, as occurred for instance in the Philippines, could precipitate military involvement in politics. The economic structure of the country—with its very heavy reliance on exports of few primary commodities—makes it prone to this. The danger in Malaysia is not a lack of allies for the industrial bourgeoisie, but a lack of a countervailing force to restrain it.

Thailand

Thailand is unusual in that there is not a wealthy class of landowners with the political power to match its counterparts in other countries. The centre of economic power in Thailand lies with large business groupings some of which are centred on banking. This financial-industrial bourgeoisie continues to be family-based although in recent years attempts have been made to encourage public incorporation. The banks do not simply control the formal financial market but extend their influence through ownership of industrial and commercial enterprises. This business class is a postwar phenomenon stimulated further by the Vietnam War and US aid, much as the Korean War was important in giving prominence to business interests in South Korea.

Although by no means as thoroughly as in South Korea, successive Thai governments have attempted to eliminate the less socially desirable forms of wealth accumulation including corruption and the suppression of informal money markets. For instance, the government engineered the collapse of the wealthy chit funds. Nevertheless, foreign loans have been pumped into unproductive investments such as urban property development and, in particular, military spending.

The political power of the finance-based bourgeoisie does not match its economic power. Political power is held by generally pro-business parties backed by sections of the military and middle classes, in addition to the bureaucracy which has provided administrative stability at a time of rapid changes in political leadership. On the one hand, this means that the government is reluctant to make any move that will upset the military leadership. On the other hand, the military is professional in the sense that it confines itself to military and political affairs rather than taking on commercial and speculative and corrupt economic ventures, as in some countries of the region. This is connected to the parliamentary form of political power in Thailand.

While a system of corruption and patronage dominated leading circles in the 1950s and 1960s, the emergence of the industrial bourgeoisie and professional classes, including the influential technocrats in government, has ensured that economic growth and development have become dominant government objectives. The independence of the state from particular economic interests, apart from the military and bureaucracy whose interests are not primarily economic, has enabled it to take some of the difficult decisions that are necessary for industrial growth. However, the relatively pluralistic nature of state power weakens the ability of government to unbalance economic power relations as industrialisation commonly requires.

Nepal

In Nepal, the wealth of the dominant classes comes first of all from land ownership. While not as widespread as in other countries, tenancy and sharecropping operate at a sufficiently broad level to provide large incomes to local elite families. As in the Philippines, provincial wealth forms the basis of political power in the capital. In addition to landed wealth, there is a powerful class of merchants who dominate the foreign trade on which the economy wholly depends.

Political power is wielded principally by the royal family and the nobility, with the Palace Secretariat being the senior partner in an "alliance" with the official parliamentary government. Economic and political power coalesce in an alliance of the landlord and commercial classes with the ruling nobility; indeed, individuals generally are members of more than one of these groups. Landlords are often engaged in commerce. The royal family has a stake in most of the largest commercial activities including the airline, hotels, and trading companies. Foreign aid, which in comparative terms is very great, also provides a major source of income for the dominant classes.

The principal sources of wealth accumulation, then, are land ownership, foreign trade, and local businesses based on tourism and foreign aid. There is no significant industrial capitalist class and only minor industrial output of jute goods, cement, and iron products. Industrial expansion is severely constrained by the stranglehold on the economy held by Indian manufacturers and trading houses, and a reluctance by Nepalese commercial interests to jeopardise their own trading revenues by encouraging possibly independent domestic producers. On the other hand, there is emerging an increasingly influential cadre of "modern" bureaucrats mostly with overseas education who, despite being drawn predominantly from the ruling classes, have a stronger commitment to economic development. These technocrats are in a better position to understand the precarious future of the present structure, but are not powerful.

While the state may be strong enough to take measures to create an industrial bourgeoisie, it shows little willingness to do so since it serves so assiduously the interest of the aristocratic landowning and commercial classes. Land reform, which would be only a very first step in breaking the power of the land-based oligarchy and expanding agricultural productivity, is not on the agenda. There is no significant class of capitalist farmers that could spearhead moves for rural transformation. Nepal's extraordinary level of dependence on foreign powers—India for trade, and aid donors for revenue, military support and basic infrastructure—also works against major economic reform.

Bangladesh

In Bangladesh, despite legislative attacks on the landlord-tenant relationship there has been no widespread development of capitalist agriculture. Landlords remain the dominant economic class in the countryside, especially in the north and west of the country. While landownership is the principal form of wealth, the limited prospects for productive accumulation have led rural wealth into a variety of unproductive activities in addition to further land purchases and sharecropping. These include usury and mortgages on land, petty commodity trading, and conspicuous consumption.

The industrial-commercial classes are very weak in Bangladesh. The political power of the landlord and business classes was seriously weakened after separation from West Pakistan in 1971 since these classes were closely associated with West Pakistani dominance of East Bengal. With the taint of collaboration, these interests could have little influence in nationalist political parties. Some redistribution of land occurred after independence but the landlord class, while shaken, retained its economic power under the rule of the Awami League.

The industrial-commercial capitalist class suffered through large-scale expropriations. The state took over banking, insurance, transport, and large industries, mostly owned by non-Bengalis, but big Bengali-owned companies were nationalised too. The "socialism" of the Awami League weighed most heavily on the class of industrial-commercial capitalists. The shift to a policy of economic liberalisation after 1975 has, however, included some serious attempts to revive private investment through incentives and disinvestment by the state. The Ershad government is particularly keen to promote manufacturing and has pursued policies reminiscent of early South Korea and Taiwan. Growth of manufacturing has been at the reasonable annual rate of about 4 percent since the late 1970s, but by starting at such a low base and with a high population growth rate, significant progress will be slow.

While the industrial capitalist class in Bangladesh remains small, its lack of political influence on a government that is nevertheless seriously committed to promoting industry is potentially conducive to industrial growth. However, the repression dealt out by the present regime is a reflection of its weak position rather than its strength. While political parties wrangle over the transition to civilian rule, the military remains the basis of political power. In these circumstances, it is likely that the centre of wealth accumulation in Bangladesh will remain land ownership, usury, and the profits from foreign aid.

Pakistan

In Pakistan, land reform has failed to bring about significant transfers of land to the poorest farm workers. Nevertheless, the various attempts at land reform in the 1970s reflect the conflict in the countryside between landlords, tenants, and a newly emergent class of capitalist farmers responding to the Green Revolution. While this conflict found expression in the populist Bhutto years in attempts at land reform, the Zia regime since 1977 had seen the dominance of a military-bureaucratic apparatus that had been largely independent of particular sections of the propertied classes both rural and urban yet not sufficiently strong to override them. The regime had, however, continued to encourage the spread of capitalist farming.

The principal sources of wealth accumulation are in agriculture—both in land ownership and through capitalist production—and industry-commerce, with a strengthening class of manufacturing capitalists particularly in food processing and textiles. These manufacturers received a serious blow with partition of the country in 1971, as not only were their assets in East Pakistan seized but the lucrative flow of export revenues, from jute products especially, was cut off. However, industrial-commercial capital had received important support from the Zia regime through disinvestment in public enterprises and tax reductions. This class has not acquired sufficient size and economic power for it to become a major political influence on the government, but it is viewed sympathetically by the new technocrats in the bureaucracy.

In addition to these relatively productive sources of wealth, many fortunes have been made and reproduced through illegal and speculative activities, some connected with the war in Afghanistan, the spoils of which are the objects of conspicuous consumption. The prevalence of illegal activities and the degree of violence on the streets are indicative of the current regime's lack of control over the country. Despite the large commitment of resources to the military, the state is not strong. The government has difficulty maintaining civil order and cannot wholly suppress organised political opposition.

The military-turned-civilian regime draws some support from right-wing, urban petty bourgeois elements and claims the allegiance of Islamic fundamentalists. However, the loyalty of these groups is by no means uncritical. The Zia regime had also alienated big landlords, particularly in provinces other than Punjab, so that its social foundations appear quite unstable. This is compounded by serious regional conflicts which destabilise the whole country. US support has been very important in propping up the military and funding the rapid growth rates of recent years.

India

The economically dominant classes in India today are the industrial and commercial capitalists and wealthy capitalist farmers. A sizeable industrial bourgeoisie grew up in the period of import-substituting industrialisation in the 1950s and 1960s, although many industrial and commercial sectors are controlled by state enterprises. Capitalist farmers now dominate the countryside with the decline of landlordism under the pressures of land reform and the Green Revolution. This locates the predominant forms of wealth accumulation in industrial and commercial as well as agricultural production. In the absence of the more prominent forms of zero-sum activity found in other countries, these factors would suggest that India has good prospects for rapid industrial advance. However, this is not the case.

Political power is shared principally by industrial-commercial capital and wealthy capitalist farmers in conjunction with a class of bureaucrats which administers government and government enterprise. This is an uneasy alliance since there are serious structural conflicts between them. Note, however, that capitalist farmers tend to wield their political power in state governments, where most agricultural policy is made, rather than centrally. They come into conflict with industrial capital over matters such as the agriculture-industry terms of trade. Bureaucrats see their role as one of regulating and constraining industrial-commercial capital in particular. In practice, industrial-commercial capital is not strong enough to dominate state policy but it is strong enough to avoid most of the impact of the bureaucracy's regulatory measures.

This power-sharing arrangement, operating within parliamentary democratic forms, means that the state is not sufficiently powerful and independent to enforce the difficult measures that rapid industrial development requires. While the principal sources of wealth accumulation outside agriculture are in private and public industrial and commercial enterprises, neither of these is very efficient. Public enterprises generally do not generate a reinvestible surplus and thereby impose a drain on the economy. This is partly because they provide subsidised inputs, including finance, to private businesses. Private businesses are not rapid accumulators on the whole because they have been able to protect themselves from the competitive forces that would make them more efficient.

If the private sector were more dynamic and productive it would make sense, in terms of developing a more powerful class of industrial capitalists, to hand over public enterprises to private business as in South Korea and Taiwan. The important factor is not the *level* of state intervention and control but the degree of effectiveness it is permitted. South Korea and India have similar levels of state participation in national economies. The difference is that in South Korea, government intervention is used to discipline private businesses, whereas in India government economic management is not insulated from particular sectional interests and serves to cosset domestic industry rather than forcing it to be efficient. As long as the government accurately reflects the interests of the dominant classes, the hard decisions necessary for rapid industrialisation will not be taken. The recent liberalisations are unlikely to have a significant impact on this situation.

CONCLUSIONS

One of the important analytical points to emerge from this study is the error of "policy voluntarism." It is correct to conceive of the problem of growth in capitalist societies as one of choosing the correct set of government policies. Economic (and other) policies arise out of particular social conditions. This is a trite statement, but it is extraordinary to find large numbers of economists who make policy prescriptions that are doomed to failure from the beginning because they are not consistent with the pattern of class dominance. The fundamental thrust towards industrial growth and development grows out of the impersonal and largely uncontrollable social forces that make up history. Within these constraints economic policies can make a difference, sometimes an important difference, and as hinted in the country case studies above, the state can help *to create* the classes that will carry out industrialisation. But this leaves us with the questions of the *sort* of state that will be interested in such acts of creation, why they are interested, and whether they can be successful. In this light it is little wonder that the simple-minded World Bank formula of "get the prices right" has more often than not foundered on the rock of hostile class interests.

The error of policy voluntarism is allied with another error of received economic opinion of the World Bank variety, that of the negative influence on growth of government involvement in the economy. The simple data of Table 6, column 1 and a wealth of further evidence demonstrate that economic growth is not necessarily inhibited by government involvement. We have previously pointed to the case of South Korea where the extent of government ownership and regulation at detailed levels of the economy have been used to maximise the efficient growth of the economy. It is not the quantity of government intervention and planning that matters but its quality. In the successful NICs the quality has been consistently high while the quantity has varied considerably. The quality of government intervention and planning is less a product of the educational levels of government officials than of the independence of these officials and their political masters from sectional influences. Corruption, nepotism, undue outside influence, the lack of an overall vision and motivation, bureaucratic parochialism, officiousness, and political weakness all contribute to low-quality planning.

The present study has had two purposes. The first has been to lay down an analytical framework for making sensible assessments of the growth prospects of nations. The second has been to apply this framework to the eight selected countries. A summary of the arguments for each country can be found in Table 8, where each factor is denoted favourable (F) or unfavourable (U) in its likely impact on future growth. An overall assessment of future prospects on a scale of 1 to 5, from "poor" to "good," appears for each country at the foot of the table.

Both Indonesia and the Philippines have poor overall growth prospects, principally because of the economic and political dominance of classes which derive wealth from unproductive activities and the structural unwillingness of their governments to attack these classes. The growth prospects of Nepal are poor for similar reasons, although there the problem is compounded by the relative absence of opportunities for productive investments.

TABLE 8   **Summary of Economic and Political Conditions**

	Indonesia	Philippines	Malaysia	Thailand	Nepal	Bangladesh	Pakistan	India
1. State of world economy	U	—	U	F	—	U	F	F
2. Availability of savings								
Domestic savings rate	F	F	F	F	U	U	U	F
Access to foreign loans	F	U	F	—	U	—	U	F
Financial intermediation	U	U	F	F	F	F	F	F
3. Productiveness of investments								
Quality of workforce	—	F	F	—	U	U	U	F
Control of workforce	F	U	U	F	F	F	F	U
Labour costs	U	F	U	U	F	F	U	F
Quality of management	U	F	F	—	U	U	F	F
Infrastructure	F	U	F	U	U	—	F	—
4. Sympathy of agriculture	F	F	F	F	U	U	F	F
5. Political conditions								
Dominance of unproductive classes	U	F	F	F	U	F	F	F
Independence of state	U	U	F	—	U	U	F	U
Strength of state	F	U	U	F	F	—	U	U
Proven commitment to growth	U	U	U	F	U	F	U	U
Overall growth prospects	2	1	4	5	1	2	3	3

NOTE: U = unfavourable; F = favourable; 1 = poor; 3 = doubtful; 5 = good.

In Bangladesh, while faced with economic difficulties similar to Nepal's, including the unsympathetic character of agriculture, the prospects are a little better in so far as the state is more independent of the interests of unproductive classes. India has fewer of the political advantages of Bangladesh but has improved chances due to high availability of savings and productive investment opportunities, and an agricultural system that is more amenable to the rapid structural changes that industrialisation brings about.

Pakistan has overall prospects similar to India's but for different reasons. Agriculture is sympathetic to industrial development, and recent industrial and infrastructural growth provide a foundation for future growth. While the government is relatively independent of wealthy interests it does not have firm control over civil order and economic policy. As a result, sufficient savings to finance industrial expansion are likely to be increasingly difficult to obtain.

Malaysia is rated as having better prospects. It has a political system that is relatively independent of the influence of unproductive classes, although there remains doubt over whether the government is sufficiently strong to take the steps necessary to restrain the emergent Malay capitalist class. The agricultural system has the required flexibility but the degree of control over labour is questionable.

Thailand appears to have the best prospects of the eight countries surveyed, with a strong political structure and a demonstrated willingness to make hard decisions. There remains some danger that finance capital may, in times of difficulty, withdraw from industrial investments, particularly since there is some doubt about available investment opportunities. While the flexibility of agriculture and current debt problems raise further doubts, the quality of Thai planning should see it through.

NOTES

1. Clive Hamilton, "Price Formation and Class Relations in the Development Process," *Journal of Contemporary Asia*, 17, 1, (1987) pp. 2–18.
2. World Bank, *World Development Report 1986*, Washington, D.C. 1986.
3. ILO, *Yearbook of Labour Statistics*, Geneva 1985.
4. Clive Hamilton, "Capitalist Industrialisation in East Asia's Four Little Tigers," *Journal of Contemporary Asia*, 13, 1 (1983).
5. F. Halim, "Rural Labour Force and Industrial Conflict in West Malaysia," *Journal of Contemporary Asia*, 11, 3 (1981).
6. Anne Booth and R. M. Sundrum, *Labour Absorption in Agriculture* (Oxford: Oxford University Press, 1986).
7. Ibid.
8. Ibid.

9. J. A. C. Mackie, "Economic Growth in the ASEAN Region: The Political Underpinnings," paper prepared for the Industrialisation Workshop, NCDS, Australian National University, Canberra ACT.
10. Hamilton, "Capitalist Industrialisation," op. cit.
11. Mackie, "Economic Growth," op. cit.
12. Richard Robison, *Indonesia: The Rise of Capital* (Sydney: Allen and Unwin, 1986).
13. Hamilton, "Capitalist Industrialisation," op. cit.

22

The State and Industrial Strategy

Helen Shapiro
Harvard Business School, Boston, Massachusetts
and
Lance Taylor
Massachusetts Institute of Technology, Cambridge

1. INTRODUCTION

The debate about industrial strategy in the economic development literature has always been charged. During the past decade, the voltage rose as
planners faced a rapidly changing global economy at the same time as their
ability to act domestically was curtailed by fiscal constraints. Meanwhile,
two neoclassically based attacks against state intervention were vigorously
mounted in the 1970s and 1980s, and a reaction is getting under way. These
shifts in objective circumstances and intellectual foundations notwithstanding, the fact remains that industrial strategies continue to be pursued—all
governments intervene to shape their economies' productive structures by
default or design.

  The goal of this paper is to set out guidelines not only about how governments should select industrial strategies, but also how they should make
the difficult transition from one policy regime to another when that
becomes desirable or necessary. We begin our discussion by reviewing
"old" views (circa 1960) of the role of the state, and the two waves of neoclassical attack. A countercritique is put forth, emphasizing the specificity
of each country's industrial experience. "Boundary conditions" to successful policies are addressed, which lead to generalizations about the strategy
lines different kinds of economies might pursue.

The arguments in Sections 2 and 3 are presented in more detail in Shapiro (1988) and the ones
in Sections 4 and 5 draw on a paper prepared by Taylor for UNU/WIDER conference on medium-term adjustment held in Helsinki, August 8–11, 1988. Comments by George Lodge and
Thomas McCraw on a previous draft are gratefully acknowledged. From *World Development*,
18, 6 (1990), pp. 861–78. Copyright © Pergamon Press. Printed in Great Britain.

2. THE ROLE OF THE STATE

Industrial strategy rests upon directed public interventions at the sectoral or firm level, aimed at stimulating particular lines of economic endeavor. Microeconomic "targeting" of policies toward particular sectors is necessarily involved. The state may also undertake economy-wide actions complementary to the sectoral thrusts. *All* governments engage in industrial strategy in this sense. Historically, no country has entered into modern economic growth without the state's targeted intervention or collaboration with large-scale private sector entities.

(a) Industrial Strategy: The Development Theorists' View

Alexander Gerschenkron (1962) was among the first to postulate conditions that lead economies to follow different strategy lines. Based on his study of European industrialization, he argued that a country's economic position relative to more advanced nations directly influenced the nature of the state's intervention in its development process. In particular, the English industrial revolution was not a model for those that followed. Its own success guaranteed that all subsequent attempts would significantly vary.

Because it came first and embodied relatively unsophisticated technology, England's industrialization was more gradual and less capital intensive than its followers. The rapid pace of technical change and the widening disparities between their actual and potential rates and levels of economic development dictated other paths for countries in the then-periphery. Germany, Italy, and Russia were likely to jump immediately into the most modern industrial sectors, characterized by capital intensity and scale economies. In these economies, however, capital was scarce and diffused, and the entrepreneurial class either risk averse or financially weak.

Different initial conditions engendered diverse institutional forms and sectoral compositions when industrial growth got under way. In the follower countries, Gerschenkron suggested that the state itself had to substitute for the market and "force" industrialization. Whereas the government's role in an "autonomous" development effort was largely restricted to creating a suitable environment for private capital, in the followers the state became more directly involved with the extraction and allocation of resources, and the establishment and management of firms. Greater "relative backwardness" led to more widespread public intervention to overcome economic inertia.

Throughout the 1960s, economists more directly concerned than Gerschenkron with development policy shared a consensus favoring state intervention, based on different but related criteria. The Keynesian revolution, which cast doubt on the market's ability to achieve optimal results, was used to legitimize economic planning. Keynes's emphasis on domestic economic prosperity as opposed to international concerns was extended to support national industrialization strategies in the Third World.

Development economics arose as a separate field of study following these Keynesian precepts. It also incorporated Schumpeter's (1934) distinction between structural economic change (or "development" in his usage) and mere growth. General equilibrium theory, it was argued, could not describe the dynamic heart of the process—long-run development would not automatically flow from decentralized, optimal decision making in the short run. Hirschman (1958) and others saw development as a sequence of punctuated disequilibria. An investment project could create opportunities for others elsewhere, either by raising profits for industries downstream by lowering their costs of production or by making it possible to take advantage of scale economies by expanding the market or inducing greater specialization among firms. An individual investor's profit and loss calculus could not adequately capture such social benefits (or costs). As Allyn Young (1928) had emphasized early on, dynamic externalities arising from investment could move the system away from equilibrium in ways that comparative static analysis could never take into account.

Scitovsky (1954) explained the conditions required for the price mechanism to achieve optional dynamic allocation: complete and functioning markets, an absence of increasing returns, and complete tradability. Empirical study showed that these conditions did not obtain in less developed countries (LDCs). Those economies were plagued with structural rigidities. Wages and exchange rates were singled out as not reflecting true opportunity costs. Private costs to investors supposedly exceeded social opportunity costs, understating industry's social return. Beginning with the work of Prebisch (1950), the Latin American structuralist school emphasized institutional barriers preventing free factor mobility and productivity growth. Development, therefore, would require creating the conditions under which capitalism could work, i.e., functioning labor and capital markets and national market integration.

From a planning perspective, Chenery (1961) and others showed how optimality of a free trade regime depended on the absence of market imperfections (including economies of scale). Singer (1950) and Prebisch (1959) embellished this work by arguing that static comparative advantage as revealed by current prices could not capture secular trends. Differences in price and income elasticities for primary and manufactured goods meant that raw material exports could not pay for manufactured imports in the long run. The supposed inevitability of future foreign exchange shortages provided an argument for industrialization not easily read from current relative prices.

Distinct viewpoints are evident in the 30-year-old literature, but a perception of development as a process of dynamic, nonmarginal change united all the authors. Required investments are lumpy and (in a poor country) large in comparison to savings flows or even the national capital stock. Although it may provide adequate signals for marginal changes, the price mechanism cannot guide "big" industrial decisions, nor can it be relied upon to induce the resource transfer necessary for industrialization. Public interventions are required both to support investors (via protection, subsidies, cheap credits, etc.) and to invest directly to break critical bottlenecks. A greater extent of market failure in less developed as opposed to richer economies provides the basic rationale for expanding the scope of state intervention.

These theoretical arguments also justified import-substitution schemes already in process. Export-led growth was inconceivable to Third World technocrats and politicians who had witnessed (and seen their economies strongly affected by) the collapse of raw material prices and world trade in the 1930s. Trade expansion continued to look bleak in the mid-1950s while Europe was rebuilding and its currencies were still not fully convertible. Confronting foreign exchange constraints, many countries shifted their economic focus to the domestic market. Industrialization was also in the interest of the political coalitions that emerged in newly formed states. In this environment, development banks, state-owned enterprises, and industrial targeting arose naturally in the developing world.

(b) Neoclassical Reactions

There were at least two major problems with the literature just reviewed. One is that while it was rich with diagnoses of why backward economies do not develop, it offered limited guidance as to how the government was to intervene to set things right. Planning tools such as social cost-benefit analysis and programming models soon proved unable to blueprint industrial growth. More fundamentally, the development theorists tacitly assumed that the state had unlimited capacity to intervene in the economic system. Its failure to carry out its assigned developmental role(s) became apparent, almost equally quickly. While doubt about the adequacy of the market was the main thrust of the first wave of dissent, the development economists' unstated beliefs about the nature of the state and its capacity to intervene became the target of the second attack.

P. T. Bauer (1972, 1984) was prescient in pointing out these problems. Generalizing from his experience in India, he had articulated most of the 1980s vintage criticisms of an expanded public sector 20 years before. He not only considered government failure, i.e., corruption and mismanagement, more critical than market failure, but reversed the direction of causality: intervention *caused* and did not cure market imperfections. Implicitly, he assumed the market mechanism capable of self-correction. Bauer was especially fearful of the adverse political consequences he thought were associated with concentration of economic power by the state.

Toye (1987) is correct in dubbing Bauer "a pioneer of the counterrevolution," but Bauer was distinctly a lone wolf until the first neoclassical reaction put traditional development economics squarely on the defensive. This initial blow was aimed at the state's capacity to guide structural change. Using new analytical tools from trade theory such as effective rates of protection and domestic resource costs, Little, Scitovsky, and Scott (1970) showed that industrial strategies were inefficient—the incentives they created were highly unequal for different economic actors. These authors and their successors sought (how successfully is taken up below) to correlate "distorted" policy regimes with poor economic performance. Read between the lines, they advocated laissez faire as the only viable alternative to an incentive mare's nest.

This neoclassical critique was bolstered by the success of export-oriented countries such as South Korea and Taiwan, which at the time were thought to have noninterventionist states. Their rapid growth in comparison to economies which followed import-substitution strategies seemed to provide empirical validation for Harry Johnson's (1967) earlier claims that dynamic gains could be had from free trade. An avid follower, Anne Krueger (1984) later explained that: "From a theory without any evidence in the early 1960's suggesting departures from free trade for dynamic reasons, the tables are turned; empirical evidence strongly suggests dynamic factors that may be associated with export-led growth" (p. 139). Export expansion somehow spurred by market liberalization became the industrialization strategy of choice.

Work around the turn of the decade by Krueger, Balassa (1971), and others was not so much anti-intervention as anti-import substitution. The debate between old-style development economists and more orthodox theorists still centered on market failure. It focused on whether to intervene, and with the exception of Bauer and a few isolated voices from the Left—Galbraith (1964) and Myrdal (1970)—the protagonists stopped well short of denying the state's political and institutional capacity to fulfill its prescribed role. That more radical claim came with the second phase of counterrevolution.

The "neoclassical political economy" of the 1980s explicitly attacks the early development economists' implicit belief in the efficacy of government intervention. Lal (1983) is a representative introduction. Echoing Bauer, he contends that "bureaucratic failure" may be worse than "market failure." Other authors set up formal models of the interaction between state and economy to show how government intervention is likely to produce inefficiencies. State policy is endogenized to the general equilibrium system by depicting it as the outcome of individual optimizing behavior in the political realm. Srinivasan (1985) classifies this effort under three heads: Mancur Olson's collective action framework, Buchanan's public choice school, and related work on trade, development, and economic history.

Olson (1982) argues that due to bargaining costs and the problem of free riders, individuals are unlikely to organize in their collective interest unless they are in small groups and/or can impose selective incentives on group members. Such coalitions of self-interested persons are likely to try to redistribute income toward themselves instead of working to raise efficiency and national income, the full benefits of which they will not receive. In stable (or static) societies, politics will increasingly be organized to cater to these interests. Efficient resource allocation will be inhibited, and by extension there will be no incentives for Schumpeterian entrepreneurs to seek out technical innovations that might speed overall growth.

While Olson is primarily concerned with the implications of his coalitions for growth and social change, Buchanan (1980) is specific about the economic losses that result from profit seeking in the presence of the state. The "public choice" school argues that the emergence of monopoly and other distortions from public policy does more than impose a deadweight loss on the economy (as measured by the famous "little triangles" of comparative statics). Competition for rents which accrue to the winners of government largesse turns into widespread "directly unproductive profit-seeking" (DUP, pronounced dupe) activities, in Bhagwati's (1982) phrase. Examples include lobbying, active politics, bribe paying, etc. Since almost any state intervention opens space for a rent (import quotas, traffic cops, defense contracts—the list is endless), the risk is that seeking government favors will override normal market activity. Rational rent seeking by individuals can produce extreme suboptimality for the economy as a whole.

Krueger's (1974) article on rent seeking and Buchanan's extension of deadweight loss calculations have been widely applied in the trade and development area. Krueger emphasized quantitative restrictions placed on imports. Firms will compete for import licenses and their attached rents: "To the extent that rent-seeking is competitive, the welfare cost of import restrictions is equal to the welfare cost of the tariff equivalent *plus the additional cost of rent-seeking activities.*"

More recent contributions have attributed DUP activity to those seeking to set up particular policies in the first place. Actors within the government itself may enter the fray, as do bureaucrats in Bardhan's (1984) extension of this line of thought to the Indian state. In his view, conflicts between bureaucrats and industrialists over appropriation of rents interact with India's traditional rural-urban disparities to perpetuate stagnation. Like other explanations of the slow "Hindu rate of growth," Bardhan's theory is to an extent belied by the improved performance of the large, distorted, and closed Indian economy after the early 1980s.

With regard to industrial strategy, rent seeking has strong implications. Inward-oriented development, by definition, relies upon market restrictions and state intervention, which supposedly create an environment more congenial to DUP than a more open, export-promoting policy line. The theory thus arrives at another explanation for the relative success of export-promoting strategies: the state is less involved so the economy is less prone to DUP. A generalization is that freer trade and factor mobility reduce rent seeking by restraining the interests and making cartels harder to maintain. The success of South Korea, where everyone now admits that the government has been extremely interventionist, is explained by its use of policy tools associated with external orientation which allowed for greater market play. The pressures of international competition are supposed to mitigate the worst sort of rent seeking observed in countries practicing pure import-substituting industrialization (ISI).

Douglass North's (1981) work on economic history can serve as a final example of the new neoclassical approach. The state, for North, becomes its own "vested interest group," creating a tradeoff between economic efficiency and state power. Paul Kennedy's (1987) subsequent best-selling discourse on military spending twists this line of thought into a vicious circle—the effort to be a great power induces internal economic tensions which make great power status ever harder to sustain.

North argues that specification of property rights is the key explanatory variable for economic performance, subject to technological constraints. He arrives at this view via the well-known Coase (1937) theorem, which shows that if property rights are well-specified and transaction costs are zero, individuals will face correct incentives and free trade will lead to efficient resource allocation among them. North endogenizes institutional change and a theory of the state to account for the persistence of inefficient property rights: economic and political efficiency are equivalent only when this condition coincides with the state's objectives. For example, because of transaction costs such as monitoring, the state may choose to raise its revenue by creation and taxation (or direct management) of a monopoly. The state may marshal ideological arguments to support its ends, but be opposed by nonfavored firms or people who strive for an alternative regime. Tension is inevitable in the presence of a Northian (or Bardhanian) state.

To summarize, there is no question that the DUP school is correct in emphasizing that state intervention, for reasons both intended and unforeseen, does not necessarily lead to efficient outcomes, in either a static or dynamic sense. Moreover, the state's enormous presence means that its actions change the environment in which firms and people operate in unexpected (and unexpectable) ways. Ironically, the early development economists did not perceive these problems because they accepted the traditional neoclassical separation of the economic and political spheres. Basically, they did not contemplate a theory of the state.

Before the new critique surfaced, neoclassical theory at least assumed that markets function, presupposing a minimal "night watchman" role for the government. In contrast, the omission of the state as an explicit actor is a fundamental flaw in the development theorists' argument, since they relied upon the state as an agent of change and presumed that it had the requisite political autonomy and administrative tools to carry out the task. In the presence of widespread market failure, the superior capacity of government functionaries to allocate resources became an article of faith. The state's ability to undertake sectoral targeting and its fiscal capacity for direct intervention were taken for granted.

The question remains, however, whether the neoclassical political economy model is any more relevant than the one it seeks to discredit.

3. ELEMENTS OF A CRITIQUE

The new literature reveals a number of shortcomings. We take up the economics of public intervention first, then go on to criticize the positive theory of the state that the neoclassical authors propose, and finally bring in perspectives on industrial strategy from other social sciences.

(*a*) The Economics of State Interventions

As we observed in connection with Little, Scitovsky, and Scott's (1970) book, two linked ideas are central to the neoclassical perspective: (1) elimination of distortions will enhance economic efficiency in Pareto's sense, and (2) increased efficiency will in turn lead to better macroeconomic performance, conventionally measured by the rate of growth of GDP. Solid support for either proposition is difficult to find.

With regard to "getting the prices right," a balanced judgment is that such a step frequently may be a necessary condition for enhanced microeconomic supply performance, but is scarcely ever sufficient. For example, such findings appear in 18 country studies of stabilization and adjustment programs organized by the World Institute for Development Economics Research (WIDER), reviewed by Taylor (1988). Several country cases of trade improvements were associated with price reform *in conjunction with* public interventions such as aggregate demand manipulation, export subsidies, public investment, and barter trade deals, but in other countries price reform alone produced poor results.

At issue is Gerschenkron's long-forgotten point about backwardness and inertia: more than a market signal is required to displace the previous "equilibrium" in order to make nontraditional export markets and investment projects attractive. An established rule of thumb among agricultural economists is that an anticipated 30–40 % rate of return plus other incentives are required to make farmers switch to a new, untried crop. Similar generalizations no doubt apply in industry; especially in poor countries, the state is (or was, in many parts of the world) the only entity with deep enough pockets to make beyond-market incentives sufficiently sweet. It is also the only entity with broad enough coercive powers to make credible threats to actors throughout the economy when they fail to perform.

Whether enhanced micro efficiency, if attained, significantly raises the growth rate is a methodologically thorny issue to address. Any quantitative judgment requires a counterfactual reference point. Little triangle estimates of the welfare gains from eliminating distortions have remained stubbornly small ever since Harberger (1959) broached the question in a serious way. One side effect of the invention of rent seeking was to increase the welfare gains by widening their base (*vide* the Krueger quotation above), but the Ptolemaic fallacy begins to arise: you add epicycles to the model to get the result you desire. Any moderately clever general equilibrium modeler can also make the triangles shrink.

As discussed in more detail below, econometric results are also not informative. Relating growth performance to increased exports (as a proxy for liberalization?) has become an active cottage industry. However, most regressions of the GDP growth rate on the export growth rate come up with a coefficient about the size of the export share (as would follow from differentiating the national product identity). Raising the coefficient by making export growth "explain" a Solow-Denison technical progress residual à la Feder (1983) is a regression fallacy: one trending variable relates to any other with close but meaningless goodness of fit.

More fundamentally, the neoclassical isomorphisms between absence of distortions, efficiency, and growth are ahistorical and timeless. They fail to account for the experience of the advanced capitalist economies, as Schumpeter with his emphasis on entrepreneurs and innovations recognized long ago. During the industrialization push in all now-rich countries, public interventions were rife. Horowitz (1977) shows that US courts restricted individuals' control over property; decisions came to favor community property over absolute domain. While the court actions served the general welfare, they violated Buchanan's strict conditions for Pareto optimality. The Handlins (1969) and Hartz (1948) demonstrate that although they were constrained by the constitution in their choice of instruments, US state legislatures controlled exports and granted monopoly power to public corporations.

At the federal level, industrial interventions in the United States during the nineteenth century were huge. The government targeted railroads and farmers with land give-aways (millions of acres to the railway companies and 240 acres to the farm families who avoided speculation), and was highly protectionist until after World War II. Following the Meiji Restoration, the Japanese state set itself up as entrepreneur, financier, and manager in several manufacturing lines. Its activist role continued throughout the militarist period and after World War II in the famous industrial programming of MITI. Although different in form and character, interventionist policies continue in the United States. Despite its pro-market rhetoric, the government continues to direct American production capacity and technical advance to support both military and economic ends. Boeing would not be Boeing, nor would IBM be IBM, in either military or commercial endeavors, without Pentagon contracts and civilian research support.

Returning to the developing economies, the key issue is what form the Gerschenkronian challenge to industrialize may take. At present, the international arena presents new opportunities (and constraints) to LDCs, but they can only be seized (and evaded) by timely and versatile policy moves. Dynamic gains from trade may not be available to, nor the export-promotion strategy warranted for, every economy. Fishlow (1986) and Cline (1982) propose a series of counterarguments about the institutional requirements for export-led growth, the nature of traditional exports (the elasticities, and much more important, as argued below, the possibilities of extending industrial activity downstream), and the potential fallacy of composition if all LDCs attempt trade expansion.

The success of an outward-oriented development scheme is contingent on structural conditions that cannot be taken for granted. Boratav's (1988) WIDER study shows that Turkey's export "miracle" in the first part of the 1980s rested upon a preexisting industrial base created by ISI, policies leading to contraction of domestic demand for manufactures, attempts at general price reform, subsidies of up to one-third of export sales plus related incentives, and rapid growth in demand for the products the country could produce by culturally compatible buyers in the region (the Gulf countries and both sides in the Iran-Iraq war). Had any one of these factors been missing, the boom probably would not have occurred.

Turkey's and other experiences with ISI suggest that this strategy need not lead to results as dismal as is often claimed. Fishlow (1986) shows how disaggregation reveals divergent histories in Latin America. During 1965–73, Brazil's GDP grew at 9.8% annually; Mexico's grew at 7.9%. For 1970–80, the rates were 8.4 and 5.2% respectively. Median growth rates for East Asia (South Korea, Taiwan, Indonesia, Malaysia, the Philippines, and Thailand) during these periods were 8.3 and 8.0%. More fundamentally, evaluating performance by comparing growth rates does not make a lot of sense—"fast" or "slow" growth depends on the basis for comparison and the relative stage of development. Brazil is not Korea; in another popular contrast, India is not Korea or even China.

The international environment also complicates the task of neoclassical political theory. In particular, domestic DUP activity is not the only distortion of free markets that occurs. The existence of transnational corporations (TNCs), strong oligopolies in certain world markets, unequal access to technology, and other factors contradict the basic assumptions of free trade. Helleiner (1990) and other exponents of the strategic trade models that have recently appeared show how economic rents need not be competed away in the presence of economies of scale, and how intervention may be Pareto superior to laissez faire. Empirical studies demonstrate that these complications affect industrial structure and performance. The ways in which leading sectors develop change with the context, and correspondingly have different macro-level effects. The implications for DUP models are manifold. The need for the state to bargain effectively with the TNCs complicates North's story: the case studies in Newfarmer (1985) give a good feel for the difficulties that can arise. DeVries (1983) points out in criticizing Olson that coalitions may arise to meet challenges during periods of stagnation and not cause them.

The basic problem is again one of counterfactuals: in attacking the government, neoclassical political economy posits an idealized market in its stead. This easily manipulable base for comparisons simply does not exist, as numerous counterexamples show. TNCs may (or may not) enhance efficiency, but they surely carry economic and political clout. Chicago-based literature on regulation stresses that the market itself generates its own rent seeking entities and redistributions of income. There is a peculiar asymmetry in the DUP models, whereby individuals coalesce to force a political redistribution, but do not do the same in the marketplace. The political arena is depicted full of lobbyists and cartel builders, while the economy is presented as being more or less subject to competition. Despite greater putative openness under a liberal trade regime, there is no guarantee that an export-promotion strategy is any less subject to DUP activity than import substitution. So-called fictional exports mushroomed in Turkey during the 1980s, as firms bought up emigrant remittances to turn in the hard currency along with doctored invoices to skim extra profits off the spate of export subsidy flows.

(b)   The Absent Neoclassical State

As they reify the market, the neoclassical political economists elide an explicit discussion of the state, despite their claim to making public action an endogenous variable. Their argument presupposes a passive, pluralist state that is acted upon by interest groups with equal access to its largesse. Indeed, the characteristics of the favors that it distributes are often not fully specified, although general equilibrium implications differ. Blomqvist and Mohammad (1986) show how levels of efficiency loss are affected by the line of production in which rent receivers engage, while Barbone (1985) argues that changes in the level of wealth implicit in the claim to an import quota affect aggregate demand.

Besides the nature of the state's favors, the specific groups to whom they are distributed will have economic and political implications. Bowles and Eatwell (1983), Barry (1983), and Cameron (1983) all argue that neoclassical political economy posits a peculiar counterfactual combining a nonpolitically organized society with an ideal liberal state, completely neutral with regard to distribution. Potential conflicts between universal suffrage and capitalism as well as the importance of liberal, democratic institutions for social (and therefore economic) stability are ignored.

The pluralist model is inapplicable to many developing countries, e.g., Brazil. There, throughout this century the state has never been the passive favor dispenser of the DUP literature. In the 1950s, it attempted to insulate itself from interest group pressure, but also created new interest groups by virtue of its interventions (Shapiro, 1988). If the state has some degree of autonomy, it need not resort to authoritarianism to eliminate DUP activity, as neoclassical authors like Lal (1983) suggest. Stable policy is another tool: if the government establishes credibility in its commitment to a particular policy line (e.g., expansion of the automobile industry in Brazil), DUP activity in that area will be ineffective and tend to wane.

Under certain conditions, the state itself may be able to extract rents from the private sector and shape investment behavior, possibilities that neoclassical political economy does not recognize (see Shapiro, 1988). Its standard assumption that individuals foresee the future perfectly with at most random errors flies in the face of the rigidities and risks of the Third World, where consequences of political and economic change are largely unknown. An important intervention, discussed more fully below, is public investment. Recent evidence suggests that public projects "crowd in" private investment via complementarities, rather than crowding it out by driving up interest rates (a market signal). In another area, one has to explain how both directed incentives and public investment have been orchestrated to transform ISI into export promotion in South Korea and elsewhere. Externalities and the uses of policies to reduce fundamental uncertainty about economic affairs have to be built explicitly into any credible theory of the developing country state.

As mentioned above, neoclassical authors lean toward authoritarianism as a device to preclude special interests from taking over the state. Lal's judgment is famous: "A courageous, ruthless, and perhaps undemocratic government is required to ride roughshod over these newly-created special interest groups" (1983, p. 33). Findlay (1986) blurs the issue but without explicitly discussing the nature of the state; he implies that the emergence of authoritarianism in South Korea and Brazil explained their shift toward export orientation. By contrast, from the field of political science, O'Donnell's (1973) bureaucratic-authoritarian model for Latin America at least tried to explain *why* military regimes were inclined to open their economies to international finance, and why democracy was no longer compatible with economic growth.

The underlying neoclassical suspicion that democracy is not compatible with economic growth unwittingly echoes some Marxist theories of the state. Offe (1974) and Offe and Ronge (1975) have analyzed the inherent contradiction between the capitalist state's primary concerns: accumulation of capital and political legitimacy. Fiscal crises along O'Connor's (1973) lines are brought forth. For example, an argument heard often in Brazil is that keeping up investment and satisfying popular demands under a fiscal constraint may simply be beyond the competence of the state (Weffort, 1978; Malloy, 1987).

The subtle difficulty with both the Marxist and neoclassical frameworks is that recognizing a potential contradiction between democracy and economic expansion in no way implies a logical affinity between authoritarian states and capitalist growth. Nor is democracy necessarily correlated with a poor growth record—there are at least moderately successful social democracies at all income levels around the world. The combination of dictatorship and outstanding economic performance, when it appears, is due to particular conditions in particular states, which must be specified. In his classic study of dictatorship and democracy, Barrington Moore (1966) saw affinities between the rise of democratic institutions and capitalism. Recent authors find an indeterminate relationship between economic policy and political regime, e.g., Haggard (1985) on the linkages between political regimes and the sorts of economic stabilization programs they apply.

The neoclassical faith in authoritarianism finally proves inconsistent in several ways. Lal (1983) is the first to point out that bureaucrats have no special talent for running an economy, but presumably they would be called upon to do so (at least at second hand) in his authoritarian state. They would have to be nonarbitrary in their use of concentrated power. Authoritarian regimes as actually observed do not behave in such ideal fashion. Latin American military rulers were not notably efficient, and demonstrated that the distribution of spoils is not a civilian monopoly. Olson (1982), predictably, sees the difficulties of Latin American states in exercising control as arising from excessively powerful interest groups seeking industrial protection to the detriment of agriculture. A more plausible view is that despite superficial regime changes, Latin America suffers from too much stability in its class and institutional structure.

(c) Other Perspectives

Briefly, it is worth noting that the social science literature outside of economics had drawn a whole different set of conclusions from the experience of later industrializers such as Japan (Johnson, 1982) and South Korea. This body of work frequently argues that sensible policy and the institutional means by which to implement it are the keys to a successful industrial strategy. In the tradition of Gerschenkron, effective institutional change is the critical explanatory factor for self-sustaining growth. From this angle, the debate about state intervention becomes sterile when it is waged entirely in market vs. nonmarket terms. Those who credit the invisible hand in all success cases have biased vision: if an economy grows rapidly, they see market forces in action; if it grows slowly, bad public policy is at fault. Those at the other extreme reduce economic development to a problem of domestic institution building. Structural constraints may be posed by the domestic and international economies, but they are ultimately nonbinding.

Such narrow frameworks are reminiscent of the earlier debate on mercantilism. Whether fiscalism built up national states at the expense of economic development was defined by Heckscher as a tradeoff between "power versus plenty." Along North's lines, a conflict of interest between the crown and the merchant class was presumed. But as Wilson (1967) remarks:

> It seems doubtful whether the controversy is a very fruitful one. For it becomes plain as soon as we try to define what "mercantilists" meant by "power" that they were thinking of a political system which rested on an economic base and had certain economic ends. Equally, "plenty" was thought of in relation to politics and strategy. "Wealth" was not merely an economic conception; it had to be of a character that would coincide with and reinforce the strength of the nation and its capacity to defend itself . . . "Power and Plenty," that is to say, were not mutually exclusive conceptions but complementary conceptions (p. 495).

The question becomes one of what conditions created the "fiscal desperation" (p. 494) of Spain, or the British fiscalism that "seemed to move in parallel with powerful private and public interests and was less evidently damaging to economic development . . . " (p. 521). What applies to visible fiscalism applies to the invisible hand as well.

4. BOUNDARY CONDITIONS

There are examples of successful industrial strategies in both the developed and developing economies, but many such initiatives have failed for both political and economic reasons. Some of the successes seem to be associated with authoritarian regimes, others with democratic institutions. Institutional responsiveness seems central to success. Can anything more definite be said about sensible strategies in specific contexts in the developing world?

In this section, arguing mainly on economic grounds, we try to describe more concretely the circumstances in which certain industrial policies may (or may not) have a chance for success. The argument is organized in terms of context-dependent "patterns" of industrial change that have been observed, and associated "boundary conditions" delimiting the sort of policies that it makes sense to use in specific national cases. We concentrate on seven sets of conditions, discussed roughly in order of ease of quantification: country size, internal vs. external orientation, labor skills, wages and income distribution, the fiscal and managerial capacity of the state, the economy's industrial heritage, and productivity growth and access to technology. Other factors such as the nature of the bureaucracy also influence the prospects for successful policy implementation, as discussed by Evans (1989).

(*a*) Country Size

The size of a country, best measured by population, influences its industrial prospects. This insight is old (dating to Werner Sombart at least) and has been elaborated econometrically by Hollis Chenery and coauthors, e.g., Chenery, Robinson, and Syrquin (1986). Chenery's statistical approach relies on both continuous relationships and sample splits. His most fruitful division has been between "large" and "small" nations, with the frontier at a population of (say) 20 million. The equations fit better for large countries: they seem to follow a more uniform pattern of industrial change. This observation is consistent with the importance of specialized, niche-oriented industrial strategies for small, open economies, as discussed below.

The econometric results for a big country can be summarized as follows: it typically enters earlier into import substitution and has a higher manufacturing share of GDP than does a small country at the same per capita income level; it pursues import substitution further into intermediate and capital goods and producers' services. The statistically "typical" large country's import and export shares of GDP are likely to be around 10% (with a standard deviation of about the same size; Korea is far more open than the norm) while a small country's shares may be more than one-half.

Both the regressions and (more importantly) country histories suggest that big countries exploit import-substitute-then-export (ISTE) strategies in manufacturing. The basic premise is that big, protected markets permit economies of scale and scope. At the same time, they allow the luxury of allocative inefficiency for extended periods of time—high-cost production creates economic loss, but does not represent a binding restriction on inward-oriented growth. In a favorable context, a statically inefficient industrial sector may become the base for breaking into the world trade with import-substituting products, as Turkey's example in the 1980s suggests.

With due regard to our warnings about facile country comparisons, South Korea and Brazil make an interesting contrast. Korea, with its unusually high trade shares, has successfully designed policies to direct the transformation of domestic production for a protected local market into export capability. A highly skilled labor force and rapid growth of a capital stock embodying world-class technology have played a central role. Brazil has historically directed more of its output toward the domestic market and has lower trade shares, e.g., Brazilian commodity exports were about 8% of GDP in the early 1980s, as opposed to South Korea's 38%.

Brazil's industrial strategy has relied on rapid demand growth in the domestic market to generate scale economies and technical change. One disadvantage is that sales prospects at home are more limited than for the world as a whole, and a concentrated income distribution (as discussed below) may be required to support purchases of modern goods. Indeed, there is always a risk that the domestic market will become saturated. Without access to external credit, domestic demand in an ISI strategy cannot grow much faster than exports in the medium to long run, i.e., there are lower bounds on the ratio of imports to GDP. If foreign resource flows decline, the state may be forced to tighten fiscal policy as a "third gap" binds (Bacha, 1980, Taylor, 1989); we take up this problem below. Foreign obligations may be especially vexing if (as in Brazil's case) much technology was imported via TNCs.

An advantage of an inward-oriented industrialization strategy is that it may pay off in terms of an autonomous growth path (less subject to external shocks) in the long run, as Hughes and Singh (1987) emphasize in the cases of India and China. When they occur, external shocks can be offset via domestic recessions which force firms to seek export markets abroad, so long as they have enough dynamism to maintain international competitiveness. This is one of several areas in which industrial and macroeconomic policies interact, favorably in the short run but unfavorably in a longer period if continued recession holds down capital formation, making local production facilities increasingly noncompetitive in the world market (as may have happened in the late 1980s to automobile plants in Brazil).

Since small countries are far more open to foreign trade, they are likely to find the ISTE approach less fruitful. Sector-level inefficiencies can easily degenerate into a binding foreign resource constraint. With benefit of hindsight, one can see that now-prosperous small economies earned foreign exchange by exploiting niches in which they could be efficient producers for export trade, e.g., downstream expansion of forest products plus high-skill/high-tech manufacturing in Canada, Sweden, and Finland, shipping in Norway (before oil), high-tech industry and financial services in Switzerland, etc.

Following the Canadian "staple school" of economic historians (Innis, 1962; Watkins, 1963), Hirschman (1977) raised the practically important question of the growth potential of the resource base. Timber and oil may favor downstream industrial and marketing expansion more than, say, sugar and bauxite. In the long run, local production of such raw materials can lead to capacity to manufacture the relevant capital goods, e.g., paper machines and components for oil refineries or petrochemical plants with associated engineering skills. The policy issues center around manipulating effective protection for downstream activities so that they can develop in an effective fashion.

Building upon a "staple" service is also an option to be explored. Entrepôt trade can be an extremely productive base, as exemplified recently by Hong Kong, a small economy which skipped much import substitution (in part because the Shanghai textile industry migrated there in the wake of the Chinese revolution) and rapidly attained export capability in many lines. Its experience is hard to replicate, however, since Hong Kong follows a prosperous city-state model of great antiquity which is not open to the overwhelming majority of poor countries in the world. For a large nation, an industrial city selling largely to the internal market is a mixed blessing (because of regional disparities, migration flows, etc.) but it is also an omen for general growth—inwardlooking industrialization seems to need an "engine." Hong Kong's metropolitan economic numbers are not more striking than São Paulo's or Bombay's, even though the hinterlands of Brazil and India grow far more slowly than their national city-states.

A special political economy underlies the successful small country approach, as Katzenstein (1985) points out for the prosperous European economies. Historically, the private sector took the lead and absorbed the failures in opening niches, but bankruptcies were cushioned by "oligarchic" politics (close linkages among large industrial firms, labor unions organized from the top down, and a stable state) plus publicly supported safety nets. Small prosperous countries initially practiced protection, but now maintain undistorted trade regimes and adjust to rapid technical change through close cooperation among public, corporate, and labor elites. In Switzerland, Sweden, and the Netherlands, nationally based TNCs are the entrepreneurs in international markets, but depend on the rest of the system. These countries exploit niches not only in manufacturing, but also in financial and other services. Very few small developing economies have started such a transition—Singapore and Hong Kong are the recent success cases (entrepôt trade, finance, and low wage manufacturing) and, for internal political reasons, Lebanon appears to have failed.

(b)   Internal vs. External Orientation

The degree of "openness" of an economy has at least two interpretations: the levels of its trade shares (obviously affected by the nation's size), and the comparative absence of interventionist commercial policies. On both definitions, openness has implications for industrial strategy. But, as we have already seen, just how it influences industrialization and growth is a topic of intense debate.

The mainstream view is that high foreign trade shares—especially exports—in GDP help industrialization; hence, policy should be directed toward eliminating barriers to trade. There is also an increasing body of literature supporting the opposite point of view, e.g., papers from WIDER on the topic include Taylor (1987), Chakravarty and Singh (1988), and Helleiner (1990). The best summary so far is that the debate is inconclusive: an a priori case for either an open or closed trade policy regime can never be fully proved.

As we observed above, this Scotch verdict also applies to the empirical evidence on the relationship between openness and growth (based largely on cross-sectional regressions and computable general equilibrium models in the absence of comparative historical studies). Chenery, Robinson, and Syrquin (1986) present cross-country regressions showing that within country groups based on population and trade specialization in manufactures and primary products, the early GDP growth rates of export-oriented economies were a few tenths of a percent above the overall average during the period 1950–83. Using another grouping based upon per capita GNP and observed growth rates, McCarthy, Taylor, and Talati (1987) show that fast-growing countries did not on average have either high or increasing shares of exports in GDP between 1962 and 1984. Examples are easy to cite: among middle-income countries, Jamaica (12%), Uruguay (5%) and Portugal (16%) have high industrial export shares of GDP and grow slowly; Colombia and Brazil have shares of 2 or 3% and their growth has historically been fast. Poorer countries' growth rates are more subject to the vagaries of capital inflows and primary product trade, but similar observations hold: Cameroon and Egypt have grown fairly rapidly with industrial export shares of about 1%, while slow-growing India (until recently) and Honduras both have shares of 3% or more.

Despite these inconclusive results, the empirical literature does present five boundary conditions that appear to apply fairly widely:

First, and least controversial, the ratios of manufactured to primary products both produced and exported tend to rise as per capita GDP goes up. In a broad sense, industrialization *is* concomitant to economic growth.

Second, trade and output data suggest that at the two-digit level of industrial classification, import substitution usually precedes production for exports, as we have already observed. The lag may be very short as in the case of South Korea (except for automobiles, where the transition took 20 years), but normally one must think in terms of quinquennia or decades. But this sector-average generalization does not rule out the possibility of a country's exporting a particular product the day it begins to be produced.

Third, both production and trade shares vary within narrower ranges in large countries than in small ones, emphasizing the importance of niche-seeking strategies for the great majority of economies in the world. The relatively few large economies that exist shape their industrial structures more in line with domestic demand.

Fourth, countries poor (rich) in natural resources tend to have high (low) shares of industry in both exports and GDP. Japan and Korea on the one hand, and the United States and Brazil on the other are obvious examples.

Finally, Fishlow (1985) raises a useful distinction between "export-led" and "export-adequate" growth. In terms of broad regional distinctions, the labels describe Asian (externally oriented) and Latin American (internally oriented) strategies. The current problem for countries pursuing the latter line is how to regain a viable growth process under fiscal duress.

To summarize, empirical regularities linking country size, observed trade shares, and economic performance help set limits on how policy can affect openness and growth. Boundary conditions suggest that the trade and production patterns of Costa Rica will never resemble Brazil's, for a variety of reasons. The implication is that policy should not be formed in one economy taking a vastly different one as a model. However, if some intervention is effective in (say) Jamaica, it might pay off in Costa Rica as well, since both small, open countries share many of the same limits to growth.

(c)   Labor Skills

There is no question that high skills are required of workers in industrial modes of production—substantial literacy and numeracy are required to produce commodities ranging from Green Revolution wheat to computer codes for microprocessors. Successful industrializers since World War II exemplify the pattern—Korea has virtually complete literacy and world-class ratios of engineers and technically trained persons to the overall population.

The real policy question is how both formal education and on-the-job training can be geared toward industrialization, in a period of tightened budget constraints for most governments in the Third World. Quoting UNESCO data, Schultz (1988) observes that public expenditure on education per child more than doubled during the period 1970–80 in all developing regions, and then decreased in 1982. A fair guess is that educational spending in most poor countries in the late 1980s continued this tendency toward stagnation or decline. Even if industrial jobs can be successfully created, these data suggest that skill constraints may increasingly bind. In a time when most governments are short of cash, policies to encourage the private sector to shoulder a greater share of the national educational effort may be required. Regulatory action supporting on-the-job training and similar activities may partially counteract the state's inability to tax the private sector in this regard.

(d)   Wages and Income Distribution

Evidence from the WIDER studies and elsewhere suggests that progressive income redistribution is likely to stimulate aggregate demand (Taylor, 1988). Compositional shifts may also occur, although country-level evidence suggests that the new commodity basket may be either more or less labor intensive (i.e., wealthier segments of the population who lose in the redistribution may bias their consumption toward either labor-intensive services or capital-intensive commodities, depending on context). There is also likely to be a reduction in import intensity of demand.

These compositional shifts are all relatively weak, so that the short-run effect of redistribution on industrial strategy can probably be ignored. The important conjunctural factor is the change in aggregate demand. It suggests that redistribution can only be pursued up to a certain point, beyond which balance of payments and/or inflation problems arise.

Beyond the conjuncture, dynamic feedbacks become important. Real wages are often central to the distributional process, and their secular growth may be necessary for industrialization in the long run. Now-popular efficiency wage arguments (Bowles and Boyer, 1988, give the radical version) suggest that worker motivation and efficiency depend on good pay. The bulk of demand for advanced products must come from exports or wage income. These linkages mean that which classes gain from productivity increases is an important question. On the one hand, worker motivation and internal demand require real wage increases; on the other, if real wages rise more slowly than productivity, unit labor costs fall, which can help trade. But it is clear that aiming for low wages alone is *not* a viable or sustainable strategy. South Korea would never have shifted its exports from human hair and cheap garments to automobiles and electronics had its wages stayed at the levels of 1955.

(e)   Fiscal and Managerial Capability of the State

The WIDER studies emphasized how in many countries public investment stimulates private capital, via complementarities; the same point is also recognized by the International Monetary Fund (Blejer and Khan, 1984). Recent econometric results support the observation, e.g., Chakravarty (1987) estimates that the "crowding-in coefficient" for public on private investment in Indian agriculture lies between one and two, while Ortiz and Noriega (1988) find a Mexican economy-wide coefficient of one. For a 72-country international cross section, Barro (1989) gets a coefficient of one.

Despite the importance of crowding in, many governments currently find public investment impossible because (even with improved tax performance and current spending cuts) they are fiscally constrained. In the major debtor countries, the public sector owes 5% or more of GDP in external obligations each year—new projects are a luxury impossible to afford. In macro models with three or four gaps (investment crowding in and inflationary pressure can be added to the traditional savings and foreign exchange constraints), Bacha (1990) and Taylor (1989) show that reducing state capital formation may be the only plausible response to output losses and inflation stemming from a tightened foreign exchange constraint. The implications for long-term growth are, needless to say, poor.

Besides fiscal problems, an important empirical question is whether the state can in fact handle all the obligations we have discussed. Theories of how it functions aside, finding an existing government capable of making use of the local resource base, utilizing the advantages and avoiding the problems inherent in the country's size, maintaining an intelligent stance between import substitution and export promotion, seeking export niches, hastening skill creation, and dealing effectively with new technologies like microprocessors is not an easy task. Optimal performance in all areas is impossible. The question is whether the state can effectively cope. Its managerial capacity—even to supervise a regime of laissez faire—is perhaps the most important boundary condition of all.

Here, we can only flag the issue—Evans (1989) takes up some of the problems it creates. But one observation (especially relevant for Africa) follows naturally from the discussion earlier in this paper: arguments for liberal policies may be based on desperation about the capacity of the state. Since the public sector does so badly, the reasoning goes, an unfettered private sector couldn't possibly do worse. This view ignores the objective difficulties—unfavorable ecological conditions, plummeting export volumes and prices, political turmoil—that African and other poor countries have faced, as well as the historical fact that industrialization does not flourish in a fully free-market regime. However, the fact that the private sector is unlikely to create industrialization on its own does not answer the question about how state capacity can be improved. Even under favorable macroeconomic conditions, a painful learning process is likely to be involved.

(f) Industrial Heritage

As we have stressed, industrialization is a historical process: each country must be seen as traversing a particular dynamic path. For a poor country, its initial conditions obviously matter. South Korea in the 1950s had a low per capita income and little capital stock. However, there had been a recent, successful land reform, and the population was well educated and had been exposed to industrial culture during the colonial period under the

Japanese. Ample human capital, generous foreign aid, privileged access to American and Japanese markets, and other intangible factors set the stage for the Korean industrial miracle. The contrast with African countries which still struggle with relics of a much more exploitative form of colonialism could not be sharper. Their lack of educational infrastructure and even rudimentary industrial experience stand out.

As a country pursues industrialization, transitions continue to occur. Toward the end, fully developed economies enter more or less competitively into world markets with levels of export subsidies, import barriers, and activities like dumping restrained to "normal" levels (with normality being a flexible concept, *vide* Japanese import restrictions and the increasing interest of the United States in "strategic trade"). In the developing world, the import-substitute-then-export strategy means that large economies may hold themselves (or at least many of their products) away from international competition for periods measured in decades. Small countries are necessarily more open to trade, and arguably have fewer opportunities for dynamic gains from distorting prices in the short run. Conceivably, their size deficiencies could be offset by regional production/trading groups, although their record of success so far is bleak. Flexible manufacturing processes as discussed by Piore and Sabel (1984) may also provide opportunities for surmounting problems posed by economies of scale, but they are just beginning to be applied in the developing world.

Neither import substitution nor the return toward international competitiveness is typically led by the invisible hand. Internally, as the small, prosperous European economies exemplify, an interlocking institutional network allows negotiation among well-organized groups—unionized labor, transnational companies, and big government. *Chaebol* and *zaibatsu* confronted by labor and activist states demonstrate the same tendencies in Korea and Japan. A key long-term result of a successful industrial strategy is a set of institutions conducive to high levels of investment and saving (undertaken, as Keynes observed, by different institutional groups whose actions have to be coordinated), absorption of technical change, and demand control mechanisms through which the government can support a steady pace of output growth.

Externally, an export push may be required to compensate (so to speak) for a period of import substitution. As we have observed, successful newly industrialized countries (NICs) often follow this pattern, although there are historical exceptions—the United States remained quite closed throughout its industrialization and India is now. But would both these economies improve their performance by pushing sales abroad?

The benefits of more exports are easy to enumerate. They can support the current account as imports are liberalized (except when there are negative domestic resource costs), and by simple arithmetic raising a modest export share of GDP toward unity is likely to be a less painful process than further reducing an already low import coefficient toward zero. Also, when world trade is expanding faster than world GDP, exports tap into a rising source of demand. As we have noted, the unknown for countries making the transition over the next decades is whether or not international trade will continue to grow as rapidly in the future as it has in the recent past. As Hobson (1902) observed long ago, progressive income redistribution and creation of a welfare state can also underwrite growth in demand.

Rapid export expansion aside, the "return" involves a transition from noncompetitive to competitive trade, as Chenery (1975) pointed out. On the export side, the emphasis shifts from primary products with a small internal market to manufactures and services sold both abroad and at home. Goods initially produced to substitute for imports (often creating a further dependence on imported intermediates and capital goods) must ultimately find external markets if world-class costs and variety are to be provided to domestic consumers. There is no reason why production for appropriate niches should not initially be supported by import barriers and export subsidies; indeed "opportunity costs" of not trading have to be ignored until learning and scale effects take hold. The point is that full industrialization only occurs after infant firms grow up, and can compete more or less effectively on international terms. The issues raised by DUP theorists are important in this context—why should a firm try to compete with foreigners instead of seeking national rents? Directed public interventions, social consensus, and profit opportunities in world-market competition necessarily must play a role in the difficult transition from noncompetitive to more competitive trade.

(g) Productivity Growth and Access to Technology

International competitiveness depends on steadily growing productivity and access to best-practice technology. With regard to productivity, it is useful to distinguish improvements due to better resource allocation and trend increases over time. In the mainstream view, liberalized trade and industrial policy should improve allocation. However, in a recent review article, Pack (1988) concludes that ". . . to date, there is no clear confirmation of the hypothesis that countries with an external orientation benefit from greater growth of technical efficiency in . . . manufacturing. When combined with the relatively small static costs of protection [i.e., small triangles], this finding leaves those with a predilection toward a neutral regime in a quandary" (p. 353). And again, "[c]omparisons of total factor productivity growth among countries pursuing different international trade orientations do not reveal systematic differences in productivity growth in manufacturing, nor do the time-series studies of individual countries that have experienced alternating trade regimes allow strong conclusions in this dimension" (p. 372). Allocative efficiency gains do not seem to result from liberal policy moves.

With respect to sources of productivity growth over time, Pack does observe that there are often large gaps between current LDC and international best-practice technology. Moreover, along Kaldor-Verdoorn lines, Amsden (1988), in her WIDER country study of South Korea, emphasizes that rapid output growth (perhaps coming largely from exports) can feed back positively into new, late vintage capital formation and productivity increases. As we have already observed, one source of Korean cost competitiveness is the fact that labor productivity grows faster than real wages, reducing unit labor costs. The virtuous circle to more exports, additional investment in export industries, and further productivity gains is successfully closed.

After the effects of formal schooling and on-the-job learning are taken into account, it is clear that if productivity is to be raised, new technology must be acquired. Despite isolated exceptions (e.g., Korean and Brazilian design of new models of cars and armored personnel carriers), little technical innovation occurs in the developing world. New technology must be obtained through deals with international suppliers, involving licensing and royalty costs, or via direct foreign investment on the part of transnational firms. Either route involves extensive bargaining between local public and private sector firms and external suppliers, under the aegis of the state.

The conditions of these bargains vary with a country's own industrial history and time. Dealing in the 1980s with Suzuki about setting up an automobile industry, India may have been in a weaker position than was Brazil when it dealt with Ford and Volkswagen 30 years before: the corporations were groping almost as blindly as their potential host at that stage. The main similarity is that a process beginning with assembly and leading toward rising domestic content is one policy goal. The time frame for such a change may be fairly short, since NIC industrial sophistication has by now reached the point at which international productivity levels in greenfield plants can be rapidly acquired, as in production of car engines during the past decade in Mexico.

Even this comfortable generalization breaks down, however, when new technologies like those based on microprocessors are at issue. Stimulating local applications rather than production of hardware has emerged as the relevant policy objective—Sweden, the most computerized economy in the world, does minimal local manufacture. In developing countries, pursuing computer literacy and familiarity emerges as the relevant policy goal. Traditional ISI strategies do not apply, but state and privately supported educational initiatives possibly may.

5. POLICIES IN ACTION

The discussion so far shows that forming industrial strategy (or reforming policies inherited from the past while growth and industrialization proceed apace) is a complex pursuit. Small wonder that practical policy advice in the area boils down to compiling lore about interventions that have (or have not) worked in one context, and trying to extrapolate about the outcomes they might provoke in another. In this spirit, we offer a few suggestions about possible approaches to strategy.

Before turning to specifics, a word about general orientations is in order. Industrial strategies can follow three broad lines—proactive state guidance of the economy, *laissez faire*, and a middle way.

The proactive industrializing state has fallen from fashion in recent years, especially in its traditional central planning attire. With party cadres calling the shots throughout the system under guidance from the top, planning did aid industrialization in big countries with simple economies and strong states—the Soviet Union in the 1930s and China two decades later. However, when production processes become more interlinked and technically harder to organize and consumers grow more sophisticated, absence of personal freedom and room for initiative handicaps adoption of new techniques and products, braking productivity growth. A rule-bound, rent-seeking bureaucracy becomes an additional fetter on change. The current wave of reforms in (ex?) socialist nations is aimed precisely at removing these obstacles to modern economic growth.

Proactive guidance can also take the form of widespread, intense industrial targeting. Such policies have been practiced with some success by the NICs in both their import-substitution and export-promotion phases. However, they fit less well into an economy that is small, open, and lacks industrial sophistication. In such a context, public participation in, but not direction of, the economy runs naturally between the free market and centrally planned extremes. As noted above, this road was taken by small country development "success cases" such as those in East Asia since World War II and in European social democracies after the turn of the century. For the reasons just discussed, elements of the strategies appropriate to large and small countries are best described through empirical generalizations rather than the abstract model used by neoclassical economic theory. They include the following:

1. Even with successfully interventionist strategies, the government generally guides but does not directly manage decentralized, market-responsive decision making at the firm level. Especially in developing economies where middle-level cadres are weak, highly able people to do the guiding from the top of both the state and key enterprises are essential. There do not have to be large forces

of "planners," but they need political backing, which in turn rests upon effective state mediation among interest groups. Guidance takes place through continual consultation among the state and producer, export and labor organizations. It may be centralized as in the famous presidential Blue House export targeting in Korea or in MITI in Japan, or more widely spread as around the development banks, planning ministry, and producers' organizations in Brazil. The point is that flexible, institutionally appropriate channels are created.

2. Through the consultation process there is feedback from producers to the state, which centralizes information and selectively shares it among firms. National solidarity and an ideology of growth sanction such bureaucratic transgressions of the rules of the market game. If such forces do not coalesce behind an industrialization push, it is much more likely to fail.

3. The state also provides venture capital for new enterprises, often at highly favorable interest rates. This is a form of lending that traditional, garden-variety banks are usually not willing to undertake. Development banks, if aggressive, can play a key role in providing venture capital and long-term investment finance in general. Their project search and identification procedures have to take place at the micro level—among the 20,000 commodities in the seven-digit SITC. Economists' two-digit level computations of effective protection rates and domestic resource costs are not of great use in identifying potentially profitable niches and sources of productivity growth in detail. Market knowledge and intuition are essential to the decision process. A publicly backed private sector is the institution best suited to carry it out.

4. Targeting is universal, with the state giving support to "thrust industries." However, in success cases, incentives can be (and are) withdrawn if firms do not meet performance criteria such as export expansion or incorporation of best-practice techniques. When scale economies are possible, protection plus barriers to entry through firm licensing may be combined. If too many producers are in an already protected market, cost reductions due to rising output volume at the firm level may never be realized unless the state or a large private sector agent brings about consolidation. For an industry starting *ab initio*, the relative merits of a quota cum licensing and a tariff regime have to be weighed; the former may be essential only when an existing sector has to be rationalized.

5. The most effective incentives depend on context. Some drain and others add revenue to the treasury, and this dimension must be weighed. Some are administratively difficult, provide especially

strong incentives for rent seeking, etc. Large countries on an ISTE path may opt for a Brazil-type "law of similars," banning any imports that compete closely with items produced at home; smaller economies might suffocate under such blanket provisions, but then they have to manage detailed import tariffs or quotas. Cheap credit is often an effective, easily administered incentive, but the government has to have the power (and the will) to cut it off if firms do not satisfy performance criteria.

6. The criteria themselves should be straight-forward and transparent—exports and technical advance. More theoretical considerations such as potential economies of scale may be used in selecting industries for targeting, but firms should perform according to simpler rules. "White elephants" grazing happily on state subsidies are not permitted to thrive in a well-run economy. In many cases, the monsters' pale hue is due to poor management, which can be changed. In situations where a bad investment decision was initially made or a good one was overtaken by external competition (e.g., Swedish shipyards), the government accepts an obligation to retrain and reemploy workers discharged in white elephant liquidations. Rapid overall growth lets this sort of transition hurt less.

7. The issue of who bears the costs of the policies just sketched must be addressed. Vicious DUP circles involving the government and specific social groups can always appear—a successfully industrializing state will cut such knots and with luck compensate the losers from the fruits of productivity growth (e.g., Korean real wages rise less rapidly than productivity, but they do rise). External circumstances may make interventionist strategies more feasible in some contexts than others. A government that is fiscally constrained because it pays interest on external debt has few degrees of freedom; indeed, pushing exports via domestic recession to transfer resources abroad may distort the whole economic system. Successful growth may be impossible in debtor economies without reduced payments, in which case foreign institutions would pay part of the adjustment cost.

8. There is often division of control, implicit or regulated through licensing, of sectoral production among national public and private enterprises and sometimes transnational corporations (or TNCs). Public enterprises do best in infrastructure, "base" industries, and sectors like oil and high-tech services in which, largely for social reasons, labor and management come to share a strong ethos of performance. Parastatals become bureaucratized and do poorly in sectors where performance depends on complex product and process changes; private enterprise often does a better job of keeping up.

9. "Infrastructure" broadly construed includes health and education. As already noted, small European countries specializing in high productivity exports, Korea, and Japan all score high on indicators such as ratios of technical people to the overall population, student scores on international science examinations, and overall well-being of their residents. The educational system in many economically successful nations is geared more toward high average performance than individual brilliance.

10. In the rich small countries and the NICs, synergy between state and private sector extends to capital formation. As noted above, public investment often does not crowd out private investment from its assigned sectors, but in fact crowds it in. The implication is that state investment programs should be designed to raise productivity in both the public and private sectors. As noted above, a state-directed phase of growth is not likely to end successfully unless private institutions appear to sustain high investment levels and generate and channel savings flows to finance them.

11. Orthodox economic theory suggests that distortions should just be avoided—in practice this recommendation reduces to little more than common sense. Successful industrializers hold distortions in line, but their efforts in this direction should not be exaggerated. The NICs are not models of laissez faire; nor were the generations of successful economies preceding them. Long-term, large divergences from market signals are costly; in a shorter run they may stimulate entrepreneurship and productivity growth. Neoclassical theory mostly gives static allocation rules. They boil down to a list of "don'ts," useful curbs to exuberance in decision making but secondary to dynamic processes of change.

6. SUMMARY AND CONCLUSIONS

The early optimism of development economics was misplaced—in the competence of the state, in the effectiveness of its interventions, in the independence of the national growth project from international trade, technology, and capital markets. In contrast to their predecessors, the legacy of 1980s vintage development economists will be documentation of imperfect policy making. The operating assumption of imperfect markets has been replaced by the presumed inevitability of imperfect states. Many have concluded that the former is the lesser of two evils, the implication being that governments should get out of development altogether.

The difficulty with this largely neoclassical recommendation is that its attempt to frame the question of the role of the state as a choice between evils is fundamentally flawed. This perspective only reinforces the profession's tendency to view economics and politics as distinct spheres. When economists finally discovered the state, they found it wanting and tried to reason it away. In the new neoclassical synthesis, the political and economic sciences are once again divorced.

But the state cannot be dismissed so easily. As we have noted repeatedly, virtually all cases of successful economic development have involved state intervention and improvisation of an industrial strategy. Mainstream economists deny this reality, arguing that no political arrangement can exist under which the state's actions will not be vitiated by DUP. But on the other hand, they want that state to act by disengaging itself from the economy. A much more sophisticated political economy is required, to *explain* and not just postulate the relationship between state and society.

Beyond these theoretical issues, changing conditions also have to be recognized. Constraints on public action have become more binding in recent years. Both foreign debt obligations and policy pressures such as International Monetary Fund and World Bank conditionality impose limits and generate internal political realignments. Fiscal costs of subsidies become more irksome at the same time as globalization of industrial activity makes it harder to attract foreign investment simply to serve an internal, albeit protected, market.

The general lesson to be learned from experience is that there are no bags of policy tricks that work regardless of context. However, that does not mean the policy decisions are contingent only on internal and external political and economic conditions of individual countries. Comparative analysis helps explain *why* particular strategies perform well or poorly in particular contexts. We have seen that successful industrial strategies have respected the boundary conditions limiting economies in which they were applied, and have incorporated the context-dependent structures discussed above. They were also flexible and adaptive. By describing boundaries and institutional dynamics within a consistent framework, we have attempted to move the intellectual debate about the state's role in development toward a synthesis that policy makers can use.

REFERENCES

Amsden, Alice. "Republic of Korea." Stabilization and Adjustment Policies and Programmes Country Study No. 14. Helsinki: WIDER, 1988.

Bacha, Edmar L. "A Three-Gap Model of Foreign Transfers and the GDP Growth Rate in Developing Countries." *Journal of Development Economics* 32 (April, 1990), pp. 279–296.

Balassa, Bela. "Trade Policies in Developing Countries." *American Economic Review, Papers and Proceedings,* 61 (1971): 178–187.

Barbone, Luca. "Essays on Trade and Macro Policy in Developing Countries." Ph.D. dissertation. Cambridge, Mass.: Department of Economics, Massachusetts Institute of Technology, 1985.

Bardhan, Pranab K. *The Political Economy of Development in India*. Oxford: Basil Blackwell, 1984.

Barro, Robert. "A Cross-Country Study of Growth, Saving, and Government." NBER Working Paper No. 2885. Cambridge, Mass.: National Bureau of Economic Research, 1989.

Barry, Brian. "Some Questions about Explanation." *International Studies Quarterly*, 27 (1983): 17–27.

Bauer, P. T. *Reality and Rhetoric: Studies in the Economics of Development*. London: Weidenfield and Nicolson, 1984.

Bauer, P. T. *Dissent on Development*. London: Weidenfield and Nicolson, 1972.

Bhagwati, Jagdish N. "Directly Unproductive Profit Seeking (DUP) Activities." *Journal of Political Economy*, 90 (1982): 988–1002.

Blejer, Mario, and Mohsin Khan. "Government Policy and Private Investment in Developing Countries." *IMF Staff Papers*, 31 (1984): 379–403.

Blomqvist, Ake, and Sharif Mohammad. "Controls, Corruption, and Competitive Rent-Seeking in LDCs." *Journal of Development Economics*, 21 (1986): 161–80.

Boratav, Korkut. "Turkey," Stabilization and Adjustment Policies and Programmes Country Study No. 5. Helsinki: WIDER, 1988.

Bowles, Samuel, and Robert Boyer. "A Wage-Led Employment Regime: Income Distribution, Labor Discipline, and Aggregate Demand in Welfare Capitalism." Helsinki: WIDER, 1988.

Bowles, Samuel, and John Eatwell. "Between Two Worlds: Interest Groups, Class Structure, and Capitalist Growth." in Dennis C. Mueller (ed.), *The Political Economy of Growth*. New Haven, Conn.: Yale University Press, 1983.

Buchanan, James. "Rent Seeking and Profit Seeking." In J. M. Buchanan, R. D. Tollison, and G. Tullock (eds.), *Toward a Theory of Rent-Seeking Society*. College Station, TX: Texas A&M University Press, 1980.

Cameron, David R. "Creating Theory in Comparative Political Economy: On Mancur Olson's Explanation of Growth." Paper presented at the Annual Meeting of the American Political Science Association, Chicago: 1983.

Chakravarty, Sukhamoy. *Development Planning: The Indian Experience*. Oxford: Clarendon Press, 1987.

Chakravarty, Sukhamoy, and Ajit Singh. "The Desirable Forms of Economic Openness in the South." Helsinki: WIDER, 1988.

Chenery, Hollis B. "The Structuralist Approach to Development Policy." *American Economic Review, Papers and Proceedings*, 65 (1975): 310–16.

Chenery, Hollis B. "Comparative Advantage and Development Policy." *American Economic Review*, 51 (1961): 18–51.

Chenery, Hollis B., Sherman Robinson, and Moshe Syrquin. *Industrialization and Growth*. New York: Oxford University Press, 1986.

Cline, William. "Can the East Asian Model of Development Be Generalized?" *World Development*, 10 (1982): 81–90.

Coase, Ronald. "The Nature of the Firm." *Econometrica*, 4 (1937): 386–405.

DeVries, Jan. "The Rise and Decline of Nations in Historical Perspective." *International Studies Quarterly*, 27 (1983): 11–16.

Evans, Peter. "Predatory, Developmental and Other Apparatuses: A Comparative Analysis of the Third World State." *Sociological Forum*, 4, 4 (1989).

Feder, Gershon. "On Exports and Economic Growth." *Journal of Development Economics*, 12 (1983): 59–73.

Findlay, Ronald. "Trade, Development, and the State." Paper presented at the 25th Anniversary Symposium on the State of Development Economics. New Haven, Conn.: Economic Growth Center, Yale University, 1986.

Fishlow, Albert. "Brief Comparative Reflections on Latin American Economic Performance and Policy." Helsinki: WIDER, 1986.

Fishlow, Albert. "The State of Latin America Economics." In *Economic and Social Progress in Latin America*. Washington, D.C.: Inter-American Development Bank, 1985.

Galbraith, John Kenneth. *Economic Development in Perspective*. Cambridge, Mass.: Harvard University Press, 1964.

Gerschenkron, Alexander. *Economic Backwardness in Historical Perspective*. Cambridge, Mass.: Harvard University Press, 1962.

Handlin, Oscar, and Mary Flug Handlin. *Commonwealth: A Study of the Role of Government in the American Economy: Massachusetts 1774–1861* (revised edition). Cambridge, Mass.: Belknap Press of Harvard University Press, 1969.

Haggard, Stephan. "The Politics of Adjustment." *International Organization*, 39 (1985): 505–34.

Harberger, Arnold. "Using the Resources at Hand More Effectively." *American Economic Review, Papers and Proceedings*. 49 (1959): 134–46.

Hartz, Louis. *Economic Policy and Democratic Thought: Pennsylvania 1776–1860*. Cambridge, Mass.: Harvard University Press, 1948.

Helleiner, G. K. "Trade Strategy in Medium-Term Adjustment." *World Development*, 18, 6 (1990).

Hirschman, Albert O. "A Generalized Linkage Approach to Development, with Special Reference to Staples." *Economic Development and Cultural Change*, 25, Supplement (1977): 67–98.

Hirschman, Albert O. *The Strategy of Economic Development*. New Haven, Conn.: Yale University Press, 1958.

Hobson, John. *Imperialism: A Study*. London: J. Nisbet, 1902.

Horowitz, M. *The Transformation of American Law*. Cambridge, Mass.: Harvard University Press, 1977.

Hughes, Alan, and Ajit Singh. "The World Economic Slowdown and the Asian and Latin American Economies: A Comparative Analysis of Economic Structure, Policy and Performance." Helsinki: WIDER, 1987.

Innis, Harold A. *The Fur Trade in Canada* (revised edition). New Haven, Conn.: Yale University Press, 1962.

Johnson, Chalmers A. *MITI and the Japanese Miracle*. Stanford, Calif.: Stanford University Press, 1982.

Johnson, Harry G. *Economic Policies Toward Less Developed Countries*. Washington, D.C.: The Brookings Institution, 1967.

Katzenstein, Peter. *Small States in World Markets: Industrial Policy in Europe*. Ithaca, N.Y.: Cornell University Press, 1985.

Kennedy, Paul. *The Rise and Fall of the Great Powers*. New York: Random House, 1987.

Krueger, Anne O. "Comparative Advantage and Development Policy 20 Years Later." In Moshe Syrquin, Lance Taylor, and Larry Westphal (eds.), *Economic Structure and Performance: Essays in Honor of Hollis B. Chenery*. New York: Academic Press, 1984.

Krueger, Anne O. "The Political Economy of the Rent-Seeking Society." *American Economic Review,* 64 (1974): 291–303.

Lal, Deepak. *The Poverty of "Development Economics."* London: Institute of Economic Affairs, Hobart Paperback No. 16, 1983.

Little, Ian M. D., Tibor Scitovsky, and Maurice Scott. *Industry and Trade in Some Developing Countries: A Comparative Study.* London: Oxford University Press, 1970.

Malloy, James J. "The Politics of Transition in Latin America." In James M. Malloy and Mitchell A. Seligson (eds.), *Authoritarians and Democrats: Regime Transition in Latin America.* Pittsburgh: University of Pittsburgh Press, 1987.

McCarthy, F. Desmond, Lance Taylor, and Cyrus Talati. "Trade Patterns in Developing Countries, 1964–82." *Journal of Development Economics,* 27 (1987): 5–39.

Moore, Jr. Barrington. *Social Origins of Dictatorship and Democracy.* Boston: Beacon Press, 1966.

Myrdal, Gunnar. "The 'Soft State' in Underdeveloped Countries." In Paul Streeten (ed.), *Unfashionable Economics: Essays in Honor of Lord Balogh.* London: Weidenfield and Nicolson, 1970.

Newfarmer, Richard (ed.). *Profits, Progress, and Poverty: Case Studies of International Industries in Latin America.* Notre Dame, Ind.: University of Notre Dame Press, 1985.

North, Douglass. *Structure and Change in Economic History.* New York: W. W. Norton, 1981.

O'Connor, James. *The Fiscal Crisis of the State.* New York: St. Martin's Press, 1973.

O'Donnell, Guillermo. *Modernization and Bureaucratic-Authoritarianism.* Berkeley, Calif.: Institute of International Studies, University of California, 1973.

Offe, Claus. "Structural Problems of the Capitalist State." In K. von Beyme (ed.), *German Political Studies,* Vol. 1. London: Sage, 1974.

Offe, Claus, and Volker Ronge. "Theses on the Theory of the State." *New German Critique* (1975).

Olson, Mancur. *The Rise and Decline of Nations.* New Haven, Conn.: Yale University Press, 1982.

Ortiz, Guillermo, and Carlos Noriega. "Investment and Growth in Latin America." Washington, D.C.: International Monetary Fund, 1988.

Pack, Howard. "Industrialization and Trade." In Hollis B. Chenery and T. N. Srinivasan (eds.), *Handbook of Development Economics,* Vol. 1. Amsterdam: North-Holland, 1988.

Piore, Michael J., and Charles F. Sabel. *The Second Industrial Divide: Possibilities for Prosperity.* New York: Basic Books, 1984.

Prebisch, Raul. "Commercial Policy in the Underdeveloped Countries," *American Economic Review,* 49 (1959): 257–69.

Prebisch, Raul. *The Economic Development of Latin America and Its Principal Problems.* Lake Success, N.Y.: United Nations Department of Social Affairs, 1950.

Schultz, T. Paul. "Education Investment and Returns." In Hollis B. Chenery and T. N. Srinivasan (eds.), *Handbook of Development Economics,* Vol. 1. Amsterdam: North-Holland, 1988.

Schumpeter, Josef A. *The Theory of Economic Development.* Cambridge, Mass.: Harvard University Press, 1934.

Scitovsky, Tibor. "Two Concepts of External Economies." *Journal of Political Economy,* 62 (1954): pp. 143–51.

Shapiro, Helen. "State Intervention and Industrialization: The Origins of the

Brazilian Automobile Industry." Ph.D. dissertation. New Haven, Conn.: Department of Economics, Yale University, 1988.

Singer, Hans. "The Distribution of Gains between Investing and Borrowing Countries." *American Economic Review*, 40 (1950): 473–485.

Srinivasan, T. N. "Neoclassical Political Economy: The State and Economic Development." New Haven, Conn.: Economic Growth Center, Yale University, 1985.

Taylor, Lance. "Gap Disequilibria: Inflation, Investment, Saving, and Foreign Exchange." Cambridge, Mass.: Department of Economics, Massachusetts Institute of Technology, 1989.

Taylor, Lance. *Varieties of Stabilization Experience*. Oxford: Clarendon Press, 1988.

Taylor, Lance. "Economic Openness: Problems to Century's End." Helsinki: WIDER, 1987.

Toye, John. *Dilemmas of Development*. Oxford: Basil Blackwell, 1987.

Watkins, Melville H. "A Staple Theory of Economic Growth." *Canadian Journal of Economics and Political Science* 29 (1963): 141–58.

Weffort, Francisco, *O Populismo na Politica Brasileira* (Rio de Janeiro: Paz e Terra, 1978).

Wilson, C. H. "Trade, Society, and the State." *Cambridge Economic History of Europe: Part IV*. Cambridge: Cambridge University Press, 1967.

Young, Allyn. "Increasing Returns and Economic Progress." *Economic Journal*, 38 (1928): 527–42.

PART SIX

THE HUMAN DIMENSION
OF DEVELOPMENT

Development is fundamentally about human welfare. It is also about social change; either encouraging social change or accepting its inevitability with the hope that the effect on human welfare can be positive.

Each of these concepts, human welfare and social change, is quite complex and multidimensional in its own right, and efforts to understand, measure, encourage, and assess either are fraught with difficulties. Those difficulties are compounded when we try to deal with them together, under the rubric of development.

The earlier chapters have shown both sides of development, but it is now time to focus specifically on the prime objective of development, the human beings involved in the process of social change, and their welfare.

The ambiguities and difficulties of social change are captured in the article by Goulet and Wilber, "The Human Dilemma of Development." They note that there have been more than a few cases in which a generation has been sacrificed for the bright promise of future development. And there have been many more cases in which the basic values of peoples have been cavalierly disregarded in the quest for development—they have been denied "cognitive respect." The realization of the magnitude of these costs is the cause of the reaction to development that was so clearly documented in the Wiarda article of Part One; this can lead to an effort to turn back the clock or to creative attempts to mold the process of change into a more beneficial form.

Those who would simply resist the change implied by development are guilty of overlooking the very real costs of underdevelopment. Goulet and Wilber point out that 1.4 million African infants die every year who would not have died had the infant mortality rate of Africa been that of the developed countries.

They are victims of underdevelopment; respect for human life calls out for dealing with this loss. Similarly, certain cultural practices of underdevelopment are objectionable on broad human grounds beyond simple ethnocentrism, for example, use of infanticide as a means of population control or disfiguration of females as a means of social control. At a minimum, development can provide opportunities for dealing with the underlying issues and can encourage alternative behavior, while not removing cognitive respect.

Goulet and Wilber conclude that the costs of underdevelopment outweigh the costs of development, and so development must be accepted at the same time decisionmakers must attempt to minimize social costs and to find standards of acceptability. The same conclusion is reached by following Albert Hirschman and accepting that social change is a reality in our world, and has been since the fifteenth century, and that the challenge of development is to find possible approaches to move it in a positive direction (Wilber and Jameson, 1991).

Beck provides a case study of the costs of underdevelopment by focusing on the strategies that have to be adopted by the poorest members of a West Bengal village, simply in order to survive. His findings correspond with those of most studies on the poorest of the poor: they are generally landless or have few if any assets; are often in debt, illiterate, isolated, and ill; and are most often in female-headed households. They are resourceful and will migrate, take on debts, or sell assets to keep themselves and their families in existence. Beck finds another set of strategies among the people he interviewed that included changing their eating patterns, using common property, share-rearing of livestock, and mutual support. Despite these efforts, their life of poverty and underdevelopment remains precarious. Beck suggests a strategy of finding ways to work in the power gaps in villages to provide better choices for the poorest of the village, always listening to their own description of their needs. Social change and development is a complex process, but the potential benefits to the poor of the village are substantial, even though not every development process would benefit them.

The article by Dorfman on the Matacos people of "the impenetrable" scrub forest of Argentina deals more directly with how the process of social change affects a people who would rather maintain their traditional life. Political and economic pressures from Argentina and Argentinians made that impossible and the Matacos seemed "headed for a dead end" of virtual extinction as their situation deteriorated year after year. With the help of outsiders, many of the Matacos have attempted to engage social change and development on their own terms. It has forced dramatic adjustments on them as they have moved toward sedentary occupations of farming, fishing, and lumbering with some success, though their dependency on outside aid has become heavy. And the process has caused major changes in their understanding of themselves as they have begun to lose their own symbols and traditions despite the "cognitive respect" they have been given. So Dorfman's conclusion about the effect of social change is ambiguous and very much in the middle ground suggested by Goulet and Wilber.

The costs of both development and underdevelopment are borne more heavily by women. They are overrepresented among the poorest, and as change comes, especially in rural areas, their burden often grows as they are required to take on additional tasks in the home as well as in the production sphere, while their existing efforts must be intensified. These observations were made most persuasively by Ester Boserup (1970), and in a book recently celebrated and updated by Tinker (1990). Boserup's work spawned extensive work on what came to be called women in development (WID). Kandiyoti's article provides an overview of the WID work and catalogues the effect of development processes on women in rural areas. This article complements Standing's in Part Five on women in manufacturing employment. Kandiyoti is critical of the work that has been done to date, however, because it is technocratic and unclear about assumptions, claims, and goals. Her own assessment is that the problems and the effects of different policies vary greatly with geography; for example, 87 percent of African women in the labor force are in agricultural production, compared with only 14 percent in Latin America. In addition, most assistance to women is stopgap and does not deal with the structures that affect their well-being. This leads to contradictory policy treatments where WID policy emphasizes basic human needs, while national agricultural policy emphasizes market-based strategies—which may be detrimental to satisfying women's basic needs. The implication is that women must take charge of the development process rather than having it guided by technicians from donor agencies. So again the issue of social change and human welfare is seen as a complex one.

The final article by Peter Gall, "What Really Matters—Human Development," describes an attempt to deal with these complexities and to measure, at a national level, human welfare–human development, and to suggest the factors that go into the differential experience of human development across countries. A human development index was created, based on measures of life expectancy, literacy, and purchasing power, and a ranking of countries resulted, showing that some countries with low incomes do better in human development terms than countries whose incomes are higher. There are a number of suggestions of factors which generate these differences. The article closes by examining the drag of military expenditures on human development and exploring the contribution of freedom to human development.

This article brings us full circle to Goulet and Wilber. Both development and underdevelopment have their costs. The challenge is to understand and accept this "tragic" nature of development, while attempting to find approaches that lie in the middle ground of improving human welfare while maintaining cognitive respect.

REFERENCES

Boserup, Ester, *Women's Role in Economic Development*. New York: St. Martin's Press, 1970.

Tinker, Irene. ed. *Persistent Inequalities: Women and World Development*. New York: Oxford University Press, 1990.

Wilber, Charles K., and Kenneth P. Jameson. "Albert O. Hirschman: An Economist in Dissent." In Warren Samuels, ed., *Contemporary Economists*. London: Edward Elgar, 1991.

23

The Human Dilemma
of Development

Denis Goulet and Charles K. Wilber

Some argue that, because economic development exacts tremendous social costs, it should be undertaken slowly, only with great deliberation, so as to minimize social disruption. In this light, the orthodox agenda of *rapid* economic growth as the surest route to the elimination of poverty is seriously questioned. The strategy of implementing major economic structural reforms designed to increase output in agriculture and industry is judged against the high price of social change which accompanies rapid development.

Although social change, especially when associated with industrialization, has always entailed a high price, the price of *not* developing is also very high. Historian E. H. Carr notes that "the cost of conservation falls just as heavily on the underprivileged as the cost of innovation on those who are deprived of their privileges."[1] Underdevelopment's high costs include chronic disease, hunger, famine, premature death, and degradation of the human spirit generation after generation. Thus is a painful dilemma posed for development agents conscious of the high social costs of sudden structural changes, yet dedicated to reducing underdevelopment's miseries as rapidly as possible.

THE HIGH SOCIAL COSTS OF DEVELOPMENT

Few writers are more insightful than the sociologist Peter Berger in exposing the high social price of development. The title of Berger's landmark book, *Pyramids of Sacrifice: Political Ethics and Social Change,* is an apt metaphor: The Great Pyramid at Cholula, Mexico, testifies in stone to what Berger calls "the relation among theory, sweat and blood."[2] The pyramid

Note: Manuscript prepared for this volume.

was built as an altar of sacrifice, and the theory legitimizing its construction was brutally simple: "If the gods were not regularly fed with human blood, the universe would fall apart."[3] Although the Aztecs bear the stigma of being history's chief executioners at Cholula, Berger concludes that later generations of leaders everywhere—politicians, military commanders, planners, and revolutionaries, abetted by social theorists—continue to immolate innocent, and usually silent, victims in needless sacrifices to insatiable gods.

Berger views development (in both its capitalist and socialist incarnations) and revolution as contemporary Molochs who devour the living flesh of millions, all in the name of a "better life" for *future* generations. One thinks here of Sartre's play *Dirty Hands* in which Hugo asks: "What is the use of struggling for the liberation of men if we despise them to the point of brainwashing them?" The conversation between Hugo and Hoederer is revealing:

> "If we don't love men, we can't struggle on their behalf."
>
> "I am not interested in what men are but in what they are capable of becoming."
>
> "I, on the contrary, love them for what they are. With all their sloppiness and filth, with all their vices. I love their voices, their warm hands . . . the worried look on their faces and the desperate combat they wage."

Pyramids of Sacrifice needs to be read as a *cri de coeur* against the perpetration of monstrous cruelties—and their legitimization by intellectuals—on living generations of men, women, and children in myriad lands. The criminals are the hosts of planners, social theorists, and change agents who purport to speak *for* the people. Tragedy is compounded by their assumption that their own perception of reality is more correct than that of the masses. Berger denounces that special blend of arrogance and benevolence which too many development enthusiasts and revolutionaries share with missionaries of old, the transformational zeal which denies to poor people that "cognitive respect" of their own perceptions of reality which is theirs as a basic right.

If any aspiration may be said to be universal, across lines of cultural space and individual personality, it is this: Every person and society wants to be treated by others as a being of worth, for its own sake and on its own terms, regardless of its utility or attractiveness to others. Therefore, Berger is right in demanding that planners, revolutionaries, and social scientists show "cognitive respect" for all populations. He himself deserves "cognitive respect" for defending this view against the mainstream of experts who glibly decree the superiority of their own diagnosis of oppression and misery and thereafter proceed to prescribe "appropriate" remedies: economic growth, or revolution and socialist transformation. The stakes are high and in no way can be reduced to the risk of a series of laboratory experiments. Experts who touch people's lives irresponsibly may damage them beyond repair.

Such warnings will remain necessary so long as development keeps confronting societies in distress with a cruel choice between bread and dignity. The facile slogan states that bread can be had with dignity; the harsh reality, however, is that dignity must often be sacrificed to obtain bread, or that the very aspiration after greater dignity becomes distorted as a quest for more bread. *Pyramids* pungently reminds us of two truths: (1) "Not by bread alone does man live," and (2) upon closer examination even the bread may be a stone!

No ethical issue is so resistant to easy answers as that of generations sacrificed now in exchange for the possibility of future development. This agonizing question leads many close to despair. Here one evokes two additional works which closely parallel Berger's own: Barrington Moore's *Reflections on the Causes of Human Misery* and Robert Heilbroner's *An Inquiry into the Human Prospect.*[4] All three authors end their foray into the history of social change on a note of rational pessimism tempered by an appeal to the transrational duty of not despairing. Uniformly they conclude that as much human suffering results from trying to "improve mankind" as from cynically exploiting it; therefore, they tend toward a "hands off history" stance to minimize suffering.

Thus Berger's brief against sacrificing present generations to prepare a better future for their children should be read as one instance of a more generalized disaffection among Western believers in progress. All facile optimism must now be rejected, every easy belief in the necessarily upward movement of history as well as the very imagery of improvement and evolutionary (or revolutionary) emancipation of the human race. Nevertheless, it would be puerile to react by swinging to the other side of the pendulum, since any serious view of history grasps the irreducibly *tragic* nature of social change.

One senses that Berger has grown discouraged over the inability of social science, development theory, or revolutionary action to deliver its promised "cargo" at a tolerable human cost. But it is an initial mistake ever to suppose that genuine development can be gained, fully or even in part, at "tolerable" human costs. Therefore, Berger should conclude not by saying "avoid social change (developmental growth and revolution) like the plague." Rather he should say: "Let us engage in an unending struggle against present structural injustices (with their train of alienation, misery, underdevelopment, worship of material well-being, etc.) so as to construct history while we bear witness to transcendence."

Although Berger is right in denying that revolution or development can be ethically pursued at *any* price, he is wrong in omitting the third element in the argument: Doing nothing also makes intolerable exactions in sacrificed generations. Writing before the 1964 military coup, Brazilian economist Celso Furtado described the enormous sacrifices paid by generations of his country people living in conditions of "underdevelopment": unnecessary deaths, continued abuse of the poor by privileged classes, constant frustration in efforts to improve their lot. Small wonder, he adds, that

> the masses in the underdeveloped countries have not generally put the same high valuation on individual liberty that we do. Since they have not had access to the better things of life, they obviously cannot grasp the full meaning of the supposed dilemma between liberty and quick development. . . . The liberty enjoyed by the minority in our society is paid for by a delay in general economic development; hence [it] is at the expense of the welfare of the great majority. . . . Very few of us have sufficient awareness of these deeply inhuman characteristics of underdevelopment. When we do become fully aware, we understand why the masses are prepared for any sacrifice in order to overcome it. If the price of liberty for the few had to be poverty of the many, we can be quite certain that the probability of preserving freedom would be practically nil.[5]

Furtado's words remind us that most men and women live in conditions far below those objectively demanded by human dignity. Thus, throughout history generations have always been "sacrificed." Why, then, should Berger condemn in absolute terms the prolongation of certain generational sacrifices a little longer while the progressive emancipation of a populace is being wrought? The point is this: although Berger correctly laments the high sacrifices demanded in the names of development and revolution, he wrongly ignores the equally high costs required by the stance of "keeping things as they are."

THE HUMAN COSTS OF UNDERDEVELOPMENT

Table 1 presents two indicators of the human costs of underdevelopment. To illustrate, of 12 million children born each year in sub-Saharan Africa, approximately 1.5 million die before they reach their first birthday. If these countries had the infant mortality rate of the industrialized market economy countries, the mortality of infants would be approximately 0.1 million. This means that because of underdevelopment 1.4 million infants die *each year* in sub-Saharan Africa alone.

The "mathematics of suffering" may be morbid, but it does lend perspective to the human costs of economic *underdevelopment*. Economist Franklyn Holzman faces the problem of human costs squarely; his consideration of the problem is worth quoting at length.

TABLE 1   **The Human Costs of Underdevelopment**

Countries Grouped by National Income per Capita	Infant Mortality Rate per Thousand Live Births	Life Expectancy at Birth in Years
Low-income countries		
(less than $400)		
Sub-Saharan Africa only	129	48
All except China and India	114	52
China and India only	59	63
Low-middle-income countries		
($400 to $1,700)	83	58
Upper-middle-income countries		
($1,700 to $7,500)	56	65
Industrial market economies	9	76
East European nonmarket economies	19	68

SOURCE: The World Bank, *World Development Report 1986* (New York: Oxford University Press, 1986), pp. 180–81, 232–35.

Let us now turn to the case of the nation caught in the "Malthusian trap," nations in which: (1) there has been no increase in the standard of living for centuries—perhaps there has even been a decline, (2) increases in output lead to a corresponding fall in the death rate so that no change in the standard of living occurs, i.e., those who live remain at subsistence, (3) the death rate is so high relative to the death rate in nations which have experienced secular economic progress that it is fair to say the inability to escape the "Malthusian trap" is responsible for the (premature) death of most of those born, and finally (4) escape from the "trap" requires a rate of investment so high that increases in productivity outrun increases in population. With such nations the case for a high rate of investment for a long period of time (one which enables the nation to escape the "trap") becomes much easier to justify and value judgments easier to make. The essential distinction between this case and that of the progressive economy is that loss of life can no longer be considered an "absolute," i.e., an infinite disutility. It was reasonable to consider it in this way in a progressive economy because loss of life is not comparable by any measure, with other changes in the level of individual welfare. In the case of the "Malthusian trap" nation, however, one is put in the position of having to compare losses of life between periods. That is to say, failure to attempt to escape the "trap" may be considered equivalent to condemning to death, needlessly, members of future generations. Under these circumstances, loss of life would seem to become a legitimate and measurable datum of the system. The question facing the planner is: shall we raise the rate of investment in the present to a point high enough to escape the "trap" even though this will involve a rise in the death rate of the present generation if we know that it will increase the life expectancy and raise the standard of living of countless future generations? No matter what his decision, the planner faced with such a question is responsible for imposing the death sentence on someone. When life and death are compared on this plane, escape from the trap might well seem to be the superior alternative since by simple addition it becomes obvious that more lives would be saved than lost in the process.[6]

Most of the world's populations live in conditions of poverty which are difficult for the affluent West to understand. And the effect of these conditions on the dignity of individuals, the degradation of their very being, cannot be measured.[7] One must, accordingly, contrast this urgent reality of poverty with the allegedly high social costs of development efforts to end poverty. The human cost of economic development has doubtless been very high in the past, but it does not necessarily follow that these costs are an inescapable part of all industrialization or agricultural modernization processes.

There exist several reasons why industrialization is not a painless process. First, there is the need in many countries for radical changes in social structure which often can be brought about only by a social revolution of greater or lesser violence. The old order fights to maintain its dominance while the new order defends itself against counterrevolutionary menaces. And the period of revolution is not restricted to the time of open civil war, but perdures until the inhibiting features of the old social structure are eradicated.

A second reason, closely allied to the first, is the need to develop new social institutions and to socialize people into new habits and values. Peasants must be transformed into factory workers by teaching them new kinds of discipline. People must be convinced that new ways of doing things can be good and beneficial, usually a difficult endeavor. Luddites rose up and smashed the new textile machinery during the British Industrial Revolution, and later Russian peasants tried to sabotage the kolkhoz as an institution. The type of labor discipline required in an industrial society is alien to the habits of a preindustrial society, and it is no easy thing to convince people of the need for new habits and discipline by persuasion alone. Not that the need for discipline and change is not understood, but usually what is understood is not willed ardently enough. Consequently, the passage from one set of habits and values to another is difficult, and often requires some resort to compulsion. This compulsion took the form of the *explicit coercion* of the state police power to expedite the movement from individual to collective farms and to enforce factory discipline in the Soviet Union of the 1930s. In capitalist countries the *implicit coercion* of the market mechanism, under which most must sell their labor where and when they can, transferred labor from rural to urban areas and imposed discipline through the threat of starvation and unemployment.

A third reason why industrialization is painful is the need to increase the rate of capital accumulation, a process which involves widening the margin between consumption and total output. Notwithstanding the prevalence of low consumption levels in underdeveloped countries, these levels cannot be raised substantially in development's early stages. According to Gunnar Myrdal, "Often it is argued that [the] more human approach is what distinguished economic development under democratic conditions from what would take place under a Communist regime—in my opinion a rather dangerous assertion if, realistically, living standards will have to be kept low in order to allow development."[8] The need to limit consumption in favor of capital accumulation can cause a rise in social discontent. The poorer classes will feel that after fighting for the recent revolution, and/or reforms, they are entitled to its fruits. The middle classes and upper classes will resent the curtailment of their former privileges and "luxury" consumption. To keep this unrest from upsetting the development plans or from leading to counterrevolution a powerful government policy of coercion may sometimes be needed. But coercion, as it enables capital to be accumulated, also increases the social cost of doing so. Clearly, development is no smooth evolutionary process of change. On the contrary, says Gerschenkron: ". . . the happy picture of a quiet industrial revolution proceeding without undue stir and thrust has been . . . seldom reproduced in historical reality."[9] The changes needed to initiate economic development are more likely to resemble a gigantic social and political earthquake.

TOWARD A MIDDLE GROUND

On balance, the *human costs* attendant upon capitalist and communist development are probably lower than the *human costs* attaching to continued underdevelopment. And it is particular historical circumstances, rather than the development process itself, which seem to account for the major share of these human costs. The task facing development agents thus becomes one of finding ways to minimize inevitable social costs accompanying economic development efforts and to agree upon standards for evaluating the acceptability of these costs relative to the potential benefits of the process.

Seeking refuge in some predetermined ideological position does not solve the problem, for as Richard Ohmann points out:

> A man who subscribes to a moral or social ideology runs the risk that someone will put it into practice and thereby burden it with a wretched

freight of human error and venality. The guillotine becomes an argument against libertarianism, juvenile gang wars an argument against permissive parenthood, the carpetbaggers an argument against emancipation. When this happens, the ideologist may recant; or he may save his ideology by disowning the malpractice as irrelevant perversion. A third response is possible: to accept *la guillotine* along with *la liberté*; but in a man of good will, this requires a strong stomach and a certain obstinacy.[10]

No response seems fully adequate to the problem. Quite possibly no adequate answer exists inasmuch as all relevant normal moral standards in this matter are so ambiguous. Nevertheless, the problem can be understood more clearly by a brief discussion of two factors affecting moral judgments.

The first factor is that "objective conditions control the environment in which behavior takes place."[11] One obvious example of this is a state of war. Restrictions of civil liberties, for example, are usually judged more acceptable in wartime than in time of peace. In Donald Bowles' cryptic phrase, ". . . the death of a political enemy on a battlefield is approved, the domestic execution of a political prisoner is disapproved."[12] A program of economic development is akin to a war on poverty. As such it is likewise an objective condition. Under these conditions, policies to restrict luxury goods consumption, to mobilize underemployed labor for projects such as reforestation, and to control population movements from rural to urban areas could be judged differently than if they were pursued during "peacetime."

Secondly, one must advert to the "ideology affecting the norms by which man evaluates such behavior."[13] In the example just cited, a state of war is an objective condition, while the historical tradition and system of beliefs which shape people's attitudes about civil liberties comprise the ideology or value system. Obviously these two factors interact. The objective conditions can alter the ideological commitments. Even under roughly similar objective conditions, value systems can yield diverse judgments as to the moral status of identical actions. For example, when Nicaragua abrogates democratic procedures it is condemned by some and excused by others. When South Africa, Taiwan, and South Korea do the same the response is reversed by the two groups.

In addition, of course, different value systems will judge the same actions or behavior differently. Raising the price of a good to take advantage of a temporary scarcity in its supply would have been condemned as a sin by Medieval Catholicism; in a capitalist society it would be considered good business practice.

The above discussion highlights the complexity of the problem of evaluating the social costs of economic development. Humanity seems to be faced with a dilemma. On one hand, the failure to overcome underdevelopment *allows* untold human suffering to continue. On the other hand, the process of overcoming these human costs through speeding up development will most likely *generate* some new ones; and the faster the old human costs are overcome the more severe the new. Also, there is the danger that the centralized power needed to generate rapid development will be used, as with Stalin, to consolidate personal power and establish totalitarianism.

Peter Berger issues the challenge that "We must seek solutions to our problems that accept *neither* hunger *nor* terror."[14] But this need not necessarily invalidate the difficult goals of pursuing authentic development and genuine revolution. And by definition neither authentic development nor genuine revolution makes absolutes of success. The qualified pursuit of both is an urgent duty because prevailing structures of underdevelopment perpetuate both hunger and terror.

NOTES

1. E. H. Carr, *What Is History?* (New York: Alfred A. Knopf, 1962), p. 102.
2. Peter L. Berger, *Pyramids of Sacrifice: Political Ethics and Social Change* (New York: Basic Books, 1974), p. 5.
3. Ibid.
4. See Barrington Moore, *Reflections on the Causes of Human Misery* (Boston: Beacon Press, 1972) and Robert Heilbroner, *An Inquiry into the Human Prospect* (New York: Norton, 1974).
5. Celso Furtado, "Brazil: What Kind of Revolution?" in Laura Randall, ed., *Economic Development, Evolution or Revolution* (Boston: D.C. Heath, 1964).
6. Franklyn Holzman, "Consumer Sovereignty and the Rate of Economic Development," *Economia Internazionale*, 11, 2 (1956): 15–16.
7. For illuminating views on the effect of poverty on the human spirit see Carolina Maria de Jesus, *Child of the Dark* (New York: E. P. Dutton, 1962), and Oscar Lewis, *The Children of Sanchez* (New York: Random House, 1961).
8. Gunnar Myrdal, *An International Economy* (New York: Harper & Brothers, 1956), p. 164.
9. Alexander Gerschenkron, *Economic Backwardness in Historical Perspective* (New York: Praeger, 1965), p. 213.
10. Richard Ohmann, "GBS on the U.S.S.R." *The Commonweal* (July 24, 1964), p. 519.
11. Karl de Schweinitz, "Economic Growth, Coercion, and Freedom," *World Politics*, 9, 2 (January 1957): 168.
12. W. Donald Bowles, "Soviet Russia as a Model for Underdeveloped Areas," *World Politics*, 14, 3 (April 1962): p. 502.
13. De Schweinitz, op. cit., p. 168.
14. Berger, op. cit., p. xii.

24

Survival Strategies and Power amongst the Poorest in a West Bengal Village

Tony Beck

INTRODUCTION

Recent attention to rural indigenous technical knowledge and farming systems in South Asia and Africa has concentrated mainly on agricultural technology and small farmers; and a growing literature on the causes of and responses to famine has focused on events which drastically affect large populations. Less interest has been shown in the landless and in "everyday forms of poor people's survival."

Survival strategies means the activities of poor people in times of stress which they see as crucial for the continued running of their household. This focus concentrates on their own priorities, and points to activities mainly outside the "formal economy." In this article it does not include organised and spontaneous violent and nonviolent resistance by the poor.[1] In West Bengal and no doubt in India generally, exploitative and oppressive village social structure is the main cause of poverty. For the outsider the problem is not only to document this, but to decide what action to take. Power relations cannot be ignored, but neither in many cases can they be dealt with directly. Those who advocate or examine radical alternatives at village level should be aware of the moral problems of doing so as outsiders.[2] The boundaries of empirical research on rural poverty by outsiders are perhaps marked by areas of organisation and cooperation by the poor. A practical

Note: Thanks are due to Daoud Knobi, Maya Rani Lodh and Kalipodo Pal, who assisted in field level interviews, and to Robert Chambers, Graham Chapman, Cathy Nesmith, and participants of the IDS workshop on "Coping and Vulnerability" for comments on a first draft. From *IDS Bulletin*, 20, 2 (1989), pp. 23–33. Copyright © Institute of Development Studies, Sussex.

focus, as in this article, can be to look for "gaps" or "soft areas" in the village power structure (Chambers 1983, pp. 157–63)—areas already used by the poor, that can bring benefits to them by exploiting the present system, and which, strengthened in the long term, could change the balance and structure of power.

Theoretically, concentrating on poor people's priorities is an adaptation of the idea of people's history developed by British Marxist historians such as Thompson, Hill, Samuel, and others.[3] This involves giving a "worm's eye" or "people's" view of the world, and a respect for and political sympathy with the poor as makers of their own histories.

This approach may have two possible effects. First, it can challenge a dominant view of the poor—that they are passive, irresponsible, or conservative, and its political corollary, that poor people are there to be planned for.[4] Challenging these views may change how plans are made, or even make it acceptable to propose that poor people can make their own plans. Second, this approach has policy implications, in particular how poor people's own strategies can be built upon and improved. In a different geographical context, Richards (1985, 1986) and Watts (1983) argued for backing and improving small farmer's indigenous agricultural strategies. Little has been written on the priorities perceived by poor rural landless people, on how they organise their lives, and how their more informal activities could be supported. To throw light on these questions, this article presents research findings from a village in West Bengal and explores their policy implications.

THE VILLAGE, "MENTAL-METRICISM," AND WHO THE POOREST ARE

The Case Study Village

Although only 40 km from Calcutta (or three hours by public transport) Fonogram village[5] in north 24 Parganas District remains relatively isolated. Local transport is limited, the main forms being foot and bicycle. There is a small town two and a half kilometers away which holds a twice weekly market. Most villagers do not often have the time to go further afield.

Fonogram is a Muslim village of 140 households and a population of about 830. It is mainly agricultural, "aman" being the year's main rice crop, harvested in October/November. West Bengal as a whole has a net sown area of roughly 13.6 mn acres and a rural population in the early 1980s of around 40 mn with about one-third of an acre available per person (the second lowest land-person ratio in India, next to Kerala) (Bandepadhyay 1983). Net sown area for Fonogram is about 162 acres (according to the Census of India for 1971), so its population density is even higher than the all West Bengal figure. An estimated one-third of households in Fonogram are operationally landless, and strategies for survival should be seen in the context of both scarcity and unequal holding of land.

Interviews were carried out with 22 respondent households in the winters of 1986/87 and 1987/88. In both these years the main part of the "aman" crop was destroyed by flooding, which meant little work for those usually employed as agricultural labourers, damage to several of the respondents' houses, and a period of general austerity (although the market price of rice, the main staple, did not increase noticeably in either year). In 1986/87 interviews were held as to how respondents were coping after the flood. A questionnaire designed from these interviews was used in 1987/88 concentrating on survival, and the villagers' views on social, economic, and political aspects of village life. Quantitative methods were seen to be inadequate for analysing the villagers' replies. My own findings have, therefore, been placed in the wider context of literature on poverty and survival to draw out their representativeness.

Of the 22 households, seven were female headed (all widows) and two respondents were widowers; in all, I spoke to 12 women, three men, and seven families (husband, wife, their parents and/or their grown up children). Twenty of the households were operationally landless (five without homestead land). Employment patterns of respondents were irregular, but the primary occupations of the main household earners were as follows: ten agricultural labourers, three labourers on lorries, three sharecroppers, three factory workers, one maid, one hawker, and one marginal farmer.

Mental-Metricism

Sen (1983) and Kynch and Sen (1983) have pointed out some analytical difficulties in development and poverty measurement studies based on respondents' perceptions, particularly that these may differ markedly from a more objectively measurable "reality." Sen has suggested focusing instead on "capabilities" or macro-level indicators of ill-or well-being, such as long-term mortality or literacy rates. This is part of a wider debate about the quality of poverty and whether or not it has an absolute or relative core (see Sen 1983 vs. Townsend 1985).

To concentrate solely on statistical analysis of macro-level data (or indeed similar analysis of micro-level data), however, ignores the paradigmatic basis of collection and use of such data—that it is based, in the Indian context, on a particular, dominant view of the poor and a political ideology that sees the poor as passive and dependent—a kind of statistical cannon fodder; and it is also to ignore the causes of poverty. Equally, such statistical analysis of macro- (or micro-) level data on literacy and mortality rates, for example, overlooks the "informal economy" in which the poor operate, which is crucial to their survival, and through which they conduct a large part of their affairs. It is useful and balanced to look for ways to combine macro- and micro-level statistical analysis with poor people's own perceptions and for ways in which these complement each other.

If village studies concerned with poor people's views are to be representative rather than idiosyncratic, there is a need for comparative material from which to generalise. As statistical analysis of data receives its legitimacy from its supposed accuracy, so village studies will become more credible as representative (or not) if comparable studies show similar findings (or not). Those few articles that I have come across on survival strategies in South Asia all comment on a lack of comparative material.[6] However, widespread evidence of, for example, enforced changes in consumption by the poor in times of food shortage, or of share-rearing of livestock by poor families, now suggests that these priorities and actions of the poor should be taken into account when policy is being considered.

Who Are the Poorest?

Drawing on recent work by Chambers (1988, pp. 17–18) and Lipton (1983a,b,c and 1985) on the "characteristics" of the poorest, and other sources including my field work, it is possible to suggest, in an eastern South Asian context, how the poorest act and which households they are in. They are likely:

1. To be exploited in terms of receipt of wages or credit, and to be in debt;
2. To be flexible in terms of coping, using a variety of strategies and able to work at a number of jobs (see Van Schendel 1986; p. 44; Jiggins 1986; p. 11; Caldwell 1986, pp. 682,691; Cain 1977, p. 209);
3. To be resilient and active in areas concerned with the running of the household (see below);
4. To be part of an informal village support network with other poor families (see below);
5. To be illiterate, but to want to educate their children;
6. To be landless or to have a small amount of unproductive land (see Lipton 1985), and to be irregularly employed;
7. To have relatively few assets or exchange entitlements (Lipton 1985; Sen 1982);
8. To be in clinical danger of undernutrition, and to spend at least 80 percent of their income without achieving 80 percent of minimum nutritional requirements (Lipton 1983a);
9. To have illness or have had recent illness in the household, and to be physically weak;
10. To be isolated in locational terms, and in terms of village power (Chambers 1983, pp. 111–14);

11. To be female headed (Gulati 81, p. 170; Mencher 1985, p. 364; Begum 1985, p. 231), and/or have large, young families (Lipton 1983c);
12. Not to belong to any political party (see below); and,
13. To spend substantial household time on common property resource activities (Jodha 1986).

Many of the poorest households are therefore likely to be landless labourer households with a female, physically weak, or often ill main earner, and/or several young children. This is a rough checklist which could be added to, and is dependent on regional variations, but the more of these indicators there are located in a household, the greater chance that this household is among the poorest. A single statistical indicator of poverty cannot expect to capture the depth and variety of the lifestyle of the poorest at village level,[7] nor can a concentration on the formal village economy; and policy is liable to be misdirected if based solely on such indicators.

STRATEGIES FOR SURVIVAL, AND POWER

Some survival strategies, such as taking debts, selling assets, and migration, are relatively well recognised. Others identified during the fieldwork are less so, and will be presented here: use of common property resources (CPRs); changes in eating and food preparation; share-rearing of livestock; and mutual support networks. All these are mainly undertaken by women and children, and challenge the dominant view that the poor are passive. While extreme crises such as famine are met by sequences of survival strategies (Corbett 1988), everyday survival strategies vary in relative importance at different times. They also interlink, but can for the time being be described separately.

Use of Common Property Resources

Strategies using CPRs includes gleaning, collection of fuel, and collection of wild foodstuffs.

Gleaning   Gleaning in Fonogram had been restricted by two bad agricultural years due to flooding, and also by those who owned the fields. However, 17 out of 22 respondents reported gleaning whenever there was time, and that this was an activity carried out mainly by children. In the remaining five households there were either no children, or respondents were out all day at work. Estimates of the amounts gathered ranged from "a handful," to 12 kg an acre, to 5 kg for a good day, to 25 kg a season. This can be compared to the amount of government aid received after the two floods—most respondents reported receiving 2–3 kg of wheat each year from the government.[8]

Collection of fuel   All respondents who could gathered twigs, branches, leaves, and cow dung. This collection was seasonal, mainly in the winter and summer, but not in the rainy season, as then no leaves fall and no-one pastures their livestock—a seasonal problem for the poorest not often noted. Most respondents did not quantify in their own minds the time spent on gathering fuel, but a common remark was that one person working for a morning (three to four hours) could collect enough to last for two days. For the most part where there are children in the household, they do the gathering.9 Most of the households' fuel requirements were met in this way, although all respondents said that the availability of CPR fuels had steadily decreased over time because of pressure on resources.

Jodha (1975, p. 1620, fn. 14), Caldwell (1986, p. 683), Dasgupta (1987, pp. 106–7), and Howes and Jabbar (1986) provide comparative South Asian material on the importance of gathered fuel to poor households, and Jodha (1986, pp. 1174–75) has estimated that poor households in 21 districts of seven states in dry tropical western and southern India, meet 66–84 percent of their fuel requirements from CPR activities, a finding that is mirrored in Fonogram village.

Gathering of wild foods   Almost all the respondents gather and eat wild foods, and gathering is done whenever and wherever possible and necessary—a point stressed by all respondents. Reported wild plants gathered were "shojina pata" (horse radish), "kolmi pata" (an "edible aquatic plant"), "neem pata" (margosa), "kochu" (an "esculent edible root"), "dumur" (fig), "pather pata" (jute leaves), and "helingsha" (a kind of watercress). Crow (1984, p. 1756), Greenough (1982, p. 231), Currey (1981, p. 128), and Rahaman (1981, p. 137) all report consumption of "kochu" by poor families in famine conditions in Bengal and Bangladesh. These wild foods cannot be consumed too often or they will cause health problems.

Children also gather fruits such as plums, tamarind, and mango, and Sengupta (1978, p. 9) describes "landless families living on jackfruit or mango in Malda and Coochbehar (West Bengal)." All this again suggests the inadequacy of the use of income or outlay to measure poverty.[10]

Jodha (1986) estimates that poor households spend 10–20 percent of their time on CPR activities, generating 15–25 days of work per household every three weeks in this way. Given this cumulative importance of CPRs, it might be worth questioning Lipton's assertion (1983a, p. 48) that "Hungry Indians are poor, and attempts to solve their food problems by (e.g.) persuading them to gather and cook more wild food and vegetable tops tends to neglect collection and cooking costs." It seems poor, hungry people are already active in this area, and do not need to be persuaded to gather.

Changes in Eating and Food Preparation

Changing patterns of eating and food preparation are less well known as a coping strategy than gathering. Spending by the poorest in Fonogram is irregular ("whenever money or a loan is available we get food" as one respondent put it), and so are their eating patterns.

"The stomach won't understand unless it gets rice" one respondent told me. But when ordinary rice is not available, several other substitutes are. Respondents reported eating "khud"—broken rice grains, about 25 grams of which come out of 1 kg of sieved rice, and which are sold only in the village, usually by better-off families. "Khud" costs about two-thirds of the price of the cheapest market rice. This can be fried with oil and salt and alleviates hunger. They also reported drinking the water left over after rice had been boiled in it ("bhater fan"), which is usually given to livestock, and eating parts of chaff left after threshing. Greenough (1982, p. 233) also notes the consumption of rice water during the 1943 Bengal famine.

Certain foods fill the stomach better than others. Several respondents said that they ate "par routi" (leavened bread) and then drank a lot of water to fill the stomach, or "gola routi" (flour mixed with water and fried like an omelette), which was considered more filling than "chapati." "Fatter" varieties of rice were preferred, as they were considered to give more energy; those doing manual work thought that they needed a fatter grain than "babus" (gentlemen) who wear wristwatches and trousers and sit in offices all day, and who prefer thinner varieties. Salt tea is also commonly taken, as sugar or molasses is too expensive, as is "pan" as an appetite suppressant.

A common response to the question of eating patterns after the two floods was: "we made one meal stretch into two," "we ate one day and fasted the next," or "we ate once a day and got by like that." Jodha (1975, p. 1620, fn. 15, 1978, pp. A38–9), Caldwell (1986, p. 688) and Van Schendel (1986, p. 43) all report regulation of consumption as a strategy for dealing with food shortage. Sleeping and fasting when no work was available, was quite common. Lipton (1983a, pp. 32–3) and Dirks (1980, p. 23) consider the nutritional side of this strategy, and Hartmann and Boyce (1983, p. 172) and Harari and García-Bouza (1982, p. 35) also give examples for Bangladesh and India.

Eight of the 22 respondents in Fonogram said that if they received a little more money they would save it for the next day rather than use it immediately to buy food. There is some evidence to suggest that poor people do plan for the long-term future by regulating consumption of food to protect assets. A connection between "voluntary" cuts in consumption and protection of assets may partly explain the finding of a longitudinal study over five years in four districts of the Kosi hill area of Nepal (Nabarro, Cassels et al. 1987) that land sales decreased but nutritional status did not improve. If poor households do protect assets by resorting to cuts in consumption, and where, as in Eastern India, there is discrimination against females (Harriss 1986), policies and programs to provide assets for the poor may perversely mean that women get less within the household.

Cuts in consumption are an enforced part of the lifestyle of the poorest. Within the narrow confines in which they found themselves, respondents had developed an expertise in food management. There were, however, several stories about irresponsible spending by some of the poorest households, and there is no reason to suppose that irresponsibility in spending is a characteristic solely of the rich.

One respondent, a widow with four young children and irregular income, when asked how she remained healthy on what seemed an inadequate diet, vividly described the different ways in which rich and poor people eat. She mimicked how rich persons would have five or six dishes of different foods in front of them and would take a little from each, turning up their noses at most of the dishes as being too spicy or too sweet, and therefore ending up eating only a small quantity; whereas poor persons would eat the whole of whatever was put in front of them, whatever the quality or quantity. This was a reminder that it is not only the rich who have views about how and what poor people eat.

Share-Rearing of Livestock

Twenty of the respondent households had some livestock, the two exceptions being unable to keep any as they had no courtyard to their houses. Of these 20, seven were share-rearing livestock and five others had share-reared in the previous five years. One other household wanted to share-rear but could not because of unavailability of animals. Five mentioned difficulty in getting animals.

The system is known locally as "poussani," which means to rear. The most common arrangement is that a household will raise a female goat, cow, duck, or chicken given to them by another, usually richer, household. After the animal has given birth twice, the first born and the mother are returned to the owner, and the rearer keeps the second born. In the case of a male animal, the proceeds after sale are divided equally between owner and rearer.

Livestock can be vitally important in sustaining poor households during periods of crisis (see Chambers 1983, pp. 129–30 for examples), but share-rearing and its importance to the poor have tended to be overlooked by researchers. Yet this system was operating in Bengal in the 1930s and 1940s, as Cooper (1984, p. 80) comments: "The landlord ensured that the sharecropper was provided with the means of production without actually bearing the costs of raising the livestock, even increasing his own stock."[11]

Share-rearing, in various forms, is common throughout South Asia today, and elsewhere.[12] Jodha (1986, pp. 1180, fn. 10) refers to how large farmers share-rear out of the poor, throughout seven states of western and southern India:

> Though varying in its extent, the practice of "salvaging" unproductive animals was observed in practically all the study areas. Large farmers gave their unproductive animals to the poor for maintenance as it was clearly costly to maintain them . . . When such animals became productive they were returned to the large farmer and net additions to the value of such animals (after becoming productive) were shared by the two parties. Depending on the type of animal . . . the terms and conditions governing this practice differed from region to region. In areas like Gujarat and Rajasthan such herding was an important source of income for the rural poor.

And Blaikie et al. (1979, p. 64) comment on share-rearing in West Central Nepal, noting that in several locations visited all the breeding of oxen was undertaken on this basis by labouring and artisan households. Bearing in mind that share-rearing potentially benefits both owner and rearer, it is perhaps not surprising that it is so widespread.

Mutual Support Networks and Power

Power relations in the village from the poor person's perspective would seem to be central in understanding the problem of poverty, but this perspective is usually avoided in favour of others less controversial. As Breman (1985, p. 34) has observed:

> In India there is a great scarcity of literature in which those living in the lowest echelons of society themselves speak out. For South Gujarat the region towards which my research has been directed for more than two decades now, I do not know of a single publication in which exploitation and repression is reported on the basis of experience from within.

I now proceed to deal with power relations with an awareness of the paradox involved in such research—that these relations are central to village life, but an area around which the researcher can only skirt.

Discussions were held with the respondents on the reasons for their poverty, how it feels to be poor, the characteristics of rich and poor people, whether the poor help each other or are helped by the rich, whether the rich cheat the poor, why the poorest do not get organised, and the importance of self-respect. Respondents themselves made the division into rich and poor—"gherastao" and "gorib." (For a similar definition of village differentiation based on poorer villagers' views, see Van Schendel, 1981, 90.)

None of the respondents belonged to a political party, and only one was familiar with government laws on sharecropping or homestead rights. In a wider, more formal sense, therefore, respondents could be considered apolitical. But their lack of involvement in formal politics did not mean that they did not hold strong "political" ideas about what was happening in their village.

As to how most respondents viewed their poverty, most replied in this manner: "Do you think I like being poor—don't you think I'm unhappy being poor?" Poverty also meant a loss of respect which was worse than hunger; apart from three who differed, all other respondents did not hesitate in saying that for them respect was more important than food, and that "without respect food won't go into the stomach." If this feeling is widespread among the poor in India, then planners' and academics' exclusive interest in income and nutrition is inadequate for understanding poverty.

When asked whose fault ("doash") it was that they were poor, all 22 respondents saw their poverty in terms of a similar apolitical causality— either they had lost their land or other assets, or were unable to work, or had not inherited any property, or they said that the population was increasing whereas land was not, or blamed the weather, or bad luck. As one woman put it: "We are poor because we have no land and my husband can't work . . . We had six 'bighas' of land before and plough cows and my husband could work five years back." Not one of the respondents thought their poverty was the fault of the rich in the village.

At the same time, respondents had definite ideas about the characteristics of the rich (and it should be remembered that it is Fonogram's poorest villagers' views that are presented here). Two respondents thought rich people helped poor ones, but the rest were adamant that they received no help ("shahajo") from the rich. About this, there was almost unanimous animosity. As one elderly widow put it:

> Rich people don't mix with the poor at all—even if we were dying and
> called them they wouldn't come. J. is going by motorcycle, A. by lorry
> and H. by cycle. I'm going by foot, shoeless. In the rainy season the rich
> eat well, but we have to eat fig leaves and get sick.

And a young landless labourer said more vividly: "Rich people are drinking poor people's blood, talking to them but not giving them anything."

Almost all agreed that rich people cheated poor people by giving too low wages, by making them work too hard, or giving too low prices for land or other assets. But no respondents made a causal connection between their own poverty and others' wealth. As another landless labourer said: "It's my own fault we are poor, not the fault of rich people."[13] However, the poor did not stop at insulting the rich. One newly wealthy family in particular, as well as other richer families, was the subject of theft and attack. Theft of pump sets and power lines were also common in the three years after 1985, when electricity had been introduced into the area. No-one familiar with the long history of "peasant" protest in Bengal will be surprised at the use of these "weapons of the weak."

Equally, almost all respondents thought that poor people helped and did not cheat each other. This help consisted mainly of small loans of either money, rice, or other edibles. This was despite the fact that there had been some disputes between the respondent households and between household members over relatively large loans and other serious matters such as "theft" of land.[14] While loans between poor households were considered as help, loans from rich to poor were not: everything depended on the attitude of the lender. K. Jansen (1986, pp. 19 and 25; table 5) has also commented on the importance of intrafamily loans in six villages in Noakhali District of Bangladesh, where such loans make up 32 percent of total village lending and were mainly used for household subsistence purposes.

One of the questions asked of respondents was why poor people did not cooperate with each other. The example was given of forming a buying cooperative which would cut prices at the local market, as buying could then be done in bulk. The most common reply was that there was no unity among the poor, that they all got money at different times, and that those who received money first would try to buy the best quality goods. While the rich were powerful, the poor were too jealous of each other to work together. The word jealousy or envy ("hingsha") was used several times. As one landless labourer said: "The poor work together sometimes when farming. But they can't work together usually because of lack of resources. They can't go shopping together because some people go later and some earlier."

Although adequate resources may be necessary if poor people are to cooperate rather than compete, it did seem as if there was a strong tradition of mutual support amongst the poorest in the village, based on the informal system of loans, and that they were also united in their animosity towards the rich, an animosity that was often strongly voiced.

There is an extensive literature on mutual support systems among the rural poor. Caldwell (1986, p. 694) points out from his work in Karnataka "the importance of marriage networks as a central mechanism in the insurance system against disaster," and Jiggins (1986, p. 16) notes: "One feature which stands out is the resilience of female household networks to seasonal stress and calamity; far from being among the most vulnerable, more critical study of the advantages of their organisational and economic flexibility may show that they are the 'survivors'."

Other recent evidence (see Van Schendel 1986, pp. 48–9; Howes and Jabbar 1986, p. 25; and Dasgupta 1987, p. 114 for South Asian material; and see also fn. 15) suggests that Lipton's assertion (1983a, p. 66), may be open to question: "Traditional rural compensations, the institutions of mutual help, were often exaggerated, and anyway are under pressure from both population growth and economic modernisation."

Respondents in Fonogram reported going from house to house asking for "khud" and "bhater fan" as well as for building materials. But the main kind of loans between poorest households was in the form of small amounts of money or foodstuff, which all respondents mentioned giving or taking. Other forms of mutual support were looking after children or live-stock. There is a complicated system of exchange, borrowing, receiving, and giving in Fonogram village. But a distinction is made between a "loan" between poor people which is an expression of support, friendship, and sol-idarity, and a loan begged from either another poor person or someone bet-ter-off, which involves a subordinate relationship.

Policies to Support Poor People's Strategies

What scope is there for policies to support these strategies of the poor? This can only be answered in context. Other strategies such as migration and sale of assets may be more the concern of men, but those discussed here focus mainly on the home and women and children's labour. Various fac-tors affect these strategies. The cultural environment is one determinant of consumption patterns (K. Jansen 1986), and also of whether or not poor women go outside the house to work. Strategies are perhaps more likely to vary by gender and ability than by age. The political setting in which they find themselves will, obviously, also influence the actions of the poorest. Mechanisation may affect strategies such as gleaning (Scott 1985, pp. 118–19). Environmental factors will also affect how the poorest people sur-vive; those living in an area with a high person/land ratio and scarce CPRs may have strategies very different from those living in the low person/land area described by Richards (Richards 1985). There are also overt and covert political strategies, with which the student of English agrarian history is familiar—trade union activity, "spontaneous" violence, or breaking of agri-cultural machinery. Individual and community strategies for survival may also differ. Given this variety of possible actions by poorest people, perhaps the most useful way of analysing survival strategies would be to identify those most likely to be supported by NGOs or governments, and to consid-er how poor people's efforts and those of outsiders can be linked.

Any consideration of policy in eastern South Asia has to take into account a high degree of centralisation of planning, a male-dominated and inefficient bureaucracy, and an overburdening of extension and village-level workers (for the latter, see NIRD 1985, pp. 80–81, 286–91). Scarcity of land and CPRs are also major constricting elements for policy, as are the competing interests of landless labourers, sharecroppers, and marginal farmers. Also, the strategies of the poorest described here, because they are part of an informal, and sometimes invisible, economy, may not be as amenable to government support as are those more informal agricultural activities carried out by small farmers and described by Richards and Watts. The possibility of "reformist" outsider policy should be viewed in the light of these constraining contexts.

Use of CPRs and Famine Foods

Use of CPRs is a thorny policy area. Changes in policy priorities towards an interest in CPRs can be seen in a recent World Bank publication which deals briefly with how rural households try to cope with transitory food insecurity (World Bank 1986, p. 26):

> In extreme cases in India, Ethiopia and Bangladesh, the starving eat a drought resistant legume, known as kessari dal, even though it can lead to paralysis. Since poor families draw on these famine foods in times of need, more research is needed to identify all sources of such foods, to understand fully how they are used, to determine what can be done to ensure their availability during periods of stress, and to develop a non-toxic variety of kessari dal or a processing method that will eliminate the toxic effect.

Indigenous methods of detoxification available for other plants (see Corkhill 1949; p. 7; Bhandari 1974, p. 77; and Leakey 1986; p. 38) suggest that it may be possible to develop such detoxification processes using village knowledge. A shift in research priorities towards "famine foods," as suggested, would surely benefit the poorest who are the main users of such foods.

Share-Rearing of Livestock

The system of share-rearing livestock described above raises questions about the Government of India's central poverty alleviation program, the Integrated Rural Development Programme (IRDP), which provides subsidy and loans to the poor to enable them to buy assets—often livestock. Problems with IRDP include leakages away from intended beneficiaries, unavailability of good quality livestock at reasonable prices, and lack of green and dry fodder (Rath 1985; Singh 1985, p. 335; Seabright 1987).

IRDP is based on top-down planning approaches—a scheme is devised, beneficiaries identified, and loans and subsidies given. At the same time the indigenous share-rearing method of loaning livestock that is widespread throughout South Asia has been ignored by planners, who may not even be aware of its existence. As share-rearing can benefit both (richer) loaner and (poor) borrower, it presents a "gap" where reformist policy can feasibly build upon strategies used by the poor. Most respondents in Fonogram village said that it had become increasingly difficult to find live-stock to share-rear. If this scarcity is widespread (and the demand for live-stock for the IRDP may be one cause of scarcity), incentives may be neces-sary to persuade livestock owners to lend—perhaps in the form of loans to the rearer to buy good quality feed. Backing up and improving this indige-nous method might help reduce the problem of too few good quality live-stock, and market "imperfections" that have meant IRDP recipients pur-chasing overpriced, poor quality animals.

Mutual Support Networks

To move to mutual support networks, various commentators have suggest-ed agricultural cooperative development as the next step forward for the Communist Government of West Bengal. But little attention seems to have been given to either agricultural labour union activity or more informal kinds of poor people's organisation and cooperation. Yet BRAC has shown in Bangladesh (Chen 1983) that it is possible to organise groups of poor landless women, using their skills for productive work, as long as the groups are homogeneous, and there is an economic incentive for the women to participate. While the poorest may "exploit" each other (partly because they have no other choice than to do so), it does seem that there is a strong existing indigenous system of cooperation among the poorest, based partially on an animosity towards the rich, that could act as a basis for the formation of groups to receive loans. Yet Government intervention in this area has up until now been at best unpromising.[16]

Policy in General

In the case of policy in general, much depends on the view the policy maker takes of the poor person. This is particularly relevant in the case of nutrition and poor people's preferences in food. Rich people's interest in what poor people eat is nothing new. Attempts to control the diet of the poor for polit-ical reasons date back, in Britain, at least until the late eighteenth century (Hammond and Hammond 1948; p. 119). Historically, little research on nutrition has looked at the preferences of poor people and how these might be included in nutrition policy, nor the political consequences of conduct-ing nutritional studies. One of the major debates about poverty in India—on the level of nutrition and income necessary for a poor person to sur-vive—has followed this historical pattern. This debate has focused almost exclusively on "scientific" and statistical estimates, and various participants have performed various forms of statistical acrobatics to support their argument. Practically no-one has asked poor people how much they think they need to eat, or attempted to measure this against "scientific" estimates. Yet poor people's preferences might be vitally important in deciding on the type and quality of food to be dispensed in times of emergency, or through ration shops. This form of "intellectual colonialism"—viewing the poor as those to be measured, weighed and planned for, rather than as people who make choices and decisions—needs to be challenged by empirical research which accepts that the poor have a voice.

CONCLUSION

This article has attempted to show that the poorest people, especially women and children, rather than being passive or apolitical, are active in their household survival strategies. While, in a South Asian context, the poorest live in an oppressive social system, which partly defines their actions, they also exploit that system for their own benefit. Measures to support and improve their present strategies may be of more use to them than externally imposed schemes (which include intermediate technology such as solar power or biogas), the benefits of which are likely to be appropriated by those at village level who have more power.

Although more comparative empirical evidence is needed to argue against the dominant paradigm that the poor are passive or followers, there is also a need for outside researchers to be aware that their solutions to poverty are likely to be marginal to its main causes. Equally, those who have never been active in cooperatives or trade unions should perhaps be wary of advising poor women and men to join or form such organisations. While poor people may want political support and sympathy, they may not want advice. So it may be that research concerned with the rural poor should be less about identifying their characteristics and giving advice, and more about listening to and presenting poor people's views. As one poor woman in Mymensingh District, Bangladesh, told someone who suggested she cook more green leafy vegetables (McCarthy 1984, p. 55):

> Don't worry about what I feed my family. You just give me some money and I will take care of it. You don't have to assume that I don't know what to feed my family. The problem is that I happen to be poor, and if you can't do anything about that then get out of here. Don't waste my time.

NOTES

1. For the moral and social difficulties of dealing with power at Indian village level, see Breman (1985).

2. This is meant with reference to empirical research, and not other more historical or academic forms of research.

3. For a similar use of such theory, on a much broader historical scale, see Watts (1983). For use of this theory in relation to Bengal, see Van Schendel and Faraizi (1984), and to Madras 1876–78, Arnold (1984). My focus here is on people rather than history.

4. For a further discussion of the political connection between ideology, planning, and the characteristics of the poor, see Beck (1988).

5. A pseudonym.

6. There is, however, a large survival literature from the Second World War, much of it by labour camp prisoners—Eugenia Ginzburg, Bruno Bettelheim, and Primo Levi, for example—and inhabitants of cities under siege, such as Olga Friedenberg and Vera Ibner on Leningrad. Interesting parallels could be drawn between strategies used by (intellectual) survivors and those used by the rural poor in South Asia today.

7. The inadequacies of statistical measurement of poverty are discussed at further length in Beck (1988).

8. Sengupta (1978, p. 7) has described Santal children collecting grain from rat holes and other kinds of gathering in Birbhum district of West Bengal. For Bangladesh, see also Siddiqui (1982, p. 358) for gleaning, Cain (1977, pp. 204, 209) who refers to children opening rat holes and gleaning, and Begum (1985, p. 235) for regional differences in gleaning practices.

9. Children also collect snails to feed to poultry. Date palm leaves are left on the side of ponds with most of the leaf submerged, and the snails crawl onto the leaves. Other livestock fodder is also gathered, as are various household materials, and livestock are taken regularly to graze on fallow land.

10. Most of the comparative literature on gathering wild foods deals with famine situations rather than periods of regular stress. For a list of famine foods in Nigeria, see Watts (1983, pp. 432–33) and for a more detailed discussion in Ethiopia, Rahmato (1988, pp. 8–10). For a review of other literature see Longhurst (1986; p. 32), and for a general discussion, Leakey (1986).

11. Sunil Sengupta has told me that "poussani" was operating several generations before the 1940s.

12. For references to share-rearing (technically known as agistment) in villages in Bangladesh see Howes and Jabbar (1986, pp. 24–25), Hartmann and Boyce (1983, p. 163), Westergaard (1983, pp. 52–57), Chen (1983, pp. 3, 148, 163), Siddiqui (1983, p. 357), Van Schendel (1981, pp. 90, 112, 167, 172, 331 fn. 7), and E. Jansen (1986, p. 44). For India, as well as Jodha see Epstein et al. (1983, p. 121), Bose (1984, pp. 100, 104), and Dasgupta (1987, p. 110). Paul Seabright has told me the system also operates in Tamil Nadu. For West Africa see White [1986, p. 24 (Niger)], and Chambers et al., eds. [1981, p. 86 (Mali)], and for Ethiopia, Rahmato (1988, p. 16). In Botswana, the system is known as "mafisa." Andrew Turton has told me that it operates widely in Northern Thailand, Jon Rigg has referred me to agistment in the highlands of Papua New Guinea and pointed out that government "buffalo banks" using agistment system are common in Thailand, and David Nabarro has told me that the system is found throughout Nepal.

13. Arens and Van Beurden make a similar point about "class consciousness" in

Bangladesh (1977, p. 77). For different views see BRAC (1979) and Epstein et al. (1983, p. 127). See also Van Schendel (1981, p. 92).

14. A subject not discussed here is intrafamily sale of assets and land leading to greater intrafamily differentiation, which may be common in West Bengal. Poverty and violence are closely interlinked, and there were many examples of intrafamily violence in Fonogram.

15. See also Longhurst for Northern Nigeria (1986, p. 30), Toulmin for Mali (1986, p. 66), and Rahmato for Ethiopia (1988, p. 7). Dirks (1980, p. 113) has suggested that such networks will break down in times of extreme stress. Splitting of families is also common. Lest these strategies be thought exclusive to the Third World, see McKee (1987, p. 113) on households with unemployed males in present day Britain. "Neighbours were variously described as providing help with household goods, furniture, child-minding or children's clothes. Women's networks were often the key to these exchanges."

16. For the failure of such groups to take off under the government's Development of Women and Children in Rural Areas programme in Bankura and Purulia districts of West Bengal, see Ghatak (1985), who attributes failure mainly to inefficient administration.

REFERENCES

Arens, J., and J. Van Beurden. *Jhagrapur: Poor Peasants and Women in Bangladesh.* Arens and Van Beurden. Amsterdam (distributed by Third World Publications), 1977.

Arnold, D. "Famine in Peasant Consciousness and Peasant Action in Madras 1876–8." In R. Guha (ed.), *Subaltern Studies,* 3, Oxford University Press, 1984.

Bandopadhyay, N. *Evaluation of Land Reform Measures in West Bengal: A Report.* Calcutta: Center for Studies in Social Sciences, 1983.

Beck, T. "Beyond Enumeration: Survival of the Poorest and Poverty Measurement in India." Paper given at IDS. London: Sussex, and the Institute of Commonwealth Studies, 1988.

Begum, S. "Women and Technology in Rice Processing in Bangladesh." In *Women in Rice Farming,* IRRI/Gower, 1985.

Bhandari, M. M. "Famine Foods in the Rajasthan Desert." *Economic Botany,* 28, 1 (1974).

Blaikie, P. M. et al. *The Struggle for Basic Needs in Nepal.* Paris: OECD, 1979.

Bose, P. K. *Classes in a Rural Society: A Sociological Study.* Calcutta: Ajanta, 1984.

BRAC. *Peasant Perceptions: Famine.* Dhaka: Bangladesh Rural Advancement Committee, 66 Mohakhali C.A., 12, 1979.

Breman, J. "Between Accumulation and Immiseration: The Partiality of Field Work in Rural India." *Journal of Peasant Studies,* 13, 1 (1985).

Cain, M. T. "The Economic Activities of Children in a Village in Bangladesh." *Population and Development Review,* 3, 3 (1977).

Caldwell, J. et al. "Periodic High Risk as a Cause of Fertility Decline in a Rural Environment: Survival Strategies in the 1980–83 South Indian Drought." *Economic Development and Cultural Change,* 34, 4 (1986).

Chambers, R. *Rural Development: Putting the Last First.* Longman, 1983.

————. "Poverty in India: Concepts, Research and Reality." *Discussion Paper* 241 Sussex: IDS, January 1988.

———— et al. (eds.). *Seasonal Dimensions to Rural Poverty.* London: Frances Pinter, 1981.

Chen M. *A Quiet Revolution: Women in Transition Rural Bangladesh.* Salenkman, 1983.

Cooper, A. "Sharecropping and Sharecropper Struggles in Bengal, 1930–50." Ph.D. diss. University of Sussex, 1984.

Corbett, J. "Famine and Household Coping Strategies." *World Development,* 16, 9 (1988): 1099–112.

Corkhill, N. C. "Dietary Change in a Sudan Village Following Locust Visitation." *Africa,* 19, 1 (1949).

Crow, B. "Warning of Famine in Bangladesh." *Economic and Political Weekly* (EPW), no. 40, October 6, 1984.

Currey, B. "The Famine Syndrome: Its Definition for Relief and Rehabilitation." In John R. W. Robson (ed.), *Famine, Its Causes, Effects and Management.* Gordon and Breach, 1981.

Dasgupta, M. "Informal Security Mechanisms and Population Retention in Rural India." *Economic Development and Cultural Change,* 36, 1 (1987).

Dirks, R. "Social Responses during Severe Food Shortages and Famine." *Current Anthropology,* 21, 1 (1980).

Epstein, T. S. et al. *Basic Needs Viewed from Above and Below: The Case of Karnataka State.* India, Paris: OECD, 1983.

Ghatak, M. "Development of Women and Children's Rural Areas of Bankura and Purulia Districts: An Evaluation." Calcutta: CRESSIDA (Mimeo), 1985.

Greenough, P. *Prosperity and Misery in Modern Bengal.* Delhi: OUP, 1982.

Gulati, L. *Profiles in Female Poverty.* Delhi: Hindustan Publishing Corporation (India), 1981.

Hammond, J., and B. Hammond (1st ed. 1912). *The Village Labourer.* Guild Books, 1948.

Harari, D., and Jorge García-Bouza. *Social Conflict and Development: Basic Needs and Survival Strategies in Four National Settings.* Paris: OECD, 1982.

Harriss, B. "The Intrafamily Distribution of Hunger in South Asia." Paper given at the Institute of Commonwealth Studies postgraduate seminar series, October 1986.

Hartmann, B., and J. K. Boyce. *A Quiet Violence: View from a Bangladesh Village.* London: Zed Press, 1983.

Howes, M., and M. A. Jabbar. "Rural Fuel Shortages in Bangladesh: The Evidence from Four Villages." *Discussion Paper* 213, Sussex: IDS, 1986.

IDS, "Seasonality and Poverty." *IDS Bulletin,* 17, 3 (July 1986).

Jansen, E. *Rural Bangladesh: Competition for Scarce Resources.* Norwegian University Press (distr. OUP), 1986.

Jansen, K. 1986. "Survival Strategies of the Rural Poor in Bangladesh." Centre for Development Research, Copenhagen (Mimeo).

Jiggins, J. "Women and Seasonality: Coping with Crisis and Calamity." In IDS, op. cit., 1986.

Jodha, N. S. "Famine and Famine Policies: Some Empirical Evidence." *EPW,* no. 41, October 11, 1975.

————. "Effectiveness of Farmers' Adjustments to Risk." *ERW,* Review of Agriculture no. 26, June 1978.

————. "Common Property Resources and Rural Poor in Dry Regions of India." *EPW* no. 27, July 5, 1986.

Kynch, J., and A. K. Sen. "Indian Women: Well-Being and Survival." *Cambridge Journal of Economics*, 7, 3/4 (1983).

Leakey, C. "Biomass, Man and Seasonality in the Tropics." In IDS, op. cit., 1986.

Lipton, M. "Poverty, Undernutrition and Hunger." *World Bank Staff Working Paper*, no. 597. Washington D.C.: World Bank, 1983a.

————. "Labour and Poverty." *WBSWP*, no. 616. Washington D.C.: World Bank, 1983b.

————. "Demography and Poverty." *WBSWP*, no. 623. Washington D.C.: World Bank, 1983c.

————. "Land Assets and Rural Poverty." *WBSWP*, no. 744. Washington D.C.: World Bank, 1985.

Longhurst, R. "Household Food Strategies in Response to Seasonality and Famine." In IDS, op. cit., 1986.

McCarthy, F. "The Target Group: Women in Rural Bangladesh." In E. J. Clay and B. B. Schaffer (eds.), *Room for Manoeuvre: An Exploration of Public Policy in Agricultural and Rural Development*. Gower, 1984.

McKee, L. "Households during Unemployment: The Resourcefulness of the Unemployed." In J. Brannen and G. Wilson (eds.), *Give and Take in Families: Studies in Resource Distribution*. Allen and Unwin, 1987.

Mencher, J. "Landless Women Agricultural Labourers in India: Some Observations for Tamil Nadu, Kerala and West Bengal." In *Women in Rice Farming*, IRRI, Gower, 1985.

Nabarro, D., C. Cassels, et al., "The Impact of Integrated Rural Developments: The Kosi Hill Area Rural Development Programme, East Nepal." Department of International Community Health, Liverpool School of Tropical Medicine, October 1987.

NIRD. "Administrative Arrangements for Rural Development: Proceedings of the National Workshop held at the National Institute for Rural Development (Hyderabad)." Government of India Publications, 1985.

Rahaman, M. M. "The Causes and Effects of Famine in the Rural Population. In John R. K. Robson (ed.), *Famine: Its Causes and Management*, Gordon and Breach, 1981.

Rahmato, Dessalegn. *Peasant Survival Strategies*. Geneva: International Institute for Relief and Development, Food for the Hungry International, 1988.

Rath, N. "Garibi Hatao: Can IRDP do it?" *EPW*, no. 6. February 2, 1985.

Richards, P. *Indigenous Agricultural Revolution*, Hutchinson, 1985.

————. *Coping with Hunger*, Allen and Unwin, 1986.

Scott, J. *Weapons of the Weak: Everyday Forms of Peasant Resistance*. New Haven, Conn.: Yale University Press, 1985.

Seabright, P. "Identifying Investment Opportunities for the Poor, Evidence from the Livestock Market in South India." Cambridge: Department of Economics (Mimeo), 1987.

Sen, A. K. *Poverty and Famines*. Oxford: Clarendon Press, 1982.

————. "Poor, Relatively Speaking." *Oxford Economic Papers*, 35 (1983).

Sengupta, S. (with M. G. Ghosh). "State Intervention in the Vulnerable Food Economy of India and the Problem of the Rural Poor." Paper for workshop on problems of public distribution of foodgrains in Eastern India, March 7–9, 1978. (Mimeo)

Siddiqui, K. "The Political Economy of Rural Poverty in Bangladesh." Dhaka: National Institute of Local Government, 1982.

Singh, K. "Eradicating Rural Poverty: Lessons of IRDP Experience." In NIRD, op. cit., 1985.

Toulmin, C. "Access to Food, Dry Season Strategies and Household Size amongst the Bambara of Central Mali." In IDS, op. cit., 1986.

Townsend, P. "A Sociological Approach to the Measurement of Poverty—A Rejoinder to Professor Amartya Sen." *Oxford Economic Papers,* 37 (1985).

Van Schendel, W. "Peasant Mobility: The Odds of Life in Rural Bangladesh." Assen: Van Gorcum, 1981.

———. "Self Rescue and Survival: The Rural Poor in Bangladesh." *Journal of South Asian Studies,* 9, 1 (1986).

———, and Faraizi, A. H. *Rural Labourers in Bengal 1880–1980,* Comparative Asian Studies Programme, Rotterdam: Erasmus University, 1984.

Watts, M. *Silent Violence: Food, Famine and Peasantry in Northern Nigeria,* University of California Press, 1983.

Westergaard, K. *Pauperization and Rural Women in Bangladesh: A Case Study,* BARD, Comilla, 1983.

White, C. "Food Shortages and Seasonality in WoDaaBe Communities in Niger." In IDS, op. cit., 1986.

Whitehead, A. "Women's Solidarity—and Divisions Among Women." *IDS Bulletin,* 15, 1 (1984).

World Bank. *Poverty and Hunger: Issues and Options for Food Security in Developing Countries.* Washington D.C.: World Bank, 1986.

25

Into Another Jungle: The Final Journey of the Matacos?

Ariel Dorfman

As a child, one of my friends thought the Matacos were some sort of animal. He had been brought up on a sugar mill in the province of Tucumán, Argentina, where at night the adults would tell stories. One story dealt with something called Matacos, which were hunted down by the hundreds in the jungles of the Gran Chaco forest. He remembered, above all, an evening when a guest of his father related how Matacos had been picked off one by one by soldiers from the back of a moving train. This confirmed his impression that the victims were monkeys or other wild beasts.

That idea persisted until several years later. One morning he went out into the yard and saw his grandmother standing in front of two small, bronze-faced children, an impassive brother and sister. With a pair of large scissors, she began to shear off their black, dirty hair. "These Matacos," she announced, "are full of lice. This is the only way to get rid of them."

It was only then that my friend realized that the Matacos were Indians.

❊   ❊   ❊

There is a vast region in the Argentine province of Chaco, some two million hectares of dry scrub forest, known as El Impenetrable. I found nobody who could fix the date when the phrase first came into use, but everybody agrees that it describes no ordinary jungle. A thick, intertwined bramble of vegetation stretches densely for miles, with an occasional solitary tree jutting above the low bush, to form a suffocating wall of thickets you can neither enter without a guide nor leave alive were that guide to abandon you.

But it is not the forest alone that isolates the zone. The land cannot

From *Grassroots Development*, 12, 2 (1988), pp. 2–15.

absorb all the water that flows into it. Water from the sky during months of rain. Water swelling from rivers that are fed by the remote Andes when they thaw, rivers overflowing their boundaries and changing course unpredictably. For days, often weeks, the roads are cut off—they can be navigated for miles as if they were narrow lakes. Afterward, withering months of dry heat, even of drought, will come, but that does not matter—the local people know that soon enough they will have more water than they know what to do with.

Most people would find such a place, alternating between swamp and arid scrubland, not only impenetrable but, frankly, uninhabitable. What to others is inhospitable and menacing is to the remaining Matacos—15,000 of the extant 23,000 are concentrated in this area—a last refuge and, perhaps, a last opportunity to survive.

It is here, on the northern frontier of El Impenetrable, bordering the brown, muddy currents of the tumultuous Bermejo River, that the village of El Sauzalito lies. It is here that a remarkable experiment is being carried out to try to save a people from extinction.

❅   ❅   ❅

In 1879, at the exact moment when the Indians in the United States were being massacred by superior firepower, Julio Roca, then Argentina's minister of war and soon to be its president, defined a new strategy toward the Indians who still controlled vast territories of the republic. "It is necessary," he said, perhaps thinking of the newly invented Remington rifle, "to directly search out the Indian's hiding place and make him submit or expel him." The resulting offensive against the Indians of the Pampas was known as *La Campaña del Desierto* (the Campaign of the Desert), and it all but exterminated the nomadic warriors who roamed the rich, fertile plains that were needed for grazing cattle and raising wheat. At the same time, though with less resources and urgency, the Gran Chaco (called the Green Desert) was conquered, and the remaining tribes of Indians were pushed back. This culminated, finally, in the expedition to the river Pilcomayo in 1912 and the massacre that was probably at the source of those stories my friend once heard around the bonfire in Tucumán.

The Matacos have their own version of what happened. Andrés Segundo is a 54-year-old Mataco who learned how to write 40 years ago. One of the first things he wrote down was his grandparents' memory of that expedition against his people, a recollection repeated today by his own children and grandchildren. He reads from his notebooks, and because his words are difficult to follow, I try to understand better by focusing on the print. Though the words are Spanish, the small, scrubby letters look almost indecipherable. As his fingers trace the hieroglyphics across the page, his voice is slurred, repetitive, incantatory.

> We did not know where those soldiers came from or why. They found
> where the aborigines [the Matacos never use the words "Indians" or
> "natives" to refer to themselves] lived and came with rifles, with bullets,
> beating people up. The Matacos went into the *monte* [the bush]. There
> was one woman with a child. She was hurt. She threw the child away.
> That is what my grandfather told me. They hunted the aborigine as if
> he was a tiger. . . . We were not harming anyone. We lived from the
> land, gathering the things that belonged to nobody. I do not know why
> the soldiers came.

The reason is, in fact, quite simple. They came because by then Argentina was producing goods for export to foreign markets—and a lot of
Indian land was there for the taking. "The settlers would come," Manuel
Fernández, another Mataco chronicler, told me, "and ask for permission to
clear land or settle down. They might give the tribe a cow." The Indians
interpreted this as a gesture of gratitude. The settlers understood that they
had bought the land. To the Matacos, that was absurd: How could you sell
the land? The Army arbitrated the disputes.

Their territory began to dwindle—but even so, the Matacos were not to
be left alone on what remained. The Argentine economy needed not only
their land—but their bodies as well.

Andrés Segundo has also recorded this event. His uncle told him of the
day that a stranger arrived. He had been sent by the owner of a remote
sugar mill in search of field hands to cut cane. The long journey that followed is recorded on yellowing scraps of paper—how they walked for a
month, whole families, until they reached the train. Andrés Segundo tells
the tale in a monotone, almost without emotion, as if these catastrophes
were natural and not manmade. It rained along the route, it seems (I write
"it seems" because the details are blurred, as if it were still raining and
there were mud on the words themselves). The little ones cried from the
cold. A terrible wind swept down, trees fell, people were killed.

That was to be the first, but not the last, trip. Trapped in a system of debt
bondage, increasingly dependent on manufactured goods, the Matacos kept
returning to the sugar plantations (cotton would come later). Part of the year
they were seasonal workers, hiring out for low wages and cheap merchandise; the rest of the time they hunted and fished, and ate fruits and berries.

But even this divided, miserable life was endangered. By the 1960s,
fewer workers were being hired—the era of mechanization had set in. (On
the plane back from the Northeast, I happened to sit next to a major
Argentine cotton exporter. Texas Instrument in hand, he calculated, for my
benefit—punching plus and minus buttons, doling out percentages—how
mechanization had made the migrants increasingly obsolete.)

The Matacos found themselves in a precarious situation. The monte
was eroding, animal species were disappearing, the ecological equilibrium

of the region had been fractured, wages were insufficient. ("There was no work," Andrés Segundo explained, "but we had to eat anyway.") Along with malnutrition, diseases like tuberculosis, Chagas, and parasitosis became prevalent. Infant mortality rose.

As the 1970s began, the future looked still bleaker for the Matacos. They had survived natural floods and disasters for centuries, but they could not withstand the manmade flood of modern civilization. Like so many other contemporary tribes of aborigines, the Matacos seemed bound for extinction.

✳   ✳   ✳

There was no road to El Sauzalito 12 years ago. Had you been able to get there, you would have found a scattering of thatched huts in the middle of a clearing overgrown with weeds. Remove the steel machetes, some clothing, a couple of bottles and tin cans, and you might have thought you were visiting the Stone Age.

Today El Sauzalito is connected by a dirt road to Castelli, 200 miles away, and by radio to the outside world. In the center of the town is a plaza, with benches, planted flowers, gravel pathways. Nearby is a bungalow where the elected mayor and aldermen meet, along with an office for the justice of the peace and a civil registrar. A hospital, a grade school, and a high school have been built. Most, though not all, of the inhabitants live in brick houses. And there is electricity.

More important, instead of losing population, El Sauzalito is growing. Couples are marrying, children are being born. I met several young men who had left to log trees but were now returning home for good. The movement is centripetal, not centrifugal as before.

Just a few miles away, you can still find small settlements that remind you of El Sauzalito's recent past: sparse collections of huts barely differentiated from the surrounding monte. But the real distance is not measured in miles. To transform El Sauzalito, thousands of hours of energy have been expended by the Matacos, and resources have poured in from the outside. If the resources were to dry up, if the Matacos were to sink into apathy, this new version of El Sauzalito would probably slip back in time, slip away into the waiting overgrowth, and once again begin to die.

✳   ✳   ✳

At the beginning of this century, a doctor by the name of Maradona wrote a book, *Através de la Selva* (Crossing the Jungle), in which he narrates his visits to various Indian communities of the Gran Chaco. "The Indian," he writes of the Mataco, "speaks softly and is even gentle in the way he treats you, but his savage, suspicious, and egoistic nature quickly prevails."

On other pages, he mentions their criminal personality, their readiness to destroy. Other adjectives he uses are "indolent," "decadent," "ridiculous," "sanguinary."

The Argentine Constitution, of course, uses none of these words to describe the Indian. But by mandating that the Indian be converted to Catholicism as a way of guaranteeing peace (Article 67, Item 15), it legally affirms the inferiority of native civilization and culture and denies Indians the right to their own beliefs. It is not surprising, therefore, that a 1978 decree put the undersecretary for Indian affairs also in charge of the welfare of minors, the elderly, and the handicapped.*

Indians are lumped together with those who are not adults, with those who have already lived out their usefulness and are waiting for death.

❋   ❋   ❋

When Diego Soneira arrived in El Sauzalito in 1973 as the representative of the Instituto del Aborigen, a sort of Bureau of Indian Affairs, he had already spent several years working in the area and was convinced that only a dramatic alteration in their way of life could save the Matacos. They had been, until then, constantly on the move, either as nomads in the jungle or as migrants on the plantations. Neither form of subsistence offered any guarantee of stability. What the Matacos needed was to become the legal owners of their own land so they would never again be expelled from it. But this meant they had to till that land and become sedentary.

This was not going to be easy. Though they had learned something about growing subsistence crops from the outreaches of the Incan empire many centuries ago and later picked up a bit more from the whites, the Matacos were primarily hunter-gatherers. What had taken the human race many thousands of years, the Matacos would have to achieve in a generation.

Soneira, however, was not the kind of bureaucrat who comes to visit the poor or the Indians armed with theories and suggestions that others must enact and then leaves for a comfortable home. He knew that if this change were to have any chance of success, it would have to be carried out by the Matacos themselves and could not be imposed from the outside. And he knew this meant accompanying the Matacos, living as they did. A former priest who lost none of his missionary zeal when he gave up the priesthood, Soneira arrived in El Sauzalito to stay. Six other white people— experts in health, agriculture, education—joined him, among them his new wife, Nene, and her mother, Clemencia Sarmiento, known to one and all from then on as Mami.

---

*Editor's note: Since this article was written, new legislation was passed in 1987 that calls for sweeping reforms in the treatment of Indians in Argentina.

Of course, the Matacos were suspicious. They had no way of knowing that Diego was different from the other white men who had brought ambitious proposals and then went away richer than when they arrived and certainly better off than the Indians who they left behind. In their first meeting with Soneira—which has assumed a sort of legendary, almost foundational status in the memory of El Sauzalito and is now narrated in a confused tangle of versions—eight Matacos were ready to cooperate; 150 others opposed his presence. (Each Mataco I spoke to included himself among the eight.) What *is* clear is that, in spite of a majority who wanted to refuse them entry, the group managed, after hours of discussion during a deluge, to pitch three tents in the middle of the bush, in the exact spot where the central plaza now proudly stands. As the days slipped by, Soneira and his companions gradually won the confidence of the Matacos, though he would be expelled twice from the town when they did not receive everything they wanted. Soneira eventually created the Asociación Promotores Chaco, which brought in outsiders to help the Matacos develop agricultural projects. Today, there are 40 *promotores* throughout El Impenetrable.

To focus only on the outside advisors, however, is unfair to the many Matacos who had concluded on their own that they were heading for a dead end. Without these Matacos, Soneira's plans would never have worked.

Ernesto Reynoso, for one, the *cacique*, or chieftain of the Matacos, had watched his people's situation deteriorate year by year. Like Soneira, he had come to believe that land ownership was the best hope for the Matacos. Nobody had elected Reynoso to his post; no other candidate wanted the job. While he may tend to exaggerate his own role ("I made this place; I am the *tata*, the big father of this place; I am the authority here"), all agree that he *was* indispensable. Over the years, he was to prove himself a wily advocate: tirelessly pestering authorities to exact promises of aid, then knocking on doors to hold them to those promises. A stubborn rock of a man, he knew that if aid were to be continued, his people would have to show results. Behind him and beside him, therefore, stand many other Matacos. His pride in what has been accomplished is their pride. "These are the machines that did everything," he says, lifting up his arms. "And these legs, they did the walking. Everything you see—the plaza, the hospital, the fields—we made it all."

His great-grandfather did not know a word of Spanish. He lived off the honey and the iguana and the fish. With machete, pickax, and shovel, his grandfather helped to build the railroad from Formosa to Salta. His father was a *bracero* on the plantations. Reynoso himself began to pick cotton when he was five years old. His wife died on one of those month-long treks to the cotton fields.

"Someday," he told me, "we will have Mataco doctors. Who knows? Perhaps someday my grandchild will pilot a plane."

❋   ❋   ❋

But the confluence of these two streams—the whites devoted to the
Matacos and the Matacos' faith in themselves—might have been insuffi-
cient if another sort of downpour had not taken place. In 1975, the
Argentine military overthrew the government of Isabel Perón.

How ironic that this event would help the Matacos, who when they
vote at all, tend to vote Peronist. The military government, as history has
shown, was not overly interested in helping those who lived on the margins of society. Obsessed with security, however, they worried that the
Gran Chaco was so underdeveloped and isolated that it would be vulnerable to foreign attacks. And the very notion that something "internal" could
also be "impenetrable" was an insult to the geopolitical, macho pride of the
military.

The armed forces therefore supplied an enormous quantity of resources
to the region, most quite useless. In the middle of the jungle, for instance, in
an area with few natives, a small concrete town was built from scratch,
replete with telephone lines, satellite-dish television, and air-conditioned
buildings staffed by government employees with nothing to do all day but
wait for the next showcase visit.

But in El Sauzalito, funds could be used for plans that were already
under way. Thus when the governor of the province came for a visit and
noted that a great deal had already been accomplished with little outside
support, he offered Diego Soneira the post of mayor, or *intendente*. Though
the military government's national policy ran directly counter to his own
democratic ideals, Soneira saw the chance to further develop the area, pay
the promotores' salaries, and channel municipal money into essential
infrastructure.

As Soneira reports it, he told the governor that there were two ways to
approach the development of El Impenetrable. One alternative was to see it
as an enormous enterprise. "In that case," he said, "your purpose is to make
money, and you exploit things to produce an immediate benefit. Or you can
see a vast school here. This means that, like any form of education, you will
run a deficit in the short run, with the benefits coming many years from
now. I am not an entrepreneur. If you want me and my people to work
here, we must be allowed to make this place into a school that will give the
Indians a chance to learn how to live on their own and not be condemned
to live off welfare forever."

The governor, surprisingly, agreed.

❋   ❋   ❋

It was inevitable that someday the vast school of and for the Matacos
would run into trouble because this effort is made up of two separate, and

one might almost say contradictory, learning processes. The first, which has had priority until now, is to modernize the Mataco economy, allowing its members to cope with an overwhelming foreign civilization that technologically and organizationally is far more powerful than theirs. The second, which was only implicit and thus far has found no institutional expression or funding, is to help the Matacos save their identity and sustain what makes them unique as they become integrated into a world whose rules they did not make.

The problem is that to become modern and have an economic base of their own, the Matacos must break their traditional patterns of social organization. For hunter-gatherers, Nature is the provider: The future depends on reading the natural world carefully, not on the systematic planning of one's work. You collect enough to last for a brief period, and when that stock has been depleted, you go out and get more. Such a culture does not conceive of the idea, for example, that a crop can be ruined if you leave the fields for a week, that there are such things as capitalization, or credit to be repaid. The future is really not in one's hands. "This may happen," the Matacos told me. "And then again, perhaps it may not."

Nor are the Matacos accustomed to fulfilling collective obligations. Formerly in their community, each family could leave without permission. Decisions were not made by a majority and imposed upon a minority. This is a perfectly logical structure if the renewable forest is always there—but it invites disaster if the earth must be worked, tractors allocated, seed and fertilizer distributed, if survival depends on taming Nature through mutual cooperation.

The Matacos have been relatively successful in this venture. This is evident in the number of buildings and facilities, in the increased standard of living, in the many hectares (still insufficient) now under irrigation, in the crops exported and the timber sold, and above all, in their capacity to organize. They control and regulate their own economic activities through the Asociación Comunitaria, with a subcommission for each industry—agriculture, lumber, tree-felling, repair work, and soon, fishing. The association allows the Matacos to plan their work, distribute the benefits, do the accounting, discuss and solve their difficulties.

The promotores, to be sure, are still on hand with suggestions, expertise, techniques—as an unavoidable bridge to a confusing outside world—and they may remain until a new generation is educated. Yet, the Matacos are obviously weaving their uncertain way to relative autonomy.

Achieving this first educational objective, however, has forced the Matacos to deal with the second, which has been perpetually postponed. The promotores did not initiate this experiment as a way to painlessly ingest one more aboriginal tribe into the stomach of the twentieth century. The idea was that the Matacos should modernize without losing their values and perspectives, their own culture.

The difficult question, of course, is the same one that is heard in many other places in the Third World: "Can it be done?"

❊   ❊   ❊

The day I arrived in El Sauzalito, a little Mataco girl had just died. She was the sixteenth child to die in the last four months.

A few hours later, I met the doctor who at the time was supposedly in charge of the community's health. I had heard vague stories about him—a man who turned away the sick if they called outside the regular schedule, a man who did not visit the other communities, a man who supposedly had said that the only way to make an Indian work was to fire a couple of shots at him. But even those stories did not prepare me for the person who swaggered through the door. He began by verbally abusing the whole experiment: It was, he said—his eyes protruding from a thin, bony face—"a total failure." Instead of advancing, the Matacos were going backwards. He branded the recent decision to plant cotton as ludicrous and stated that what was needed was a *criollo* landowner to establish some order. Finally, he turned around, crouched slightly, and using his buttocks as a metaphor, wiped them with his hand to show how worthless he considered everything.

"Why are you here then?" I asked.

His answer chilled me. "I am not human," he said. Perhaps he meant "humanitarian"—but the word he may have used mistakenly suited his manner quite well. "I didn't come here to save anybody, but for my own benefit. I'm almost 60. If I had retired as an ordinary doctor, I would be a beggar. That's why I agreed to come to this place. So I could retire with the pension of a hospital director."

I would not mention the doctor except that he personifies, in my opinion, two undeniable facts about the Mataco condition: First, many outsiders come to such places not to help those who live there but to help themselves. Second, and perhaps more significantly, the Matacos had been trying to get the doctor replaced ever since he arrived three years earlier. They had received repeated assurances that he would soon depart, but there he sat, symbol of all the things—far too many things—that the Matacos do not control and yet are essential to their well-being. The Matacos can do little about the world economic crisis or that of the Argentine economy—even though these crises mean that their products fetch lower prices, that inflation eats up their benefits, and that subsidies and services become even scarcer.

The apparent hostility and complexity of the outside world creates among the Matacos an added dependency on the external buffers that protect and benefit them. Without the promotores or outside aid, the Matacos could not have begun their journey toward autonomy; but now they tend to think of those factors as permanent. With some embarrassment, wherever I went, I had to submit to a long litany of needs and petitions and complaints, as if each person were demanding that I solve his problems.

This is not, of course, unique to the Matacos. The dilemmas of paternalism and dependency are present in most development projects. It is not my purpose to explore here how those problems can be overcome. What does matter at this point is to note that if all power—both evil and good—seems to come from outside, then the Matacos' sense of self-worth is weakened. Everything they learn tells them that the road to autonomy, the road to success, passes through the abrogation and eradication of their past identity.

❄   ❄   ❄

The anthropologist Edward Spier, in his classic study of the Yaqui Indians, coined the phrase "enduring peoples" to designate those human groups who have "experienced incorporation into nation-states, and have existed within or outlasted nation-states." He examines "the Cataláns and Basques of Spain; the Welsh and the Irish, formerly of Great Britain; the Cherokees, the Hopis, and the Senecas of the United States; the lowland Mayas of Mexico; and finally, the Jews of many different states."

In all of these cases, he finds that a people will persist—despite drastic changes in genetic constitution, place of residence, language, customs, and beliefs—if they continue to hold a common identity, that is, a stock of symbols and experiences that allow them to have a common understanding of the world and of their relationship to other cultures. Peoples who are unable to maintain the consciousness of their ethnicity are unable to remember their past collectively or use it to interpret the present and will probably be absorbed.

Can the Matacos endure?

Do they have within their culture the resilience and flexibility to go through the rites of modernization without disintegrating as an independent cultural entity?

There is at this point no way of telling for sure. What I saw and heard was not overly encouraging.

In 1944, the Matacos were converted to Christianity by missionaries of the Anglican Church. For the first time, the Indians received some elementary education, health care, and protection from the incursions of the army and the white settlers who would often kill a Mataco or two for fun. But the Indians were also taught to forget their own legends and stories, to feel ashamed of their past, and to stop dancing and singing their traditional music.

I asked the Matacos I met to tell me stories and myths from their past. They either pretended not to understand my question or told me they could not remember. When I repeated several legends or described beliefs about the dead and their spirits—things I had read in collections edited by foreign anthropologists—people nodded, agreeing that these were stories they knew. They did not, however, admit to telling their own children these tales, to sharing that body of sacred law that contains moral guidance and the threads of communal identity. Some promotores told me that something similar happens with songs and dances: The Matacos sing hymns at church, but the old instruments and melodies are being put aside and forgotten.

The only Mataco I met who was prepared to recount and discuss the old myths was—strange as it may seem—Ernesto Avendaño, the Anglican pastor of El Sauzalito. Perhaps he was sure enough of the divine origins of his own beliefs to be able to admit knowing those stories. He explained, in any case, that they were mere superstitions and were no longer necessary to his people. The songs, he added, were learned as apprenticeship to witchcraft, but all that was a thing of the past.

Since this rejecting attitude is the basic belief of most Matacos—or at least what they profess to believe—the situation is delicate for the promotores. Patricio Doyle, a former Catholic priest who has focused on the cultural future of the Matacos, does not want to interfere with their religious beliefs or their forms of worship. But he does want to discover what remains of their values, skills, and legends, what the Matacos can build on as they become part of the Western world and the Argentine nation.

He is now working on a *revistita,* a small magazine in Mataco and Spanish that will belong to the community itself and serve as a vehicle for amplifying the multiple voice of the Matacos. He hopes the Matacos will begin to express their present problems as well as what belongs to their past and their collective memory.

He has also managed to persuade two experts in the development of art and recreation among marginal groups to come from Buenos Aires and work with the local people.

And yet Patricio Doyle, who has spent many years among the Matacos, does not speak their language. Nor, for that matter, does any other promotor, not even Diego Soneira. Nor do any of the white children. Some words are understood, some conversations can be followed vaguely, but not one of the people who have come to help the Matacos survive as a cultural entity is fluent in their language. No matter how they have tried, they have been unable to learn it or even find Matacos who will teach them.

I heard the language often during my stay. Once, I remember, I was at a meeting that Mario Pisano, a promotor, held with the residents of nearby Vizacheral to discuss future fishing activity. After some words had been exchanged in Spanish, one of the men suddenly switched to Mataco, and the rest soon joined in with a flowing antiphony. Before one person had ended, another had begun, as if speaking to himself and yet to all of them, as if somebody inside were listening, murmuring very low—only ears accustomed to the bush could distinguish each sound—and on it went, a honied, intertwining superimposition of voices, until they stopped. They had reached some sort of conclusion, one and all of them, and Spanish was once again the language to be used. I felt, during these moments, as if they were defending their last refuge on earth, those thickets of syllables that only they could understand.

It almost seems as if the Matacos are unwilling to teach the promotores their language. Once you give strangers your language, it is as if you have given them your jungle, your land, your trees. It is in the language, after all, that places and birds, animals and customs are named and invoked.

Perhaps I had caught a glimpse of the real Impenetrable—the language, the one place in the world that belongs only to the Matacos.

❃ ❃ ❃

The Matacos have beautiful legends.

Like those of all peoples, they narrate the origins of the universe, the reason why there are men and women, how the animals appeared, why it rains and why honey exists, the struggles of heroes and the voyages of tricksters.

Some of their legends seem to be recent because they exhibit a considerable awareness of white, dominant people.

In one of these, the Matacos explain why they are so few and other tribes so populous. According to this tale, the different races and nations crawled out from underground through a hole dug by an armadillo. All the men and women of each race were able to escape and populate the earth. But when the Matacos' turn came, only a few appeared before a pregnant Mataco woman got stuck in the hole and was unable to move. And so, many Matacos remain unborn.

Another legend says Christians and Matacos resided together long ago in one house "where everything could be found." Everything that was good—the axes, tools, horses, cattle, beautiful clothes for women—was taken by the ancestors of the Christians, and the Matacos were left with only clay pots, dogs, and "other inferior things."

The clay pot, which the Matacos make with great skill and elegance, is the protagonist of another short tale. It began to compete with the iron pot, saying that it could cook as well and as quickly over fire. But the iron pot won, and so the pot made of earth cracked, and was thrown away.

The Matacos have beautiful legends, but they feel defeated. A people will survive only if they are able to take pride in their own culture.

❃ ❃ ❃

Between 1821 and 1982, almost 6.4 million immigrants came to Argentina. In 1895, immigrants made up 25.5 percent of the population, and by 1914, this figure had risen to 30 percent, the highest proportion in the world.

No statistics record how many Matacos there once were. So we cannot know what proportion is now left.

❋   ❋   ❋

Some 420 miles south of El Sauzalito is the city of Resistencia, the capital of the province of Chaco.

In the central plaza of Resistencia—christened with that name because it triumphantly *resisted* the assaults of the savages—there is a statue. It is the copy of a statue I have seen often in art and history books and whose original I once contemplated in Rome itself. It was given to the city of Resistencia by the resident Italian-Argentine community, and it portrays the twins Romulus and Remus suckling a she-wolf.

That is how Rome saw its origins, as if there had been no previous tribes on its peninsula, no previous inhabitants. And the immigrants who came to the Argentine northeast saw themselves opening supposedly virgin territory just like the Romans did: each of them a Romulus, each a Remus coming to establish tiny empires in a foreign land.

There is no statue in Resistencia to the ancestors of Andrés Segundo or Ernesto Reynoso.

There is no statue of their ancestors anywhere.

❋   ❋   ❋

By a strange coincidence I heard Rome mentioned the first morning I arrived in El Sauzalito. Although the reference had nothing to do with immigration, it may have had something to do with empires.

I asked Patricio Doyle why he had left Buenos Aires, what he was doing in this remote place.

"Christ was not born in Rome," Doyle answered. "He was born in Bethlehem. Who knows what will be born in this faraway land and radiate, by example, elsewhere?"

❋   ❋   ❋

Most of the Matacos I spoke with seemed unaware of their purported transcendence or of the cultural crossroads they have come to.

I hesitated before writing down the previous sentence. I really cannot be certain that it is true.

The problem is that I was barely able to communicate with the Matacos during my brief stay. We talked, of course, extensively. Yet there was, except for one occasion, no deep contact—no moment when two people come together and know they are sharing something, that there is some understanding. I lacked their language, and they used mine without eloquence, though often with great dignity. Their Spanish, moreover, besides not being their native tongue, is the language of those who dominate them, and they must have supposed that what I would write about them might be essential for future aid or grants. They were careful, therefore, of what they said. Nor did it help that I lacked an interpreter: Translations at least pretend that there is some equality in the interchange. And there was the incredible reserve and intractability of the women, with whom I was never able to speak at all and whose importance in the conservation and transmission of an oral, autochthonous culture cannot be overstated.

I was not frustrated by this lack of connection. I interpreted it as a sign that the Matacos had secret paths in their forests to which I had no access, treasures they would not yield easily. I was glad they had something hidden—and only hoped that behind their silence, or the words that are like silence, there are strengths upon which they can build as their experiment continues. As they become more self-assured, they should be able to engage in an ever more significant dialogue with the outside world.

But there was, as I suggested, one exception. His name is Ramón Navarrete. As the *primer consejal,* or deputy mayor, of the *municipio,* he had attained the highest political and administrative post a Mataco ever held. I had tried to speak to him on several occasions, and he was always busy. Only on my last day in El Sauzalito—as the afternoon turned into what I can only describe as a green-hot evening—were we able to talk.

When democracy and elections returned to Argentina in 1983, Diego Soneira decided to step down as *intendente.* The concentration of so much power in his hands had allowed the community to take gigantic steps forward, but it had also created confusion and seemed a bit artificial. It was time, Soneira believed, for the people themselves to administer their own institutions, to be less sheltered from the outside world. They had to learn not to look to him for all the answers. Though the Matacos constituted a large majority of the population, they did not propose one of their own as mayor, preferring a criollo who was sympathetic to them and had administrative experience. They did, however, elect three *consejales,* or aldermen, and Navarrete is one of them. He is not a leader, as is Ernesto Reynoso, but he is—of all the Matacos—the one who best understands how language and Argentine society work. He is the closest example to an "intellectual" that I found in the Mataco community.

Like intellectuals everywhere, Navarrete is anguished. He must cope with burdens he only vaguely comprehends—budgets, sick leaves, papers in triplicate, the wonders of modern-day bureaucracy—and at the same time respond to the increasing demands of Matacos who believe the municipio exists to provide jobs and food.

To live between two worlds, where tradition and newness constantly mingle and conflict, is after all one of the primary experiences of modernity in the Third World. It is as if, he said, he had given me a quick lesson in Mataco and then sent me into the bush to fend for myself. Would I easily survive?

Navarrete has become an explorer, the Mataco who has ventured farthest into what Mami calls "the white jungle," the jungle of civilization where people play according to different rules, where newcomers can easily get lost among other swamps and traps that await and tempt them.

Navarrete learned Spanish from an Anglican missionary when he was seven years old; but it was only when he reached his first year of high school and studied grammar—many years later as an adult—that he realized Mataco, just like Spanish, must have certain rules and categories. Since then he has been studying his own language, trying to discover its inner laws.

This is not a detached intellectual pursuit. Navarrete has seen tribes in Salta who no longer speak their original tongue. He feels that each time an old man dies, a universe of words and stories dies with him. So Navarrete plans to teach the language to the Mataco children, as part of their curriculum. He is also interested in helping the promotores learn the language. He patiently explained several words I wanted to learn, but in spite of his excellent Spanish, our attempts often broke down at a loss for the proper usage.

He has not, however, been able to teach Mataco at school, although the law specifically recommends bilingual education. A previous school director let him work, but the next administrator opposed his presence there, saying he was unqualified. (Who, though, is qualified to certify teachers of Mataco?)

Navarrete's problem is symptomatic. If the Matacos are to become self-sufficient, the school must prepare the children for the future while the parents are learning in the fields and the offices—and this must be done in a way that shows respect for their culture. Instead, the Mataco children feel unwelcome in school. The dropout rate is outrageously high.

One of Navarrete's older daughters, now 18, had to repeat first grade three times and finally decided to stop wasting her time. It is true that in those times, she and the rest of the family had to periodically migrate to pick cotton. Now things seem better. Several Matacos have graduated from high school—and now work in the Asociación Comunitaria. They are essential to Patricio Doyle's plan to publish the revistita. Navarrete's nine-year-old daughter has already completed three years of elementary school without repeating a grade and will herself enter high school in just a few years.

What would he like her to be?

"A lawyer," he says. "What we most need are lawyers who can defend our interests."

Navarrete is anguished and open and doubtful. He is trying to build bridges over rivers that keep changing course.

He is the only Mataco who did not ask me for anything.

❀ ❀ ❀

I spent several days in El Sauzalito without meeting Diego Soneira. It turned out he was in the faraway village of El Espinillo, some 200 miles across El Impenetrable. I went to see him on my last day in the region.

I found him trying to put a lumbermill into operation. It had been erected a couple of years before, but the contractor had done everything wrong, and the mill had never worked. In a casual conversation with regional authorities, Soneira had mentioned what a pity such economic potential was being wasted, when the machinery could be repaired. He had been invited to try. What white technicians had failed to accomplish, or even propose, Soneira was going to do with Matacos. They had, after all, been operating a successful lumbermill for years.

If I needed a symbol of how far the Matacos have come, this was it. Instead of receiving help, Mataco operators, carpenters, and electricians were giving it to others, spreading their knowledge across El Impenetrable. And the others, in this case, were Toba Indians, rivals of the Matacos for centuries. In fact, some Matacos in El Sauzalito—who one promotor playfully calls *los rezongones,* or complainers—had told me before I left that Diego should be home with them, that he did not care for them anymore.

Meanwhile, Diego would have liked nothing better than to be back in El Sauzalito. He had brought his wife and his seven children with him because the job was supposed to be over in a few days. Then several machine parts that he needed to complete the job were delayed, and the authorities also failed to give him some unspecified aid they had promised. A few days had turned into a week. The nine Soneiras, plus the five Mataco technicians, were sleeping in an abandoned brick house, cooking over an open fire in the patio. They were without running water and were assaulted each evening—at exactly five past eight—by the most venomous, stubborn, hostile mosquitoes they had ever encountered. (And these people know an awful lot about mosquitoes.) The mosquitoes were so terrible, in fact, that they forced the Soneiras to seek refuge each evening in the sweltering heat of their sleeping quarters—and managed to infiltrate the premises anyway, if one were to believe the blood-stained walls.

And yet, the Soneiras were all cheerful, and Diego was calm, confident, tireless. Perhaps it was better to have seen him here, as if he were on another adventure, starting from scratch in a relatively strange place. It may be that in this way I was able to catch a glimpse of what the man must have been like when he arrived in El Sauzalito so many years ago. There was no doubting his strength or his magnetism.

He watched me watch him and finally smiled and said: "I know what you are going to ask me. Everybody always asks me the same thing. You want to know why I came here, why I stay here?"

It was as if he had read my mind. So I asked him something different when we finally sat down. I asked him two questions. How long did he think this experiment would last? When would he know if he had been successful?

He said he did not know the answer to the first question, but he may have responded to it in answering the second.

"I'll be successful when I'm not needed anymore," Diego said.

And then he went off, 150 miles of dirt road away, to search for the missing spare parts.

One day in El Sauzalito, under the burning noon sun, I ventured a little into the monte.

I did not go alone. My idea was to be guided by a Mataco. I wanted to experience what it would be like to be submerged in a habitat where he was the master, where his sense of smell, his ears that notice the slightest twitch of a leaf, his extraordinary eyesight and foresight would make him my superior. I wanted to be in a place where all my knowledge and skill would be useless, where his culture reigned and mine was out of place. I wanted, in a way, to experience what the Matacos must feel every day as they confront white, Western civilization: to be at a loss, displaced, defenseless.

I was not in El Sauzalito long enough to take such a trip, nor had I built up enough confidence with a Mataco so he might take me along on one of the frequent hunting expeditions.

I settled for an artificial second best. Mami called two young Matacos—8 and 11 years old, respectively—to guide me toward a still-wild area near the Río Bermejo, where the town ends.

I was not sure if they understood just what it was that I wanted, but they moved with me toward the river, and for a while I convinced myself that I was on the verge of the desired experience. They glided barefoot through a labyrinth of undergrowth, moving through the thickets, scaring flocks of pale-blue butterflies, somehow able to find their way in that tangled vegetation.

If it were not for these boys, I thought to myself, I would be lost. It was a game I was playing with myself, of course. I knew that the town was nearby and that I was in no real danger of losing my way. As if to answer me, there was suddenly a noise in the bushes and I sensed something big lurching toward us. But no wild beast emerged. It was merely a pig, one of the few remaining from a failed livestock experiment. It snorted across our path. I wondered what the two Mataco kids thought of this expedition. But they would not answer any of my questions—just a nod of their heads once in a while, a pause to look back to see if I was following.

After we reached the river, they decided to come back by another route, and they got lost. Several times we reached a wedge of canes and weeds and vines that would not let us pass. We had to backtrack. And then, again, a few more yards and the need to start over. Finally, they made their way to the river, retraced their steps to a familiar path, and managed to get me safely home.

What is the meaning of this experience?

Should I emphasize the boys' surefooted, fleeting movements at the beginning of the excursion, proving how Mataco children are still acquainted with the jungle and will somehow continue in the traditions of their forefathers? Or is the second stage more significant, when they lost their sense of direction and the bushes seemed alien to them as they would not have been to their ancestors when they were children?

Or was there no significance whatsoever in that brief exploration? Was not their conduct distorted by my very presence, their need to please me, their need to interpret my rather sophisticated and enigmatic desires?

I cannot tell. I would have to be a Mataco.

I would have to be a Mataco to know exactly where the two boys are going.

26

Women and Rural Development Policies: The Changing Agenda

Deniz Kandiyoti
Richmond College, Surrey, England

INTRODUCTION

Policy interest in rural woman started manifesting itself in the early 1970s at a time when widespread disenchantment was being felt with the effects of current development policies on the agrarian sectors of most Third World countries. These policies had, broadly speaking, resulted in stagnating levels of food production, nutritional decline, and a destructuring of rural communities, fueling massive rural to urban migration. Concern over absolute poverty, and levels of rural and urban unemployment and underemployment, increasingly started appearing on the policy agenda. As the emphasis shifted from "modernization" to the provision of the poorest people's basic needs (food, shelter, health, etc.) distributional issues came to the fore, although initially the effects of gender inequality did not receive separate attention above and beyond those of class membership. In time, and especially after the UN Decade for Women started in 1975, a growing body of research under the broad rubric of women in development (WID), started documenting the counterproductive effects of ignoring rural women's contributions and their special needs from the point of view of both agricultural productivity and the overall welfare of rural families.[1] Thus, policy proposals related to rural women became intimately linked to an ongoing assessment of strategies of rural development.

Studies on women in development have made several important contributions. They have expedited the demise of modernization or "trickledown" theories of development by illustrating how modernization has had demonstrably different effects not only on different rural strata but on men and women, often contributing to a deterioration of conditions and increased workloads for the latter.[2] They have brought women into a previously genderless (and hence myopic) consideration of the links between subsistence and peasant production and the capitalist sector in less developed countries, and questioned the nature of the relation of unpaid family labour to wage labour both in more advanced economies and the Third World. They have addressed the methodological and conceptual biases in accounting for women's work (Agarwal, 1989; Beneria, 1981; Dixon, 1982). Finally, numerous case studies have alerted us to the fact that rural development policies will not have their intended effect, or might even produce unintended negative outcomes, if the role and position of women in rural households is not explicitly taken into account.

As things stand now, an apparent consensus seems to have been generated by this accumulation of both fact and polemic such that organizations with finalities as diverse as those of the World Bank, different UN and government agencies, private foundations, and feminist groups are clamouring to relieve rural women of their drudgery, to increase their control over resources, and to equip them with credit, know-how, and appropriate technologies.

A certain style of advocacy has developed over the years which is quite technocratic in general tone and which maintains that assisting rural women—far from being a frivolous, if benevolent, exercise—is, on the contrary, certain to pay dividends in terms of "development." Thus the case for explicit support of rural women's activities is often presented as a basic-rights issue which also makes good economic or "development" sense. Part of the rationale behind this style of presentation has been that it is so hard to "sell" the idea of assisting women to governments, bureaucracies, and other male-dominated agencies, especially when they have dire problems and other priorities, that only hard-headed fact and proof that the goals of assisting women and promoting development are totally congruent with one another could have any impact at all. The result has been that the possible contradictions contained in policy proposals emanating from different, though often implicit, assumptions about both women and development are often glossed over, and are becoming much harder to identify.

The aim of this paper is to review and evaluate some of the most commonly held assumptions about the desirability of making rural women the target of direct policy measures, the goals that are sought in doing so, and the means advocated to achieve these goals. In so doing, I will attempt to show how mainstream WID research has closely followed, reflected, and responded to changing international priorities in matters of development assistance, but has seldom clarified its basic premises or spelt out the political implications of its stated objectives.

ASSUMPTIONS

The instrumentality of policy interventions aimed at rural women is generally clearly spelt out. Some of the concrete areas in which such interventions are expected to produce beneficial results are population control, health delivery, food production, nutrition, and the alleviation of absolute poverty through expanded opportunities for "income-generation." Most policy papers tend to stress the intrinsic congruence between the goals of greater equity for women and increased productivity. Their thinking is based on a set of commonly held assumptions, some of which have been well substantiated and documented and others less so. These may be summarized as follows:

1. Women are de facto food producers and active participants in the agrarian sectors of the Third World.
2. Some of the main constraints on women's productivity are related to the labour time involved in their daily household maintenance tasks.
3. A reduction or freeing of labour time from household tasks implies its possible diversion to income-generating activities.
4. Women's access to income is more likely to pay welfare dividends for the community at large (especially for children) than men's incomes.
5. Women's productivity and potential for income-generation may be raised with minimal capital outlays.

The first assumption is generally documented through extensive material from sub-Saharan Africa, where women's involvement in food production is highest and where food shortage is worst. It is a fact that African women's farming activities take place on an ever-shrinking resource base, with extremely primitive technology and with severely stretched time resources. However, at a more global level, the extent of women's involvement in subsistence production is a function of the nature of local farming systems, access to resources, and the degree of overall commoditization of the agrarian sector. There are therefore important regional disparities in women's participation in agricultural production, ranging from a high 87 percent of the female labour force in low-income African countries to a low 14 percent in Latin America (ILO/INSTRAW, 1985).

The agrarian sectors of many regions of the Third World have become commoditized to the extent that subsistence farming can account only for an absolutely minimal fraction of a household's needs. In many parts of Asia and Latin America the women of landless or near-landless households are forced to rely on wage earnings from varied and intermittent sources. This is to some extent reflected in policies directed at rural women: those relating to Africa frequently stress the need to assist subsistence farming, whereas in Asia the accent is on employment creation programs and expanded opportunities for wage-work.

Women's type and level of involvement in agricultural activities is consistently mediated by rural households' access to productive resources. These activities may range from postharvest processing and care of live-stock with relatively little involvement in fieldwork for women from rela-tively wealthy landed families, to greater participation in or actual "feminization" of fieldwork in smallholder or near-landless households, especially in areas of selective male outmigration, to exclusive reliance on wage-work for women from landless households. Since both the intensity and modality of women's cultivation and crop-related activities depend on their location in rural stratification, the type of assistance they could benefit from not only varies, but may introduce important divergences of interest among women from different strata. Although project-level documents generally acknowledge these differences, broader policy statements on assistance to rural women tend to identify them in a more amorphous man-ner and single them out as a disadvantaged and vulnerable group who shoulder the burden of feeding and maintaining families, frequently with-out any form of outside support.

In this respect there are significant regional variations in sex-selectivity of outmigration from rural areas with important consequences for women. In Africa, selective male outmigration has resulted in a high proportion of female-headed rural households, whereas in Latin America women's high-er rates of migration have resulted both in their greater representation in the urban service sector and in increases in urban-based, female-headed households. In Asia sex ratios in outmigration have tended to be more bal-anced, and there is a lower overall incidence of female-headed households. However, whether they are primarily responsible for ensuring the survival of their families or not, women's daily household maintenance tasks are uniformly singled out among the factors setting a limit to their labour pro-ductivity and income-earning ability.

The second assumption is clearly documented through a satisfactory number of time–budget studies indicating that tasks such as water fetching, fuel collection, food processing and preparation can account for the better part of an adult woman's extremely long working day. Allocating resources to better sanitation, easy access to water points, cheap sources of fuel, improved means of porterage and transportation can thus have immediate-ly beneficial effects on women's daily workloads (Carr, 1978). The introduc-tion of labour- and time-saving appropriate technologies for laborious oper-ations such as food processing may be somewhat more problematic in that it may have different consequences for different classes of rural women: an alleviation in the workload of women from landed households, and a loss of livelihood for landless women who receive wages for such processing operations performed for other households (Whitehead, 1985). However, it must be kept in mind that proposals to upgrade women's daily maintenance tasks ultimately aim at increasing their labour productivity, which brings us to the third assumption, namely that women's freed time may be diverted towards income-generating activities.

These activities consist either in upgrading the areas in which women are already involved (through the provision of improved techniques and tools for cultivation, access to farm credit, extension services, etc.), or in the creation of new sources of livelihood through rural-based cottage industries from fruit canning and soap making to textiles and brick making, depending on local skills and resources. A certain amount of training and education, as well as the creation of organizations to facilitate credit and marketing outlets (such as women producers' cooperatives) are advocated as realistic objectives. What is striking about many of the proposals for women's projects is that they seem to be relatively oblivious of similar rural development projects geared to men, and the lessons learned from their shortcomings. This, I will argue, is because the criteria for success for women's projects are much less stringent, and because they do not have exactly the same aims as projects geared to male farmers. I will return to this point in the course of the discussion of the fifth assumption, namely that significant improvements can be achieved with very meagre resources.

An important rationale behind increasing women's direct control over resources in general, and cash in particular, stems from the assumption that women are more likely to use these resources to further the immediate welfare of their families, especially the nutrition and health of their children. Certainly some of the available data tends to suggest that increases in male incomes do not automatically translate themselves into improved nutritional levels for the family as a whole, and that consumer durables and leisure activities may divert considerable income from the household budget (Hanger and Moris, 1973; Palmer, 1977; Young, 1978). This is even more true of women with migrant husbands receiving only intermittent support, and totally true of female-headed households who have no other support. Even though this position may be seen as a realistic recognition of a de facto situation, it nonetheless inscribes itself in the more general current tendency to accept women as the "responsible" reproducers assisted by public agencies, thus extending the ideology of the "good mother" to the field of legislation and assistance. While this tendency has been the subject of extensive commentary in the case of the welfare states of industrialized countries,[3] the parallels to be drawn with international aid assistance to Third World women have not yet appeared on the agenda. In Third World countries where no safety net is provided by local welfare states, and in regions where male responsibility for dependants is at least normatively present, women themselves may be likely to put up fierce resistance to measures by-passing the male household head, even though they may in practice contrive ways of increasing their own control over household income. There is very little recognition given to the fact that interventions to increase women's direct control over income are likely to have different consequences for different categories of women, depending on their age, class, and marital status.

Finally, an assumption that is never really fully spelt out, but quite persistently present, is that the goal of assisting rural women can be realistically achieved with relatively modest capital outlays, mainly through a better use of local resources, the provision of training and credit facilities, as well as reasonably priced, easy-to-maintain appropriate technologies. This is reflected in the kinds of projects that involve women. A recent report describes them as having

> suffered by being scattered, small and peripheral to the main thrust of planning processes, programmes and projects. Different agencies (international and national) have financed a plethora of small projects in various sectors with little coordination nor concern for sustained financial viability, capacity to grow and expand or replicability (Sen and Grown, 1987, p. 82).

This brings us back to a point alluded to earlier, namely that different, less stringent criteria are applied to projects for women. It might be worth looking at some of the reasons for this state of affairs before proceeding further.

First, in the case of women any increment in productivity, however modest, may easily be seen as a major advance over labour time totally taken up with daily maintenance tasks. The question, of course, remains as to whether women will have any degree of autonomy over the way they dispose of their labour, or whether they will become better and more efficiently integrated into processes deepening the subordination of small peasant producers. A very crude analogy could be made here between attitudes to male subsistence farming and women's household maintenance tasks at very different phases of accumulation. Subsistence farming received a great deal of negative attention from the colonial state in so far as it held back land and labour from commercial crops and effectively acted as a barrier to the expansion of cash cropping. Women's involvement in "nonproductive" tasks is now acting as a brake on a dangerously stagnating subsistence sector which has deteriorated to the point of not being able to reproduce itself, as is plainly the case in Africa. A frankly negative assessment of the growth of WID research in Africa suggests that women have now been identified as a problem for state and international agencies because, among other things, "They have persistently sought to manipulate alternative, parallel markets for their produce and resisted efforts by different social forces—including husbands—to labour without any foreseeable return" (Mbilinyi, 1984, p. 290). From this perspective, WID projects may be seen as attempts at tighter control and more efficient monitoring of women's activities. However, whereas men's priorities did not necessarily coincide with those of colonial governments, which often had to resort to coercive measures of labour control, there is a greater degree of congruence between women's need to reduce household drudgery and increase their income, and official interest in a more productive and efficient rural economy. Women should certainly take full advantage of this interest, whilst not losing sight of the broader picture and of the fact that projects to assist them might have different final objectives, depending on the donor agencies and the local bureaucracies administering them.

Secondly, one rapidly becomes aware of the fact that the ultimate aim of aid to rural women is to promote greater self-sufficiency rather than development in the sense of expansion and qualitative change. The subsistence production of rural women and women's poverty is now attracting attention because a growing number of Third World countries have become net importers of foodstuffs, and uncontrollable migration to urban centres in search of jobs is creating severe problems with politically unsettling implications.

Assistance to rural women often appears as part of a series of stop-gap measures to tackle some of the most visible outcomes of underdevelopment, such as hunger and malnutrition. It seems highly improbable, however, that such assistance can have lasting benefits unless it is accompanied by sweeping changes in land distribution, pricing, and credit policies; in short, an onslaught on the mechanisms that reproduce and intensify inequalities within the agrarian sector. This is an area where current trends are not necessarily conducive to optimism, not least because of the contradictory objectives which different policy choices may represent.

To give but one example on food production in sub-Saharan Africa, the Lagos Plan, the Berg Report, and the policies of the Reagan government seemed to be at odds with one another. The Lagos Plan, endorsed by governments in the region, advocated greater self-reliance in food; the Berg Report (accepted by the World Bank) argued for accelerated export production supplemented by food aid, whereas the Reagan administration cut back aid substantially, with the exception of a few countries deemed strategic to US interests. Given the external debt links of most underdeveloped countries, the likelihood that their agrarian sectors will be subject to tight monitoring by supranational agencies, such as the IMF, is extremely high. So far, most efforts towards increasing the productivity of peasant production and the real incomes of rural producers (in supervised credit schemes, smallholder projects, and other "peasant" packages) have been accompanied by an intensification of labour within the household which has primarily affected women's workloads. The unremunerated labour of women, as well as their wage-earning potential, will thus continue to represent an important economic resource for a whole series of beneficiaries, from household heads to governments. Arguments to the effect that households are not egalitarian institutions, and that some projects work to the detriment of women's and children's welfare, will be weighed against countervailing policy objectives, such as the need to maintain, protect, or even recreate a smallholder sector or other family-based forms of livelihood, as a means of increasing productivity or tempering rapid processes of differentiation among the peasantry.

There is a sense in which policy documents on assistance to rural women and broader rural development policies almost seem to emanate from different universes. The former still use the language of "basic needs," whereas the latter distinguish themselves by a strong market orientation. It is important to reflect on the meaning of this disjunction. Is it the case that they emanate from totally different sections within the international planning community? Is there some sort of division of labour, whereby women-directed policies unwittingly come to represent the "welfare" arm of monetarist policies? Or is there some other combination of factors, including the creation of a new conventional wisdom in the area of development assistance?

One policy analysis paper draws our attention to the shift from an earlier equity-oriented approach in matters of assistance to women, which stressed the widening gender gap created by development policies, to a poverty-oriented approach, which documents the importance of raising the productivity and income of poor women as a more general growth and poverty-alleviation strategy. This shift is explained as follows:

> In the face of economic theorists' and policymakers' lack of interest, the equity approach to research on women has evolved into an alternative approach that links women's issues to poverty and tries to quantify the positive effects that may result from incorporating women's concerns into economic development programs (Buvinic, 1983, p. 16).

This lack of interest, however, begs the question, and can be better interpreted in the context of yet another shift in priorities in response to the global economic trends of the 1980s. The hardships provoked by recession and the implementation of severe stabilization measures, and the grossly unequal distributive effects of structural adjustment packages are now accepted as an established fact. The accent is on crisis management and on "buffering" some of the worst excesses in human suffering terms of current international economic policies (Cornia et al., 1987).

Behind the rather bland and uniform sounding recommendations to equip and empower poor Third World women, there may lie a wide range of frankly contradictory objectives from simply making women more efficient managers of poverty, to using their claims and organizations as a political vehicle for far-reaching redistributive measures, both within and across nations.[4] With very few exceptions, policy documents on WID effectively avoid and obscure these troublesome issues by presenting assistance to women as a technical rather than a political issue.

GOALS AND MEANS

The evidence of increasing levels of female poverty and its implications for community welfare has, as pointed out earlier, been instrumental in promoting a wide-ranging reassessment of rural women's access to resources: access to land and water, to agricultural inputs, credits and services, to education, training, and extension, and to institutions and organizations. Ensuring an increase in women's rights of appropriation over resources and over their own labour has been declared a priority to be furthered through the following measures:

1. The protection of women's existing sources of livelihood.
2. The elimination of discriminatory legislation in the ownership and control of productive assets.
3. The promotion of equitable access to agricultural inputs, credit, extension services, and education.
4. The support of extra-household forms of organization of women's labour.
5. The encouragement of an increased capacity for political empowerment and organization.

An area to which development planners are invited to show special sensitivity concerns changes which actually result in the loss of women's control over earnings which were traditionally theirs. There are numerous examples of such loss of income in agriculture, food processing, manufacture, and trading (see Petritsch, 1981). One of the best-documented instances is the case of the introduction of Japanese rice-hullers in Indonesia, depriving poor women of one of their few sources of wage-work (Cain, 1981). The same applies to Bangladesh, where there is concern over the informal diffusion of custom-husking which decreases the need for hand-pounding performed by poor women. In this case the divergence in the interests of women who are wage-workers with no alternative income-generating opportunities and those who are family labourers is quite apparent.

However, even in cases where technological innovation has less class-specific results, important policy dilemmas are involved. It seems short-sighted to adopt protectionist attitudes vis-à-vis women's traditional activities and to bemoan their loss if they involve obsolete technologies and very low productivity. The real challenge would seem to lie in ensuring that the upgrading or modernization of certain areas of activity either do not result in losses for women or can be compensated for by the creation of viable local alternatives. It has so far been the case that the reorganized or modernized activities which were previously considered as women's work are redefined as male tasks, so that an actual change in personnel takes place. For instance, commercial rice milling in Bangladesh is a male occupation, and modern dairies in India have male employees, whereas traditional milk producers were women. Although innovation may in some cases produce a lower overall demand for labour, serious attempts should be made to ensure that women continue to retain control over organizationally and technologically more sophisticated versions of their farming, processing, marketing, and handicraft activities. This goal is especially hard to achieve, not only because women lack training, skills, capital, and mobility, but also because they may come up against opposition from other factional interest groups. There have been instances where women's interests were so clearly at variance with those of officials that resistance took the form of organized protest, as in the case of the Chipko movement in India, where women's interest in access to forests and forest products became part of a broader environmental conservation drive (Sharma, 1984). It seems clear that women's ability to organize and become mobilized to safeguard their livelihood is critical to the success of such policies, though such mobilization is greatly hampered, both by divergences in the interests of women of different class, caste, or ethnic membership and the low overall level of women's political participation.

The elimination of legislation barring women from access to productive assets (in terms of inheritance, ownership, and control of property) is also a clear priority. Although land reforms can improve the access of the poor, including women, to land rights, their effects on women have been shown to be quite variable depending on definitions of beneficiary status, their ability to accommodate women's customary land-use rights where they exist, and their success in integrating women into mass organizations (such as co-operatives) as full members (Deere, 1984; Tadesse, 1982; Brain, 1976; von Werlhof, 1983; Palmer, 1985). On the whole, piecemeal legal measures, especially if they are confined to title ownership only, will have a limited impact unless they are backed up by a whole package of measures covering every phase of the production process including marketing.

Separate attention has been given to women's access to agricultural inputs, credit and services, extension and education, and all have been found inadequate (see UNESCO, 1964, 1973; Ashby, 1981; Staudt, 1975/6; Berger and De Lancey, 1984; Lycette, 1984). Access to the above, and especially to favourable credit and marketing terms, are problematic for all economically and politically disadvantaged groups. In the case of rural women these problems are compounded by the fact that their recognition as legal adults has yet to be established in many places, that official sources discriminate against them, that they lack the ties of clientship and patronage which male farmers often mobilize to establish their solvency, and are required to operate in a world from which they have in many places been totally excluded. Since aid donors are well aware that local power structures will not give way and be modified to accommodate poor women's needs, the creation of special projects, programs, and funds appears to be the only way of circumventing their constraining effects. This gives rise to the frequently voiced complaint that women's projects remain marginal to the mainstream of development efforts, which is of course perfectly true, but does not in itself lead to a clear analysis of exactly what would be involved for things to be otherwise.

Another issue of concern in modifying rural women's "productive package" is what happens to their domestic responsibilities. Attempts to increase rural women's productivity in the absence of parallel efforts to reduce their reproductive work merely result either in intolerable workloads, or in a redistribution of such tasks among women of different age groups within the same household, e.g., school-age daughters withdrawn from school in order to keep house and take care of siblings. Croll's (1981) review of socialist policies in the Soviet Union, China, Cuba, and Tanzania shows that despite an explicit commitment to increase rural women's productivity, the resources allocated to alleviate women's reproductive and domestic load are inadequate and have actually declined, due to the cost of substituting services (such as crèches, nurseries, and public dining rooms) for women's unremunerated labour. Policy documents calling for the improvement of rural women's productivity in the Third World rarely make any direct reference to this problem, except in connection to appropriate technologies for heating, cooking, water and fuel collection, and food processing.

In fact, on closer inspection it appears that what is being called for is not simply an increase in women's labour productivity but an intensification and elaboration of their mothering and nurturing roles as well. For instance, the so-called participatory strategies for health delivery are predicated upon women's willingness as mothers to adopt, administer and ultimately finance the GOBI "technologies" which have a decisive impact on child survival—growth monitoring, oral rehydration therapy, breastfeeding and improved weaning practices, and immunization. Given the increasingly restricted availability of public funds in the health sector, the onus is on women to extend their traditional responsibilities as the feeders and healers of their families to include the provision of basic health care, although it is candidly acknowledged that this will make new demands on their time and financial resources (Leslie et al., 1986).

One of the persistent obstacles to increasing women's rights of appropriation over the resources they generate is seen to reside in the maintenance of production and exchange relations within the household. At least, this forms part of the reasoning behind the advocacy for extra- or suprafamilial institutions to organize rural women's productive activities. A strong case is made for instance for separate women's organizations such as women-only cooperatives, which are justified on several grounds: building on already existing female networks or modes of cooperation, avoiding confrontation with cultural patterns which oppose the mixing of unrelated men and women, and, finally avoiding a submergence of women's interests and loss of leadership to men. Organizational strategies which bring women together in collective work groups are also seen as a means of circumventing male control over resources by making it possible for women to sell goods and services directly (Dixon, 1981).

In principle, one might expect benefits from extra-household organizations in terms of increased productivity, greater control over one's labour time, and possibly enhanced bargaining power in the domestic situation. However, little detailed attention is paid to the crucial factors which could make these benefits materialize—or fail to do so. Clearly this would depend on the one hand on the nature of the work, the regularity, security, and amount of income earned and on the nature of domestic arrangements, including different modes of resource allocation within households and broader cultural expectations on the other. For some women, the fact that they become more exploitable in market terms, since they are typically organized in small-scale, low-capital, and essentially vulnerable enterprises, may not be immediately compensated by gains in their domestic status. This may be especially true in areas where the cultural disparagement of women's nondomestic work is strongest.

Since it is hard to hope for significant advances in rural women's rights of appropriation over resources and access to services without a certain measure of political empowerment, the final and most intractable question concerns their potential for organization and participation in political pressure groups. WID literature is very mixed on this issue. It ranges from a set of technocratic prescriptions operating in what appears to be a political vacuum, to a limited recognition of the political dimension of the interventions proposed. Typically, the issue of women's movements, their possible conflicts with other factional interests, and their potential for alliances with other forms of struggle are not squarely confronted. There is, on the other hand, a growing body of scholarship documenting instances of women's collective action and their increasing participation in popular protest movements (Jelin, 1987). A noteworthy feature of such movements concerns the "politicization" of women's daily struggles around issues of primary relevance to their lives—from food prices and the general cost of living, through the lack of social services to the disappearance of their children at the hands of repressive regimes. Strategies for rural women's empowerment ultimately cannot avoid the complicated set of issues posed by women's grass-roots movements and the challenges they may represent.

In conclusion, project and policy proposals for rural women as they appear in WID research frequently suffer from several shortcomings. They tend to ignore, deemphasize, or conceal the broader development context in

which women-specific projects are inscribed, and thus make it more difficult to discern who the ultimate beneficiaries of women's projects will be.
Even though there is a strong suggestion that women's projects, unlike
packages for male farmers, are more likely to benefit the whole community,
and especially its more helpless members such as children, the welfarist
tone of this body of policy does not accord well with the pervasive concern
over instituting more efficient forms of labour control over peasant producers, where the household as a production unit is still the cheapest way to
obtain the labour of an entire family. Little acknowledgement is given to the
fact that increasing women's productivity has to be matched with substantial, as opposed to cosmetic, relief from reproductive tasks, especially if this
relief involves costly alternatives such as better infrastructure and overall
sanitation. Finally, there is considerable ambiguity over the broader redis-
tributional issues that assisting poor rural women raises. It is frequently
unclear whether rural women will be better equipped to simply make do
with what they already have, or whether genuinely new resources will be
allocated to them. Most importantly, the political implications of such allocations are seldom spelt out. Ultimately, this ambiguity can only be
resolved not by examining women's projects, which are surprisingly uniform in both tone and content, but with reference to the broader policies
and goals of the agencies and policy-making bodies concerned.

NOTES

1. The following represent a few typical examples of a much broader literature:
   Palmer, 1977; IDS, 1978; Abdullah and Zeidenstein, 1982; Dauber and Cain,
   1981; D'Onofrio-Flores and Pfafflin, 1982; Lewis, 1981.
2. This reassessment was initiated by the pioneering work of Ester Boserup,
   although divergences developed in the identification of both the causes of
   women's subordination in the Third World and the means to achieve change.
   See Boserup, 1970; Beneria and Sen, 1981. For critiques of development policies
   also see Rogers, 1980; Ahmed, 1980; Chaney and Schmink, 1976.
3. For reviews of this question in West European and Scandinavian welfare states
   see Sassoon, 1987, and for the United States see Brown, 1981.
4. For instance, two texts covering very similar ground but with important differences in emphasis are Sen and Grown, 1987 and Joekes, 1987. The former is
   much more forthright about spelling out a political project centred around poor
   Third World women's claims.

REFERENCES

Abdullah, T. A., and Zeidenstein, S. A. *Village Women of Bangladesh: Prospects for Change.* Oxford: Pergamon Press, 1982.

Agarwal, B. "Work Participation of Rural Women in the Third World: Some Data and Conceptual Biases." In K. Young, ed., *Serving Two Masters,* pp. 1–26. New Delhi: Allied Publishers, 1989.

Ahmed, Z. "The Plight of Rural Women: Alternatives for Action." *International Labour Review*, 119, 4 (1980): 425–38.

Ashby, J. "New Models for Agricultural Research and Extension: The Need to Integrate Women." In B. Lewis, ed., 1981, pp. 144–238.

Beneria, L. "Conceptualising the Labour Force: The Underestimation of Women's Economic Activities." In N. Nelson, ed., *African Women in the Development Process*, pp. 279–98. London: Frank Cass, 1981.

Beneria, L., and Sen, G. "Accumulation, Reproduction and Women's Role in Economic Development: Boserup Revisited." *Signs*, 7, 2 (1981): 10–28.

Berger, M., and De Lancey, W. *Bridging the Gender Gap in Agricultural Extension*. Report prepared for USAID, Office of Women in Development, Washington, DC: ICRW, 1984.

Boserup, E. *Women's Role in Economic Development*. London: George Allen & Unwin, 1970.

Brain, T. L. "Less than Second Class: Women in Rural Settlement Schemes in Tanzania." In N. Hafkin, and E. G. Bay, eds., *Women in Africa: Studies in Social and Economic Change*, pp. 265–82. Stanford, Calif.: Stanford University Press, 1976.

Brown, C. "Mothers and Fathers and Children: From Private to Public Patriarchy." In L. Sargent, ed., *Women and Revolution*, pp. 239–67. London: Pluto Press, 1981.

Buvinic, M. "Women's Issues in Third World Poverty: A Policy Analysis." In M. Buvinic, M. A. Lycette, and W. P. McGreevey, eds., *Women and Poverty in the Third World*, pp. 14–33. Baltimore, Md.: Johns Hopkins University Press, 1983.

Cain, M. "Java, Indonesia: The Introduction of Rice Processing Technology." In R. Dauber, and M. Cain, eds., 1981, pp. 127–38.

Carr, M. *Appropriate Technology for African Women*. United Nations Economic Commission for Africa, 1978.

Chaney, E., and Schmink, M. "Women and Modernization: Access to Tools." In J. Nash and H. Safa, eds., *Sex and Class in Latin America*, pp. 160–82. New York: Praeger, 1976.

Cornia, G. A., Jolly, R. and Stewart, F., eds. *Adjustment with a Human Face: Protecting the Vulnerable and Promoting Growth*. Oxford: Clarendon Press, 1987.

Croll, E. J. "Women in Rural Production and Reproduction in the Soviet Union, China, Cuba and Tanzania: Socialist Development Experiences." *Signs*, 7, 2, (1981): 375–99.

Dauber, R., and Cain, M. L., eds. *Women and Technological Change in Developing Countries*. Boulder, Colo.: Westview Press, 1981.

Deere, C. D. "Rural Women and Agrarian Reform in Peru, Chile and Cuba." In *Women on the Move: Contemporary Changes in Family and Society*, pp. 57–81. Paris: UNESCO, 1984.

Dixon, R. B. "Jobs for Women in Rural Industry and Services." In B. Lewis, ed., 1981, pp. 271–328.

Dixon, R. B. "Women in Agriculture: Counting the Labour Force in Developing Countries." *Population and Development Review*, 18 (1982): 539–66.

D'Onofrio-Flores, P. M., and Pfafflin, S. M. *Scientific-Technological Change and the Role of Women in Development*. Boulder, Colo.: Westview Press, 1982.

Hanger, J., and Moris, J. "Women and the Household Economy." In R. Chambers, and J. Moris, eds., *Mwea: An Irrigated Rice Settlement in Kenya*, pp. 209–44. Munich: Weltform Verlag, 1973.

IDS. "Women and Green Revolutions." Paper presented at the Conference on "Continuing Subordination of Women in the Development Process," Institute of Development Studies, Sussex, 1978.

ILO/INSTRAW. *Women in Economic Activity: A Global Statistical Survey (1950–2000).* Geneva and Santo Domingo: ILO/INSTRAW, 1985.

Jelin, E., ed. *Ciudadania e Identidad: Las Mujeres en los Movimientos Sociales Latino-Americanos.* Geneva: UNRISD, 1987.

Joekes, S. *Women in the World Economy.* Geneva and New York: INSTRAW and Oxford University Press, 1987.

Leslie, J., Lycette, M., and Buvunic, M. "Weathering Economic Crises: The Crucial Role of Women in Health." Report prepared for USAID, Office of Women in Development. Washington, DC: ICRW, 1986.

Lewis, B., ed. *Invisible Farmers: Women and the Crisis in Agriculture.* USAID, Office of Women in Development. Washington, DC: ICRW, 1981.

Lycette, M. A. "Improving Women's Access to Credit in the Third World." Report prepared for USAID, Office of Women in Development. Washington, DC: ICRW, 1984.

Mbilinyi, M. "Research Priorities in Women Studies in Eastern Africa." *Women's Studies International Forum,* 7, 4 (1984): 289–300.

Palmer, I. "Rural Women and the Basic Needs Approach to Development." *International Labour Review,* 115, 1 (1977): 97–107.

Palmer, I. *The Impact of Agrarian Reform on Women.* Women's Roles and Gender Differences in Development, monograph No. 6. West Hartford, Conn.: Kumarian Press, 1985.

Petritsch, M. "The Impact of Industrialization on Women's Traditional Fields of Economic Activity in Developing Countries." UNIDO Seminar on the Role of Women in the Development of Industrial Branches Traditionally Employing Female Labour, Sofia, Bulgaria, October 15–18, 1981.

Rogers, B. *The Domestication of Women: Discrimination in Developing Societies.* London: Kogan Page, 1980.

Sassoon, A.S., ed. *Women and the State.* London: Hutchinson, 1987.

Sen, G., and Grown, C. *Development, Crisis and Alternative Visions: Third World Women's Perspectives.* New York: Monthly Review Press, 1987.

Sharma, K. "Women in Struggle: A Case Study of the Chipko Movement." *Samya Shakti: A Journal of Women's Studies,* 1, 2 (1984): 55–62.

Staudt, K. A. "Women Farmers and Inequities in Agricultural Services." *Rural Africana,* 29 (Winter 1975/6).

Tadesse, Z. "The Impact of Land Reform on Women: The Case of Ethiopia." In L. Beneria, ed., *Women and Development: The Sexual Division of Labour in Rural Societies,* pp. 203–22. New York: Praeger, 1982.

UNESCO. *Access of Girls and Women to Education in Rural Areas.* Paris: UNESCO, 1964.

UNESCO. *Study in the Equality of Access of Girls and Women to Education in the Context of Rural Development.* Paris: UNESCO, 1973.

von Werlof, C. "New Agricultural Cooperatives on the Basis of Sexual Polarisation Induced by the State." *Boletin de Estudios Latin Americanos y del Caribe,* 35 (1983): 39–50 (Amsterdam: CEDLA).

Whitehead, A. "Effects of Technological Change on Rural Women: A Review of Analysis and Concepts." In A. Ahmed, ed., *Technology and Rural Women: Conceptual and Empirical Issues*, pp. 27–64. London: George Allen & Unwin for the ILO World Employment Programme, 1985.

Young, K. "Modes of Appropriation and the Sexual Division of Labour: A Case Study of Oaxa, Mexico." In A. Kuhn and A. M. Wolpe, eds., *Feminism and Materialism*, pp. 124–54. London: Routledge & Kegan Paul, 1978.

27

What Really Matters— Human Development

Peter Gall

For years, economists, politicians, and development planners have measured average per capita income to chart year-to-year progress or decline within a country. As a result, a great deal of national development activity was focused on economic growth, often neglecting the human dimension of development. What was needed was a new way to measure development—human development—and a new strategy to meet human needs.

Now there *is* a way to measure human development. A team of leading scholars has created a new Human Development Index (HDI) for the United Nations Development Programme (UNDP). *Human Development Report (1990),* to be published annually for UNDP, quantifies the human condition and ranks countries by their success in meeting human needs. It also examines why some countries lag behind and recommends concrete steps to move countries forward. The result is a fresh and uncompromising look at how people's lives are enriched or impoverished throughout the world, in rich countries and poor. (See Table 1.)

Even countries of low per capita gross national product (GNP) may rank high on the Human Development Index—that is, their people live relatively long lives, are mostly literate, and generate enough purchasing power to rise above poverty. On the other hand countries with high per capita GNP may still have low rates of human development. The difference lies in the way national leaders set their priorities and allocate government funds, and in the degree of freedom that citizens enjoy to act on their choices and influence their own lives.

Japan comes out with the highest HDI ranking. For the most recent years for which data is available (1987 for life expectancy and income, 1985 for literacy), average life expectancy in Japan was 78 years. Adult literacy

From *World Development (UNDP),* 3, 3, pp. 4–12.

was 99 percent. The average real income level, adjusted to reflect purchasing power, was US$13,135 (lower than in nine other developed countries).

At the other end of the spectrum is Niger, with life expectancy of 45 years, literacy of 14 percent, and average adjusted real income of $452. Among poorer countries, the highest human development ranking goes to Costa Rica, which has no standing army, boasts a life expectancy of 75 years, a literacy rate of 93 percent, and average adjusted real income of $3,760.

The report zeroes in on several key questions. Does a government care more about economic development alone or about health care and education as well? Does it spend the money it controls more on armaments or on teachers? Are women just toilers in the fields or do they share in the wealth and responsibilities of a nation?

The answers tell a lot about a country. Brazil's per capita income grew over 6 percent a year in the 1970s so that the country is now considered "upper middle-income," but the distribution of that income is "among the worst in the world," says the Report. Brazil's childhood mortality rate is almost twice that of Sri Lanka, a country with one-fifth the per capita income.

Twenty-five developing countries spend more on the military than on education and health. There are eight times more soldiers in the developing countries than physicians. On the other hand, Costa Rica targeted literacy for action, and particularly women's education, so that female literacy rose from 17 percent in 1960 to 65 percent in 1980. Educating the women helped speed the decline in mortality of infants and children under five.

The book, which is being published commercially by Oxford University Press, is bound to stir controversy. Not only does it name countries that it feels have ignored human development opportunities, it recommends that international donors attach "benign conditions" as strings to development assistance, such as lower military spending or channeling more money to schools or public health.

Developing countries' military spending on arms holds a particular place of shame in the book, which discloses that annual military costs represented nearly 160 million man-years of income, three times the equivalent military burden of industrialized countries. "Obviously, the poverty of the people of the developing world has been no barrier to the affluence of their armies," the Report concludes.

The book makes two major contributions to development. The first is the creation of the triple-component Human Development Index itself. The authors selected *life expectancy* as one component not only for its own value, but because it speaks to health care delivery and the ability of people to live long enough to achieve goals. *Literacy* not only helps people to get and keep jobs, but to understand their surroundings and culture. *Purchasing power*— per capita income adjusted to account for national differences in exchange

TABLE 1

	Low Human Development Index	Human Dev. Index	GNP per Capita Rank 1987		Medium Human Development Index	Human Dev. Index	GNP per Capita Rank 1987		High Human Development Index	Human Dev. Index	GNP per Capita Rank 1987
1	Niger	.116	20	45	Egypt	.501	49	85	Malaysia	.800	80
2	Mali	.143	15	46	Lao People's Dem. Rep.	.506	9	86	Colombia	.801	72
3	Burkina Faso	.150	13	47	Gabon	.525	93	87	Jamaica	.824	62
4	Sierra Leone	.150	27	48	Oman	.535	104	88	Kuwait	.839	122
5	Chad	.157	4	49	Bolivia	.548	44	89	Venezuela	.861	95
6	Guinea	.162	31	50	Myanmar	.561	11	90	Romania	.863	84
7	Somalia	.200	23	51	Honduras	.563	53	91	Mexico	.876	81
8	Mauritania	.208	40	52	Zimbabwe	.576	45	92	Cuba	.877	66
9	Afghanistan	.212	17	53	Lesotho	.580	35	93	Panama	.883	88
10	Benin	.224	28	54	Indonesia	.591	41	94	Trinidad and Tobago	.885	100
11	Burundi	.235	18	55	Guatemala	.592	63	95	Portugal	.899	94
12	Bhutan	.236	3	56	Viet Nam	.608	16	96	Singapore	.899	110
13	Mozambique	.239	10	57	Algeria	.609	91	97	Korea, Rep. of	.903	92
14	Malawi	.250	7	58	Botswana	.646	69	98	Poland	.910	83
15	Sudan	.255	32	59	El Salvador	.651	56	99	Argentina	.910	89
16	Central African Rep.	.258	29	60	Tunisia	.657	70	100	Yugoslavia	.913	90
17	Nepal	.273	8	61	Iran, Islamic Rep. of	.660	97	101	Hungary	.915	87
18	Senegal	.274	43	62	Syrian Arab Rep.	.691	79	102	Uruguay	.916	86
19	Ethiopia	.282	1	63	Dominican Rep.	.699	51	103	Costa Rica	.916	97
20	Zaire	.294	5	64	Saudi Arabia	.702	107	104	Bulgaria	.918	99
21	Rwanda	.304	26	65	Philippines	.714	46	105	USSR	.920	101
22	Angola	.304	58	66	China	.716	22	106	Czechoslovakia	.931	102

Rank	Country	Value		Rank	Country	Value		Rank	Country	Value	
23	Bangladesh	.318	6	67	Libyan Arab Jamahiriya	.719	103	107	Chile	.931	73
24	Nigeria	.322	38	68	South Africa	.731	82	108	Hong Kong	.936	111
25	Yemen Arab Rep.	.328	47	69	Lebanon	.735	78	109	Greece	.949	98
26	Liberia	.333	42	70	Mongolia	.737	57	110	German Dem. Rep.	.953	115
27	Togo	.337	24	71	Nicaragua	.743	54	111	Israel	.957	108
28	Uganda	.354	21	72	Turkey	.751	71	112	USA	.961	129
29	Haiti	.356	34	73	Jordan	.752	76	113	Austria	.961	118
30	Ghana	.360	37	74	Peru	.753	74	114	Ireland	.961	106
31	Yemen, PDB	.368	39	75	Ecuador	.758	68	115	Spain	.965	105
32	Cote d'Ivoire	.393	52	76	Iraq	.759	96	116	Belgium	.966	116
33	Congo	.395	59	77	United Arab Emirates	.782	127	117	Italy	.966	112
34	Namibia	.404	60	78	Thailand	.783	55	118	New Zealand	.966	109
35	Tanzania, U. Rep. of	.413	12	79	Paraguay	.784	65	119	Germany, Fed. Rep. of	.967	120
36	Pakistan	.423	33	80	Brazil	.784	85	120	Finland	.967	121
37	India	.439	25	81	Mauritius	.788	75	121	United Kingdom	.970	113
38	Madagascar	.440	14	82	Korea, Dem. Rep. of	.789	67	122	Denmark	.971	123
39	Papua New Guinea	.471	50	83	Sri Lanka	.789	38	123	France	.974	119
40	Kampuchea	.471	2	84	Albania	.790	61	124	Australia	.978	114
41	Cameroon	.474	64					125	Norway	.983	128
42	Kenya	.481	30					126	Canada	.983	124
43	Zambia	.481	19					127	Netherlands	.984	117
44	Morocco	.489	48					128	Switzerland	.986	130
								129	Sweden	.987	125
								130	Japan	.996	126

rates, tariffs, and tradable goods—demonstrates the relative ability to buy commodities and meet basic needs. The Report also recommends policy options for UNDP's own field officers, for leaders in both industrialized and developing countries, for nongovernmental organizations, and for academics who both study and help shape development policies.

One of the keys to enlarging human development lies in deciding how to allocate scarce resources—between expensive hospitals and primary health care, between urban and rural services, between subsidies to powerful groups such as wealthy landowners and weaker groups such as the absolute poor and the homeless. "Such a restructuring of budget priorities will require tremendous political courage," warns the Report.

As a guide for governments and all those involved with development issues, the study yielded a number of conclusions and policy messages. Among them:

- Removing the immense backlog of human deprivation remains the challenge for the 1990s. It is true that developing countries have made very significant progress towards human development in the last three decades. Life expectancy rose from 46 years in 1960 to 62 years in 1987. The under-five mortality rate was halved. Adult literacy rose from a rate of 43 percent to 60 percent. But there are still more than a billion people in absolute poverty, 800 million who go hungry every day, and 14 million children who die each year before their fifth birthday.

- Average measures of progress in human development conceal immense disparities within developing countries, between urban and rural areas, between men and women, between rich and poor. Rural areas have half the access to health services and safe drinking water that urban areas have. High-income groups often preempt many of the social service benefits.

- Respectable levels of human development are possible even at fairly modest levels of income, or as the Report says: "Life does not begin at $11,000, the average per capita income in the industrialized world." Chile, Costa Rica, Jamaica, Sri Lanka, Tanzania, and Thailand do far better in human development than in raising incomes, "showing that they have directed more of their economic resources towards human progress."

- Social subsidies are absolutely necessary for poorer income groups. "Simply stated, economic growth seldom trickles down to the masses." Although not too costly—generally less than 3 percent of GNP—subsidies establish a safety net. When removed without an alternative net, as in Morocco and China during recent periods of high growth, "the ensuing political and social disturbance has cost far more than the subsidies themselves."

- Technical cooperation must be restructured if it is to help build human capabilities in developing countries. Instead of development budgets going to the salaries and travel of foreign experts, much more must go to help train national personnel and build institutions that can take on the burden of human development and become self-sufficient. "The yardstick for measuring the success of technical assistance programmes," says the Report, "must be the speed with which they phase themselves out." Also, nongovernmental organizations, or NGOs, must be used much more to help people help themselves. The reason: "NGOs are generally small, flexible, and cost-effective."

- A significant reduction in population growth rates is essential for improvements in human development levels. The share of developing countries in world population is expected to grow from 75 percent in 1980 to 84 percent by 2025. The growth, above all in Africa and South Asia, reflects an "urgent need to strengthen programmes of family planning, fertility reduction and maternal and child health care." And if population growth continues while access to international assistance lags and trade outlets continue to shrink in the industrial countries, "the compulsion to migrate in search of better economic opportunities will be overwhelming—a sobering thought for the 1990s."

- Sustainable development strategies mean more than the protection of natural resources and the physical environment. Any form of debt—financial debt, the debt of human neglect, or the debt of environmental degradation—is like borrowing from future generations. Sustainable development should aim at limiting all these debts.

The book concedes shortcomings in the first Human Development Index. There is not enough data, for example, to pinpoint income distribution in all countries studied. Nor is there an accepted way to measure personal freedom. But the first Report does address the issue of freedom, and lists 15 developing countries which have achieved relatively high levels of human development within a reasonably democratic political and social framework. These countries are Costa Rica, Uruguay, Trinidad and Tobago, Mexico, Venezuela, Jamaica, Colombia, Malaysia, Sri Lanka, Thailand, Turkey, Tunisia, Mauritius, Botswana, and Zimbabwe.

In any concerted international effort to improve human development, says the Report, "priority must go to Africa." Even if the international community earmarks an overwhelming share of resources for Africa and patiently helps to rebuild African economies and societies as the Report urges, it will take Africa "at least 25 years to strengthen its human potential, its national institutions and the momentum of its growth."

Africa is the hardest region of the world in which to live. It has the lowest life expectancy, the highest infant mortality rates, and the lowest literacy rates—and women's literacy is only 61 percent that of men. Average per capita income in Africa fell by 25 percent during the 1980s. To be poor in Africa is to command little in the way of resources and to have little power to change things. To be a poor woman in Africa is to have still less of either.

The Report specifically calls for changing laws to provide women equal access to incomes, employment opportunities, credit, and technology, and to offer women far more education and health care, particularly maternal health care. Funds should be directed to safety nets for the poor, such as nutritional support programs in health clinics and school feeding programs. To boost the flow of resources to rural areas, more decisions must be made locally and not by central governments. "Such decentralization of decision-making," says the Report, "may be one of the most important ways of reducing rural-urban income gaps."

While most of the Report concentrates on the developing world, the rich, industrialized nations come in for attention, too, as examples of development which often goes astray. In the United States, the number of homeless people has risen tremendously in the past five years, and in the United Kingdom income gaps widened during the 1980s, leading to deepened poverty.

It is the element of freedom, which is immeasurable, that the Report calls "the most vital component of human development strategies." People must be free to actively participate in setting development priorities, formulating policies, implementing projects, and choosing who shall run their country so that social goals "do not become mechanical devices in the hands of paternalistic governments."

ANNEX 1: STRUCTURAL ADJUSTMENT—THE HUMANE APPROACH

In developing countries, structural adjustment programs often receive a mixed welcome. Many leaders understand the need to balance budgets, to cut public spending, and to free market forces in order to get their economies on track. But they are also aware of the negative consequences, including rising unemployment, declining wages, and cuts in spending on social services that often accompanied the adjustment programs of the 1980s.

The challenge is to balance budgets without unbalancing human lives, and some countries have found ways to adjust with less pain than most. Chile undertook massive public works programs, at one time employing as much as 13 percent of the work force. In Botswana, needy infants and children were monitored carefully, and supplied with food and other support as necessary.

One of the countries that coped best was Zimbabwe. Not long after its independence in 1980, Zimbabwe suffered a series of economic shocks which required adjustment. Some measures taken were orthodox, such as restraining credit growth, reducing subsidies, devaluing the currency, and raising interest rates. But the government also took steps that were unusual, restraining dividend payouts, continuing import controls, and adopting a more expansionary economic policy than most such packages approved by the International Monetary Fund.

Indeed, for much of the 1980s Zimbabwe adjusted on its own because it failed to reach agreement with the IMF. At the same time, it continued to protect Zimbabwe's most vulnerable groups.

- Loans were channeled to low-income farmers, whose share of credit from the Agricultural Finance Corporation more than doubled from 17 percent in 1983 to 35 percent in 1986. Those loans and other marketing reforms nearly quadrupled low-income farmers' share of marketed maize and cotton from 10 percent to 38 percent.
- Spending on health and education rose from 22 percent of total government spending in 1980 to 27 percent in 1984, while allocations for defence and administration dropped from 44 percent to 28 percent. Spending on primary education rose from 38 percent to 58 percent of the education budget. More money went to preventive health care during those years as well.
- Special food programs provided drought relief and a supplementary feeding program for undernourished children. More than 250,000 children received food supplements at the peak of the drought in 1984.

Because of these conscious policy decisions, the economic costs of adjustment did not become human costs. The infant mortality rate continued to decline, primary school enrollment rose sharply, and malnutrition did not rise despite the drought.

ANNEX 2: WHERE DOES THE MONEY GO— TO SOLDIERS OR TEACHERS?

Money that could be used for human development often goes to military budgets instead, even in the poorest countries. Military expenditures in developing countries have multiplied by seven times over the last 25 years to almost $200 billion, compared with a doubling by the industrialized countries. Three-quarters of the global arms trade today takes place in developing countries.

In the industrialized countries there are, on average, 105 soldiers for every 100 teachers, suggesting greater support for war than wisdom. In

TABLE 2

	Armed Forces as Percentage of Teachers
High soldier–teacher ratio	
Ethiopia	494
Iraq	428
Oman	275
Chad	233
Democratic Yemen	200
Pakistan	154
Low soldier–teacher ratio	
Costa Rica	0
Mauritius	10
Côte d'Ivoire	13
Ghana	14
Jamaica	20
Brazil	24

TABLE 3 **Fifteen Countries with Relatively Democratic Human Development**

	HDI Rank, 1–130[a]
Latin America, Caribbean	
Costa Rica	103
Uruguay	102
Trinidad and Tobago	94
Mexico	91
Venezuela	89
Jamaica	87
Colombia	86
Asia	
Malaysia	85
Sri Lanka	83
Thailand	78
Middle East, North Africa	
Turkey	72
Tunisia	60
Sub-Saharan Africa	
Mauritius	81
Botswana	58
Zimbabwe	52

Of the 130 countries ranked, ranks 1–44 were listed as being of "low" human development, 45–84 of "medium," and 85–130 of "high" human development.

developing countries, there are on average only 68 percent as many soldiers as teachers. But as with any indicator, averages can disguise enormous disparities. Costa Rica has no standing army, while Ethiopia, which is
engaged in a bitter civil war, has almost five times the number of soldiers as
teachers.

The *Human Development Report 1990* has produced a statistical table
(Table 2) reflecting some of the highest and lowest ratios of soldiers to
teachers.

ANNEX 3: WHAT VALUE FREEDOM?

The Report puts a higher value on human development achievements in
countries with a reasonable degree of democracy and a lower value on
those with authoritarian governments. "Human freedom is vital for human
development," says the Report. "People must be free to exercise their choices in properly functioning markets, and they must have a decisive voice in
shaping their political future."

The Report's authors intend to fashion a quantitative measure of
freedom, to be included in a future index. Until then, it has listed 15
top countries whose high human development levels have been achieved
"within a reasonably democratic political and social framework" (see
Table 3).

PART SEVEN

WHAT IS TO BE DONE?

The readings in the book have covered the many elements of the political economy of development and underdevelopment, ranging from methodology and history to the specific questions of industry's and agriculture's roles in the development process. Part Six placed all these concerns squarely in the context fundamental to the development question: the human costs of development and underdevelopment.

Social change will occur, is occurring, and conscious effort to guide it in a positive direction can have benefits to the human beings involved. Since the effort to encourage development started after the Second World War, we have learned a great deal about the process, though this has not inoculated us from "conventional foolishness." The task still remains daunting and the purpose of this part of the book is to suggest the directions that must be taken to overcome the loss of development momentum during the 1980s and to avoid the false paths that have been followed in the past. The greatest task, perhaps, is one that is beyond the scope of this book. Albert Hirschman, in his assessment of development economics as a subdiscipline of economics (1983), found the major failure of development economists in their loss of hope for the possibility of development. In reaction they retreated to narrow technical issues or abandoned the field entirely. Hirschman has retained his "bias for hope," based upon his experience with the development process and his clear sense that social change cannot be avoided. So one key task is to accept social change and the possibility that it can be for the better; and that is something each of us must do for him- or herself. With that accomplished, the articles in this section can help us see "what is to be done."

Denis Goulet, in a classic article, provides a vision of what true development would be, a world of justice and of new forms of behavior that reflect liberation from oppression. His vision is utopian, perhaps, but can there be hope without some such utopian vision of a better world? Can development become a hinge word in that effort and can development/liberation become truly a victory cry for all human beings?

Freire's classic article places the focus on those who have borne the costs of underdevelopment, the oppressed, and on the fundamental change in their lives and attitudes required in any true process of development/liberation. He points to the difficulties involved, the fear of freedom, the tendency to paternalism, the tendency of the oppressed to become oppressors, and their desire to be like the oppressors. Freire strongly expresses the hope that social change that takes seriously its pedagogical dimension and incorporates cointentional education can unmask the dimensions of oppression and counter the myths that sustain it, and in this process development/liberation can occur.

These visions of development/liberation must confront the objective reality of underdevelopment and the possible steps that can be taken to confront it. The next three articles focus on three of these elements: the issues of human development, the conflict between the arms race and development, and the ecological limit of development efforts.

Griffin and Knight provide a contemporary treatment of one of the main themes of development highlighted in Part One by Sen: the mobilization of underemployed manpower. Their context is the concentration on "human development" introduced by Gall in Part Six, and they use Sen's earlier ideas of capabilities and entitlements. Their survey of performance on capability measures—life expectancy, infant mortality, and education access—reiterates the important advances that development has brought. But the 1980s, with slower growth, higher unemployment, and widespread government fiscal crisis has endangered these gains and made any further gains contingent on careful thinking and policy development. They emphasize three aspects that policymakers must take into account. The first is that policy should encourage the development of human capabilities through the mobilization of local resources and of participation as well as through traditional human capital formation through health, education, and sanitation. Second, the link between human development and the distribution of income, of wealth, and of power should be taken into account, with policies designed to ensure improved distribution. Finally, while the alleviation of poverty has an ethical imperative, it is also functional in increasing long-run growth performance in countries. So resources spent on the military would be far better used in alleviating poverty, and government restrictions on grassroots and private activity should be reduced.

Thorsson, and the United Nations, point out that "the arms race and underdevelopment are not two problems; they are one. They must be solved together, or neither will ever be solved." Both must be linked to the issue of security, realizing that true security can be provided through development better than through military expenditures. The points made in the article have taken on a new dimension with the cooling of the Cold War and the possibility of diverting resources from nuclear weapons and deterrence. It is not clear that this will free up world resources for development efforts; as the Iraqui invasion of Kuwait and the subsequent armed reaction indicated, one result may simply be an intensification of conflict in Third World areas. Nonetheless, there is no denying the need to assess military expenditures in a developmental context.

With Cartwright's article, the issue of sustainable development raised by Helleiner in Part One appears again. He points out that the difficulties of the 1980s have led to an intensification of the exploitation of natural resources as a means of satisfying debt obligations. He documents the costs of these steps and argues for the intrinsic value of conservation. Finally, he suggests that one favorable element in the debt overhang is the possibility, realized in a number of cases, of using those blocked resources to further conservation efforts. There is clearly much more to be done, however.

The final article by Sklar focuses on Africa, but has a far wider range of applicability. Its starting point is that the "binary belief system" that an economy must be either capitalist or socialist is not conducive to innovative advances in social theory or in organization. All too often development thinking is cast in those terms, and thus the possibilities for development are narrowed. Perhaps the developmental genius of South Korea and Taiwan was to avoid those binary categories and to find a mode which combined strong government activity with private enterprise, always in a context in which basic social justice was maintained. In Africa, as well as in Latin America, the Caribbean, South Asia, and most probably Eastern Europe as well, socialist efforts require capital formation but are unable to provide an incentive structure that will encourage successful growth. However, capitalism needs the state, especially to socialize the losses which occur in social change, but it lacks any theory of social responsibility that will limit the injustices created. Sklar suggests that successful development will require a hybrid formation that will encourage social invention and lead to a release of social energy. Although it appears that capitalism is on the march in the Third World, Sklar is quite correct in pointing out that the social injustice which follows in its wake will limit its success. It is no accident that the World Bank's *World Development Report, 1990* focused on the issue of poverty, for the Bank's model of development which has dominated policy during the 1980s has clearly had little beneficial impact on poverty. Thus Sklar leads us into the problem of development with a call to break from these binary categories, and implicitly with a bias toward hope that new ways of thinking can lead to new approaches toward development, and that the 1990s can see a rekindling of hope for development.

REFERENCES

Hirschman, Albert O. "The Rise and Decline of Development Economics." In his *Essays in Trespassing: Economics to Politics and Beyond.* Cambridge: Cambridge University Press, 1981.

World Bank. *World Development Report, 1990.* Oxford: University Press, 1990.

28

"Development" . . . or Liberation?

Denis Goulet

Latin Americans in growing numbers now denounce the lexicon of development experts as fraudulent. To illustrate, Gustavo Gutierrez, a Peruvian theologian and social activist, concludes that "the term development conveys a pejorative connotation . . . (and) is gradually being replaced by the term liberation . . . there will be a true development for Latin America only through liberation from the domination by capitalist countries. That implies, of course, a showdown with their natural allies: our natural oligarchies."[1]

Gutierrez is a major spokesman for "theology of liberation." Numerous seminars and conferences have already been held on the theme in Colombia, Mexico, Uruguay, Argentina, and elsewhere. For Gutierrez—as for Gustavo Perez, René Garcia, Rubem Alves, Juan Segundo, Camilo Moncada, Emilio Castro,[2] and others—"liberation" expresses better than "development" the real aspirations of their people for more human living conditions. Gutierrez does not attempt to review all the changes in the definition of development since the Marshall Plan was launched in 1947. This task has already been performed by others.[3] Instead he focuses his critical gaze on three perspectives with one of which most experts in "developed" countries identify.

THREE VIEWS OF DEVELOPMENT

For many economists development is synonymous with economic growth measured in aggregate terms. A country is developed, they hold, when it can sustain, by its own efforts and after having first reached a per capita

Reprinted from the *International Development Review*, 13, 3 (September 1971), by permission of the publisher. Copyright © 1971 by the Society for International Development.

GNP (Gross National Product) level of $500 (for some observers) or $1000 (for others), an annual rate of growth ranging from 5% to 7%. According to these criteria, certain countries are highly developed, while those on the lowest rungs of the ladder are either underdeveloped or undeveloped. Similar comparisons can also be established between different regions and sectors within a single economy. Although this view is generally repudiated today, it still retains some vestigial influence, thanks to the impact of works like Walt Rostow's *The Stages of Economic Growth* and to the dominant role still played by economists in planning. Even when they give lip-service to other dimensions in development, many economists continue to subordinate all noneconomic factors to the practical requirements of their growth models.

The second outlook, far more prevalent today, was summarized at the start of the United Nations' First Development Decade in U Thant's phrase, "development = economic growth + social change." The trouble with this formula is that it either says too much or says too little since not any kind of growth will do, nor any kind of change.

Most social scientists adopt some variant of this conception as their own working definition of development; it is broad enough to embrace a variety of change processes emphasizing economic, social, cultural, or political factors. Nearly always, however, social scientists subordinate value judgments about human goals to the achievement of economic growth, to the creation of new social divisions of labor, to the quest for modern institutions, or to the spread of attitudes deemed compatible with efficient production. The last point is well illustrated by those who affirm that "modernity" is not the presence of factories, but the presence of a certain viewpoint on factories.

Behind an array of theories and special vocabularies, however, lingers the common assumption that "developed" societies ought to serve as models for others. Some observers, eager to minimize culture bias, reject the notion that all societies *ought* to follow patterns set by others. Nevertheless, they assert that modern patterns are inevitable, given the demonstration effects and technological penetration of modern societies throughout the world.

A third stream of development thinkers stresses ethical values. This group has always constituted, in some respects, a heretical minority. Its position centers on qualitative improvement in all societies, and in all groups and individuals within societies. Although all men must surely have enough goods in order to be more human, they say, development itself is simply a means to the human ascent. This perspective, at times called "the French school," is linked to such names as economist François Perroux, social planner Louis Lebret, theorist Jacques Austruy, and practicing politicians like Robert Buron and André Phillip. According to these men and their disciples, social change should be seen in the broadest possible historical context, within which all of humanity is viewed as receiving a summons to assume its own destiny. Their ideas have influenced United Nations agencies in some measure, but they have made their greatest inroads in religious writings on development: papal encyclicals, documents issued by the World Council of Churches and the Pontifical Commission on Justice and Peace, pastoral letters drafted by bishops in several countries. The single geographical area where the French school has achieved considerable penetration is Latin America.

This is why the conclusion reached by Gutierrez is particularly significant. According to Gutierrez, the French school, because of its historicity and its insistence on norms for social goals, is the least objectionable of the three perspectives he criticizes. Nevertheless, he argues, the realities barely hinted at by the French are better expressed by the term "liberation" than by "development." By using the latter term the French school does not dramatize its discontinuities with the other perspectives sharply enough. Worse still, its spokesmen employ such notions as foreign aid, technical cooperation, development planning, and modernization in ways which remain ambiguous at best. Consequently, in the eyes of many Latin Americans "development" has a pejorative connotation: it does not get to the roots of the problem and leads to frustration. Moreover, "development" does not evoke asymmetrical power relations operative in the world or the inability of evolutionary change models to lead, in many countries, to the desired objectives. Therefore, says Gutierrez, it is better to speak of liberation, a term which directly suggests domination, vulnerability in the face of world market forces, weak bargaining positions, the need for basic social changes domestically and for freer foreign policies.

THE LANGUAGE OF LIBERATION

To substitute for "development" the term "liberation" is to engage in what Brazilian educator Paulo Freire calls "cultural action for freedom."[4] Liberation implies the suppression of elitism by a populace which assumes control over its own change processes. Development, on the other hand, although frequently used to describe various change processes, stresses the benefits said to result from them: material prosperity, higher production and expanded consumption, better housing or medical services, wider educational opportunities and employment mobility, and so on. This emphasis, however, errs on two counts. First, it uncritically supports change strategies which value efficiency above all else, even if efficiency must be gained by vesting decisions in the hands of elites—trained managers, skilled technicians, high-level "manpower." A second failing, analyzed by Harvard historian Barrington Moore in *Social Origins of Dictatorship and Democracy*, is the dismissal of violence as unconstructive and the refusal to condemn the violence attendant upon legal change patterns.

Not theologians alone, but social scientists, planners, educators, and some political leaders in Latin America prefer the terminology of liberation to that of development. They unmask the hidden value assumptions of the conventional wisdom and replace them with a deliberate stress on self-development as opposed to aid, foreign investment, and technical assistance. Since I have written a detailed critique of the Pearson, Peterson, Jackson, and other development reports elsewhere,[5] there is no need to repeat here what is there said regarding the value assumptions and critical omissions of these reports. What is germane to the present discussion is the confirmation given these criticisms by Third World spokesmen in UNCTAD (United Nations Conference on Trade and Development) and GATT (General Agreement on Tariffs and Trade) meetings.[6] Not surprisingly, more and more leaders from underdeveloped areas are coming to regard "development" as the lexicon of palliatives. Their recourse to the vocabulary of liberation is a vigorous measure of self-defense, aimed at overcoming the structural vulnerability which denies them control over the economic, political, and cultural forces which impinge upon their societies. Even to speak of liberation, before achieving it, is a first conquest of cultural autonomy. Ultimately what is sought is to alter relationships between director and directed societies, between privileged elites and the populace at large within all societies. Ever more people are coming to understand that "to be underdeveloped" is to be relegated to a subordinate position in history, to be given the role of adjusting to, not of initiating, technological processes.

The language of liberation is being nurtured in societies where a new critical consciousness is being formed. For these societies, the models of genuine development are not those billed by U.S. aid agencies as success stories—South Korea, Greece, Taiwan, and Iran. Industrialization and economic growth have no doubt taken place in these lands, but no basic changes have occurred in class relationships and the distribution of wealth and power; the larger social system remains structurally exploitative. Moreover, economic gains have been won under the tutelage of repressive political regimes. Finally, as one European has observed, "U.S. aid seems to work best in countries which are lackeys of American foreign policy."

Revolutionary Latin Americans reject this kind of development. They look instead to China, Cuba, and Tanzania as examples of success. In China, mass starvation has been abolished and a feudal social system overthrown. Elitism in rulers is systematically uprooted whenever it reappears, and technological gains are subordinated to the cultural creation of a new man capable of autonomy. Cuba, notwithstanding its economic mistakes, freely admitted, has overcome its servile dependence on the United States and asserts itself increasingly in the face of the Soviet Union, upon whom it still relies heavily for financial, technical, and military assistance. Moreover, Cuba has abolished illiteracy in sensational fashion, decentralized investment, and reduced the gap in living conditions between the countryside and the cities. And Tanzania is admired because it rejects mass-consumption as a model for society, practices self-reliance in its educational system (choosing to grant prestige to agricultural skills rather than to purely scientific ones geared to large-scale engineering projects), accepts foreign aid only when the overall impact of the projects financed will not create a new elite class within the nation itself, and in general subordinates economic gains to the creation of new African values founded on ancient communitarian practices.

For liberationists, therefore, success is not measured simply by the quantity of benefits gained, but above all by the way in which change processes take place. Visible benefits are no doubt sought, but the decisive test of success is that, in obtaining them, a society will have fostered greater popular autonomy in a nonelitist mode, social creativity instead of imitation, and control over forces of change instead of mere adjustment to them. The crucial question is: Will "underdeveloped" societies become mere consumers of technological civilization or agents of their own transformation? *At stake, therefore, is something more than a war over words; the battle lines are drawn between two conflicting interpretations of historical reality, two competing principles of social organization.* The first values efficiency and social control above all else, the second social justice and the creation of a new man.

Western development scholars are prone to question the validity of the new vocabulary of liberation. As trained social scientists, they doubt its analytical power, explanatory value, and predictive capacities. Yet their scepticism is misplaced inasmuch as empirical social science has itself proved unable to describe reality, let alone to help men change it in acceptable ways. Of late, however, a salutary modesty has begun to take hold of social scientists. Gunnar Myrdal (in *Asian Drama*) confesses the error of his early days as an "expert" on development, and challenges (in *Objectivity in Social Research*) the assumptions behind all value-free theories and research methods. More forcefully still, Alvin Gouldner, in *The Coming Crisis of Western Sociology*, argues the case for a new Utopian, value-centered radical sociology for the future. And economist Egbert de Vries[7] reaches the conclusion that no significant breakthroughs in development theory have been achieved in the last decade. Western development scholars, therefore, themselves lost in deep epistemological quagmire, are ill-advised to scorn the new theories.

One finds in truth great explanatory power, analytical merit, and predictive value in the writings of Latin American social scientists on development, dependence, and domination.[8] The new liberation vocabulary is valid, even empirically, because it lays bare structures of dependence and domination at all levels. Reaching behind the neutral "descriptive" words of developmental wisdom, it unmasks the intolerably high human cost to Latin Americans of economic development, social modernization, political institution-building, and cultural westernization. The reality described by these writings is the pervasive impotence of vulnerable societies in the face of the impersonal stimuli which impinge upon them. Furthermore, their vocabulary enjoys high prescriptive value because it shows this powerlessness to be reversible: if domination is a human state of affairs caused and perpetuated by men, it can be overthrown by men. Finally, the highly charged political language of liberation has great predictive value to the extent that it can mobilize collective energies around a value which is the motor of all successful social revolutions—HOPE. Liberated hope is not the cold rational calculus of probability à la Herman Kahn or Henry Kissinger, but a daring calculus of *possibility* which reverses the past, shatters the present, and creates a new future.

"DEVELOPMENT" AS A HINGE WORD

In spite of its absolute superiority, however, the language of liberation remains, for many people in the "developed" world, tactically unmanageable. The historical connotations of the word sometimes lead them to resist mobilization around its theme, especially if these people are not themselves oppressors, but inert beneficiaries of impersonal oppressive systems. A second category of people may also find it difficult to respond, namely those insurgent professionals who can subvert "the system" only by mastering its tools and serving as a fifth column in alliance with revolutionary groups on the outside. Understandably, these persons will need to continue using the currently available "professional" terminology. It is considerations such as these which lie behind the question: Can "development" serve a useful hinge role in mobilization? The answer is affirmative if one agrees with political scientist Harvey Wheeler that

> . . . we don't possess a *revolutionary* social science to serve the utopian needs of the revolution. And those learned enough to create it are divorced from the activists who must prepare the way for the new utopianism. . . . Somehow, the radical activists and the radical scientists—the utopians—must come together.[9]

Desired changes within "developed" societies can ensue only in the wake of concerted (and much unconcerted) action emanating from a variety of change agents. There can be no objection on principle, therefore, to granting tentative validity to "development" as a hinge word.

For the benefit of those who have not yet been weaned from the sweet milk of palliative incrementalism,[10] "development" needs to be redefined, demystified, and thrust into the arena of moral debate. If critically used as a hinge word, it may open up new perspectives and render the leap into "liberation" possible for many people. Nevertheless, only from the third per-

spective on development summarized above can one find a suitable platform whence to make this leap of faith. The reason is that, of the three viewpoints, only this ethical, value-laden, humanist approach is rooted in history, and not in abstract theory. Before the language of liberation can sound
convincing to the categories of people I have described, it must be shown
that "development," as normally understood, alienates even its beneficiaries in compulsive consumption, technological determinisms of various
sorts, ecological pathology, and warlike policies. Worst of all, it makes
those who benefit from development the structural accomplices of the
underdevelopment of others. Surely this cannot be what authentic development is. As one reflects on its goals, he discovers that development, viewed
as a human project, signifies total liberation. Such liberation aims at freeing
men from nature's servitudes, from economic backwardness and oppressive technological institutions, from unjust class structures and political
exploiters, from cultural and psychic alienation—in short, from all of life's
inhuman agencies.

A new language, able to shatter imprisoning reality, must be born from
the clash between vocabularies nurtured in different soils. The first will ges-
tate in a Third World matrix and express the emerging consciousness of
those who refuse to be objects, and declare their intent to become subjects,
of history. The keys to this vocabulary are the conquest of autonomy and
the will to create a new future. At the opposite pole, out of "developed"
societies, must arise a subversive redefinition of development itself. Its
function will be to destroy the First World's uncritical faith in the universal
goodness of its notions of progress, achievement, social harmony, democracy, and modernization. Confrontation between the two is required because
neither "development" alone nor "liberation" alone fully transcends both
cultural domination and purely negative responses to oppression.
Moreover, both terms can be used by symbol manipulators to mystify reality or rationalize palliative change strategies.

Nevertheless, it is clear that competing terminologies of development
and liberation are not equally subject to distortion. On the scales of human
justice, the interests which they express do not balance each other out.
There is indeed, as Camus writes, universal meaning in the rebel's refusal
to be treated as something less than a man. And as Marx put it, the
oppressed masses are the latent historical carriers of universal human values. The battle to free men is not comparable to the struggle to maintain or
expand privilege. Consequently, every trace of elitism and cultural manipulation must be purged from the development vocabulary and replaced with
the symbols of liberation. Even then history will not give men any respite;
rather, it will propel them into asking: Liberation for what? Ancient teleo-
logical questions reappear, concerning the good life, the good society, and
men's final purposes. That they should keep arising is no sign of the weakness of men's words, but merely a clue to the grandeur of their historical

task. That task is to strive endlessly to outstrip not only alienating material conditions but all particular images of the ideal society as well.

Intellectuals who discuss revolution and violence often utter irresponsible words which place bullets in other people's guns. As they debate development and liberation, the danger they face is less dramatic but no less destructive in the long run. For most of them resort to persuasive political definitions, thereby preempting all the intellectual ground upon which descriptive and evocative definitions might find their place. Such habits render genuine liberation impossible since true cultural emancipation admits of no sloganism, no sectarianism, no simplism. Revolutionary consciousness is critical of self no less than of others; and it brooks no verbal cheating even to achieve ideological gains. In final analysis, any liberation vocabulary must do two things. The first is to unmask the alienations disguised by the development lexicon: the alienation of the many in misery, of the few in irresponsible abundance. The second is to transform itself from the rallying cry of victims alone into the victory chant of all men as they empower themselves to enter history with no nostalgia for prehistory.

Success proves difficult because men have never fully learned the lesson implied in a statement by the Indian mystic Rabindranath Tagore that, ultimately, only those values can be truly human which can be truly universal.

NOTES

1. Gustavo Gutierrez Merino, "Notes for a Theology of Liberation," *Theological Studies*, 31, 2 (June 1970): 243–61.
2. The writings of these men are found largely in papers circulated by documentary services such as LADOC (Latin American Bureau, U.S. Catholic Conference), ISAL (Iglesia y Sociedad en América Latina), and the Theology of Liberation Symposium (in Spanish), Bogota.
3. Cf. the excellent work by Jacques Freyssinet, *Le Concept de Sous-Dévelopment*, Mouton, 1966. A brief review of the different meanings attached to the word "development" can be found in Denis Goulet, "That Third World," *The Center Magazine*, I, 6 (September 1968): 47–55.
4. Cf. Paulo Freire, *Cultural Action for Freedom*, Harvard Educational Review and Center for the Study of Development and Social Change, Monograph No. 1, 1970. One may also consult the same author's *Pedagogy of the Oppressed*, Herder and Herder, 1970.
5. Cf. Denis Goulet and Michael Hudson, *The Myth of Aid: The Hidden Agenda of the Development Reports*, IDOC Books, 1970. This work contains two essays, one by Goulet entitled "Domesticating the Third World," and a second by Hudson on "The Political Economy of Foreign Aid."
6. On this cf., e.g., Guy F. Erb, "The Second Session of UNCTAD," *Journal of the World Trade Law*, 2, 3 (May–June 1968): 346–59. For a Latin American view, see the document entitled, "The Latin American Consensus of Viña del Mar," dated May 17, 1969.

7. Egbert de Vries, "A Review of Literature on Development Theory," *International Development Review*, 10, 1 (March 1968): 43–49.

8. Cf., e.g., such works as F. Cardoso and E. Falleto, *Dependencia y Desarrollo en América Latina*, Santiago, 1967; Theotonio dos Santos, *El Nuevo caracter de la dependencia,* Santiago, 1968; Celso Furtado, *Dialéctica Do Desenvolvimento*, Rio de Janeiro, 1964; numerous essays by Alberto Guerreiro Ramos (a Brazilian now teaching at UCLA), et al.

9. Harvey Wheeler, "The Limits of Confrontation Politics," *The Center Magazine*, 3, 4 (July 1970): 39.

10. The difference between palliative and creative incrementalism is explained in Denis Goulet, *Is Gradualism Dead?*, Council on Religion and International Affairs, 1970.

29
Pedagogy of the Oppressed

Paulo Freire

While the problem of humanization has always, from an axiological point of view, been man's central problem, it now takes on the character of an inescapable concern.[1] Concern for humanization leads at once to the recognition of dehumanization, not only as an ontological possibility but as an historical reality. And as man perceives the extent of dehumanization, he asks himself if humanization is a viable possibility. Within history, in concrete, objective contexts, both humanization and dehumanization are possibilities for man as an uncompleted being conscious of his incompletion.

But while both humanization and dehumanization are real alternatives, only the first is man's vocation. This vocation is constantly negated, yet it is affirmed by that very negation. It is thwarted by injustice, exploitation, oppression, and the violence of the oppressors; it is affirmed by the yearning of the oppressed for freedom and justice, and by their struggle to recover their lost humanity.

Dehumanization, which marks not only those whose humanity has been stolen, but also (though in a different way) those who have stolen it, is a *distortion* of the vocation of becoming more fully human. This distortion occurs within history but it is not an historical vocation. Indeed, to admit of dehumanization as an historical vocation would lead either to cynicism or to total despair. The struggle for humanization, for the emancipation of labor, for the overcoming of alienation, for the affirmation of men as persons would be meaningless. This struggle is possible only because dehumanization, although a concrete historical fact, is *not* a given destiny but the result of an unjust order that engenders violence in the oppressors, which in turn dehumanizes the oppressed.

Because it is a distortion of being more fully human, sooner or later being less human leads the oppressed to struggle against those who made them so. In order for this struggle to have meaning, the oppressed must not, in seeking to regain their humanity (which is a way to create it), become in turn oppressors of the oppressors, but rather restorers of the humanity of both.

This, then, is the great humanistic and historical task of the oppressed: to liberate themselves and their oppressors as well. The oppressors, who oppress, exploit, and rape by virtue of their power, cannot find in this power the strength to liberate either the oppressed or themselves. Only power that springs from the weakness of the oppressed will be sufficiently strong to free both. Any attempt to "soften" the power of the oppressor in deference to the weakness of the oppressed almost always manifests itself in the form of false generosity; indeed, the attempt never goes beyond this. In order to have the continued opportunity to express their "generosity," the oppressors must perpetuate injustice as well. An unjust social order is the permanent fount of this "generosity," which is nourished by death, despair, and poverty. This is why the dispensers of false generosity become desperate at the slightest threat to its source.

True generosity consists precisely in fighting to destroy the causes which nourish false charity. False charity constrains the fearful and sub-dued, the "rejects of life," to extend their trembling hands. True generosity lies in striving so that these hands—whether of individuals or entire peo-ples—need be extended less and less in supplication, so that more and more they become human hands which work and, working, transform the world.

This lesson and this apprenticeship must come, however, from the oppressed themselves and from those who are truly solidary with them. As individuals or as peoples, by fighting for the restoration of their humanity they will be attempting the restoration of true generosity. Who are better prepared than the oppressed to understand the terrible significance of an oppressive society? Who suffer the effects of oppression more than the oppressed? Who can better understand the necessity of liberation? They will not gain this liberation by chance but through the praxis of their quest for it, through their recognition of the necessity to fight for it. And this fight, because of the purpose given it by the oppressed, will actually consti-tute an act of love opposing the lovelessness which lies at the heart of the oppressors' violence, lovelessness even when clothed in false generosity.

But almost always, during the initial stage of the struggle, the oppressed, instead of striving for liberation, tend themselves to become oppressors, or "sub-oppressors." The very structure of their thought has been conditioned by the contradictions of the concrete, existential situation by which they were shaped. Their ideal is to be men; but for them, to be men is to be oppressors. This is their model of humanity. This phenomenon derives from the fact that the oppressed, at a certain moment of their exis-tential experience, adopt an attitude of "adhesion" to the oppressor. Under these circumstances they cannot "consider" him sufficiently clearly to objec-tivize him—to discover him "outside" themselves. This does not necessarily mean that the oppressed are unaware that they are downtrodden. But their perception of themselves as oppressed is impaired by their submersion in the reality of oppression. At this level, their perception of themselves as opposites of the oppressor does not yet signify engagement in a struggle to overcome the contradiction,[2] the one pole aspires not to liberation, but to identification with its opposite pole.

In this situation the oppressed do not see the "new man" as the man to be born from the resolution of this contradiction, as oppression gives way to liberation. For them, the new man is themselves become oppressors. Their vision of the new man is individualistic; because of their identifica-tion with the oppressor, they have no consciousness of themselves as per-sons or as members of an oppressed class. It is not to become free men that they want agrarian reform, but in order to acquire land and thus become landowners—or, more precisely, bosses over other workers. It is a rare peasant who, once "promoted" to overseer, does not become more of a tyrant toward his former comrades than the owner himself. This is because the context of the peasant's situation, that is, oppression, remains unchanged. In this example, the overseer, in order to make sure of his job, must be as tough as the owner—and more so. Thus is illustrated our previ-ous assertion that during the initial stage of their struggle the oppressed find in the oppressor their model of "manhood."

Even revolution, which transforms a concrete situation of oppression by establishing the process of liberation, must confront this phenomenon. Many of the oppressed who directly or indirectly participate in revolution intend—conditioned by the myths of the old order—to make it their private revolution. The shadow of their former oppressor is still cast over them.

The "fear of freedom" which afflicts the oppressed,[3] a fear which may equally well lead them to desire the role of oppressor or bind them to the role of oppressed, should be examined. One of the basic elements of the relationship between oppressor and oppressed is *prescription*. Every pre-scription represents the imposition of one man's choice upon another, transforming the consciousness of the man prescribed to into one that con-forms with the prescriber's consciousness. Thus, the behavior of the oppressed is a prescribed behavior, following as it does the guidelines of the oppressor.

The oppressed, having internalized the image of the oppressor and adopted his guidelines, are fearful of freedom. Freedom would require them to eject this image and replace it with autonomy and responsibility. Freedom is acquired by conquest, not by gift. It must be pursued constantly and responsibly. Freedom is not an ideal located outside of man; nor is it an idea which becomes myth. It is rather the indispensable condition for the quest for human completion.

To surmount the situation of oppression, men must first critically recognize its causes, so that through transforming action they can create a new situation, one which makes possible the pursuit of a fuller humanity. But the struggle to be more fully human has already begun in the authentic struggle to transform the situation. Although the situation of oppression is a dehumanized and dehumanizing totality affecting both the oppressors and those whom they oppress, it is the latter who must, from their stifled humanity, wage for both the struggle for a fuller humanity; the oppressor, who is himself dehumanized because he dehumanizes others, is unable to lead this struggle.

However, the oppressed, who have adapted to the structure of domination in which they are immersed, and have become resigned to it, are inhibited from waging the struggle for freedom so long as they feel incapable of running the risks it requires. Moreover, their struggle for freedom threatens not only the oppressor, but also their own oppressed comrades who are fearful of still greater repression. When they discover within themselves the yearning to be free, they perceive that this yearning can be transformed into reality only when the same yearning is aroused in their comrades. But while dominated by the fear of freedom they refuse to appeal to others, or to listen to the appeals of others, or even to the appeals of their own conscience. They prefer gregariousness to authentic comradeship; they prefer the security of conformity with their state of unfreedom to the creative communion produced by freedom and even the very pursuit of freedom.

The oppressed suffer from the duality which has established itself in their innermost being. They discover that without freedom they cannot exist authentically. Yet, although they desire authentic existence, they fear it. They are at one and the same time themselves and the oppressor whose consciousness they have internalized. The conflict lies in the choice between being wholly themselves or being divided; between ejecting the oppressor within or not ejecting him; between human solidarity or alienation; between following prescriptions or having choices; between being spectators or actors; between acting or having the illusion of acting through the action of the oppressors; between speaking out or being silent, castrated in their power to create and re-create, in their power to transform the world. This is the tragic dilemma of the oppressed which their education must take into account.

[This paper] will present some aspects of what the writer has termed the pedagogy of the oppressed, a pedagogy which must be forged *with*, not *for*, the oppressed (whether individuals or peoples) in the incessant struggle to regain their humanity. This pedagogy makes oppression and its causes objects of reflection by the oppressed, and from that reflection will come their necessary engagement in the struggle for their liberation. And in the struggle this pedagogy will be made and remade.

The central problem is this: How can the oppressed, as divided, unauthentic beings, participate in developing the pedagogy of their liberation? Only as they discover themselves to be "hosts" of the oppressor can they contribute to the midwifery of their liberating pedagogy. As long as they live in the duality in which *to be* is *to be like*, and *to be like* is *to be like the oppressor*, this contribution is impossible. The pedagogy of the oppressed is an instrument for their critical discovery that both they and their oppressors are manifestations of dehumanization.

Liberation is thus a childbirth, and a painful one. The man who emerges is a new man, viable only as the oppressor-oppressed contradiction is superseded by the humanization of all men. Or to put it another way, the solution of this contradiction is born in the labor which brings into the world this new man: no longer oppressor nor no longer oppressed, but man in the process of achieving freedom.

This solution cannot be achieved in idealistic terms. In order for the oppressed to be able to wage the struggle for their liberation, they must perceive the reality of oppression not as a closed world from which there is no exit, but as a limiting situation which they can transform. This perception is a necessary but not a sufficient condition for liberation; it must become the motivating force for liberating action. Nor does the discovery by the oppressed that they exist in dialectical relationship to the oppressor, as his antithesis—that without them the oppressor could not exist[4]—in itself constitute liberation. The oppressed can overcome the contradiction in which they are caught only when this perception enlists them in the struggle to free themselves.

The same is true with respect to the individual oppressor as a person. Discovering himself to be an oppressor may cause considerable anguish, but it does not necessarily lead to solidarity with the oppressed. Rationalizing his guilt through paternalistic treatment of the oppressed, all the while holding them fast in a position of dependence, will not do. Solidarity requires that one enter into the situation of those with whom one is solidary; it is a radical posture. If what characterizes the oppressed is their subordination to the consciousness of the master, as Hegel affirms,[5] true solidarity with the oppressed means fighting at their side to transform the objective reality which has made them these "beings for another." The oppressor is solidary with the oppressed only when he stops regarding the oppressed as an abstract category and sees them as persons who have been unjustly dealt with, deprived of their voice, cheated in the sale of their labor—when he stops making pious, sentimental, and individualistic gestures and risks an act of love. True solidarity is found only in the plenitude of this act of love, in its existentiality, in its praxis. To affirm that men are persons and as persons should be free, and yet to do nothing tangible to make this affirmation a reality is a farce.

Since it is in a concrete situation that the oppressor-oppressed contradiction is established, the resolution of this contradiction must be *objectively* verifiable. Hence, the radical requirement—both for the man who discovers himself to be an oppressor and for the oppressed—that the concrete situation which begets oppression must be transformed.

To present this radical demand for the objective transformation of reality, to combat subjectivist immobility which would divert the recognition of oppression into patient waiting for oppression to disappear by itself, is not to dismiss the role of subjectivity in the struggle to change structures. On the contrary, one cannot conceive of objectivity without subjectivity. Neither can exist without the other, nor can they be dichotomized. The separation of objectivity from subjectivity, the denial of the latter when analyzing reality or acting upon it, is objectivism. On the other hand, the denial of objectivity in analysis or action, resulting in a subjectivism which leads to solipsistic positions, denies action itself by denying objective reality. Neither objectivism nor subjectivism, nor yet psychologism is propounded here, but rather subjectivity and objectivity in constant dialectical relationship.

To deny the importance of subjectivity in the process of transforming the world and history is naïve and simplistic. It is to admit the impossible: a world without men. This objectivistic position is as ingenuous as that of subjectivism, which postulates men without a world. World and men do not exist apart from each other, they exist in constant interaction. Marx does not espouse such a dichotomy, nor does any other critical, realistic thinker. What Marx criticized and scientifically destroyed was not subjectivity, but subjectivism and psychologism. Just as objective social reality exists not by chance, but as the product of human action, so it is not transformed by chance. If men produce social reality (which in the "inversion of the praxis" turns back upon them and conditions them), then transforming that reality is an historical task, a task for men.

Reality which becomes oppressive results in the contradistinction of men as oppressors and oppressed. The latter, whose task it is to struggle for their liberation together with those who show true solidarity, must acquire a critical awareness of oppression through the praxis of this struggle. One of the gravest obstacles to the achievement of liberation is that oppressive reality absorbs those within it and thereby acts to submerge men's consciousness. Functionally, oppression is domesticating. To no longer be prey to its force, one must emerge from it and turn upon it. This can be done only by means of the praxis: reflection and action upon the world in order to transform it.

Making "real oppression more oppressive still by adding to it the realization of oppression" corresponds to the dialectical relation between the subjective and the objective. Only in this interdependence is an authentic praxis possible, without which it is impossible to resolve the oppressor-oppressed contradiction. To achieve this goal, the oppressed must confront reality critically, simultaneously objectifying and acting upon that reality. A mere perception of reality not followed by this critical intervention will not lead to a transformation of objective reality—precisely because it is not a true perception. This is the case of a purely subjectivist perception by someone who forsakes objective reality and creates a false substitute.

A different type of false perception occurs when a change in objective reality would threaten the individual or class interests of the perceiver. In the first instance, there is no critical intervention in reality because that reality is fictitious; there is none in the second instance because intervention would contradict the class interests of the perceiver. In the latter case the tendency of the perceiver is to behave "neurotically." The fact exists; but both the fact and what may result from it may be prejudicial to him. Thus it becomes necessary, not precisely to deny the fact, but to "see it differently." This rationalization as a defense mechanism coincides in the end with subjectivism. A fact which is not denied but whose truths are rationalized loses its objective base. It ceases to be concrete and becomes a myth created in defense of the class of the perceiver.

Herein lies one of the reasons for the prohibitions and the difficulties . . . designed to dissuade the people from critical intervention in reality. The oppressor knows full well that this intervention would not be to his interest. What *is* to his interest is for the people to continue in a state of submersion, impotent in the face of oppressive reality. . . . "To explain to the masses their own action" is to clarify and illuminate that action, both regarding its relationship of the objective facts by which it was prompted, and regarding its purposes. The more the people unveil this challenging reality which is to be the object of their transforming action, the more critically they enter that reality. In this way they are "consciously activating the subsequent development of their experiences." There would be no human action if there were no objective reality, no world to be the "not I" of man and to challenge him; just as there would be no human action if man were not a "project," if he were not able to transcend himself, to perceive his reality and understand it in order to transform it.

In dialectical thought, word and action are intimately interdependent. But action is human only when it is not merely an occupation but also a preoccupation, that is, when it is not dichotomized from reflection. Reflection, which is essential to action, is implicit in Lukács' requirement of "explaining to the masses their own action," just as it is implicit in the purpose he attributes to this explanation: that of "consciously activating the subsequent development of experience."

For us, however, the requirement is seen not in terms of explaining to, but rather dialoguing with the people about their actions. In any event, no reality transforms itself,[6] and the duty which Lukács ascribes to the revolutionary party of "explaining to the masses their own action" coincides with our affirmation of the need for the critical intervention of the people in reality through the praxis. The pedagogy of the oppressed, which is the pedagogy of men engaged in the fight for their own liberation, has its roots here. And those who recognize, or begin to recognize, themselves as oppressed must be among the developers of this pedagogy. No pedagogy which is truly liberating can remain distant from the oppressed by treating them as unfortunates and by presenting for their emulation models from among the oppressors. The oppressed must be their own example in the struggle for their redemption.

The pedagogy of the oppressed, animated by authentic, humanist (not humanitarian) generosity, presents itself as a pedagogy of man. Pedagogy which begins with the egoistic interests of the oppressors (an egoism cloaked in the false generosity of paternalism) and makes of the oppressed the objects of its humanitarianism, itself maintains and embodies oppression. It is an instrument of dehumanization. This is why, as we affirmed earlier, the pedagogy of the oppressed cannot be developed or practiced by the oppressors. It would be a contradiction in terms if the oppressors not only defended but actually implemented a liberating education. . . .

The pedagogy of the oppressed, as a humanist and libertarian pedagogy, has two distinct stages. In the first, the oppressed unveil the world of oppression and through the praxis commit themselves to its transformation. In the second stage, in which the reality of oppression has already been transformed, this pedagogy ceases to belong to the oppressed and becomes a pedagogy of all men in the process of permanent liberation. In both stages, it is always through action in depth that the culture of domination is culturally confronted.[7] In the first stage this confrontation occurs through the change in the way the oppressed perceive the world of oppression; in the second stage, through the expulsion of the myths created and developed in the old order, which like specters haunt the new structure emerging from the revolutionary transformation.

The pedagogy of the first stage must deal with the problem of the oppressed consciousness and the oppressor consciousness, the problem of men who oppress and men who suffer oppression. It must take into account their behavior, their view of the world, and their ethics. A particular problem is the duality of the oppressed: they are contradictory, divided beings, shaped by and existing in a concrete situation of oppression and violence.

Any situation in which "A" objectively exploits "B" or hinders his pursuit of self-affirmation as a responsible person is one of oppression. Such a situation in itself constitutes violence, even when sweetened by false generosity, because it interferes with man's ontological and historical vocation to be more fully human. With the establishment of a relationship of oppression, violence has *already* begun. Never in history has violence been initiated by the oppressed. How could they be the initiators, if they themselves are the result of violence? How could they be the sponsors of something whose objective inauguration called forth their existence as oppressed? There would be no oppressed had there been no prior situation of violence to establish their subjugation.

Violence is initiated by those who oppress, who exploit, who fail to recognize others as persons—not by those who are oppressed, exploited, and unrecognized. It is not the unloved who initiate disaffection, but those who cannot love because they love only themselves. It is not the helpless, subject to terror, who initiate terror, but the violent, who with their power create the concrete situation which begets the "rejects of life." It is not the tyrannized who initiate despotism, but the tyrants. It is not the despised who initiate hatred, but those who despise. It is not those whose humanity is denied them who negate man, but those who denied that humanity (thus negating their own as well). Force is used not by those who have become weak under the preponderance of the strong, but by the strong who have emasculated them.

For the oppressors, however, it is always the oppressed (whom they obviously never call "the oppressed" but—depending on whether they are fellow countrymen or not—"those people" or "the blind and envious masses" or "savages" or "natives" or "subversives") who are disaffected, who are "violent," "barbaric," "wicked," or "ferocious" when they react to the violence of the oppressors.

Yet it is—paradoxical though it may seem—precisely in the response of the oppressed to the violence of their oppressors that a gesture of love may be found. Consciously or unconsciously, the act of rebellion by the oppressed (an act which is always, or nearly always, as violent as the initial violence of the oppressors) can initiate love. Whereas the violence of the oppressors prevents the oppressed from being fully human, the response of the latter to this violence is grounded in the desire to pursue the right to be human. As the oppressors dehumanize others and violate their rights, they themselves also become dehumanized. As the oppressed, fighting to be human, take away the oppressors' power to dominate and suppress, they restore to the oppressors the humanity they had lost in the exercise of oppression.

It is only the oppressed who, by freeing themselves, can free their oppressors. The latter, as an oppressive class, can free neither others nor themselves. It is therefore essential that the oppressed wage the struggle to resolve the contradiction in which they are caught; and the contradiction will be resolved by the appearance of the new man: neither oppressor nor oppressed, but man in the process of liberation. If the goal of the oppressed is to become fully human, they will not achieve their goal by merely reversing the terms of the contradiction, by simply changing poles.

This may seem simplistic; it is not. Resolution of the oppressor-oppressed contradiction indeed implies the disappearance of the oppressors as a dominant class. However, the restraints imposed by the former oppressed on their oppressors, so that the latter cannot reassume their former position, do not constitute *oppression.* An act is oppressive only when it prevents men from being more fully human. Accordingly, these necessary restraints do not *in themselves* signify that yesterday's oppressed have become today's oppressors. Acts which prevent the restoration of the oppressive regime cannot be compared with those which create and maintain it, cannot be compared with those by which a few men deny the majority their right to be human.

However, the moment the new regime hardens into a dominating "bureaucracy"[8] the humanist dimension of the struggle is lost and it is no longer possible to speak of liberation. Hence our insistence that the authentic solution of the oppressor-oppressed contradiction does not lie in a mere reversal of position, in moving from one pole to the other. Nor does it lie in the replacement of the former oppressors with new ones who continue to subjugate the oppressed—all in the name of their liberation.

But even when the contradiction is resolved authentically by a new situation established by the liberated laborers, the former oppressors do not feel liberated. On the contrary, they genuinely consider themselves to be oppressed. Conditioned by the experience of oppressing others, any situation other than their former seems to them like oppression. Formerly, they could eat, dress, wear shoes, be educated, travel, and hear Beethoven; while millions did not eat, had no clothes or shoes, neither studied nor traveled, much less listened to Beethoven. Any restriction on this way of life, in the name of the rights of the community, appears to the former oppressors as a profound violation of their individual rights—although they had no respect for the millions who suffered and died of hunger, pain, sorrow, and despair. For the oppressors, "human beings" refer only to themselves; other people are "things." For the oppressors, there exists only one right: their right to live in peace, over against the right, not always even recognized, but simply conceded, of the oppressed to survival. And they make this concession only because the existence of the oppressed is necessary to their own existence.

This behavior, this way of understanding the world and men (which necessarily makes the oppressors resist the installation of a new regime) is explained by their experience as a dominant class. Once a situation of violence and oppression has been established, it engenders an entire way of life and behavior for those caught up in it—oppressors and oppressed alike. Both are submerged in this situation, and both bear the marks of oppression. Analysis of existential situations of oppression reveals that their inception lay in an act of violence—initiated by those with power. This violence, as a process, is perpetuated from generation to generation of oppressors, who become its heirs and are shaped in its climate. This climate creates in the oppressor a strongly possessive consciousness—possessive of the world and of men. Apart from direct, concrete, material possession of the world and of men, the oppressor consciousness could not understand itself—could not even exist. Fromm said of this consciousness that, without such possession, "it would lose contact with the world." The oppressor consciousness tends to transform everything surrounding it into an object of its domination. The earth, property, production, the creations of men, men themselves, time—everything is reduced to the status of objects at its disposal.

In their unrestrained eagerness to possess, the oppressors develop the conviction that it is possible for them to transform everything into objects of their purchasing power; hence their strictly materialistic concept of existence. Money is the measure of all things, and profit the primary goal. For the oppressors, what is worthwhile is to have more—always more—even at the cost of the oppressed having less or having nothing. For them, *to be* is *to have* and to be the class of the "haves."

As beneficiaries of a situation of oppression, the oppressors cannot perceive that if *having* is a condition of *being,* it is a necessary condition for all men. This is why their generosity is false. Humanity is a "thing," and they possess it as an exclusive right, as inherited property. To the oppressor consciousness, the humanization of the "others," of the people, appears not as the pursuit of full humanity, but as subversion.

The oppressors do not perceive their monopoly on *having more* as a privilege which dehumanizes others and themselves. They cannot see that, in the egoistic pursuit of *having* as a possessing class, they suffocate in their own possessions and no longer *are;* they merely *have.* For them, *having more* is an inalienable right, a right they acquired through their own "effort," with their "courage to take risks." If others do not have more, it is because they are incompetent and lazy, and worst of all is their unjustifiable ingratitude towards the "generous gestures" of the dominant class. Precisely because they are "ungrateful" and "envious," the oppressed are regarded as potential enemies who must be watched.

It could not be otherwise. If the humanization of the oppressed signifies subversion, so also does their freedom; hence the necessity for constant control. And the more the oppressors control the oppressed, the more they change them into apparently inanimate "things." This tendency of the oppressor consciousness to "in-animate" everything and everyone it encounters, in its eagerness to possess, unquestionably corresponds with a tendency to sadism.

> The pleasure in complete domination over another person (or other animate creature) is the very essence of the sadistic drive. Another way of formulating the same thought is to say that the aim of sadism is to transform a man into a thing, something animate into something inanimate, since by complete and absolute control the living loses one essential quality of life—freedom.[9]

Sadistic love is a perverted love—a love of death, not of life. One of the characteristics of the oppressor consciousness and its necrophilic view of the world is thus sadism. As the oppressor consciousness, in order to dominate, tries to deter the drive to search, the restlessness, and the creative power which characterize life, it kills life. More and more, the oppressors are using science and technology as unquestionably powerful instruments for their purpose: the maintenance of the oppressive order through manipulation and repression.[10] The oppressed, as objects, as "things," have no purposes except those their oppressors prescribe for them.

Given the preceding context, another issue of indubitable importance arises: the fact that certain members of the oppressor class join the oppressed in their struggle for liberation, thus moving from one pole of the contradiction to the other. Theirs is a fundamental role, and has been so throughout the history of this struggle. It happens, however, that as they cease to be exploiters or indifferent spectators or simply the heirs of exploitation and move to the side of the exploited, they almost always bring with them the marks of their origin: their prejudices and their deformations, which include a lack of confidence in the people's ability to think, to want, and to know. Accordingly, these adherents to the people's cause constantly run the risk of falling into a type of generosity as malefic as that of the oppressors. The generosity of the oppressors is nourished by an unjust order, which must be maintained in order to justify that generosity. Our converts, on the other hand, truly desire to transform the unjust order; but because of their background they believe that they must be the executors of the transformation. They talk about the people, but they do not trust them; and trusting the people is the indispensable precondition for revolutionary change. A real humanist can be identified more by his trust in the people, which engages him in their struggle, than by a thousand actions in their favor without that trust.

Those who authentically commit themselves to the people must reexamine themselves constantly. This conversion is so radical as not to allow of ambiguous behavior. To affirm this commitment but to consider oneself the proprietor of revolutionary wisdom—which must then be given to (or imposed on) the people—is to retain the old ways. The man who proclaims devotion to the cause of liberation yet is unable to enter into *communion* with the people, whom he continues to regard as totally ignorant, is grievously self-deceived. The convert who approaches the people but feels alarm at each step they take, each doubt they express, and each suggestion they offer, and attempts to impose his "status," remains nostalgic toward his origins.

Conversion to the people requires a profound rebirth. Those who undergo it must take on a new form of existence; they can no longer remain as they were. Only through comradeship with the oppressed can the converts understand their characteristic ways of living and behaving, which in diverse moments reflect the structure of domination. One of these characteristics is the previously mentioned existential duality of the oppressed, who are at the same time themselves and the oppressor whose image they have internalized. Accordingly, until they concretely "discover" their oppressor and in turn their own consciousness, they nearly always express fatalistic attitudes toward their situation.

> The peasant begins to get courage to overcome his dependence when he realizes that he is dependent. Until then, he goes along with the boss and says "What can I do? I'm only a peasant."[11]

When superficially analyzed, this fatalism is sometimes interpreted as a docility that is a trait of national character. Fatalism in the guise of docility is the fruit of an historical and sociological situation, not an essential characteristic of a people's behavior. It almost always is related to the power of destiny or fate or fortune—inevitable forces—or to a distorted view of God. Under the sway of magic and myth, the oppressed (especially the peasants, who are almost submerged in nature)[12] see their suffering, the fruit of exploitation, as the will of God—as if God were the creator of this "organized disorder."

Submerged in reality, the oppressed cannot perceive clearly the "order" which serves the interests of the oppressors whose image they have internalized. Chafing under the restrictions of this order, they often manifest a type of horizontal violence, striking out at their own comrades for the pettiest reasons.

> The colonized man will first manifest this aggressiveness which has been deposited in his bones against his own people. This is the period when the niggers beat each other up, and the police and magistrates do not know which way to turn when faced with the astonishing waves of crime in North Africa. . . . While the settler or the policeman has the right the livelong day to strike the native, to insult him and to make him crawl to them, you will see the native reaching for his knife at the slightest hostile or aggressive glance cast on him by another native; for the last resort of the native is to defend his personality vis-à-vis his brother.[13]

It is possible that in this behavior they are once more manifesting their duality. Because the oppressor exists within their oppressed comrades, when they attack those comrades they are indirectly attacking the oppressor as well.

On the other hand, at a certain point in their existential experience the oppressed feel an irresistible attraction toward the oppressor and his way of life. Sharing this way of life becomes an overpowering aspiration. In their alienation, the oppressed want at any cost to resemble the oppressor, to imitate him, to follow him. This phenomenon is especially prevalent in the middle-class oppressed, who yearn to be equal to the "eminent" men of the upper class. Albert Memmi, in an exceptional analysis of the "colonized mentality," refers to the contempt he felt toward the colonizer, mixed with "passionate" attraction toward him.

> How could the colonizer look after his workers while periodically gunning down a crowd of colonized? How could the colonized deny himself so cruelly yet make such excessive demands? How could he hate the colonizers and yet admire them so passionately? (I too felt this admiration in spite of myself.)[14]

Self-depreciation is another characteristic of the oppressed, which derives from their internalization of the opinion the oppressors hold of them. So often do they hear that they are good for nothing, know nothing, and are incapable of learning anything—that they are sick, lazy, and unproductive—that in the end they become convinced of their own unfitness.

> The peasant feels inferior to the boss because the boss seems to be the only one who knows things and is able to run things.[15]

They call themselves ignorant and say the "professor" is the one who has knowledge and to whom they should listen. The criteria of knowledge imposed upon them are the conventional ones. "Why don't you," said a peasant participating in a culture circle, "explain the pictures first? That way it'll take less time and won't give us a headache."

Almost never do they realize that they, too, "know things" they have learned in their relations with the world and with other men. Given the circumstances which have produced their duality, it is only natural that they distrust themselves.

Not infrequently, peasants in educational projects begin to discuss a generative theme in a lively manner, then stop suddenly and say to the educator: "Excuse us, we ought to keep quiet and let you talk. You are the one who knows, we don't know anything." They often insist that there is no difference between them and the animals; when they do admit a difference, it favors the animals. "They are freer than we are."

It is striking, however, to observe how this self-depreciation changes with the first changes in the situation of oppression. I heard a peasant leader say in an *asentamiento*[16] meeting, "They used to say we were unproductive because we were lazy and drunkards. All lies. Now that we are respected as men, we're going to show everyone that we were never drunkards or lazy. We were exploited!"

As long as their ambiguity persists, the oppressed are reluctant to resist, and totally lack confidence in themselves. They have a diffuse, magical belief in the invulnerability and power of the oppressor.[17] The magical force of the landowner's power holds particular sway in the rural areas. A sociologist friend of mine tells of a group of armed peasants in a Latin American country who recently took over a latifundium. For tactical reasons, they planned to hold the landowner as a hostage. But not one peasant had the courage to guard him; his very presence was terrifying. It is also possible that the act of opposing the boss provoked guilt feelings. In truth, the boss was "inside" them.

The oppressed must see examples of the vulnerability of the oppressor so that a contrary conviction can begin to grow within them. Until this occurs, they will continue disheartened, fearful, and beaten.[18] As long as the oppressed remain unaware of the causes of their condition, they fatalistically "accept" their exploitation. Further, they are apt to react in a passive and alienated manner when confronted with the necessity to struggle for their freedom and self-affirmation. Little by little, however, they tend to try out forms of rebellious action. In working toward liberation, one must neither lose sight of this passivity nor overlook the moment of awakening.

Within their unauthentic view of the world and of themselves, the oppressed feel like "things" owned by the oppressor. For the latter, *to be* is *to have*, almost always at the expense of those who have nothing. For the oppressed, at a certain point in their existential experience, *to be* is not to resemble the oppressor, but *to be under* him, to depend on him. Accordingly, the oppressed are emotionally dependent.

> The peasant is a dependent. He can't say what he wants. Before he discovers his dependence, he suffers. He lets off steam at home, where he shouts at his children, beats them, and despairs. He complains about his wife and thinks everything is dreadful. He doesn't let off steam with the boss because he thinks the boss is a superior being. Lots of times, the peasant gives vent to his sorrows by drinking.[19]

This total emotional dependence can lead the oppressed to what Fromm calls necrophilic behavior: the destruction of life—their own or that of their oppressed fellows.

It is only when the oppressed find the oppressor out and become involved in the organized struggle for their liberation that they begin to believe in themselves. This discovery cannot be purely intellectual but must involve action; nor can it be limited to mere activism, but must include serious reflection: only then will it be a praxis.

Critical and liberating dialogue, which presupposes action, must be carried on with the oppressed at whatever the stage of their struggle for liberation.[20] The content of that dialogue can and should vary in accordance with historical conditions and the level at which the oppressed perceive reality. But to substitute monologue, slogans, and communiqués for dialogue is to attempt to liberate the oppressed with the instruments of domestication. Attempting to liberate the oppressed without their reflective participation in the act of liberation is to treat them as objects which must be saved from a burning building; it is to lead them into the populist pitfall and transform them into masses which can be manipulated.

At all stages of their liberation, the oppressed must see themselves as men engaged in the ontological and historical vocation of becoming more fully human. Reflection and action become imperative when one does not erroneously attempt to dichotomize the content of humanity from its historical forms.

The insistence that the oppressed engage in reflection on their concrete situation is not a call to armchair revolution. On the contrary, reflection—true reflection—leads to action. On the other hand, when the situation calls for action, that action will constitute an authentic praxis only if its consequences become the object of critical reflection. In this sense, the praxis is the new *raison d'être* of the oppressed; and the revolution, which inaugurates the historical moment of this *raison d'être,* is not viable apart from their concomitant conscious involvement. Otherwise, action is pure activism.

To achieve this praxis, however, it is necessary to trust in the oppressed and in their ability to reason. Whoever lacks this trust will fail to initiate (or will abandon) dialogue, reflection, and communication, and will fall into using slogans, communiqués, monologues, and instructions. Superficial conversions to the cause of liberation carry this danger.

Political action on the side of the oppressed must be pedagogical action in the authentic sense of the word, and, therefore, action *with* the oppressed. Those who work for liberation must not take advantage of the emotional dependence of the oppressed—dependence that is the fruit of the concrete situation of domination which surrounds them and which engendered their unauthentic view of the world. Using their dependence to create still greater dependence is an oppressor tactic.

Libertarian action must recognize this dependence as a weak point and must attempt through reflection and action to transform it into independence. However, not even the best-intentioned leadership can bestow independence as a gift. The liberation of the oppressed is a liberation of men, not things. Accordingly, while no one liberates himself by his own efforts alone, neither is he liberated by others. Liberation, a human phenomenon, cannot be achieved by semihumans. Any attempt to treat men as semihumans only dehumanizes them. When men are already dehumanized, due to the oppression they suffer, the process of their liberation must not employ the methods of dehumanization.

The correct method for a revolutionary leadership to employ in the task of liberation is, therefore, *not* "libertarian propaganda." Nor can the leadership merely "implant" in the oppressed a belief in freedom, thus thinking to win their trust. The correct method lies in dialogue. The conviction of the oppressed that they must fight for their liberation is not a gift bestowed by the revolutionary leadership, but the result of their own *conscientização*.*

The revolutionary leaders must realize that their own conviction of the necessity for struggle (an indispensable dimension of revolutionary wisdom) was not given to them by anyone else—if it is authentic. This conviction cannot be packaged and sold; it is reached, rather, by means of a totality of reflection and action. Only the leaders' own involvement in reality, within an historical situation, led them to criticize this situation and to wish to change it.

Likewise, the oppressed (who do not commit themselves to the struggle unless they are convinced, and who, if they do not make such a commitment, withhold the indispensable conditions for this struggle) must reach this conviction as Subjects, not as Objects. They also must intervene critically in the situation which surrounds them and whose mark they bear; propaganda cannot achieve this. While the conviction of the necessity for struggle (without which the struggle is unfeasible) is indispensable to the revolutionary leadership (indeed, it was this conviction which constituted that leadership), it is also necessary for the oppressed. It is necessary, that is, unless one intends to carry out the transformation *for* the oppressed rather than *with* them. It is my belief that only the latter form of transformation is valid.

The object in presenting these considerations is to defend the eminently pedagogical character of the revolution. The revolutionary leaders of every epoch who have affirmed that the oppressed must accept the struggle for their liberation—an obvious point—have also thereby implicitly recognized the pedagogical aspect of this struggle. Many of these leaders, however (perhaps due to natural and understandable biases against pedagogy), have ended up using the "educational" methods employed by the oppressor. They deny pedagogical action in the liberation process, but they use propaganda to convince.

It is essential for the oppressed to realize that when they accept the struggle for humanization they also accept, from that moment, their total responsibility for the struggle. They must realize that they are fighting not merely for freedom from hunger, but for

---

*The term *conscientização* refers to learning to perceive social, political, and economic contradictions, and to take action against the oppressive elements of reality.—Ed.

> . . . freedom to create and to construct, to wonder and to venture. Such freedom requires that the individual be active and responsible, not a slave or a well-fed cog in the machine. . . . It is not enough that men are not slaves; if social conditions further the existence of automatons, the result will not be love of life, but love of death.[21]

The oppressed, who have been shaped by the death-affirming climate of oppression, must find through their struggle the way to life-affirming humanization, which does not lie *simply* in having more to eat (although it does involve having more to eat and cannot fail to include this aspect). The oppressed have been destroyed precisely because their situation has reduced them to things. In order to regain their humanity they must cease to be things and fight as men. This is a radical requirement. They cannot enter the struggle as objects in order *later* to become men.

The struggle begins with men's recognition that they have been destroyed. Propaganda, management, manipulation—all arms of domination—cannot be the instruments of their rehumanization. The only effective instrument is a humanizing pedagogy in which the revolutionary leadership establishes a permanent relationship of dialogue with the oppressed. In a humanizing pedagogy the method ceases to be an instrument by which the teachers (in this instance, the revolutionary leadership) can manipulate the students (in this instance, the oppressed), because it expresses the consciousness of the students themselves.

> The method is, in fact, the external form of consciousness manifest in acts, which takes on the fundamental property of consciousness—its intentionality. The essence of consciousness is being with the world, and this behavior is permanent and unavoidable. Accordingly, consciousness is in essence a "way towards" something apart from itself, outside itself, which surrounds it and which it apprehends by means of its ideational capacity. Consciousness is thus by definition a method, in the most general sense of the word.[22]

A revolutionary leadership must accordingly practice *cointentional* education. Teachers and students (leadership and people), cointent on reality, are both Subjects, not only in the task of unveiling that reality, and thereby coming to know it critically, but in the task of re-creating that knowledge. As they attain this knowledge of reality through common reflection and action, they discover themselves as its permanent re-creators. In this way, the presence of the oppressed in the struggle for their liberation will be what it should be: not pseudoparticipation, but committed involvement.

NOTES

1. The current movements of rebellion, especially those of youth, while they necessarily reflect the peculiarities of their respective settings, manifest in their essence this preoccupation with man and men as beings in the world and with the world—preoccupation with *what* and *how* they are "being." As they place consumer civilization in judgment, denounce bureaucracies of all types, demand the transformation of the universities (changing the rigid nature of the teacher-student relationship and placing that relationship within the context of reality), propose the transformation of reality itself so that universities can be renewed, attack old orders and established institutions in the attempt to affirm men as the Subjects of decision, all these movements reflect the style of our age, which is more anthropological than anthropocentric.

2. As used throughout this paper, the term "contradiction" denotes the dialectical conflict between opposing social forces.—Translator's note.

3. This fear of freedom is also to be found in the oppressors, though, obviously, in a different form. The oppressed are afraid to embrace freedom; the oppressors are afraid of losing the "freedom" to oppress.

4. See Georg Hegel, *The Phenomenology of Mind* (New York, 1967), pp. 236–37.

5. Analyzing the dialectical relationship between the consciousness of the master and the consciousness of the oppressed, Hegel states: "The one is independent, and its essential nature is to be for itself; the other is dependent, and its essence is life or existence for another. The former is the Master, or Lord, the latter the Bondsman." Ibid., p. 234.

6. "The materialist doctrine that men are products of circumstances and upbringing, and that, therefore, changed men are products of other circumstances and changed upbringing, forgets that it is men that change circumstances and that the educator himself needs educating." Karl Marx and Friedrich Engels, *Selected Works* (New York, 1968), p. 28.

7. This appears to be the fundamental aspect of Mao's Cultural Revolution.

8. This rigidity should not be identified with restraints that must be imposed on the former oppressors so they cannot restore the oppressive order. Rather, it refers to the revolution which becomes stagnant and turns against the people, using the old repressive, bureaucratic State apparatus (which should have been drastically suppressed, as Marx so often emphasized).

9. Eric Fromm, *The Heart of Man* (New York, 1966), p. 32.

10. Regarding the "dominant forms of social control," see Herbert Marcuse, *One-Dimensional Man* (Boston, 1964) and *Eros and Civilization* (Boston, 1955).

11. Words of a peasant during an interview with the author.

12. See Candido Mendes, *Memento dos vivos—A Esquerda católica no Brasil* (Rio, 1966).

13. Frantz Fanon, *The Wretched of the Earth* (New York, 1968), p. 52.

14. *The Colonizer and the Colonized* (Boston, 1967), p. x.

15. Words of a peasant during an interview with the author.

16. *Asentamiento* refers to a production unit of the Chilean agrarian reform experiment.—Translator's note.

17. "The peasant has an almost instinctive fear of the boss." Interview with a peasant.

18. See Regis Debray, *Revolution in the Revolution?* (New York, 1967).
19. Interview with a peasant.
20. Not in the open, of course; that would only provoke the fury of the oppressor and lead to still greater repression.
21. Fromm, op. cit., pp. 52–53.
22. Alvaro Vieira Pinto, from a work in preparation on the philosophy of science. I consider the quoted portion of great importance for the understanding of a problem-posing pedagogy and wish to thank Professor Vieira Pinto for permission to cite his work prior to publication.

30

Human Development: The Case for Renewed Emphasis

Keith Griffin
University of California at Riverside
and
John Knight
Oxford University Institute of Economics and Statistics

The process of economic development can be seen as a process of expanding the capabilities of people.[1] The ultimate focus of economic development is human development. That is, we are ultimately concerned with what people are capable of doing or being. Can they live long? Can they be well nourished? Can they escape avoidable illness? Can they obtain dignity and self-respect? Are they able to read and write and communicate and develop their minds?

According to this view, development is concerned with much more than expanding the supplies of commodities.[2] The enhancement of capabilities often requires changing technologies, institutions, and social values so that the creativity within human beings can be unblocked. This, in turn, results in economic growth, but growth of gross domestic product (GDP) is not the same thing as an expansion of capabilities. The two are, of course, linked but they are not identical.

Economic growth can be seen as a means to the end of enhancing people's capabilities. Yet, economists traditionally have concentrated on the production of goods and services and on its rate of growth. Increased physical output, in turn, has been assumed to give rise to greater economic welfare.

More recently, it is true, greater emphasis has been placed on the distribution of goods among people and on considerations of need and equity. The philosopher John Rawls defined deprivation in terms of the availability

From *Journal of Development Planning*, 19 (1989), pp. 9–40.

of "primary goods" or "things it is supposed a rational man wants whatever else he wants,"[3] and the International Labour Organisation attempted to translate the concept into operational terms with its advocacy of "basic needs."[4] Basic needs, however, remains a goods-oriented view of development, whereas what is wanted is a view that puts people first.

This is the great merit of the human capabilities approach, pioneered by Amartya Sen.[5] The connection between goods and capabilities can readily be illustrated. A bicycle, for instance, is a good; by providing transport, it gives a person the capability of moving from one place to another. It is the concept of capabilities that comes closest to our notion of the standard of living and, more generally, to our notion of development. Goods may provide the basis for a high standard of living, but they are not in themselves constituents of it. A person's standard of living has some components that his money cannot buy. An illiterate person in poor health would not enjoy the same capabilities, and thus the same standard of living, as an otherwise identical person, not only because he would be likely to have a lower income but also because literacy and health directly affect capabilities.

Although there is some relationship between income per capita and human well-being, as the term is commonly understood, the statistical association is not close and divergences from the general tendency are at least as striking as the general tendency itself.[6] Human fulfilment is about whether people live or die, whether people eat well, are malnourished or starve, whether women lead healthy and tolerable lives or are burdened with annual childbearing, a high risk of maternal mortality, the certainty of lifelong drudgery, whether people can control their lives at work, whether their conditions of work are tough and unpleasant, whether people have access to work at all, whether people control their political lives, whether they have the education to be full members of society with some control over their destiny. These are all aspects of the standard of living—but only loosely included or not included at all in the measure of GNP per capita.

Any approach that puts people first must come to terms with the fact that in the Third World the average age of the population is low, although it is tending to rise slowly. In 1980 in the developing countries as a whole, 39.1 percent of the population were less than 15 years of age as compared to 23.1 percent in the developed countries. Conversely, only 4.0 percent of the population of the Third World is over 65 years, whereas in the developed countries 11.3 percent of the population is older than 65.[7] Thus, human development in the Third World is necessarily concerned in large part with enhancing the capabilities of the young.

It is natural to inquire whether economic growth during the past two decades has been accompanied by increased human capabilities. Certainly there has been growth: in no group of countries did per capita income fail to rise during the period 1965–1985 (see Table 1). Some groups of countries did much better than others, however. The developing countries as a whole

TABLE 1   **Growth of GNP per Capita, 1965–1985**
(Annual Percentage)

Low-income economies	2.9
China	4.8
India	1.7
Other low-income	0.4
Middle-income economies	3.0
Lower middle-income	2.6
Upper middle-income	3.3
High-income oil exporters	2.7
Industrial market economies	2.4

SOURCE: World Bank, *World Development Report 1987* (Oxford, Oxford University Press, 1987).

grew faster than the industrial market economies (3.0 percent a year compared to 2.4 percent a year). But within the Third World there was a tendency for the poorest countries to fall relatively further behind the less poor. Thus, GNP per capita in the middle-income economies increased 3.0 percent a year, whereas in India the rate of growth of income per capita was 1.7 percent and in the "other low-income countries" only 0.4 percent. China, where GNP per capita increased 4.8 percent a year, was the great exception. Among the middle-income countries, East Asia did much better than Latin America. As shown below, human capabilities increased relatively most rapidly in both China and East Asia.

The general rise in average incomes could be a misleading guide to the income gains of the poor. In some countries, including large ones, the incidence of poverty remains high. This often is due in part to a high and even rising degree of inequality in the distribution of income. A large number of cross-sectional studies of countries have been undertaken and these have been used to provide support for the hypothesis of growing inequality.[8] Moreover, a number of studies of individual countries, based on time-series data, have shown that inequality was increased along with a rise in average incomes. Indeed, some authors have attempted to show that not only has inequality increased but that in some countries for quite long periods the absolute standard of living of some sections of the poor has declined.[9] It cannot be assumed, therefore, that the basic human capabilities have risen to the same extent as average incomes.

The debate today is not over whether inequality within countries has increased but whether increased inequality is inevitable. The balance of recent evidence suggests that the degree of inequality is not closely related to the level of income per capita, as was once thought, but to factors dependent upon the strategy of development that is followed. These factors include the distribution of productive assets (particularly land), the distribution of educational opportunities, the employment intensity of the development path, and the general policy stance of government. It is possible, therefore, for governments successfully to pursue distributive equity objectives as well as growth objectives. Similarly, governments have it within their power to promote the enhancement of human capabilities by means of their education, health, nutrition, participation, and other policies. Moreover, the twin objectives of distributive equity and human development will often involve the same policies.

Taking a long view, there is no doubt that the basic human capabilities have indeed increased in the third world. Perhaps the best indicator of this is the increase in life expectancy at birth since around 1950. In the poorest countries, life expectancy at midcentury was between 30 and 40 years; today it is at least 50 years in most countries and rises to 70 or more for females in such countries as China, Malaysia, Sri Lanka, Chile, and Argentina.

The data on infant mortality tell a similar story to that of life expectancy. There has been a long-run decline everywhere and in some countries the decline has been dramatic, with the rate falling by 50 percent or more. This is true in Latin America for Argentina, Chile, and Colombia and in Asia for China, Malaysia, the Philippines, and Sri Lanka. However, infant mortality rates remain very high, that is, above 100 per 1,000 infants less than one year old, in Bangladesh, Pakistan, the United Republic of Tanzania, and Côte d'Ivoire. As with life expectancy, there is only a weak correspondence between infant mortality rates and per capita incomes.

Data on life expectancy and infant mortality for the period 1965 to 1985 are included in Table 2. Figures 1 and 2 show similar movements since 1955, but by region, in life expectancy, and infant mortality, respectively. The long-run improvements in both indexes are apparent for all regions. However, as with income, averages may overstate somewhat the gains to the poor whose access to health services is marginal in many countries. There is considerable evidence that health delivery systems (oriented toward hospital-based, high-technology, specialized services) provide limited population coverage and contribute to an unequal distribution of health services.

Turning now to primary education, it is evident that this is one of the great success stories of the Third World, at least in quantitative terms (see Table 3). It is less certain that there have been improvements in the quality of education. School enrolments have expanded rapidly in the past 20 years and in most countries primary education for boys is universal or nearly so. The position of girls is less good, but even so, in over half the countries more than 90 percent of girls attend primary school, although they are less likely than boys to complete their primary education. Less favourable treatment in educating young girls continues to be a problem, especially in

TABLE 2 Life Expectancy, Infant Mortality, and GNP per Capita

| | LIFE EXPECTANCY AT BIRTH (YEARS) | | | | INFANT MORTALITY (DEATHS PER 1,000 AGED UNDER ONE YEAR) | | GNP per Capita (US Dollars) |
| | MALE | | FEMALE | | | | |
	1965	1985	1965	1985	1965	1985	1985
Low-income countries	47	60	50	61	127	72	270
India	46	57	44	56	151	89	270
China	54	68	55	70	90	35	310
Other low-income	44	51	45	53	150	112	200
Middle-income countries	53	60	56	64	104	68	1 290
Lower middle-income	47	56	50	60	132	82	820
Upper middle-income	58	64	62	69	84	52	1 850
High-income oil exporters	48	61	51	65	115	61	9 800
Industrial market economies	68	73	74	79	23	9	11 810

SOURCE: World Bank, *World Development Report 1987* (Oxford, Oxford University Press, 1987).

FIGURE 1   **Life expectancy.**

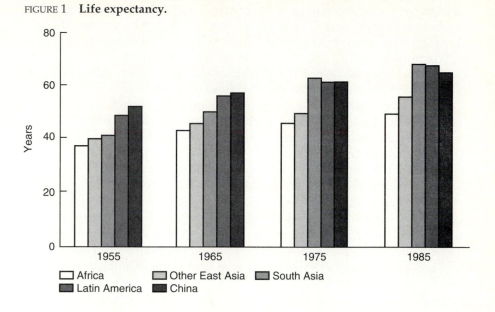

FIGURE 2   **Infant mortality (deaths per 1,000 live births).**

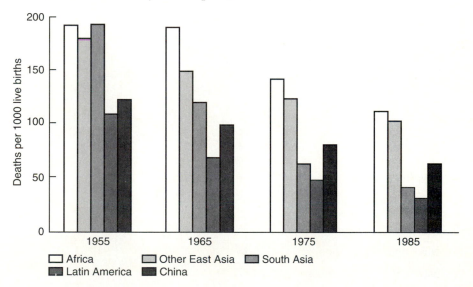

SOURCE: United Nations Secretariat.

Pakistan (where twice as many boys as girls attend school) but also in India, Bangladesh, Egypt, and Côte d'Ivoire. Although illiteracy rates still are more than 52 percent in Africa and South Asia, one can anticipate that they will continue to fall as the proportion of the population with a primary school education rises. None the less, the absolute number of illiterate persons will probably increase for years to come.

Secondary education has also grown rapidly, although often from a small base (see Table 3). Still, between one-third and two-thirds of the relevant age group attends a secondary school in most Third World countries, including the two largest, India and China. The third largest—Indonesia—has expanded its secondary school system rapidly and has overtaken the two Asian giants. Serious shortcomings remain in Pakistan and Bangladesh (where expansion of the system has been slow) and in sub-Saharan Africa (where, apart from the United Republic of Tanzania, expansion has been fast). Given the difficulties encountered in Asia and Africa at the time of independence, progress in secondary education has been remarkable.

Thus, the indicators suggest that there has been a long-term increase in human capabilities in the Third World. The growth not only in output but also in capabilities reflects the application by society of cumulative collective knowledge. Never before has the stock of knowledge in the world increased so rapidly or been so widely disseminated as it has in the past 40 or 50 years. Nonetheless, world-wide access to science and technology is unequal. The diversity of the world's languages is a source of enrichment and cultural plurality and within many countries language is a unifying force. But within some countries linguistic heterogeneity is a source of disunity and conflict and between countries language can act as a barrier

TABLE 3   **Primary and Secondary School Enrollment Ratios**
(Percentage of Age Group)

	PRIMARY		SECONDARY	
	1965	1984	1965	1984
Low-income countries	74	97	21	32
India	74	90	27	34
China	89	118	24	37
Other low-income	44	70	9	23
Middle-income countries	85	104	22	47
Lower middle-income	75	103	16	40
Upper middle-income	96	105	29	56
High-income oil exporters	43	75	10	45
Industrial market economies	107	102	63	90

SOURCE: World Bank, *World Development Report 1987* (Oxford, Oxford University Press, 1987).

restricting access of hundreds of millions of people to world knowledge. Yet, the barriers are slowly being overcome, not least because language teaching has greatly increased the number of people who can speak more than one language.

Nationally and internationally there have been dramatic changes in the ways information and culture are transmitted. There was a time in human history when most education occurred within the family. Gradually, however, the transmission of knowledge became institutionalized, first within the church and other religious organizations and later within state schools and, to a lesser extent, private schools. More recently, superimposed on these inherited means of spreading knowledge, information, and cultural values, the mass media have become increasingly prominent. Both deliberately and unintentionally, in both formal and informal ways, the mass media now exercise an enormous influence over what people know, how people interpret and understand the world, and what values people adopt and act upon.

HUMAN DEVELOPMENT IN THE CURRENT ECONOMIC CONTEXT

We have seen that, viewed in long-term perspective, there has been remarkable progress in human development in the Third World. Recent short-term developments, however, have been unfavourable and in some countries a full-scale crisis has emerged. The most obvious sign of crisis is the dramatic slowing down in the rate of growth of per capita GDP between the last half of the 1970s and the present. The deceleration of growth occurred in all regions of the Third World (excluding China), and in every region, except South Asia and East Asia, average incomes fell markedly (see Table 4).

Parallel to the decline in growth rates has been a fall in the rate of growth of the productivity of labour. The phenomenon is widespread throughout Asia, Africa, and Latin America and, indeed, in Africa and Latin America, the average level of productivity declined, not just the rate of growth of productivity. During the period 1980–1985, the average productivity of labour declined 1.5 percent a year in Africa and 2.7 percent a

TABLE 4   **Rate of Growth of GDP per Capita, 1976–1987**
(Annual Percentage)

	1976–1980	1981–1985	1986	1987
Africa	1.9	−3.5	−4.9	−2.6
Latin America	2.8	−1.8	1.6	0.4
Western Asia	0.8	−3.9	−0.3	−3.9
South Asia and East Asia	4.1	2.9	3.2	2.7

SOURCE: Department of International Economic and Social Affairs, United Nations Secretariat.

year in Latin America.[10] This reflects the fact that in Africa and Latin America total output increased less rapidly than the size of the labour force, and in Latin America total output actually declined. A reduction in value added per employed worker is, of course, desirable in a period of recession in so far as it allows large numbers of people to continue to secure a livelihood rather than become openly unemployed. On the other hand, a fall in output per person-year inevitably puts downward pressure on the real wages and incomes of those who remain in employment and on the level of profits (and hence on investment and long-term growth of output and employment).

In practice, rates of urban unemployment in the major cities of Latin America tended to rise (see Table 5) and nonagricultural real wages in Africa and parts of Latin America tended to fall (see Table 6). In Latin America and the Caribbean the rate of open urban unemployment rose from 6.8 percent in 1970, to 7.1 percent in 1980, to an estimated 10.3 percent in 1986. In some countries, of course, unemployment rates were considerably higher than this, for example, in Colombia, Chile, Peru, and Venezuela.

In Chile, real industrial wages in 1986 were 7.9 percent lower than they had been in 1980. In Mexico, the fall was 33.9 percent and in Peru, 34.5 percent. The situation in parts of Africa was equally as bad. In Kenya, for example, real nonagricultural wages in 1985 were 22 percent lower than they had been in 1980, whereas in the United Republic of Tanzania in 1983 the fall was 40 percent.

Slow growth, declining productivity, rising unemployment, and falling real wages and average incomes have resulted in increased poverty and an acceleration in the number of hungry people in the world. According to the World Food Council, between 1970 and 1980, hunger grew by 15 million people, or an average of 1.5 million people a year. The first half of the 1980s

TABLE 5   **Open Urban Unemployment, 1970–1986**
(Percentage)

	1970	1980	1986
Argentina	4.9	2.9	5.2
Brazil	6.5	6.2	3.6
Chile	4.1	11.7	13.1
Colombia	10.6	9.7	13.8
Mexico	7.0	4.5	4.8
Peru	8.3	10.9	11.8
Venezuela	7.8	6.6	11.8

SOURCE: International Labour Organisation, *Overview of the Employment Situation in the World* (Geneva, November 1987), table 9, p. 39.

TABLE 6   **Real Wages in Nonagricultural Activities**
(Index: 1980 = 100)

	Year	Index
Africa		
Kenya	1985	78
Malawi	1984	76
United Republic of Tanzania	1983	60
Zambia	1984	67
Zimbabwe	1984	89
Latin America[a]		
Argentina	1986	103.5
Brazil	1986	112.8
Chile	1986	91.9
Colombia	1986	116.5
Mexico	1986	66.1
Peru	1986	65.5
Venezuela	1985	104.6

[a]The data refer to wages in industry.

SOURCE: International Labour Organisation, *Background Document,* High-level Meeting on Employment and Structural Adjustment, Geneva, November 1987, tables 9 and 10, pp. 28 and 32.

added almost 40 million hungry people, or close to 8 million per year—a fivefold increase in the average annual growth rate.[11] The absolute number of undernourished people increased in every region of the Third World, but only in Africa did the proportion of undernourished people rise, namely, from 29 percent in 1979–1981 to 32 percent in 1983–1985.[12] Changes in nutrition deficiency during the period 1971 to 1985, using data and standards from the Food and Agriculture Organization of the United Nations (FAO), are presented in Figure 3.

Problems of environmental, ecological, and political deterioration exacerbate the long-term economic problem in some parts of the Third World. In the Sahel, the Himalayas, and the Andes, economic progress is hampered by desertification or erosion, partly the result of climatic change and partly of population pressure. In other areas, deforestation is upsetting the ecological balance, to the detriment of poor people. In many developing countries, war and political instability exacerbate the poverty problem by withdrawing confidence in the currency, diverting scarce resources, destroying assets, disrupting assistance programmes and sapping incentives and motivation at family and community levels.

The world economy has evidently undergone a profound change in recent years. This change was not planned and in fact has been highly disorderly. World financial markets expanded rapidly for several years and

FIGURE 3   **Nutrition deficiency (calorie intake below 1.2 BMR threshold).**

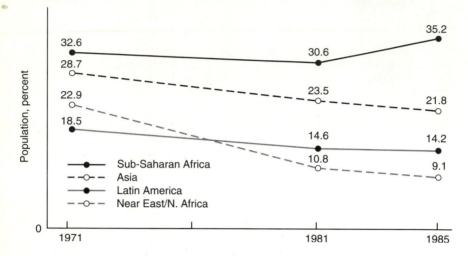

SOURCE: Food and Agriculture Organization of the United Nations.

then collapsed in October 1987; remedial measures have brought with them the threat of economic recession; exchange rates have been unstable and have moved in unpredictable ways. These changes have had disruptive consequences for economic progress and have inflicted severe damage on the real economies of many Third World countries.

It is important to recognize that the current economic crisis is policy induced. It is not an arbitrary act of nature but a consequence of changes in economic philosophy and in government policies. The policies introduced during the past decade reflect both a revised view of the proper role of the State and changed governmental preferences as between inflation and a higher level of economic activity.

The debt crisis is yet another manifestation of massive world economic imbalances. By 1985 a number of Third World countries were deeply in debt to the international banking system and multilateral financial institutions. In absolute terms the largest Third World debtors were Brazil ($106.7 billion), Mexico ($97.4 billion), Argentina ($48.4 billion), the Republic of Korea ($48 billion), and Indonesia ($35.8 billion).[13] In per capita terms, however, a great many other countries have very large external borrowings and have been having enormous difficulties servicing their debts (see Table 7). In Mali, Senegal, Zambia, Bolivia, Côte d'Ivoire, and Chile, the per capita external debt is greater than the per capita income and in a number of other countries per capita external debt is more than half as large as per capita GNP. Already, several countries have had to suspend payments of interest on the debt and postpone repayment of capital.

TABLE 7   **Per Capita Income and per Capita External Indebtedness in 25 Countries, 1985**
(US Dollars)

	Per Capita GNP	Per Capita External Debt
Ethiopia	110	44.2
Bangladesh	150	64.9
Mali	150	195.9
Niger	250	180.5
India	270	46.3
Kenya	290	206.8
United Republic of Tanzania	290	162.6
Senegal	370	271.8
Pakistan	380	132.0
Zambia	390	669.1
Bolivia	470	620.6
Indonesia	530	220.5
Philippines	580	478.7
Egypt	610	501.9
Côte d'Ivoire	660	836.2
Zimbabwe	680	255.1
Nigeria	800	184.0
Peru	1 010	735.9
Colombia	1 320	494.5
Chile	1 430	1,671.2
Brazil	1 640	787.1
Mexico	2 080	1,236.4
Argentina	2 130	1,588.3
Republic of Korea	2 150	1,854.3

SOURCE: World Bank, *World Development Report 1987* (Oxford, Oxford University Press, 1987).

The banks find themselves in the position of having to make greater provision in their balance sheets for bad debts, while extending additional loans to the Third World so that at least some of the interest can be repaid. The time may come when both creditors and debtors recognize that an orderly program of debt forgiveness would be to everyone's advantage. Meanwhile, the developing countries have become net suppliers of resources to the rich countries. In 1980 the capital-importing developing countries received a net transfer from the rest of the world of $39.4 billion, but by 1985 resources were flowing in the opposite direction and these developing countries transferred $31 billion to the rich countries.[14]

Many governments have been forced by an outflow of resources to cut investment, reduce public expenditure, and impose a deflationary contraction on the economy. At the same time, in order to service at least part of the debt, attempts have been made to shift resources in favour of the export sectors. This process is described as structural adjustment. It also reflects the need for long-term development strategies that do not assume substantial resource inflows in the future.

Structural adjustment has forced governments to reveal their expenditure priorities and, unfortunately, many governments have shown that, in practice, human development receives very low priority. Indeed, in many countries, central government outlays on the social sectors have decreased relative to total government expenditure and in real per capita terms. Education and health have been particularly hard hit. In contrast, the proportion of central government expenditures on general public administration has risen between 1972 and 1985 from 36 to 39 percent in the low-income countries, from 24 to 36 percent in the lower middle-income countries, and from 18 to 32 percent in the upper middle-income countries. Some data for selected countries are presented in Table 8.

In each of the three groups of countries included in Table 8, central government expenditure on education and health in 1985 was proportionately lower than it was in 1972. In the low-income countries, for example, education accounted for 13.2 percent of central government expenditure in 1972 but only 7.6 percent in 1985; health accounted for 4.9 percent in 1972 but only 3.7 percent in 1985. Expenditure on defence, in contrast, actually rose, from 17.2 percent of government expenditure in 1972 to 18.6 percent in 1985. That is, in the latter year, expenditure on the military in the poorest countries of the world was nearly 65 percent higher than spending on education and health combined.

In the low-income countries the share of education in central government expenditure fell 42.4 percent between 1972 and 1985, whereas the share of health fell 20.4 percent. The pattern of cuts was reversed in the middle-income countries: in the lower middle-income countries the share of education declined 15.9 percent compared to a cut of 26.9 percent in health expenditure, and in the upper middle-income countries there were cuts in shares of 13.8 percent and 41.8 percent in education and health, respectively.

The share of education fell in six of the seven low-income countries selected for the table. Indeed, in Zaire, government expenditure on education virtually ceased. The situation regarding health expenditure was as bad or, considering the initial conditions, even worse. In most Third World countries, government expenditure on health services was low even in 1972. By 1985 the share of health in total public expenditure had fallen in each of the groups of countries and in almost all the countries listed.

Overall, then, the picture is not encouraging. There seems to be a clear bias within the political system towards a reduction of public expenditure on human development in times of distress. This possibly reflects underlying changes in currents of thought about the appropriate role of govern-

TABLE 8   Central Government Expenditure on Education and Health as Percentage of Total Government Expenditure

	EDUCATION		HEALTH		PUBLIC ADMINISTRATION	
	1972	1985	1972	1985	1972	1985
Low-income countries, e.g.:	13.2	7.6	4.9	3.7	36.2	39.1
Burkina Faso	20.6	16.9	8.2	5.5	37.6	37.9
Malawi	15.8	12.3	5.5	7.9	36.7	36.4
Zaire	15.2	0.8	2.3	1.8	56.1	86.2
Kenya	21.9	19.8	7.9	6.7	30.2	35.3
United Republic of Tanzania	17.3	7.2	7.2	4.9	22.6	48.6
Sri Lanka	13.0	6.4	6.4	3.6	37.7	66.2
Lower middle-income countries, e.g.:	16.4	13.8	5.2	3.8	24.0	36.1
Bolivia	31.3	12.2	6.2	1.5	31.2	70.2
Indonesia	7.4	11.3	1.4	2.5	41.2	33.9
Turkey	18.1	10.0	3.2	1.8	18.3	54.1
Tunisia	30.5	14.3	7.4	6.5	25.1	25.7
Chile	20.0	13.2	10.0	6.1	20.0	18.4
Upper middle-income countries, e.g.:	12.3	10.6	7.9	4.6	18.3	32.3
Brazil	8.3	3.2	6.7	7.6	18.3	38.0
Mexico	16.4	12.4	5.1	1.5	15.2	44.4
Argentina	20.0	9.5	0.0	1.8	20.0	21.3
Venezuela	18.6	17.7	11.7	7.6	24.8	31.1

NOTE: Public administration covers expenditure on the general administration of government not included in other categories of economic and social services. Especially in large countries, where lower levels of government have considerable autonomy and are responsible for many social services, central government expenditure on education and health may account for only a small fraction of the total.

SOURCE: World Bank, *World Development Report 1987* (Oxford, Oxford University Press, 1987).

ment, as mentioned earlier. This change in economic philosophy appears to have originated in the advanced industrial economies, particularly in the United States of America, the Federal Republic of Germany, and the United Kingdom of Great Britain and Northern Ireland, and to have spread from there to many developing countries. However, in addition to the change in currents of thought, the reduction in expenditure on human development appears to have been a short-run and, as we shall see, a short-sighted response to the series of crises in which governments found themselves. Given the need for structural adjustment, many governments considered it was easier or more expedient to reduce expenditure on human development than on other items in the central government's budget.

The situation, however, is not altogether bleak. Indeed, there has been continued improvement in countries that have been able to maintain economic growth and avoid the worst impact of the 1980s recession. The above average performance of the South Asian and East Asian countries of 2.7 percent GDP growth per capita per year during the period 1981–1985 was accompanied by continuing progress, and even some acceleration, in health and nutritional trends. Sectoral policies emphasizing the need for accelerating agricultural production in formerly food-importing countries and for expanding low-cost, wide-coverage programs in health, nutrition, and water supply have been important contributory factors.

Moreover, several countries in Africa, other parts of Asia, and Latin America have been able to sustain expenditure on human development even while implementing structural adjustment programs. For instance, targeted programs in the area of child health and nutrition throughout the 1970s and early 1980s enabled Chile to achieve a continuous decline in infant and child mortality despite serious economic fluctuations; an example of a successful sectoral program during adjustment was the drought relief program in Botswana, backed up by a comprehensive system of monitoring nutritional status.[15] Indonesia is one of the countries that managed to expand expenditure on education and health as a proportion of total government expenditure, from 8.8 percent in 1972 to 13.8 percent in 1985 (see Table 8).

There are policy choices to be made; there are a number of alternative responses open to governments. Even in times of economic crisis and reduced public resources, governments can make the following choices:

1. A reduction in the quantity of services provided, for example, by curtailing the volume of food distributed through public channels such as food-for-work programs or government-owned ration shops;

2. A deterioration in the quality of services provided, for example, by allowing teacher-pupil ratios to fall sharply or, because of foreign exchange shortages, by reducing expenditure on school textbooks;

3. Reducing inefficiency within the public services, for example, by eliminating the wasteful use of construction materials or by inviting suppliers to tender bids;

4. An improvement in targeting to favour the poor, for example, by switching health expenditure from large urban hospitals to rural clinics or by reallocating educational expenditure from university to primary education;

5. Greater cost recovery of publicly provided services, for example, by introducing tuition fees for university studies (combined with scholarships for the poor) or by charging for certain types of medical care.

In our view, the objectives of policy during periods of structural adjustment should be to safeguard human development programs whenever possible and, if curtailment of public expenditure is unavoidable, to ensure that the burdens of adjustment are borne by those most able to do so. In many Third World countries the opposite has occurred: human development programs have been savagely cut and the brunt of the adjustment has fallen on the poor. This has weakened long-run prospects for development, while increasing inequality and poverty. It would instead have been much better to restructure human development programs, to reduce inefficiency, to improve targeting and, where necessary, to maintain the existing level of services, to introduce discriminatory user charges. The case for this approach will be made at greater length below.

DEVELOPMENT OF HUMAN CAPABILITIES: SCOPE AND DEFINITIONS

The development of human capabilities should be seen not as an objective with a definitive end-point but as a process continuing in time without end. It is an approach to overall development that puts the well-being of people first and that regards human beings simultaneously as both means and ends of social and economic policy. It is not, of course, a formula that can be applied mechanically, but it does contain ingredients that distinguish it from commodity-centred approaches to development. It places considerable emphasis on local resource mobilization as a way of allowing people to develop their capabilities and on participation as an agent of constructive change.

In many Third World countries, government is highly centralized and authoritarian. The people often are relegated to the status of subjects and come to fear and distrust government. Particularly in rural areas, and above all among the poor, government officials are seen more as coercive than as persuasive agents. Thus, the relationship between the State and the majority of the people is not conducive to the mobilization of large numbers of people for development. At the very least, a strategy that gives priority to the development of human capabilities requires decentralized administration to the local level and administration at that level by officials who enjoy the confidence and support of the great majority of the population.

Beyond this is the need to organize the population so that it can participate in its own development. Participation, or the opportunity to participate if one wishes, is, of course, an end in itself, but participation also has a number of instrumental values that make it attractive to a process of human development. First, participation in representative community-based organizations can help to identify local priorities, to determine which needs are essential or basic and which are of secondary importance, and to define the content of development programs and projects so that they reflect accurately local needs, aspirations, and demands. Next, having identified priorities and designed the programs that incorporate them, participation in functional organizations (service cooperatives, land reform committees, irrigation societies, women's groups) can be used to mobilize support for national and local policies and programs and local projects. Lastly, participation can be used to reduce the cost of public services and investment projects by shifting responsibility from central and local government (where costs tend to be relatively high) to the grass-roots organizations (where costs tend to be low). In some cases, for example, it may be possible to organize the beneficiaries of an investment project and persuade them to contribute their labour voluntarily to help defray construction costs. In other cases some of the public services (clinics, nursery schools) can be organized, staffed, and run by local groups rather than by relatively highly paid civil servants brought in from outside. Thus, in an appropriate context, participation can flourish and in so doing contribute much to development.

The instrumental value of participation and human development is not limited to the economic sphere; they also are of value in other spheres of life. There is, for example, a political dimension to human development. If formal democracy is not to be an empty shell, then people must have an education and information so that all groups in society are aware of the issues facing the country and can participate effectively in the political process.

Human development is of intrinsic value too. In some respects the development of human capabilities is increasingly regarded as a right to which all people are entitled. This right, in many societies, includes the ability to read and write, access to basic health care, and freedom from starvation. In addition, certain aspects of human development are akin to consumption goods in the sense that they are sources of satisfaction or pleasure. Education is desired in part for its own sake; employment, too, provides direct satisfaction by giving a person the recognition of being engaged in something worth his while[16]; and a clean and healthy environment can be a source of aesthetic pleasure.

We are particularly concerned, however, with the ability of human development expenditure to increase the productive capacity of an economy and raise the level of material prosperity. There are several ways it can do this.[17] First, human development expenditure can raise the physical, mental, and cognitive skills of the population through education and training. Secondly, public policy that focuses on human development can assist in the efficient deployment and full utilization of knowledge and skills; it can increase entrepreneurial and managerial capabilities, and it can transform theoretical knowledge into applied technology through research and development programs. Thirdly, public policy can establish an institutional framework that enhances incentives, removes impediments to resource mobility and resource mobilization, and increases participation in decision-making, which, in turn, can help to improve economic efficiency.[18]

Many programs could be classified as human development programs, but in the discussion below we shall restrict consideration to three broad categories: education and training; health services, water supply and sanitation; and food security and nutrition policies. It must be stressed, however, that although these programs can be listed separately there are in fact a great many complementarities among them.

For example, a program of school meals, intended to improve the nutrition of young people, often leads to reduced school drop-out rates and hence to an increase in the quality of the education system. Similarly, reduced infant mortality rates combined with greater education for women and greater nonfarm employment opportunities for women are associated with lower fertility rates and a lower rate of increase of the population.[19] Women, indeed, play a key role in human development not only because they account for half or more of the total population but also because they have a major responsibility in most societies for ensuring adequate nutrition for the family, caring for the sick, and educating the young before they enter the formal education system. In addition, recent research has shown that the weight at birth and the subsequent development of young children are affected by the state of health of the mother during pregnancy. Hence, there is complementarity between the health of the mother and that of the child.

In most developing countries women have substantially less access to education, to jobs, to income, and to power than men. Women's levels of health and nutrition are often inferior to men's. Women generally account for the largest proportion of deprived people. The improvement of human capabilities requires in particular that the capabilities of women be improved. In some countries attitudes and customs will have to change; governments can play a role in this process, for example, through programs directed at women.

Employment, too, is complementary to many human development programs. Employment evidently requires and is dependent upon skills being present in the labour force. But employment also generates skills in a process of learning by doing and, conversely, lack of employment can easily lead to the loss of skills. Unemployment represents not only a loss of potential output in the present, but by destroying skills, it represents a loss of future output as well.

In countries where unemployment is high, perhaps because of the way structural adjustment policies have been implemented, there may be scope for the direct mobilization of labour on capital formation projects. Underutilized human resources in the form of unemployed labour can sometimes be transformed into investment which can help to sustain long-run economic growth. Labour-intensive construction projects can be used to expand irrigation facilities, to create reservoirs and sources of safe water, to provide dirt farm–to-market roads, to undertake field terracing, anti-erosion works, and tree planting projects, and to build schools, clinics, and community centres.[20] In principle, such programs have the capacity to mobilize local resources that might otherwise remain unused and thereby raise the level of output and the rate of growth. Moreover, if they are properly administered, they do this by creating sources of income, in the form of employment, for some of the poorest members of society and thereby lead to a redistribution of income in favour of those most in need. In this way the creation of employment can lead directly to an enhancement of human capabilities.

HUMAN CAPITAL FORMATION, PHYSICAL INVESTMENT, AND ECONOMIC GROWTH

Expenditures on improving human capabilities have the potential to yield a return to society no less than the return from physical capital formation. Take the example of education. The standard technique for determining priorities for educational expenditure is social rate of return analysis. Some broad conclusions can be drawn from the many studies on this question that have been conducted in developing countries (see Table 9). First, the private rate of return to all levels of education is normally extremely high, reflecting in part the government subsidization of education. These high private rates of return help to explain the strength of private demand and of political pressure for education, which in turn have contributed to its rapid expansion in recent decades. Secondly, the social rate of return to all levels of education, although consistently lower than the corresponding private return, is generally no less than average rates of return on fixed capital investments. Thus, despite the rapid expansion, there are many developing countries in which education is still under-provided. Thirdly, the estimated social rate of return is generally highest at the primary level and lowest at the tertiary level of education.

Such estimates have to be treated with caution. There is a limit to what one can learn about the social benefit of educational expansion from cross-section estimates of private earnings streams. The earnings differences

TABLE 9   **Returns to Investment in Education, by Region, Type, and Level**

Number of Countries Reporting	Region	SOCIAL		
		Primary	Secondary	Tertiary
16	Africa	28	17	13
10	Asia	27	15	13
10	Latin America	26	18	16
45	Developing countries	24	15	13
15	Developed countries	—	11	9

Number of Countries Reporting	Region	PRIVATE		
		Primary	Secondary	Tertiary
16	Africa	43	26	32
10	Asia	31	15	18
10	Latin America	32	23	23
45	Developing countries	31	19	22
15	Developed countries	—	12	12

SOURCE: World Bank, *Financing Education in Developing Countries. An Exploration of Policy Options* (Washington D.C., 1986), p. 7.

between different educational levels may be attributable to various non-causal correlates of education, such as intelligence and determination, rather than, or in addition to, education itself. In so far as this is important, social rate of return estimates are biased upwards. On the other hand, there are various reasons why such estimates may understate the social value of education. They do not take into account the various "externalities" to which education can give rise, such as the potential effect of educated people on the productivity of those around them or on the health of their families. Nor do they take account of the power of education to enrich the lives and capabilities of people in ways other than by raising the production of goods and services. Moreover, a recognition that investment in human beings makes less use of scarce foreign exchange than does investment in machinery and equipment would similarly favour educational expenditures.

The social return to expansion of primary education depends largely on its effects on the productivity of peasant farmers. The evidence suggests that this in turn depends on whether farmers are operating in a traditional or a modernizing environment—one in which change is rapid. Education assists farmers to obtain and evaluate information about improved technology and new economic opportunities, and thus to innovate.[21] The level of education required depends on the levels of technology currently in use and potentially suitable.[22] Education being complementary to other inputs, its value cannot be assessed in isolation. It depends on the degree of access to credit, extension services, new seeds, and other inputs. The greatest impact on rural development can thus be made where education is part of a package of measures.

Perhaps because of the rapid expansion of education in many developing countries, the quality of education is frequently unsatisfactory. The same educational attainment may require more years of schooling in a developing than in a developed economy. In part, this reflects a lack of early environmental stimulation of children and the inadequacy of their health and nutrition. However, it also reflects the quality of teacher training and the strain on resources—often associated with rapid quantitative expansion—such as overcrowded classrooms, high pupil-teacher ratios, lack of textbooks, and ill-equipped facilities. In time of fiscal restriction, expenditure on physical inputs is squeezed more than salaries. In some countries there is also a problem of incentives. If the priorities of pupils and their teachers are to perform well in examinations in order to secure good jobs, and if examinations test rote-learning, then repetition, memorization, and rigid book-learning are encouraged in the schools—the so-called diploma disease.[23] Empirical research has suggested that in Brazil the social rate of return on expenditure for improving the quality of primary schooling would exceed that for increasing its quantity.[24]

In a sense, governments, perceiving a choice between high-quality education for a few and low-quality education for many, have opted for the latter. Indeed, the decision may not have been a conscious one in that educational expansion has often proceeded uncontrolled, impelled along by political pressures. Yet, low educational quality is not inevitable.[25] In the first place, improvements in quality may be possible without raising costs, for example, through curricular and examination reform or less reliance on seniority rules in promotions. Secondly, some expenditures on qualitative improvements may yield high rates of return, for example, training courses in leadership and management for head teachers. Thirdly, the use of pupil fees for particular purposes such as additional textbooks and the involvement of parents and communities in supportive actions may harness the enthusiasm for educational improvements.

There has been a long-run improvement in the various indicators of health in the developing countries over the post-War period. Thus, for instance, the infant mortality rate for the developing countries as a whole fell from 180 per 1,000 in 1950–1955 to 137 in 1960–1965, to 104 in 1970–1975, and to 88 in 1980–1985.[26] However, there is a wide variety of experience, and the gains in many countries have been modest if seen in relation to the improvements that could have been made on the basis of existing knowledge of primary health care and basic nutrition. Progress since 1980 has been more limited. The available evidence suggests that the decline in infant mortality was halted and even reversed during the 1980s in many Latin American and African countries. Indicators of child malnutrition increased in African countries after 1980. By contrast, malnutrition and mortality continued to decline in the majority of South and East Asian countries.

At present, there are economically feasible solutions to most of the health and nutrition problems that afflict many millions of people in the poor countries. The basic ingredients of primary health care would include the following: a simple pregnancy management program; oral rehydration therapy to cure digestive tract infections and improved water supply, sanitation, and health education to prevent them; immunization against the six communicable diseases; and an essential drug program covering some 15–20 basic products.

The reduction of malnutrition is more difficult: people are hungry because they lack resources to grow enough food or to buy it. The fundamental solution to protein-energy malnutrition may thus require a redistribution of resources, but directed food subsidies and direct feeding schemes can assist. Recent improvements in food technology can help to overcome micronutrient deficiencies, for example, by fortifying the country's salt with iron or iodine.

Studies have shown that improvements in water supply can have dramatic effects on the incidence of diarrhoeal diseases. The cost of providing vaccine doses against six main vaccine-preventable diseases is about $1.20 per child. The per capita cost of 15 essential drugs needed at the village health post level is only some $0.50–0.60 per year, and an episode of diarrhoea can be treated with oral rehydration salt available commercially at $0.15–0.20. The costs of combating micronutrient deficiencies are low: vitamin A capsules cost $0.10, the cost of iodizing salt is $0.05, and iron fortification of salt or centrally processed grains costs $0.05–0.09, all per person per year.[27]

The costs of providing primary health care are low, and yet provision is not as widespread as it could be. According to a World Health Organization (WHO) estimate, some three quarters of all health spending in the developing world is being used to provide expensive medical care for a relatively small urban minority.[28] Moreover, modern hospitals and costly medical technology absorb the great majority of health-related foreign aid to developing countries. There is a case for reallocating resources towards low-cost, high-impact primary health care measures.

Health expenditures of this sort can be justified not only by their effect on peoples' capabilities to enjoy life, but also by their effect on productivity. There is evidence that dietary energy improvements have an immediate effect on the performance of workers and that supplementation of micronutrients can have an even more dramatic effect on anaemic workers. Growth retardation at an early age, caused by dietary deficiency or infection, is a powerful mechanism for perpetuating the vicious circle of poverty, malnutrition, and stunting. Severe malnutrition of children under five leads to lifelong impairment of cognitive and physical performance. If children can be protected from these harmful effects, their long-run productivity and income could be greatly enhanced, and the resources required for their subsequent health care could be reduced. Moreover, the benefits need not stop there: primary health care lends itself to social mobilization and community participation in the design and delivery of programs, and this is likely to result in communities being better organized, more self-reliant, and more vocal.

The creation of human resources is one thing; their effective utilization is another. It is important that there be the right environment and incentives for human resources to be used fully and productively. Their effective use requires that factor prices reflect their scarcities. The failure of markets to secure this outcome can result in economic inefficiency, associated with, for example, mismatch of supply and demand, unemployment of labour, and brain drain. A potential problem is that the free market outcome may well conflict with income distribution objectives of government. In that case, the better solution may be to pursue income distribution objectives by means of other instruments.

Human capabilities can be dormant, waiting to be tapped, lacking perhaps in organizational initiative. Sometimes these capabilities can be tapped through greater participation of people at the grass-roots level. Obstacles may arise from gross inequalities in power, wealth, and incomes between different groups and classes in society. The lack of freedom of association and organization may constitute a barrier in some cases. There are also societies in which discriminatory practices based on gender, race, caste, religion, status, etc. effectively preclude equal economic or social participation by some groups. Illiteracy, limited education and knowledge, lack of confidence, passivity, and so on also constitute barriers to participation of individuals and groups in society.

Some of these obstacles are more amenable to policy than others. The role of government has to be examined carefully. Experience suggests that local people will not be motivated if group activities are both controlled and taxed by government. Perhaps the effective role of government is to provide information and an organizational framework, to ensure that the incentives are right, and let the people do the rest.

HUMAN DEVELOPMENT AND THE DISTRIBUTION OF INCOME

It is widely believed that expenditure on human development programs either is distributionally neutral or else discriminates in favour of the poor. This view, however, is not generally correct. Concerning Asia and the Pacific, one study reports that

> Inequality in opportunities to benefit from human resources development is pervasive in the developing countries of the region. There is

inequality between sexes, among regions within each country, between rural and urban areas and among persons in different economic and social groups.[29]

What is true of Asia and the Pacific is equally true of Africa and Latin America. The major beneficiaries of human development programs tend to be males, households living in the large urban areas, and people with middle or high incomes. Females, residents in the rural areas and those with relatively low incomes benefit proportionately less than others from the resources allocated to human development. This is due in part to "urban bias" in the provision of services, in part to a failure, for cultural and sociological reasons, of some of the intended beneficiaries to use the public services and facilities that are provided, but above all to a pattern of unequal subsidies among programs that effectively favours upper-income groups. The per capita subsidy of human development programs used disproportionately by the relatively better off (such as university education) tends to be much higher than the per capita subsidy of programs used largely by the poor (such as health clinics in rural areas). Consequently, the potential of expenditure on human development to reduce social rigidities, increase social mobility, and thereby ameliorate inequality remains large.

There is thus a need, particularly in times of structural adjustment, for governments to change the composition of their human development expenditure programs to ensure that, on balance, most of the benefits accrue to those in the lower half of the income distribution.[30] This can be done, for example, by switching resources from expenditure on urban hospitals to expenditure on primary health care (particularly in countries where hospitals account for 50–60 percent of government health funds), and by switching resources from university education to primary and secondary education (particularly since expenditure per university student often is 30–40 times greater than expenditure per primary school student).

In addition to a change in the composition of public expenditure, there may be a case in some countries for introducing user charges to help cover part of the cost of human development programs. If the tax system were optimal and progressive, and if the benefits of public expenditure programs were equitably distributed, the case against user charges would be quite strong and the case in favour of universal free education and health services would be attractive. But since tax systems in the developing countries often are in practice regressive, and since the benefits of many human development programs are reaped disproportionately by the better off, there may be an argument on grounds of equity for charging for services. In addition, where the alternative to imposing charges is to cut services, there may be an argument on grounds of long-term development for requiring users to cover at least part of the cost.

It is, of course, essential that if user charges are introduced they are designed in such a way that they do not add to the regressivity of the tax system. This can be done in several ways. First, user charges should be avoided as much as possible on services largely used by the poor, for example, primary education, primary health care, and public water points. Secondly, in the case of services and facilities used by both the poor and the rich, for example, secondary education, non-basic health services, and piped water, user charges should be selective, discriminating among users according to per capita income. Thirdly, full-cost charges should be imposed on services used largely by upper-income groups, for example, university education and sophisticated medical treatment available only to a few. But, fourthly, where full-cost charges are imposed, low-income groups should be entitled to scholarships (e.g., for university education) or exempted from the charge or subject to only a nominal charge. In this way, a system of user charges can actually be used to create a more egalitarian society.

No system of user charges, however, can counteract discrimination in access to services. This is something that requires positive intervention by the State. One of the clearest cases of discrimination is that against women. In some countries, namely, Bhutan, Nepal, India, and Pakistan, discrimination is so blatant that, contrary to the pattern everywhere else, the life expectancy of women is less than that of men. This reflects in part a lower regard for the health of female infants than for male infants. In education, too, there is great discrimination. On average, the illiteracy rate among females in the developing countries is 75 percent higher than among males, that is, 48.9 percent illiteracy among women as compared to 27.9 percent among men.[31] In primary school, women account for 44 percent of the pupils in the developing countries; in secondary schools, 39 percent; in tertiary education, 36 percent. In the least developed countries, the situation is even worse: women account for only 20 percent of those studying in tertiary education and 11 percent of the teaching staff in tertiary education.

In addition to discrimination based on sex, there is discrimination based on race (as in South Africa, Fiji, and Malaysia) and on religion (as in the Islamic Republic of Iran). Finally, there are specific problems associated with people of a particular age. In some countries the problem takes the form of child labour, that is, of some children entering the labour force, for example, in the carpet-making industry, before they have received primary and secondary education. In others it is reflected in a disproportionately high incidence of unemployment among the urban youth, a high incidence of long-term unemployment and consequently of unemployability among some sections of the young and, partly as a result of this, a sense of hopelessness accompanied by social disorders such as criminality and drug addiction.

The distribution of the benefits of human development programs among the social classes is slightly paradoxical. Most of the absolute benefits of public services in health, nutrition, education, housing, and transport accrue to the nonpoor, but even so, public subsidies and benefits in kind account for a higher proportion of the total income of the poor than of the nonpoor. Everything else being equal, therefore, a reduction in public expenditure is likely to fall most severely on the poor.

To avoid this, we have suggested that governments alter the composition of public expenditure and, possibly, introduce discriminatory user charges. In the next section we shall discuss the possibility of more accurate targeting of benefits in favour of the poor. It must be recognized and confronted squarely, however, that a redistribution of public resources in favour of the poor may in some circumstances be at the expense not of the rich but of the lower-middle classes. This could easily occur, for example, as a by-product of a switch of expenditure from urban to rural areas. Such a reallocation of resources might well be politically difficult to achieve, particularly if the urban population is more vociferous and better organized than the scattered rural population. In other words, the political economy of public expenditure cannot be ignored when designing human development programs—politics do impose constraints on policy makers—but at the same time it must be recognized that in many developing countries large sections of the poor have been denied an equitable share of the benefits of government programs.

HUMAN DEVELOPMENT AND THE ALLEVIATION OF POVERTY

There is a temporal dimension to the alleviation of poverty. It is important to know whether policies that alleviate poverty in the short term do so at the expense of long-term success. Sustained economic growth is crucial to reducing poverty in the long run. Among the decisive factors will be the rates at which resources such as physical and human capital accumulate and technical progress occurs, in relation to the growth of the population and labour force. The converse relationship may also be true, however. That is, immediate poverty alleviation may be good for growth. For instance, in so far as measures to enhance human capabilities through improved knowledge and health help people to escape from a vicious circle of poverty, they may make possible further, long-run improvements in their condition. The normal view that capital expenditures promote growth whereas current expenditures raise only current welfare need not hold for such measures.

While economic growth is not sufficient to ensure human development, sustained growth is likely to be central in the long run to policies intended to expand the capabilities of all people in the Third World. The austerity currently experienced in many parts of Latin America and Africa is likely, if continued for much longer, to be incompatible with the maintenance of democratic political processes and with the continuation of human development programs at acceptable levels. In Latin America, for example, the debt crisis has forced countries to undergo a massive contraction in aggregate demand, substantial depreciation of exchange rates, and often, after more than a decade of trade liberalization, a reimposition of nontariff barriers to trade and very high tariffs on imports. The result has been a decline in the real value of imports by more than 45 percent between 1980 and 1985 (as well as a fall in the real value of exports because of lower commodity prices). Employment, investment, and growth have all suffered severely. Unfortunately, the adjustment measures that have had to be adopted in many parts of Africa and West Asia have been even more deleterious. A revival of growth is essential in all three of these regions.

Nonetheless, it may be possible to adopt medium-term measures to contain poverty during the period of financial and economic crisis. One way to do this is to target the benefits of human development programs to favour the poor. Targeting presupposes, of course, that it is possible to identify the poor in general or those with specific needs, for example, for improved nutrition. This, in turn, requires that data be available and in a form that permits analysis in terms of relevant social categories, for example, by level of income, occupational group, social class, and age.

The difficulties and costs of accurate targeting should not be underestimated and in some cases it may be cheaper and more efficient to provide a universal service rather than attempt to discriminate in favour of particular groups. Moreover, there is a danger, indeed a virtual certainty, that every targeted program will fail to reach some of the intended beneficiaries while providing services to some unintended beneficiaries. A study of the Indian integrated rural development program, for example, showed that 20 percent of the actual beneficiaries had incomes above the poverty line and hence, in principle, were not eligible for participation in the scheme.[32]

Targeted programs that rely on the exercise of discretion by government officials are vulnerable to corruption and abuse. Programs targeted at people with an income below some arbitrary minimum or with food consumption below some arbitrary daily caloric minimum fall into this category. More likely to be successful are programs that rely on self-targeting or else are universally available within a restricted category. Examples of the latter include free lunches to all primary school children or rationed food supplies available only to inhabitants of rural areas. The chances of corruption in such cases are pretty low, but conversely the chances of providing benefits to many who are not poor are pretty high.

Self-selection of beneficiaries has great appeal because in principle it is possible to offer universal coverage while in practice designing the program in such a way that it is attractive primarily to those most in need of assistance. Food-for-work programs, for instance, can be open to all, yet it is obvious that they will appeal primarily to the unemployed from households where average food consumption and incomes are low. Similarly, it is possible to design a limited food rationing system to which everyone has access but which in practice favours the poor, the rest of the community voluntarily obtaining its supplies elsewhere.[33] The easiest way to do this is by concentrating on varieties of foodgrains and qualities of products that are of special interest to low-income groups and that are characterized by low or even negative income elasticities of demand.

The general point is that it may be possible to redesign human development programs, for example, by better targeting, to ensure that, particularly in times of increased hardship, a higher proportion of total benefits accrues to the poor. This general point can be extended by considering whether it is possible within a context of falling public expenditure to change the composition of public expenditure in order to give higher priority to reducing poverty. This, of course, raises the issue of the importance given by policy makers to human development as compared to the claims for spending by other government services.

Military expenditure can be used to illustrate the choices facing governments. In extreme cases, expenditure on defence is a multiple of expenditure on education and health. The data must be interpreted with caution as statistical conventions appear to vary from one country to another, but the figures may provide a rough indication of orders of magnitude (see Table 10). In the low-income countries as a whole, average expenditure on defence was 18.6 percent of total central government expenditure, whereas education and health combined accounted for 11.3 percent of government spending. In the lower middle-income countries the proportions were 14.2 and 17.6 percent respectively.[34]

Governments need to ask themselves whether reduced expenditure on the military would lead to reduced national security. In many cases, perhaps a majority, it is doubtful that it would. Governments should also consider whether slack and inefficiency in the armed services is greater than in other areas of public expenditure. Anecdotal evidence suggests that it often is. Similarly, defence procurement policies could be reconsidered: the market for military equipment is in general oligopolistically organized and hence not very competitive and the price mark-up on supplies is high. The scope for financial savings in the defence budget may be much greater than in other areas of public spending and, if so, it may be possible to release resources for human development programs without impairing a country's ability to defend itself.

Finally, it may be possible, particularly during a relatively short period of economic crisis, to use some of the resources allocated to the military services to support human resources, antipoverty, and public investment programs. It is common for the armed forces to be used to help the civilian

TABLE 10   **Defence Expenditure as Percentage of Total Central Government Expenditure in Selected Countries, 1972 and 1985**

	1972	1985
Low-income countries	17.2	18.6
Burkina Faso	11.5	18.2
Nepal	7.2	6.2
Malawi	3.1	5.7
Zaire	11.1	5.2
Burma	31.6	18.5
Kenya	6.0	12.9
United Republic of Tanzania	11.9	13.8
Ghana	7.9	7.5
Pakistan	39.9	32.3
Sri Lanka	3.1	2.6
Uganda	23.1	16.7
Lower-middle-income countries	15.7	14.2
Bolivia	18.8	5.4
Indonesia	18.6	12.9
Morocco	12.3	14.9
Philippines	10.9	11.9
Dominican Republic	8.5	8.4
Thailand	20.2	20.2
El Salvador	6.6	20.3
Paraguay	13.8	10.2
Turkey	15.5	10.9
Mauritius	0.8	0.8
Ecuador	15.7	11.3
Tunisia	4.9	7.9
Costa Rica	2.8	3.0
Chile	10.0	11.5
Upper-middle-income countries	14.4	9.7
Brazil	8.3	4.0
Uruguay	5.6	10.8
Yugoslavia	20.5	54.8
Mexico	4.2	2.7
Argentina	10.0	8.8
Republic of Korea	25.8	29.7
Venezuela	10.3	6.1
Israel	40.0	27.8
Oman	39.3	43.0
Singapore	35.3	20.1

SOURCE: World Bank, *World Development Report 1987* (Oxford, Oxford University Press, 1987).

population when natural catastrophes such as floods and earthquakes occur. The question being raised here is whether the armed forces could play a constructive role over a longer period when economic catastrophes occur. The manpower and construction equipment of the armed forces might be used to sustain public investment in infrastructure (roads, bridges) and to construct the physical facilities needed for human resource programs (rural clinics, primary schools). Equally, the training facilities of the armed forces could be used to train the civilian labour force in useful skills (electricians, mechanics). In this way, the conflict in priorities between military expenditure and human resource development could at least be reduced.

There may also be opportunities to reduce poverty by mobilizing slack local resources. The ease with which this can be done depends in part on the degree of grass-roots participation, a topic that was briefly discussed earlier. Particularly in the rural areas, and particularly during the off-peak seasons, the supply of labour is likely to be highly elastic and its opportunity cost low. If this labour is combined with technology of low capital intensity, it should be possible to generate substantial employment, raise the incomes of the working poor, and produce productive assets of lasting value. The organizational intensity of a strategy of local resource mobilization, however, is likely to be high. In effect, the mobilization of labour is used as a substitute for physical capital. But again, the cost of mobilizing slack local resources can be kept to a minimum if the local population already has been organized around institutions intended to promote their well-being.

The capability of small-scale, locally based development to be self-sustaining is often underestimated. If resource mobilization is successful in raising rural incomes, experience shows that a significant proportion of the additional income may be ploughed back into investment, which then raises incomes further in the next period. In other words, marginal savings rates are potentially quite high even among very low-income households. Thus, human development programs based in rural areas should not be regarded as income transfers to the poor but as an efficient way of raising the incomes of the poor on a sustained basis.

In the urban areas, particularly in what is known as the informal sector, it may be possible to mobilize slack resources and release entrepreneurial initiative simply by removing government-imposed obstacles to progress. Quite often government policy towards the urban informal sector contains too few elements of inaction, restriction, and harassment.[35] The punitive demolition of squatter settlements merely destroys the housing of the poor; it does not result in better health or a more sanitary environment. Similarly, trade licensing systems create monopoly rents for license holders while discouraging investment in the informal sector. The effect of this is to harm the lower-income groups by reducing employment as well as the supply of goods and services originating in the informal sector which the poor consume. From Kenya to Peru,[36] the informal economy is usually thought of as a problem rather than as a reservoir of frustrated initiative and untapped talent and a way out of underdevelopment for many of the poor.

Yet, especially at a time when public expenditure is falling, and expenditure on human development is falling faster than average, a strong case can be made for removing laws and regulations that make it difficult for the poor to help themselves, to put a roof over their heads, to obtain a job, to establish a small shop or enterprise. If the ability of the State to help the poor in a time of economic crisis is declining, the least that can be done is to make certain that the State does not aggravate the problem of poverty or obstruct the efforts of low-income groups to improve their situation through their own exertions.

CONCLUSIONS

The peak of enthusiasm for "investment in human beings" occurred during the 1960s. Since the first oil crisis, the pendulum has swung in the other direction. The question has become: how to manage the economic crisis and return to economic growth? There is again a tendency to consider education, health, and social services as consumer goods—luxuries to be afforded in good times but not in bad. The pendulum has swung too far towards the neglect of human resource development.

Our object has been to provide a counterweight. When governments face a severe dilemma of having to choose between adjusting to short-term economic and fiscal constraints and pursuing long-run human resource goals, there is a danger that the former will dominate the latter. For instance, the costs of neglecting the former are more calculable, and more attributable, than the long-run costs to the development process of neglecting the latter. Nevertheless, the solution to the short-term problems of the present may contribute to a series of equally pressing short-run problems in the future.

We advocate that a broader view be taken of the development process than is normal—a view that encompasses not only the growth of national income per head and improvements in its distribution but also the enhancement of the capabilities of people to be and to do more things and to lead fuller lives. Education, health, and nutrition have an important role to play in helping people to develop their capabilities. The enhancement of human capabilities is both an end in itself and a means to higher production and income. There is evidence that the economic returns for expenditures on education and health can be high. There is thus a good case for protecting such expenditure against the fiscal squeeze that generally accompanies economic recession and structural adjustment programs.

Although the distributional effects of government taxation and expenditure are often regressive, with richer households receiving larger benefits, it is the poor who may suffer most from public expenditure cuts, in that the smaller absolute benefit to the poor is nevertheless a more important part of their income. The basic public services, such as primary education and basic health care, in particular need to be protected, for reasons both of efficiency and of equity. There is a case for greater targeting of subsidized public services on the poor, for example, by concentrating on poor rural areas and using self-selective schemes such as food-for-work. If it is naïve to expect that, in a period of curtailment, additional funds will be provided or that funds will be diverted from other activities, such as defence, for those activities that enhance human capabilities, then at least the basic services should continue to be generally provided free and, where it would not be a regressive move, selective cost recovery might be introduced to maintain and enlarge programs providing nonbasic services.

NOTES

1. Amartya Sen, "Development: Which Way Now?" *Economic Journal*, 93, 372 (December 1983): 755.
2. Amartya Sen, "Goods and People," in *Resources, Values and Development* (Oxford: Basil Blackwell, 1984), pp. 510 and 511.
3. John Rawls, *A Theory of Justice* (Cambridge: Harvard University Press, 1971), p. 92.
4. International Labour Organisation, *Employment, Growth and Basic Needs: A One-World Problem* (Geneva, 1976).
5. Amartya Sen, *Resources, Values and Development* . . ., pp. 315–16.
6. See Amartya Sen, "Public Action and the Quality of Life in Developing Countries," *Oxford Bulletin of Economics and Statistics*, 43, 4 (November 1981); and Keith Griffin, *Alternative Strategies for Economic Development* (London: Macmillan, 1988), chap. I.
7. World Bank, *World Development Report 1984* (Oxford: Oxford University Press, 1984), table 4.2, p. 67.
8. See, for example, Felix Paukert, "Income Distribution at Different Levels of Development: A Survey of Evidence," *International Labour Review*, CVIII, 2–3 (August–September 1973); and Montek S. Ahluwalia, "Inequality, Poverty and Development," *Journal of Development Economics*, 3, 3 (September 1976).
9. Keith Griffin and Azizur Rahman Khan, "Poverty in the World: Ugly Facts and Fancy Models," *World Development*, 6, 3 (March 1978); and Irma Adelman and Cynthia Taft Morris, *Economic Growth and Social Equity in Developing Countries* (Stanford: Stanford University Press, 1973).
10. International Labour Organisation, *Overview of the Employment Situation in the World* (Geneva, November 1987), p. 2.
11. World Food Council, *The Global State of Hunger and Malnutrition and the Impact of Economic Adjustment on Food and Hunger Problems* (April 1987), p. 3.
12. Ibid., table 1, p. 16.

13. World Bank, *World Development Report 1987* (Oxford, Oxford University Press, 1987), table 16, pp. 232–33.

14. United Nations Children's Fund, *Adjustment with a Human Face* (Oxford: Oxford University Press, 1987). The net transfer is calculated as the difference between loans, direct investments, and grants received and profit repatriation, interest, and capital repayments.

15. United Nations Children's Fund, *Adjustment with a Human Face* . . ., Vol. 1, pp. 289–94.

16. Amartya Sen, *Technology, Employment and Development* (Oxford: Clarendon Press, 1975), p. 5.

17. See Louis Emmerij, "The Human Factor in Development," *Human Development: The Neglected Dimension* (United Nations publication, Sales No. 86.III.B.2), p. 20.

18. For evidence that participation raises the return on physical capital and increases the productivity of labour, see Conrad Phillip Kottak, "When People Don't Come First: Some Sociological Lessons from Completed Projects" (Washington, D.C.: World Bank, 1985); and David C. Korten, "Community Organization for Rural Development: A Learning Process Approach," *Public Administration Review* (September–October 1980).

19. Robert Cassen, "Population and Development: A Survey," *World Development*, 4, 10–11 (1976): 788–96.

20. See J. Gaude and others, "Rural Development and Labour-Intensive Schemes: Impact Study of Some Pilot Programmes," *International Labour Review* (July–August 1987).

21. M. E. Lockhead, D. T. Jamison, and L. J. Lau, "Farmer Education and Farm Efficiency: A Survey," *Economic Development and Cultural Change*, 29 (1980). 37–76.

22. Daniel Cotlear, "The Effects of Education on Farm Productivity: A Case Study from Peru" (1987).

23. R. P. Dore, *The Diploma Disease, Education, Qualification and Development* (London: George Allen and Unwin, 1976).

24. Jere Behrman and Nancy Birdsall, "The Quality of Schooling: Quantity Alone May Be Misleading," *American Economic Review*, 73, 5 (1983): 928–46.

25. Jocelyn Dejong and John Oxenham, "The Quality of Education in Developing Countries" (1987).

26. *World Population Prospects. Estimates and Projections as Assessed in 1984* (United Nations publication, Sales No. E.86.XIII.3).

27. Figures from G. A. Cornia, "Investing in Human Resources: Health, Nutrition and Development for the 1990s" (November 1987).

28. Cited in Cornia, op. cit., p. 23.

29. *Economic and Social Survey of Asia and the Pacific 1986* (United Nations publication, Sales No. E.87.II.F.1), part two, p. 171.

30. See G. A. Cornia, "Social Policy Making During Adjustment," in Khadija Haq and Uner Kirdar, eds., *Human Development, Adjustment and Growth*, (Islamabad, North-South Round-table, 1987), pp. 85–88.

31. United Nations Educational, Scientific and Cultural Organization, Office of Statistics, *The Current Literacy Situation in the World* (Paris, May 1987), p. 4.

32. N. J. Kurian, "IRDP—How Relevant Is It?" (May 1987), p. 7.

33. See Keith Griffin and Jeffrey James, *The Transition to Egalitarian Development* (London: Macmillan, 1981), chap. 4.

34. World Bank, *World Development Report 1987* . . .

35. International Labour Organisation, *Employment, Incomes and Equality: A Strategy for Increasing Productive Employment in Kenya* (Geneva, 1972), p. 226.

36. See Hernando de Soto, *El Otro Sendero: La Revolución Informal* (Lima: Editorial El Barranco, 1986). See also Victor Tokman, "The Informal Sector Today: A Policy Proposal." Paper presented to the Round-table in Managing Human Development, Budapest, September 6–9, 1987.

31

The Arms Race and Development: A Competitive Relationship

Inga Thorsson

THE SECRETARY-GENERAL'S REPORT ON DISARMAMENT AND DEVELOPMENT

In the Final Document of the 1978 Special Session on Disarmament, the General Assembly requested the Secretary-General, with the assistance of a group of experts, to prepare a study on the relationship between disarmament and development. An Expert Group was appointed and, under the able leadership of Inga Thorsson, held ten meetings between 1978 and 1981. The Expert Group was aided in its work by forty research reports which it was able to commission.

The Report of the Secretary-General on the "Study of the Relationship Between Disarmament and Development" was issued on October 5, 1981. The Secretary-General described the study as "an important attempt by the international community to thoroughly investigate the proposition that a balanced and generally acceptable pattern of economic and social development is inextricably related to disarmament". He continued, "The clear and widely shared understanding of this relationship may provide a basis for the formulation of practical measures by Governments that would both promote disarmament and further development". . . . We have presented here excerpts from Inga Thorsson's presentation of the Report in the 2nd Committee of the General Assembly.

Reprinted from *Development*, 1 (1982), pp. 12–15, 20, the quarterly journal of the Society for International Development.

Common sense alone tells us that military preparations are an economic burden. The arms race and development are to be viewed in a competitive relationship, particularly in terms of resources. Or to put it another way: the arms race and underdevelopment are not two problems; they are one. They must be solved together, or neither will ever be solved.

It is a historical fact that governments have, over the past 30 years, spent vast resources on armaments, resources which—on grounds of morality, on grounds of equal human justice, on grounds of enlightened self-interest—ought to have been directed to ending world poverty and building for human and material development. In this way world armaments are among the causes of poverty and underdevelopment.

The 1972 U.N. study on this same theme concluded that disarmament and development "stand fundamentally apart." Taking their point of departure, this statement is still true. Ten years ago and, as duties of the industrialized countries went, development was simply equated with development assistance. But since then, the development discussion has been broadened to involve basic structural changes in all societies, within states and among states, including more equitable distribution of income, access to the means of production and greater participation by all groups in decision making, and progress towards the establishment of a New International Economic Order.

In the present study we have introduced a new conceptual framework, defined in a dynamic triangular interrelation between disarmament, development, and security. We have taken a broader approach to the problem of security. In our era, national security can no longer be equated with military might. Even less can international security, i.e., security *for all*, do so. Also, we demonstrate that threats to security may be made and aggravated in many ways, including those that go far beyond purely military threats. It was recognized by the first Special Session on Disarmament that the arms race itself has become a threat to the security of nations. Thus, disarmament, particularly nuclear disarmament, would directly enhance security, and, therefore, prospects for development.

National security is not a goal in itself. Its ultimate purpose must be to secure the independence and sovereignty of the national state, the freedom of its citizens—freedom and the means to develop economically, socially, and culturally, which defines exactly what we mean by "development." In today's world this can never be achieved by any state at the expense of others. In a world of interdependence, only through global, or international, security will it be possible to reach the objective of national security for the ultimate goal of freedom, well-being, and human dignity for people throughout the world.

Today there is an array of intensifying nonmilitary threats which aggravate the security problems of states. Such nonmilitary threats can be described as:

- Widespread reductions in prospects for economic growth;
- Existing or impending ecological stresses, resource scarcities—notably in the field of energy and certain nonrenewable raw materials—and a growing world population. Today's stresses and constraints may translate into tomorrow's economic stresses and political conflicts;
- The morally unacceptable and politically hazardous polarization of wealth and poverty.

The appalling dimensions of poverty, the destruction of the environment, the accelerating race for arms, and the resulting global economic malaise are largely problems of our own making. The Group states that it is well within our collective capabilities and within the earth's carrying capacity to provide for basic needs for the world's entire population, and to make progress towards a more equitable economic order, at a pace politically acceptable to all. The Group reaffirms that the arms race is incompatible with the objectives of a New International Economic Order. Of course, also in the future, economic growth is possible even with a continuing arms race, but it would be relatively slow, and very unevenly distributed both among and within regions of the world. We show, on the other hand, that a cooperative management of interdependence can be in the economic and security interests of all states. But the adoption or rather the evolution of such an outlook is quite improbable if the arms race continues.

It is imperative that nonmilitary challenges to security are treated as nonmilitary. If this is not recognized, if states fail to accept and persevere in tackling these challenges through voluntary measures and cooperation, there is a grave risk that the situation will deteriorate to the point of crisis where, even with a low probability of success, the use of military force could be seen as a way to produce results sufficiently quickly. This is far from being a remote possibility. In recent time there has been a marked and increasing tendency in international relations actually to use or threaten to use military force in response to nonmilitary challenges, not only to "security," but also to the secure supply of goods and the well-being of the nations which face these challenges.

The study has documented that at least 50 million people are directly or indirectly engaged in military activities world-wide. This figure includes, *inter alia,* an estimated 500,000 qualified scientists and engineers engaged in research and development for military purposes.

Military research and development remains by far the largest single objective of scientific enquiry and technological development. Approximately 20 percent of the world's qualified scientists and engineers were engaged in military work at a cost of around 35,000 million dollars in 1980, or approximately one-quarter of all expenditure on research and development. Virtually all this R and D takes place in the industrialized countries,

85 percent in the USA and the USSR alone. Adding France and Britain would push this share above 90 percent.

It stands to reason that even a modest reallocation to development objectives of the current capacity for military R and D could be expected to produce dramatic results in fields like resource conservation and the promotion of new patterns of development, better adapted to meeting the basic needs of ordinary people. This is, *inter alia* evident from the fact, which is also among our findings, that, on an average, a military product requires 20 times as much R and D resources as a civilian product.

The 1972 report on the subject identified more than 70 possible alternative uses. Our present investigations suggest, in more elaborated and detailed ways, for instance, that production workers in the military sector could quite easily transfer their skills to the development, production, and installation of solar energy devices. Environment, housing, and urban renewal are other areas likely to gain from the possible rechanneling of military R and D. New transport systems, particularly in urban areas, are sorely needed and have long been regarded as a major civilian alternative for the high technology industries in the military sector.

In purely financial terms, world-wide military expenditures by 1981 exceed, as we all know, the astounding level of 520,000 million dollars, representing 6 percent of world output. Member States certainly realize that this amount is roughly equivalent to the value of all investible capital in all developing countries combined.

The effect on the economic and social spheres in our societies of the arms race extend far beyond the fact that 5 to 6 percent of the world's resources are not available to help satisfy socially productive needs. The very fact that these resources are spent on armaments accentuates the inefficient allocation of the remaining 94 to 95 percent, within and between nations. Three fundamental characteristics of the arms race reinforce this disallocation: *first*, the sheer magnitude of the volume of resources; *second*, the composition of expenditure, most particularly the stress on R and D, affecting investment and productivity in the civilian sector; and *third*, the fact that this massive effort has now been sustained for over 30 years.

As an illustration of the contribution which can be made by disarmament measures, even limited, to world development, one study submitted to the Group projects global economic prospects under three types of hypothetical scenarios, viz., a continued arms race, an accelerated arms race, and modest disarmament measures involving the release of some resources for reallocation to the developing countries. Utilizing the United Nations input-output model of world economy it is calculated that an acceleration of the arms race would adversely affect global economic well-being in all but one of the regions of the world. A wealth of numerical data is presented in chapter III of the report. I will here highlight some general results. Besides the negative impact on per capita consumption, an accelerated arms race will also result in a decline of the world's stock of capital, reduce the value of nonmilitary exports, and entail reductions in industrial employment in the poorest regions of the world.

In contrast, a scenario of even modest disarmament measures is shown to yield higher per capita consumption for different regions and in addition bring about a higher world GDP, a larger capital stock, a general increase in the agricultural output, to mention only a few of the obvious economic gains. Besides these global economic gains, a scenario of modest disarmament would also yield significant benefits for the poorest regions of the world. This conclusion is by itself of considerable significance when it is remembered that in many cases, increases in military outlays by industrial countries have been accompanied by a decline in their aid transfers, despite the repeated request for the fulfilment of the UN targets for official development assistance and despite the fact that existing volumes of assistance are grossly inadequate to meet the basic aid requirements for the poorer countries. The report shows that even a minor part of savings from modest disarmament has the potential of dramatically enhancing present levels of assistance.

We can make similar calculations for the past. For instance, if half the funds spent on armaments throughout the world from 1970 to 1975 had instead been invested in the civilian sector, it has been calculated[1] that annual output at the end of that period would have been 200,000 million dollars higher than it actually was—a figure in excess of the aggregate GNP of Southern Asia and the mid-African regions. And mark well, this growth would most likely have been achieved without any extra demand for investible resources.

Military outlays fall by definition into the category of consumption and not investment. As a consequence, steadily high or increasing military outlays tend to depress economic growth. This effect may be direct through displacement of investment, and indirect through constraints on productivity.

A study conducted in the late 1960s by Emile Benoit is much cited as showing that military outlays do not have negative effects on economic growth for developing countries. In reality Benoit's own conclusion was more modest.[2] He said:

> Thus we have been unable to establish whether the net growth effects of defence expenditures have been positive or not. On the basis of all the evidence we suspect that it has been positive for the countries in our sample, and at past levels of defence burden, but we have not been able to prove this.

This suspected positive relationship of Benoit's has been contested as spurious, since it was simultaneously correlated with other important socioeconomic factors in the economies of those developing countries, particularly a high net inflow of foreign assistance. Based on today's level of research, it can now be confidently refuted. In our study we do recognize that the availability of unutilized and underutilized resources in developing countries may produce short-term results, suggesting a parallelism between high rates of growth and significant military spending, a situation which is, by the way, frequently associated with foreign dependence. In the long run, however, the totality of the socioeconomic consequences of sizeable military outlays outweighs any immediate economic spinoffs into the civilian sector.

On the basis of the present report, and the research commissioned for it, we can confidently conclude that military budgets are deadend expenditures in all kinds of economies, be they market, centrally planned, or mixed; be they industrialized or developing. Military expenditures do *not* foster growth. Through their inflationary effects—thoroughly analysed in the study—and the general economic and political malaise to which they contribute, military spending *inhibits* the capital investment required for development. Through the drain on the most valuable research talents and funds, it *restrains* productivity gains and *distorts* growth in science and technology. The military sector is not a great provider of jobs. On the contrary it is shown that military spending is one of the least efficient kinds of public spending. It drains away funds that could relieve poverty and distress. The very nature of military spending heightens tensions, reduces security, and underpins the system which makes even more arms necessary.

This study has in my view strengthened the economic and social case for the disarmament-development relationship by identifying military spending as an impediment to economic growth and social development and the arms race as an obstacle to the establishment of a New International Economic Order.

The Group has indicated the political and economic potentials of rationally imperative alternatives in suggesting that policies aimed at implementing the disarmament-development relationship are likely to broaden the base of East-West détente and put the North-South dialogue in a mutually advantageous frame of reference.

Its report should not be considered an individual project. I should like to express a hope for an effective follow-up process, to the benefit, first of all, of the billions of human beings inhabiting this world of ours.

NOTES

1. United Nations Disarmament Fact Sheet, no. 9, "Cost of the Arms Race," 1979.
2. Emile Benoit, *Defence and Economic Growth in Developing Countries* (Lexington, Mass.: Lexington Books, 1973), p. 4.

APPENDIX

[The following are the recommendations from the report of the group of experts on disarmament and development.]

On the basis of its findings and conclusions, implicit in this entire report and more explicitly summarized above, the Group makes the following recommendations:

1. That all Governments, but particularly those of the major military Powers, should prepare assessments of the nature and magnitude of the short- and long-term economic and social costs attributable to their military preparations so that their general public be informed of them.

2. That Governments urgently undertake studies to identify and to publicize the benefits that would be derived from the reallocation of military resources in a balanced and verifiable manner, to address economic and social problems at the national level and to contribute towards reducing the gap in income that currently divides the industrialized nations from the developing world and establishing a new international economic order.

3. A fuller and more systematic compilation and dissemination by Governments of data on the military use of human and material resources and military transfers.

4. That the disarmament-development perspective elaborated in this report be incorporated in a concrete and practical way in the ongoing activities of the United Nations system.

5. That Governments create the necessary prerequisites, including preparations and, where appropriate, planning, to facilitate the conversion of resources freed by disarmament measures to civilian purposes, especially to meet urgent economic and social needs, in particular, in the developing countries.

6. That Governments consider making the results of experiences and preparations in their respective countries available by submitting reports from time to time to the General Assembly on possible solutions to conversion problems.

7. That further consideration be given to establishing an international disarmament fund for development and that the administrative and technical modalities of such a fund be further investigated by the United Nations with due regard to the capabilities of the agencies and institutions currently responsible for the international transfer of resources.

8. That the Secretary-General take appropriate action, through the existing inter-agency consultative mechanism of the Administrative Committee on Coordination, to foster and coordinate the incorporation of the disarmament and development perspective in the programmes and activities of the United Nations system.

9. That the Department of Public Information and other relevant United Nations organs and agencies, while continuing to emphasize the danger of war—particularly nuclear war—should give increased emphasis in their disarmament-related public information and education activities to the social and economic consequences of the arms race and to the corresponding benefits of disarmament.

32

Conserving Nature, Decreasing Debt

John Cartwright

Two crises haunt the Third World today: the debt burden and environmental degradation. The debts arising from the borrowing which took place in the 1970s in order to produce economic growth, and which failed to cover its costs have brought to Third World countries a legacy of run-down infrastructure and reduced social services, a situation compounded by the insistence of Western lenders that they curtail expenses still further in order to keep paying. At the same time, and in part because of these pressures, many Third World countries are rapidly running down their stock of natural resources—forests, fisheries, minerals, and grazing lands—with the result that they suffer frequent droughts and floods, erosion, landslides, and other "natural" disasters, and face the loss of a patrimony which could provide their future generations indefinitely with a comfortable and secure means of living.

While there are no simple or easy solutions to either of these crises, the industrialised countries are beginning to realise that Third World environmental degradation will adversely affect their own long-term well-being, and that they should therefore be contributing to Third World environmental protection or restoration out of self-interest. Herein lies an opportunity for the Third World to achieve a measure of debt relief, while protecting key natural ecosystems and moving towards more environmentally sustainable modes of economic activity. This article will focus on one widely discussed approach: the reduction of debts owed to Western lenders in exchange for the conservation of natural ecosystems.

THE ECONOMIC CRISIS: WHAT DOES IT INVOLVE?

Few observers really believe that the Third World can repay the debt, of over one trillion dollars, that it owes to Western private lenders, govern-

From *Third World Quarterly*, 11, 2 (April 1989), pp. 114–27.

ments and international institutions; certainly the banks, which have quiet-
ly written off substantial portions of their overseas loans and sold others at
heavy discounts, do not seem to consider repayment to be possible. A combination of the ability of modern technology to create substitutes for most
of the Third World's raw materials, the increase in value added through
processing, protectionist barriers against Third World manufactures, and
high US interest rates aimed to cushion the devaluation of the dollar make
it almost inconceivable that heavily indebted Third World countries could
pay off their debts on terms anywhere near as stringent as those currently
imposed upon them. These factors are clearly beyond the Third World's
control, and thus in a morally just world these countries might well be for-
given their debts. However, in our present world it is unlikely that Western
bankers and governments will drop all their claims for repayment, no matter how severe the cost to debtor countries in terms of health and educational facilities, communications, environmental protection, and even
human lives,[1] although one can argue that the Third World countries were
sold a bill of goods in the 1970s by Western bankers anxious to recycle
"petrodollars" and by development "experts," who now insist that the
Third World pay the price for their bad advice.

At the same time, the exploitation of natural resources is intensified in
order to finance interest repayments on the debt. Much of this "resource
development" is carried out by foreign-owned businesses, although some
of the benefits go to a rather limited number of nationals. Almost always it
is a "once-off" activity, whether it be creating a nickel mine in the
Dominican Republic or logging a virgin forest in Indonesia, and because to
a large extent it is a forced sale, countries are not realising as much gain
from liquidating their capital as they might under less urgent circumstances.

NATURAL ECOSYSTEMS IN THE THIRD WORLD:
WHAT IS BEING LOST?

The destruction of natural ecosystems through agriculture, urbanisation,
and resource extraction has always been a facet of human progress.
However, until this century it generally took place against a background of
substantial blocks of natural areas which remained intact. What is new in
the present situation is that all the areas comprising major ecosystems may
be destroyed within the next fifty years, and this would result in costs even
higher than those imposed by, for example, dumping toxic wastes into the
ground or the oceans.

I use the term "natural ecosystems" here to refer to those ecosystems
not significantly altered by human intervention. Such human activity as
does occur (such as gathering nuts or fruit, collecting building materials, or
hunting game) does not result in substantial changes in the ecosystem. Any
ecosystem, of course, is undergoing constant change, but on a biological

time-scale measured in centuries or millenia: a plant develops a poison such as caffeine or nicotine to ward off attacks by insect predators, an insect species develops an enzyme which can dispose of this poison and thus allows it to eat the plant. Out of these processes of adaptation come countless substances which we have found beneficial. "Conservation" involves maintaining a sufficient amount of each natural ecosystem so that these processes of evolution can continue undisturbed. Conservation also entails using those parts of the world that we do alter in ways that will allow future generations to continue to use them. In short, conservation is about foreclosing the fewest possible options for future generations.

Among the natural ecosystems being destroyed today through logging, clearing for agriculture, pollution and drainage, tropical moist forests (or "rainforests") are the most significant. These forests contain at least half the species of living organisms on our planet, as well as the greatest quantity of living material, or biomass, per unit of space. Estimates by Norman Myers on the basis of data from the early 1980s suggest that just under 200,000 km^2 a year were being destroyed or grossly disrupted[2]; more recent data suggest that the rate of destruction has increased sharply, with Brazilian Amazonia alone losing 125,000 km^2 in both 1987 and 1988.[3] Even at the slower rate, all the world's remaining eight million km^2 of tropical forest would have disappeared by the year 2035 at the latest, and lowland forests, which are most accessible for logging, would be gone much sooner.

The most obvious costs of this destruction are borne by the people who rely on the forests for their homes and livelihoods; and the world economy loses products such as rubber, Brazil nuts, and rattan. Loss of large blocks of forest means a 50 percent reduction in rainfall around and within them. The montane forests hold soil and water, thus providing year-round water supplies, and protection against landslides and the silting of hydro-electric and irrigation dams. These services are considered to be "free," but there is a substantial economic cost if any of them are taken away. For example, in Honduras the unit cost of providing drinking water for the capital from a protected forest source was calculated at 0.04 the cost of providing water from a deforested watershed.[4]

But the more serious consequences of losing these forests will not arise until well into the future, and are payable by people far removed from the scene of destruction. In order to cope with the diverse predators and pathogens that could destroy them, tropical plants protect themselves by means of an astounding range of genetic adaptations. Substances such as curare, the Amazonian hunters' poison now widely used in surgery as a relaxant, and vincristine, derived from the rosy periwinkle of Madagascar and which has vastly improved the survival chances of children suffering from leukemia, are widely known examples of the pharmaceutical drugs which have already been discovered in this cauldron of life. There are potentially hundreds, if not thousands of such substances in the tropical forests—if we can find them before they are wiped out.[5] Similarly, there is an immense potential range of industrial substances, from petrol substitutes to gums and rubbers to canes and edible oils.[6] With the developments of modern biotechnology, the possibility of incorporating genes that provide resistance to plant diseases (which, of course, are also constantly evolving ways to overcome the plants' resistance) has greatly increased; but the genetic material is needed in order to accomplish these "miracles." This particular cost of the destruction of tropical rainforest will be borne, therefore, by future generations throughout the world in the form of more costly or less diversified foods and industrial materials, as well as illnesses and deaths that might have been prevented. Since the wealthier and more technologically advanced countries of the North would be the first to benefit from this genetic pool, they should be prepared to pay for its survival.

A further cost of tropical deforestation may be a change in global weather patterns and climate, extending to the major food-growing zones of the northern hemisphere. One source of change could be the increased albedo (reflection of the sun's energy from the Earth's surface) as forest is transformed into cropland or pasture; this could lead to a weakening of the tropical heat engine which affects air circulation patterns as far north as the mid-latitudes of Canada and the Soviet Union, and in particular to decreased rainfall in the world's major grain belts.[7] But the albedo effect is minor compared to the potential problems arising from the "greenhouse effect": carbon dioxide and other gases trap increased amounts of the sun's energy in the atmosphere, with the resulting increase in world temperatures probably producing inland droughts and rising sea levels, as well as other unpredictable effects. The replacement of tropical forests by the much lower biomass of farm crops and secondary growth has been estimated to release at least two billion tonnes of carbon (in the form of carbon dioxide) into the atmosphere each year, and while this is less than the five billion tonnes released world-wide each year by the burning of fossil fuels, it still approximately equals the 2.3 billion tonnes net annual increase of atmospheric carbon that has been measured.[8] In other words, bringing a total halt to tropical forest destruction (or halving the consumption of fossil fuels) would be enough to reduce the total output of carbon dioxide to a level that could be absorbed by the earth's "carbon sinks."

There are, in short, strong motivations of self-interest that ought to lead the Western industrial states to support effective conservation measures. Even at that supremely self-satisfied gathering of major Western political leaders, the 1988 economic summit in Toronto, Chancellor Helmut Kohl of Germany proposed that they ought to reward developing countries that protected their forests by forgiving some of their debts,[9] although there was no mention of this proposal in the final communiqué by all the leaders.

But while protection of tropical ecosystems may be of interest to the North, which already has largely devastated its own natural ecosystems, what do Third World countries stand to gain? On the face of it, there would seem to be a great deal of logic in the "conventional wisdom" that these ecosystems contain the main resources they possess, such as timber, hydro-electric power, fertile land for agriculture, and so on, and that they should follow the same path as the already rich nations by exploiting these resources on a once-off basis to build up their wealth, which they could then gradually channel into other more industrial activities.

There are several good reasons why the protection of these ecosystems would be more beneficial to Third World countries than their destruction. First, the noneconomic benefits of conservation are significant to many indigenous peoples, who find sacred or spiritual qualities in their natural surroundings. Although these people generally hold only marginal political power within their states, their desire to conserve these areas will continue to gain more and more support, even if for more aesthetic and recreational reasons, from an increasingly numerous and prosperous urban middle class, as one can already see happening in such newly industrialising countries as Malaysia. Nigel Collar has argued persuasively that to wipe out these ecosystems and the species in them is to curtail the freedom of individuals, by denying them the opportunity to enjoy the existence of such species in the future[10]; and on a more materialistic level, a loss of ecosystems cuts down future options for all human activities, economic as well as social.

Second, while volcanic and floodplain soils are capable of sustaining agriculture for centuries, the majority of tropical soils are not. Most forest clearing in Amazonia and in Africa can provide only a few years of cleared-land farming before the farmers are forced to move on. Sustainable farming in single locations involves getting farmers to adopt often labour-intensive methods, such as the "matengo pit" system of alternating pits to catch water and heaped-up soil in order to grow plants on dry hillsides,[11] or the "chinampas" system of agroforestry in tropical moist forests,[12] whose benefits may not be apparent until there is no new land to clear.

Finally, the economic argument that exploiting one's natural resources to the full will provide the wealth to finance more technological development depends on some rather shaky assumptions. First, it assumes that somewhere there are the raw materials available to support this industrialisation, and in particular, adequate food supplies that a country can import. Second, it assumes either that the country will be able to sell its industrial products on world markets, or else that it has a big enough domestic market to absorb the increasing range of products from its industrialisation. Third, it assumes that the money it can get from its present exploitation of natural resources is in fact sufficient to finance this industrialisation.

The case for conservation, then, involves both the positive arguments that it offers long-term sustainable economic benefits and a range of noneconomic benefits; and a negative one—that the alternative to exploiting one's natural ecosystems on a one-shot basis in order to build up financing for more advanced technological development is a mirage. The struggle to protect natural ecosystems continues to be an uphill battle, which leads to the question: who benefits from their destruction, and in what ways?

THE POLITICS OF CONSERVATION: THE LOCAL ARENA

A clear answer is suggested by examining who benefits from such ecologically destructive "development" activities such as the current logging practices in Southeast Asia and Africa, and the clearing of forest for settlement and ranching projects in Brazil. In logging, while some local people are employed to fell and haul logs, the bulk of the money goes to the timber concessionaires and their overseas backers; and since raw logs are still shipped overseas, much of the final value, added through processing, goes to Japanese and other overseas industries.[13] In Brazil, poor settlers in Amazonia have cleared their patch of land, discovered in two or three years that it would not yield a living, sold to large-scale speculators and moved on to try elsewhere, conveniently taking the pressure for land reform off their regions of origin. In short, the major benefits from development activities tend to go to an already affluent group and to companies from the industrialised states. Some poorer citizens may improve their situation, such as the Javanese resettled as a result of Indonesia's transmigration scheme, but for many settlers the gains are only short-term and the local inhabitants are almost invariably left worse off by the destruction of their homeland. Many of these activities give the appearance of benefiting the poor and the landless, but it is an illusion.

Even when they are not benefiting in financial terms from the exploitation of natural ecosystems, the privileged sectors of society are generally very much aware that the alternative to allowing the poor to exploit these areas is to permit major land reforms. It is therefore only to be expected that their willingness to support the conservation of these areas will generally be limited. Add to this the fact that they can benefit as *compradors* in the logging, mining, and other exploitative activities undertaken by foreign companies, and one sees a very potent source of opposition to any large-scale conservation effort.[14]

Beyond these economic pressures favouring the quick exploitation of natural resources, Third World political leaders generally share with their counterparts in the North the view that natural ecosystems simply represent "free" resources to be exploited as expeditiously as possible, and that the best measure of well-being for a people is the extent to which it can transform these resources into material goods for consumption without limit. Few leaders yet seem ready to accept the view of the Prime Minister of Norway, Harlem Brundtland, or President Oscar Arias of Costa Rica, that "growth" and "conservation" need not be conflicting goals, but can indeed be complementary ones.[15] Third World leaders, whether popularly based or self-appointed, tend to face less domestic pressure than their Northern counterparts to consider environmental alternatives because their environmental movements generally are relatively weaker; they also are under stronger pressure to achieve economic development because of population growth, demands for land, and desire for more material wealth, in addition to the demands of their creditors.

Unfortunately, those who benefit from the protection of natural areas such as parks or reserves are not necessarily those who lose out under development schemes. I have already noted that one important long-term benefit of conserving Third World natural ecosystems—the preservation of a diversity of genetic resources—will probably be most fully exploited by the more technologically advanced societies. Also, both scientific researchers and tourists visiting reserves and parks are likely to come from the more affluent countries (although we should note that the results of some of this research will trickle down to the local population). Within the country which is setting aside protected areas, the people most likely to visit are the members of the middle class, a pattern already clearly established in India and to a lesser extent in Latin America. The services provided for visitors have generally been organised by large outside operators, although there are a few parks where local people manage the concessions, as in Amboseli Park, Kenya.[16] The local inhabitants, in fact, have all too frequently been pushed aside or ignored when a reserve has been established, with the result that the reserve begins to resemble an armed fortress fending off the outside world.[17] Alternatively, where the central government operates the facilities, collects entrance fees, and generally takes any revenue arising from conservation activities, little monetary benefit comes back to either the park or the local people.

A reserve existing in a sea of local hostility is not likely to survive for long, especially if the central government wishes to gain popularity among the local populace. There is another biological reason for involving the local people in the maintenance of reserves. Few countries can set aside the blocks of 1,000 km^2 that many biologists consider desirable for the long-term survival of an ecosystem as complex as a tropical rainforest.[18] This does not necessarily mean that there will be massive impoverishment of the biota if primary forests are reduced to a series of smaller fragments; a number of studies[19] suggest that a modest primary forest core surrounded by a larger buffer which provides suitable habitat for larger or more sparsely distributed species should probably not lose too many species, provided that the buffer zone is only utilised in relatively low-impact ways (such as controlled hunting and selective logging). Such an arrangement is being tested in Bolivia's Beni World Biosphere Reserve, and also in the Korup Park in Cameroon. This approach of allowing the local human inhabitants to carry out a range of monitored activities within a protected area offers two key benefits: it expands the area in which a natural ecosystem can continue to function, with all that this implies for the maintenance of species and genetic diversity; and it does not threaten the lifestyles of the local inhabitants.

CONSERVATION: THE INTERNATIONAL DIMENSION

Even if a national political leader were willing to confront both his own national business class and powerful foreign corporations by seeking to protect key portions of ecosystems, he would have other problems to overcome. The most pressing problem would be debt relief: how could the money be found to meet the annual interest payments? This is where the debt crisis has temporarily opened a "window of opportunity" for some conservation measures. While such measures can only make a small dent in the total debt problem (even Rubinoff's grand scheme of compensation for a world-wide system of tropical forest reserves involved only some $3 billion a year, less than one-fiftieth of the total annual debt service bill),[20] they do offer a mutually face-saving compromise on the debt issue, while providing a substantial benefit in terms of conservation. Some purists will object that since the debts themselves were illegitmately foisted on the Third World, any action which legitimates them ought to be repudiated (just as hard-liners among the banking fraternity dismiss any action which appears to "forgive" debtors), but it seems to me unrealistic to expect that creditor governments and private institutions will ever accept a total repudiation of these debts, and thus it would be sensible to seek a myriad of modest actions that could be undertaken relatively quickly, and that could contribute to an overall reduction of the debt burden.

Among conservation nongovernmental organisations (NGOs) in the West, "debt-for-conservation" swaps have attracted wide attention. The sale by creditor banks of debts at a discount in the secondary market has allowed Western conservation NGOs to buy up some of the debts, and then arrange to write off the debt in exchange for the debtor country putting some local currency (and effort) into conservation. Three widely publicised agreements were reached in 1987. In Bolivia, the government had created the Beni Biological Reserve of 134,000 hectares in 1982, but lacked the funds to develop and safeguard it effectively. Seeking the resources to make the reserve effective, a US foundation, Conservation International, in 1987 acquired a Bolivian debt of $650,000, discounted to $100,000, from a Swiss bank. Conservation International then cancelled the $650,000 debt, and in exchange the Bolivian government set up a zone of 1.4 million hectares around the reserve and a $250,000 endowment, to be managed by a Bolivian foundation, and asked Conservation International to advise on the management of the reserve for the next five years. Steps are currently under way to draw up a management plan which will involve the local people in the buffer zone around the reserve.[21] In Costa Rica and Ecuador somewhat different arrangements were made with World Wildlife Fund-US and the Nature Conservancy. These NGOs acquired debts at a heavy discount, and cancelled them in return for long-term local currency bonds issued by the governments concerned, in order to finance conservation activities. In each of these cases, the specific scheme arose out of a broad commitment by the national government to protect the area concerned, and the implementation arrangements are under the control of a locally based foundation: this has so far succeeded in deflecting the charge that foreigners are forcing the country to do what they want. Other similar arrangements are under nego-tiation, aided by a US Internal Revenue Service ruling which allows US banks to claim as a tax deduction the value given by the debtor country in its own currency to the conservation NGO for the debt instrument, even though it had sold the instrument to the NGO for a good deal less.[22]

Limited in scope though they are, these arrangements have enabled governments to protect critical areas to which they might not otherwise have been able to allocate resources. The fact that such areas have been operated through national conservation foundations and have been fitted within the context of overall government conservation objectives has reduced the perception that foreigners are dictating the government's prior-ities.[23] Unlike debt-for-equity swaps, they do not give ownership of a coun-try's resources to a foreign entity. However, it remains to be seen whether such schemes could be worked in a situation where powerful business interests or other government departments have different goals, such as, for example, Peru's Manu Park or parts of Sumatra or Irian Jaya in Indonesia. It is also cause for concern that so far the emphasis has been on the immediate task of setting aside and protecting specific areas; yet if these areas are to avoid biological isolation and continual encroachment, the people living around them must be provided with access to alternative land, fuelwood, and other resources. This could be achieved through some kind of sustain-able agroforestry on lands already altered by human activity, but would be both costly and time-consuming.

Private arrangements between NGOs and Third World countries make only a very small impact on the two problems of ecosystem destruction and debt payments. For example, the Costa Rican scheme involves some $5.4 million of debt, and the country has put a limit of $50 million on all such schemes whereas it owes a total of $4 billion. As far as conservation is con-cerned, the total need is equally beyond the capabilities of the private NGOs. To protect only 10 percent of the world's tropical forests would involve creating some 800 reserves of 1,000 km^2 each, and even if such blocks could be found, the countries concerned might plausibly argue that selling the timber in one such reserve could earn them $5–10 billion.[24]

The financing for conservation on a scale that will match these poten-tial earnings and thus protect viable portions of the tropical world's natural ecosystems will have to come through schemes either backed by or financed directly by governments. The use of debt swaps here raises a number of much greater difficulties, beginning with the willingness of Western governments to fund such actions (which will require a major lobbying effort by their NGOs). The World Bank and the International Monetary Fund (IMF) say that they are at present precluded by their charters from "forgiving" debts through such arrangements, although lobbying is under way in the USA and elsewhere to change these rules.

From a Third World perspective, the fact that Western governments have the power to exert greater pressure on them than that of Western NGOs means that the danger of their priorities being set by outsiders is increased. To be sure, this is already being done on a far larger scale through the IMF, but this hardly justifies accepting what could easily be seen as yet another form of neocolonialism. Then too, there is the question of whether Western governments would try to pass off debt-for-conservation swaps as an alternative to more fundamental changes in the international economy, or use them to justify curtailing aid programs, in which case there would be no new money coming into the Third World.

Third World NGOs also have further justifiable concerns: whether the government in question would in fact involve local people in any conservation arrangements, and more broadly, who within the country would reap what kind of benefits from the deal; what type of control the government might be able to exercise over the activities of the NGO as part of its monitoring of the arrangements; and whether the government would use this revenue to justify cutting back other funding for conservation programs. There is also considerable concern that massive plans worked out by Western and Third World governments acting in concert are likely to be aimed at further exploitation of natural areas rather than at their protection. The major example of such a scheme, the Tropical Forest Action Plan (backed by the World Bank) is sufficiently ambiguous in its goals to have led the NGOs concerned to believe that it will simply commercialise forests in ways that reduce poor peoples' access to them, and turn primary forests into plantations.[25]

Finally, for both governments and NGOs there is the moral question underlying any attempt at long-term conservation while short-run needs remain unfulfilled. As one Latin American conservationist explained: "The banks are asking us to put aside land for the future, while people are dying of hunger and ill health." The only answer to this, he suggested, was to ensure that conservation was carried out in ways that did provide benefits for people, and to make clear to people the nature of these benefits.[26]

Despite these cautions, Third World countries concerned about their long-term self-interest would do well to examine such arrangements with institutions from the North, both private NGOs and also government agencies. The value of biological reserves—particularly tropical rainforests—can only increase as our need for, and our ability to use, genetic materials grows. There is a sharpening awareness, among the public and even among politicians in the West, of the importance of these genetic reservoirs as well as of the potential climatic impact resulting from the destruction of tropical forests. Such awareness gives Third World states an opportunity to obtain wealth from these areas without necessarily cutting them down and selling them to the industrialised states. Provided that they also bargain for the financing to establish alternative ways of living on the land for their people, Third World states *can* have their forests and live off them too, for a price a good deal lower than they will have to pay once they have exhausted them by present methods of exploitation.

It can be objected that debt swaps of any sort tacitly grant the legitimacy of the Third World's debts, and therefore should be totally shunned. I suggested above that such a view is unrealistic, and in any case, even if there were some eventual possibility of achieving a full repudiation of these debts, the threat to natural ecosystems is severe enough that action needs to be taken even at the cost of principles. (I could draw a parallel here to the readiness of African front-line states to buy food from South Africa when faced with famine.)

Many people in both the North and the South now recognise that the contribution of tropical ecosystems to the welfare of mankind is so great that everyone ought to contribute to their survival. With sufficient prodding from their own NGOs, Third World governments can press for financial support, in order to help them to protect major ecosystems from further damage; and they can certainly expect support in this demand from Northern NGOs. Since most states can be moved to act when their own well-being is threatened, the present situation provides a promising opportunity for Third World governments to seek an improvement on both their environmental and economic front.

NOTES

1. Even such an apolitical body as UNICEF has charged that the deaths of at least 500,000 children in 1988 could be attributed to the cuts in health care forced by countries' struggles to pay their foreign debt charges. *Globe and Mail* (Toronto), December 21, 1988.
2. N. Myers, "Tropical Deforestation and a Mega-extinction Spasm," in M. Soulé, ed., *Conservation Biology: The Science of Scarcity and Diversity* (Sunderland, Mass.: Sinauer Associates, 1986), p. 399. See also N. Guppy, "Tropical Deforestation: A Global View," *Foreign Affairs*, 2, 4 (Spring 1984): 929.
3. *Guardian Weekly* (London) October 30, 1988.
4. C. Queseda Mateo, "La Tigra National Park: A Source of Concern," *IUCN Bulletin*, 18, 10–12 (October–December 1987): 14.
5. See N. Myers, *The Primary Source: Tropical Forests and Our Future* (New York: W. W. Norton, 1985), pp. 210–23.

6. Ibid. pp. 226–59.
7. For differing views in this debate, see C. Sagan et al., "Anthropogenic Albedo Changes and the Earth's Climate," *Science*, 206 (1979): 1363–68, and G. L. Potter et al., "Albedo Change by Man: Test of Climatic Effects," *Nature*, 291, (7, May 1981): 47–49.
8. G. M. Woodwell, "The Carbon Dioxide Question," *Scientific American*, 238, 1 (January 1978): 37.
9. *Globe and Mail* (Toronto) June 20, 1988.
10. N. J. Collar, "Species Are a Measure of Man's Freedom: Reflections after Writing a Red Data Book on African Birds," *Oryx*, 20 (1986): 18.
11. R. Dumont and M. F. Mottin, *Stranglehold on Africa* (London: André Deutsch, 1983), p. 151.
12. J. D. Nations and D. I. Komer, "Central America's Tropical Rainforests: Positive Steps for Survival," *Ambio*, 12, 5 (1983): 232–38.
13. Data in a detailed study of Malaysia's industry indicate that more than three-quarters of the sawlogs are exported unprocessed. See R. Kumar, *The Forest Resources of Malaysia*, (Singapore: Oxford University Press, 1986), pp. 91, 100. He also notes that while it contributes more than 5 percent of GDP, the forest industry employs less than 3 percent of the labour force, and most of that is in saw-milling and other processing activities (pp. 9, 154).
14. The conflicts in Brazil between Indians, rubber tappers, and others who depend upon or live in the Amazonian forest, and the large ranchers who wish to clear it, are a case in point. See, for example, *International Wildlife*, (July–August 1988): 24–28. In fairness, we should note that a few large companies, such as the Brazilian mining company CVRD and the Sabah Foundation in Malaysia, have done excellent conservation work—but they are exceptional.
15. For Gro Brundtland's views, see H. Brundtland, *Our Common Future* (New York: Oxford University Press, 1987) (hereafter *Brundtland Report*).
16. D. Western, "Amboseli National Park: Enlisting Landowners to Conserve Migratory Wildlife," *Ambio*, 11 (1982): 302–308.
17. For examples from Africa, see D. Turton, "The Mursi and National Park Development," and R. H. V. Bell, "Conservation with a Human Face: Conflict and Reconciliation in African Land Use Planning," both in D. Anderson & R. Grove, eds., *Conservation in Africa* (Cambridge: Cambridge University Press, 1987); also S. Oldfield, ed., *Buffer Zone Management in Tropical Moist Forests: Case Studies and Guidelines* (Gland, Switzerland: IUCN Tropical Forest Programme, 1988), p. 16.
18. I. Rubinoff, "A Strategy for Preserving Tropical Rainforests," *Ambio*, 12, 5 (1983): 255–58.
19. For example, A. D. Johns, "Selective Logging and Wildlife Conservation in Tropical Rainforest: Problems and Recommendations," *Biological Conservation*, 31 (1985): 355–75.
20. I. Rubinoff, "A Strategy for Preserving Tropical Rainforests," 257–58.
21. For details of this and other debt swaps, see B. Bramble, "How Debt Can Be Swapped for Trees," Washington D.C.: US National Wildlife Federation, unpublished paper, May 1988; and for a more general examination, see her "The Debt Crisis: The Opportunities," *Ecologist*, 17, 4–5 (1987): 192–99.
22. US Internal Revenue Service, *Advance Ruling 87–124*, November 12, 1987.

23. Various Latin American delegates at the International Union for the Conservation of Nature General Assembly in Costa Rica, February 1988, told me that there was surprisingly little objection in their countries to the debt-for-nature swap approach; a few intellectuals thought Latin Americans should be undertaking these measures themselves without outside help, but there was little objection to the idea of conserving these areas.

24. For example, the Danum Valley reserve of the Sabah Foundation contains an estimated $750 million worth of timber in its 9,300 hectares, or about $8 million per km^2, a figure in line with other Asian dipterocarp forests. African primary forests would be worth about the same, while Amazonian ones would be worth somewhat less.

25. The TFAP is described in *Tropical Forests: A Call for Action*, 3 volumes, Washington D.C.: World Resources Institute, 1985. For critiques, see especially V. Shiva, "Forestry Myths and the World Bank: A Critical Review of *Tropical Forests: A Call for Action*," *Ecologist*, 17, 4–5 (July–November 1987): 142–49; M. Renner, "A Critical Review of *Tropical Forests: A Call for Action*," ibid. p. 150; and various letters in ibid. 18, 1 (1988): 35–40.

26. Eric Cardich Briceño of Peru, at IUCN General Assembly, San José, Costa Rica, February 3, 1988.

33

Beyond Capitalism and Socialism in Africa

Richard L. Sklar

Ideological conflict between capitalism and socialism is more than 150 years old in the industrial countries of Europe and North America. Its gradual extension to other parts of the world during the twentieth century has entailed a basic alteration of the terms of debate. Within the leading industrial countries, partisans have debated both the economic merits of privately owned productive capital, and the justice of profit-taking as a right of such ownership. In socialist thought, "social justice" has meant that the whole product of labour belongs to those who actually produce it; hence its value should be realised by the producers themselves, either individually, or collectively through public institutions. On that basis, socialists have promised to construct an efficient, humane, and just social order. With equal conviction, proponents of capitalism hold that no alternative economic system produces as large a volume of goods, jobs, and other material benefits for as high a percentage of the population; that social inequality is inevitable, regardless of the property system in effect or the organisation of economic production; and that justice, in any case, is always individual, never "social."

With the extension of this debate to a far wider world, consisting mainly of societies that are late-comers to industrialisation, the question of a "just" distribution of wealth has been overshadowed by the urgent need for its creation in countries that are relatively poor. To be sure, an extreme maldistribution of national wealth is always an economic liability, as well as a moral blight; for those who live in abject poverty contribute minimally to their country's capacity to produce wealth for all. Still, the issue of extremely unequal economic development on a world scale is far more

Professor of Political Science, University of California, Los Angeles. The author is grateful to Geoffrey Bergen for his expert research assistance.
From *The Journal of Modern African Studies*, 26 (March) 1 (1988), pp. 1–21. Reprinted with the permission of Cambridge University Press.

salient in ideological discourse today than any question of redistribution within individual nation-states, regardless of philosophical debates that rage around the concept of social justice.

In Africa, the poorest continental region of the world, capitalism has been associated with the humbling experience of alien domination. In the European settler states of Eastern, Central, and Southern Africa, black Africans were driven from their lands and compelled by despotic forms of rule to supply cheap labour for a white capitalist master-class. Elsewhere, as in the "colonial estates" of Western Africa, "indirect" forms of rule were relied upon to provide cheap labour for the colonial business system.[1] In the struggle against colonial rule, ambivalence toward capitalism has been the hallmark of every nationalist movement in Africa, including both black and white nationalism in South Africa. On the one hand, egalitarian ideologies were virtually irresistible because they justified the claims of subject nations and races. On the other hand, national and racial freedom often appeared to involve the conquest of economic power by capitalist means. The names of Nnamdi Azikiwe, Jomo Kenyatta, and D. F. Malan evoke the careers of radical nationalists who became proponents of capitalism when they perceived that socialistic policies were incompatible with the drive for national economic strength in their respective countries.

Three decades of African independence have all but disqualified textbook socialism as an economic strategy for Africa. The failures of collectivism and economic statism in Congo-Brazzaville, Guinea, Tanzania, and elsewhere, have been noted and absorbed by policymakers in avowedly socialist régimes from Algeria to Zimbabwe.[2] Following the example of Deng Xiaoping, socialist leaders and thinkers in many Third World countries now acknowledge the importance of a free-market system, private investment, and entrepreneurship during the early stages of economic development. The economic success stories of South Korea, Brazil, Côte d'Ivoire and, potentially, Kenya,[3] are associated with the repudiation of socialism. In a bygone era, communist régimes were able to accelerate the pace of industrialisation by investing large amounts of capital extracted ruthlessly from the intensified labour of rural producers—the "internal colony." That form of exploitation has been rendered obsolete for purposes of economic development by the effects of exponential population growth in the Third World, and the ever rising costs of essential imports. It is no longer possible to squeeze nearly enough "surplus" production out of agriculture to feed the urban population and defray the costs of imported fuel, chemicals, and machinery, not to mention the service charges for external debts. Furthermore, agricultural collectivisation as a strategy for economic development in Africa can be expected to founder on the rocks of rural resistance.[4] African socialists today have no useful socialist models of high economic achievement for Third World countries in the late twentieth century.

Yet socialism in Africa persists with vigour as a political movement and philosophy of social protest. Nearly 40 percent of all African states are governed by leaders of political parties that are at least formally dedicated to the establishment of socialism.[5] However, the issue of capitalism versus socialism is no more relevant to the pattern of international relations than it is to the problem of economic development. For example, in the turbulent Horn of Africa, Marxist-Leninist Ethiopia's only reliable ally is capitalist Kenya, while its sworn enemies include secessionists in Eritrea and irredentists in Somalia led by Marxist-Leninists. Similarly, in West Africa, the Marxist-Leninist rulers of Benin are much closer to the capitalist rulers of Togo than to the "revolutionary" leaders of Burkina Faso. In two cases, Angola and Ethiopia, the persistence of doctrinaire Marxism-Leninism as an official ideology can be partly explained as a consequence of each régime's dependence for its survival on military assistance from the Soviet Union. In Angola and six other avowedly Marxist-Leninist régimes—Benin, Congo, Madagascar, Mozambique, Somalia, and Zimbabwe—the official ideology is little more than a cloak of legitimation for the ruling party. Dissidents in those countries are not free to question the system of rule, but they are free to espouse unorthodox and pragmatic economic strategies. Outside of Ethiopia, African intellectuals in the self-styled Marxist-Leninist states, like their counterparts in China and Hungary, are even expected to engage in debates on the relative merits of private versus public-sector strategies for development.[6]

In African social thought, capitalism, and socialism coexist as binary concepts implanted during the era of colonial rule and anticolonial struggle. Each can also be reconciled with a partial selection of precolonial economic practices and systems of belief, but neither copes effectively with Africa's postcolonial poverty and relative economic decline. The binary belief system has not been conducive to innovative advances in social theory and organisation.

Each part of the binary system corresponds to a political tendency or movement. Political and social "movements" are metaphorical expressions that signify purposeful combinations of thought and action. The terms "capitalist" and "socialist" identify the elements of an ideological conflict in Africa, and other regions of delayed development. Is it necessary for Africans and other late-starters in the march toward industrialisation to choose between capitalism and socialism? Should theorists of development favour one movement or the other in that great competition?

THE SOCIALIST MOVEMENT

Social movements are abstract objects of thought rather than concrete social realities. Scholars infer their presence from selected combinations of ideas and actions, and they do not otherwise exist as separate or distinct social

realities. For example, in colonial Africa, the emergence of a socialist movement has been inferred from the thought and action of nationalists. In turn,
national independence movements have often been described with reference to events in everyday life.

Insofar as political thought and action have been avowedly socialistic,
scholars have been able to classify and periodise elements of the socialist
movement in specific countries, and for Africa as a whole. At a fairly high
level of generalisation, the subject is divisible into three major thematic categories which are roughly congruent with successive periods of time. For
the purpose of this survey, they shall be identified as ethical, revolutionary,
and democratic socialism.

In opposition to European imperialism, African nationalists often
appealed to the authority of their cultural heritage for moral support.
African social theorists uniformly affirm that African intellectual traditions
elevate the ideals of cooperation and service to the community far above
the value of competition motivated by a desire for individual gain.[7]
Socialism has been widely supported by African intellectuals on the ground
that its adoption would signify the revival of a valued cultural tradition.
Thus did Léopold Sédar Senghor, renowned poet, philosopher, and states-
man of francophone Africa, expound an African mode of socialism, based
on the communal traditions and spiritual heritage of the African people.
His intellectual counterpart in anglophone Africa, Julius Nyerere, has
argued that Africa's socialist future should and will restore the humane values of an idealised communitarian past, in which the social order vouch-
safed dignity to all and guaranteed the satisfaction of basic human needs.[8]
However, the political careers of Senghor and Nyerere also show that ethical socialism is not proof against political paternalism and the denial of
democratic rights. In Senegal, Senghor presided over a relatively liberal oligarchy that permitted dissent within narrowly defined limits. In Tanzania,
Nyerere's one-party state has been faulted for its frequent resort to preventive detention, regimentation of trade unions, intolerance of dissent, and
other coercive public policies.[9]

Revolutionary socialism in the continent connotes the application of
Marxism—mainly its sociological theory—to African social problems.
Unlike ethical socialists, who believe that it would be possible to build
modern socialist societies on traditionalist moral foundations, revolutionaries contend that class struggles will be unavoidable. As a rule, they set store
by Leninist tenets, including the notion of a vanguard party (presumed to
represent the real interests of working people), and a preoccupation with
the alleged menace of capitalist imperialism. A transition from ethical to
revolutionary socialism is evident in the thought of Kwame Nkrumah,
whose last published essays include polemics against "two myths," namely
"African socialism" as a distinct social form, and the notion of a "third

world" that would not have to choose between the rival worlds of capitalism and socialism.[10]

Nkrumah's contribution to revolutionary socialism in Africa—a by-product of national and personal tragedy—should be coupled with that of Amílcar Cabral, whose revolutionary realism is justly acclaimed.[11] His famous challenge to the postcolonial *petite-bourgeoisie*-in-power—would they be willing to commit "suicide as a class" in order to be "reborn" as a class of revolutionary workers?[12]—strongly suggests the impossibility of socialist revolution in countries which lack sturdy industrial foundations. Cabral's deeply pessimistic analysis was confirmed by his own assassination in 1973 (the result of a conspiracy within his party), and by the opportunism of subsequent leaders in Guinea-Bissau. Since his death, revolutionary socialism in Africa has reappeared in the anti-apartheid doctrine of racial capitalism.

In South African history, capitalism and racism are inextricably related. Racial capitalism is a revolutionary idea that affirms the essential identity of class struggle and the struggle for racial liberation. Its primary political significance in South Africa lies in the reconciliation, that it both foretells and fosters, of revolutionary Marxism with the racial nationalist philosophy of black consciousness. In 1978, the Azanian People's Organisation (Azapo) was created to pursue the goals of several black consciousness organisations which had been banned the year before. Azapo's 1983 manifesto begins thus:

> Our struggle for national liberation is directed against the historically evolved system of racism and capitalism which holds the people of Azania in bondage for the benefit of the small minority of the population, i.e., the capitalists and their allies, the white workers and the reactionary sections of the middle class.[13]

The term "racial capitalism" has also been used by various Marxists who allege that black consciousness thought is a form of racial chauvinism. Such persons gravitate toward the broadly based and multi- or nonracial African National Congress (A.N.C.). However, most political thinkers associated with the A.N.C. are wary of the racial-capitalism concept because it is widely understood to imply the goal of a specifically socialist revolution. Although the A.N.C. is closely allied with the South African Communist Party, it is also a nondoctrinaire liberation movement, and takes care to avoid ideological tags, such as racial capitalism, that would compromise its multiclass posture by too much of a tilt to the side of class struggle. In response to leftist criticism, the A.N.C.'s director of public information has declared: "The ANC is not a socialist party. It has never pretended to be one, it has never said it was, and it is not trying to be. It will not become one by decree or for the purpose of pleasing its 'left' critics."[14] In fact, there is broad agreement among astute analysts of South African politics that majority rule with A.N.C. leadership would not necessarily entail a socialist revolution.[15]

Democratic socialism unites the ideal of social justice with that of government by the people. The latter ideal is seriously compromised when either traditionalists or vanguard élitists take power. Nyerere's *ujamaa* socialist orthodoxy can stultify the nonconformist mind just as surely as Leninist orthodoxy. Democratic socialists maintain that popular government is inseparable from the protection of individual political rights. With liberals, they guard against the evils that accompany statist forms of public ownership and control, while they seek nonstatist alternatives through community organisation and voluntary cooperation.

Where in Africa has a genuine movement for democratic socialism taken shape as an alternative to both capitalism and dictatorship? Senegal merits consideration, given the democratic practice of its avowedly socialist ruling party. However, Senegal today is securely capitalist; socialist objectives are merely incidental to public policies in that country. Meanwhile, potentially powerful movements for democratic socialism are discernible in the complex societies of Nigeria and South Africa.

In 1992, the 32nd year-to-be of its history as a sovereign state, Nigeria will be restored to civilian rule for the second successive time. Few doubt the intention of Nigeria's caretaker-military government to redeem its pledge of withdrawal from political office. Indeed, this process has already begun with (1) the report of an appointed study commission (Political Bureau) to the Armed Forces Ruling Council, and (2) the subsequent announcement by the President, Major-General Ibrahim Babangida, of a phased transition, beginning with local government elections in 1987, and culminating in federal legislative and presidential elections in 1992.

The Political Bureau's report, 14 months in preparation, was intended to initiate a public debate on the future of political life in Nigeria. Its numerous recommendations range from the choice of social goals and values to the construction of political institutions, reform of the economy, and reorganisation of the territorial system.[16] A remarkable feature of the report is its unequivocal endorsement of socialism for selection as the official "national philosophy." Preference for a democratic form of socialism is manifest in the espousal of a comprehensive bill of political rights, its fidelity to the federal form of constitutional government, and its rejection of any type of civilian-military "dyarchy," or shared rule. However, the democratic integrity of this socialist blueprint is marred by its recommendation of a mandatory two-party system, and the further stipulation that each of the recognised political parties would be required to endorse the "national philosophy." In democratic thought and practice, the link between freedom of expression and the freedom of citizens to form political parties is indissoluble. Failure to respect the principle of that relationship does not bode well for democratic socialism in Nigeria. In fact, the Armed Forces Ruling Council subsequently accepted the two-party recommendation without reference to the proposed national policy of socialism.[17]

Whatever the outcome of the national debate, now in progress, the report of the Political Bureau does reflect an undoubted partiality for socialism among Nigerian intellectuals. In Nigeria, as elsewhere, the strength of socialism as a creed for intellectuals varies directly with the growth of capitalism and its baneful side effects, principally urban poverty, high unemployment, and profiteering at the public expense. With socialist conviction, the Political Bureau advocates nationalisation of the entire oil industry and other "commanding heights" of the economy:

> public utilities; enterprises which require heavy capital expenditure; enterprises and property which are tied up with the political integrity and security of the nation and other monopoly-type enterprises which generate imperfection in the market and prevent resources from being put to their most efficient use such as the distribution of essential commodities.[18]

However, private enterprise would be retained in both agriculture and the small-to-medium-sized business sector.

All told, this avowedly socialistic blueprint envisions the coexistence of capitalist, socialist, and democratic thought and practice. But each of these idea systems would be diluted in the mixture. It could be argued, justly if not persuasively, that the blueprint is neither capitalist, socialist, nor democratic; that its economic orientation is merely statist (rather than truly socialist), while its proposed form of political representation is illiberal. In fairness, however, it should also be observed that the blueprint is genuinely constitutionalist: it would divide the powers of government, and render officials accountable for their actions under the rule of law. Wherever they function, constitutional forms of government open the door to movements for democracy and social justice.

In South Africa, a strong affinity for democratic socialism motivates the rapidly growing, organised black labour movement. The two principal black labour federations—the Congress of South African Trade Unions (C.O.S.A.T.U.) and the National Council of Trade Unions (N.A.C.T.U.)—are clearly so inclined. C.O.S.A.T.U.'s formal endorsement of the 32-year-old Freedom Charter in July 1987 signifies dedication to political democracy, an attachment to the African National Congress in national politics, and support for the belief that mines, banks, and monopoly industries should be publicly owned. In 1986, C.O.S.A.T.U., the A.N.C., and the latter's own trade-union arm issued a joint communiqué to express, *inter alia*, their "common understanding that victory [over the *apartheid* system] must embrace more than formal political democracy."[19] That elliptical phrase could imply a leaning toward socialist measures. C.O.S.A.T.U.'s president has expressed his own belief in both multiparty democracy and "socialism as practiced by the Labour Party in England."[20] Neither C.O.S.A.T.U. nor its rival, N.A.C.T.U. (aligned with Azapo and the black consciousness philosophy), is in the least inclined to relinquish its autonomy of action as a worker's organisation to any political party. Each prides itself on the democratic practice of worker control that has characterised the phenomenal growth of black trade unionism since 1969. Trade union autonomy is a prime marker for the great divide between democratic and Leninist socialism.

THE CAPITALIST MOVEMENT

The phrase "capitalist movement" will seem odd to many of those who readily accept the idea of a socialist, or worker's, movement. Various other movements also pass muster easily in historical and social studies—for example, movements of farmers, teachers, and women. No less familiar are racial, religious, conservative, and reform movements. But the idea of a capitalist movement is rarely suggested and liable to be challenged as a figment of borderline imagination. After all, it will be objected, capitalists constitute "interests" rather than "movements."

However, Martin Sklar has described an irrepressible capitalist movement in the United States of America during the era of "corporate reconstruction."[21] From the vantage point of social history, he observes, capitalists, like workers and farmers, are "people with goals, values, ideas and principles . . . with a way of life to develop, defend and extend."[22] Their objectives and achievements will be caricatured and misunderstood if they are portrayed as disembodied interests, contained and isolated for sterile analysis within the concept of "capital."

In this section, Martin Sklar's concept of a capitalist movement will be used to interpret currents of thought and related actions in support of economic enterprise based on the private ownership of productive property. In view of a common ideological tendency to counterpose private and state enterprise as antithetical activities, let it be said that capitalist movements have never been antagonistic to a supportive rôle for public or state investment and economic management. In its early mercantilist stage, western capitalism justified state direction of the economy as a matter of principle. Ever since, when capitalist movements have been either ascendant or growing in strength and influence, the state has been called upon routinely to undertake economic projects that are needed to foster private enterprise albeit beyond the capacity of profit-seeking private firms to pursue. As Robert Heilbroner has written:

the state foists upon the public the costs of those activities that would result in monetary "losses" if they were carried out by the economic sphere. . . . This socialisation of losses applies to much of the network of canals, railways, highways, and airways that have played an indispensable part in capitalist growth, as well as the provision of literate and socialised work forces through public education programs, the protection of public health and the like.[23]

In every capitalist economy, as Heilbroner observes, "the normal operation of the market system would be unsustainable without the socialising, protecting, and stimulating state activities that further the regime of capital."[24] During the early stages of industrialisation, public management and regulation tends to overshadow the effects of private initiatives regardless of a government's ideological preference. In sub-Saharan Africa today, state enterprise bulks larger in proportion to total economic activity than it does in any other market-economy region of the Third World. The extent of sub-Saharan Africa's economic statism is summarised in a 1986 report of the World Bank thus:

> Public sector employment is half of all modern sector employment, compared with only one-third in Asia. Allowing the country size, public enterprises are more numerous than in most other developing countries, and they engage in a wider array of activities. Public investment accounts for the bulk of investment in the formal sector.[25]

Many analysts of the economic crisis in Africa have targeted the inefficiency and mismanagement of this allegedly "over-extended" public sector as a primary cause of economic stagnation.[26] Consequently, the policy of "privatisation," involving divestiture by the state, has been featured in debates on development. But reform strategies designed to increase public-sector efficiency, may be more practical where natural resource and utility companies are concerned. As A. M. Hawkins has observed:

> It is doubtful whether private sector funding exists in most countries to take over state-owned enterprise. A more promising approach would be to restructure economic policy along market-oriented lines and to revise the guidelines within which public enterprises will operate in the future.[27]

Beyond that kind of residual commitment to state enterprise, and apart from occasional deviant proposals to extend the public sector (*vide* the Nigerian advisory commission's socialistic report of 1987), there does now appear to be a continent-wide consensus on the centrality of private enterprise to African economic recovery and progress. Not since the era of formal decolonisation have political conditions for the emergence of African capitalist movements been as auspicious as they are today. Nor, since that time and with very few exceptions, have political scientists studied African business-interest groups objectively and without pejorative or restrictive categorisation.[28] Hence it is surprisingly difficult to adduce scholarly evidence of capitalist political organisations in black Africa; and without such facts and figures it is impossible to infer the existence of a capitalist movement. However, the insufficiency of scholarly data for propositions that accord with common knowledge should not deter theoretical consideration of their significance. In subjects that are highly liable to ideological distortion, the order of thought often diverges from the order of things. African business movements are not alone in the shadow of scholarly neglect. With several notable exceptions, it is also fair to say that "the political aspects of labor movements [in Africa] have not been deeply researched."[29]

Political research on the capitalist movement in Africa might begin with analyses of the thought of capitalist planners and theoreticians. A starting point could be the pathfinding Conference on the Enabling Environment for Private Sector Contributions to Development held in Nairobi, in October 1986, and attended by some 150 delegates, including African ministers and civil servants, business executives (both African and international), and officials of voluntary development assistance agencies.[30] The opportune concept, "enabling environment," had been proposed by Prince Sadruddin Aga Khan (formerly U.N. High Commissioner for Refugees), spiritual leader of the Ismailis, a Shiite Muslim sect with varied communal, commercial, and educational interests in East Africa.[31] Organised by the Aga Khan Foundation, this conference allowed for the confluence of various currents of African capitalist thought. The main themes and conclusions have been summarised in an insightful report by Goran Hyden, to which this precis is indebted.[32]

Development planners of diverse ideological persuasions now believe that individual initiatives in the private sector are required to arrest and reverse Africa's current economic decline. In their collective view,

> The key to the solution of the current African malaise is a release of the energies of the many million African producers, both men and women. The encouragement of African entrepreneurship is essential. Where indigenous entrepreneurship flourishes and markets develop, it will also become easier to attract foreign capital. Thus, there is a synergy between indigenous and international business.[33]

Hence they advocate movement "toward freer markets and more realistic prices for products, capital, labour, and foreign exchange." In the short run, however, such policies may be expected to impose hardships on poor urban dwellers, which could lead to political unrest. Therefore, it will be necessary "to mitigate the potential negative consequences associated with the shift toward greater reliance on market mechanisms." In this connection, voluntary agencies are designated to assume growing responsibilities for the provision of community services, while the World Bank conducts continent-wide research in support of governmental attempts "to monitor the changing conditions of different socio-economic groups." High points of the capitalist agenda include these items:

- Elimination of price controls in conjunction with measures to increase competition and avoid monopolies and cartels, "whether by parastatals or by private business";
- Gradual reduction of exchange controls balanced by reduced protectionism in the industrial countries;
- Elimination of counterproductive "red tape" in regulatory systems devised by governments for business enterprise;
- Reform of the parastatal sectors, including privatisation as a "tool" and not "as an end in itself";
- Credit facilities and technical assistance for small businesses and farming;
- Product specialisation among countries and other devices to enhance the viability of regional markets.

Several years ago, Crawford Young wrote, with reference to African states, "The capitalist pathway in Africa has numerous followers but few partisans."[34] Today, the spirit of capitalism in Africa is abroad, and away from the shadow of desiccating doubt. It is manifest in the privatisation policies of many governments, the virtual abandonment of socialistic economic strategies by once-doctrinaire régimes (e.g., Benin, Congo, Angola, and Mozambique), the growing emphasis on business management as a subject of study in postsecondary education, a concerted effort to promote the creation of small enterprises in francophone countries,[35] and in many other ways. What twist of irony brings the ruling party of Guinea-Bissau, at its fourth congress, to launch a "second struggle for national liberation" under the banner of incentives for the development of private enterprise? "Twelve years of nationalisation have been the hallmark of the former Portuguese colony, and have left it in a state of almost total collapse."[36] Amílcar Cabral, revolutionary realist, might have changed course more rapidly and with less rhetorical ado.

TRANSCENDENCE

In the "great competition" between capitalism and socialism for influence in Africa, no final decision can be rendered during the current era of extreme disparity between Africa and the industrial countries with respect to wealth, income, scientific knowledge, and overall power in the world. Few sophisticated socialists today rate the "developmental merits" of socialism above those of capitalism; fewer still would dispute the short-term advantages of capitalism for societies at early stages of industrial development. Instead, they argue that socialism is morally superior to an economic system, such as capitalism, that depends upon the domination and exploitation of working people by a privileged class.[37] Socialism persists as an ideological and political movement, regardless of its failures, because capitalism is unalterably identified with social injustice. Personal insecurity, social disorganisation, and urban unemployment are the spectral witnesses of African capitalism from Abidjan to Nairobi.

Still, three decades of trial and error, in Africa and elsewhere in the Third World, have also acquainted social reformers with the pitfalls of socialism. The hardest lesson for socialists to learn is one that Karl Marx taught better than anyone else. Plainly stated, there is no substitute for capital; it is the driving force of economic development. Twentieth-century socialists in capital-scarce countries became statists, not because they had an especially hearty appetite for regulation, but to compensate for shortages of private capital that were either inherited or created by their own policies. Ironically, socialists in the industrialised West, where capital was abundant, subordinated their own thinking to the statist doctrines of socialists in the capital-scarce countries. Hence the ideological confusion of western socialists today, as development theorists from left to right, including many socialists in the capital-scarce countries, become increasingly critical of the doctrines and methods of economic statism.

With the resurgence of development strategies centred on private-sector initiatives, it has become important to distinguish carefully between ideological criticisms of economic statism and those which are practical in their conception. The former disparage state enterprise on the ground that it threatens democracy, either because the state, itself, resists democratisation, or because it becomes an object of acquisitive and rapacious private attention. The latter caution against methods of economic management that are insufficiently productive and result in stagnation. For pragmatists, who seek to reverse Africa's economic decline, strictly moral condemnations of economic statism are quite beside the point.

A second important lesson for socialists, one that cannot, alas, be learned from Marx, is that socialism lacks an adequate theory, or example, of incentives. Before Marx, Robert Owen grappled with the problem in a socialist community by means of education and manipulation of psychic rewards by paternalistic managers. In this century, revolutionary socialists from Trotsky and Stalin to Mao Zedong, Castro, and Sékou Touré have tried to compensate for the weakness of socialist incentives for both workers and managers by resorting to combinations of moral suasion and coercion—poor substitutes for personal motivation. At the executive level, studies of economic management in socialist countries almost invariably reveal its ingrained conservatism. Alec Nove's reflection on the problem is as realistic as it is picturesque: "many managers seek a quiet life, have not the slightest desire, or aptitude, for facing the cold winds of markets or (God forbid!) competition."[38] His counsel for transition from the socialism-we-know to "developmental socialism" includes the maintenance of "a market environment" to stimulate "individual and group initiative."[39]

While socialists need to acknowledge the developmental merits of capitalism, those who favour capitalism ought to be equally candid about the "socialisation of losses" that underlies every development program in the continent. As Richard Sandbrook observes, with reference to African development:

> a range of economic conditions must be fostered by the state. Services that directly facilitate production—roads, railways, ports, airports, electricity, water and telecommunications—is one of these. Essential public services that directly assist production as they promote a skilled, healthy, motivated labour force are also important; these include schools, technical education, public housing, sanitation and facilities for sports and health. The public sector may also intervene directly through subsidy or investment in industries which are essential to expansion of complementary industries but are too risky to attract private investors. Publicly owned steel or transport or cement may sometimes play a significant economic role even if they are not profitable in themselves.
>
> Finally, the state should regulate foreign economic relations in order to maximize the local benefits.[40]

Lest it be imagined that state participation in the development of capitalism is largely confined to background investments in the infrastructure, basic industries, and public services, let us reflect with Sayre Schatz that "capitalist success stories" in Korea, Japan, Mexico, Brazil, and elsewhere were all made possible by state intervention "by way of subsidies, protection, guaranteed markets, and other forms of 'price distortion' in order to create an abundance of profitable investment opportunities."[41] The socialist counterpoint to our previous observation that "there is no substitute for capital" is the incontestable retort that there is no substitute for an actively interventionist state.

To balance the scales of developmental merit, socialists may seek to offset the gravity of their problem with incentives by weighing the deficiencies of capitalism in regard to the well-being of poor people in poor countries. The statistical evidence, regularly presented by the World Bank, is sobering. In 1980, an estimated 780 million people in Third World countries with capitalist economies—between 35 and 40 percent of their total population—

lived in "absolute poverty," defined to mean "a condition of life so characterised by malnutrition, illiteracy and disease as to be beneath any reasonable definition of human decency."[42] In 1984, the World Bank assessed Africa's economic plight thus: "No list of economic or financial statistics can convey the human misery spreading in sub-Saharan Africa." Child mortality was "double the average" for all developing countries, while the estimated number of "severely hungry and malnourished people" in Africa was 100 million.[43]

None of this would persuade proponents of capitalism to concede advantages to socialists on the equitarian ledger. In our time, the correlation of socialism to improvement in the physical quality of life is no more likely to be positive than that of capitalism. For example, in South Korea's "middle class society" (average per capita income approximating $2,500 in 1987, while the average young adult had 12 years of formal education), most people are far better off materially than their occupational counterparts in communist North Korea, despite the continuing depression of South Korean wages relative to gains in productivity.[44] In Africa's leading instance of long-term experimentation with socialist methods—that of Tanzania—economic stagnation has largely negated the beneficent effects of equitarian policies, despite an unusually high degree of dependence on foreign aid for domestic investments.[45] Relatively few Kenyans, today or in the foreseeable future, would trade places with Tanzanians. Yet socialist economic failures contrasted with capitalist success stories, in Africa and elsewhere for that matter, afford small comfort to millions in Kenya, Nigeria, and other exemplars of Third World capitalism, whose lives are blighted by growing poverty, recurrent unemployment, debilitating illness, and inadequate education.

Just as socialism sputters and stalls in practice for want of a realistic theory of incentive, so too does capitalism marginalise concern for human need while the factors of production are being combined to form efficient economic organisations. In the advanced capitalist democracies, social stability is predicated on "trade-offs" between "equality and economic efficiency." Arthur Okun ventures the view that capitalism and democracy "need each other—to put some rationality into equality and some humanity into efficiency." On that basis, he argues, it is now "within the grasp" of industrial capitalism to eradicate poverty.[46] No such claim would be remotely credible for capitalism in the Third World, where the relatively modest challenge of "more efficiency without less equity" appears to indicate the minimum requirement for effective political order,[47] if not, indeed, the very survival of national political communities. To aim higher—at the dual goal of capitalist economic development and substantial improvement in the quality of life for a growing proportion of those who benefit marginally, if at all, from the spread of capitalism—it would be necessary to balance increases in efficiency with even greater proportionate increases in equity. However, it is difficult to imagine how that could be accomplished without a nonideological theory of public and collective responsibility for the well-being of all citizens regardless of their economic circumstances. "Welfare capitalism," the sturdy foster-child of industrial capitalism, has no home in the Third World. Like socialism, it is ill-adapted to formative and variable economic environments.

In sum, socialism needs capital and lacks a theory of incentive; capitalism needs the state and lacks a theory of social responsibility. The African economies need private capital, purposeful state participation, powerful incentives, and public responsibility for the general standard of living. These common requirements for social progress can only be met by judicious mixtures of capitalism and socialism. However, the so-called mixed economy signifies an armed truce in the enduring state of ideological belligerency, or righteous warfare, between its principal elements.

In theoretical as well as practical concerns, "necessity is the mother of invention." Challenged by social problems of unprecedented severity, development theorists in Africa need to question the validity of restrictive political conceptions. Narrowly construed, "the great competition" between capitalism and socialism may prove to be one such barrier to a breakthrough in theory and practice.[48] In Africa, outside of South Africa, the premise of competition between capitalism and socialism has very little significance outside intellectual circles, where it does impair the ability of theorists to contribute new ideas to the campaign for development. Meanwhile it scarcely affects the attitudes or judgments of government officials or business executives. Moreover, empirical studies indicate that this conception of ideological conflict no longer serves as a guide to policy or statecraft in African countries—apart from South Africa, where government policies still exacerbate tendencies toward ideological holy war with devastating effects.

As Gerald Bender has observed, it is impossible to differentiate systematically between Marxist-Leninist and other African states in regard to their policies for development or their political structures.[49] In those countries with avowed Marxist-Leninist régimes—Angola, Benin, Congo, Ethiopia, Madagascar, Mozambique, Somalia, and Zimbabwe—empirical studies reveal no less, and often more, political and religious freedom than in the vast majority of other states, including the one-party capitalist bastions of Gabon, Côte d'Ivoire, Kenya, Malawi, Togo, and Zaïre. With the possible exception of President Mengistu Haile-Mariam, no Marxist-Leninist chief executive in Africa has as much personal autonomy as do Presidents Omar Bongo, Felix Houphouët-Boigny, Daniel arap Moi, Kamuzu Banda, Gnassingbe Eyadema, or Mobutu Sese Seko.

Bender has also noted that no real difference can be discerned between Marxist-Leninist and other African régimes regarding the rôle of the state in the economy.[50] "Communist" Congo has long boasted a freer commercial system than "capitalist" Zaïre.[51] There *has* been a significant degree of deviation from the norm for small-scale enterprise in those "socialist" states which have tried, with ruinous and tragic consequences, to either abolish or severely curtail private trading. Virtually all such policies have been repudiated by the governments concerned as acts of folly. Thus, Samora Machel, the late President of Mozambique, is reported to have declared in a speech that Marxism-Leninism does not require the state to sell tomatoes or matches.[52]

From his vantage point on Angolan policies, Bender has observed that the régime's continued adherence to Marxism-Leninism as an official ideology is the direct consequence of South Africa's undeclared war, and that its termination would signal the end of Angola's military dependence on Cuba and the Soviet Union. Many Angolan leaders "feel an urgency to move away from socialism and toward a free-market economy." Meanwhile, he concludes, "South Africa is the biggest obstacle to Angola's movement away from both Marxism-Leninism and dependence on the Soviet Union."[53] Peaceful relations between South Africa and its neighbours would be conducive to the growth and spread of capitalism in three countries that are now ruled by Marxist-Leninist régimes as a result of revolutionary struggles against white supremacy.

However, the indispensable condition of international peace in Southern Africa is the democratisation of government in South Africa—specifically, the acceptance of common (nonracial) political institutions by the white population. The removal of race as a barrier to the enjoyment of common rights by all citizens would allow the currents of ideological and social renewal to course through the arteries of a social system that is already quickened by its industrial heart. In South Africa, a capitalist movement of class-conscious entrepreneurs, corporate organisers, and committed intellectuals has been evident for at least a century.[54] South Africa is the sole African country where a relatively mature capitalist movement is ahead of its socialist counterpart in ideas and organisation. Needled and stimulated by socialist gadflies, South African capitalists could contribute handsomely to the creative processes of hybrid formation and social invention.

Every national economy in Africa, from the least industrial to the most, is presently crippled by the effects of widespread poverty and low levels of human nurture—health care, nutrition, basic education, and occupational training. The challenges of economic development call for policies and practices that are difficult to pursue simultaneously because each is selectively identified with either capitalism or socialism and, conversely, incompatible with the other. Thus social service policies equal to the requirements of human nurture far exceed the capacity of capitalism in Africa. Similarly, incentive mechanisms suitable for the mobilisation of human resources and maximisation of productivity elude the grasp of socialists in power. These and other prerequisites of sustained economic development are weakened by the absence of synthesising ideas that could supersede the great capitalist-socialist competition. Progress toward a unified theory might also release developmental energies that are scarcely imagined by those who practise the art of economic development today.

NOTES

1. Ronald Robinson and John Gallagher, *Africa and the Victorians: The Official Mind of Imperialism* (New York, 1961), pp. 379–409.
2. On the pitfalls of socialism in Africa, see Crawford Young, *Ideology and Development in Africa* (New Haven, 1982).
3. Nicholas Harman, "East Africa: Turning the Corner," in *The Economist* (London), June 20, 1987.
4. Michael F. Lofchie, "Agrarian Socialism in the Third World: The Tanzanian Case," in *Comparative Politics* (New York), 8, 3, April 1976, pp. 479–99; and Dean E. McHenry, Jr., *Tanzania's Ujamaa Villages: The Implementation of a Rural Development Strategy* (Berkeley, 1979).
5. Twenty out of 52 sovereign African states are so governed, based on this writer's modification of enumerations in Claude S. Phillips, *The African Political Dictionary* (Santa Barbara, 1984), pp. 75 and 83.
6. In a major address, President José Eduardo dos Santos of the People's Republic of Angola has called for scientific balance in the teaching of economics at the national university, in conjunction with a comprehensive program of economic restructuring, to include expansion of the private-enterprise sector, removal of price controls, contraction of the state sector, and affiliation with the International Monetary Fund. "The teaching of economics," he declared, "should be seen as a branch of science involving responsibilities similar to those demanded of physics, biology, or medicine. This means that the excessive burden of political content in the study of economics must be counterbalanced with diversified and up-to-date information on the various currents of modern economics." *Jornal de Angola* (Luanda) (August 18, 1987), translated by Gerald J. Bender.
7. Onigu Otite, "Introduction. The Study of Social Thought in Africa," and "Issues in African Socialism," in Otite, ed., *Themes in African Social and Political Thought* (Enugu, 1978), pp. 9–11 and 138–56.
8. For an insightful comparison of Nyerere and Senghor, see Paul Nursey-Bray, "Consensus and Community: The Theory of African One-Party Democracy," in Graeme Duncan, ed., *Democratic Theory and Practice* (Cambridge, 1983), pp. 96–111.
9. Rhoda E. Howard, *Human Rights in Commonwealth Africa* (Totowa, N.J., 1986), chaps. 6, 7, and passim.
10. On Nkrumah's intellectual evolution, see Paulin J. Hountondji, *African Philosophy* (Bloomington, 1983), chaps. 6 and 7.
11. See Patrick Chabal, *Amilcar Cabral: Revolutionary Leadership and People's War* (Cambridge, 1983).
12. Ibid., p. 177.

13. Reproduced in Michael Sinclair, *Community Development in South Africa* (Washington, D.C., 1986), appendix iii.

14. Quoted in John Saul, "South Africa: The Question of Strategy," in *New Left Review* (London), 160, November–December 1986, p. 11.

15. Heribert Adam and Kogila Moodley, *South Africa without Apartheid: Dismantling Racial Domination* (Berkeley and Los Angeles, 1986), pp. 248–63; Saul, loc. cit.; Thomas G. Karis, "South African Liberation: The Communist Factor," in *Foreign Affairs* (New York), 65, 2 (Winter 1986–87): 267–87; and Tom Lodge, "State of Exile: The African National Congress of South Africa, 1976–86," in *Third World Quarterly* (London), 9, 1 (January 1987): 1–27.

16. This discussion of the Political Bureau's report to the Armed Forces Ruling Council is based on its summary and analysis in *Newswatch* (Lagos) (April 13, 1987), which was confiscated by the authorities in Nigeria, who forbade the further publication of this weekly magazine for six months as punishment for the unauthorised disclosures. For a comprehensive analysis of the report, based on *Newswatch*, see Larry Diamond, "Nigeria: Pluralism, Statism and the Struggle for Democracy," in Diamond, Juan Linz, and Seymour Martin Lipset, eds., *Democracy in Developing Countries*, Vol. II, *Africa* (Boulder, 1988). For the government's own views and analysis, see Federal Republic of Nigeria, *Government's Views and Comments on the Findings and Recommendations of the Political Bureau* (Lagos, 1987).

17. Ibid., p. 43.

18. *Newswatch*, 13 April 1987, p. 16.

19. "Statement: COSATU, SACTU, and the ANC," in *Sechaba* (Lusaka) (May 1986): 11.

20. "Interview: Elijah Barayi," in *Africa Report* (New Brunswick), 31, 2 (March–April 1986): 18.

21. Martin J. Sklar, *The Corporate Reconstruction of American Capitalism, 1890–1916: The Market, the Law, and Politics* (Cambridge, 1988).

22. Ibid., pp. 2–3; also pp. 11–14 and 20–33.

23. Robert L. Heilbroner, *The Nature and Logic of Capitalism* (New York, 1985), p. 102.

24. Ibid., p. 104.

25. The World Bank, *Financing Adjustment with Growth in Sub-Saharan Africa, 1986–90* (Washington, D.C., 1986), p. 21. The term "formal sector" refers to economic activity that is "effectively subject to `formal' rules" embodied in "contracts, licenses, labor inspection," and similar legally enforceable devices. International Labour Organisation, *World Labour Report* (Geneva, 1984), p. 25.

26. World Bank, *Accelerated Development in Sub-Saharan Africa: An Agenda for Action* (Washington, D.C., 1981), pp. 5 and 40–4; for the ensuing debate see, *inter alia*, Robert S. Browne and Robert J. Cummings, *The Lagos Plan of Action vs. The Berg Report* (Lawrenceville, Va., 1984); and John Ravenhill, ed., *Africa in Economic Crisis* (New York, 1986). Cf. Larry Diamond, "Class Formation in the Swollen African State," in *The Journal of Modern African Studies* (Cambridge), 25, 4 (December 1987): 567–96.

27. A. M. Hawkins, "Can Africa Industrialize?" in Robert J. Berg and Jennifer Seymour Whitaker, eds., *Strategies for African Development* (Berkeley, 1986), p. 299.

28. The writings of Donal Cruise O'Brien on Senegal constitute a significant exception. He describes a theocratic-entrepreneurial élite (the *sufi marabouts*) that acts

as a democratic force in so far as its ability to procure disciples depends on its use of the political process to satisfy their economic needs. "Wails and Whispers: The People's Voice in West African Muslim Politics," in Patrick Chabal, ed., *Political Domination in Africa: Reflections on the Limits of Power* (Cambridge, 1986), pp. 71–83.

29. Richard L. Sklar, "Developmental Democracy," in *Comparative Studies in Society and History* (Cambridge), 29, 4 (October 1987): 700.

30. *Financial Times* (London), November 1, 1986. This conference was sponsored by three governmental and three nongovernmental organisations; namely, the World Bank, African Development Bank, Government of Kenya, Kenya Association of Manufacturers, Voluntary Development Assistance (Kenya), and Inter-Action (U.S.A.). Goran Hyden, "Business and Development in Sub-Saharan Africa," in *UFSI Reports* (Indianapolis), 25 (1986), Africa/Middle East, p. 8, n. 12.

31. Ibid.

32. Ibid., pp. 6–7. Quotations from Hyden's lucid summary.

33. Ibid., p. 6.

34. Young, *Ideology and Development*, p. 183.

35. *Africa Research Bulletin: Economic, Financial, and Technical* (Exeter), 23, 1 (February 28, 1986): 8067.

36. Ibid., 23, 22 (December 31, 1986): 8468.

37. For the idea of "developmental merits" in relation to the choice between capitalism and socialism, see Sayre P. Schatz, "Postimperialism and the Great Competition," in David G. Becker, Jeff Frieden, Schatz, and Richard L. Sklar, *Postimperialism: International Capitalism and Development in the Late Twentieth Century* (Boulder and London, 1987), pp. 197–98.

38. Alec Nove, *The Economics of Feasible Socialism* (London, 1983), p. 177.

39. Ibid., pp. 183–96 and 199.

40. Richard Sandbrook with Judith Barker, *The Politics of Africa's Economic Stagnation* (Cambridge, 1985), p. 34.

41. Sayre P. Schatz, "Laissez-Faireism for Africa?" in *The Journal of Modern African Studies*, 25, I (March 1987): 138.

42. World Bank, *Poverty and Human Development* (Oxford, 1980), pp. v and I.

43. World Bank, *Toward Sustained Development in Sub-Saharan Africa* (Washington, D.C., 1984), p. 9.

44. Hahn Been Lee, "Korean Development: Lessons, Problems and Prospects," David Dollar and Kenneth Sokoloff, "Economic Growth and Income Inequality in South Korea," and Aidan Foster-Carter, "A Comparison and Assessment of the Two Koreas," Conference on "The Role of the State in Economic Development: Republic of Korea" University of California, (Los Angeles: August 14–16, 1987).

45. Foreign aid accounted for two-thirds of Tanzanian gross domestic investment in 1979. Howard, op. cit., p. 76.

46. Arthur M. Okun, *Equality and Efficiency: The Big Tradeoff* (Washington, D.C., 1975), pp. 117 and 120.

47. I am imdebted to Jeff Frieden for this formulation. "Equity"—defined here to connote social and economic justice—is a more realistic goal/value for social reformers in the Third World than Okun's "equality."

48. Sayre P. Schatz, whose thesis—"the character of the contemporary era depends upon the superiority of either capitalism or socialism" for "development tasks" in the Third World—has stimulated the argument of this section, does not, by any means, construe the "great competition" narrowly. Yet his thesis does diverge, avowedly so, from that of David G. Becker and the present writer, who reject the proposition that competition between capitalism and socialism is a fundamental issue for development in the Third World. See Schatz, "Postimperialism and the Great Competition," pp. 193 and 197, and Becker, "Postimperialism: A First Quarterly Report," in Becker, Frieden, Schatz, and Sklar, op. cit., pp. 215–17. See also the historical investigation of this issue in another context by Martin Sklar, op. cit., whose encouragement of the transcendence thesis in this section is indistinguishable from its origin.

49. Gerald J. Bender, "The United States and Africa," Presidential Address to the Twenty-Ninth Annual Meeting of the African Studies Association, Madison, Wisconsin, October 31, 1986.

50. Personal communication.

51. *The Wall Street Journal* (New York), July 2, 1980, Jonathan Kwitny.

52. Elliot Berg, "The World Bank's Strategy," in Ravenhill, ed., op. cit., p. 57.

53. Bender, "The United States and Africa," and personal communication.

54. For the rise of a capitalist intelligentsia in South Africa, see Belinda Bozzoli, *The Political Nature of a Ruling Class: Capital and Ideology in South Africa, 1890–1933* (London, 1981).

BIBLIOGRAPHY

PART ONE / Theory and Method in Economic Development

BARAN, PAUL. "Economic Progress and Economic Surplus." *Science and Society*, 17, 4 (Fall 1953): 289–317.

CEBOTAREV, E. A. "Women, Human Rights and the Family in Development Theory and Practice." *Canadian Journal of Development Studies*, 9, 2 (1988): 187–200.

CHENERY, HOLLIS, et al. *Redistribution with Growth: An Approach to Policy*. Oxford: Oxford University Press, 1974.

———, and M. SYRAQUIN. *Patterns of Development: 1950–1970*. London: Oxford University Press, 1975.

DONALDSON, LORRAINE. *Economic Development: Analysis and Policy*. Mineola, N.Y.: West Publishing Co., 1984.

FEI, JOHN C. H., and C. RANIS. *Development of the Labor Surplus Economy: Theory and Policy*. Homewood, Ill.: Irwin, 1964.

FRANK, ANDRE GUNDER. "Sociology of Development and Underdevelopment of Sociology." In *Latin America: Underdevelopment or Revolution?* New York: Monthly Review Press, 1969, pp. 21–94.

GOULET, DENIS. *The Cruel Choice*. New York: Atheneum, 1971.

———. "An Ethical Model for the Study of Values." *Harvard Educational Review*, 41, 2 (May 1971).

HELLEINER, G. K. "Conventional Foolishness and Overall Ignorance: Current Approaches to Global Transformation and Development." *Canadian Journal of Development Studies*, 10, 1 (January 1989): 107–18.

HIRSCHMAN, ALBERT O. *The Strategy of Economic Development*. New Haven: Yale University Press, 1958.

JAMESON, KENNETH, and CHARLES K. WILBER, eds. *Directions in Economic Development*. Notre Dame, Ind.: University of Notre Dame Press, 1979.

KUZNETS, SIMON S. *Modern Economic Growth*. New Haven: Yale University Press, 1966.

MEIER, GERALD M. "Do Development Economists Matter?" *IDS Bulletin* 20, 3 (July 1989): 17–25.

MOORE, MICK. "Interpreting Africa's Crisis: Political Science versus Political Economy." *IDS Bulletin*, 18, 4 (October 1987): 7–15.

MYRDAL, GUNNAR. *Asian Drama: An Inquiry into the Poverty of Nations*. New York: Pantheon, 1968.

———. *Economic Theory and Underdeveloped Regions*. New York: Harper & Row, 1971.

NURKSE, RAGNAR. *Problems of Capital Formation in Underdeveloped Countries*. Oxford: Basil Blackwell, 1958.

PANTIN, DENNIS. "Long Waves and Caribbean Development." *Social and Economic Studies*, 36, 2 (June 1986): 1–20.

RANDALL, MARGARET. "When the Imagination of the Writer Is Confronted by the Imagination of the State." *Latin American Perspectives*, 16, 1 (Winter 1989): 61–115.

RANIS, GUSTAV, et al., eds. *Comparative Development Perspectives: Essays in Honor of Lloyd G. Reynolds*. Boulder, Colo.: Westview Press, 1984.

REYNOLDS, LLOYD G. *Image and Reality in Economic Development*. Yale University Economic Growth Center Series. New Haven: Yale University Press, 1977.

SEN, A. K. "Development as Capability Expansion." *Journal of Development Planning*, 19 (1989): 41–58.

STREETEN, PAUL. "Economic Models and Their Usefulness for Planning in South Asia." In Gunnar Myrdal, ed., *Asian Drama: An Inquiry into the Poverty of Nations*. New York: Pantheon, 1968.

TODARO, MICHAEL. *Economic Development in the Third World*. 4th ed. New York: Longmans, 1989.

UL HAQ, MAHBUB. *The Poverty Curtain: Choice for the Third World*. New York: Columbia University Press, 1976.

WILBER, CHARLES K., ed. "The Methodological Foundations of Development Economics." *World Development* (Special Issue), 14, 2 (February 1986).

PART TWO / Economic Development and Underdevelopment in Historical Perspective

ANDERSEN, ROBIN. "Images of War: Photojournalism, Ideology, and Central America." *Latin American Perspectives*, 16, 1 (Winter 1989): 61–96.

BAIROCH, PAUL. *The Economic Development of the Third World Since 1900*. Translated from the fourth French edition by Cynthia Postan. Berkeley: University of California Press, 1975.

BARAN, PAUL. "On the Roots of Backwardness." In *The Political Economy of Growth*. New York: Monthly Review Press, 1957, 134–62.

BARRET-BROWN, MICHAEL. *The Economics of Imperialism*. Baltimore: Penguin, 1974.

BHATT, V. V. "Economic Development: An Analytic-Historical Approach." *World Development*, 4, 7 (July 1976).

BRYCESON, DEBORAH F. "Peasant Cash Cropping vs. Food Self-Sufficiency in Tanzania: A Historical Perspective." *IDS Bulletin*, 19, 2 (April 1988): 37–46.

FURTADO, CELSO. *Economic Development of Latin America: A Survey from Colonial Times to the Cuban Revolution*. Cambridge, England: Cambridge University Press, 1970.

GERSCHENKRON, ALEXANDER. *Economic Backwardness in Historical Perspective*. New York: Praeger, 1965.

GOULD, JOHN D. *Economic Growth in History: Survey and Analysis*. London: Methuen, 1972.

GRIFFIN, K. B. *The Underdevelopment of Spanish America*. London: G. Allen, 1969.

JUNEJA, MONICA. "The Peasant Image and Agrarian Change: Representations of Rural Society in Nineteenth Century French Painting from Millet to Van Gogh." *Journal of Peasant Studies*, 15 (1987–88): 445.

KITCHING, GAVIN. *Development and Underdevelopment in Historical Perspective: Population, Nationalism and Industrialization*. New York: Methuen, 1982.

LOGAN, BERNARD I. "The Reverse Transfer of Technology from Subsaharan Africa to the United States." *Journal of Modern African Studies*, 25, 4 (December 1987): 597–612.

MORAWETZ, DAVID. *Twenty-Five Years of Economic Development: 1950 to 1975*. Washington, D.C.: World Bank, 1977.

POLANYI, KARL. *The Great Transformation: The Political and Economic Origins of Our Time*. Boston: Beacon Press, 1957.

REYNOLDS, L. G. *Economic Growth in the Third World, 1850–1980*. Economic Growth Center Series. New Haven: Yale University Press, 1985.

RODNEY, WALTER. *How Europe Underdeveloped Africa*. Dar es Salaam: Tanzania Publishing House, 1972.

ROSTOW, W. W. *Stages of Economic Growth*. 2d ed. New York: Cambridge University Press, 1971.

ROWE, WILLIAM, and T. WHITFIELD. "Thresholds of Identity: Literature and Exile in Latin America." *Third World Quarterly*, 9, 1 (January 1987): 229–45.

THOMAS, C. *Dependence and Transformation*. New York: Monthly Review Press, 1976.

PART THREE / Economic Development in a Revolutionary World: Trade and Dependency

AMIN, SAMIR. *Imperialism and Unequal Development*. New York: Monthly Review Press, 1977.

APTER, DAVID, and LOUIS GOLDMAN, eds. *The Multinational Corporation and Social Change*. New York: Praeger, 1976.

ARRIGHI, G. "Labor Supplies in Historical Perspective: A Study of the Proletarianization of the African Peasantry in Rhodesia." *Journal of Development Studies*, 6 (April 1970): 197–234.

BATH, G. RICHARD, and DILMUS JAMES. "Dependency Analysis of Latin America." *Latin American Research Review*, 11, 2 (1976).

CAPORASO, JAMES A. "Dependence, Dependency, and Power in the Global System: A Structural and Behavioral Analysis." *International Organization*, 32, 1 (Winter 1978).

CARDOSO, FERNANDO HENRIQUE. "The Consumption of Dependency Theory in the United States." *Latin American Research Review*, 12, 3 (1977).

———, and ENZO FALETTO. *Dependency and Development in Latin America.* Berkeley: University of California Press, 1978.

CULPEPER, ROY. "The Debt Crisis and the World Bank." *Canadian Journal of Development Studies,* 9, 2 (1988): 285–301.

DARRAT, A. F. "Are Exports an Engine of Growth? Another Look at the Evidence." *Applied Economics*, 19, 2 (February 1987): 277–83.

DESTA, ASAYEHGN. "Africa's External Debt in Perspective." *Journal of African Studies*, 15, 1 & 2 (Spring–Summer 1988): 23–32.

DHONTE, PIERRE. *Clockwork Debt: Trade and the External Debt of Developing Countries.* Lexington, Mass.: Heath, 1979.

DOS SANTOS, THEOTONIO. "The Structure of Dependence." *American Economic Review*, 60, 2 (1970).

EMMANUEL, ARGHIRI. *Unequal Exchange: A Study of the Imperialism of Trade.* New York: Monthly Review Press, 1972.

FRANK, ANDRE GUNDER. *Capitalism and Underdevelopment in Latin America: Historical Studies of Chile and Brazil.* New York: Monthly Review Press, 1967.

GIRLING, ROBERT HENRIQUES. *Multinational Institutions and the Third World: Management, Debt, and Trade Conflicts in the International Economic Order.* New York: Praeger, 1985.

GOTUR, PADMA. "Interest Rates and the Developing World: Interest Rates in the Developed World Have Pervasive and Important Effects on Debt, Growth and Commodity Exports in Developing Countries." *Finance and Development*, 20 (December 1983): 33–36.

HELLEINER, G. K., ed. *A World Divided: The Less Developed Countries in the International Economy.* New York: Cambridge University Press, 1976.

HYMER, S., and S. RESNICK. "International Trade and Uneven Development." In J. Bhagwati, R. Jones, R. Mundell, and J. Vanek, eds., *Trade, Balance of Payments and Growth.* Amsterdam: North Holland, 1971.

KIM, EUN MEE. "Foreign Capital in Korea's Economic Development, 1960–85." *Studies in Comparative International Development*, 24, 4 (Winter 1989–90): 24–45.

KIM, YUNG MYUNG. "Patterns of Dependency and Development: A Comparative Analysis of Radical and Conservative State Policies in Peru, Egypt, Brazil and South Korea." *Korea and World Affairs*, 8, Winter 1984: 812–44.

KWON, J. K., and Y. G. YOO. "Welfare Inequality among Urban Households in South Korea: 1965–83." *Applied Economics*, 19, 4 (April 1987): 497–510.

LOONEY, ROBERT E. "The Impact of Arms Production on Income Distribution and Growth in the Third World." *Economic Development and Cultural Change*, 38, 1 (October 1989): 145–54.

MAGDOFF, HARRY. *The Age of Imperialism.* New York: Monthly Review Press, 1969.

MOSS, JOANNA, and J. RAVENHILL. "Trade Diversification in Black Africa." *Journal of Modern African Studies*, 27, 3 (September 1989): 521.

MULLER, EDWARD N. "Dependent Economic Development, Aid Dependence on the U.S. and Democratic Breakdown in Third World." *International Studies Quarterly*, 29 (December 1985): 445–69.

PARSONS, JOHN E. "Bubble, Bubble, How Much Trouble? Financial Markets, Capitalist Development and Capitalist Crises." *Science and Society*, 52, 3 (Fall 1988): 260–89.

PETRAS, JAMES, and H. BRILL. "Latin America's Transnational Capitalists and the Debt: A Class Analysis Perspective." *Development and Change*, 19, 2 (April 1988): 179.

PREBISCH, RAOUL. "The Role of Commercial Policy in Underdeveloped Countries. *American Economic Review*, 49, 2 (May 1959).

SINGER, H. W. "The Distribution of Gains Between Investing and Borrowing Countries." *American Economic Review*, 40, 2 (May 1950).

STEIN, LESLIE. "Third World Poverty, Economic Growth and Income Distribution." *Canadian Journal of Development Studies*, 10, 2 (1989): 225–40.

TSAKLOGLOU, P. "Development and Inequality Revisited." *Applied Economics*, 20, 4 (April 1988): 509–32.

PART FOUR / Agricultural Institutions and Strategy

ADAMS, DALE W. "The Conundrum of Successful Credit Programs in Floundering Rural Financial Markets." *Economic Development and Cultural Change,* 36, 2 (January 1988): 355–68.

AGARWAL, BINA. "Who Sows? Who Reaps? Women and Land Rights in India." *The Journal of Peasant Studies,* 15 (1987): 531.

ALIER, JUAN MARTINEZ. *Haciendas, Plantations and Collective Farms.* London: Frank Cass, 1977.

BARKIN, DAVID. "Cuban Agriculture: A Strategy of Economic Development." *Studies in Comparative International Development,* 7, 1 (Spring 1972).

BARRACLOUGH, SOLON, ed. *Agrarian Structure in Latin America.* Lexington, Mass.: Heath, 1973.

BERRY, R. A., and W. CLINE. *Agrarian Structure and Productivity in Developing Countries.* Baltimore: Johns Hopkins University Press, 1979.

BRASS, TOM. "Unfree Labor and Capitalist Restructuring in the Agrarian Sector: Peru and India." *The Journal of Peasant Studies,* 14, 1 (1986): 50–77.

CLAY, E. J., and B. B. SCHAFFER, eds. *Room for Manoeuvre: An Exploration of Public Policy Planning in Agricultural and Rural Development.* Cranbury, N.J.: Associated Universities Press, Inc., 1984.

DEJANVRY, A., et al. "Land and Labor in Latin American Agriculture from the 1950s to the 1980s." *The Journal of Peasant Studies,* 16 (1988): 396.

FIGUERA, A. "Agrarian Reformisms in Latin America: A Framework and an Instrument of Rural Development." *World Development,* 5 (1977).

GANAPATHY, R. S. "The Political Economy of Rural Energy Planning in the Third World." *Review of Radical Political Economics* 15 (Fall 1983): 83–95.

GHAI, D., et al., eds. *Agrarian Systems and Rural Development.* New York: Holmes and Meier, 1979.

GLADWIN, C. H., et al. "Providing African Women Farmers Access: One Solution to the Food Crisis." *Journal of African Studies* 13, 4 (Winter 1986–87): 131–41.

GOLDSMITH, ARTHUR. "The Private Sector and Rural Development: Can Agribusiness Help the Small Farmer?" *World Development* 13 (October–November 1985): 1125–38.

GRIFFIN, KEITH. *The Political Economy of Agrarian Change.* London: Macmillan, 1974.

———. *Land Concentration and Rural Poverty.* 2d ed. London: Macmillan, 1980.

GURLEY, JOHN. "Rural Development in China 1949–1972, and the Lessons to Be Learned from It." *World Development,* 3, 7–8 (July–August 1975).

HEYER, R., P. ROBERTS, and G. WILLIAMS, eds. *Rural Development in Tropical Africa.* London: Macmillan, 1981.

JOHNSTON, BRUCE F., and JOHN W. MELLOR. "The Role of Agriculture in Economic Development." *American Economic Review,* 51, 4 (September 1961).

———, and P. KILBY. *Agriculture and Structural Transformation: Strategies in Late-Developing Countries.* New York: Oxford University Press, 1975.

———, and W. C. CLARK. *Redesigning Rural Development: A Strategic Perspective.* Baltimore: Johns Hopkins University Press, 1982.

LIPTON, MICHAEL. *Why Poor People Stay Poor: A Study of Urban Bias in World Development.* Cambridge, Mass.: Harvard University Press, 1977.

LONGHURST, RICHARD. "Cash Crops, Household Food Security and Nutrition." *IDS Bulletin,* 19, 2 (April 1988): 28–36.

MORALES, EDMUNDO. "Coca & Cocaine Economy and Social Change in the Andes of Peru." *Economic Development and Cultural Change,* 35, 1 (October 1986): 143–62.

MURALT, JURGEN VON, and J. SAJHAU. "Plantations and Basic Needs: The Changing International and National Setting." *IDS Bulletin,* 18, 2 (April 1987): 9–14.

MUTSAERS, ANTONY. "Industrial Development: A Natural Growth if Rooted in Agricultural Demand." *CERES,* 21, 2 (March–April 1988).

OTSUKA, KEIJIRO, and Y. HAYAMI. "Theories of Share Tenancy: A Critical Survey." *Economic Development and Cultural Change,* 37, 1 (October 1988): 31–68.

PEARSE, ANDREW. *Seeds of Plenty, Seeds of Want: Social and Economic Implications of the Green Revolution.* New York: Oxford University Press, 1980.

SPOONER, NEIL. "Does the World Bank Inhibit Smallholder Cash Cropping? The Case of Malawi." *IDS Bulletin,* 19, 2 (April 1988): 66–70.

STAVENHAGEN, RODOLFO, ed. *Agrarian Problems and Peasant Movements in Latin America.* New York: Doubleday, 1970.

TEUBAL, MIGUEL. "Internationalization of Capital and Agroindustrial Complexes: Their Impact on Latin American Agriculture." *Latin American Perspectives,* 14, 3 (Summer 1987): 316.

PART FIVE / Industrial Institutions and Strategy

CHUDNOVSKY, DANIEL, and MASAFUMI NAGAO. *Capital Goods Production in the Third World: An Economic Study of Technological Acquisition,* Dover, N.H.: Frances Pinter (Publishers) Ltd., 1983.

CODY, JOHN, et al. *Policies for Industrial Progress in Developing Countries.* New York: Oxford University Press, 1980.

CUKOR, GYORGY. *Strategies for Industrialization in Developing Countries.* New York: St. Martin's Press, 1974.

DEYO, F. C. *Dependent Development and Industrial Order: An Asian Case Study.* New York: Praeger, 1981.

GOULET, DENIS. *The Uncertain Promise: Value Conflicts in Technology Transfer.* New York: IDOC North America, 1977.

HIRSCHMAN, ALBERT O . "The Political Economy of Import-Substituting Industrialization in Latin America." *Quarterly Journal of Economics,* 82, 1 (February 1968).

KIM, WON-BAE. "Industrial Restructuring and Related Labour Issues in Korea." *IDS Bulletin,* 20, 4 (October 1989): 32–36.

KIRKPATRICK, C. H., and F. I. NIXSON, ed. *The Industrialisation of Less Developed Countries.* Dover, N.H.: Manchester University Press, 1983.

LEE, E. *Export-Led Industrialization and Development.* Geneva: International Labour Office, 1981.

LEFF, NATHANIEL H. "Disjunction between Policy Research and Practice: Social Benefit-Cost Analysis and Investment Policy at the World Bank." *Studies in Comparative International Development,* 23, 4 (Winter 1988): 77–87.

MATTHEWS, RON. G. "The Development of a Local Machinery Industry in Kenya." *Journal of Modern African Studies,* 25, 1 (March 1987): 67–94.

MENGISTU, BERHANU, and Y. HAILE-MARIAM. "Public Enterprises and the Privatization in Sub-saharan Africa." *Third World Quarterly,* 10, 4 (October 1988): 1565–90.

MYTELKA, LYNN K. "The Unfulfilled Promise of African Industrialization." *African Studies Review,* 32, 3 (December 1989): 1–76.

NANKANI, HELEN. "The Lessons of Privatization in Developing Countries." *Finance and Development,* 27, 1 (March 1990): 43–45.

NEWHAM, MARK. "Power Generation." *South,* (May 1988): 85–87.

ROCA, SERGIO G. "State Enterprises in Cuba under the New System of Planning." *Cuban Studies,* 1986: 153–80.

ROEMER, M. "Resource-Based Industrialization in the Developing Countries: A Survey." *Journal of Development Economics,* 6 (1976).

SUBBARAO, A. V. "Influence of Political Structure on Worker Participation in Developing Asian Countries." *Canadian Journal of Development Studies,* 8, 1 (1987): 97–115.

PART SIX / The Human Cost of Development

ADAMS, J. D. "The Threat to Education from Structural Adjustment: A Realistic Response." *IDS Bulletin,* 20, 1 (January 1989): 50–54.

ADELMAN, I., and C. T. MORRIS. *Economic Growth and Social Equity in Developing Countries.* Stanford, Calif.: Stanford University Press, 1973.

BARRIOS DE CHUNGARA, D. *Let Me Speak!: Testimony of Domitila, A Woman of the Bolivian Mines.* New York: Monthly Review Press, 1978.

BERGER, PETER. *Pyramids of Sacrifice: Political Ethics and Social Change.* New York: Basic Books, 1974.

BRUNDENIUS, C. and M. LUNDAL. *Development Strategies and Basic Needs in Latin America: Challenges for the 1980's.* Boulder, Colo.: Westview, 1982.

DE. ALMEIDA-FILHO, NAOMAR DE. "The Psychosocial Costs of Development: Labor, Migration, and Stress in Bahia, Brazil." *Latin American Research Review,* 17, 3 (1982).

DE JESUS, MARIA CAROLINA. *Child of the Dark.* New York: Dutton, 1962.

DE SCHWEINITZ, KARL DE, JR. "Economic Growth, Coercion, and Freedom." *World Politics,* 9, 2 (January 1957).

ELLIOT, CHARLES. *Patterns of Poverty in the Third World: A Study of Social and Economic Stratification.* New York: Praeger, 1975.

HOLZMAN, FRANKLYN. "Consumer Sovereignty and the Rate of Economic Development." *Economia Internazionale,* 11, 2 (1958).

LEWIS, W. ARTHUR. "Is Economic Growth Desirable?" In *The Theory of Economic Growth.* Homewood, Ill.: Irwin, 1955.

MENGISTU, BERHANU, and Y. HAILE-MARIAM. "The Status and Future of Privatization in Sub-Saharan Africa." *Journal of African Studies,* 15, 1 & 2 (Spring–Summer 1988): 4–9.

NAIR, KUSUM. *Blossoms in the Dust.* New York: Praeger, 1962.

O'DONNELL, GUILLERMO. *Modernization and Bureaucratic Authoritarianism: Studies in South American Politics.* Berkeley: Institute for International Studies, University of California, 1973.

SCHULTHEIS, MICHAEL. "Refugees: A Special Issue." *African Studies Review,* 32, 1 (April 1989).

SELL, RALPH R., and S. J. KUNITZ. "The Debt Crisis and the End of an Era in Mortality Decline." *Studies in Comparative International Development,* 21, 4 (Winter 1986–87): 3–30.

WAAL, ALEX DE. "Is Famine Relief Irrelevant to Rural People." *IDS Bulletin,* 20, 2 (April 1989): 63–67.

WOLF, DIANE L. "Daughters, Decisions, and Domination: An Empirical and Conceptual Critique of Household Strategies." *Development and Change,* 21, 1 (January 1990): 43–74.

PART SEVEN / What Is To Be Done?

AGARWALA, RAMGOPAL. "Planning in Developing Countries: Using the Lessons of Experience to Formulate a Workable Approach." *Finance and Development,* 22 (March 1985): 13–16.

AVRAMIC, DRAGOSLAV. "Development Policies for Today." *Journal of World Trade,* 17 (May–June 1983): 189–206.

FRANK, ANDRE GUNDER. "Capitalist Underdevelopment or Socialist Revolution?" In *Latin America: Underdevelopment or Revolution?* New York: Monthly Review Press, 1969.

FREIRE, PAULO. *Pedagogy of the Oppressed.* New York: Herder and Herder, 1972.

GRAN, GUY. *Development by People: Citizen Construction of a Just World.* New York: Praeger, 1983.

GUTIERREZ, GUSTAVO. *A Theology of Liberation.* Maryknoll, N.Y.: Orbis Books, 1972.

HIRSCHMAN, ALBERT. *A Bias for Hope.* New Haven: Yale University Press, 1971.

LASZLO, E. *Regional Cooperation Among Developing Countries—The New Imperative of Development in the 1980s.* New York: Pergamon, 1981.

LEONTIEF, W., ANNE CARTER, and PETER PETRI. *The Future of the World Economy.* New York: Oxford University Press, 1977.

MEIER, GERALD M. *Emerging from Poverty: The Economics that Really Matters.* Fair Lawn, N.J.: Oxford University Press, 1984.

MYRDAL, GUNNAR. *The Challenge of World Poverty: A World Anti-Poverty Program in Outline.* New York: Pantheon Books, 1970.

NYERERE, JULIUS K. *Freedom and Development.* Oxford: Oxford University Press, 1974.

O'DONNELL, GUILLERMO. "Brazil's Failure: What Future for Debtor Cartels." *Third World Quarterly,* 9, 4 (October 1988): 1157–66.

RAVENHILL, JOHN. "Adjustment with Growth: A Fragile Consensus." *Journal of Modern African Studies,* 26, 2 (March 1988): 179–210.

ROY, SANJIT. "The Tilonia Model: A Successful Indian Grassroots Development Strategy." *Canadian Journal of Development Economics,* 8, 2 (1987): 355–74.

RUTTAN, VERNON W. "Cultural Endowments and Economic Development: What Can We Learn From Anthropology?" *Economic Development and Cultural Change,* 36, 3 (April 1988 Supplement): s247.

SEIDMAN, ANN. "Towards Ending IMF-ism in Southern Africa: An Alternative Development Strategy." *Journal of Modern African Studies,* 27, 2 (March 1989): 1–22.

SINGH, YYOTI SHANKAR. *A New International Economic Order: Towards a Fair Redistribution of the World's Resources.* New York: Praeger, 1977.

SIPOS, SANDOR, and H. SITARSKA. "Technological and Organizational Change: A Challenge to Eastern Europe." *IDS Bulletin,* 20, 4 (October 1989): 37–43.

WYNNE, BRIAN. "The Toxic Waste Trade: International Regulatory Issues and Options." *Third World Quarterly,* 11, 3 (July 1989): 120–46.